D1233575

John Marshall Harlan

JOHN MARSHALL HARLAN

Great Dissenter of the Warren Court

TINSLEY E. YARBROUGH

New York Oxford
OXFORD UNIVERSITY PRESS
1992

Oxford University Press

Oxford New York Toronto
Delhi Bombay Calcutta Madras Karachi
Petaling Jaya Singapore Hong Kong Tokyo
Nairobi Dar es Salaam Cape Town
Melbourne Auckland

and associated companies in
Berlin Ibadan

Published by Oxford University Press, Inc.,
200 Madison Avenue, New York, New York 10016

Library of Congress Cataloging-in-Publication Data
Yarbrough, Tinsley E., 1941–
John Marshall Harlan : great dissenter of the Warren Court /
Tinsley E. Yarbrough.
p. cm. Includes bibliography references and index.
ISBN 0-19-506090-3
1. Harlan, John M. (John Marshall), 1899–1971.
2. Judges—United States—Biography.
I. Title. KF8745.H33Y37 1992 347.73'2634—dc20 [B]
[347.3073534] [B] 91-16145

2 4 6 8 9 7 5 3 1

Printed in the United States of America
on acid-free paper

To
Mary Alice,
Sarah,
and Cole

Preface

It was one of John Harlan's favorite stories. A large photograph of his grandfather, the first Justice John Marshall Harlan, adorned a wall of his chambers. One day he identified the photograph to a visiting Japanese dignitary. "I did not realize, Justice Harlan," the visitor replied, respectfully, "that the post was hereditary."

During his thirty-four-year tenure on the U.S. Supreme Court (1877–1911), the first Justice John Marshall Harlan acquired a well-deserved reputation as the Court's "great dissenter." When a majority in the *Civil Rights Cases* of 1883 struck down a Reconstruction-era statute banning racial discrimination by inns, theaters, restaurants, and public conveyances, Harlan I vigorously dissented. To the majority's conclusion that equating such discrimination with the sort of slavery and involuntary servitude Congress was empowered to forbid under the Thirteenth Amendment "would be running the slavery argument into the ground," he asserted that Congress had power to eliminate not merely slavery itself but also "its badges and incidents," including denial of service by places of public accommodation. To the Court's conclusion that Congress's power to enforce the Fourteenth Amendment extended only to "state action" that denied equal protection and other rights the amendment's provisions guaranteed, he responded that the amendment's conferral of U.S. citizenship on all persons born or naturalized in the United States had clothed Congress with authority to protect the rights implied by that citizenship, including freedom from racial discrimination in public accommodations, from private as well as governmental interference. Even accepting the majority's state action thesis, he added, inns and other businesses serving the public should be considered quasi-state agencies and thus subject to congressional control. When the Court upheld state segregation laws in *Plessy* v. *Ferguson*, moreover, he registered his most famous dissent, defending the nation's "color-blind" Constitution and asserting both eloquently and prophetically that

> the judgment this day rendered will, in time, prove to be quite as pernicious as the decision made by this tribunal in the *Dred Scott* case. . . . The destinies of the two races, in this country, are indissolubly linked together, and the interests of both require that the common government of all shall not permit the seeds of race hate to be planted under the sanction of law. What can more certainly arouse race hate, what more certainly create and perpetuate a feeling of distrust between these races, than state enactments which, in fact, proceed on the ground that colored citizens are so inferior and degraded that they cannot be allowed to sit in public coaches occupied by white citizens?[1]

Nor were the first Justice Harlan's differences with his brethren confined solely to race cases. In a period when his fellow justices repeatedly rejected claims that the Fourteenth Amendment embodied within its meaning the guarantees of the Bill of Rights, which would make the great liberties of the first eight amendments fully binding on the states, Harlan I argued with equal vehemence and persistence that the Fourteenth Amendment's framers intended its provisions to have precisely that construction. In a 1907 dissent, moreover, he forcefully rejected the view of the majority "that the legislature may impair or abridge the rights of a free press and of free speech whenever it thinks that the public welfare requires that to be done." When, on the other hand, the Court accorded extensive constitutional protection to "liberty of contract" and related property rights mentioned nowhere in the Constitution's text, Harlan I generally urged greater deference to the judgments of the political branches of government, condemning the majority's assumption of the role of a "super-legislature" and efforts to read laissez-faire and Social Darwinian economic theories into the nation's supreme law.[2]

The second Justice John Marshall Harlan, the subject of this book, is equally deserving, however, of the appellation "great dissenter." During his sixteen years on the supreme bench (1955–71), a tenure less than half the length of his illustrious grandfather's, Harlan II wrote 613 opinions, more than any other justice of his era. One hundred and sixty-eight were opinions for the Court and 149 were concurrences; but nearly half, an impressive 296, were dissents. In the Court's 1963–67 terms, the core period of Warren Court activism in civil liberties litigation, he averaged 62.6 dissents per term.

Somewhat ironically, however, the second Harlan embraced little of his grandfather's jurisprudence. Harlan I regularly dissented in a era of judicial restraint in the field of personal, noneconomic rights. Harlan II, on the other hand, became a leading dissenter during the Court's greatest period of civil liberties activism, and many of his opinions, whether in dissent or with a majority, rejected significant elements of Harlan I's constitutional philosophy. While he concurred in the Warren Court's rejection of state-mandated racial segregation, Harlan II challenged the notion that Congress's authority to enforce the Fourteenth Amendment extended to private forms of racial discrimination. He could not agree, either, that the discriminatory practices of privately operated places of public accommodation amounted to quasi-state action subject to the Fourteenth Amendment's reach. The second Harlan was also an eloquent and persistent critic of the Warren Court's incorporation into the Fourteenth Amendment's meaning, and extension to state governments, of most provisions of the Bill of Rights. To a considerably greater degree than his grandfather, moreover, he believed that the enjoyment of freedom of expression could be curtailed by considerations of public need, especially society's interest in national security. Indeed, in the last opinion he registered as a member of the Court, a dissent in the *Pentagon Papers Cases*, he argued that courts should defer to the executive's determination that a publication would impair national security so long as the head of the appropriate executive department had personally made such a judgment and the publication at issue lay within the realm of foreign relations. In his view, the judiciary had no business "redetermin[ing] for itself the probable impact of disclosure on the national security."[3]

Finally, Harlan II was less deferential than the elder Justice to government's regulatory authority over business and industry. By the time of his appointment to the Court in 1955, the laissez-faire doctrines against which his grandfather had contended had been so firmly repudiated that Harlan II would have been unlikely to attempt to resurrect them, even had he wished to. But Harlan II's reputation as a lawyer, unlike his grandfather's, rested primarily on his skillful representation of substantial financial interests. It was not surprising, therefore, that he frequently voted to limit the reach of antitrust laws and other federal regulatory legislation. Nor was it remarkable that when Justice Hugo L. Black sought to write an opinion for the Court rejecting entirely the application of substantive due process in economic cases, and thus the power of courts to rule at all on the "reasonableness" of economic legislation, Harlan II refused to join his senior colleague's effort, even after its tone had been considerably moderated. The elder Harlan had not entirely rejected the power of courts to rule on the reasonableness of economic controls via due process either. But when measured in the context of the very different Courts on which each served, Harlan I's willingness to defer to legislative judgments in cases involving economic controls over individual freedom may have been greater than his grandson's.[4]

Harlan II's restraintist posture was not limited, of course, to the sorts of issues the first Harlan had confronted. In reapportionment and other cases, for example, he objected to the Warren Court's use of the equal protection guarantee in subjecting nonracial forms of discrimination to strict judicial scrutiny and in protecting rights not recognized elsewhere in the Constitution. He vehemently dissented when in 1967 the Court overturned a 1958 precedent he had joined and held that Congress had no power to strip United States citizens of their citizenship, even for acts of loyalty to other nations.[5]

Not surprisingly perhaps, given his experience as a federal and state prosecutor and as counsel to the New York State crime commission, he was also exceptionally deferential to government in criminal procedure cases. In his first full term on the Court, he dissented when a majority held in *Griffin* v. *Illinois* that indigent defendants were entitled to free transcripts or comparable assistance in appealing their convictions; the potential implications of such a decision for other elements of the criminal justice system were simply too daunting for him to accept. His dissents in *Mapp* v. *Ohio*, requiring the suppression of unconstitutionally seized evidence in state trials, and *Miranda* v. *Arizona*, imposing standards on the interrogation practices of law-enforcement officers, among numerous other cases, also reflected his concern that the Warren Court was imposing constitutionally unwarranted restrictions on the ability of police to maintain an orderly society. In these and other contexts, he accorded the political branches of government, especially those of the states, great latitude.[6]

But neither was Justice Harlan entirely predictable in his approach to issues confronting the Court. In *Cumming* v. *Richmond County Board of Education*, decided just three years after his *Plessy* dissent, the first Harlan spoke for a unanimous Court in permitting a Georgia school board to discontinue operation of its black high school for financial reasons while existing white schools remained open. Given the broad traditional authority of the states in the area of education, Harlan I had concluded, the federal courts could intervene in such cases only in the event of a "clear and unmistakable disregard" of constitutional rights.[7]

There were also exceptions to Harlan II's restraintist stance in civil liberties cases. His 1958 opinion for the Court in *NAACP* v. *Alabama* was the first to extend constitutional protection to freedom of association. He first questioned the constitutionality of Connecticut's now notorious ban on contraceptives in *Poe* v. *Ullman* (1961), four years before the Court's historic decision in *Griswold* v. *Connecticut* which invalidated the statute on privacy grounds. Arguably, the substantive due process rationale on which Harlan based the right of privacy in his *Poe* dissent and in a Griswold concurrence was much more the precursor of the Court's recognition of a right of abortion in *Roe* v. *Wade* than the "liberal-activist" Justice Douglas's opinion in *Griswold*. Indeed, Douglas's attempt there to tie the right of privacy to specific guarantees of the Bill of Rights prompted Justice Harlan to repudiate any doctrine limiting the scope of constitutional guarantees to those stated in the document's text. Harlan also joined the Court in extending the Fourth Amendment's protection against unreasonable search and seizure to police eavesdrop practices, and in his last term on the Court he spoke for the majority in upholding the individual's right to display expletives in public places and in striking down on due process grounds filing fees for indigents seeking to initiate divorce proceedings.[8] In short, his constitutional jurisprudence, like his grandfather's, was decidedly more complicated and discerning than his generally restraintist posture might suggest.

Indeed, it is fair to say that the second Justice Harlan was one of the most thoughtful and perceptive jurists ever to occupy a seat on the nation's supreme bench. In his foreword to a collection of the Justice's writings, Professor Paul Freund observed:

> Justice Harlan's special quality is precisely this gift of conjoining the particular with the general, or rather of finding the general implanted within the particular. Thus one reads his opinions with the secure feeling that they will convey an understanding of the exact controversy to be resolved and will disclose the philosophical wellsprings of the Justice's position. . . .
>
> This accomplishment, I believe, is what principally attracts law school students to Justice Harlan's opinions. The positions he takes on constitutional issues, stressing continuity and tradition more strongly than is fashionable with many students, do not cloud their appreciation of the opinions themselves. Indeed, the very students who more often than not regret the Justice's position freely acknowledge that when he has written a concurring or dissenting opinion they turn to it first, for a full and candid exposition of the case and an intellectually rewarding analysis of the issues. They sometimes regret that their heart's desire has not been supported with equal cogency in the Court's prevailing opinion, sharing as they do an aversion to what a certain English judge called well-meaning sloppiness of thought.[9]

Admittedly, Professor Freund's impressions may have been colored somewhat by his essential agreement with major elements of Justice Harlan's jurisprudence. But few, if any, would dispute his central premise. Even Justice William Brennan, one of Harlan's principal jurisprudential antagonists, has praised the Justice's "massive scholarship."[10]

That Justice Harlan to date has been the subject of relatively little scholarly attention is not, however, particularly surprising. Following his appointment in 1955, he became a prominent member of the shifting restraintist bloc Justice Felix Frankfurter had attempted to lead since his elevation to the bench in 1939. He and Frankfurter were friends before Harlan's appointment; they became close friends and frequent allies during their years together on the Court; and Harlan embraced the high regard for precedent, separation of powers, federalism, and deference to the judgments of elected policymakers, which formed core elements of his senior colleague's jurisprudence. It has been natural, therefore, for students of the Court to view Harlan largely as Frankfurter's protégé and Harlan's opinions as essentially extensions of Frankfurter's own views.

Harlan's personality may be another factor helping to explain his failure to date to receive the attention he deserves. In an interview with a reporter shortly after his death, Justice Potter Stewart, another of Harlan's close friends and frequent allies, praised his colleague's judicial abilities, but added: "What truly set him apart was his character, not his scholarship. His generous and gallant spirit, his selfless courage, his freedom from all guile, his total decency."[11] Justice Black, one of Harlan's principal jurisprudential antagonists in many arenas but also a close personal friend, expressed the same sentiments more colorfully and succinctly. "John Harlan," the New Deal Democrat once remarked, "is one of the few people who convince me that there is such a thing as a good Republican."[12] But whoever first referred to Harlan as "Frankfurter without mustard" perhaps best captured his personality. Harlan was a gracious, decent man, well regarded by jurisprudential allies and opponents alike, almost never involved in Court intrigues. Such figures rarely whet the interest of biographers or other Court observers. Nor do self-effacing figures who lack the self-confidence of their counterparts. Nathan Lewin, who served as Justice Harlan's clerk during the the Court's 1961–62 term, has written:

> Justice David Brewer, who sat on the Supreme Court with the senior Harlan for twenty years, said of his colleague that he "goes to bed every night with one hand on the Constitution and the other on the Bible, and he sleeps the sweet sleep of justice and righteousness." The grandson was not given to such certitude, and neither the words of the Constitution nor the lessons of Holy Scripture made his sleep less troubled. Skepticism and open-mindedness were his characteristics, and they fit in well with his philosophy of the judiciary and with is own innate modesty. In this, he stood in sharp contrast to Justice Black, to whom right was right and wrong was wrong, and the Constitution could be counted on to mark the difference.[13]

A story Professor Charles Alan Wright relates about the second Harlan is equally instructive. At one of the Court's sessions toward the end of his tenure, Harlan announced the majority's decision in an obscure and complicated case involving federal milk marketing regulations. As he began a summary of the opinion he had drafted for the Court, he observed apologetically that "this case does not lend itself well to oral summarization." "He was right," Professor Wright recalls. "I should be surprised if there was a person in the courtroom not already familiar with the case who understood what the Court had done, or why, when Justice Harlan finished." In summarizing his dissent in the case, on the other hand, Justice Black "brought the case alive."

> The issue, in his view, was whether the courts should overrule the judgment of the Secretary of Agriculture and take a substantial sum of money away from the dairy farmers close to Boston and give it to the dairy farmers farther away. To do so, he thought, was to change the historic practice of the industry, to go against the will of Congress, and to disregard the view of the administrator charged with running the program. It was a few weeks before Christmas, and Justice Black concluded that he was not willing to be a party to "giving an $8 million Christmas present to the farmers farther away." For all I know, the majority may

> well have been right in the result they reached but Justice Black certainly persuaded those who heard him that morning that a great injustice had been done.[14]

The point, of course, is not that Justice Harlan was inarticulate. He registered numerous eloquent opinions during his tenure on the Court; his oral summaries were often similarly impressive, especially after 1963, when rapidly failing eyesight obliged him to deliver them entirely from memory, a task he performed with consummate skill. Harlan simply lacked the certitude which enabled Hugo Black to paint with a broad brush, cutting through the complexities of a case to its essential core—even at the risk of oversimplifying the facts and distorting the language and history of relevant law.

Harlan no doubt respected the first Justice Harlan. His instructions that his gravestone read "John M. Harlan," carrying only his middle initial rather than his middle name,[15] probably reflected that respect as much as any desire to perpetuate his own separate identity. He regularly wore on his vest a gold watch the elder Harlan's colleagues had given his grandfather in 1896, and furniture from the elder Justice's chambers occupied prominent places in his own chambers and home. But Harlan II also conceded that his grandfather was given to "overstatement"[16] and sought to tie his own judicial pronouncements closely to the facts of individual cases. His lack of certitude and innate modesty led him to forge a complex judicial and constitutional philosophy which does not lend itself readily to extensive generalization or easy analysis.

Whatever the reasons for such inattention, however, the second Justice Harlan's career and jurisprudence are clearly deserving of extensive examination. When he went on the Court, the outstanding legal reputation he had earned in more than thirty years with one of New York's most prestigious firms prompted those most familiar with his career to term him a "lawyer's lawyer." On his retirement and death in 1971, he was praised as a "judge's judge." Nor is it fair or accurate to dismiss him as essentially Felix Frankfurter's shadow. It is true, as his sister Edith once put it, that Harlan "took many pages from Justice Frankfurter's book."[17] But their jurisprudential positions were hardly identical. Harlan may have been an even more eloquent, balanced, cautious, and ultimately effective defender of their mutual positions than Frankfurter himself. Most critically perhaps, Frankfurter left the Court in 1962, at the beginning of the most "liberal-activist" period in the Court's history to date. In fact, Frankfurter's retirement and the appointment of Arthur J. Goldberg to replace him was a principal catalyst for the rapid expansion of constitutional liberties by the Warren Court in the middle and late sixties. It was thus John Harlan, not Felix Frankfurter, who was the principal Court critic of Warren era trends.

Nor is Justice Harlan's significance limited to the Warren period. When David Souter was appointed to the Court in 1990, he cited Harlan's approach to constitutional interpretation as his own model.[18] And while Harlan arguably displayed a higher regard for precedent and a more balanced response to civil liberties claims than most members of the current Court have demonstrated, developments on the Burger and Rehnquist Courts have reflected more the Justice's thinking than that of his jurisprudential antagonists.

The relative infrequency with which scholars have focused on Harlan's jurisprudence has thus left a sginificant gap in the literature on the Supreme Court and American constitutional law. In some small measure, it is hoped, the pages which follow will help to fill that void.

Greenville, N.C.
April, 1991

T. E. Y

Acknowledgments

Responsibility for what follows is of course mine alone. This book would not have been possible, however, without the assistance of numerous individuals and agencies. I am especially grateful to members of Justice Harlan's family; to J. Edward Lumbard, senior chief judge of the U.S. Courts of Appeals for the Second Circuit and Justice Harlan's intimate friend for more than forty years; to John Twarda, longtime caretaker of the Harlan family home at Weston, Connecticut; and to Paul Burke, Harlan's messenger during most of his years on the Supreme Court, who shared their valuable memories. Mr. Twarda loaned me several photographs, and Judge Lumbard was a constant source of encouragement and advice, assisting me in securing financial support for the project, providing me with numerous leads to Harlan contemporaries, and carefully reviewing the manuscript.

The Justice's only child, Eve Dillingham, shared with me her memories of her father, as well as his World War II diary and many valuable family photographs, and also read the manuscript. His sisters Janet White, now deceased, and Edith Powell graciously agreed to be interviewed, and Mrs. Powell provided me with additional photographs. Justice Harlan's nephew Roger A. Derby gave me access to important Harlan family papers, read the manuscript, and furnished excellent insights into the family's history.

Grants from the Earhart Foundation, the William Nelson Cromwell Foundation, the Southern Regional Education Board, and the East Carolina University Research Committee provided critical financial support. Assistance provided by the archival staffs of the Seeley G. Mudd Manuscript Library at Princeton University, repository for the John Marshall Harlan papers; the manuscript division of the Library of Congress; the law libraries of the University of Virginia and Dewey Ballantine, the Justice's law firm; and the Joyner Library of East Carolina University is deeply appreciated. Equally helpful were the Justice's clerks and contemporaries who agreed to be interviewed. I am also extremely grateful to Mrs. Paul M. Bator, who shared with me transcripts of interviews that her late husband, one of the Justice's earliest clerks, conducted in connection with his research for a biography of Justice Harlan.

Finally, I wish to extend my sincere thanks to Cynthia M. Smith and Violet Blackwelder, whose clerical assistance was flawless; to my superb Oxford editor Valerie Aubry and her assistants Niko Pfund and Carol Solis-Cohen for encouragement and guidance throughout the project; to Linda Grossman for outstanding copyediting; and to my wife, Mary Alice, and our children Sarah and Cole, to whom this book is lovingly dedicated.

Contents

John Marshall Harlan

1

Buckner's "Boy Scout"

Family Roots

Like that of most families, John Harlan's family history lacks the factual precision he was reputed to have admired. John Harlan, a seventeenth-century English gentleman, had four sons. In 1687, two of them, George and Michael, sailed from Liverpool to the New World to escape the persecution Quakers were then suffering in England. George had a son, James, born in Maryland in 1692; James a son George born in Pennsylvania in 1718; and George a son James born in Virginia in 1755. In 1774 James and his brother Silas were part of a company of thirty men who traveled to the Kentucky frontier and built cabins at Harrodsburg. In 1778, they built a stockade fort seven miles up the Salt River from Harrodsburg. Called Harlan's Station, the fort would appear on the first map of Kentucky. Eventually, a stone house was built there also.[1]

In 1779, Silas joined George Roger Clark in the Illinois Indian campaigns. He was killed on August 19, 1782, at the Battle of Blue Lick Springs. But while Silas died without ever having married, his younger brother James married Sarah Caldwell, Silas's sweetheart, and that couple had nine children. One of their sons, also named James, became a leading Kentucky lawyer and politician, serving, at various stages of his career, as a member of the Kentucky legislature, as the state's secretary of state and attorney general, as a two-term member of Congress, and as United States attorney for Kentucky, an appointee of President Lincoln.

James Harlan's son John Marshall Harlan, born in Boyle County in 1833 and named for the great Chief Justice, was also destined to have an active public and political life. Twice a candidate for Kentucky's governorship and, like his father, the state's attorney general from 1863 to 1867, the first Justice Harlan originally became active in national politics at the Republican national convention of 1876, where he helped secure Rutherford B. Hayes's nomination to the presidency. And while he was overlooked in a bid to become Hayes's attorney general, in 1877 he accepted an appointment to a seat on the Supreme Court. His thirty-four-year tenure on the Court, from December 10, 1877, until his death on October 14, 1911, was exceeded, until William O. Douglas, only by justices Stephen Field and John Marshall. Also, from 1889 to his death, he taught constitutional law at what is now George Washington University. And in 1893 he served as one of the American arbitrators at a Paris conference convened to settle disputes between the United States and England over Alaskan seal fisheries.

Although James and John Marshall Harlan were not abolitionists, the elder Harlan emancipated certain of his slaves before the Civil War. Once the nation erupted in war, he and his son were instrumental in preventing Kentucky, where opinion was sharply divided, from joining the Confederacy. When Kentucky refused to furnish its quota of conscript soldiers to the Union, the younger Harlan volunteered to fight for the North and organized a regiment of militia, which he led in combat against the South. He began as a colonel of the Tenth Kentucky Infantry, but by 1863 was acting commander of a brigade. In fact, at the time his father's death made it necessary for him to return home, his nomination by President Lincoln to the rank of brigadier general was pending before the Senate.

However, the first John Marshall Harlan would always maintain southern sympathies. Family lore relates that during the war he captured Lucius Quintus Cincinnatus Lamar, a Mississippian with whom he would later serve on the Supreme Court, and then permitted Lamar to escape while transporting the Confederate officer to a military prison.[2] As a member of the Louisiana Commission, created by President Hayes shortly before Harlan's appointment to the Court, Harlan opposed the return of federal troops to that state. Years later, when the Court heard argument in a case growing out of a heated, at times violent, election dispute between Kentucky Republicans and Democrats, during which the former's gubernatorial candidate apparently shot his Democratic opponent, "the sympathies of Justice Harlan" for his troubled and beloved state "were so awakened that he shed tears."[3]

But Harlan I's constitutional loyalties were to the Union, the Thirteenth, Fourteenth, and Fifteenth amendments, and the principles of Reconstruction. During his long tenure as a justice, he repeatedly dissented from the Court's repudiation of Reconstruction doctrine.

John Marshall Harlan and his wife, Malvina F. Shanklin of Indiana, whom he married in 1856, had three daughters and three sons—James Shanklin, a lawyer who was to serve as attorney general of Puerto Rico and chairman of the Interstate Commerce Commission; Richard Davenport, a Presbyterian minister and university administrator; and John Maynard Harlan, the second Justice Harlan's father. Of the three sons, John Maynard Harlan was to prove the most colorful, dynamic, and enigmatic. Born in Frankfort, Kentucky, in 1864, John Maynard was educated at Princeton, where he played center and guard on the football team and was also a member of its baseball team as well as Ivy, Princeton's most exclusive eating club. Following graduation from Princeton in 1884, graduate study at the University of Berlin, the study of law at George Washington University, and a stint as his father's legal secretary, he moved in 1888 to Chicago and began a lengthy legal practice there with a series of partners, including his brother James.

John Maynard's parents often vacationed at Block Island, an exclusive resort off Long Island. On one of the family's summer holidays there, during or shortly after his years at Princeton, John Maynard met Elizabeth Palmer Flagg of Yonkers. Like the Harlans, Elizabeth Flagg's ancestors had migrated to America from England. The first Flagg to arrive in this country, a middle-class Englishman, settled in Massachusetts about 1640. Much to his parents' dismay, he married a servant girl who had followed him to America on a separate boat. Elizabeth's father, Ethan Flagg, was a prominent and wealthy citizen with extensive landholdings in Westchester County. Shortly after their first meeting in Block Island, Elizabeth and John Maynard fell in love; in 1890, they were married.[4]

John Maynard established a successful law practice in Chicago, but his abiding interest was politics. Harold J. Ickes, then a young Chicagoan who later was to serve in Franklin Roosevelt's cabinet, has described Chicago's city council of that period as "forever on the auction block—ready to go to the highest bidder." The "Gray Wolves" was the popular label for Chicago councilmen most susceptible to the temptations of graft. Their leader was Martin B. Madden, a Republican alderman. And the council's chief corrupter, by Ickes's account, was one Charles T. Yerkes, who had earlier served a prison sentence for municipal wrongdoing in Philadelphia. After his arrival in Chicago, Yerkes acquired substantial control of the city's four traction, or streetcar, lines, and no device, apparently, was beneath him in his efforts to secure favorable franchise arrangements from those aldermen most receptive to his favors.[5]

But not all Chicagoans or members of the council condoned Yerkes's corrupting influence. Several alderman spoke out against Yerkes, Madden, and their henchmen; a Municipal Voters' League was organized to support the election of good-government candidates. In 1896 John Maynard Harlan was elected to the council from the twenty-first ward and quickly became the recognized leader of the city's Republican reform elements. His term on the council, a political opponent later wrote, was "full of pyrotechnics" as he "eagerly poured vials of wrath on Yerkes and his ilk."[6]

Bolstered by the support his council activities generated among reform elements, in 1897 John Maynard became a candidate for mayor. His reformist zeal made Republican regulars uncomfortable, and they denied him the party's nomination, opting instead for a respectable, "safe" lawyer and judge. But John Maynard was to be a candidate anyway. A movement "encouraged and supported" by reformist newspapers, Harold Ickes later recalled, "sprang into being almost overnight, intent upon running knight-errant Harlan as an independent candidate. Civic enthusiasm shot up. Nominating petitions were circulated and signed in vast numbers, and Harlan entered the race as an independent Republican."[7] It soon became clear, moreover, that the official GOP candidate and another hopeful had no chance—the leading contenders were to be Harlan and his Democratic opponent, Carter H. Harrison, the son of a former mayor.

Harlan ran a poorly financed but strong race. The former football player, who was six feet tall, had the sturdy build of an athlete, and boxed two or three times a week to keep in shape, struck an impressive figure on the campaign platform. He was also a pugnacious opponent. "Should anyone be bold enough to venture a rude interruption of him," Carter Harrison later wrote, "it was his habit to advance truculently to the footlights, invite the obstructer to the platform, there to fight it out."[8] Family lore includes similar stories.[9] In Harrison's view, the admiration of the "army of lusty young two-fisted chaps" his opponent attracted "was based more on his reputation as a scrapper than on the things for which he stood ready to fight." But Harlan's voter appeal was not a product simply of his contentious spirit and combative reputation. He was also a superb speaker. Over the opposition of his brother James, Ickes, and other members of his campaign organization, John Maynard decided to hold a series of noonday meetings at the Central Music Hall in downtown Chicago. Staff members were fearful that few people would be willing to attend a lunch-hour political speech, but the crowds the colorful, eloquent, and bombastic candidate drew were larger than the music hall could accommodate. He not only lashed out at Yerkes and Madden, he also secured a list of the prominent businessmen who served as directors of Yerkes's traction companies and demanded that they assume some responsibility for Yerkes's crooked dealings. In Ickes's judgment, not even William Jennings Bryan's "Cross of Gold" speech matched Harlan's last speech of the campaign, delivered at a rally the night before the election. "John Harlan lifted that crowd out of its seats that night. My backbone had never had such a workout as that scene gave it. How I envied Harlan his power, which was the power of sincerity and truth—the power to advocate boldly the just cause—in strong, forceful speech, expressed in brilliant phrases and beautiful English."[10]

Harlan would prove a master, moreover, at controlling and manipulating hostile audiences, and not merely through intimidation. This was amply demonstrated even before the mayoral race. In 1896, when William McKinley was running for the presidency, Harlan presided at a political rally before which the industrialist Mark Hanna, McKinley's key financial supporter and adviser, was to be the principal speaker. Feelings had run high between labor and capital during the campaign, and Hanna was considered by labor sympathizers as capitalism's "most vicious representative." A crowd of workers had organized to wreck the rally, and when Harlan rose to introduce Hanna, the mob jeered. When

John Maynard began to speak, someone in the audience shouted, "Louder!" "If the angel Gabriel tried to speak," Harlan retorted, "some damn fool would yell 'louder!' " The crowd started to laugh. "I never knew a public speaker," a friend later wrote Harlan's son, "who could handle himself more skillfully with an unfriendly audience. When John Maynard got control of the crowd and he called for fair play and courtesy . . . [t]he crowd listened . . . and the planned rough-house subsided."[11] In the 1897 mayoralty campaign, Harlan would have the same effect on his audiences.[12]

Finally, during the race for mayor Harlan could draw on his growing reputation as one of Chicago's more respected citizens.[13] An example of the respect Chicagoans had for him is reflected in an incident which occurred years after the election. When Barney Balaban of Paramount Pictures and his brother built the Tivoli Theater there, unfounded rumors circulated that the balcony was structurally defective and the theater a menace. When the rumors reached alarming proportions, the brothers retained Harlan to represent their interests. They selected Harlan not only because of his legal skill, but because he was a man, Barney Balaban later wrote Harlan's son, "whose reputation for integrity was beyond reproach, and whom the public would believe, simply because they believed in [his] forthrightness." Harlan actually occupied the theater stage on several occasions, telling audiences the story of the vicious rumor campaign. Public fears were allayed, and the rumors soon ceased—a consequence, the Balaban brothers were certain, of the high esteem in which Harlan was held by Chicagoans.[14]

All these factors served him well in the mayor's race. But not well enough. Carter Harrison, by his own admission, was no match for his opponent on the stump. To offset Harlan's robust football-hero image, Harrison took up bicycling, the most popular exercise of the period, completed several "centuries," or 100-mile bicycle treks, had posters circulated picturing him in cycling garb mounted on a bike, and campaigned as the "cyclers' champion." Harrison also had the support of Chicago's Democratic political machine, as well as Yerkes and company, who were apparently never able to corrupt Harrison, but obviously considered him less a threat than the reformist zealot Harlan. "Charles T. Yerkes issued his instructions to his employees yesterday morning," the *Chicago Record* reported on April 6. "They were told to vote against John Maynard Harlan and for Carter H. Harrison. . . . These orders were delivered to the men by the [streetcar] barn bosses in every barn in the west and north sides yesterday before the men went to work." Harlan, the paper added, was not surprised. "Why should not Yerkes try to defeat me? His franchises are about to expire, and he knows that he will have to pay [the city] for what he gets if I am elected mayor." The outcome was hardly a surprise either. In the end, Harrison won a clear majority; Harlan came in a distant third.[15]

Harlan did not seek re-election to the city council. In 1903, he again sought the Republican nomination for mayor, but did not mount an independent race when his party again chose another candidate. By 1905, according to Harold Ickes, the Republicans had apparently decided that the only way to purge the would-be reformer from their ranks was to make him the party's candidate for mayor, and Harlan received their nomination. At this point in Chicago's history, public support for municipal ownership of the traction systems was high, and a campaign based on that issue seemed a certain vote-getter. But to Ickes's horror, and apparently to James Harlan's dismay as well, John Maynard began to equivocate, adopting a conciliatory stance toward the private traction interests he had earlier condemned. The effect on his campaign was disastrous. Late in the race, he began to attack his Democratic opponent's ties with a particularly unsavory ward politician. But that tactic was too little, too late. Harlan's opponent won by 23,000 votes, and the abrupt modification of Harlan's stance on the traction question left many of his reform-minded supporters permanently disillusioned.[16]

The 1905 campaign by no means ended John Maynard Harlan's involvement in politics. He once ran on an independent ticket for the Illinois governorship. He had a role in Woodrow Wilson's selection as the Democratic presidential candidate in 1912, supported the aborted attempt to mount a Progressive party presidential campaign with Theodore Roosevelt in 1916, and stumped in 1928 for Al Smith on the ground that national prohibition, which Smith vowed to end, was the issue of the day. Earlier, in 1924, he proposed a national plebiscite to determine the public's position on the Eighteenth Amendment's nationwide ban on the sale of alcoholic beverages. At various points during his career, he drafted proposals for improving international harmony and security. But he never again was to attract the voter enthusiasm his initial mayoralty campaign had generated. Nor was politics ever again to assume the central role in his life that it had played during his early years in Chicago.[17]

Particularly in light of the fact that he played a prominent part in Chicago's enactment of traction legislation, Harlan's switch on the issue was probably influenced most by financial considerations and little, if at all, by any basic shift in his political leanings. Harlan's wife, Elizabeth, was, by all accounts, a more practical person than her husband. There is little evidence that she found his political career particularly distasteful. But his political activities were expensive and took valuable time away from his law practice. Elizabeth might well have preferred that her husband concentrate more on the law and less on politics. Harlan had no inherited wealth, and while Elizabeth's father had been a wealthy man, her oldest sister's husband, who had been given control over management of the Flagg daughters' inheritance, had proven to be a poor trustee. John Maynard's law practice was thus the family's principal source of income,[18] and his involvement in politics a strain on the family's finances.

It was not surprising, then, that when Harlan yielded to his supporters' pleas that he make a second run for mayor in 1903, he had remarked, "I'll make the fight, but I don't know how I am ever going to square it with Mrs. Harlan."[19] The day after the 1905 election, he told Ickes that he had been offered a $10,000 retainer and $2,000 monthly by federal judge Peter S. Grosscup to represent the "people's interest" in receivership proceedings affecting Yerkes's traction holdings, then pending in Grosscup's court. Knowing of the judge's ties to Yerkes and believing that Grosscup saw Harlan as merely a "respectable front" for the protection of the traction interests, Ickes urged his friend to decline the judge's offer.

> I pleaded with him not to destroy the faith of those thousands of young men and others in the city who had followed him in his fights and who still believed that he had been right. On this subject, I became emotional, because I felt it deeply. Tears trickled down my fast leathering cheeks and I noticed some in my former leader's eyes, too. All afternoon I wrestled with him, but his mind was made up. He had already committed himself to Mrs. Harlan. He assured me that he would continue to fight to protect the people. I told him that he couldn't and at the same time serve his real clients—the traction companies.[20]

But Harlan persisted in his decision, and in the ensuing years he represented the traction interests in protracted, and lucrative, litigation.[21]

The Early Years

Whatever the state of their finances, the Harlans mingled with Chicago's financial and social elites; and their son John Marshall, born May 20, 1899, and daughters Elizabeth, Janet, and Edith, enjoyed a comfortable upper-class childhood. The family's spacious three-story home was situated on Division Street, a few blocks from Lake Shore Drive, in one of the city's more fashionable residential areas. The Harlans' eldest daughter Elizabeth made her debut in Chicago, and as a young child John attended the exclusive Chicago Latin School, located across the street from the Harlan home.[22]

John was close to both his parents but particularly fond of his mother, whom he resembled in both facial features and temperament. But while his personality lacked his father's bombastic, pugnacious qualities, he was not, his sister Janet recalled, "a goody, goody little boy at all." Instead, he was full of devilment. Janet was only three years younger than her brother, and they played—and plotted mischief—together constantly. In the Harlan household, the children were served supper before their parents. John Marshall and Janet relished teasing the maids who served them. "When the maids would pour us milk," Janet recalled, "we would lift up our glasses, ostensibly to help the maid doing the pouring.

Then, when the pitcher was in full swing, we'd pull our glasses away, causing the milk to spill. We caught them time and time again that way. I think they thought we didn't know what we were doing—but we did. It was great fun!" On another occasion, they were playing "Pullman Porter" on a very tall clothes bureau, using its drawers as steps, when Janet caused the bureau to tip over onto her brother. "It didn't really hurt him," she remembered. "But mother rushed upstairs terribly alarmed, when she heard the noise."

Whether always intended or not, John was also a regular source of humorous remarks. At the suggestion of their son Richard, Justice and Mrs. Harlan had begun spending their summers at Pointe-au-Pic, Quebec, on the lower St. Lawrence River, or Murray Bay, as the area was more generally known. Eventually, the elder Harlans built a house, which they named "Braemead," there, in a sunny meadow on a high bluff. Richard's wife, Margaret, also had a house there, and John Maynard and his family rented a cottage there each summer as well. The Murray Bay church, which the Justice served as one of two trustees, held Anglican services one Sunday, Presbyterian services the next. The Harlans were Presbyterian, but one Sunday John and the other children attended an Anglican service, conducted in Latin. When they returned home, Justice Harlan asked his grandson, "How was church?" "Oh, it was all right," John replied. "The minister dressed in a sheet and spoke Chinese."[23]

While John would continue to spend his childhood summers in Murray Bay, his days in Chicago were to be brief. Although mischievous and fun-loving, John was a delicate and sickly child. In time, his mother became extremely concerned about his health, and his father, his sister Elizabeth remembered, "looked askance at him and wondered if he was going to grow up to be a brownie or [a man]. . . . My father was not very understanding of children at all and very stern with the men." A Chicago physician advised Mrs. Harlan, according to Elizabeth, that it "was kill or cure with my brother"—that "he should go to a very rigorous climate which would either establish his health or [cause him to] get a great deal sicker and probably die."

When John was eight, his parents placed him in the preparatory school of Upper Canada College, in Toronto. Naturally, he was soon very homesick. In a poignant early letter to his father, he wrote:

> I wish very much that you would come up to school and see me so that I can talk to you. I wish that I could go home.
>
> Write to me often so that I shall have something to look forward to.
>
> I am your loving and
> Devoted
> Son,
> John[24]

Shortly after his arrival in Toronto, he also contracted scarlet fever. "And my mother went rushing up there," Elizabeth later recalled. "She wasn't allowed to see him—she had never had scarlet fever . . . and she used to spend every day trying to talk to him through the window . . . [while] this little boy [stood there] with tears streaming down his face." Once their son had recovered, the Harlans brought him back to Chicago for the balance of the school year. The next year, however, he returned to Canada. And when J.S.H. Guest, the Toronto school's headmaster, opened the Appleby School in Oakville, Ontario, in September of 1911, John accompanied Guest to Appleby, where he remained for four years.

To the extent possible, Guest modeled Appleby after the English public (or private) schools, and John thrived there.

> In qualities of leadership [Guest later wrote] he has always been distinguished. While here, he made a most efficient Prefect, and, in his last year, a very capable Head Boy. This last position is, in this school, one of great responsibility, and I do not think that a holder of it has ever surpassed the tact, strength, and conscientiousness, which John Harlan displayed.
>
> In athletics, he was always keen, capable of very considerable endurance, and sufficiently distinguished to be chosen to represent the school in two of the games which we play, namely Cricket and Rugby Football.[25]

John's parents were pleased with Appleby, but they realized that his Canadian schooling had offered their son little opportunity to make American friends. Consequently, for his last year of preparatory school they enrolled him in New York's prestigious Lake Placid School. There he studied and played with young men from some of the nation's leading families. The school's fall and spring terms were held in Lake Placid and the winter term in Coconut Grove, Florida. Its elite student body totaled about forty-five, with ten to twelve in each class. While there, John played basketball, football, and baseball, and also acted the role of Julius Caesar in a school play.[26]

In 1916, John entered Princeton, his father's alma mater, where he developed a distinguished academic and extracurricular record. Like his father, he was a member of Ivy. He was also chairman of the *Daily Princetonian* and president of his class for three of his four years there. On occasion, he became involved in the political debates of that era. In early 1920, he and a fellow student debated the League of Nations covenant then pending in the Senate, with Harlan supporting the reservations proposed by Senator Henry Cabot Lodge. Lodge, Harlan argued, did "not seek to deny the responsibility of the United States to the rest of the world," he simply conditioned that duty on another, "more fundamental one—the right of our people to say what those responsibilities shall be." No League arrangement should be adopted, he insisted, which would undermine the Monroe Doctrine and permit the extension of foreign influences in the Western hemisphere. Properly limited, however, the treaty, in his view, was "worth a try-out as the best thing at hand."[27]

Harlan's closest associates at Princeton, like those at Lake Placid, were the scions of prominent and powerful families. When he was chairman of the *Princetonian*, Charles Scribner of the publishing family was the paper's president and Harvey Firestone, Jr., its secretary-treasurer. Somewhat ironically, given his Republican leanings and the ultimate direction of his career, another of his college friends was Adlai E. Stevenson, the future Illinois governor, two-time Democratic presidential candidate, and United Nations ambassador. Harlan dated Stevenson's sister Buffie regularly during his Princeton years; he and Adlai also served together in the Princeton Naval Unit, an organization for students who wished to enter the Navy but were not yet of enlistment age. Harlan and Stevenson joined the unit, which was headed by a retired admiral and numbered about 250 cadets, when it was first organized in the fall of 1918; at one point they held the unit's top two command positions. To provide all the members with rudimentary officers' training, however, the admiral decided to rotate all command positions, and Harlan and Stevenson soon found themselves back in the rear ranks—"a readjustment," as Harlan later put it, "that required some readjustment."

Hoping to salvage some measure of unit status and independence for themselves, the two then persuaded the admiral to form a band. Although neither could play a note of music, Harlan wrangled an appointment as band leader and Stevenson became his deputy. The band and its conductors practiced assiduously every afternoon, and eventually they mastered two tunes—"I've Been Working on the Railroad" and "Smiles." Later that fall, the naval units of several Ivy League schools marched in a combined parade in Manhattan. With Harlan and Stevenson leading them, the Princeton bandsmen marched up Thirty-fourth Street and into Fifth Avenue. Harlan later described what happened next.

> Adlai and I, both with batons, turned right on Fifth Avenue and we struck up [our first] tune and finished it, and then we moved into our second number, and suddenly the volume of music got dimmer and dimmer and dimmer, until I looked behind [us] . . . and found that we [two] were marching majestically down Fifth Avenue while the entire battalion had gone the other way, including the band. . . . We ignominiously turned around and re-established ourselves at the head of the battalion.[28]

His bandsmanship notwithstanding, Harlan's record at Princeton placed him in contention for a Rhodes Scholarship at Oxford University. J.S.H. Guest, his Appleby headmaster, wrote Princeton's Rhodes committee:

> I do not think . . . that of all the boys who have passed through my hands, I could name one who fulfills more completely the requirements called for by the conditions of the Rhodes Trust, than John Harlan. . . . When [he] left us, it would have been easy for him . . . to have entered

> Oxford or Cambridge without any special preparation. With five years further intellectual work, he should . . . be assured of taking a high place in any course at Oxford that he may choose.[29]

His other references were equally glowing, and in 1920, his last year at Princeton, Harlan became a Rhodes Scholar and began a three-year course of study in law and jurisprudence at Oxford's Balliol College, the university's law school.

Harlan's years at Oxford confirmed the high regard for things British he had begun to acquire at Appleby. The British insistence on form and structure for their own sake both annoyed and amused him, but later descriptions of him as an Anglophile were essentially accurate. Perhaps as a counterpoint to his combative, volatile father, Harlan was an extremely gracious, likeable young man who made friends wherever he happened to be. England was no exception. He forged permanent friendships with many of his Oxford classmates and faculty and visited with his classmates' families in England and Scotland during Oxford holidays. He also enjoyed, his sister Edith later recalled, the luxurious treatment accorded Oxford students. Their living quarters were spartan at best, but numerous servants were available to attend to their needs. Such indulgences were apparently no obstacle to his scholarship, however. David H. McAlpin, a Lake Placid and Princeton classmate who was to become one of Harlan's closest friends, visited him at Oxford, then went on a holiday with him and other friends to France and Spain. Even on that trip, McAlpin later recalled, Harlan worked. "John had a whole case full of books [with him. In Spain,] everyone would take a siesta from about twelve until four in the afternoon. . . . Most people would sleep [during] siesta. John worked. John was very conscientious always." He finished his years at Oxford with a "First" in jurisprudence, seventh in a class of 120.[30]

Root, Clark, and Emory Buckner

On his return from England, Harlan sought a position with a New York law firm. His sister Elizabeth had married Roger A. Derby. Derby, who was very fond of his brother-in-law, was acquainted with Grenville Clark and Elihu Root, Jr., two of the senior partners in one of the city's most prestigious firms, Root, Clark, Buckner, and Howland. Derby took Harlan to the firm's 31 Nassau Street offices and introduced his brother-in-law to his two friends.[31] But the member of the firm who was to have the greatest influence on both Harlan's association with Root, Clark and his entire career was another senior partner, Emory R. Buckner.

John Harlan and Emory Buckner were both midwestern by birth; otherwise, they came from very different backgrounds. Buckner was born in 1877 on a Pottawattamie County, Iowa, farm, the son of a circuit-riding

Methodist minister. When he was in high school, the family lived in Nebraska. One day Buckner's father suggested that Emory take a course in shorthand during the summer at a business college. After completing such a course, his father explained, a friend's son had secured a position as a stenographer earning $80 a month, a handsome sum in those days. Emory took his father's advice and after high school also attended a teacher's institute. Following a year teaching eighth-grade classes in Oklahoma territory, he drew on his shorthand training to become court reporter for the chief justice of the Oklahoma Supreme Court. He worked with the chief justice three years, traveling about the court's jurisdiction and gathering valuable insights into the law and, especially, human nature. Emory enjoyed his work, the pay was more than adequate, and had it not been for his father, he might have given up plans to become a lawyer and remained a court reporter the rest of his life. But the elder Buckner was determined that Emory would attend college, and eventually he did, graduating Phi Beta Kappa from the University of Nebraska in 1904. In 1907, he received a law degree from Harvard, worked a few months for a New York firm, then became an assistant U.S. attorney. In 1912, he resigned his federal position to become counsel to the Aldermanic Police Investigating Committee, established to inquire into corruption in the New York police department. Then he joined Root, Clark.[32]

When he and John Harlan first met, Buckner had become Root, Clark's chief litigator and one of New York's foremost trial lawyers. A master at trial preparation, who marshalled every fact of conceivable relevance and skillfully anticipated his opponents' every ploy, he was equally adept in the courtroom—eloquent in oral argument, formidable at cross-examination. He had developed, too, a reputation as a man of high honor, with a deep commitment to justice and fair play. One day in 1923, the year he and John Harlan met, Buckner's father wrote a letter to a newspaper, announcing that he could no longer believe any passage of the Bible which reflected adversely on the goodness of God. Methodist leaders, as the elder Buckner's bishop put it, were "both amazed and shocked" at his "unprovoked and unwarranted" heresy. But the church hierarchy made no public charge, ordered no hearing. Instead, the Methodist conference at its next meeting simply placed the controversial cleric on its list of retired clergy, citing no reason for its action. Emory Buckner moved quickly to his father's defense, preparing and circulating—at a personal expense of $18,000—documents attacking the church's stance. "Buckner's campaign," according to a contemporary account, "drove his father's enemies first to explanations—which did not explain—and then to embarrassed silence. It made the Buckner case a *cause célèbre* from one end of the country to the other. It left the fundamentalists . . . without a leg to stand on."[33] In his legal career, Buckner displayed the same sort of conviction.

"Buck," as he was called, also possessed what John Harlan would later characterize as a "remarkable gift . . . for training and inspiring young lawyers and launching them on their careers."[34] As Root, Clark's chief recruiter of new talent and the partner in charge of its large litigation section, Buckner had extensive contact with the firm's younger lawyers. His courtroom skills, exemplary character, and sincere interest in the development of their careers invariably inspired their respect, loyalty, and affection. John Harlan was no exception. "[F]rom a professional standpoint," he once wrote, "Emory Buckner was the greatest single influence in my life. His standards of objectivity, integrity, and professional skill were the most valuable exposure that I think any young man could possible have had."[35] In numerous other settings, he made the same point. Harlan was to be devoted to "Buck" and so aware of his tremendous impact on his life, in fact, that while serving on the Supreme Court, he helped to raise funds for an admiring account of his mentor's life, for which he wrote its introduction. For years after Buckner's death in 1941, Harlan also helped to manage the affairs of his friend's widow and daughters.[36]

Their first meeting, however, was not an entirely happy encounter for Harlan. Buckner believed that Oxford's program in jurisprudence, as John E. F. Wood, one of the university's products and a later Root, Clark recruit, put it, was "a thoroughly impractical course of study which even in England would not have qualified a man for admission to the bar."[37] Buckner was thus concerned that Harlan's studies at Oxford, however intrinsically edifying, would not have equipped him for the practice of law in New York. "When Buckner saw me," Harlan was to recall, "his comment was, 'Well, you'd better go to law school.' I said, 'Well, if I've got to do that, I'll go into business. I've had enough of studying.' "[38] Ultimately, though, it was agreed that Harlan would work for the firm, but be given afternoons off for courses at the New York Law School. On September 24, 1923, *The Bull*, the office bulletin Emory Buckner sponsored, recorded that Harlan became an associate in the firm.[39] Later, Harlan described his New York Law School experience as "more of a 'filler-in' . . . than an integral part of my legal education, which was the product of the jurisprudential approach of Oxford and the practical approach afforded by sitting at the feet of a great lawyer."[40] But the training he received there undoubtedly better equipped him for the New York bar examinations than his years at Oxford had; in 1924, after completing the school's two-year program in a year, he was admitted to the bar.

As he has in other settings, Harlan quickly became a popular addition to the Root, Clark staff. Herbert Brownell, who entered the firm in 1927 and, as President Eisenhower's attorney general, was to play a key role in Harlan's appointment to the federal judiciary, first met Harlan at an annual office party to celebrate the staff's Christmas bonuses. Like others in the firm, Brownell found him "a delightful companion . . . warm-hearted, witty, erudite—a considerate and cultured gentleman." To appear more mature than his twenty-eight years, Harlan had affected a slight stoop and, Brownell would recall, was already "dignified in appearance, even at that early date." But appearances could be deceiving. During dinner, Harlan rose and, in his best Oxford English, "unexpectedly burst into song."

He was just a tender law clerk
Pure and unstained was his name
When a partner made an error
And the poor clerk got the blame.

It's the same the whole world over
It's the clerk that takes the blame
It's the partner gets the gravy
Ain't it all a bleeding shame.

Then the clerk became a partner
And he had a clerk as well
But his heart was still a 'smarting
So he gave his poor clerk hell.[41]

Buckner and the firm's other partners also concluded that the new associate's selection had been a superb professional choice. Buckner was uncertain, as he wrote Felix Frankfurter whimsically in 1925, how much of Harlan's talent was "due to innate ability and how much more or less capacity he would have if he had taken the Harvard Law course, instead of the Oxford course." Buckner and Felix Frankfurter, who was then teaching law at Harvard, were close friends. In fact, Frankfurter had been the first person with whom Buckner dined on his arrival in New York. Buckner would later recruit many of the firm's young associates from Harvard. However, beginning with Harlan, Root, Clark's first Rhodes Scholar, he would also draw them from Oxford. Buckner was convinced that Harlan was "an extremely valuable man,"[42] it was thus hardly surprising that when Buckner agreed to become U.S. attorney in New York, Harlan went along and became a leading member of his staff.

Buckner's "Boy Scouts"

Emory Buckner would serve as U.S. attorney from March 1925, to April 1927. During his tenure, 75 percent of his office's work would be devoted to such matters as fraudulent bankruptcies and mail fraud, only a quarter to Prohibition cases and enforcement of the Volstead Act. But Buckner's encounters with bootleggers were to be by far the most publicized and controversial battles of his tenure. And John Harlan, whom Buckner named to head his office's Prohibition division, was to play an important role in those efforts.[43]

Like most New Yorkers, Buckner hated the Eighteenth Amendment and the very idea of national control over a matter so eminently suited for state and local regulation as the sale of liquor. But he was determined to enforce all statutes, even those he thought foolish. "I am not going to stick my hand in the air," he told reporters shortly after his appointment, "and take an oath for nothing!" Buckner's pledge extended to his personal life. He swore off all intoxicants for the duration of his tenure and exacted the same sacrifice from his staff. Shortly after taking office, he also poured the contents of his ample cellar of bootleg wine and whiskey down the drain—much to the consternation of Harlan and other staffers, who suggested, to no avail, that he simply leave his cellar unlocked, permitting his valued stock to be "stolen." Both summers he was in office, Buckner and several staffers took a fishing trip to the Harlan summer home in Murray Bay, Quebec. While in Canada, his assistants were released from their vows of temperance, but not Buckner. He even resigned all his club memberships, including his beloved Harvard Club, rather than risk being obliged to raid one of his own clubs.[44]

John Harlan was equally skeptical of national prohibition—and committed to its enforcement. "He thought it was ridiculous," his sister Edith has recalled. "We all did. Here we were making gin in our own bathtubs. I made some myself lots of times. We all had our own bootleggers." Harlan became a prolific contributor to *Scraps*, the newsletter Buckner began, publishing in the U.S. attorney's office. One of Harlan's tongue-in-check pieces examined "Opinion Evidence to Establishing Intoxicating Character of Beverages," another the "Diversion of Intoxicating Liquor." Colleagues of that period would later write that he "always made a study, in depth, of anything whereof he wrote."[45]

When Edith graduated from Vassar, Harlan asked her what she would like as a graduation gift. "A bottle of scotch would be very nice," she promptly replied. Her brother obliged, and Edith and several friends proceeded to drink the entire quart, after which, she recalls, they made a terrible scene at the class supper, interrupting each of the Vassar president's after-dinner remarks with gay shrieks of approval. Up to that time, degrees had been conferred at Vassar before the class supper. Following Edith's graduation, by her account, the order of those events was reversed. But her graduation, and Harlan's gift, given in 1930, occurred several years after Harlan's tenure as assistant U.S. attorney. While he was in office, Edith remembers, "he was very scrupulous about attending to the law . . . and of course he never took a drink. He was very careful about that."[46]

But commitment to the Volstead Act was one thing, its effective enforcement quite another. After passage of the federal statute, New York had repealed its own liquor laws. When Buckner took office, two thousand Prohibition cases were pending in the federal court in New York, and that number was increasing at an amazing rate. Every week, New York police officers made thousands of arrests for Volstead Act violations and took about a thousand of those arrested to the federal building—followed by a veritable army of bail bondsmen and lawyers. For the most part, those arrested were waiters, porters, bartenders, bellhops, and assorted other "small fry." Rarely were their employers or the sources of their liquor brought to court. But whatever the status of those arrested, the U.S. attorney's staff and the office of the federal commissioner were no match for what Buckner termed the "Niagara Falls of liquor cases roaring upon them"; only one of the district's six judges devoted even part of his time to the Prohibition docket. If the situation he had inherited continued, Buckner predicted, "I would find myself at the end of my four-year term about 500 years behind the calendar."[47]

The young associates Buckner recruited from Root, Clark and other firms—"Buckner's Boy Scouts" they were quickly dubbed—would be singularly loyal and dedicated. During his two years as U.S. attorney, moreover, Buckner increased the number of his assistants from thirty-three to fifty. But only Harlan and eleven others were assigned to Prohibition cases—Buckner realized that, given his office's limited budget, a more selective enforcement policy, and one designed to curtail use of the time-consuming jury trials which federal courts were obliged to accord criminal defendants, was imperative if he was to be at all effective in the enforcement of Prohibition. In the West, especially in Chicago, a padlock policy permitted under the Volstead Act had proved to be reasonably successful, and Buckner decided to adopt a similar approach. Instead of focusing on criminal prosecutions, he and Harlan decided to seek injunctions that ordered the closing as public nuisances of nightclubs and other establishments found to be in violation of the law, and forbidding use of the premises for any other purpose as well. Those who ignored a padlock order would be subject to jail and/or fine for contempt of court.[48]

Such a policy offered at least two advantages. First, it focused law enforcement and the glare of publicity on club managers and the owners of real estate on which offending establishments were situated, instead of on waiters, cashiers, and other minor employees. More important perhaps, time-consuming jury trials were required for neither injunction nor contempt proceedings. The new policy would thus relieve the backlog of Prohibition cases clogging the U.S. attorney's office and the federal court.[49]

Buckner embarked upon the padlock policy, in a sense, even before officially assuming his duties as U.S. attorney. Dipping into his own pockets, he gave young Root, Clark associates $1,500 and instructed them to go out and purchase liquor. Not surprisingly, they had no difficulty accomplishing their task. In one club, their waiter had the headwaiter look them over before agreeing to serve them scotch highballs. At another, one of the group was treated coolly until he showed the headwaiter his Phi Beta Kappa key and identified himself as a University of Virginia student. But only two establishments refused to serve them liquor, and in short order all Buckner's money had been spent. On the basis of the evidence thus gathered, he and Harlan initiated padlock proceedings against fourteen Manhattan clubs and restaurants. Numerous additional actions followed, and the press announced that Buckner had plans ultimately to move against some five hundred establishments. Nor was he any respecter of social class; the businesses targeted included many of the district's most exclusive.[50]

In addition to initiating the padlock program, Buckner sought to expedite the processing of minor Prohibition prosecutions. To eliminate the backlog of such cases, he held what the press dubbed "bargain days" for Prohibition violators, promising them fines and no jail term in exchange for guilty pleas. With Harlan's assistance, he also proposed creation of a system of federal police courts empowered to hear Prohibition cases without a jury and appeared before the Senate judiciary committee to argue that such an innovation would permit effective enforcement of the Volstead Act without massive increases in the Prohibition budget. In an accompanying memorandum, which Harlan had probably drafted and both signed, Buckner set the estimated cost of effective enforcement in New York State at approximately $70 million a year if jury trials continued to be required, but at only $20 million annually if they were abolished for petty cases. In response to committee members' questions, he also asked Felix Frankfurter to prepare a memorandum assessing whether jury trials could be eliminated in such cases without adoption of a constitutional amendment.[51]

Buckner and Harlan were to be embroiled in controversy throughout their tenures in the U.S. attorney's office. Under the Supreme Court's 1914 ruling in *Weeks* v. *United States*,[52] evidence seized unconstitutionally by federal agents was inadmissible in federal criminal trials, but the "silver platter" doctrine embedded in the *Weeks* case permitted federal prosecutors to use evidence provided them, on a "silver platter" so to speak, by state officers. During a hearing on a motion to exclude from trial evidence seized during a warrantless raid on a West Sixty-seventh Street speakeasy, the defendants' counsel, who had preceded Harlan as head of the Prohibition division, argued that there was such extensive cooperation between local law enforcement and the U.S. attorney's office in Prohibition cases that any seizure of evidence by police in such cases was tantamount to a federal seizure and thus subject to the *Weeks* rule. In an effort to deflect the defense's contention, Harlan testified that the cooperation of local police with his office had not been "nearly so good" following the appointment of a new police commissioner. Harlan's assistant, J. Edward Lumbard, who had been assigned to work with local officers, also testified that the police had not always followed his instructions. But Lumbard could not cite a single instance in which the police had failed to follow his suggestions, and only two months earlier Emory Buckner had told reporters he was "receiving better cooperation from the Police Department than ever before." The trial court admitted the disputed evidence, but Police Commissioner George V. McLaughlin declined comment on Harlan's testimony and was apparently incensed at any suggestion his office was providing federal authorities anything less than full cooperation.[53]

That evening Harlan issued a press release. Emphasizing the context within which his remarks had been made and that he had been subpoenaed as a witness by counsel for defendants in a Prohibition prosecution, he attempted to clarify his position.

> When I talked about cooperation in my testimony, I used that word in the sense of a centralized and coordinated activity between the United States Attorney's office and the police in the enforcement of prohibition, a meaning which the counsel for the defense relied upon as establishing their proposition [that] the police in enforcing national prohibition were in all cases acting as Federal agents. By way of illustration I pointed out that since the abolition of the special service division by Commissioner McLaughlin, in which were at one time centered all the prohibition enforcement activities of the New York City Police Department, the contact between the police and the United States Attorney's office had become less centralized and more diffuse.

His division, he stressed, had "at all times had the fullest measure of cooperation from Police Commissioner McLaughlin and all his subordinates."[54]

Other court challenges were also mounted. In the fall of 1925, the West Forty-third Street Elks Club sought an injunction against the U.S. attorney's office subpoena of club records for a grand jury investigation. Complaining that Buckner and Harlan were on a "fishing expedition pure and simple," counsel for the organization argued that the residential club was, in reality, "a home, not a hotel" and that its papers should be subject to seizure only with a warrant based on evidence that the club was involved in Volstead Act violations. The mere fact that beer had been delivered to the premises, he contended, did not mean that his clients were responsible for its delivery.

For John Harlan, however:

> The question [was] not one of the inviolability or otherwise of the home. It is a simple question whether or not there is a privileged class in this country. The question, squarely put, is: Shall the criminal law, and particularly the Prohibition law, be enforced against saloons, cabarets, places of amusement where any one may go, and ordinary individuals generally, and yet be restrained from enforcement when it comes to private clubs, fraternal organizations or secret societies?[55]

Buckner's use of young associates in his firm to secure evidence of Volstead Act violations was another target of criticism. One of the four lawyers given money by Buckner to purchase illegal booze was Leo Gottlieb, who was to become one of Harlan's closer friends and attorney for the Justice's estate. When Gottlieb applied for membership in the Association of the Bar for the City of New York, several members threatened to oppose his admission, charging that he and his confederates had acted in an unethical manner in gathering evidence at restaurants and clubs while posing as patrons. Such tactics, they argued, smacked of entanglement.

Coming to Gottlieb's defense, Buckner issued a statement indicating that he had instructed his young associates not to indulge in enticements or coaxing, to visit only establishments where they were known, and, if asked, to present cards containing their names, calling, and firm address. In addition, he pointed out that not one of the fourteen club and restaurant keepers against whom the attorneys' tour had led to legal proceedings had complained about the tactics used to obtain incriminating evidence.[56]

Buckner's statement conflicted with press accounts of the assistants' maneuvers. But Judge Augustus Hand, the senior judge of the U.S. District Court for the Southern District, along with his cousin Learned Hand, the jurisdiction's most distinguished jurist, also defended Gottlieb. Both judges were friends of Buckner. In a letter to Elihu Root, Jr., Augustus Hand explained the difference between entrapment and the simple purchase of an illegal product in an establishment openly violating the law. If the bar association wished to attack anyone, the judge added, "they ought to bring Buckner before the Appellate Division and not badger a young man who performed a public service at his request."[57]

Somewhat ironically, it was the nation's "dry" lobby and congressmen sympathetic to Prohibition who became Buckner's most vehement foes. They attacked not only his decision to focus on major offenders rather than attempt to reach all violators but also his recommendation that special inferior courts be created to handle minor cases without jury trial and his conclusion that, without such a modification in the federal judiciary, massive increases in the Prohibition budget would be necessary to secure anything approximating effective enforcement. They also objected to his proposal for a popular referendum in New York and other states to determine how Prohibition should be enforced in each state, as well as his suggestion that the legalization of light wines and beer might help to reduce the demand for hard liquor.[58]

Wayne B. Wheeler, general counsel for the Anti-Saloon League, was Buckner's most vocal critic among "dry" forces. After one meeting with President Coolidge, Wheeler issued a statement to the press in which he contended that the U.S. attorney was encouraging violations of the law, accused New York of having "run up the white flag" and surrendered to "liquor criminals," and scorned

> the attitude of some Federal officials who say that they will not enforce parts of the national prohibition act against a certain class of liquor law violators. Such a position is untenable, and in States which had no State

> or local enforcement laws it is notice to liquor lawbreakers that they may violate [the] law with Federal immunity from arrest. No Federal officer who respects his oath of office will say that he will not enforce any part of a Federal law.[59]

On that and other occasions, Wheeler also warned that Buckner's proposal to establish inferior federal police courts had aroused concern in Congress that such a move would impair the dignity of the federal judiciary. Those misgivings and Buckner's claims that effective enforcement of Prohibition would require huge budget increases (unless jury trials were suspended) might jeopardize, Wheeler feared, congressional support for the "dry" effort. In New York, state Anti-Saloon League officials echoed Wheeler's charges and questioned Buckner's credentials as a defender of their faith. "His very attitude," exclaimed one, "shows his lack of sympathy for the friends of Prohibition and his sympathy, by inference, with the 'wet' cause. The last time I talked with him he referred to us repeatedly as 'you drys.' The inference is plain enough." Congressional "drys" were equally critical. On the floor of the Senate, William E. Borah, the powerful Idaho Republican maverick, condemned Buckner's proposal for state referenda on the Prohibition issue. Observing that state variations in the enforcement of federal law would lead to endless confusion and that the Civil War had been fought over a similar proposition, Borah declared: "To my mind it is treason. It is evasion of the Constitution." He was prepared, he added, to walk "through blood and fire" to maintain the Constitution "as it is."[60]

But Buckner also had his defenders. When the general secretary of the Methodist church's Board of Temperance, Prohibition, and Public Morals attacked the U.S. attorney's stance—and New York City's morals—a prominent Methodist cleric warned the secretary "to keep his tongue off New York and . . . Emory Buckner" and promised that the Methodist church, in New York at least, was "going to stand behind the great work that Mr. Buckner is doing." Another clergyman, who headed the New York Civic League, which had cooperated with Buckner in padlocking more than two hundred clubs and restaurants, cited the severe budget constraints confronting the Prohibition effort and the president's lack of commitment to the issue. "[I]f the President remains a 'Silent Cal' upon so important an issue," he asserted, "then we who believe in the strict enforcement of the Prohibition law have a right to criticize him as a poor Executive."[61]

The U.S. attorney, however, was perfectly capable of defending himself. In a letter to Wheeler, released to the press, Buckner agreed that "we must have rigid enforcement against all violations of the law, big and little, with jail sentences promptly imposed, or else modify or repeal the law." But he insisted that the federal police courts he had proposed were the only way to secure full enforcement without more than tripling the Prohibition budget:

> Please come over to New York and tell me concretely just what Judges are to try the petty violators of the law whom you want to prosecute, just where the court rooms are to be located, and just where I am to get the assistants to prosecute them without, at the same time, abandoning my drive on the wealthy bootleggers who have grown rich from law-breaking. If you will show me . . . I shall be only too happy to prosecute the little fellows.[62]

In an earlier letter to Wheeler, Buckner challenged opposition to his proposal for police courts. "The bogey about Federal judges being appointed for life has," he asserted, "defeated prohibition enforcement for the past five years and will continue to defeat it until Congress is willing to provide the obvious machinery which not only the prohibition law but the narcotics law, petit larceny [in] interstate commerce, navigation laws, petit larceny from the Post Office, and every other kind of crime which is dealt with by Special Sessions judges, or traffic courts, or police magistrates [in] our cities and states, require." That such judges would be appointed for life and preside without juries was of no import to Buckner either.

> Do not the Prohibitionists expect that the law will continue for life? And if the law does continue for life we have a score of other laws which should be handled without jury trials, and which are breaking the backs of the Federal machinery.[63]

Buckner had written this letter while apparently still hopeful that the League might support his approach to Prohibition. Across the top of a copy he sent Felix Frankfurter, he had scrawled a request: "If he [Wheeler] is a friend of yours, write him what you think of me. He ought to get action." But Frankfurter obviously had no influence on Wheeler, and Buckner's defense of his stance had fallen on deaf ears not only in the League's offices but in other "dry" quarters as well. Following his testimony before the Senate judiciary committee, for example, the national convention of the Women's National Committee for Law Enforcement adopted a resolution urging his removal from office "on the ground that his ideas will not tend to uphold the Constitution and enforce the law of the land."[64]

The Bathtub Venus

Enforcing Prohibition in New York City was no easy task, even under the best of conditions. Indeed, one man was arrested while attempting to sell liquor to an employee of the Boy Scouts of America at the organization's Manhattan headquarters! All but the most zealous "drys," however, must have appreciated Buckner's and Harlan's efforts. While Buckner was attempting to cope with his office's critics, John Harlan was principally responsible for the preparation of cases and, considering the circumstances, developed an impressive record. Not only were hundreds of clubs and restaurants padlocked, but thousands of criminal prosecutions were also processed. During Buckner's tenure, over seventy defendants were acquitted after trial, the jury deadlocked in ten, and nearly seven hundred were dismissed. But 3,880 guilty pleas were secured as well as forty-eight convictions after trial.[65]

Among the criminal prosecutions were six, involving numerous defendants, which Harlan considered major cases. William V. ("Big Bill") Dwyer, one of the most notorious bootleggers of the period, received a two-year sentence and a $10,000 fine. The mayor of Edgewater, New Jersey, and twenty-two confederates drew prison terms on a variety of charges, the mayor for facilitating the landing of booze on the New Jersey coast. Other major defendants met similar fates, and only one such trial ended in a deadlocked jury.[66]

The most celebrated of their Prohibition prosecutions, however, involved Earl Carroll, the colorful theater owner and producer. At midnight on February 22, 1926, after his *Vanities* showgirls' last performance of the evening, Carroll hosted what the staid *New York Times* was to characterize as an "all-night bacchanalian orgy" at his Manhattan theater. Two jazz bands provided dance music for five hundred guests, who were also treated to two large tables of food and drink and three large tubs of "iced liquid," as the paper put it. Those in attendance were asked to sign "release cards," which read:

> Know all men by those present, that whereas, I . . . am about to participate in a certain party, entertainment, feast or bacchanalia given by Earl Carroll. . . , and whereas I am doing so entirely at my own initiative, risk, and responsibility. . . ; now, therefore . . . I do hereby for myself, my heirs, executors, administrators and assigns, release and forever discharge the Earl Carroll Vanities and the beauties contained therein from any and all claims, demands, actions or causes of action arising out of injury or death that may occur to me by reason of the said revel, irrespective of how such injury or death may occur.

Guests were also encouraged to memorize a number printed on the card—the telephone number of a neighboring mortuary.[67]

Carroll's guests ate and drank through the night, a Charleston dance contest was held, and several *Vanities* showgirls cavorted about the theater stage in bathing suits and negligees. But the party's *pièce de résistance* occurred about 4:00 A.M., when the showman directed his guests to the theater's orchestra seats, where they watched as a chorus girl stepped nude into a bathtub which had been placed on the stage and proceeded to bathe in what appeared to be an illicit beverage. Carroll then invited the audience to fill their glasses from the tub, announcing with a flourish, "Gentlemen, the line forms at the left"—an invitation fifteen to twenty male guests readily accepted.[68]

A reporter present that evening asked Carroll if he could print a story about the party. "Go as far as you like," the showman, by the newsman's account, replied. When numerous stories began to appear, however, Carroll issued a statement denying their more potentially damaging details. "It might have been held in a church, for all the revelry there was among the guests," he claimed. "It was a party which any man, even a minister, might have attended with his wife." The tub, he asserted, was filled only with "harmless fruit compounds." And no woman had stepped into or bathed in a tub on his stage.[69]

Buckner and Harlan were not convinced. When Buckner, on beginning his tenure as U.S. attorney, had first initiated proceedings against the clubs and restaurants which sold liquor to his young Root, Clark associates, the proprietors of several had flatly denied any wrongdoing to reporters. Buckner promised to put them and his young colleagues on the witness stand and allow a judge to decide whom to believe—"the proprietors, who have something to lose, or the young lawyers, actuated only by a desire to see the law enforced." If those in question swore under oath that they were correctly quoted in the press, he warned, he would institute perjury proceedings against them.[70]

Buckner and Harlan took the same tack with Carroll. The showman was called before a grand jury, where he again denied that liquor had been served or that a woman had bathed on his stage, as well as other details furnished by witnesses to the incident. That grand jury ended its session without making any findings in the case. But a subsequent grand jury handed up an indictment charging Carroll with six counts of perjury. He had lied to each grand jury, the indictment charged, when he testified that no liquor was served, that no one was in the bathtub, and that no list of the guests had been compiled.[71]

In late May, the Carroll case went to trial in a packed courtroom, with a new array of fetching *Vanities* girls gracing the front row of the spectator section each day of the proceedings. After opening statements of opposing counsel, John Harlan first had the defendant's grand jury testimony read to the jury and called witnesses to verify Carroll's appearances before the two grand jury proceedings. He then called to the stand Arthur F. Irwin, night editor of the *Daily Mirror*, who testified that he had attended the party, had taken two drinks which "tasted like champagne" from the bathtub, and had seen a young girl in the tub. Three other *Mirror* staffers confirmed Irwin's account. "Well," one testified, "I saw a nude woman—a woman without any clothing on at all—get into the tub. I saw her climb over the side of the tub." A member of the *Vanities* chorus line agreed that a woman had indeed bathed in the tub, and another witness said he had observed several guests signing a book in the rear of the theater.[72]

During cross-examination, Carroll's counsel, Herbert C. Smyth, challenged the prosecution witnesses' assertions that they could distinguish wine and liquor from certain nonalcoholic beverages. A representative of the Canada Dry company testified for the defense that his firm paid the defendant for the privilege of serving free ginger ale to *Vanities* audiences and that sixty to seventy thousand pints of the product had been consumed at Carroll's theater in the past year. Several defense witnesses supported Smyth's claim that the party guests had been served ginger ale rather than wine or champagne. One claimed, in fact, that he had searched in vain for a drink of whiskey and, unable to locate one, had left the party before the bathtub incident. There was also no firm evidence to support Harlan's contention that Carroll had lied when he told the grand jury inquiry that no guest list had been maintained at the party.[73]

The showman's conviction or acquittal appeared to hinge, then, on his denials regarding the bathtub incident, and Harlan's star witness on that point was to be Joyce Hawley—the "bathtub Venus," as Harlan and the press dubbed her. Miss Hawley had come to New York from Chicago. She had lived for several months at a hotel, as she had previously in Chicago, but recently had moved in with a nurse and the nurse's husband. Her employer card at Carroll's theater listed her as a "D.D." or "Dumb Dora"—theater slang for a girl who could neither sing nor dance, possessed no other stage qualifications, but did qualify as a "showgirl" or "model."[74]

Harlan hoped to portray Miss Hawley as a much-abused innocent and thereby neutralize any sympathy the New York jury might harbor for the defendant in a Prohibition-related prosecution. His task was difficult. Miss Hawley was only seventeen, but she had been posing nude as an artist's model since age fourteen. The day before she was to take the witness stand, she produced a phony-looking birth certificate and told Harlan that her real name was Teresa Daugelos. Harlan had also learned that the defense planned to claim that she was actually twenty-one and that the birth certificate in her possession was her sister's.[75]

Painfully aware that a witness of doubtful credibility could prove disastrous, particularly in a perjury prosecution, Harlan hurriedly telephoned James H. Douglas, a Chicago attorney, who sent him a certified copy of the Miss Hawley/Daugelos birth certificate. The certificate verified the witness' claim that she was only seventeen, as did her parents, with whom Douglas also spoke. Harlan could thus call Miss Hawley to the witness stand confident of her tender age, if not limited experience.[76]

In the courtroom, Harlan effectively depicted his witness as Carroll's victim. She not only concurred in the accounts of other prosecution witnesses but she also testified that one of the defendant's employees "got me drunk" before the bathtub performance, that she was indeed nude in the tub, and that when she began crying as fifteen to twenty men lined up around the tub, Carroll "bawled me out." Later, she added, the showman reneged on his promise to pay her $700 to $1,000 for her appearance.[77]

Miss Hawley did not fare so well under Smyth's scornful cross-examination. Was not she "so drunk" that night, he asked, that she could not possibly remember details of what happened at the party? "I remember things," the witness replied, no doubt to Harlan's consternation, "but I was feeling very good. I had to feel very good to do a thing like that." Smyth also attempted, with some success, to establish that Miss Hawley had sought to have Carroll purchase her silence with a theatrical contract, and he drew admissions from her regarding her work as a model and that, however traumatic the bathtub performance might have been for her, she was now performing the same act nightly at a Greenwich Village theater.[78]

Before and during the trial, Smyth had argued that the grand juries' questions regarding the bathtub incident were totally irrelevant to their inquiry into possible Volstead Act violations and that his client's response thus should not have been the basis for perjury charges. Judge Henry W. Goddard had repeatedly denied Smyth's motions to dismiss those counts of the indictment against Carroll and strike from the record any testimony relating to them. In his summation to the jury, however, the defense lawyer repeated his contention and charged that the Volstead Act's author "never had any idea in his wildest imaginings that it would be used to obtain a conviction based on a girl in a tub without any clothing. . . . Mr. Buckner has often complained of the clogged wheels of justice, yet he has taken up a great deal of time . . . to try this kind of case. If liquor was not in the bathtub, the incident was not material. The Grand Jury inquiry was under the national prohibition law." In any event, if his client had lied about the bathtub incident, he "lied like a gentleman"—protecting his guests' privacy and a young woman's reputation. Not that Smyth thought Miss Hawley's reputation deserved protection. "There is nothing more charming than a pretty woman," he reminded jurors, "yet how often pretty women without consciences will go any length to wreak their vengeance upon men."[79]

John Harlan had been principally responsible for presenting the prosecution's case up to that point. But Emory Buckner would give the government's summation. The defendant had not "lied like a gentleman," the U.S. attorney charged; he had "lied to protect his bootlegger. On two occasions he took [the] oath, then spat on the Bible and deliberately lied to protect commercial bootlegging. He did it because he thinks he is above the law. But he is not." Smyth's concession that his client had lied was, to Buckner, "virtually a plea of guilty." And if the jury agreed with the defendant's counsel that Carroll had lied about the bathtub incident, he asserted, it must find him guilty of perjury, whether or not the tub contained wine or champagne. Nor, Buckner exclaimed, should the jurors be influenced by Miss Hawley's reputation. "Miss Hawley is not mine," he shouted. "I didn't put her in a bathtub. She's Carroll's. . . . Any time that Earl Carroll puts a better woman in one of his bathtubs . . . then I'll bring a better woman to this courtroom." Sounding more like his preacher father than a Wall Street lawyer, he then concluded: "This case has not so much to do with prohibition, but [with] what is to become of God, of our oaths, our courts and institutions if Carroll is to be permitted to boot the Bible out of this building, have his attorney apologize for him and get away with it."[80]

When a defense witness had assured the court during the trial that Miss Hawley's bath contained no booze, Judge Goddard brought broad smiles to the prosecutors' faces when he asked incredulously, "And were these men all standing around that bathtub just to get a drink of ginger ale?" But the jurors were not so cynical or perceptive. They acquitted Carroll of lying about the consumption of liquor at the party. They convicted the defendant, however, of lying about the bathtub incident. Carroll faced a possible maximum sentence of ten years in prison and a $4,000 fine. Judge Goddard gave him a year and a day and a $2,000 fine. But John Harlan considered a conviction on any of the counts "a great triumph, particularly in view of the nature of the case and the popular reaction in New York City towards Prohibition." Harlan had been convinced that one juror in particular would never vote for conviction in a Prohibition case and had resigned himself to a hung jury. When Carroll was found guilty, Harlan sought out the juror. "I'd never convict anyone of violating any damfool Prohibition law," the juror readily conceded, confirming Harlan's impressions. "But," he added, "when a guy goes out and lies about it under oath, well, now, that's something else again."[81]

In October, while an appeal of his conviction was pending, Earl Carroll applied for a passport, explaining that he was planning an indefinite stay in Europe, subject to the call of the court. After conferring with Buckner, John Harlan told State Department officials that his office had no objections to the showman's request. The "Bathtub Venus" was not so fortunate. In late May, the mayor of Northampton, Massachusetts, declined to issue a permit authorizing Miss Hawley's appearance in an "exhibition act," as the *Times* termed it, at a local theater. "Any young woman who will jump into a bathtub nude, before a crowd of men," the mayor explained, "is not the type of attraction we want in Northampton." Cincinnati was no more hospitable. Yielding to a storm of protest, city fathers rescinded a permit for her scheduled performance there. If city officials did not act, one matron had warned a police lieutenant, "the decent women of Cincinnati would."[82]

While his reception was more cordial, Harlan fared little better at the annual reunion of his Princeton class that year. "At the height of the alumni parade," a friend has recounted, "his classmates forcibly deposited him in a bathtub bearing captions commemorating his efforts to enforce prohibition."[83]

The Queens Sewer Scandal

However gratifying the convictions of Carroll and Volstead Act violators, as well as the padlocking of hundreds of illicit establishments, might have been, Buckner was sensitive to the complaints of his critics that he was enforcing Prohibition too enthusiastically—or not vigorously enough. He was also offended by charges of politics in the conduct of his office. Various critics complained that he had his eye on the New York governor's mansion and that his Prohibition campaign was designed to bolster his popularity with New York voters. Buckner was heavily involved in Republican politics, and Felix Frankfurter thought he could have been elected governor in 1928, when Franklin Roosevelt barely survived a campaign against a weak GOP candidate. The idea that Buckner's defense of the "dry" faith would endear him to most New Yorkers, however, was debatable at best, and Buckner repeatedly denied that he had gubernatorial aspirations, telling one Republican group he was a candidate only for "31 Nassau Street," his law firm's address.[84]

Buckner undoubtedly found charges growing out of his prosecution of two principals in the Harding administration scandals even more objectionable. In 1926, he tried Harding's attorney general Harry M. Daugherty and Alien Property Custodian Thomas W. Miller on charges of conspiring to defraud the government. After the defendants' first trial ended in a deadlocked jury, Thomas J. Heflin (D-Ala.) charged on the floor of the Senate that Daugherty would never have gone to trial "until he knew somebody on the jury would hang there until doomsday or acquit him or make a mistrial." Buckner, Heflin added, had been appointed by the same administration which had produced Daugherty, Harding's interior secretary Albert B. Fall, and other officials later ensnared in the Teapot Dome scandal and related wrongdoing. Daugherty's counsel dismissed Heflin's rhetoric as "hot air, like a lot of other speeches made in the Senate." And while Buckner himself made no comment, a member of his staff pointed out that the U.S. attorney had been appointed by President Coolidge, not Harding, and that a retrial of Daugherty and Miller was imminent. During that retrial, however, the defendants' lawyers complained that politics had played a part in their clients' prosecution.[85]

These latter charges were apparently the final straw. At the beginning of his summation to the jury in the case, which ended in a conviction for Miller, but not Daugherty, Buckner announced that he was resigning his position as U.S. attorney. Explaining his decision to reporters later, he cited "my three girls to educate and support." He also conceded, however, that he had been influenced by opposing counsel's assertion that he was trying to "injure a fellow-being for myself or my own preferment."[86]

When asked whether his resignation would mean a major personnel shake-up in the U.S. attorney's office, Buckner replied that he knew then of only one member of his staff who would definitely be leaving with him—John Harlan, who had left his position as head of the Prohibition division to play a key role in the Daugherty-Miller prosecutions, as he had in the Earl Carroll case.[87] Neither was to return to Root, Clark for long, however, before being called back into public service. In 1928,

Buckner agreed to an appointment as a special assistant attorney general for the state to investigate charges of official corruption in the borough of Queens; John Harlan was again to be his chief assistant.

Maurice E. Connolly had been elected president of the Queens borough government in 1911 as a reform Democrat. By the fall of 1927, he had held the position longer than any other New York City politician had ever held a single elective office. His tenure had been extremely lucrative as well as lengthy. The construction of sewers had proven a much more costly undertaking in Queens than in other boroughs. Calls for sewer construction bids were based on specifications provided by a company with which Connolly and John M. Phillips, a major Democratic contributor, had close ties, and the borough president's detractors smelled kickbacks and bribery—especially when Connolly financed a new home, loans to friends, and other expenditures entirely in cash, none of which went through his bank account. In recent years, too, seven incinerators had been built by the city by a single firm controlled by one of Connolly's friends—at a cost a third higher than that for similar facilities in other cities. Statistics regarding borough expenses for paving told a similar story. An attorney for a Queens alderman and a group of disgruntled taxpayers asserted that, in the past ten years, the borough had paid $10 million in excess of fair and reasonable prices for asphalt and concrete pavements. Concrete pavements cost $2.50 per square yard more in Queens than in Brooklyn, asphalt from $1.75 to $2.50 more.[88]

Queens residents urged Governor Al Smith to initiate an investigation of Connolly's stewardship. Smith, like Connolly, was a Democrat; he was also seeking his party's presidential nomination and the Queens borough president was a political ally. The governor designated Justice Townsend Scudder, a member of the state supreme court's appellate division, to conduct an inquiry. To limit any damage the Queens scandal might do his presidential aspirations, Smith named Buckner, a Republican of impeccable reputation, to be the judge's chief investigator. Buckner rented a suite of offices, had Smith also name John Harlan a special assistant attorney general, and recruited five of the "Boy Scouts" who had worked with him in the U.S. attorney's office to serve as his core staff. He would also draw on the expertise of a large body of engineering and statistical specialists.[89]

On beginning the inquiry, Buckner told reporters that he did not know what evidence might ultimately be produced, adding:

> What I do know is this, that the inquiry won't start until I and my assistants are familiar with every single fact and figure pertaining to the letting of contracts in Queens while Mr. Connolly has been President of the borough. When I go to work on a case I build it up exactly as bricklayer builds a house, and I number every brick. When the case gets into court, I have all my bricks ready to go into the exact places arranged for them.

If Buckner would be the inquiry's chief contractor, however, Harlan was to be its principal bricklayer. J. Edward Lumbard, who had become one of Harlan's closer friends and would later serve as chief judge of the Court of Appeals for the Second Circuit, had worked with Buckner and Harlan in the U.S. attorney's office and joined them again for the Queens investigation. "Buckner would come in from time to time," Lumbard has recalled, "to see how we were getting along. But Harlan kind of ran the show." The "show" involved interviews with numerous witnesses—nearly three hundred during the inquiry's first few months alone—and the compiling of a massive collection of records and other documents.[90]

In an attempt to stop further investigation into his activities, Connolly resigned from the borough presidency. But a grand jury investigation was then ordered, and Buckner had Harlan present the government's case before that body. Characteristically, Buckner's young assistant had prepared the case exceptionally well. A truckload of file cabinets crammed with evidence was brought to the county courthouse for presentation to the grand jury. Even with that impressive display of documentation and the testimony of witnesses, Buckner and Harlan could not convince the grand jury to charge Connolly with accepting bribes. But they did secure an indictment on charges of conspiracy to defraud the city of property, obstruction of the due administration of the law, and neglect of legal duties.[91]

The case went to trial on September 25, 1928. "John Harlan's thorough and imaginative conduct of the investigation," as J. Edward Lumbard later wrote, clearly "disclosed Connolly's approval of contracts at grossly exorbitant prices" and made Buckner's presentation of the case at trial a relatively simple task. To underscore the story of municipal corruption that Harlan's carefully gathered data revealed, the prosecution erected a four-by-thirty-foot chart in the courtroom. Each time another incriminating contract price was entered into the record, the figure was added in chalk to the chart. Connolly, who never explained the large sums of cash in his possession, was convicted. "We sat up all night," Lumbard remembers, "waiting for the jury to come in." But Harlan had little doubt about the outcome; the court's bailiff, who was listening at the door to the jury room, had provided him with frequent reports of the jurors' progress.[92]

Connolly would appeal his conviction, but without success. Despite his youth and limited experience, John Harlan had become exceptionally skilled not only at preparing for trial and examining witnesses, but also in the preparation of briefs. After he and Buckner returned to Root, Clark following their work in the U.S. attorney's office, they had been in heavy demand as counsel for the owners of real estate subjected to padlock proceedings, who claimed that they had been unaware that their property had been put to illicit uses. In one such case, Harlan wrote a 150-page brief which Buckner then presented to Learned Hand, the presiding judge and Buckner's close friend. "Is this your brief?" the distinguished jurist asked Buckner. When Buckner conceded it was, Hand retorted, "Well, I'm not going to read it. It's too long." "Well, it will be your loss, your Honor," Buckner replied. "It's a very good brief. My assistant wrote it and I put my name on it." Hand then threw the document across the bench and onto the counsel's table where Buckner and Harlan were seated. "You can imagine how I felt," Harlan later recalled. "Then, after the case had been decided, Hand called me in and said, 'Just wanted to say it was a damn good brief.' "[93] Apparently, the appellate brief Harlan wrote in the Queens case was equally effective; it blocked Connolly's appeal.

Judge Hand, of course, was hardly the only one impressed with young Harlan's work. When Emory Buckner had first designated Harlan to head the Prohibition division of the U.S. attorney's office, he had described his young assistant as "Poise in Motion" and "Persistence Embodied." J. Edward Lumbard and other members of Buckner's troop of "Boy Scouts" were just as favorably impressed. "At twenty-six he [already] had all the qualities of leadership; it was easy to work with a man who treated his colleagues as equals and partners. We knew him at once to be a man of integrity, dedicated to the job at hand; a man of tolerant and generous spirit, possessed of a sense of humor and unable to take himself too seriously." Harlan's tenure as Prohibition division head and in the Queens inquiry had served merely to enhance his mentor's and peers' impressions. On his return to Root, Clark, he was clearly established, as one of his younger colleagues in the firm would put it, as Emory Buckner's "most valued assistant." Soon, he would become one of the firm's most important members and one of New York's outstanding litigators—a "lawyer's lawyer."[94]

2

Lawyer's Lawyer

"My brother's success in life," John Marshall Harlan's sister Edith has written, was "perhaps due in part to [the] total supportive role played by his three adoring sisters, his mother, and his wife. In their view he could do no wrong."[1] The latter woman in his life, Ethel Andrews, who in 1928 would become Harlan's wife, was the daughter of a Yale Colonial History professor. Her marriage to Harlan was not her first. Originally she was married to Henry K. Murphy, a New York architect twenty years her senior. Ethel and Murphy, one of the first architects to blend American and Chinese styles, lived for most of their marriage in China, where he designed several buildings at Peking University. Ethel was a beautiful, charming, artistic woman who found her husband and their lives in China fascinating. But Murphy, as the Harlans' daughter, Eve, later put it, "just couldn't stay away from other women." Ethel's parents, distraught at the emotional and physical distress Murphy's philandering caused their daughter, urged her to obtain a divorce. Ethel ultimately complied, but with considerable reluctance. "I think she would have stayed with him," Eve Harlan has said, "except that my grandparents put a great deal of pressure on her to leave him. I think he always loved her from what she heard later on. He was married five times, and mother knew one or two of his subsequent wives. They would get together for tea and discuss Henry Murphy."[2]

Ethel's divorce was granted in September of 1927. The following March, her brother John, a young Root, Clark associate, asked his sister to accompany him to a firm party, where she met John Harlan. Over the next several months, she and John saw each other regularly, but Ethel apparently had little inkling of his growing feelings for her. Then one week she was confined to her apartment ill, and a friend who lived several blocks away was sending her trays of food. "My father," their daughter later related, "stopped by to pick up a tray for mother's friend, carried it several blocks and up four flights of stairs to her apartment, sat and talked to her for two hours about trout fishing, in which she had no interest whatever, and then popped the question—to her utter astonishment."[3]

Ethel accepted John's proposal. Now Harlan was obliged to tell his very proper mother that her only son was about to marry a divorcée. Extremely nervous at that prospect, he waited until Mrs. Harlan had departed for a summer visit to the family home at Murray Bay, then wrote her a long, handwritten letter.

> Dearest Mother—
>
> Prepare yourself for a shock. I'm engaged to be married. The lady is Ethel Andrews, and of course she's the most wonderful girl in all the world. You'll love her as much as I do when you meet her.
>
> All this happened a week ago tonight, and I just couldn't tell you before you left. We both wanted to make quite certain about it before we told anyone, and now that we are why our respective families must have our secret right away. . . .
>
> Now you'll want to know all about her, but I'll have to be brief because it's very late. Her father and mother are New Haven people. Mr. Andrews is Professor of Colonial History at Yale. John Andrews her brother is in Root-Clark. Ethel is 31 years old—her birthday is on May 30—so we almost have the same birthday. She went to school in Switzerland and for a year to Bryn Mawr.

Without a skip, he then broached the more sensitive element in his fiancée's background

> When she was 21 she married a man over 40, one Henry Murphy, an architect in New York. She lived with him for two years and then of course such a match proved impossible and they separated. She finally concluded to get a divorce which she did last year. The rest of it is she's a perfect darling, and there you have it. I never thought I *could really* fall in love, and I tried like the devil to avoid doing it now. But I couldn't.
>
> Our plans are a little vague. We want to get married sometime before Christmas. We think that this is about the right period in which to subject our present feelings about each other to some sort of test. We both feel very much the same way about getting married—namely that if we can avoid it we're not going to do it. She's had one unfortunate experience, and you know the way I have felt about marriage. So we're not going to do anything foolish. I may say that at present we are both agreed that we can't possibly avoid getting married.
>
> Well, it's late Mother dear, but I am so happy time doesn't seem to count. I shall await eagerly your congratulations. You'll love her when you see her.

In August, John and Ethel visited his mother in Murray Bay. A friend of the Andrews family, a prominent historian, also took it upon himself to visit Mrs. Harlan for tea and vouch for Ethel's—and her parents'—character. With his mother's blessing, they were married on November 10, 1928, in Farmington, Connecticut.[4]

A Family Dispute

At this point, John Marshall Harlan was not merely the head of his immediate household; in a very real sense he had become the head of his parents' family as well. In 1911 or 1912, John Maynard Harlan's family had moved from Chicago to Washington, where they remained until 1924, when they moved to New York. During this period and later, John Maynard maintained a law practice, at various times, in Chicago, New York, and Washington, while Elizabeth Harlan and their daughters traveled often to Paris and other parts of Europe and spent their summers at Murray Bay.

The Harlans were never to be legally separated, much less divorced. As their daughter Edith characterized their relationship, however, "they weren't together a great deal." Harlan's law practice required extensive travel. Over the years, however, his marriage had also become increasingly turbulent. "They did quarrel a lot," Edith has remarked. "And I often made the comment . . . that I would live with either one or the other, but not with them together. . . . It was too unpleasant."[5]

A number of factors had apparently contributed to the growing strains in the Harlans' marriage. While John Maynard's income had improved considerably during the years he represented Chicago's traction interests, he was continually pressed for money. The tremendous time, energy, and expense he devoted to politics in the critical early years of his law practice may also have taken their toll. According to their daughter Elizabeth, moreover, Mrs. Harlan "hated Chicago [and] whenever she could . . . ran away" with the children to Yonkers and her mother, for whom John Maynard had little affection.

The contrast between John Maynard's bombastic, temperamental personality and his wife's reserved demeanor probably had an impact as well. Harlan was in many ways a kind and indulgent husband and father. But his brother James, who was even more given to displays of temperament than John Maynard, remarked that his brother had "wonderful telephone battles with office boys and toll operators and notable engagements with waiters in restaurants." And John Marshall Harlan would recall once arriving at a hospital where his father lay ill to find members of the hospital staff gathered around his bed while the elder Harlan harangued them about the bad egg he had been served for breakfast that morning. "The use of plain language," one relative has said, "was characteristic of the family." Indeed, John Maynard's daughter Elizabeth, who was charming but could also be "difficult," wrote an unpublished autobiography which emphasized this Harlan family trait.

And it seems undoubtedly to have taken its toll on the elder Harlans' marriage.[6]

But John Maynard's involvement in a protracted, bitter, and embarrassing battle with his two brothers, family members suggest, created perhaps the greatest strain in his marriage. John Maynard's brother Richard had been valedictorian of his Princeton class, served as minister of New York's First Presbyterian Church from 1886 to 1890, was president of Lake Forest College for five years, and later held an administrative position with George Washington University. He also regularly wrote eloquent letters to the *New York Times* and other major papers.[7]

Like his brother John Maynard, however, Richard Harlan was a poor financial manager. In fact, he had resigned from the Lake Forest College position after, as the *New York Times* characterized it, "a disagreement with the trustees over financial policies." In his will, Richard's father-in-law, Phinehas Prouty, had established a trust for each of his three daughters—Margaret Harlan, Adelaide, and Anna. Initially, Prouty's widow, Adelaide's husband, and Richard were named as trustees. But Prouty's will had given Richard virtually unlimited discretion in matters relating to his wife's trust, which, according to a 1903 accounting, had an inventory value of $120,000 in securities, and by 1907, Richard had become its sole trustee.[8]

Richard's investments proved exceedingly unwise. Two companies in which he risked $10–$15,000 of his wife's funds failed. In an attempt to recoup those losses, he invested heavily in high-risk securities, buying on margin to finance the purchases, borrowing from banks when additional margin became necessary, and pledging the trust securities as collateral. During the panic of 1907, the banks closed out his loans and sold his collateral. By 1909, the trust had been almost totally depleted, and members of Margaret's family—who stood to inherit the balance of the trust should Margaret, then about fifty and childless, die "without issue"—were pressing the distinguished clergyman and educator for an accounting. "You cannot blame us," Margaret's sister Adelaide wrote her brother-in-law in early 1911, "for wondering how the Executor's account stands, because nothing has been explained for the past eight years."[9] But Anna's husband, E. K. Beddall, angry that he was not also a trustee, was most persistent and suspicious.

Shortly before Christmas in 1909, Richard revealed the consequences of his handiwork to his brothers and his wife. James Harlan was then with the Interstate Commerce Commission, John Maynard a prominent lawyer, Richard a cleric and college administrator, and each the son of a Supreme Court justice. "All the parties feared," as legal papers would later put it, "that if the losses should become known they would be given wide and sensational publicity." In a desperate attempt to avoid such a scandal and the anguish it would cause their parents, the brothers settled upon a scheme in which they would begin to replenish the trust and also prepare a false accounting to placate members of Margaret's family. John Maynard had no funds to contribute at that point but promised to help his brother whenever his own financial situation improved. But James, who had no children and whose wife was independently wealthy, raised $58,000, and Margaret contributed $25,000, which she received from the sale of all her property except personal effects to James.

Ultimately, the scheme was to prove as complicated as Richard's investments had been unsound. As an interstate commerce commissioner, James Harlan could not legally repurchase the railroad securities which had been the core of Margaret's trust. John Maynard was thus designated to manage the fund. Richard and Margaret were packed off to Montreal to live so that they could avoid embarrassing questions, and as the date for filing the false accounting approached, they began an extended tour of Europe, ostensibly for Margaret's health. To guard against the possibility that letters regarding the matter might fall into the wrong hands, the brothers also devised a set of pseudonyms for use in their correspondence. James, for example, was to be "Silas," John Maynard "Tom," and Richard "David." An elaborate code for communicating with Richard and Margaret during their European trip was adopted for the same purpose. It was also apparently agreed that some of the money raised would be used to pay off Richard's considerable personal debts. Otherwise members of the Prouty family, John Maynard later explained, might have "become doubtful as to [Richard's] qualifications as a trustee, or even . . . suspect his integrity."

Anna Prouty Beddall's marriage had begun to collapse at about the time the false accounting was filed. Eventually, E. K. Beddall divorced his wife in Nevada, and several years later it was discovered that he had squandered nearly $90,000 of Anna's trust. Beddall was thus eliminated as a threat to the Harlan brothers' scheme. For a time, moreover, the brothers and Margaret were also apparently content with the arrangement. But following the deaths of Justice and Mrs. Harlan in 1911 and 1915, respectively, and disagreements arising out of several business dealings and personal disputes, James and John Maynard became bitter enemies. "What I wish now to know," John Maynard wrote James on one occasion, for example, "is whether you circulated or sent to *any* member of the family copies of your letter to me in which you refer to what Richard apparently has said to you about what I said to him of a telephone talk with a woman while I was at the Belmont [hotel]. I said no such thing to Richard. Did you send a copy of that letter to Elizabeth?"[10]

In 1917 and 1918, as the brothers' enmity grew more intense, James began to claim that the securities he had provided for Margaret's trust were a loan, not a gift, and that the $25,000 he had given Margaret, presumably in return for most of her property, had also been a loan. Now no longer an interstate commerce commissioner, James demanded, too, that his brother give him custody of the securities; when John Maynard initially refused, James began to withhold the monthly checks he had sent to Margaret over the years.

Eventually, John Maynard delivered securities valued at $68,637 to his brother, explaining that the $14,362 difference between that amount and the $83,000 James and Margaret raised was exhausted in transactions James had approved, including $11,115 used in 1910 to pay Richard's debts and $3,246 lost on the sale of stock. In a series of memoranda which he mailed to family members in 1919 and 1920, however, James accused his brother of diverting the shortage to his own use, condemning him as a "sneak" and worse. From that point on, he would refer to John Maynard as "the broker brother, a name my younger brother has now fairly earned and established in our family history through his successful and profitable adventures in the merchandizing of his brotherhood." "Such betrayal of one brother by another," he charged, "strikes at the fundamentals of family life."[11] For his part, John Maynard denied any wrongdoing and contended that his brother's withholding of income from Margaret amounted to a scheme to "blackmail" him into compliance with James's demands.

By 1921, the festering squabble had become the subject of a series of lawsuits. In June of that year, James sued John Maynard in the Illinois courts, claiming that he had loaned his brother the funds merely for investment purposes, that he had been given no accounting since 1917, and that he had reason to believe that some of the money had been used to pay off personal debts. Early the following month, John Maynard secured an injunction from a District of Columbia court, restraining James from further prosecuting the Illinois suit. But in an opinion the second Justice Harlan might have applauded, the U.S. Court of Appeals for the District of Columbia reversed the trial court, holding that without specific statutory authorization, federal courts had no power to enjoin pending state proceedings.

By the time an appeal of that ruling was ready for decision, James and John Maynard had agreed to litigate their differences in a third suit, that one also to be heard in Washington. The background for the third suit was thus. In 1921, John Maynard had completed the purchase of securities sufficient to completely restore the trust principal. From these, he deposited securities valued at $14,362, the amount of the shortage James had claimed, with the court in an interpleader suit which he brought against James and Richard in Washington, and the balance in a Washington bank, which was to serve as custodian for Richard in his capacity as trustee. Thus, when the original District of Columbia suit reached the Supreme Court, it could dismiss that case as moot, thereby avoiding a full-dress opinion in a case involving the descendants of one of its more outstanding former members.[12]

In 1924, yet another suit was filed, this time by Richard's wife and sister-in-law against the Harlan brothers and a Washington bank named as receiver during the litigation in the District of Columbia courts. Margaret Harlan claimed that the $25,000 she had contributed to cover her husband's losses, as well as James Harlan's contribution, had been entrusted to John Maynard. She further asserted that up to September of 1919, James had received the bulk of the income derived from the fraud, claiming that he needed money to meet loans he had obtained to secure his contribution to the trust. She had received only $13,120 from the fund although, she contended, her limited financial resources had caused her "hardships and sufferings" and she had "begged" James, without success, for her fair share of any income the fund generated. The sisters asked that all the remaining money be placed in a trust fund in their names and that a trustee be designated.[13]

In his answer to the complaint, James Harlan sought to place blame for the entire matter on John Maynard. He had not consented, he insisted, to the way in which his brother had managed the funds and had objected to John Maynard's use of a portion of the money to pay Richard's debts. John Maynard, he contended, had offered to raise $27,000 if James put up the balance needed to replenish Margaret's trust. Yet James had learned in 1921 that his brother "had not put up a dollar of his own money, and claims that he had never agreed to do so." He was determined, James asserted, to "bring John [Maynard] Harlan face to face with his wickedness."[14]

Ultimately, Root, Clark attorneys arranged an out-of-court settlement of the dispute which the brothers, Margaret, and members of her family were willing to sign. Given the financial pressures to which John Maynard was regularly subject, he no doubt viewed his brother's trusteeship as a potential source of funds. Not long after Richard's appointment as a trustee, for example, Richard had been obliged to inform his brother: "It would not [be] feasible for the Trustees of [the] trust to make any loan on the property you mention. There are reasons why it would not be expedient to raise the questions with my co-trustees just now."[15] But such an expression of interest was hardly evidence of any inclination toward embezzlement. Under the terms of the settlement, James agreed to surrender his claim to the securities and to settle with Margaret for back income. He thus dropped his contention that John Maynard had mishandled the funds entrusted to his care. Even so, the embarrassing affair had created further discord in the Harlans' marriage. That situation and John Maynard's increasingly pressing financial problems had meant, too, that members of his family had begun to look more to the son than the father for guidance.

John Marshall Harlan no doubt realized the further strain the lawsuits in which his father and uncles were embroiled had created for the family. For that reason, he largely avoided direct participation in Root, Clark's efforts to settle the dispute—efforts undertaken largely by Emory Buckner and Leo Gottlieb. He was deeply concerned, however, about both his parents' difficulties and the protracted controversy over Margaret's trust. In a 1924 letter to his sister Elizabeth, for example, he expressed frustration that "this d—n suit" was absorbing all their father's attention and the hope that his parents' situation could soon be improved. "I gather," he wrote,

> that you and mother have been going over the family situation a good deal. I have been living with it pretty constantly, and while I see the many angles and difficulties which beset the path of a final solution, I am optimistic enough to believe that a real solution can be had. It will demand not merely a change in the family fortunes in the material sense, but more fundamentally a radical re-adjustment of mental and psychological processes, particularly in mother and father. The point of departure I have taken in all my talks with mother and father is that we must get together again as a family. In my view of it that is the important thing, and the place where it may be is entirely secondary. Everyone is now agreed that New York is the goal, and it is therefore unnecessary to discriminate between the primary and secondary factors.
>
> The most hopeful thing to me is that both mother and father have come to realize this.

While his parents' difficulties would continue until his father's death of liver cancer in 1934, John Harlan remained the dutiful, loyal son, attempting to maintain close relations with his father and assist him in resolving his continuing financial problems, difficulties aggravated by the severe economic depression of the late 1920s and early 1930s. In May of 1931, for example, a Chicago associate of his father wrote John, urging him to persuade John Maynard to sell off a parcel of Murray Bay property to satisfy mortgage obligations the elder Harlan had been unable to meet. "I have every reason to believe," the friend suggested, "that John's financial condition is at a very low ebb and that he can take care of no part of this obligation. I must therefore look to the Murray Bay property for the amount due." In that situation and others, Harlan provided his father financial support. After John Maynard's death, moreover, John Marshall and his sisters Elizabeth and Edith paid off their father's debts and were sole financial support for their mother until her death in 1957.[16]

In spite of this, until shortly before his death, the elder Harlan would remain increasingly distant not only from his wife and other family members, but from his only son as well. Characteristically, the younger Harlan's correspondence with his father during this period was discreet and cryptic. It suggests, though, a relationship in which the son was seeking to reach out to his father, but with little apparent success. "Check mailed this morning air mail," read one 1930 telegram to the elder Harlan's residence at the Chicago Club; "am depositing two hundred your account here today," read another. "Won't you please answer my last letter?" he urged his father in several telegrams; in another, he pleaded, "Have not heard from you for a long time. Please write." "This card is evidently for you," he wrote at Christmas in 1931. "We had a very pleasant Christmas and hope that you did." When his only daughter, Evangeline, was born on February 2, 1932, Harlan telegraphed his father, "Your granddaughter arrived early this morning. Everyone fine." When Eve was to be christened in April of that year, he wrote his father, urging him to attend the service.

John Maynard's failure to correspond regularly with his son did not necessarily mean strains in their relations. In a 1907 letter to his own father, for example, John Maynard had explained that his failure to write his parents regularly was simply "a case of either pure 'cussedness' on my part or of a surrender to natural disinclination to write letters." From the time his final illness was diagnosed in 1933 until his death the following year, moreover, he lived with his wife and youngest daughter in New York, and after his death, his son drafted an admiring memorial tribute to him, copies of which would be available to visitors to his law office and judicial chambers. It is doubtful, though, that father and son were ever entirely reconciled. "I knew," the Harlans' daughter Edith later remarked, "that my brother and my father at times had differences. . . . My brother was . . . very annoyed by father at times because he felt that father had been inept and stupid about some things. . . . [Father] was visionary and not practical. He always had some scheme or other that he wanted to work on that was much more a [matter] of his own self-expression than [something] with any chance of achievement. . . . And John never had any visions about anything."[17]

The Eccentric Wendels

If the course in Harlan's family life was at times rocky, however, the progress of his career was rapid and impressive. On January 1, 1931, he was made a junior partner at Root, Clark. The formal letter making the offer, as Elihu Root, Jr., wrote him, included the usual "provisions designed to prevent the kind of trouble which sometimes comes up when men die and leave unreasonable executors." In a more informal letter, Root assured his young colleague "that the making of this offer is one of the happiest and pleasantest things we have ever done," adding:

> The determination to make the offer was not based on personal friendship. We decided long ago that if the firm was to live and prosper as an institution and keep up its morale, admission to partnership would have to be held sternly to a basis of ability and it is on that basis that we are proceeding now, but having made our determination we find that the result of it is delightful to us because you have gotten to be a friend and a comrade.[18]

As Emory Buckner's health declined and his responsibilities were shifted increasingly to his young colleague, Harlan also became Root, Clark's chief trial lawyer. His first major case in that capacity was also to be his most bizarre. It would involve the estate of one of New York's wealthiest and most eccentric families, the Wendels.

In the 1920s, Manhattan tour buses stopped regularly at the corner of Fifth Avenue and Thirty-ninth Street, where guides pointed out the "House of Mystery," the only remaining residence in an area of office buildings and businesses. 442 Fifth Avenue was the home of Ella Virginia von Echtzel Wendel. Ella's grandfather Johann Wendel, the first of the family to migrate to the United States in the 1830s, had been in the fur business with John Jacob Astor and married Astor's half-sister Elizabeth, but had made his fortune largely in real estate. His credo was, "Buy, but never sell, New York real estate." His only son, John D., Ella's father, had enthusiastically honored the elder Wendel's wishes, as had John D.'s son John Gottlieb, who had steadily added to the family's holdings and attempted to prevent Ella and her six sisters from marrying, thereby threatening to disperse the Wendel property. Of the sisters, only the rebellious Rebecca had successfully defied her brother's wishes. In 1899, another sister Georgiana, then fifty, ran away from the family's summer home at Irvington-on-Hudson. But when she was discovered at a Park Avenue hotel, John Gottlieb had her committed to the psychiatric ward of Bellevue Hospital and persuaded a sheriff's jury to declare her insane. When a state court later found Georgiana's commitment invalid, she sued her brother for $50,000. That suit was eventually dropped, but in 1903 Georgiana ran away to Europe. After five years abroad, she returned to the family fold, where she remained until 1919, when she was committed to a mental institution until her death. A third sister died relatively early in life, and the compliant Ella and her sisters Mary, Josephine, and Augusta apparently gave their brother no difficulty.[19]

John Gottlieb died in 1915, Josephine and Augusta several years earlier. In 1925, Mary also died, leaving Ella the sole mistress of 442 Fifth Avenue and the forty-acre Irvington property. When Ella's sister Rebecca, who lived on Long Island, died in 1930, estimates of the Wendel fortune ranged from $30–$100 million. The property taxes on the Fifth Avenue house and adjoining lot alone amounted to $250 a day, and the family had probably paid a genealogist handsomely for documents justifying the addition of "von Echtzel"—"a pretension to the Prussian nobility utterly without foundation"—to the family name. But John D. Wendel and his son had insisted that the sisters live sheltered and extremely spartan lives; that pattern persisted after the patriarch's death. The five-story Fifth Avenue house had been built in 1856, and few improvements had been made since. There was no elevator or dumbwaiter, and in 1931 the kitchen was still serviced by its original coal-burning stove. Only the dining room was wired for electricity; gas lamps and candles provided light for the rest of the house. The house had no telephone and only one large zinc bathtub, which Ella, whose scalp and ears were encrusted with dirt, rarely occupied. Educated at home by governesses, the spinster Wendel sisters presumably never attended a ball, entertained suitors, visited a nightclub or theater, or owned any jewelry. They were dressed in ankle-length, high-necked black dresses, which they wore until the dresses became shabby and green from age and filth. By one account a "very simple, timid, shy person, without wit or charm," whose mind "was childish and undeveloped," Ella never listened to a phonograph or radio, never read a newspaper. Neither did her spinster sisters. While he lived, it was said, their brother insisted that someone from the family real estate office come to the house each morning for breakfast because he could not endure his sisters' peasantlike chatter.[20]

Nor had the sisters abandoned their parsimonious life-styles when freed of their brother's domination. Since she considered meat unduly expensive, Ella ate mainly vegetables grown on the Irvington estate. She complained that she could not afford to install an oil furnace in the Fifth Avenue house, and when her attorney suggested that she sell the house and move to a penthouse with an elevator, she was horrified at his spendthrift proposal. The two family automobiles were stored on blocks, activated only for the summer trips to and from Irvington.[21]

Like most of the Wendels, Ella was more than a trifle eccentric. Convinced that all disease was absorbed into the body through the feet, she wore rubber rain shoes with thick soles every day of the year. When she wished to purchase a dish towel or a bar of chocolate, she sent a letter to the appropriate tradesman. When she wanted to leave the house for a short trip, she wrote her sister Rebecca's chauffeur on Long Island, who then made a 150-mile drive for an excursion of several blocks.[22]

Most of Ella's day was devoted to the care of the latest in a series of eighteen Maltese poodles, all named Tobey, which she had owned for years. The current Tobey slept in Ella's bedroom in a small four-poster bed which matched her own. Each morning at 9:00, she took Tobey for a long walk in the lot adjoining the Fifth Avenue house, which served as a dog run and was spotted with flagstone so that the poodle's paws would not become muddy or its mistress' feet exposed to disease-transmitting soil. After the walk, the poodle was bathed and served a breakfast of liver or a chop, with Ella acting as cook. In the afternoon, she and Tobey took another walk, after which the two ate dinner in the dining room, Tobey at his own small brass table, complete with velvet tablecloth and napkin. Afterwards, Ella bathed Tobey a second time, took the poodle on yet another walk, then talked to the animal until both fell asleep. The same elaborate routine, repeated daily both at the Fifth Avenue house and on the Irvington estate, occupied much of Ella's time. Most of the remainder she spent sorting and resorting the contents of 157 trunks filled with family effects and scattered about the house. When a Tobey died, Ella had a damp-proof, watertight underground vault and varnished oak casket with brass handles, lined in satin, constructed. Each poodle was buried in a graveyard on the Wendel property; each gravesite was marked with a tombstone, with notes from Ella left on each coffin.[23]

Ella Wendel died on March 13, 1931. When her sister Rebecca had died eight months earlier, she had bequeathed a portion of her estate to Ella and the balance to a number of charities. Ella's will left the bulk of the Wendel fortune to those identical institutions. The largest portion of the estate, initially estimated after her death at $75 million, was to further the teachings of the Methodist church and was equally divided among the Drew Theological Seminary in New Jersey and seminaries in Nanking, China. Other recipients included two hospitals and a children's home situated near the family's Irvington estate.[24]

Since Ella had associated only with children during her summers in Irvington, the bequest to the children's home near there seemed rational enough, as did those to societies for the prevention of cruelty to animals. But the will's contents also raised a number of intriguing questions. First, it was unlike Ella to have left anything, much less the bulk of her estate, to religious and charitable organizations. She had not attended church for at least the last thirty years of her life and often referred to charities as "grafters." A Wendel lease form indicated, in fact, that "None of our property is leased for churches, theaters or other forms of cheap entertainment." In the past, she had shown only contempt for the head of Drew Seminary, and after Rebecca had married a clergyman, John Gottlieb Wendel had discouraged his sisters from attending church at all. Ella's attorney, Charles G. Koss, explained that Ella had instructed him to prepare a will "like Beckie's" and Rebecca, who had devoted much of her life to religious and charitable causes, had been generous to such institutions in her will. Given Ella's deep aversion to them, however, it was difficult to imagine her having pursued the same course.[25]

Second, Ella had not only left extremely valuable property to attorney Koss and his daughter Isobel, but she had recently increased Isobel's share substantially by eliminating Joseph Lundy, the son of the devoted family coachman, entirely from her will. Ella and Isobel were close, but she had also been fond of Lundy and his late father. When a family maid recalled that Ella had told Koss repeatedly that she could not be bothered with the preparation of a will, and had capitulated only after a long afternoon of arguing with the attorney in the family library, suspicions grew about the eccentric recluse's inordinate generosity to Koss and his daughter. Most perplexing of all, the will made no provision at all for the surviving Tobey, the only creature, the *New York Times* reported after her death, for whom Ella had ever "displayed any kindness."[26]

Shortly after her death, Charles Koss and his associate George F. Warren told reporters that Ella Wendel had left "no relatives whatever." But given the intriguing features of her will, her manifold eccentricities, and the truism—attributed to W. Barton Leach, a Harvard law professor and John Harlan II's close friend—that "No one with money dies without heirs," a challenge to Ella's final testament seemed inevitable. What no one could have expected was the sheer number of claimants who were to emerge. Some of those seeking a slice of the pie made no pretext to a legal entitlement. There was, for example, the refugee from the Russian revolution, then living in Paris, who wrote New York's comptroller, seeking a thousand dollars from the estate. That amount, she assured the city official, would make her and her elderly mother "happy" and enable her to start a business. "[W]e would live and bless until death," she added, "the memory of Miss Wendel and the magnanimity of the nobleness of soul of the American people." Ultimately, over 2,300 persons, represented by hundreds of lawyers (two alone appearing for 291 claimants), would make a legal claim to a portion of the Wendel estate.[27]

Except for one brief period, the firm with which Charles Koss was associated had represented the Wendels' interests since the Civil War. But as the number of claimants continued to climb—and attracted some of New York's ablest litigators, including Arthur Garfield Hays and Samuel Untermyer—Koss and his associate Warren quickly realized that they were no match for the growing assault on Ella Wendel's will. Initially, they retained Emory Buckner to represent the estate and its heirs. When Buckner suffered a slight stroke in early 1932, however, they turned to his chief assistant, John Harlan. "It was a judgment," the author of a fascinating study of the Wendel litigation concluded, which Harlan "brilliantly vindicated. His chief skills as a lawyer, along with his intellect, were his painstaking attention to detail and exhaustive preparation; his mastery of facts and ability to articulate them; and his skill in cross-examining witnesses." In the Wendel case, he would put all those talents, honed at the feet of his mentor Buckner, to superb use. Assisted by a battery of twenty-five Root, Clark associates and attorneys representing the heirs, Harlan prepared a file for every bit of evidence he planned to present in defense of Ella Wendel's will, marshalling arguments as to their relevance and admissibility, anticipating possible challenges, and amassing legal authorities to support his position. For every item of evidence the opposition was expected to introduce, he followed the same meticulous procedure, in reverse. The whole experience was to be supremely satisfying for him and his principal assistant, Henry J. Friendly, a future chief judge of the Second Circuit. In later years, Friendly would recall, the two often remarked "that the Wendel estate litigation was the most enjoyable forensic experience of our lives. It combined the elements of drama with—what is not always available—the financial resources needed to do a truly thorough professional job."[28]

Not surprisingly, the first courtroom battles in the case were to be essentially jurisdictional. In the early fall of 1931, Rosa Dew Stansbury, an elderly Vicksburg, Mississippi, spinster who claimed to be a fifth-degree heir and Ella's nearest surviving kin, filed a suit in federal court against the estate's executors. Following Ella's death, Charles Koss had paid Miss Stansbury $1,000, with a promise of $24,000 more, to sign a waiver of any further claim to the Wendel fortune. Miss Stansbury's attorney, Arthur Garfield Hays, urged Judge Julian W. Mack to void the waiver and enjoin its use in probate proceedings. Koss, Hays contended, had persuaded the claimant to sign the document before she retained counsel and had failed to inform her that there were grave doubts as to Miss Wendel's competency and that her will was certain to be contested.[29]

Henry Friendly, who had studied with Felix Frankfurter and clerked for Justice Louis D. Brandeis, was regarded as an expert on questions of jurisdiction and was assigned to write a brief opposing Hays's petition. Friendly's position prevailed. While a federal court obviously had jurisdiction to hear a suit between citizens of different states, Judge Mack dismissed the case, giving the doctrine of abstention what, Friendly believed, must have been one of its earliest applications. Probate of Ella's will had begun in New York's surrogate or probate court before Miss Stansbury's federal suit was filed, and her waiver had been made part of the state court's record. For that reason, Mack refused to intervene. He agreed that the mere filing of the waiver in the state court had not given it exclusive jurisdiction over the document. He decided, however, that the waivèr was "so vitally . . . involved in and so akin to the very probate itself as to make it . . . highly desirable that all of the issues affecting it be determined by the court having the exclusive probate jurisdiction." In that way, conflicts over judicial interpretation of the waiver's validity could be avoided.[30]

The jurisdictional disputes were hardly over, however. Ella's executors had submitted her will to probate in New York County before Judge James B. Foley, one of the county's most distinguished jurists and its principal surrogate. In her will, however, Ella had listed her residence as Westchester County, in which the Wendel family's Irvington estate was situated. Surrogate Foley typically sided with the terms of a will in probate disputes, and John Harlan was determined that Foley preside over the disposition of the Wendel fortune. For precisely the same reason, attorneys for the claimants hoped to move the case to the Westchester surrogate court. But Surrogate Foley was not about to permit such a juicy and intriguing set of disputes to slip from his hands. To Harlan's relief, Foley concluded that Ella Wendel's legal residence was New York County, largely because that was where the bulk of her wealth was located.[31]

Ultimately, settlements amounting to nearly $3 million would be reached among the alleged heirs having the strongest claims to a portion of the Wendel wealth. Emory Buckner played the primary role in those sensitive negotiations. But the allure of unearned riches had also attracted a multitude of fraudulent claimants, and John Harlan was the principal figure in defending the estate from their clutches. The phony heirs included several who erected a tombstone bearing altered birth and death dates in a West Virginia cemetery, as well as Ilinois claimants who produced letters from Ella's father, dated 1836 and 1841, but written on paper purchased from Woolworth's and manufactured not earlier than 1930. Another set of impostors faked two cards purporting to provide evidence of an 1819 marriage, then planted them in the files of the Maryland land office, while others presented forged "Good Samaritan" letters, allegedly from Ella, her brother, and grandfather, promising them the entire Wendel estate![32]

The most audacious and, for those named in Ella's will, potentially dangerous impostor to surface in the case, however, was one Thomas Patrick Morris, a frail Scotsman in his fifties. Morris claimed that he was the son of Ella's brother, John Gottlieb Wendel, the progeny of a secret marriage in 1876 of Wendel to Mary Ellen Devine of Edinburgh. As a youth, Morris had been taken to live with foster parents, Peter and Margaret Morris, in Dundee. But beginning in 1885, he asserted, John Wendel had made the first in a series of annual visits to the Morris home. "He would pick me up and hug and kiss me, and let me play on his knee. He told me to call him Papa Wendel, and I did."[33]

The annual visits ended in 1897, when young Thomas Patrick enlisted in the militia. In 1901, however, John G. made another summer trip to Dundee. On this occasion, according to Morris, he gave his son a watch and chain and a book, wrapped in paper. "In the book you will find some writing," John G. told him. "Read it and don't ever show it to anybody." Inscribed on the inside front cover and flyleaf of the book, a novel entitled *The Blockade of Phalsburg,* was a letter which read:

March 1st, 1901

My Dear Son,

I am writing you this to clear up any doubt you might have in your mind as to your parentage.

I, John G. Wendel of 442 Fifth Avenue, New York City and Mary Ellen Devine of Edinburgh, Scotland, were married at Castle Garden, June 11, 1876, promising to marry her later on in the church of her faith, Roman Catholic. My family being Methodist I refused to carry it through. I was kept busy through the death of your grandfather, straightening out matters, and in the latter part of May, 1879, your mother and I quarreled, and being with child [she] fled to friends, a Mr. and Mrs. Morris living at 4 John St., Dundee Scotland. I followed and tried to make a reconciliation but allowed religious scruples to stand in the way.

You were born the 3rd of January, 1880. Your mother still refusing to be reconciled about two weeks after your birth disappeared leaving you in bed while our friend was out shopping. Fearing the scandal and that the news might drift back to my family in the States I failed to report it. I arranged with our friends to register your birth as their own and care for you, living in hopes your mother would return. My hopes were in vain. You were registered as Thomas Patrick Morris the first two names the wish of your mother whom you dearly loved.

The foregoing statement is true,
So help me God.

Your loving Father,
JOHN G. WENDEL

On the back flyleaf, Morris found a will in which John G. left his entire estate "to my Son Thomas Patrick Morris Wendel." John G. had taken this approach to declaring his wishes, the will stated, because of his "sisters, especially Mary and Ella's objections and refusal to recognize my son by a secret marriage and their threats to publicly expose me."[34]

In 1906, according to Morris, he was serving as a "chief greaser" on a passenger line when he jumped ship in New York to find a job. By accident, he later met John G. in a city park, and thereafter the two saw each other several times each week. One day in March 1907, his father suggested that he meet his aunts at the Wendel's Fifth Avenue house. But Ella had berated her brother for bringing "your brat" to the house and ordered them to leave. Except for one brief glimpse in Arizona some years later, Morris testified, that was the last time he saw his father.[35]

In late July of 1932, Morris told his story on the witness stand in Surrogate Foley's court. His attorney also introduced the book containing John G.'s purported will and letter, as well as a document claimed to be John G.'s and Mary Devine's marriage certificate, a letter from Morris's foster mother, who claimed that he was not her natural son, and an 1897 letter to the Morrises, in handwriting similar to that in the book, in which John G. inquired about "my son Thomas Patrick Morris." Joseph Lundy, whose father, Richard, the Wendels' coachman, had been one of three witnesses to the will, could not testify that his father's signature on the document was or was not in Richard Lundy's handwriting. But the grandniece of Michael Lynch, a longtime family employee who also witnessed Wendel's signing of the will, testified that Lynch's signature was in his hand. Her great-uncle had once admonished her, she also testified, "Helen, never be ashamed of being a Catholic. John G. Wendel was ashamed of his wife and child because they were Catholics." Several witnesses asserted, moreover, that Morris bore a striking physical resemblance to John G. Wendell, and one of them, a stationer whose shop Wendel frequented for nearly thirty years, said Wendel had once told him about his son, adding, "You ought to see my big boy." Ann Gordon, a registered nurse who had attended John G. Wendel between 1898 and 1903, when he had a serious attack of pneumonia, also testified that Wendel had revealed his son's existence to her in the presence of two physicians and her sister. Finally, and perhaps most effectively, Morris's counsel, Raymond L. Wise, introduced into evidence a life-sized bust of John G. Wendel which a sculptor had designed from two photographs. "We were stunned," Arthur Garfield Hays would later write, "at the likeness between the bust of John G. Wendel and Thomas Patrick Morris. As witnesses had said, 'Morris was the spitting image of Wendel.' "[36]

Wise had made an impressive case for his client. When he had finished, Hays recalled, the estate's "lawyers had lost their air of amused indifference." But John Harlan was hardly unprepared for rebuttal. While he had been in Scotland taking depositions and otherwise investigating Morris's claims, Henry Friendly and other assistants had checked out some twenty-three of Morris's assertions. By the time Harlan returned, Friendly had established that Morris had lied at least twenty-one times. "When I reported my success," Friendly later reported, Harlan, "undaunted by my exuberance and his own achievements in Scotland, suggested that we should concentrate on the remaining two points." Nor, for the meticulous Harlan, were such suggestions exceptional. When another claimant based her position on an obviously forged entry in a German church register, Harlan suggested that an associate investigating the claim engage a handwriting expert. When the associate responded that the forgery was so obvious no expert was needed, Harlan wired a prompt reply: "Get the handwriting expert." And when he confronted Patrick Morris in the courtroom, according to one contemporary account, he "tore" the claimant's case "to shreds."[37]

First, Harlan introduced a chart of the family of Peter and Margaret Morris, Thomas Patrick's alleged foster parents, on which he listed the birth dates of their various children. The chart indicated that the Morris union had produced progeny at regular intervals and that there would have been an unusual break in that pattern were Thomas Patrick not the Morris' child. Second, he persuaded Surrogate Foley to exclude certain testimony of Morris's witnesses. If this appeal had been overruled, Harlan was prepared to counter testimony about John G. Wendel's frequent sexual liaisons with servant girls, several of whom were obliged to induce abortions, with a memorandum showing that such promiscuity was legally irrelevant to Morris's claim that he was John G.'s legitimate offspring.[38]

Through skillful cross-examination and the introduction of documentation and testimony, Harlan was also able to challenge critical factual details in Morris's story, especially his chronology of meetings with Wendel. Harlan did not badger Morris. Instead, Henry Friendly would remember, his "questions were put in such a sympathetic manner that Morris got the impression he was being afforded an opportunity to strengthen his case and furnished supporting detail in abundance—most of which afforded further opportunities for us to prove his inability to tell the truth." Then, Harlan would ensnare his victim. "Would it surprise you to know," he asked Morris gently at one point, "that John G. Wendel did not leave New York from 1879 to 1914, that during July of 1901 [when, by Morris's account, Wendel visited Scotland and presented him the novel containing his letter and will] he signed checks here in New York and wrote letters to his employees from Quogue, Long Island—would it surprise you to know that?" When Morris conceded his surprise, Harlan continued. "I want to give you every opportunity to fix the dates right. I tell you that Mr. Wendel was in New York during the part of July that you say you saw him in Scotland. Does that change your recollection about the date?" Later, Harlan led the witness back over his earlier testimony about his confrontation with Ella Wendel in, Morris claimed, March of 1907. "And if I tell you," he then asked, "that on February 16, 1907, Miss Ella Wendel and her sisters sailed for Europe and were gone until July, does that change your testimony?" And on it went, as Harlan repeatedly exposed serious gaps between Morris's testimony and conflicting evidence.[39]

A handwriting expert Harlan called to the witness stand weakened Morris's case still further. Elbridge W. Stein concluded that the letter John G. Wendel had purportedly written Peter and Margaret Morris in 1897, as well as the letter and will in the copy of the novel Wendel was alleged to have given Morris, were not in Wendel's handwriting. The signatures of the witnesses to the will, Stein further asserted, were also forgeries. In fact, in his judgment, the letter, will, and signatures had all been written by the same person—and years after 1901. Scribner's had published *The Blockade of Phalsburg,* he explained, in 1900, and the copy in Morris's possession was yellowed with age. Yet places where the pen used to write the letter and will had cut the paper were white, which indicated they had been made years after the book's publication and Wendel's alleged inscription.[40]

Harlan's most devastating assault on Morris's case, however, was directed at the marriage certificate the claimant had produced as evidence of Mary Ellen Devine's betrothal to John G. Wendel. Harlan and his associates were convinced the certificate was a fake, but proving their suspicions was another matter. Then one day as Harlan and Friendly sat in the Root, Clark library, examining a long table of documents relating to the case, an attorney from Charles Koss's firm happened by on an unrelated errand. "That is just like the certificate in our family Bible at home," he remarked when he spotted the marriage certificate. His remark launched Harlan on an exhaustive search of publishing houses and book dealers with family Bibles for sale; eventually he found what he was looking for.[41]

On November 18, 1932, Harlan called to the stand William H. Holman, a representative of A. J. Holman and Company, a firm which had printed Bibles since 1870. The Holman Bibles contained marriage certificate forms featuring illustrations of a large wedding ring and a bell tower at the top of the certificate. Bibles in which the "bell" and "ring" certificates appeared were not first published until 1885. Samples Holman produced, moreover, indicated that the certificate on which Morris was relying—which, an expert witness testified, had been torn from a book—had been printed in 1913. John G.'s alleged marriage to Mary Devine in 1876 was thus recorded on a certificate printed thirty-seven years after the event![42]

Holman's revelation demolished what had remained of Morris's case. On Harlan's motion, Surrogate Foley dismissed the Scotsman's claim. Thoroughly convinced that Morris was a fraud, Foley also turned the record and exhibits over to the district attorney. At Morris's later trial for fraud, expert witnesses called to testify in his behalf conducted experiments which convinced them that the Holman Bible certificates had differed in important respects from the marriage certificate on which the defendant had based his claim. Even so, Morris was found guilty and given a three-year sentence.[43]

On a motion for a new trial, his counsel argued that Mary Ellen Devine, whom Surrogate Foley had termed a "wraith or ghost," was not actually Patrick's mother, that instead she had merely been a fiction used by John G. Wendel to hide the fact that the boy was really the product of John G.'s incestuous relationship with his sister Mary. But to no avail. Morris's conviction was affirmed, and he served his sentence, at all times continuing to protest his innocence.[44]

In later years, Henry Friendly espoused the view that Harlan's and his efforts in the Wendel case had perhaps served the public interest. "Surely it was better that Miss Wendel's vast estate should go to hospitals, institutions of learning, and other charities, even though there was almost no evidence she had ever taken an interest in them, than to distant relatives she had never known," much less to "fakers." Friendly doubted, however, whether such considerations had occurred to Harlan and was certain he himself had never entertained them. "Our pleasure came from the *gaudium certaminis*, the joy of battle, and from pride in a task well done. Today's young lawyers are missing something if they have lost this."[45]

But whatever Harlan's motives beyond the simple representation of his clients' interests, his defense of the Wendel estate had further bolstered his growing reputation as a lawyer's lawyer. In 1934, a friend wrote Emory Buckner regarding Surrogate Foley's impressions of the young attorney's work:

> [He] told me that of all the cases he has tried it was infinitely the best prepared. In fact he used the word "perfect" with reference to John Harlan's work. As a result of hard study, so he said, he thought he knew the case pretty well himself, but John's mastery of every detail and his instant perception of just where the pieces fitted into the whole picture were a revelation. He expressed especial amazement that a man obviously so fatigued and sleepless as John could be so crystal-clear in matters of memory and so lucid in all his mental processes.[46]

The Chair of Indecency

As John Harlan's legal career blossomed, he and Ethel settled into a lifestyle common to those of their social background and his developing professional standing. Harlan enjoyed golf and tennis, winning awards in both. During their months together in the Prohibition division of the U.S. attorney's office, he and J. Edward Lumbard and become close friends, and most Saturdays and Sundays before his marriage to Ethel, Harlan, Lumbard, and David Peck, another division staffer, played thirty-six holes of golf—and one June day, Lumbard remembers, seventy-two holes—at a club in New Jersey. After Harlan's marriage, a round of eighteen holes and an occasional game of tennis became the friends' weekend custom.[47]

During their years in New York, the Harlans would occupy a series of increasingly commodious and comfortable Manhattan apartments, first on Eighty-sixth Street, then on East End Avenue, in a building also occupied at one point by Emory Buckner and his family, and, after World War II, on East Fifty-first Street, near the United Nations building. In 1937, the Harlans built a country home in Weston, Connecticut, on twenty acres of beautiful countryside. And the Weston home became their favorite residence, especially for Ethel Harlan. Ethel was fond of fox hunting, and the couple often hosted hunt breakfasts at their Weston home, Harlan writing a friend before one such occasion to assure him that the pink coat he was planning to wear would be entirely "in order." Harlan never rode to the hounds and attempted western riding only long enough to get engaged to Ethel, "and that was it." In 1938, the Lumbards built a house in Fairfield, near the Harlans' Weston home, and John and Lumbard were frequent golf and tennis partners at the Fairfield Country Club.[48]

In 1930, Harlan had assisted Emory Buckner in defending heavyweight boxer Gene Tunney in Tim Mara's suit for a piece of the champ's earnings from the 1926 Tunney-Dempsey match. Since Tunney had written a letter and signed other documents which, on their face, supported Mara's claim, the case was a difficult one. A Bronx speakeasy operator had proved to be their best witness in the case; Harlan later would recall spending "days drinking with him before he agreed to testify." Although the trial verdict in the case favored Mara, he ultimately settled out of court for $30,000 rather than risk reversal on appeal and the uncertainties of a new trial.[49]

The Tunney case, Earl Carroll affair, Prohibition cases, and the bizarre Wendel litigation notwithstanding, Harlan's law practice was devoted largely to lucrative but dry and arcane matters of corporate law, best typified perhaps by *Randall* v. *Bailey*,[50] which involved the meaning to be assigned state statutes governing the payment of corporate dividends. Whether of general appeal or only of interest to corporate lawyers, his caseload had little relevance to the sorts of fundamental civil liberties claims he would later confront on the Supreme Court. In 1940, however, he became briefly, but significantly, involved in one such suit.

In February of that year, the Board of Higher Education of the City of New York had offered the noted British scholar Bertrand Russell a visiting professorship in mathematics and logic at City College. By that stage in his career, Russell had achieved a reputation as one of the world's foremost philosophers. But he was also an extremely controversial figure. A pacifist who opposed Allied involvement in World War I, he had been imprisoned four and a half months in 1918 for seditious writings.

Then, too, there was his unorthodox personal life. Thrice married and allegedly involved in several adulterous relationships, he and one of his wives had established a progressive experimental school where, *Life* magazine reported, "uninhibited children studied, said, did, dressed and undressed as they pleased," making the school "world-famous" as a "Paradise for Bad Children." As much a source of conservative consternation as his life-style, however, were the professor's unorthodox views on sex, morality, marriage, child-rearing, and education, especially his apparent support of sexual relations among college students and adultery as therapy for troubled marriages.[51]

Almost immediately after word of Russell's appointment surfaced, the resident Episcopal bishop, an Englishman who had been attacking his countryman's views since 1929, wrote a letter to New York newspapers in which he condemned the scholar as "a recognized propagandist against both religion and morality." A large contingent of clerics, religious organizations, and "patriot" groups soon joined the bishop. And when the Board of Higher Education, bolstered perhaps by the support of John Dewey and other leading academics of the day, reaffirmed its decision despite the growing outcry, Jean Kay, a Brooklyn housewife, filed a taxpayer suit in the state supreme court challenging the board's action on a variety of grounds. Ordinarily, such a suit would have had little chance for success. Never before, after all, had an American court held a teacher's qualifications to be a proper subject for judicial review. But Justice John E. McGeehan, the state judge who heard the case, was a staunch Roman Catholic who had once attempted to have Martin Luther's portrait removed from a courthouse mural of legal history. Straining to extend to the board's action provisions of state law traditionally applied only to primary and secondary schools, McGeehan held Russell's appointment invalid on the ground that the scholar was not a U.S. citizen and had not been subjected to an examination of his qualifications! The justice found "most compelling," however, the charges which had been raised against Russell's "notorious immoral and salacious writings." McGeehan agreed that he had authority to overturn the appointment purely because of his objections to Russell's literary "filth." He concluded that Russell had advocated adultery and other violations of the criminal law, and the judge insisted that he had both the power and responsibility to forbid the creation of a "chair of indecency" for such a sinister influence on the city's children. Later, he remarked that after reading one of the professor's books he had been obliged to "take a bath." Russell, he was certain, wanted "to make strumpets out of all our girls."[52]

As a practical matter, the wisdom of appealing Justice McGeehan's opinion seemed increasingly doubtful. Following the higher board's vote to reaffirm Russell's appointment in mid-March, Queens borough president George Harvey had announced that he would move to strike the entire 1941 appropriation for the city's colleges at the next meeting of the board of estimate. If he had his way, said Harvey, anticipating a stance similar to that school segregationists would assume in the 1950s and 1960s, "the colleges would either be godly colleges, American colleges, or they would be closed." Presumably, Harvey's extreme proposal would have gotten nowhere, whatever the ultimate result of the Kay suit. But Mayor Fiorello La Guardia also removed the allocation for Russell's post from the 1941 budget, and the board of estimate prohibited the use of any city funds for Russell's employment, thereby in essence abolishing the position.[53]

Neither Bertrand Russell nor those members of the higher board still supportive of his appointment could resist challenging, however, Justice McGeehan's assault on their reputations. Alarmed by the way the office of the city corporation counsel was handling the case for the board, Russell had retained an attorney to represent his interests in the controversy. On the advice of ACLU personnel, he chose Osmond K. Fraenkel. An ACLU director, Fraenkel would later write an article attacking McGeehan's interference and contending that people should resort to the polls, not the courts, when "officials err in the exercise of the discretion given them by law." In a companion piece, a co-author had complained that, apparently under Justice McGeehan's First Amendment, Congress could make "no law abridging the freedom of speech" only if "a man speaks good and not evil." The day after McGeehan announced his decision, but before an order had been entered in the case, Fraenkel petitioned the judge to make Russell a party to the suit and permit him to answer Mrs. Kay's allegations. Characteristically, however, McGeehan denied the petition, holding that Russell had no legal interest in the proceedings, and two appellate courts refused to reverse his judgment. By the time the New York Court of Appeals had acted in the case, Russell was giving lectures on philosophy at the Barnes Foundation in a Philadelphia suburb. Except for the foundation's offer, he later wrote, he and his family would have been obliged "to live as cheaply as possible on the charity of kind friends."[54]

Members of the higher board had also been dismayed by the city's inept representation of their interests before Justice McGeehan. Some suspected that Nicholas Bucci, the assistant corporation counsel handling the case for the higher board, was following the directions of corporation counsel William C. Chanler and Mayor La Guardia, who probably had no qualms about Russell's credentials but were concerned about the political damage the city's defense of the appointment might cause the La Guardia administration. When Chanler refused to permit his office to represent the higher board in an appeal of McGeehan's ruling and urged board members not to challenge the decision either, their suspicions were confirmed.[55]

Despite Chanler's refusal to represent them, several members of the higher board were determined to challenge McGeehan's decision. Justice McGeehan's ruling and rhetoric had particularly incensed Lauson Stone, a board member and the son of Supreme Court Justice Harlan Fiske Stone. "The board of higher education," Stone recently recalled:

> had become less conservative than it had been in the past, when it was pretty much the creature of the very conservative elements in the city, and the new board was attempting to make the universities and colleges under its supervision into something worthwhile. New people were put in charge of the various institutions, and the people at City College were looking for faculty they considered distinguished. They came up with this idea of having Russell give some mathematical lectures at City College. Many people did not agree with some of his views about sex; I'm not sure I agreed with them. But they weren't pertinent to his appointment . . . and we didn't think the judge had any power to do what he did.[56]

After Justice McGeehan announced his decision, Stone visited his father's chambers in Washington. The elder Stone was sympathetic. He suggested that his son and other board members contact Emory Buckner. They did, and Buckner and John Harlan, both of whom shared the board's outrage at McGeehan's temerity, offered to represent the board members without fee, their clients and "several kind friends," as Stone later put it, taking care of only the lawyers' out-of-pocket expenses. Since Buckner was ill (he would be dead within a year), Harlan again assumed major responsibility for the case.[57]

When Lauson Stone and other board members petitioned Justice McGeehan to substitute Harlan and Buckner as their counsel, McGeehan denied their petition. The board as an entity, he argued, was forbidden by state law to retain independent counsel; moreover, the interests of individual board members in the case, like those of Professor Russell, were too minor and remote from the immediate dispute to justify their being permitted to enter the suit except as members of the board.[58]

In the ninety-four-page brief he filed with the appellate division of the state supreme court, Harlan was thus obliged to challenge McGeehan's position on the issue of counsel as well as the judge's reversal of Russell's appointment. On the first question, Harlan cited Section 355 of the city charter, which did generally authorize the corporation counsel alone to assign counsel to represent individual agencies and officials, but also included an exception permitting officials to retain counsel of their own choosing, and at their own expense, where a judicial action might "affect . . . them individually or may be followed by a motion to commit for contempt of court." Since members of the board could be held in contempt if they disobeyed McGeehan's injunction, Harlan asserted, the exception Section 355 allowed seemed squarely applicable to his clients. Even apart from the exception, he added, William Chanler's refusal to act for the board itself authorized board members to retain their own counsel; such had been the teaching of at least two earlier cases.[59] But Harlan had an even broader objection to McGeehan's stance. Citing previous cases emphasizing the independence of state boards of education from the control of municipal authorities,[60] he reasoned that Section 355 in general was inapplicable to the higher board if it prevented the board's members from performing and defending their lawful functions.

Harlan also challenged Justice McGeehan's conclusion that state law prohibited the hiring of alien college professors. "This is the first time, as far as we know," he contended, "that it has ever been held by any Court in this State that the faculties of our public institutions of higher learning are closed to the employment of scholars from other countries. Such a result is indeed wholly out of keeping with the basic concepts of an enlightened system of higher education."[61] The citizenship requirement applied to "public schools," and its context and history demonstrated conclusively to Harlan that the provision extended only to primary and secondary schools. The requirement was included, after all, in a section of the state education law entitled "Teachers and Pupils"; the term "pupils" normally referred to children in the primary and secondary grades. The statute dealing with the Board of Higher Education referred to "students," not "pupils."[62]

Nor, Harlan contended, had McGeehan been correct in holding Russell's appointment invalid on the ground that the scholar had not been administered a civil service examination. A provision of the New York constitution did require that appointments to various positions of public employment be made on the basis of "merit and fitness to be ascertained . . . by examination," but only to the extent such examinations were "practicable." Surely, Harlan argued, the higher board could have reasonably concluded that merit examinations were not a "practicable" method for recruiting college faculty. "Professorial appointments have traditionally been made upon the basis of outstanding learning and exceptional achievement, and never upon the basis of minimum qualifications. Necessarily the qualifications of such an appointment are not the subject of precise admeasurement, and any attempt thereat, such as competitive or non-competitive examination, would be the sheerest pretense."[63] That, he assumed, was why every college and university in the country followed the higher board's approach rather than the one Justice McGeehan appeared to be imposing.

Finally, of course, Harlan took issue with the principal basis for McGeehan's reversal of Professor Russell's appointment—the judge's conclusion that the appointment of a professor who advocated illegal acts violated public policy and thus posed an arbitrary and capricious interference with public health, safety, and morals. Characteristically, Harlan declined to debate the merits of Russell's writings. He did assert, however, that "no fair appraisal of [them] can be made by selecting isolated passages and considering them apart from their context," adding, "the conclusion reached by the lower Court that Professor Russell in his writings encourages violations of the Penal Law is wholly unjustified when the books to which the Court refers are read as a whole."[64] Whatever the nature of Russell's views, he argued, the higher board had fully discussed their possible impact on City College's students before reaffirming the eminent scholar's appointment, and the court had no authority to overturn the board's collective judgment, at least where state law had imposed no standards limiting the board's discretion. "[W]here an officer or board has been vested with full and complete power to perform a particular administrative duty," he observed, detailing numerous cases to back up his position, "the courts are powerless to interfere with the action of such office or board on the ground that such action is, in the opinion of the Court, unwise, arbitrary or contrary to public policy. This being clear, it follows of necessity that a court cannot assume such power by the expedient of reading into the grant of power various implied restrictions which the Court deems to be required by the public interest."[65]

The brief which Harlan filed in the Russell case was forceful, eloquent, and tightly reasoned. On this occasion, however, his position would not prevail; both the appellate division of the state supreme court and the New York Court of Appeals affirmed Justice McGeehan. Harlan was deeply disappointed with the higher courts' reaction. Louis Lusky, who was then practicing in Harlan's firm, had assisted with preparation of the appeal. His colleague's defeat in the Russell case, Lusky has recalled, was the only time he ever saw Harlan "really angry."[66]

The War Years

As Harlan's battle over the Russell appointment was reaching its abrupt and frustrating conclusion, war erupted in Europe and the Pacific. Harlan was then in his early forties, well beyond the usual age for military service. By October of 1942, however, he was in England, heading the Eighth Bomber Command's Operations Analysis Section.[67]

The Operations Analysis Section, one of many established during the war, was the brainchild of Harvard law professor W. Barton Leach and Dr. Ward Davidson, director of research for the Consolidated Edison utility. The Japanese attack on Pearl Harbor had underscored fundamental weaknesses in American air power. Following the disaster there, Secretary of War Henry L. Stimson's special assistant Harvey H. Bundy asked Leach and Davidson to conduct a survey and make recommendations for improving U.S. air capability. The two suggested creation of research units comparable to the RAF's Operational Research Agency and composed of persons with analytical capabilities from a variety of fields, including physics, mathematics, chemistry, biometrics, genetics—and law. Lawyers, they explained, could be especially useful since, "in their profession," as Leach later put it, "they found it essential to become bridges of communication between scientific expert witnesses on the one hand and [non-specialist] judges and juries" on the other.[68]

Their recommendations were approved, and Leach was transferred from military intelligence to the Army Air Force as chief of its Operations Analysis Division. He next was obliged to select a head of the division's first section. "I knew what type of man I wanted," he later remarked, "the best trial lawyer in the country in his early 40s with dynamic force and an easy personality and also with substantial experience in dealing with the British." During several days' conversations with New York attorneys, John Harlan's name had invariably "come up—always with great admiration. So I met Harlan, whom I had not known up to that time, and he was fascinated at the thought. He felt that he ought to be in the War, and as a graduate of Oxford he loved England and the British. He dropped his law practice and reported to the Pentagon." When Arthur Garfield Hays, heartened perhaps by Harlan's stance in the Russell case, wrote Harlan in October 1942, inviting him to join a group of downtown lawyers for monthly discussions of civil liberties issues, thus giving "each member an opportunity to do his share in maintaining liberty at home," Harlan's secretary responded cryptically that he was away from the city for an indefinite period "on a position in the war effort and therefore will not be available for some time to come."[69]

After an initial visit to England, Harlan returned briefly to the States to complete recruitment of a team which included from his law firm Philip Scott, Louis Lusky, and Leslie Arps—the latter recently drafted into the infantry and thus particularly grateful for the assignment. He also organized the section into a number of compartments, among which were units concerned with bombing accuracy, radio and radar technology, battle damage, bomb damage assessment, and gasoline consumption. The section's first assignment was to examine air attacks being made on German submarine pens at Lorient and St. Nazaire on the coast of France. Based on his team's analysis of strike and post-strike photographs, as well as their knowledge of ballistics and the resistance of concrete to bombardment, Harlan reported that attacks on the pens, which had an eleven-foot concrete covering, were not, and could not be, successful with current weapons; their only real impact was to awaken U-boat crews on leave between sorties.[70]

The team also conducted a study of bombing accuracy and concluded that fewer than 5 percent of the bombs being dropped were landing within five hundred feet of their targets. The bomber crews were certain to resent and challenge such findings. Drawing on his skill as a lawyer, however, Harlan was able to soothe the crews' concerns, especially when he presented the team's partial solution to the problem. By the application of probability theory, his scientists had concluded that concentrated bombing patterns, instead of the dispersed patterns then in use, would improve the accuracy of bombing raids. Since tighter formations could provide better mutual support against German fighter planes, the crews liked the team's proposed alternative. But not every recommendation was so easily accepted. When the section concluded that bombing accuracy could be improved if all planes released their bombs at the same time the lead bombardier began dropping his load, the other bombardiers protested. A test of bombardier competence had revealed, however, that only about 5 percent of the hastily trained men had the combination of skills required for successful performance of their duties. Thus, Harlan's decision held.[71]

The team lent their scientific and engineering expertise to the war effort in other ways as well. Not only did they develop effective radar and electronics countermeasures but they also prepared a textbook on the destruction of bridges and industrial installations. Their suggestions were nearly as often based on common sense observations as on theory. When they learned, for example, that gunners were being trained on skeet-shooting ranges, where the object was to lead the "bird," they convinced the gunners that, in actual combat situations, it was more often necessary to trail a target. On one occasion, Harlan went along on a bombing raid over German industrial installations, later joking that he almost shot down one of his own planes in the process. "He was sending all these chaps out, and he never went," his sister Edith later remarked. "So he insisted on going out on one mission."[72] Following the Normandy invasion, he took a tour of France, inspecting bombed sites and interviewing German POWs.

In the last months of his active service with the section, Harlan and Leslie Arps also drafted a secret 165-page memorandum detailing the development of the British Air Ministry and Royal Air Force as a separate branch of the British military. While largely descriptive in nature, the memorandum lobbied subtly for creation of a separate department of the air force in the U.S. military hierarchy—a proposal then the subject of hot debate in military circles, which in 1947 was to be enacted into law. At one point in the memorandum, for example, Harlan and Arps concluded that the British experience had illustrated:

> the important feature of RAF organization, namely, the extreme degree of flexibility which RAF Commands have maintained in order to achieve the ultimate desire or aim of the moment. The ability of the RAF to adjust itself to meet the particular situation amply vindicates the original concept of the founders of the separate Air Force that the Air Force must be organized in such a way that it can play not only an independent role but also a supporting role, with the emphasis on whichever role is most important at the time.[73]

Harlan's experiences with the section included the usual frustrations with military red tape. Officials of the British Air Ministry were reluctant to share their data with the section despite Harlan's assurances of absolute confidentiality. On several occasions, his military superiors complained when the section's reports were not cleared through them before being distributed. And there were other similar annoyances. "Damn nonsense," he recorded in his diary after one frustrating encounter. The section's efforts proved exceptionally productive, however, with the Eighth Bomber Command's bombing accuracy alone rising from the abysmal 5 percent Harlan's team had discovered on beginning their work to an impressive 65 percent rate of successful strikes. Harlan's diary entries also recorded his deep regard and affection for his team. One diary entry noted, for example: "Talked with Lusky who has cable from Charlotte beseeching him to go home. Sent wire to Ethel asking her to talk with Charlotte and let me know her advice. Louis also discouraged about his work. Advised him that apart from Charlotte I didn't want him to go, but that his first obligation was to her." And when his successor as head of the section—whom Harlan had predicted would be an "absentee landlord"—proved to be a terrible disappointment to Leslie Arps, who initially was to have taken over leadership of the section, and to other members of the team, Harlan quietly intervened to secure another replacement. "The boys are in the best of spirits," he later wrote in his diary, "and [the] victory over Dolan has been a great thing."[74]

Harlan's second military assignment may have been less gratifying. In early August of 1944, he learned of his nomination to a committee responsible for planning for the postwar occupation of Germany. Such an assignment could have become a long-term commitment, and his orders were being processed in Washington before he had been approached about the matter. At first, he took a "dim view" of the assignment, and his initial impressions of the planning process were not favorable. By now a confirmed Anglophile, he was appalled at the limited progress of American planning for the occupation in contrast to what he found to be the "definite and well expressed ideas" of the British on what should be done. "I have rarely seen a more messed up situation," he wrote in his diary on August 9. "Too many cooks, too little understanding of the picture here by Washington, too many memoranda, no firm hand on the situation. The net will probably be that we shall find Germany surrendering without our having any well thought out plan as to what we are going to do."

The following day he wrote that "Actually there is very little difference between British and Americans, except on the zoning point, although the Air Force people over here seem to think that the British are running away with the show. It's that rather than the merits which makes them so mad; and of course it's our own damn fault for not being better organized. Saw the President's memo on the Zoning question—an extraordinary document from a chief executive."[75]

Harlan was especially concerned that American leaders were being unduly conciliatory toward the Soviet Union and neglecting traditional U.S.–British ties in the negotiations. In one diary entry, he wrote of his discouragement over "the tendency in our higher circles to play ball with the Russians rather than with the British," adding:

> This may be what we shall have to do at some point along the line, but it seems unnecessary to make that choice at once. The Russians stand a good chance of coming out with more than they would be willing to take if we forced them to trade, rather than recognizing, as the official U.S. thinking seems to do, that the Russians have the superior claims or at least must be appeased. One document from the Strategic Planning group in the JCS goes so far as to foresee the possibility of the next war being between Britain and Russia, and predicts that a combined British-American set up couldn't defeat the Russians; ergo we must play ball with the Russians or at least not get committed to the British.[76]

In the main, however, Harlan would consider his military tour among the most significant and rewarding episodes of his life. Commissioned as a colonel, he was awarded the Legion of Merit and a citation of appreciation for patriotic service. From France and Belgium, moreover, he received the *Croix de Guerre*. But Harlan had also found the experience immensely enjoyable. "He made some friends and renewed acquaintances from his days at Oxford," his sister Edith remembers. "He had some lovely British women driving him hither and yon, and he had a great old time. I think Ethel was rather relieved to get him home." In his diary entry for November 27, 1944, he noted receiving a letter from his wife. "She says," he wrote, that "I have been stringing her along" about a date for his separation from the Army Air Force. In a return cable, he assured her that he would be home for Christmas; on December 10, he received his release orders.[77]

Lawyer's Lawyer

While Harlan was in Europe, Ethel had taken a small apartment at the Hotel Langdon in New York, and their daughter, Eve, was a five-day boarder at the Thomas School. But they spent much of their time at the country house in Weston. John Harlan was a gentleman farmer at best. On one occasion when an imperfectly formed egg was brought in from the farm's henhouse, he suggested that it be placed beneath a hen again until completely developed! And he once mistook a hummingbird for a rodent. But his caretaker kept a number of chickens and goats on the place, and during the war Ethel and Eve grew a victory garden there.[78]

On Harlan's return from the war, he and his family maintained the Langdon hotel apartment for a time, then moved into a seven-room apartment overlooking the East River. As before his departure to Europe, the Harlans entertained frequently both in New York and at Weston. Many of their social acquaintances were drawn naturally from the law and the families of successful businessmen who had homes in the Weston area. But Harlan's beautiful, charming, and outgoing wife was also an aspiring playwright. "One of my chief memories of her as a youngster," Eve has said, "was of her constantly at the typewriter. Unfortunately, none of them got produced, but she came close. She was pretty good at writing and got some other things published." It was not surprising, then, that their wide social circle included friends from the arts and theater as well as from law and business.[79]

For recreation in those postwar years as well as before, Harlan enjoyed golf and tennis and was also an inveterate fisherman. Each summer for several years, he, Ethel, and Eve spent a few weeks on Amabelish, a remote Canadian island where he and several friends were partners in a fishing club. "We used to take the train to Montreal," Eve recalls, "then an overnight train to St. André, where we were met by a car and driven as far as the car would go, then we would take a horse and wagon as far as that would go, and then go the rest of the way on foot." While Ethel, like the other wives, was hardly fond of these outings, Eve enjoyed playing with the children of her parents' friends. "But mostly," she said, "I can remember sitting in the bottom of a canoe, in the rain, reading *A Tale of Two Cities,* while my father fished in a place it was known no fish had passed for thirty years." On one occasion, while Harlan was on leave from the military, the family had taken a trip to Bermuda. "One afternoon while we were there, Father was resting on the bed with a cigar in one hand, when Mother decided to give him a manicure, and suddenly got an inspiration. While he dozed, she painted his fingernails a bright red, then told him there was no way to get it off. He was really beside himself, until we finally took pity on him."[80]

Eve's childhood memories of her father are essentially pleasant ones, tinged with a child's regret at the time he devoted to reviving his law practice. "He was a marvelous father when he was around. He very seldom got angry or lost his temper. He was humorous, very witty; he could be quite a tease. Mainly, I'd say our household was a happy one." Harlan also took an interest in Eve's growing enthusiasm for music. "But," she adds, "he was a career man and lawyer all the time, and I guess I would have liked to see more of him when I was growing up. He worked all the time, and I think he found family life difficult. He left most of the day-to-day family matters to my mother."[81]

After the war as before, Harlan's practice was devoted largely to the interests of major corporate clients, including American Telephone and Telegraph and its subsidiary Western Electric, the International Telephone and Telegraph Company, and the Gillette Safety Razor firm. One of his more significant cases, in fact, extended over both the pre- and postwar periods. In a suit initially filed in 1940, he represented the American Optical Company in a federal injunction suit charging that American and other optical manufacturers had engaged in price-fixing and other restrictive trade practices. Harlan tried the case from November of 1941 to September 1942, when the secretaries of war and navy asked that proceedings be suspended for the duration of the war. After the war, he and John E. F. Wood, another of the firm's Oxford products and a close friend, negotiated a consent decree with the government.[82]

In the years following the war, Harlan also argued a number of important corporate cases in the Supreme Court. In one, he represented foreign diamond mining interests in an antitrust suit. To assure the defendants' presence for subsequent proceedings, a district judge granted the government's motion for a preliminary injunction tying up their U.S. property. Since federal law allowed appeals in such cases only of final judgments, not preliminary decrees, a successful appeal of the order seemed doubtful. By a 5–4 vote, however, the Supreme Court agreed with Harlan's argument that the Court had jurisdiction to issue an extraordinary writ of certiorari in the case and, on the merits, overturned the injunction.[83]

At least one of the cases Harlan successfully argued before the high court led to a landmark decision in the fields of corporate law and civil procedure. In *Cohen* v. *Beneficial Industrial Loan Corp.*, he represented a New Jersey company and several of its managers and directors in a stockholder suit. The plaintiff charged the defendants with numerous counts of fraud and mismanagement extending over an eighteen-year period and involving the diversion of more than $100 million in corporate funds. But he was only one of sixteen thousand stockholders in the company and owned only a hundred of its more than two million shares. In fact, his holdings, together with 150 shares held by an intervenor in the case, amounted to only 0.0125 percent of the company's outstanding stock, with a market value which never exceeded $9,000. His suit was brought to a federal district court in 1943 as a dispute between citizens of different states. But a 1945 New Jersey law required any plaintiff having a small financial interest in a case to be liable for the defendants' reasonable expenses and attorney's fees if he failed to win his suit. Harlan argued in the district court that the New Jersey law applied in such cases and that the plaintiff should be required to post a $125,000 bond. The district judge rejected Harlan's claim, but a court of appeals reversed, and the Supreme Court sided with the appeals panel, giving Harlan and his clients an important victory—and erecting a not insubstantial obstacle to suits by minor stockholders.[84]

But Harlan's principal postwar clients were members of the Du Pont family and a number of their corporate interests. In an antitrust action tried in New York, a district court rejected his arguments and held that Du Pont and other companies were involved in an international conspiracy to eliminate competition in the trade of chemical products, arms, and ammunition. In a supplemental order, moreover, the judge required the defendants to license their patents at a reasonable rate of royalties.[85] Harlan was to be more successful, however, in defending Pierre S. and Irénée Du Pont in another antitrust suit.

In the first century of its existence, E. I. Du Pont de Nemours & Co. had been a major manufacturer of military and commercial explosives. When the U.S. Army and Navy decided in 1908 to build and operate their own explosive factories, Du Pont feared a significant decline in its future market and decided to expand its operations into other commercial fields. The massive World War I demand for explosives took priority over the company's expansion plans, but only temporarily. In fact, the increases in Du Pont's capacity and plant facilities which the wartime demands necessitated made its postwar efforts to find expanded uses for its facilities even more urgent.[86]

During the first World War, Du Pont had set aside $90 million for postwar expansion, and even before United States entry into the war the company had begun to acquire several manufacturers of paint, rubber-coated fabrics, and other products used in the growing automobile industry. Not coincidentally, Du Pont also began to forge enduring ties with the General Motors corporation, which had first been organized in 1908. In 1915, while a battle for control of the automobile company was raging between its founder, William C. Durant, and a bankers' group, Pierre S. Du Pont, who was then Du Pont's president, became chairman of General Motors' board of directors. Between 1917 and 1919, Du Pont used its expansion fund to acquire 23 percent of General Motors' outstanding stock. By 1920–23, Du Pont held 38 percent of the automobile conglomerate's stock; by 1953, Du Pont's General Motors holdings were estimated at $1 billion. Over the years, moreover, Pierre S. and Irénée Du Pont, Du Pont treasurer John J. Raskob, as well as numerous other members of the Du Pont family and the company's corporate management, held important positions in the General Motors hierarchy.[87]

To the layperson at least, the motivation behind such financial and managerial connections seemed obvious. As John J. Raskob pointed out in a 1917 report recommending Du Pont's purchase of General Motors stock, Du Pont's "interest in the General Motors Company will undoubtedly secure for us the entire Fabrikoid, Pyralin, paint and varnish business of those companies, which is a substantial interest." Certainly, the arrangement's likely impact was not lost on the Flint Varnish and Chemical Works, which to that point had been General Motors' principal paint supplier. In 1918, the Flint Works president told William C. Durant that "he knew Du Pont had bought a substantial interest in General Motors and was interested in the paint industry" and that he feared his company would soon lose General Motors' business. Du Pont bought Flint and later dissolved the little company.

By August of 1921, Lammot Du Pont, a Du Pont vice president later to serve as chairman of the board of both companies, was able to report that four of General Motors' eight operating divisions bought from Du Pont their entire requirements of Fabrikoid, four divisions their entire requirements of rubber cloth, and seven their entire needs for Pyralin and celluloid. Du Pont's sales department was of the view that "the condition is improving and that eventually satisfactory conditions will be established in every branch, but they wouldn't mind seeing things going a little faster." Things did. In 1941, for example, General Motors took 93 percent of Du Pont's entire "Duro" automotive finish production; in 1947, 83 percent.

The Sherman Anti-Trust Act forbids combinations in restraint of interstate commerce, and Section 7 of the Clayton Act prohibits stock and capital acquisitions likely to have the same effect. In the years since its enactment in 1914, the Clayton Act had been applied only to the acquisition of stock in a competing corporation, that is, to so-called "horizontal" acquisitions, rather than to "vertical" acquisitions of a supplier or customer corporation's stock. And the Federal Trade Commission had given the act that construction. A 1950 amendment made it clear, however, that the law could be applied to vertical as well as horizontal transactions.

In an antitrust action filed in New York, a federal district court agreed with the government's claim that Du Pont and a British company had conspired to deny others access to a valuable nylon patent. In a second suit filed in June of 1949, the government charged that Du Pont, General Motors, and the United Rubber Company, which Du Pont had acquired in 1927, as well as individual members of the Du Pont family and two corporations with large amounts of Du Pont stock, were involved in a gigantic conspiracy to restrict trade in tires and other products associated with the automotive industry. The defendants, according to the government's complaint, had pursued three objectives: first, combined control of the three companies' management and policies; second, use of this favorable position to create and exploit protected markets for certain of their products, to the exclusion of competitive suppliers; and third, the reservation of various fields of production exclusively for the Du Pont company.

As he had in the New York phase of the litigation, John Harlan was retained to represent the interests of Pierre and Irénée Du Pont, as well as two companies with large Du Pont holdings, in the case, to be tried in Chicago before U.S. District Judge Walter L. LaBuy. Nor was Root, Ballantine, Harlan, Bushby, and Palmer, as Harlan's firm was now known, the only firm allied behind the various defendants. A huge team of lawyers, including many from several of the nation's leading firms, as well as their clerical and other assistants, descended on the city, taking over several floors of a Chicago hotel. Like the members of other firms connected with the case, Harlan and his staff realized that they had a "tough position" to defend; they had already spent months preparing for the trial. "We drove to [Du Pont's] Wilmington [headquarters] in Harlan's car every Monday and returned to New York on Friday afternoon for about eight or nine months, working hard on the case," Charles Stewart, one of the three members of Harlan's legal staff in the case, has recalled. "Then we moved to Chicago three or four months before the trial began."

Harlan and his staff had not anticipated, however, the lengthy delay between their arrival in Chicago and the trial's commencement. The government's legal contingent was to be decidedly more modest in size and resources than its opposition. After his arrival in Chicago, Harlan visited the hotel room of Willis Hotchkiss, the government attorney who, single-handedly at that point, was representing the United States of America against the defendants' impressive array of legal talent. "There he was," Harlan later recounted, "in a little basement room of the hotel, with every inch of space on the beds, chairs, tables and floors covered with mounds of documents. I asked him whether he mightn't prefer a larger room, and he said he couldn't on his government *per diem*. I felt sorry for him because he barely had room to sleep, and I offered to let him use some of our space, or any other facilities." The attorney, Harlan added, admiringly, "politely but flatly refused."[88]

Ultimately, Hotchkiss—a "rabid New Dealer" who "absolutely regarded the case as a crusade" against corporate privilege, as Harlan's daughter, Eve, later put it—was overwhelmed by the forces allied against him. At the time of opening statements by the attorneys, Hotchkiss issued a rambling, frequently incoherent brief against privilege, concluding:

> Now, at this time, and speaking in the open I am going to ask those good friends of mine at the tables of the opposition to do me a favor. I say "good friends" in no invidious sense. It is not seemly for members of our profession to carry the sword of the battle into the robing rooms.
>
> I ask these good friends to take it to those lords who reside in their palaces near the banks of the Brandywine. Take this message to those mighty lords, who stand accused here of having corrupted the high traditions of the people of this land who have been led by kindly providence into . . . this, the promised land. . . .
>
> Warn them for me, and do it with the utmost solemnity. Warn them that they must not put their hands on the holy ark of the tabernacle of justice, as they did two score years ago.
>
> The eyes of the people of this beloved land of ours are fixed on this proceeding. I say it, and I say it after long and prayerful consideration, that the wrath of that people will be terrible to behold if those mighty lords attempt again what they achieved two score years ago.

Shortly thereafter, Hotchkiss was removed from the case, the victim of a nervous breakdown.[89]

The Chicago trial lasted nearly seven months and produced an 8,283-page transcript. Fifty-two witnesses were called, over two thousand exhibits introduced into evidence, and final oral arguments alone consumed several weeks. Government counsel detailed the elaborate network of ties among the defendant corporations and members of the Du Pont family. Harlan and his associates argued, on the other hand, that such interrelationships were not alone sufficient to establish a conspiracy to restrain interstate commerce. While the original complaint had alleged that General Motors was required to take all or substantially all its supply requirements from Du Pont, it was later revised to contend that General Motors was expected only to prefer Du Pont's products over its competitors' when quality, price, and service were equal. Later, the government was also obliged to drop its claim that all Du Pont products of relevance to the automobile industry were involved in the conspiracy and allege only an attempt to restrain trade in fabrics, finishes, and antifreeze. Harlan attempted to capitalize on this "watering down" of the government's case.[90]

He also read from a message Woodrow Wilson had presented to Congress in 1919—several years after Du Pont's connections with General Motors had begun to develop—in which the president urged American development of chemical technology to make the United States independent of German expertise in that field. The Du Ponts, he contended, were motivated only by such regard for the national interest. To bolster his contention, he called eighty-three-year-old Pierre Du Pont and his seventy-six-year-old brother Irénée to the witness stand. Had Du Pont's World War I expansion, he asked Irénée, been accompanied by a desire for captive markets: "Absolutely not," the elderly industrialist replied. "I never heard of a protected market at that time." Pierre Du Pont naturally agreed. He and his brother had been motivated purely by a desire to make the nation independent of foreign expertise as well as by the belief that General Motors stock offered an excellent financial investment.[91]

In his final argument, Harlan reiterated this theme, praised his clients' services to their country, and scorned the government's attack on them "and their deceased brother, Lammot, who unfortunately is not here to look his accusers in the eye."

> If I may be permitted to make a personal remark, I have been proud to represent these two distinguished men to whom the Government has so often turned in times when our country has been in peril, and who have always responded, and I consider it shameful, if your Honor please, that such a baseless attack, without evidence, should have been made on their characters and integrity, almost at the twilight of their lives.[92]

On December 3, 1954, Judge LaBuy embraced Harlan's central premise. In a 100-page opinion, LaBuy summarized the government's extensive factual allegations in considerable detail, yet held, as Harlan had argued, that the defendants' interrelationships, however elaborate, did not establish a conspiracy to violate the Sherman or Clayton acts. LaBuy concluded, for example, that Du Pont treasurer John J. Raskob's 1917 statement that his company's acquisition of General Motors stock would "undoubtedly secure for us the entire Fabrikoid, Pyralin, paint and varnish business of those companies," had merely indicated that "Raskob, for one, thought that Du Pont would ultimately get all that business" and not that he "expected to secure General Motors trade by imposing any limitation upon its freedom to buy from suppliers of its choice." Other documents did establish "DuPont's continued interest in selling to General Motors—even to the extent of the latter's entire requirements—but they similarly [made] no suggestion that the desired result was to be achieved by limiting General Motors' purchasing freedom." Most important to Judge LaBuy perhaps, both Pierre and Irénée Du Pont had denied knowledge of any agreement binding General Motors to buy Du Pont products, and LaBuy found "it most unlikely that an agreement . . . would hav been made without the knowledge of these important officials." He reached the same conclusion regarding Du Pont's relationship with the United Rubber Company.[93]

Harlan's defense, like Judge LaBuy's decision, naturally pleased the Du Ponts and their employees. "There is singing and dancing in the streets of Wilmington today," Jane Du Pont wired Harlan from the company's Delaware headquarters the afternoon of the decision, "and we love you." In addition, following Harlan's opening statement in the case, George E. Thompson, a longtime assistant to Pierre Du Pont, had written Harlan to request an autographed copy of his remarks.

> I have been in Mr. Pierre's personal employ for twenty-three years, not a long time measured against the full span of his wonderful career but over half of my own lifetime. During that time I have heard and seen Mr. duPont attacked, slandered and villified by the United States Government, by New Deal editors and radio commentators and by others. There have been a few occasions when Mr. duPont has been defended by the words of others but these efforts were rather weak and unimpressive. So, as I sat in the courtroom in Chicago and listened to your thrilling speech in behalf of the DuPont Company and, more particularly, in direct defense of Mr. duPont personally and heard you so wonderfully and so truthfully depict the fine character and greatness of this much beloved man, I could not keep back a few tears of pride and gratification and would not if I could—I was not ashamed of them and daresay I was not alone in this respect. I am very grateful indeed for the opportunity of being present to hear your defense of Mr. duPont.[94]

The family patriarchs were equally impressed with Harlan's performance. While Harlan and his staff were in Wilmington preparing for the trial, Pierre Du Pont had entertained them and their wives at his Longwood estate. During the trial, the brothers hosted a party for the team at a Chicago hotel. And in late 1953, while Judge LaBuy's decision in the case was still pending, Irénée Du Pont invited the Harlans to visit Xanadu, his Cuban retreat. Harlan, however, had been obliged, temporarily at least, to decline the latter invitation, though assuring Irénée in a January 7, 1954, letter, "how deeply disappointed Ethel and I are at not being able to come down," and expressing the hope that they could be given "a rain check for some time in the future when our lives become more ordered." "I have been to Washington and talked with the 'powers that be,' " he explained, "as to the schedule relating to the matter which you know about."[95]

The matter discussed was Harlan's nomination to the Court of Appeals for the Second Circuit. In less than a year, President Eisenhower would also choose him for a seat on the nation's highest tribunal. Both events were hardly surprising. Indeed, for this grandson of a Republican Supreme Court justice, son of a prominent, if eccentric, Republican politician, and "lawyer's lawyer," elevation to the federal bench, even to the high court, seemed a logical and natural next step in an unusually successful career. In the Eisenhower era, his defense of the Du Pont family and its corporate interests from attack by "rabid New Dealers" in a lawsuit initiated during the Truman administration had probably done him no harm either.

3

The Appointments

Harlan's Politics

While testifying before the Senate judiciary committee during hearings on his Supreme Court nomination, John Harlan sought to minimize his ties to the political arena. "Let me say," he told members of the committee,

> that I have never been in politics myself. I think it is rather a reflection on me, because, frankly, I think that people who are citizens should take an interest in public affairs.
>
> But be that as it may, I have been a busy lawyer since a youngster, and that . . . has been the consequence. I have never been a member of a district political club. I was a member of the New York Young Republican Club. When I became a member of the district attorney's staff as a youngster under my late senior partner, Emory Buckner, I joined the Young Republican Club. My recollection is—I may be wrong about it, but I think I am accurate—I have attended, I think, one, and if more than one, it is only two or three, dinner sessions of that club in the last 35 years. I have known [New York Governor Thomas E.] Dewey pleasantly. I have never known him intimately. Unless you wish to consider my appointment as chief counsel to the crime commission as an appointment of his . . . I have never held any office to which he appointed me under him.[1]

When compared with the political backgrounds of most of the Roosevelt and Truman appointees to the high court, or that of Earl Warren, President Eisenhower's first appointment, Harlan's political activities prior to his elevation to the federal bench were indeed limited. Only rarely, however, has one reached a seat on the federal judiciary with no previous political experience, Harlan was no exception to that general rule. Indeed, his career had been honeycombed with the sorts of political, bar, public service, and related experiences normally found in the backgrounds of candidates for judicial office.[2]

Not surprisingly perhaps, given his service in the 1920s as Emory Buckner's assistant U.S. attorney and in the prosecution of the Queens sewer scandal, Harlan served from 1937 to 1941 as a member of the board of directors of the Society for the Prevention of Crime, a New York organization formed in 1878 "to promote, in all proper and suitable ways, the removal of sources and causes of crime . . . to aid in the enforcement of the laws of the State . . . and to arouse a correct public opinion in support of all laws, organizing and forming meetings and associations for instruction and discussion upon such topics." During Harlan's tenure, the group had become increasingly controversial. Its chief investigator, one Harry Sussman, made numerous arrests on lottery, narcotics, and similar charges, but his cases were often dismissed on constitutional and related grounds. In 1939, moreover, Samuel Marcus, a veteran antivice crusader, resigned his membership on the Society's board in protest, charging that the organization had "been led into playing politics."

Marcus's principal target was Harlan's friend J. Edward Lumbard, the Society's chief counsel. In a letter to Governor Herbert Lehman, a Democrat, Marcus had urged a grand jury probe into corruption in the government of Albany County, where, he claimed, daily gambling takes ran as high as $10,000, officials were accepting bribes in exchange for permits to operate gasoline stations, and the local Democratic machine was using tax assessments to reward and punish political friends and foes. When Governor Lehman asked Marcus for detailed charges, Marcus was denied access to Society files which contained incriminating information regarding corruption in the Albany County government. Lumbard was an active Republican, and Marcus was convinced that the Society's counsel planned to turn its files over to the GOP-controlled state legislature so that it could conduct an embarrassing investigation in time to affect upcoming elections. In a statement to the press, the Society's president, a prominent clergyman, denied Marcus's charges. The Society's board, not Lumbard, he contended, had made the decision to turn over its records to the legislature, and its action was based not on political considerations but on fear that the Albany political machine would exert an undue influence over any grand jury probe conducted in the county.

The extent to which Lumbard may have influenced the Society's decision, the role of politics in that decision, and John Harlan's involvement in the issue would remain unclear. After Marcus's charges appeared in the press, however, Lumbard had asked Harlan to draft a response without, apparently, considering it necessary to explain details of the issue to his friend.[3]

But Harlan's involvement in partisan politics was by no means purely a matter of conjecture. In 1945, he served as chairman of the lawyers' division of a finance committee organized for the congressional campaign of Frederick V. P. Bryan, who won the GOP primary, then lost the general election to Vito Marcantonio. He was also active in J. Edward Lumbard's unsuccessful 1947 campaign for a seat on the state supreme court. In 1948, he was chairman of the lawyers' division of a citizens' committee organized to support the Dewey-Warren presidential ticket. The following year, he served in a similar committee formed in behalf of a GOP candidate for the New York Court of Appeals, writing letters in that capacity to solicit campaign contributions. Furthermore, in 1941 he was mentioned in the press as a possible candidate for district attorney of New York County.[4]

Like most successful candidates for judicial office, the future justice was active in bar affairs, especially those of the Association of the Bar of the City of New York. From 1948–50, for example, he was vice president of the association, and at various stages of his career he served on its bill of rights and judiciary committees as well. In another related bar activity, he was long active in the National Legal Aid and Defender Association, serving at one point as a member of its board of directors although as a justice he would frequently oppose expansion of the constitutional rights of indigent defendants.[5]

For a time, in the early 1940s Harlan also held at least a nominal membership on a committee organized by his friend Whitney North Seymour at the request of the American Civil Liberties Union (ACLU) to advise the Union "in dealing with legal problems." In a letter inviting Harlan to participate, Seymour wrote, "I do not need to persuade you that lawyers owe a peculiar obligation to contribute their advice and skill in this field." Harlan apparently agreed. In his reply to Seymour, he wrote that he would be "glad" to serve. His decision was based, however, on Seymour's "assurance that the work will not be burdensome." With characteristic caution, he indicated his understanding "that the committee will function purely informally, and that there will be no publicity in connection with it," adding, "I would not wish to have my name published as a member of the committee until I know more about what the committee is supposed to do."[6]

At one point during Harlan's tenure as a member of the civil rights committee of the state bar association, Seymour circulated a report recommending that the committee file an amicus curiae brief on behalf of a Jehovah's Witness convicted for conducting his itinerant ministry in a New York town without a permit. "As much as one may disagree with the doctrine of Jehovah's Witnesses and dislike their methods of proselytizing," Seymour wrote, "their activities do present a square question of religious liberty. It is only by defending the rights of such unpopular minorities that the rights themselves can be preserved. Our Committee has in the past had no occasion to speak out officially in the field assigned to it in this State. It seems to me that this case furnishes an appropriate occasion for breaking our silence."[7] Committee members were asked to advise Seymour if they dissented from his recommendation. Harlan apparently registered no objection, but there is no evidence either that he ever played an active role in the civil rights advisory committees on which he served.

During his years of law practice, Harlan not only participated in a variety of partisan, political, and civic activities, he also enjoyed close relations with the Dewey wing of the Republican Party. Although Harlan later testified before the judiciary committee that he knew Governor Dewey "pleasantly" rather than "intimately," his correspondence and personal contacts with the governor went back to 1931, and his friendship with Dewey's close associate Herbert Brownell, who was to become President Eisenhower's attorney general, extended back to the 1920s and their early days together at Root, Clark. Brownell and John Andrews, Harlan's future brother-in-law, had been friends at Yale law school even before Brownell met Harlan. While Harlan and Ethel Andrews were dating, they had attended horse shows with Brownell and visited the future attorney general's cottage on the New Jersey shore—where, Brownell would recall years later, Harlan had become "terribly distraught" when Ethel suffered a fall. Over the years, the Harlans and Brownells had become very close friends. When Brownell ran for a state legislative seat, Harlan was "one of the very few," Brownell remembers, "who made a financial contribution" to his friend's campaign. When Dewey decided to create a state crime commission to investigate ties between organized crime and government, the governor's selection of Harlan as the commission's chief counsel in 1951 was thus hardly surprising.[8]

Governor Dewey's decision to create a state crime commission grew largely out of unfavorable publicity given New York and its organized crime elements, including the notorious Frank Costello, in hearings conducted by Tennessee Democrat Estes Kefauver's Senate Committee on the Investigation of Organized Crime. Grand jury investigations were already under way in New York, Kings, and Saratoga counties. Dewey's commission was to conduct a statewide inquiry, then make recommendations to the governor regarding his authority to remove corrupt local officials, the extent to which state power over local law enforcement should be enlarged, the desirability of establishing a uniform system of jury selection and authorizing local prosecutors to change the location of court proceedings in order to prevent local tampering with the administration of justice, and the special problems posed by multicounty and multistate criminal activity.[9]

To give the commission a nonpartisan image, Governor Dewey appointed four Democrats and one Republican as commissioners. Its chairman was Joseph M. Proskauer, a Democrat, former justice of the appellate division of the state supreme court, and an adviser to Al Smith during his tenure as New York's governor. Proskauer's colleagues on the commission were a former New York City police commissioner, a former U.S. ambassador to Norway, the dean of the Fordham law school, and a chancellor emeritus of the University of Buffalo.[10]

While Harlan was recuperating from minor surgery in a New York hospital, Governor Dewey telephoned him to explain that he was forming the commission and that before discussing the selection of commission counsel with Proskauer, he wanted to learn whether Harlan was interested, he would later say, "in the possibilities for doing a public job," at least if he would be free to withdraw should the obligations of his law practice so dictate. Later, Proskauer visited the Harlans' Manhattan apartment and offered him the position. On March 31, 1951, Governor Dewey's secretary James C. Hagerty, who would later serve as President Eisenhower's press aide, announced Harlan's appointment.[11]

Harlan would serve without pay, in the position until January of 1952, when the Du Pont–General Motors antitrust case began to require his exclusive attention. Proskauer had known Harlan, as he later expressed it, since the commission's counsel "was a youngster at the bar carrying the bag for Emory Buckner." Although they were on opposite sides of the political fence, they worked well together.[12]

After a trip to Washington for a talk with Senator Kefauver, the future Supreme Court justice recruited a talented, loyal staff. For his chief assistant, he selected Ben Matthews, a seasoned lawyer. Most of the attorneys on his staff, however, would be promising young associates—"bird dogs" they came to be called—from the city's most prestigious firms, who were anxious, as were their superiors, to work with one of New York's finest litigators. Peter Megargee Brown, a Yale law graduate who had taken a position with Harlan's firm in 1948, enthusiastically accepted an assignment. So, too, among others, did Harlan's law and wartime associate Leslie Arps, who later was to found what Brown termed New York's "biggest and . . . most vulgarly rich" firm, and Harry Weyher, a recent Harvard law graduate and associate with another of the city's largest firms. "One of the partners called me in one day," Weyher remembers, "and said that John Harlan was getting together a legal staff for the crime commission. He told me Harlan was one of the outstanding litigators in New York and that it would be very worthwhile to know him and work with him. So he sent me over to see him. I liked him instantly; he made a wonderful impression on you when you first met him. So I decided to do it for the experience and for the contact with Harlan."[13]

Augmenting the legal staff were a number of full-time investigators, including one who had worked for Tom Dewey in his investigations of organized crime and another attached to the state police. Local police were also put at Harlan's disposal for temporary assignments; at one point, in fact, nearly two hundred were involved in the commission's investigations. Harlan, Peter Brown recalls, preferred "rookie policemen because he figured they hadn't yet been corrupted." For the extensive, court-sanctioned wiretap surveillance the investigators undertook, Brown adds, detectives who spoke Italian were essential.[14]

Harlan devoted several months to organizing his office, at 270 Broadway in New York City, and training his staff. One day, he noticed one of the "bird dogs" stamping a document "Secret." "He suggested," Brown recalls, "that that wasn't a good idea, because when people rifle through your papers, they pick out the ones that say 'Secret.' " He also regularly cautioned his eager young charges "never to write or say anything that you wouldn't like to see in the *New York Times* the next day."[15]

While completing selection of a staff, Harlan instructed Matthews, Arps, and several others to conduct a thorough review of the staff's powers and the permissible scope of their investigations. He then broke the organization down into a group focusing on the New York waterfront and others investigating the influence of organized crime on Staten Island, in Ogdensburg and other communities, and on state and local judges. Once that task was completed, Harlan and his staff began conducting hearings, interrogating witnesses, and collecting documentary evidence. By early 1953, they had conducted more than six thousand interviews and called over two hundred witnesses before five public hearings. The staff's efforts would lead to creation of the New York Waterfront Commission as well as other reforms. For his efforts, Harlan, according to his daughter, was the target of death threats. While the death threats were never carried out, potential political damage was incurred by an accusation that Harlan was using the commission and its staff for partisan political purposes.[16]

The charge was raised by Herman Methfessel, a Democratic veteran in the office of the Richmond County (Staten Island) district attorney and himself district attorney there for four years. During the commission's investigation of gambling and other criminal activity on Staten Island, members of Harlan's staff had interviewed a Mrs. Anna Wentworth. In the 1940s, Mrs. Wentworth worked as a domestic in the Staten Island home of Theresa Dalessio, the mother of three reputed gamblers, the Dalessio or "Dio" brothers. A third-floor room of the Dalessio house was used for gambling on Saturday nights; when Harlan's investigators showed Mrs. Wentworth photographs of Herman Methfessel, she told them she had seen Methfessel in the Dalessio gambling den on several occasions in 1944. During later sessions with Harlan, she again identified Methfessel's photograph, and in a hearing conducted before the commission in late September of 1951, she stood by her assertions. Methfessel, who also testified at the hearing, vehemently denied Mrs. Wentworth's allegations and charged that she was a chronic liar and publicity seeker of marginal intelligence. But he declined an opportunity to cross-examine her. Instead, he asked the commission to subpoena Governor Dewey, the district attorneys of New York and Kings counties, Methfessel's Republican opponent in his last election campaign, and Judge Proskauer, among others, as his witnesses. Moreover, when the commission, on Harlan's recommendation, declined his request, pointing out that the witnesses the district attorney wished subpoenaed would have no testimony to offer of relevance to its inquiry, Methfessel ordered Mrs. Wentworth arrested on perjury charges.[17]

On learning of the district attorney's arrest of a witness who had implicated him in possible criminal activity, Harlan's eyes gleamed. "That was a terrible mistake," he calmly observed, "on the part of Mr. Methfessel."[18] He then moved to secure Mrs. Wentworth's release from jail and alerted Governor Dewey, who promptly stripped Methfessel of jurisdiction over gambling, perjury, and government corruption cases. The charges against Mrs. Wentworth were later dropped, and Methfessel found himself the target of disciplinary proceedings before the state bar. The referee conducting that investigation found insufficient evidence, however, to warrant disciplinary action, and Methfessel, who lost a reelection bid shortly after his appearance before the commission, charged that the timing of the commission's hearing—held just six weeks before the election and several months after Harlan and his assistants had first interviewed Mrs. Wentworth—was politically motivated. Harlan and Proskauer, who, like Methfessel, was a Democrat, hotly denied the allegations. But the former district attorney would persist in his charges, as will be seen later in the chapter.

Although Harlan resigned from the commission in early 1952, several months after the Staten Island hearings, he continued to serve as its general counsel even while increasingly involved in the Du Pont–General Motors litigation. In that capacity, Harry Weyher has said, Harlan continued to exert considerable influence over the commission's work. Ben Matthews, who became the commission's chief counsel after Harlan left, Leslie Arps, and the "bird dogs" visited the future Justice's Weston home on several occasions. During those sessions, Weyher has recalled of one such visit, "Harlan was the one who made the decisions" about what witnesses to call, the evidence to be presented, and whether or not to hold particular hearings.[19]

Weyher smilingly recalled years later that when Harlan took his charges to lunch one day, during his tenure as chief counsel, "he didn't volunteer to pay for the tab at the end. We even divided up the sales tax, as I remember." Whatever their concerns about their chief's generosity, however, Weyher, Brown, and the other "bird dogs" left their tenure on the crime commission with feelings for Harlan bordering on adoration. "He was always calm," Weyher recalls. "You never saw him angry unless he wanted to be angry. He could get angry, but he had complete control of himself. And you had confidence in him. He had the air of knowing what he was saying." Peter Brown has echoed Weyher's sentiments. "Harlan never would say to himself, 'I have special qualities, and I can wing it.' He never was flamboyant, he never showed off, he was meticulous about his preparation." Like Emory Buckner before him, Brown also recalls, Harlan was a superb mentor. "It was typical of him to show kindness to the juniors. . . . He would invite the 'bird dogs' to his Connecticut house and introduce us to Dewey, Brownell, Lumbard, the group around him. I thought that was the way every senior lawyer was, but that isn't the way it was or is."[20]

Nor would Brown lend any credence to Herman Methfessel's charges. "As counsel we were not allowed to say anything that was not made public, but we were allowed, on order from the [state] supreme court, to wiretap. . . . So we knew a lot about what was going on in Staten Island that was not in the newspapers. . . . Methfessel was not a person of very high character or behavior. . . . There was a lot of opportunity for Methfessel and his gang . . . to cross-examine, to raise issues, in the hearing . . . and he failed to. John Harlan was a person of extremely high integrity, and he never would have stooped to doing something reprehensible or to take advantage of another person."[21]

The Methfessel affair notwithstanding, Harlan's work with the crime commission enhanced his reputation as a public-spirited citizen as well as a distinguished corporate lawyer. Characteristically, Harlan avoided potentially damaging political controversy, including direct involvement on either side of the growing debate over Wisconsin Senator Joseph McCarthy and the tactics of "Red Scare" politics. However, at least one of his associates apparently did not consider Harlan entirely above making use of such tactics in the rough-and-tumble of a political campaign. During the fall of 1948, a functionary of the Republican state committee sought Harlan's advice about using a Socialist leader in Governor Dewey's presidential bid. In 1946, Socialist Louis Waldman had given an address supporting Dewey's re-election as governor and the election of Irving M. Ives to the U.S. Senate. "If you vote for the Democratic candidates for Governor and Senator," Waldman had asserted, "you are, at the same time voting for the candidates supported by the Communist Party. You can defeat the totalitarian forces in our midst by voting for . . . the entire Republican state ticket." The state GOP official thought Waldman had "real value, even though he may have to be somewhat curbed."[22] Although there is no evidence of a Harlan response to the proposal, the official in question apparently did not think Harlan would find such a suggestion offensive.

Nor, evidently, was Harlan willing to intervene when the McCarthyite tactics were employed against Adlai Stevenson during the 1952 presidential campaign. At one point, Eisenhower forces attempted to put to political use the fact that Stevenson had given a deposition in support of Alger Hiss, the former State Department official convicted of perjury after denying that he had engaged in espionage for the Soviet Union. On September 16, 1952, R. Keith Kane mailed Harlan a copy of a statement of lawyers who "deplore[d] any effort to criticize or reproach Governor Stevenson for testifying by deposition in the Hiss case." Stevenson, the statement asserted, had been ordered by the court to submit a deposition in the case, and his statement that Hiss's reputation for loyalty was good was based only on what he had heard others say. "[H]e said not a word as to what he himself thought of Hiss [and in] our view as lawyers, he did only what any good citizen should have done under the circumstances." Kane urged Harlan to add his signature to the petition.

> My purpose is to oppose the introduction into the campaign of an irrelevant issue which might seriously impair in practice and in popular understanding the administration of justice in our courts and the protection granted by the bill of rights in our federal and state constitutions to those accused of crime. Regardless of our political preferences, we as lawyers have a responsibility to defend the integrity of the processes of our courts.[23]

Stevenson, of course, had been Harlan's contemporary at Princeton; Harlan and Stevenson's sister Buffie had dated frequently during their college years. Even so, the petition would remain unsigned in his files. Nor would his friend Edward Lumbard find that decision surprising. "He wouldn't have gone along with using the Stevenson deposition in the campaign. If Stevenson wanted to say a good word for Hiss, it certainly didn't detract in any way from Stevenson's qualifications to be president. . . . But John probably would have taken the middle course of just staying out of it."[24]

The Circuit Appointment

By the time of Dwight Eisenhower's inauguration in January, 1953, then, John Harlan not only enjoyed a reputation as an outstanding corporate attorney whose selection to the federal bench was likely to find favor with Republican loyalists, he had also devoted a respectable share of his time and energy to party, bar, and public service causes. Of perhaps even greater significance were his ties to Thomas E. Dewey and the governor's political associates. The Dewey forces had supported Eisenhower over conservative Ohio Senator Robert A. Taft at the 1952 Republican convention. Now they were being rewarded with several top posts in the new administration. Harlan's longtime friend Herbert Brownell had become Eisenhower's attorney general and thus the key administration figure in the selection of federal judges. All that appeared to remain, were Harlan interested in a judgeship, was the fortuitous circumstance of a vacancy.

That opportunity was not long in coming. On June 30, 1953, Augustus N. Hand assumed senior status on the Court of Appeals for the Second Circuit after twenty-six years on the appellate bench. The next day, Hand's colleague Judge Thomas Swan followed suit, creating a second vacancy on the circuit. The Second Circuit's jurisdiction covered New York, Connecticut, and Vermont; for a time, John A. Danaher, a former Republican senator from Connecticut, appeared to be the prime contender for one of the vacancies. In late September, President Eisenhower appointed Danaher to the Court of Appeals for the District of Columbia, but administration spokesmen denied rumors that Harlan and Connecticut federal district judge Carroll C. Hincks were to be appointed to the

Second Circuit vacancies. Moreover, when the secretary of the Federal Bar Association for New York, New Jersey, and Connecticut, which earlier had endorsed Danaher, wrote Harlan that his name had been suggested for consideration by the association's judiciary committee, Harlan responded that he "would prefer that no action be taken . . . on the matter referred to in your letter, since I am in no sense seeking judicial office."[25]

Actually, however, Harlan was approached about a judgeship within days of the Hand and Swan announcements. A group of prominent New York lawyers had met with Attorney General Brownell and urged Harlan's nomination. By that point, the attorney general had already spoken with the president also about the "possibility of John Harlan's appointment to a future vacancy on the Supreme Court . . . since we had agreed that the appointment of an experienced trial lawyer to the next vacancy on that Court would be advisable." The president had expressed the view, too, "that some prior experience on the bench would strengthen the qualifications of the next Supreme Court appointment." Brownell was thus confident that Eisenhower would support Harlan's appointment.[26]

When Brownell and his former law partner, Sherman Baldwin, met with Harlan at New York's Commodore Hotel regarding the appointment, the attorney general later recalled, Harlan was "taken aback" by the idea, especially since he was then heavily involved in the Du Pont–General Motors antitrust suit. Even so, he apparently found the opportunity intriguing. For while the precise timing of his meeting with Brownell is unclear, a letter which Harlan's law partner Arthur Ballantine wrote him two weeks after the Hand and Swan announcements, in reply to a letter from Harlan, indicates that by July 13, the date of Ballantine's letter, Harlan had already been approached by the administration and was giving the matter serious consideration. In part, no doubt, because of Harlan's ongoing defense of the Du Pont brothers in antitrust litigation, Ballantine found the prospect of his partner's leaving the firm—and the case—less than appealing. "I was profoundly interested to have your letter," he wrote,

> although like the boys I could not be pleased with the situation. This will arrive after you have decided, at least subject to the moods of Wilmington [Delaware, site of Du Pont's headquarters]. I doubt whether Mr. W. will stand in the way, especially since Covington [and Burling, the Washington, D.C., firm representing the Du Pont company in the case] will be so eager to take over completely. Of course my good friend John O'Brien [the Covington and Burling lawyer handling the case for his firm] would rather that you kept in the case, but he will be torn two ways because of his firm's interest.
>
> It is the kind of question one wishes would never come up—but it does thrust up its ugly head, and you have to be the one to decide. I can see that you still have it in you to want to follow in the footsteps of your grandfather, notwithstanding that the Judge (in the abstract) has

depreciated like the dollar. I agree with you that such an opportunity is not likely to recur. The answer you have to work out for yourself. For myself I would not like the life . . . nor would Helen like her side of it, but then I have no judicial background—rather theological, and apparently no trace of that came down to me—thanks possibly to my mother.

Nor was Ballantine alone in his disappointment. The partners, Harlan's friend Leo Gottlieb later recalled, "were absolutely dumbfounded." In the past, Wilkie Bushby and William Palmer, in particular, had expressed concern that their chief litigator's inclinations toward public service were creating uncertainty regarding the firm's future among its most promising young associates. When informed of the judgeship offer, Gottlieb said, "Bushby made some rather indiscreet remarks about how they had been deserted by John. [And] it *was* a tremendous loss. . . . Harlan was the bright star of the firm at that time and recognized as such by the bar."[27]

The partners' feelings were soon largely assuaged. William Palmer, for example, wrote Harlan:

I wait with deep interest news as to the reaction of the DuPonts.

On the assumption that they assent and that the appointment goes through, let me say that I think you are doing the right thing. I don't think you will regret it years hence when the signing off time comes.

Don't worry about the office. There are things a man should spend himself for regardless of personal consequences.[28]

Harlan obviously gave his partners' concerns serious consideration. By this point, however, he had already decided to accept the appointment, provided only that the Du Ponts were willing to release him from his obligations as their counsel.

Ultimately, the Eisenhower administration was able to accommodate both supporters of Harlan's appointment and his powerful clients. During the fall, while Harlan completed the trial of the Du Pont suit in Chicago, the Justice Department processed the customary paperwork connected with judicial appointments. In late November, for example, a friend wrote Harlan that "[t]he F.B.I. were around and I 'trotted out' my choicest adjectives in adverting to you," adding, "The Circuit Court of Appeals sorely needs the finest of the profession and I fervently hope that the President will crown you with the appointment." "Many thanks for your kind letter," Harlan responded. "I am sorry that you were bothered, and hope that you didn't extend yourself too far."[29]

In December, Harlan made final arguments in the Chicago case. Shortly before Christmas, he wrote Attorney General Brownell that "[i]f your plans respecting me have not changed, I simply want you to know that the final arguments in the Chicago case concluded last Monday and that I am now in a position where I think I can meet whatever schedule you have in mind." On January 13, 1954, President Eisenhower sent his nomination to the Senate. In a joint statement, the president of the Association of the Bar of the City of New York and the chairman of its judiciary committee termed Harlan "a worthy successor to the long line of judges who have made this one of the greatest courts in the country," and declared that their colleague would "make a great judge." Equally ebullient, the *New York Times* predicted editorially that "[e]veryone familiar with the character, personality and public record of John Marshall Harlan . . . will rejoice in his nomination," adding that Judge Hand "could have no worthier successor." In the judgment of the *Times'* editors, "[t]here should not be, and presumably will not be, any needless delay in the Senate's confirmation of this fine appointment."[30]

On this occasion, there was to be no delay. In response to a telegram from Senator William Langer (R-N.D.), the chairman of the Senate Judiciary Committee, Edward J. Fox, chair of the American Bar Association's (ABA) Standing Committee on Federal Judiciary, of which Harlan's friend Whitney North Seymour was also a member, reported that his committee had given Harlan its highest rating, finding the nominee "exceptionally well qualified by training, experience and ability" to be an appellate jurist. John G. Buchanan, the ABA committee's first chairman, a longtime friend of both Harlan's and Judge Hand's, and, like the nominee, a Princeton graduate, also wrote Langer to endorse the appointment, as did others. "Within your recollection and mine (though we were very young)," Buchanan reminded Langer, "there was a great John Marshall Harlan once in the federal judiciary. His grandson too may be expected to perform service of great distinction and great value to his country." As one of his Oxford classmates wrote Harlan, such expressions were probably little more than "carrying coals to Newcastle." On February 4, Harlan met briefly with a subcommittee of the judiciary committee, but no hearing was conducted. On February 8, the entire committee unanimously approved the nomination. The next day, the full Senate followed suit, confirming both Harlan and Judge Hincks, who was already serving a recess appointment. In late March, Harlan took the oath of office.[31]

John Harlan would serve on the Second Circuit just over a year. During his brief tenure, he participated in approximately a hundred appeals and wrote opinions in twenty-three cases. With one notable exception, his circuit caseload bore little relation to the sorts of broad constitutional issues he was later to confront on the Supreme Court. Several cases involved constructions of the federal tax laws.[32] Others grew out of bankruptcy proceedings,[33] and still others dealt with such matters as conspiracy to defraud the government,[34] divorce decrees,[35] stockholder suits,[36] misbranded products,[37] counterfeit federal reserve notes,[38] airline safety,[39] and damages to goods shipped in foreign commerce.[40]

The one exception to this pattern was *United States* v. *Flynn*. In early 1953, Elizabeth Gurley Flynn and twelve other second-string leaders of the American Communist Party were convicted of conspiring to violate the federal Smith Act by willfully advocating the overthrow of the U.S. government by force and violence. The conspiracy charged against Flynn and her co-defendants was essentially the same as that at issue earlier in *Dennis* v. *United States,* in which the Second Circuit and the Supreme Court had rejected First Amendment and related constitutional challenges to the Smith Act convictions of eleven top Communist leaders, including Eugene Dennis. In fact, the *Dennis* defendants were named as co-conspirators in the *Flynn* case, and the evidence presented in the latter prosecutions closely paralleled that presented in *Dennis.* The appeal of the *Flynn* convictions, which Harlan's friend Edward Lumbard had overseen as U.S. attorney for New York's southern district, though he had not prosecuted the cases, thus offered an excellent opportunity for observing the new judge's application of Supreme Court precedent in a particularly sensitive constitutional field.[41]

For those who favored extreme deference to government in such cases, Harlan's maiden performance would not be a disappointment. The Supreme Court had long held that expression could be the subject of criminal punishment under a statute regulating conduct only if it created a "clear and present danger" of lawless action; in a number of cases decided in the 1940s, the Court had tightened considerably its reading of the clear and present danger test, requiring that the connection between expression and potential illegal conduct be close indeed before speech alone could be the basis for criminal prosecution. Speaking for the three-judge panel which affirmed the convictions of Eugene Dennis and his co-defendants, however, Judge Learned Hand had given the test an interpretation broadly sympathetic to the claims of government, in fact one closely resembling the long discredited "bad tendency" doctrine under which the Supreme Court had once permitted the criminal prosecution of defendants whose speech and writings might merely have had some tendency to generate lawless action at some indefinite future date. In cases involving conflicts between First Amendment claims and national security interests, Hand asserted, courts "must ask whether the gravity of the 'evil,' discounted by its improbability [of occurring], justifies such invasion of free speech as is necessary to avoid the danger." In his opinion for the Supreme Court in *Dennis,* moreover, Chief Justice Fred M. Vinson endorsed Hand's rhetoric, observing that the distinguished jurist's statement of the clear and present danger test was "as succinct and inclusive as any other we might devise at this time," and added: "It takes into consideration those factors which we deem relevant, and relates their significance. More we cannot expect from words."[42]

While justices Black and William O. Douglas vehemently dissented from the *Dennis* majority's stance, Black concluded his dissent on an optimistic note.

> Public opinion being what it now is, few will protest these convictions of these Communist petitioners. There is hope, however, that in calmer

> times, when present pressures, passions and fears subside, this or some later Court will restore the First Amendment liberties to the high preferred place where they belong in a free society.[43]

Judge Harlan was clearly not prepared, however, to anticipate such a shift in the Court's thinking. Indeed, his reading of the clear and present danger test in *Flynn* appeared to give government even greater latitude than the Hand-Vinson version permitted. "Where a conspiracy to destroy the Government by force or violence is involved," Harlan asserted in rejecting the appellants' construction of the test and challenge to its application in their case, "we think that the 'clear and present danger' concept, as defined in Dennis . . . connotes no more than that the setting in which the defendants have conspired is such as to lead reasonably to the conclusion that their teachings may result in an attempt at overthrow."

Like Judge Hand and the Supreme Court in *Dennis*, the trial judge in *Flynn* had summarized the growing postwar tensions between Communist and non-Communist nations and asserted that the United States had become the target of "invective upon invective," and was continuously being charged with having "aggressive designs" to "enslave" other nations. In such an international climate, he had concluded, "[a]ny border fray, any diplomatic incident, any difference in the construction of the modus vivendi—such as the Berlin blockade . . . might prove a spark in the tinderbox, and lead to [a] war of survival in extension of or in addition to the war in which we were engaged in Korea." Judge Harlan found such factors an ample basis for the trial judge's conclusion that the defendants' advocacy of Communist doctrine had created a clear and present danger to national security.[44]

Harlan and his colleagues also rejected the appellants' other claims. In view of the important First Amendment interests at stake in such cases, the defendants' counsel argued that the ordinary rules of evidence in conspiracy cases should be inapplicable in Smith Act prosecutions. Specifically, they contended that the government's case should rest entirely on evidence relating to the defendants' own activities, not those of alleged co-conspirators or of Communists generally. Citing *Dennis* and other precedents, Harlan rejected the appellants' contention, asserting that their "intent," like any other element of a crime, could be established by circumstantial evidence.[45]

Nor would the panel accept the challenge which the appellants mounted against evidence that Communist functionaries had abused an official who was expelled from the party's ranks. The official, who was suspected of cooperating with federal agents, had been forced to undress and, with a pistol at his head, write an incriminating statement; he was then expelled "as a traitor and enemy of the working class." The defendants and their co-conspirators had neither authorized nor participated in the official's treatment, and their lawyers argued that the probative value of such evidence was far outweighed by its tendency to inflame the jury. But Harlan and his colleagues were not persuaded. "While the episode to be sure was an unsavory one," he observed, "there is no blinking the fact that this was one of the prime reasons for its relevance on the issues to which it was directed." Earlier in his opinion, he had remarked: "In its attempt to bring out the nature of [Communist] objectives and methods the Government should not be limited to showing actions known to or authorized by the defendants."[46]

The appellants' contention that publicity surrounding their case, combined with the trial judge's refusal to postpone the proceedings, had denied them a fair hearing met the same fate. During the trial, the U.S. Senate Subcommittee on Internal Security had conducted hearings, in the same courthouse in which the *Flynn* proceedings were being conducted, on the alleged infiltration of Communists into the United Nations; the same subcommittee had also issued an anti-Communist pamphlet which referred to two of the defendants by name. In addition, a federal grand jury in the district in which the trial was being conducted had recommended that the National Labor Relations Board revoke the certificates of several labor unions whose officials had invoked the Fifth Amendment privilege against compulsory self-incrimination during the grand jury's proceedings. Flynn and her co-defendants argued, as Harlan put it, "that the climate of public opinion, induced" by such activities, "was such that any jury chosen to try them must have entered the jury box with at least a predisposition to regard the Communist Party as an illegal revolutionary conspiracy, which was one of the central issues to be tried."[47]

In addressing the appellants' claim, Harlan readily agreed "that the vast majority of the American people regard Communism with deep-seated antipathy, and that as events have unfolded since the close of World War II many people have come more and more to regard Communism as committed to the overthrow of our Government by force or violence, a belief which has found expression in" recently adopted federal legislation enacted to supplement the Smith Act. Drawing on Judge Hand's *Dennis* opinion, however, he rejected the assertion that the trials of Communists should be delayed until public animosity subsided. "In essence," he asserted, "what the appellants are asking us to do is hold that there can be no proper trial of Communist Party members until the world situation quiets down and public opinion about Communism changes. We think there is nothing in our concepts of Constitutional due process which leads us to any such weird result." No member of the jury had read the subcommittee's pamphlet, and there was "not the slightest evidence that any of this publicity affected in any degree the trial Judge" or that it "added materially to the difficulty of giving the defendants a fair trial." The problem was simply one "which under present turbulent world conditions we must recognize as inherent in any prosecution involving members of the Communist Party."[48]

While the law of conspiracy is frustrating to laypersons—and many lawyers and judges—imbued with the notion that people should be held criminally responsible only for their own acts, Judge Harlan's treatment of that troublesome field of the law was arguably consistent with prevailing precedent, as was his reading of the clear and present danger standard. One can also share his doubts as to whether any reasonable postponement of the *Flynn* trial would have eliminated the defendants' concerns about the climate in which they were tried. Even so, Harlan's *Flynn* opinion was the target of intense criticism. One commentator condemned his approval of criminal punishment for speech which "may result in an attempt at overthrow" as taking "us back to the law of constructive treason in the worst days of the English common law."[49] And following Senate confirmation of his Supreme Court nomination, Eugene Gressman, who had clerked for Justice Wiley Rutledge, one of Harlan's more liberal predecessors on the Court, would assert that under the interpretation of clear and present danger Harlan had advanced in his "uninspired" *Flynn* opinion, "the danger need not be either 'clear' or 'present' but only 'potential' to warrant Congress' interfering with free speech and free press."[50]

"A Real Pro"

Harlan's *Flynn* stance undoubtedly did no harm to his standing with the Eisenhower administration. But as the White House became an increasingly frequent target of Senator McCarthy, and McCarthy a mounting liability to the Republican Party, Harlan added his voice to the growing chorus of the senator's detractors, though characteristically avoiding specific reference to McCarthy by name. In a commencement address at the Brooklyn Law School on June 15, 1954, he warned against "false prophets" who would undermine democracy in the guise of fighting subversion. "In the years that lie ahead, perhaps as never before," he observed,

> our country will need the services of men who can stand against and rise above the hysteria and fears that are bound to beset us.
>
> We must be vigilant, not alone against those who seek to destroy or weaken us from without; we must also be alert to resist the irresponsible and superficial utterances of those false prophets among us who preach that our free institutions and processes are inadequate to protect us from the schemings of those who would undermine within.[51]

Harlan's condemnation of McCarthyism did not seem to have dampened the administration's desire to elevate him to a seat on the Supreme Court, and the opportunity to make such a move came much sooner, perhaps, than President Eisenhower, Herbert Brownell, or Harlan could have expected. On October 9, 1954, Justice Robert H. Jackson died. Jackson had been the only New Yorker on the Court, and Harlan's nomination would restore geographic representation. In addition, Harlan possessed the prior judicial experience, however limited, that Earl Warren, Eisenhower's controversial first appointment, had lacked and which the president now considered a prerequisite for nomination. Governor Dewey and Brownell were mentioned in the press as the president's possible choices for the position. But neither was interested, and Harlan was Brownell's first, and only, choice.[52]

Harlan was also the preferred candidate of Judge Learned Hand, his longtime friend. As one of the nation's most eminent judges, Hand had in the past often been a likely candidate for nomination himself. Indeed, the very enthusiasm of his partisans may have been the principal factor foredooming his chances. In 1943, for example, President Roosevelt had picked Wiley Rutledge rather than Hand for a vacancy on the Court, telling Justice Douglas, according to Douglas's memoirs, "this time Felix overplayed his hand," and adding: "Do you know how many people asked me today to name Learned Hand? Twenty, and every one a messenger from Felix Frankfurter. . . . And by golly, I won't do it." Now eighty-two and retired from the Second Circuit since 1951, Hand was no longer in contention. He endorsed Harlan's candidacy, writing Eisenhower:

> I am taking the liberty of suggesting to you the appointment to the Supreme Court of Judge John Marshall Harlan, of the Court of Appeals for the Second Circuit, in place of Justice Jackson. I am confident that he would be an ideal successor; indeed he seems to me to combine more of the necessary qualifications than anyone else I know. He is a well trained lawyer of wide experience and a clear and penetrating mind. More important than these [qualities], he has the detachment, the balance, the horizons and the sense of public duty that are essential to the character of any judge, and especially to that of a justice of the Supreme Court. . . . I believe that his appointment would give general satisfaction to all those competent to judge, and I feel sure that he would almost at once begin to add to the reputation and moral authority of the Court.[53]

If Judge Hand's endorsement lent prestige to the president's leanings, Attorney General Brownell's support was conclusive. In early November, Harlan visited President Eisenhower at the White House. Harlan had met Eisenhower once previously, when the future president, then retired from the army, visited a military crony in Connecticut. "Did President Eisenhower remember meeting you?" a family member inquired following the White House visit. "Not until I reminded him of it," Harlan replied, a twinkle in his eyes.[54] With Brownell's support, the nomination was hardly in doubt. On November 8, a month after Justice Jackson's death, the White House submitted Judge Harlan's nomination to the Senate.

Harlan's Supreme Court nomination, like his selection to the Second

Circuit, was greeted enthusiastically in most quarters. Officials of the Association of the Bar of the City of New York again expressed confidence that their fellow member would "make a great justice of a great court," and the board of directors of the New York County Lawyers Association unanimously declared him "outstandingly qualified" for the position, while a member of the ABA's judiciary committee urged his early confirmation. The New York papers were equally supportive. In two editorials published within a week of the nomination, the *Times* applauded the president's decision to draw his choice from the lower federal judiciary, termed "the principle of promoting judges . . . a good one if not followed with blind rigidity," and, while conceding Harlan's extremely limited lower court tenure, assured its readers that "his character, ability and legal experience amply justif[ied] his rapid advance."[55]

National magazines published glowing tributes to his prestigious academic credentials, outstanding career at the bar, distinguished judicial ancestry, modest, unassuming personality, warmth, and patrician bearing. "The legal profession and the judiciary were pleased," *Time* magazine reported, "that President Eisenhower did not pay off a political I.O.U. with the Supreme Court appointment but chose Judge Harlan because, as one lawyer put it, he is 'a real pro.' " The *New Yorker*, among other magazines and newspapers, also quoted extensively from an interview he granted reporters shortly after his nomination was announced. During the interview he confided that his grandfather Harlan, whom Justice Holmes had termed "the last of the tobacco-spitting Justices," could indeed "hit a spittoon dead center at thirty paces." Of his own background, he remarked, "It does sound awfully tame, doesn't it?" adding modestly, if not entirely accurately, "If it helps any . . . I don't play golf at all well." He had, he assured those present, thoroughly enjoyed his time on the bench. "The marvelous variety of it! Instead of dealing with a single case for a year, as one is apt to do in private practice, one has to deal with hundreds of cases in that time, and all so different!" By the same token, he had no doubt that his many years of trial practice were a valuable asset on the bench. "I hope it may prove helpful that I've been on the opposite side of the bench so recently. Whenever I argue cases before the Supreme Court, what I appreciated most was having a judge lean over and ask me questions. Then I'd be sure he was really interested. I mean to ask a lot of questions." Finally, he conceded mixed feelings about the recent changes in the direction of his life. "We love New York and are bound to miss it. The theatre, and the boats on the river, and all that. Then, too, younger lawyers we know are bound to be shier about asking us around for a casual drink. *Everyone* is bound to be shier, I suppose, in tribute to the dignity of the Court. To some extent, a judge is, and ought to be, a man apart." Then he added, in language reflecting his British ties, "Not that I have any intention of turning into a solemn old hermit. No, by heaven, I won't have that."[56]

Harlan's friends naturally shared the pleasure that the bar and press did with his nomination. When one well-wisher sent an effusive congratulatory letter to New York attorney John Harlan Amen, Amen forwarded it to Harlan, with a note that the writer "seem[ed] to be in a state of considerable mental confusion." Others, of course, were not confused. Adlai Stevenson, unaware perhaps that Harlan had declined to join those protesting the Eisenhower campaign's use of his deposition in behalf of Alger Hiss, hoped that he was "not the last to express my delight with at least one action of the present administration. Indeed, I am confident that they will never do anything as good again." Pierre Du Pont, III, lamented recent "purely political appointments" to the Court and asserted that Harlan's nomination was "the first ray of hope I have seen that the judiciary of the United States is finally being restored to the dignity and integrity that it lost beginning with Roosevelt." An elderly clergyman, a longtime friend of the Harlan family, expressed satisfaction that "[y]our lovely father, ever proud of your unaided achievements, would not have considered that he had lived in vain, had he been here, today." Another friend assured the nominee that he had "seldom seen an appointment that was met with such universal and enthusiastic approval," adding, "How pleased Buck would have been." Harlan's former law and wartime associate Louis Lusky predicted, approvingly if not prophetically, that Harlan would "pick up where your grandfather left off." Heavyweight champ Gene Tunney termed the appointment "wonderful" and wondered what the trial judge in his case was "thinking of it in the after life." The master of Balliol College called the appointment "splendid news." A former *Herald Tribune* reporter wrote that "[i]t may be of some solace to Mickey Dee, Pope Dee and other [law violators] it was such a pleasure to write about . . . that they were uncovered by the best." And several of Harlan's friends expressed hope that the nominee could exert influence on some of the Court's liberal members. "Now that you will be on the inside," wrote the head of a Park Avenue advertising firm and Ethel Harlan's frequent fox hunting companion, "perhaps you can get some of those fellows who go off the track—at least my track—straightened out. For instance, my old friend Bill Douglas." Yet another wrote of his pleasure that Harlan would now "be aboard to hold" Douglas "in check."[57]

Amid such positive reaction to his nomination, Harlan began to establish contacts with his future brethren. The previous May, the Court had unanimously declared segregated public schools unconstitutional. Re-argument addressing the sort of decree the Court should issue in the segregation cases had been scheduled for December 6, and Harlan was particularly interested in a thorough briefing on those tremendously important suits in the event his nomination were confirmed by the time of the re-argument date. Harlan's first overtures were apparently to Justice Harold Burton, for on November 12, 1954, Burton wrote the nominee that he had shared Harlan's note with Chief Justice Warren. "We both think highly of your plan to come promptly after confirmation for at least a visit with us and if possible to sit with us in the Segregation Cases set for the week of December 6." Later, Warren sent Harlan a memorandum on the cases which his clerks had prepared. Justice Jackson's clerk, Barrett Prettyman, Jr., whom Harlan invited to be his clerk the day after the nomination was announced, also prepared a memorandum at Harlan's request.[58]

In response to Harlan's letter accepting the nomination, President Eisenhower had predicted "early" Senate confirmation of his choice. Burton, himself a former senator, and the chief justice generally shared the president's optimism. "We have no reliable information as to the course of the Senate," wrote Burton. "It is however the Chief Justice's guess [and] mine that after some sparring around the confirmation will come before the end of this short session unless some unexpected protest should arise. We have heard of none." Neither had Justice Tom Clark. In mid-November, Clark invited John and Ethel Harlan to a small dinner party to be held at a Washington supper club on December 2. Five members of the Court were to be present, Clark acknowledged, but the club selected was "most careful on publicity and there will be none. . . . By that time," wrote Clark, "you will be confirmed I am told by friends on the Hill—and the Senate will be adjourned."[59]

Eisenhower and the justices were unduly optimistic. In fact, four months were to pass before Harlan would receive the Senate's nod. At the same time the nomination was being submitted to the Senate, its leaders were agreeing that no controversial appointments would be approved during the Congress's short fall session, convened primarily to consider disciplinary action against Senator McCarthy. And while the body voted on December 2 to censure the Wisconsin senator, by that point objections to Harlan's confirmation had begun to surface, and hearings on his nomination had been delayed until early 1955.[60]

Nor was Senate opposition to the nomination to be confined purely to disgruntled southern Democrats. William Langer (R-N.D.), William Jenner (R-Ind.), and other conservative Republicans had little affection for the Eisenhower administration, nor its officials for them. "They were," William P. Rogers, the Brownell deputy charged with shepherding the nomination through the Senate, has recalled, " 'odd-ball' characters, outrageous in their conduct, nutty, not very able. Langer was totally unpredictable." Senator Jenner had once telephoned Rogers late one evening, urging the deputy attorney general to have Eisenhower appoint a political friend to a judgeship. "His choice was totally unqualified, and I told him so. He begged and pleaded, even crying over the phone and complaining that the appointment was critical to him." The following day, Rogers encountered Jenner at the Capitol, and the senator started pressing his case again, not seeming to remember the previous night's lengthy conversation. "Were you drunk last night, Senator?" Rogers asked, only half-jokingly. "No," Jenner replied, "you're just the only SOB in the administration who will talk to me."[61] Langer, Jenner, and company were to give the Harlan nomination considerable difficulty.

Senator Langer, the judiciary committee's chairman, was the first to raise doubts about Harlan's early confirmation. When Langer wrote Harlan to inform him of the committee's approval of his Second Circuit appointment, the North Dakota Republican had penned at the bottom of the letter his expression of confidence that the new jurist would "do a good honest job!" But beginning with Earl Warren's nomination, the eccentric Langer had embarked upon what was to become a six-year campaign of opposing any and all Supreme Court nominations until someone from his state, or another state from which no appointment had yet been drawn, received the honor. When several senators were reported in the press to have suggested that the nomination of Harlan, whose Second Circuit appointment had been confirmed only nine months earlier, was hardly controversial and that Senator Langer thus might get action from his committee without a hearing or formal meeting but by simply polling its members, the chairman replied that he had "no such plans." On November 19, 1954, he announced that the committee's consideration of the nomination was being postponed until the next congressional session at the request of James O. Eastland (D-Miss.), a committee member and the Senate's most outspoken segregationist. And in early December, Langer told reporters that while he had no personal objections to Harlan, he would oppose confirmation as part of his continuing effort to force the president's appointment of persons from "small states" to major federal posts.[62]

As Senator Eastland's request made clear, however, opposition to Harlan's confirmation was not to be confined solely to those concerned about the paucity of justices from the nation's North Dakotas. Privately, Eastland told William Rogers that Harlan was a "high class fellow" who clearly deserved confirmation. But "some delay," he added, would be necessary for "political reasons." When the judiciary committee postponed action on the nomination, its counsel revealed that to date the body had received six letters opposing the appointment and complaining that Harlan had been a Rhodes Scholar; that he was a member of the advisory council of the Atlantic Union Committee, an organization established to forge closer relations among the nations of the Atlantic community; and that he was "inexperienced." Two of those concerns seemed laughable at best, the third of limited significance. By that point, though, a number of segregationists and Republican conservatives had begun to voice similar complaints, lending weight to press speculation that they were planning to oppose confirmation for a number of substantive and tactical reasons.[63]

The motivations underlying the stance of Eastland and company were not difficult to fathom. Staunch segregationists in the Senate obviously believed that obstruction of the confirmation process would mean a delay in further Supreme Court review of the school segregation cases; that assumption was entirely correct. Several days after the judiciary committee postponed consideration of Harlan's nomination, the Court issued a brief order putting off further argument of the cases indefinitely. A full-scale review of the nomination would also afford the segregationists an opportunity to probe Harlan's "social" views, attack the segregation decision and the "judicial lawmaking" it was claimed to embody, and attempt to embarrass the administration which had named the now detested Earl Warren, author of the school ruling, to the Court's center seat.[64]

The segregationists, along with other Senate conservatives, were also concerned about what the *Chicago Tribune* called Harlan's "international leanings," particularly his views regarding the treaty power and the constitutional status of international agreements. Following announcement of the nomination, Ernest K. Lindley, a Harlan classmate at Oxford and director of *Newsweek*'s Washington bureau, wrote a lengthy and flattering profile which devoted considerable attention to the nominee's years in England and was based on both Lindley's reminiscences and interviews with a dozen of their Balliol College contemporaries. Harlan's classmates recalled "a quietly agreeable companion, [who] always seemed unruffled, and was impressive in appearance," "sane, well-balanced, solid, poised, modest, even-tempered, clear-headed, well-mannered, pleasant . . . an industrious student." They remembered, too, that he had played golf and tennis and also took up rowing, "progressing through torpids and the second eight to the Balliol first eight," as well as winning, with his partner, the intercollege doubles championship in tennis with a "smashing play at the net." None of his Oxford contemporaries could recall a "prankish anecdote." But one remembered gratefully his lowering a half-bottle of scotch from his rooms down to a group of revelers one night after the pubs had closed.[65]

Probably as a result of objections to Harlan's international ties, the Oxford portion of Lindley's piece, a draft of which would be retained in Harlan's files, apparently never appeared in print. In his interview with reporters following announcement of his selection, moreover, Harlan had sought to minimize his British connections. Unlike many Rhodes Scholars, he had said, he had not been converted to "rabid Anglophilia." In fact, he had returned to England only once since his Oxford days—for his wartime service with the Eighth Bomber Command.[66]

But the objection to Harlan was not only that he was a former Rhodes Scholar. There was the matter, too, of his association with two organizations dedicated to closer U.S. ties with other nations of the world. In 1952 he had accepted the invitation of former Supreme Court Justice Owen J. Roberts, the president of the Atlantic Union Committee, to join the group's five-hundred-member national council. He was also a member of the Citizens Association for the United Nations. His membership in both had been entirely pro forma. When Justice Roberts invited him to become a member of the Atlantic Union's council, he had responded characteristically that while he was "glad" to join, his extensive involvement in the Du Pont–General Motors antitrust litigation would mean that he could not "be counted on for any work or activity in the next year"; he had never even attended a meeting of the council. In fact, he was listed on its roll as "John Maynard Harlan." His membership in the Citizens Association was equally nominal. He had paid his $25 membership fee but had attended only one meeting. Membership in each organization, moreover, was hardly suspect. The Atlantic Union's work, for example, had been praised by presidents Eisenhower and Truman; its membership, as its executive secretary informed Harlan in a letter, had included "distinguished citizens of all shades of political belief except the *extreme* right and left from [Georgia Senator] Walter George to Oveta Culp Hobby; from [Alabama Senator John] Sparkman to Senator Joseph McCarthy."[67]

For several of the Senate's most conservative members, however, mere membership in such organizations smacked of support for the "One World" movement and the subordination of national and state law to the dictates of international agreements. In early 1952, Ohio Republican Senator John Bricker had introduced his proposal for a constitutional amendment to make clear that any treaty provision which conflicted with the Constitution would have no force or effect and to provide that treaties and executive agreements would become effective as internal law "only through legislation which would be valid in [their] absence." In February 1954, the Senate had failed, by a vote of sixty to thirty-one, a single vote shy of the two-thirds majority required for constitutional amendment proposals, to adopt a modified version of the Bricker Amendment. Its supporters saw Senate consideration of the Harlan nomination as an opportunity to examine the nominee's views regarding the impact of international agreements on internal law. Also, since the United Nations Charter and other agreements to which the United States was a signatory contained language arguably inconsistent with racial segregation, Senator Eastland and his allies were naturally extremely interested in that facet of Harlan's thinking.

Statements made by Justice Roberts and President Eisenhower's secretary of state John Foster Dulles around the time of the nomination were of little help to Harlan's position either. "I don't know," Roberts had remarked, for example, "what strange poison there is in this nationalism." And in 1952 Dulles had made a speech at an American Bar Association meeting in which he claimed that treaties are

> more supreme than ordinary laws, for congressional laws are invalid if they do not conform to the Constitution, where[as] treaty laws can override the Constitution. Treaties, for example, can take powers away from Congress and give them to the President. They can take powers from the State and give them to the Federal Government or to some international body, and they can cut across the rights given to the people by the constitutional Bill of Rights.

Dulles had later moderated his stance. But conservatives had not forgotten his rhetoric or that the Eisenhower administration had ultimately opposed the Bricker Amendment.[68]

But concerns about Harlan's international leanings perhaps stemmed primarily from the Supreme Court's decision—or nondecision—in *Rice v. Sioux City Memorial Cemetery*, announced November 15, 1954, just a week after Harlan's nomination was submitted to the Senate. Mrs. Evelyn Rice, the widow of a veteran killed in Korea, had attempted to have the body of her husband, a Winnebago Indian, buried in the Sioux City, Iowa, cemetery. After graveside services were conducted and the funeral party had disbanded, cemetery officials had informed her that under the terms of their contracts "burial privileges accrue[d] only to members of the Caucasian race." Mrs. Rice then filed a suit in a state court, seeking damages to compensate her for the mental suffering caused by her humiliation at being required to halt her husband's funeral at the grave site.[69]

In her original complaint, Mrs. Rice contended that the cemetery's bar against non-Caucasians violated provisions of the Iowa constitution and the Fourteenth Amendment's equal protection clause. The Iowa courts would have the final word, however, on the reach of the state's constitutional guarantees, and the equal protection clause had been consistently construed to reach only governmentally imposed or "state" action, not the policies of private institutions such as the Sioux City cemetery. In *Shelley* v. *Kraemer*, a 1948 case, the U.S. Supreme Court had invoked the equal protection clause to bar a state court from using its injunctive powers to enforce the terms of a racially restrictive housing covenant. And in a 1953 case the Court had assumed the same stance in overturning a state damage suit participants in such a covenant filed against a person who had violated the agreement. But each of those cases had involved an attempted use of state judicial power to enforce a private discriminatory policy against persons who no longer wished to discriminate, and that ingredient was not present in the Sioux City case. Probably for that reason, Mrs. Rice's counsel later amended her complaint to claim that the cemetery's policy also violated Articles 55 and 56 of the U.N. Charter, pledging member nations to promote the observance of human rights and fundamental freedoms without regard to race or color.[70]

The Iowa courts had rejected each of Mrs. Rice's claims, and the Supreme Court, reduced to eight members by Justice Jackson's death, divided evenly in the case, thereby affirming the state courts without opinion. Later, the justices would grant a rehearing of the case after Harlan's arrival, but would then dismiss it, citing a new Iowa statute prohibiting racially discriminatory burial policies. Given the new law, Justice Frankfurter observed for the majority, over the dissents of Chief Justice Warren and justices Black and Douglas, the *Rice* case had "assumed such an isolated significance" that it no longer warranted the Court's review.[71] While Harlan's nomination was pending in the Senate, however, four justices had voted to uphold Mrs. Rice, perhaps on the ground that the Sioux City cemetery's Caucasians-only policy violated the U.N. Charter. Harlan, conservatives feared, might provide the critical fifth vote for such a position.

Finally, the press speculated that the nominee's ties to Governor Dewey and Dewey ally Herbert Brownell might be causing Harlan some difficulty.[72] Earl Warren had been Dewey's running mate in the 1948 presidential campaign, and the Dewey wing of the Republican Party was the party's most racially progressive faction. Senate partisans of Robert A. Taft, who had died in 1953, had not forgotten either that the Dewey forces had sided with Eisenhower rather than Taft at the 1952 Republican convention. Such animosities were likely to generate at least mild sniping during the confirmation proceedings. And syndicated columnist Drew Pearson had added fuel to that issue in one of his columns. Pearson charged that Dewey had arranged Harlan's nomination to the federal bench so that the governor could step into Harlan's position in the nominee's law firm. Pearson also questioned "whether Dewey . . . did a little whispering to New York State banking authorities to secure tentative advance approval of [a] merger" of the Manhattan and Chase National banks in which the Harlan firm was involved—a merger effort which had failed in 1951 because, the columnist claimed, "the approval of the appropriate authorities" could not be secured.[73]

As the Senate judiciary committee moved toward hearings on the nomination, Harlan's supporters attempted to deflect the concerns being raised about his confirmation. When the Pearson column appeared in a St. Paul newspaper, Douglas F. Thornjo, a Minnesota lawyer who had recently worked in Harlan's former law firm, drafted a forceful rebuttal for the paper's editor. Calling the column a "slanderous attack upon the name of an honorable judge and an ethical law firm," Thornjo pointed out that Harlan had left his law practice in March of 1954, while Dewey had not entered the firm—now called Dewey, Ballantine, Bushby, Palmer, and Wood—until the following January. "It is clear, therefore, that Justice Harlan had long been out of the firm and that if Governor Dewey was stepping into any position in the firm . . . it was not the position formerly held by Justice Harlan." Nor had the bank merger initially failed because it did not have the approval of state banking officials. Instead, a clause in the 1799 charter of one of the banks had led to the failure of the 1951 negotiations. Besides, "while Justice Harlan was a member of the Root firm in 1951, during the merger negotiations [he] was a litigator engaged in fighting the DuPont anti-trust case. In his huge law firm Justice Harlan had little or nothing to say about the banking and corporate problems which were present and foremost in the 1951 Manhattan-Chase merger." Privately, though never publicly, the nominee also responded to Pearson's speculations. "They're entirely plausible," he remarked during a family gathering on the terrace of his Weston home. "There is only one thing wrong with them. There isn't a shred of truth in them."[74]

Harlan partisans also lobbied members of the Senate in the nominee's behalf. Thornjo mailed copies of his letter to Minnesota's senators and to Senator Langer, and Harlan's Princeton and Oxford classmates were especially active. Most indefatigable among them was Axel B. Gravem, who had been a student at Oxford during Harlan's years there. A Massachusetts attorney with business interests in several states, Gravem had been one of the first to write President Eisenhower to congratulate the president on his choice of justices. "There is only one thing wrong with Mr. Harlan," wrote the colorful Gravem, "when he plays golf he does not use a tee, but puts the ball down on the bare ground, swats it with a long and co-ordinated swing which propels the damn thing about five feet above ground but always to a disconcerting distance of about 250 yards." In his correspondence with various senators, Gravem made the most of his business connections. "As you know," he wrote Senator Joseph C. O'Mahoney of Wyoming, "I have drilled oil wells in Wyoming . . . and we still have important interests in your good state." To West Virginia Democrat Harley M. Kilgore, who had succeeded Senator Langer as chairman of the judiciary committee when the November 1954, elections returned a Democratic majority to Congress, he wrote: "I am almost a resident of your good state . . . having an office in Elkins where I am engaged—I am glad to say successfully—in the drilling of natural gas wells. I feel as if I am one of your good constituents. . . . In our small way, my little company is doing all it can to alleviate some of the economic stringency in your state which has come about through the difficult coal situation and we also hope to be of some help in starting up new industry in the area." Gravem praised his classmate as a man "of the highest integrity, with a judicial mind in keeping with the highest traditions of our Supreme Court and with a devotion to his country so well attested by his activities in World War II." Nor was he able to fathom how anyone could fault Harlan's Oxford experience. "The fact that he was a Rhodes Scholar should add, rather than detract, from his fitness. He was chosen because of his scholastic ability, the judgment of the faculty as to his character and because he was considered an 'all round' American worthy of representing his Country abroad. He has more than fulfilled that judgment." To "reports that, because his illustrious grandfather, Justice Harlan, delivered a famous dissenting opinion on the negro question, Mr. Harlan's stand on that difficult question may be colored (no pun intended!)," Gravem rejoined that the Supreme Court had already decided the issue and that, in any event, it was "quite ridiculous to foist the opinions of one's ancestors on the descendant!"[75]

Harlan's Princeton classmate David J. Winton, who, like the nominee, had roomed at the university's Hampton Hall, was almost as prolific a correspondent as Gravem. A Minnesotan, Winton focused his efforts mainly on Minnesota Senator Hubert Humphrey, a leading proponent of civil rights reform, who assured his constituent that he was "for Harlan one-hundred percent and . . . will do what I can to hasten his confirmation," albeit adding, "You know, however, that when a fellow isn't on the committee that handles these confirmations there is a limit to what he can do." Harlan's Democratic friends also tried to place New York Senator Herbert H. Lehman in the nominee's corner. "As a Democrat," Henry Rothschild, a professional and social friend of Harlan's for more than twenty years, wrote Lehman, for example, "I believe it would be unfortunate if the Republican Party could, in the future, claim sole credit for supporting this appointment. I believe," he added, forcefully if not entirely accurately, "support of Judge Harlan's appointment to be in the best interests of the Democratic Party."[76]

While Lehman would make no commitments, assuring Rothschild and others only that he would give their recommendations "careful consideration," Lehman's Republican colleague Irving M. Ives was naturally an early supporter. New Jersey Senator H. Alexander Smith, who had first met Harlan at Princeton in 1920 while chairing a committee reorganizing the university, also attempted to push his colleagues toward favorable action. "With many other members of the Senate," Smith wrote Harlan on February 10, "I am very much disturbed in the delay in your confirmation to the Supreme Court. I am trying to do all I can to get the Judiciary Committee to act as soon as possible." Since Smith expected to appear before the committee, he also wanted "to get the facts straight" regarding his friend's career. "Any background information you can give me will be helpful and I want to assure you that I will do all I can to expedite your prompt confirmation." Harlan quickly obliged, providing the senator a biographical profile and correcting inaccuracies in Smith's understanding of his background.[77]

Leaders of the bar also urged his confirmation. Within days of the nomination, Edward J. Fox of the ABA's judiciary committee had written Senator Langer, reminding him that the committee had given Harlan its highest rating for the Second Circuit seat and adding:

> Everything which has happened during his service on the Bench has justified that favorable report.
>
> Courteous, scholarly, practical and with an enormous capacity for work Judge Harlan is, by education, experience and tradition, ideally equipped for membership on the Supreme Court and the Standing Committee on Federal Judiciary recommends without qualification that his nomination be confirmed.[78]

When Langer was replaced as Senate judiciary committee chairman, Fox reaffirmed the ABA's confidence in a letter to Senator Kilgore. The ABA committee's first chair, John G. Buchanan, wrote Kilgore, too, with a copy to Harlan and his congratulations ("Quod bonum felix faustumque sit!"). Former solicitor general John W. Davis—perhaps the nation's most prominent advocate and counsel for South Carolina in the school segregation cases—also wrote the committee in Harlan's behalf.[79]

Not all the letters to members of the Senate, of course, supported confirmation. In early February, Oregon Democrat Richard L. Neuberger received fifty identical letters, all on the letterhead of a Portland foundry, opposing the appointment. The foundry's manager said he had sent them to Washington after a local American Legion post had reported that Harlan "supports one world and things like that." A few days before, the Georgia House of Representatives adopted a resolution condemning Harlan's selection as a "direct slur to the people of the South" and asserting that he was "born, reared and has lived in an atmosphere seeking reformation of the Constitution of the United States by judicial fiat." The liberal Americans for Democratic Action, on the other hand, urged the judiciary committee to act swiftly or risk giving credibility to reports that some senators were postponing the confirmation process in order to delay school desegregation.[80]

While supporters and opponents debated the merits of his appointment, Harlan attempted to prepare for the hearings. In anticipation of questions members of the judiciary committee seemed bound to raise about his Atlantic Union membership, he had secured a copy of its charter and related material from its executive secretary. He also was obliged to decide whether to attend the hearings and, if so, how to respond to the committee's questions. Until the Roosevelt era, nominees had generally not testified personally before the committee. In 1949, moreover, Sherman Minton, an ex-senator then serving on the Court of Appeals for the Seventh Circuit, had declined the committee's request for testimony, citing his position as a jurist facing potential questions relative to cases then pending in his court. With the assistance of Eisenhower's solicitor general Simon E. Sobeloff—who addressed his correspondence, "Dear Mr. Justice," adding, "Certainly I may address you so today—it is not too premature"—Harlan studied the records of predecessors and decided to make an appearance before the committee.[81]

He also obtained the advice of his future colleagues regarding the sorts of responses he should give the committee's questions. Justice Frankfurter sent him a transcript of his testimony before the committee, and Chief Justice Warren polled his brethren, later writing the nominee that

> Most of them were of the opinion . . . that, if called, it would probably be desirable to respond and answer any questions that would not later embarrass you in your work on the Court. Most of them were of the opinion that if they were in your place, they would not answer questions relative to their views on the Constitution, statutes or legislation. Two of the Justices stated they would answer very general questions in this field but nothing that was specific.
>
> It seems to me that if the Committee attempted to probe your mind on legal matters, it would be for a definite purpose and they would not be satisfied with general questions and answers if the matter was opened

> up at all. Somehow or other, I feel that having been confirmed so recently you will be spared this kind of ordeal.

Justice Douglas shared the Chief Justice's general optimism. The committee's decision to hold executive, or closed, hearings, Douglas wrote the nominee, "means to us here that the protests are of such minor character they are not going to be dignified and blown up by public hearings. . . . I understand from Herb Brownell that the complaints are piddling." In the main, however, Harlan simply waited, writing one friend, "Frankly, and for your own information, I don't know what is going on except what I read in the newspapers."[82]

In late February, the waiting ended. When Senator H. Alexander Smith wrote Harlan for details on the nominee's background, he predicted that "the matter will be disposed of right after the February 22nd holiday"; Smith was correct. Hearings on the Harlan nomination were held on February 24 and 25, with the nominee present both days and appearing as a witness the second day of the proceedings.[83]

Witnesses testifying in Harlan's behalf included Senator Smith, who informed his colleagues that the nominee had sought his "advice as to whether, in my judgment, a chap who had a chance to go to Oxford under a Rhodes scholarship to study law, would be wise to do that before he studied in this country." Smith had "advised him strongly to do it." Was Smith willing, an amused Senator Thomas C. Hennings (D-Mo.) asked, to asume responsibility for Harlan's years at Oxford? "I am willing to take the credit for it," Smith replied. "I think he did a very wise thing, and I am proud of the fact that I had that little part in the development of what I think is one of the outstanding jurists in this country." John W. Davis, who would die in March, had been unable to attend the hearings. But Edward J. Fox and John G. Buchanan of the ABA extolled the nominee's virtues, as did Whitney North Seymour, who appeared in behalf of New York City's bar association; Joseph Proskauer, the New York crime commission chairman who represented the New York County Lawyers Association; the president of the state bar association; and a Georgetown University law professor who had been among those representing the government in the Du Pont litigation and concluded "that no company received any better, more skillful representation."[84]

Wendell Berge, a veteran Justice Department attorney who began his career as a junior law clerk with Root, Clark, testified that even as a junior partner Harlan had been an inspiration to young lawyers in the firm. "[T]hey have all had the utmost admiration for him as a lawyer, as a brilliant intellect, as a man of kindly and genial disposition. His character appealed to us as being of the highest." Berge also spoke favorably of his contacts with Harlan during Berge's years as head of the Justice Department's antitrust division.

> Mr. Harlan always represented his clients' interests appropriately, he did everything that was proper and reasonable. . . . On the other hand,

> he was not one of those lawyers, of whom we had many, who would come before the Division protesting that their clients could do no wrong . . . that it was an outrage for the Government to proceed in this matter, and who banged on the table and wanted to exert such pressure as they could to get recognition for what they wanted.

Berge preferred resolution of antitrust cases through negotiation rather than trial and considered Harlan a superb broker in such settings. Berge recalled one trial in which Harlan had participated. The nominee had made "a most effective and statesmanlike argument in his client's behalf."[85]

Most of the committee's attention was devoted, however, to the nominee's testimony and to the contentions of his opponents. Several representatives of obscure conservative and patriotic organizations offered testimony and written statements. In a prepared statement, Mrs. Joseph S. Huxley, regent of the Maryland State Society of the Order of the American Revolution, expressed concern over Harlan's Oxford ties, international views, association with the Atlantic Union, and his defense years before of "Bertram" Russell, the "well-known leftist and advocate of many theories that we reject and look upon with horror." Several 1940 issues of the *Congressional Record* made clear, she declared, "the influence of Rhodes Scholars in the overall plan to form a union between England and America," a union, she was certain, in which "America will be the loser." Nor, to her mind, was it "at all farfetched to predict that [Harlan] might well swing the Court as the fifth member affirming far-reaching powers under alien treaties to override our Constitution whenever the whim occurs to an all-powerful Executive. We are not attacking our present Executive, for whom we have great respect," she assured the committee, "but we are looking to the future."[86]

The remarks of most other opposition witnesses were similar, combining opposition to the nominee's assumed internationalist leanings with veiled and not so veiled expressions of doubt about racial desegregation. Mervin K. Hart, president of the National Economic Council, deplored the Supreme Court's declining prestige, asserting that "[t]oo often in the past 20 years the Court has become a political body" and offering as evidence "the segregation decision in which the Court usurped the functions of the Congress." Members of his group thought it "incredible that any American should be willing to surrender to aliens the control of themselves and their descendants and their country." But he assured the committee that "particularly on the Atlantic seaboard . . . there are many persons who would be willing to see the United States rendered subject to the vote of the 60 nations that compose the U.N., although most of them are vastly inferior to the United States in resources, manpower, and in many other ways, including traditions." A Baltimore insurance broker and director of the American Citizens Association wanted the committee to ask Harlan whether he was "an advocate of catapulting 160 million Americans in with about 3 billion outside the United States, where we would be outnumbered, outvoted, raped, robbed, and ruined?" A woman who was a frequent witness before congressional committees and who represented the obscure Wheel of Progress, an affiliate of the equally obscure Women's Patriotic Conference, asserted, moreover, that while "there should be no particular group, sectional, geographical, or color," influencing judicial appointments, she and her followers were "deeply concerned that there is a great deal of that going on." To support her claim, she quoted from an article in a black magazine, which praised Harlan's appointment.[87]

Of political fringe witnesses, however, George Racey Jordan, a former Air Force major, was the most forceful, articulate, and colorful. Several years earlier, Jordan had accused Roosevelt confidant Harry Hopkins of shipping atomic materials to the Soviet Union. More recently, he had coordinated an unsuccessful campaign to secure ten million signatures on a petition opposing Senator McCarthy's censure. Executive director of the right-wing group the American Coalition of New York, Jordan argued that as a member of the Supreme Court, Harlan "would be in a position to bring to a successful conclusion the legal conspiracy that a treaty is superior to the Constitution—the fraudulent shortcut to the destruction of our sovereignty advocated by the internationalists." He added, "There are plenty of able jurists available with no connections with world government—real jurists who know that the framers of the Constitution never intended by any stretch of the imagination to make it possible to destroy our independence as a nation by mere treaty." The Atlantic Union council, he explained to members of the committee, was, "I suppose . . . very much like the foreign relations council of the Rockefeller empire. They sit around a table like this and try to figure out how to outsmart you fellows."[88]

With the exception of their questioning of Harlan, though, committee members gave their most extensive attention to Herman Methfessel, the former Staten Island district attorney who blamed the nominee's crime commission activities for his re-election defeat. Methfessel, then practicing law in Miami, assured the committee "at the outset that any opposition to Judge Harlan is not a matter of his personal integrity," then proceeded to accuse the nominee of converting the commission into a political tool. The witness had never, he claimed, even visited the Dalessio gambling house where Anna Wentworth's testimony had placed him; Mrs. Wentworth was a "psychopathic liar." Yet the commission, on Harlan's recommendation, had denied him the right to cross-examine her or call his own witnesses.

> I think if he was convinced that easily, if he was willing without any investigation of the truth of the statements or the source from which they came, to call that woman at a public hearing with the whole State and the whole country listening in . . . and then to oppose the right of

a man to defend himself in the same forum where he had been attacked . . . I feel that attitude made him unsuitable for a justice of the court of last resort in this country.

Methfessel complained again, too, that commission agents had coached Mrs. Wentworth in her identification of him and that the scheduling of the commission's hearing and of her testimony was designed to damage his re-election chances.[89]

When Proskauer was called to the witness chair, he asserted that the commission, not Harlan, had scheduled the hearing, "and we had no more idea about connecting it with an election than with the state of the weather on Mars." He also assailed Methfessel's arrest of Mrs. Wentworth on perjury charges following her testimony before the commission as "the most outrageous thing I ever knew of a lawyer to do." The Staten Island investigation, he added, had proved very fruitful: fifteen gamblers and eight police officers had been indicted; all the bookmakers and four of the officers pled guilty to the charges. The Dalessio brothers were indicted for federal and state tax violations; ultimately, the federal government recovered $442,000 in taxes from them, and New York $91,000. In Proskauer's judgment, "far from being any blot on . . . John Harlan, his conduct in this crime commission investigation ought to bring him another Croix de Guerre in addition to the two that he has and another Legion of Merit. Never can I sufficiently thank him for myself personally and for the people of the State of New York for his continued and self-sacrificing devotion."[90]

On returning to the witness chair, Methfessel was somewhat more subdued. He stuck to his general position, however, and rejected any implication in Judge Proskauer's testimony that criminal activity uncovered by the commission had developed only after he became district attorney.[91]

During Methfessel's testimony and that of other opposing witnesses, the questions of most committee members suggested that their sympathies lay clearly with the nominee. When, for example, Methfessel questioned Judge Proskauer's dismay at the district attorney's arrest of Mrs. Wentworth, implying that the judge and Harlan had only objected to her arrest without a warrant, though warrantless arrests were commonplace, Senator John McClellan (D-Ark.) interrupted the witness.

Not to imply any criticism of you but as I understand [it, Proskauer] in testifying made the distinction about it being unusual by reason of the fact that her arrest grew out of a controversy between you and her, a dispute as to which was telling the truth.

That is what I think he meant to cite as the unreasonable procedure, and not the mere fact that she was arrested without a warrant for a felony.

And when one of the witnesses concerned about Harlan's international leanings lectured the committee at length on the dangers confronting the nation, including its rejection of the gold standard ("Any country that is on the gold standard can't be socialistic"), a mildly exasperated McClellan finally remarked, "I would like to hear something relevant to what we have at issue here." Although taking little part in the interrogation, Senator Kefauver, who had not only assisted the New York crime commission in its work but was a supporter of the Atlantic Union, also intervened in the nominee's behalf at various points in the proceedings, as did Illinois Republican Everett Dirksen, among others.[92]

Of Republicans on the committee, only William Jenner of Indiana and Herman Welker of Idaho, both strong Bricker Amendment proponents, seemed very inclined to elicit potentially adverse comments from supportive and opposing witnesses. When Wendell Berge, the former head of the Justice Department's antitrust division, praised Harlan's skills as a corporate lawyer, for example, Senator Welker remarked of the division, "I know that they have done some ax work on some of my people, the small Coca-Cola bottlers and gas workers, when DuPont and all the rest went scot free." But even Welker and Jenner took issue with some of the Harlan critics' more extreme statements. When one witness connected the nominee to the "World Federalist" movement, Senator Welker retorted, "Now, that is a conclusion. Do you have any facts to base that on?" When the witness explained that a speaker at a recent meeting of "World Federalists" was, like Harlan, a Rhodes Scholar, Welker did not press the point, though Senator McClellan dryly observed, "Let us find out if he implies that all Rhodes scholars are World Federalists." But when another witness used excerpts from a black magazine to suggest that Harlan was the candidate of the nation's blacks and might vote to strike down state bars against interracial marriage, Welker rejoined: "[P]ersonally I hate to see a lady of your stature . . . come here before the committee and read some magazine . . . because, you know, it is very easy to charge and very hard to disprove."[93]

Among Democrats, Senator Eastland seemed least enthusiastic about the Harlan appointment. Through what Herbert Brownell later termed a "comedy of errors," Eastland had initially planned to reveal evidence of the nominee's supposed ties with the Communist Party—only to discover that the material in question related to another John Harlan, a Baltimore resident! But the senator did his best with what he had. While invariably courteous and respectful of the nominee's professional credentials, the Mississippi Delta Democrat sought repeatedly to focus the committee's attention on information and assertions unhelpful to the nominee's cause. At one point in Major Jordan's testimony, for example, Eastland asked the witness whether the organization he represented enjoyed an exemption from federal taxation.

MR. JORDAN:
Senator, that is a very embarrassing question. We are not exempt because we are considered a political organization.

SENATOR EASTLAND:
What about the Atlantic Union Committee?

MR. JORDAN:
They are tax exempt, naturally, because they are educating people on how to get around the Constitution. . . .

SENATOR EASTLAND:
. . . Is Judge Harlan on the governing body of that?[94]

When Herman Methfessel complained of partisan politics in the New York crime commission's handling of its investigation of him, Eastland, assisted by Senator Welker, pursued the same tack.

SENATOR EASTLAND:
. . . You think it was a trick of the Dewey machine to purge you; is that correct?

MR. METHFESSEL:
Definitely.

SENATOR WELKER:
. . . Your main objection to Judge Harlan's confirmation . . . is based upon the fact that he had a very important part in [an] election campaign to destroy you as district attorney in the county or in the district you represented?

MR. METHFESSEL:
And a little worse than that—my reputation . . .

SENATOR WELKER:
You feel that the justice then, was a party tortfeasor in this frameup against you?. . .

MR. METHFESSEL:
The frameup was worked by Mr. Harlan's subordinates, and some outsiders. I can't say, and I don't think I should attempt to—I don't think it would be right because I don't think Mr. Harlan would have taken part in the frameup—but I do think that since it was going on under his charge, there is a certain responsibility which must attach itself to Mr. Harlan for having permitted it to happen. On the very day of the hearing, their chief investigator brought Mrs. Wentworth to the door of the courtroom when I was testifying, and asked her who I was, and she couldn't say, and he put his arm around her and said, "Well, that is Methfessel, the district attorney."

There were two witnesses who overheard that. Unfortunately

one is dead now, but one still remains. And I think Mr. Harlan must assume responsibility for what the people under him did.[95]

Eastland and company were to be Judge Harlan's toughest inquisitors. In early January, the nominee had written Justin Blackwelder, the Atlantic Union's executive secretary, indicating that he planned to resign from the organization if confirmed to the Supreme Court, "since I do not feel that a member of the Court should be identified with any organization espousing particular political action, however worthy it may be." But Harlan assured Blackwelder that he had "no apologies to make for [his] membership in the Union, whose objectives should command the support of all who understand what they are." Under questioning from senators Eastland, Welker, and Jenner, among others, however, he emphasized the limited, pro forma character of his association with the Union and scant knowledge of its goals. He had never met Justice Roberts, the Union's president, nor had he played any role in its work. "I do not think I even paid my dues. I attended no meetings of the committee. . . . I have never spoken on behalf of the committee, nor have I discussed the affairs with anybody even informally. If you want me to be completely frank about my relationship to it, until this matter came up in connection with my nomination, I am afraid that if anybody had asked me if I was a member of the Atlantic Union Committee I might have been mistaken in saying 'No.' " When Senator Jenner quoted a statement attributed to Justice Roberts, including among the Union's goals a common citizenship, economic and military policy, and currency, as well as a free exchange of goods and services, among member nations, Harlan retorted that, if Roberts's statement were an accurate quote, he would "disassociate" himself from the Union, "because I don't believe in it." He had joined the Union council, he said, merely because he considered it "one of the instrumentalities that was trying to bring about collective action in the defense against the Communist front." He was not an isolationist. "I think that in the complications of this world situation today, with the leadership of the world thrust at our doorsteps, it behooves us to write and take leadership on behalf of the free world, which means drawing into our group by the things that we stand for and so spearhead against the menace threatening us." At the same time, he insisted, he was also "not an internationalist. I am not a one-worlder. I am not a unionist now. I have never joined any of those organizations." Nor would he yield to anyone in his devotion to American institutions. "God knows, they are the things which make us stand out so far above these people in the Communist countries and the dictator countries where the salvation of the people is dependent upon the whim of one man."[96]

Following suggestions of his future colleagues and his own instincts, Harlan refused to respond except in the most general terms to questions touching on issues which were, or might become, the Court's concern. When, for example, Senator Eastland asked him whether, in his view, a treaty, as Secretary of State Dulles had suggested, could "cut across the Bill of Rights, whether it can override the Constitution of the United States, and whether under a treaty rights given under the treaty will be paramount to the domestic laws of the State," Harlan replied that, "as to the scope of the treatymaking power which has had a long history . . . those involved questions which have been before the Supreme Court, which are likely to come again before the Supreme Court in one fashion or another, and as to that, I must ask your indulgence in saying that I would not in my position be entitled to comment on that." But Eastland was not deterred. "Would the same answer go to the question that a treaty can supplant the domestic laws of the State?" Again, the nominee declined to answer, merely declaring somewhat ambiguously at a later point in his testimony "that the Constitution is the thing that stands over us all."[97]

For Eastland, of course, the treaty question was merely part of a broader, more significant issue—race. He had several questions for the nominee which, he said, "I am [not] propounding, but . . . that I have been asked to propound by a Senator."

SENATOR EASTLAND:
. . . Question No. 1: Do you believe the Supreme Court of the United States should change established interpretations of the Constitution to accord with the economic, political, or sociological views of those who from time to time constitute the membership of the Court? . . .

JUDGE HARLAN:
. . . To lay the inquiry bare, as I understand it, you are asking me how I would have voted on the segregation issue?

SENATOR EASTLAND [apparently with a straight face]:
No, sir. That has not anything to do with it. What he is asking you is this—it is not my question—do you think that a judge should interpret the Constitution in accordance with the personal views of that judge on economic, political, or sociological questions?

JUDGE HARLAN:
That gives a different thrust to the question. No, sir. I believe that so far as human frailties permit, that one who goes on the United States court, for that matter on the court that I am now on, lays aside under his oath of office his personal predilections so far as it is possible humanly to do so and to decide issues before him according to the law and the facts and the Constitution.

SENATOR EASTLAND:
Of course, I knew you would answer it that way. Here is the second question: In your opinion, does the difficulty of amending the Constitution or the delay which is incident to the use of

the amendment process prescribed in the Constitution ever justify the Supreme Court in changing established interpretations or provisions of the Constitution? . . .

JUDGE HARLAN:
. . . I think I can answer that question with propriety, and my answer is, categorically, I do not believe that to be the case.

SENATOR EASTLAND:
Here is the third and last question: In your opinion is the legislative power as effectually denied to the courts of the United States by the Constitution as it is to the Executive? . . .

JUDGE HARLAN:
Well, the framer of that question is perhaps inartistic in framing it, because obviously the Constitution vests the legislative power in Congress, the judicial power in the courts of the United States, and the executive power in the Executive.

That is the whole scheme of our arrangement of government.[98]

While the hearing thus gave Senator Eastland and his colleagues an opportunity to probe the more potentially controversial elements in Harlan's background and, obliquely at least, as in the foregoing colloquy, to attack recent decisions of the Supreme Court, the proceedings also enabled the nominee to challenge statements of other witnesses as well as certain press reports. He expressed particular dismay at those witnesses who appeared to question his loyalty to the nation, asserting, "I do not recall even having met any of these witnesses, ever heard of them, and still less having been given the courtesy before they appeared here to ascertain what my views on any of these questions were." He also denied many of their factual allegations, some of which had already been alluded to in the press. He had not, he said, attended a recent dinner of the Atlantic Union, "of any kind, nature, or description," with or without Senator Kefauver, a Union supporter. Press reports and the testimony of witnesses to the contrary, he had never even met, much less sponsored a function honoring, Serge Rubenstein, a Russian-born financier who had recently been murdered in New York while deportation proceedings were pending against him. "I am at a loss to account how such a story could have been circulated."[99]

Like Judge Proskauer, moreover, Harlan disputed Herman Methfessel's allegations. Quoting frequently from a transcript of the crime commission's Staten Island hearing, he insisted that the former district attorney had never asked to cross-examine Mrs. Wentworth, even though the commission's own rules of procedure gave every witness, indeed any person mentioned during a hearing, the right to question witnesses. Methfessel's claim that Harlan had objected to Mrs. Wentworth's arrest only because it had been made without a warrant was, he declared, a "red herring." He and his staff were concerned only with whether "a district attorney, who was then being investigated, had the right during the progress of the commission's hearing to intimidate by arrest a woman who had testified against him." Nor had the timing of the commission's hearing been politically motivated; the commission had simply completed hearings elsewhere in the state before conducting the Staten Island proceedings. Harlan was perhaps most vehement, however, in repudiating Methfessel's assertion that Mrs. Wentworth had initially been coached by the commission staff to identify the district attorney from photographs shown to her.

> Let me . . . give you my most solemn assurance that that never happened. These young men that I took were men who were not connected politically. They came out of law offices in New York where people were willing to release them, and they were selected because they were lawyers and for no other reason. And that was the character of the investigation that we tried to conduct.
>
> . . . if I had thought that I was being associated with men, either at the top, or my selectees, in an enterprise of the character that Mr. Methfessel suggests, I can assure you that I would not have left my busy law office and given about 9 months of my time without compensation at the expense of my activity in my own law firm. I can assure you of that.[100]

The previous December, when some of Senator Eastland's doubts about the Harlan appointment surfaced in the press, a friend wrote the nominee of his disgust at the Mississippi Democrat's machinations, adding, "Congress does seem to attract the lowest form of human life." After the judiciary committee hearings, another friend suggested a number of questions the committee should have asked:

> 1. (a) Is it not a fact that in the United States you went to a college founded by the Presbyterians and that you are therefore anti-Catholic? (b) How will this bias affect your decisions?
>
> 2. (a) Is it not a fact that in England you went to a college founded by the Catholics and can therefore be expected to be anti-Protestant? (b) How will this bias affect your decisions?
>
> How silly can people get?[101]

On March 9, the judiciary committee voted ten–four to recommend that the Senate confirm Harlan's nomination. But Eastland and his allies were not yet finished. On March 16, the Senate devoted three hours to floor debate on the question. After Senator Kilgore summarized Harlan's credentials and Senator Smith extolled his virtues, Eastland—assisted intermittently by Senator Jenner as well as a number of southern Democrats—began his attack. Eastland was certain that, if confirmed, Harlan would "be the ablest lawyer on the Court. He will be an improvement over most of the Justices." But Eastland opposed confirmation, he said, primarily on three grounds: "First, the nominee would not agree to protect the sovereignty of the United States in the fight which now is being waged by powerful, organized pressure groups on the Atlantic seaboard to" subordinate the Constitution to the dictates of treaty arrangements, making "the United Nations Charter, with its taint of communism . . . paramount" to the nation's fundamental law. Second, "the nominee lacks judicial experience, this is a political appointment, dictated by Thomas E. Dewey and his henchmen. . . . [Third,] Judge Harlan is from the State of New York, and . . . the people of this great State possess views and philosophies which are different from those entertained by the rest of the country. . . . It has had, and now has entirely too much influence, for one State, upon the Government of the United States and the policies of our country."[102]

The segregation issue and the position of the nominee's grandfather on that issue, Eastland assured his colleagues, had not entered into his decision.

> I believe that Judge Harlan is an able lawyer. He has certainly been a successful lawyer. I think he is too smart and is too able an attorney to accept the views held by a number of Justices as to the effect of the 14th amendment to the Constitution in segregation matters. I do not believe he will be subject, in segregation cases, to pressure by organized pressure groups. I believe that he will follow what was evidently the intent of the Founding Fathers who wrote the Constitution, and the real intent of those who framed and passed the 14th amendment. . . . I believe that he would cite the law as he sees it, and would not rely for authority upon the writings of Communist-front sociologists and psychologists.

No, Eastland was simply concerned that, given Harlan's internationalist views, his confirmation might further jeopardize national security.

When asked about the Bricker Amendment before the judiciary committee, Harlan had pleaded ignorance of its provisions, citing the press of his busy law practice. Eastland was appalled.

> Mr. President, here is an able lawyer, a man who represented the DuPonts in a great antitrust case, a man who was on the bench of the circuit court of appeals, a man who is highly educated, a graduate of Oxford University. He stated that he did not know what the Bricker amendment was. . . . [P]ractically every schoolchild in the United States knew about the great fight which the senior senator from Ohio [Mr. Bricker] was making. It seems peculiar to me that that fact did not trickle down to this nominee, who is a great lawyer and an American of high intelligence.

The Mississipian also scorned the nominee's ties with the Atlantic Union and United Nations committee, as well as his reluctance to discuss constitutional issues. "The character and nature of his evasive answers lends weight to the conclusion that he sides with those who would forfeit our sovereignty. This, plus what I will charitably term his 'naïveté' in being wholly oblivious to, and holding no opinion or convictions concerning, great public issues that characterize the life of our times."

Not even New York City's bar association and Judge Proskauer were spared. The association, which had endorsed its member's confirmation, was the only bar group in the country, the senator asserted, which actively opposed the Bricker Amendment. Joseph Proskauer, moreover, was at "the San Francisco convention where the United Nations was organized, making . . . inspiring speeches for the insertion" in the U.N. Charter of the controversial Articles 55 and 56, which Mrs. Rice had attempted to use to override the sanctity of a private contract. Proskauer, too, had signed an amicus curiae brief in *Shelley* v. *Kraemer*. Alger Hiss, he added, had signed the same brief. "The antithesis that now confronts the world," Eastland exclaimed, "is Christ versus the antichrist. For a court to attempt to graft the United Nations Charter into the body politic of this country is no more, nor no less, than an attempt to introduce the antichrist. Need I say more."

As he had in the judiciary committee, Harlan would also have his defenders on the Senate floor. Before the floor debate, he had suggested to Deputy Attorney General Rogers, who had accompanied him to the committee hearing, that Rogers provide Senator Dirksen and other prominent Republicans with excerpts from his committee testimony for possible use in rebutting Eastland and his other adversaries during the floor debate. Rogers had thought Harlan's idea a good one and acted promptly on it, albeit substituting another senator for John Bricker, one of those Harlan had suggested Rogers contact. The mellifluous-voiced Senator Dirksen proved particularly effective.[103]

Dirksen agreed with his "distinguished friend, the Senator from Mississippi" that the nominee's integrity, character, judicial temperament, and sense of civic responsibility were above reproach and indeed had "not [been] impeached by any witness" or "in any letter or communication which has come to my attention." Nor was he disturbed by Harlan's "formal but almost casual" membership on the Atlantic Union's council. Prominent persons, including members of Congress, were often persuaded to join organizations about which they knew little more than what was contained in the "idealistic language" of the group's literature. And after all, Harlan's invitation had come from a former Supreme Court justice, and the committee's membership included an "imposing list" of generals, admirals, ambassadors, and business leaders, among other prominent figures. Harlan, moreover, could hardly be blamed for the U.N. Charter, a document approved by eighty-nine senators and thus part of national law. "[T]he issue, in my judgment, is not John Marshall Harlan.

I think the issue is the failure of the United States Senate to take action on a provision of the Constitution which permits a loophole," making treaties part of the supreme law of the land whether or not consistent with the Constitution's provisions. Dirksen hoped that Congress would reconsider the Bricker Amendment at an early opportunity. But, he insisted, "John Marshall Harlan cannot do it. That is a job for the Senate and the House of Representatives." And what of the nominee's refusal to answer certain questions put to him by the judiciary committee? "I think," said Dirksen, "I would have been very cautious if I had been in a similar position. . . . I would have been thinking whether a case involving that point might come before the court for resolution, and whether perhaps I would tie my own hands."

While he had not been among those supplied excerpts from Harlan's committee testimony, Senator Estes Kefauver also spoke in the nominee's behalf, although Harlan's temporizing on the Atlantic Union issue caused him some regret. Similarly, in a memorandum to the Atlantic Union Committee's board of governors, Union secretary Justin Blackwelder predicted that board members would be disappointed by press reports of Harlan's testimony, but assured them that the accounts were "grossly unfair." Senator Eastland had taken statements from Union literature and Justice Roberts's remarks out of context, Blackwelder explained, "so that they appeared to say things which they were never intended to mean. Judge Harlan stated that *if* those statements represented the true purposes of the Committee (which, of course, they did not) he wished to disassociate himself from those views." Even so, Senator Kefauver expressed regret that Harlan had been "slightly apologetic for his interest in the United Nations or in the Atlantic Union Committee," adding, "I would think more of Judge Harlan if he had straightforwardly and enthusiastically presented his support of those two great efforts." At the same time, Kefauver thought Harlan should be applauded, not criticized, for whatever efforts he had made in behalf of world peace and asserted that nothing revealed by the judiciary committee proceedings had convinced him that Harlan was "not capable, that he does not have the proper concept with reference to the Constitution, or that as a private citizen he has not done his duty to his community and to the country." Other Democrats, including Alben Barkley, a Kentuckian like Harlan's grandfather, also endorsed the nomination.[104]

When the March 16 debate ended, the Senate voted overwhelmingly to confirm the nomination. For all the rhetoric, Harlan's opponents could muster only eleven votes, with seventy-one senators voting to approve the appointment and fourteen not voting. Of those voting against confirmation, only two—senators Langer and Welker—were Republican and non-southerners. During the Senate debate, senators Richard Russell (D-Ga.), John Stennis (D-Miss.), and Sam J. Ervin (D-N.C.) had expressed concern about the nominee's limited judicial experience, Russell contending that years on the bench would instill a "willingness to decide questions as the judge finds the law to be, rather than to attempt to write the law as the judge feels it should be." Presumably, they and fellow southerners who voted against confirmation shared Senator Eastland's other objections to the nomination.

In truth, of course, Harlan's confirmation was never in serious doubt. The proceedings had simply given senators concerned about the school desegregation ruling and rejection of the Bricker Amendment opportunity for further debate. Whatever the motivations of individual senators, few apparently could be convinced that John Harlan represented a threat to the nation's security. In fact, Senator Bricker himself was among those voting for confirmation.

The nominee, however, had found the confirmation process, as he wrote Justice Frankfurter shortly before the Senate vote, a frustrating "experience—one that should never have [been] associated with a nomination to that great Court." He had even considered having his nomination withdrawn, or declining the appointment if confirmed. In a letter of March 8, 1955, to William T. Lifland, his Second Circuit clerk, he had made an unusual request.

> In addition to the piece of research about which I telephoned you the other day, I wonder whether you could run down the following item for me: On page 44 of [Chief Justice Charles Evans] Hughes' book on "The Supreme Court of the United States", he makes the statement that John Quincy Adams and Roscoe Conkling both declined nomination to the Court after they had been confirmed by the Senate. I would like to know what the grounds were, and get copies of their declinations if you can find them in the official records. Don't draw any alarming implications from this. I am just interested.[105]

The "piece of research" Harlan had initially requested apparently concerned Senate votes on previous Supreme Court nominations. For in a letter to the nominee of March 7, Lifland had included a summary of such data. He and Barrett Prettyman had obtained the information, Lifland wrote, from the Supreme Court library. The library was their quickest source. "It is their practice," he added, "to treat all requests for information in strict confidence, and they assured [Prettyman] that his request would be treated in that way." On March 11, Lifland wrote Harlan another letter, discussing the Adams and Conkling withdrawals and enclosing copies of their statements. "We've been keeping in touch with the Senate Clerk's office," he further disclosed, "but they have not yet been able to tell us when the nomination will be acted upon. Here's hoping."[106]

Amid the euphoria of confirmation, any thoughts Harlan might have entertained of declining the appointment must have vanished. Or perhaps he simply came to share President Eisenhower's attitude. After the Senate vote, the president wrote Harlan to express regret that he had been subjected to "harassment and delay," adding, "I assure you, however, that as I have grown wiser, I hope, in the ways of political life, such things tend to bother me less—or perhaps I merely become inured to them."

On March 17, the day following the Senate's vote, Eisenhower signed Harlan's commission. When the Supreme Court next convened on March 28, he took the oath of office from Chief Justice Warren, becoming the eighty-ninth justice to occupy the high bench. "I am glad beyond words," Adlai Stevenson had written him several days earlier, "that at last justice has been done to the new Justice!"[107]

4

The Justice and Company

Ethel Harlan, especially, was always to prefer the Weston, Connecticut, countryside to Washington, D.C., and the frustrations of the Senate confirmation process had obviously done nothing to enhance the city's appeal. But the spacious and comfortable house at 1677 31st Street which her husband purchased in the fashionable Georgetown section did much to ease his wife's adjustment to Washington life. "Georgetown and our own house," she wrote Marion Frankfurter, wife of Justice Frankfurter, in late April following Justice Harlan's confirmation, "have done a lot to make me feel better. We have had so many small amusements along our street and pleasant experiences getting settled that the first rather alarming impact of Washington has worn off. People have, as you said, been kind and cordial, and I am feeling much gayer."[1]

The official atmosphere into which Justice Harlan had now been thrust was not so benign, however. The elevation of Harlan Fiske Stone—a fine jurist but poor chief—to the Supreme Court's center seat in 1941 had created a leadership vacuum on the Court, with Stone unable or unwilling to maintain the social harmony and decisional pace necessary for the court's effective functioning, and justices Frankfurter and Black vying for their brethren's jurisprudential souls. In recent terms, Frankfurter's "restraintist" bloc—including the able, articulate, and acerbic Justice Jackson, as well as Chief Justice Vinson, Stone's successor, appointed in 1946, and justices Clark, Minton, Burton, and Reed—had generally prevailed in First Amendment and other civil liberties cases over the vehement dissents of justices Black and Douglas. But the 1953 appointment of Chief Justice Warren to replace Vinson had begun to narrow the restraintist bloc's margin, and Jackson's death had further depleted its ranks.[2]

The tension between Black and Frankfurter, and their allies, of course, was not purely a consequence of their competing philosophies of constitutional law and judicial function. The untimely death of Black's wife Josephine in 1951 had plunged the Justice into a deep melancholy ("She ought to be the last of her generation to die," he had mournfully told a friend, "not one of the first. Life is wrong—it's just wrong."), which appeared to intensify the tone of his dissents and aggravate his isolation from the Frankfurter bloc. Then, too, there were Black's protracted, well-publicized, and embarrassing battles with Justice Jackson. In a congratulatory note on the occasion of Black's 1937 appointment to the Court, Jackson had expressed "high confidence" in the new Justice's "capacity to translate into law our aspirations for a better social order." Following Jackson's 1941 appointment to the bench, however, philosophical differences, a clash of personalities, and abrasive competition for the leadership Chief Justice Stone failed to provide the Court led to increasingly strained relations.

In the controversial *Jewell Ridge* case, those tensions bubbled to the surface. In disputing the majority's reading of the Fair Labor Standards Act in a suit between the Jewell Ridge coal company and a United Mine Workers local, Jackson quoted remarks Justice Black had made while a member of the Senate. Black, who had joined the *Jewell Ridge* majority, was incensed, charging in a memorandum to his colleagues, "If the dissent goes down as now printed, it will not be a fair representation of the true facts." In spite of this, Jackson filed his dissent without deleting the offensive passages. When the Court denied the coal company's petition for a rehearing—a motion based on the claim that Justice Black, whose former law partner had represented the union in the case, should have recused himself from participation—Jackson joined the Court's denial of a rehearing, but filed a brief concurrence, joined by Justice Frankfurter, in which he emphasized that it was the responsibility of the individual justice, rather than the Court, "to determine for himself the propriety of withdrawing in any particular circumstances," adding, "There is no authority known to me under which the majority of this Court has power under any circumstances to exclude one of its duly commissioned Justices from sitting or voting in any case."[3]

Jackson's concurrence, of course, was more than a lesson on recusal policy. In context, it was a thinly veiled implication that Black should not have participated in the *Jewell Ridge* proceedings—and a particularly offensive one in Black's eyes, since his recusal would not have affected the final outcome of the litigation. But Jackson was not finished. On the day that the concurrence appeared, Jackson departed for Nuremberg, where he was to serve as a prosecutor of Nazi war criminals. When Chief Justice Stone died in April of 1946, while Jackson was still in Europe, stories began circulating in the American press that Justice Frankfurter was promoting Jackson as Stone's replacement, while Black was threatening to resign should President Truman make Jackson chief justice. When Truman nominated Fred M. Vinson to succeed Stone, Jackson's frustrations overwhelmed his judgment. In a 1,500-word cablegram to members of the Senate and House judiciary committees, copies of which he provided the press, Jackson bitterly denounced Black, accusing him of "bullying" tactics, scoring his "publicized threats to the President" to resign were Jackson nominated, and implying that Black was the source of the news reports suggesting that "offensive behavior on my part is responsible for the feud on the Court." Recalling the *Jewell Ridge* affair, Jackson also condemned "the employment of justices' ex-law partners to argue close cases," warning: "I want that practice stopped. If it is ever repeated while I am on the bench I will make my Jewell Ridge opinion look like a letter of recommendation by comparison."[4]

When the Jackson cablegram hit the papers, Black's former law clerk John Frank wired Black that: "This outburst begins the final triumph. Congratulations on winning a real if bloody victory in the unmasking of a bad man." The telegram was filed unanswered, and Black declined public comment. Jackson also made no further public statements, and when he returned to the Court the following October, he and Black resumed outwardly cordial, if essentially aloof and formal, relations. But Jackson's feelings, like Black's presumably, had hardly mellowed. At one point, apparently in 1949, Jackson drafted two scathing attacks on his colleague, one framed in the first person, the other in the third person. In the latter, he applauded his own record and condemned Black's, observing in one passage that "Stone and Jackson . . . had endangered their own interests by standing up for free speech, free press, and minority rights when Black was getting to the top of Alabama politics by joining the Klan and exploiting racial and religious bias." A friend with whom Jackson shared the second draft was only guardedly sympathetic, suggesting that the Justice's references to Black's exploitation of prejudice was "a little strong." Perhaps for that reason, Jackson decided against another public display of his feelings.[5] But he would go to his grave resentful of Black and convinced that his colleague's opposition had denied him the chief justiceship.

Justice Frankfurter apparently had a higher personal and professional regard for Justice Black than Jackson had, and when Frankfurter was appointed to the bench Black had written the new Justice that he was "looking forward with unusual pleasure to our association in the [Court's] important work—work which my experience here has convinced me, more than ever, is vital to the causes in which we believe." Frankfurter was also relatively assiduous in his efforts to maintain cordial relations with his colleague. After joining the Jackson concurrence in the *Jewell Ridge* rehearing motion, for example, Frankfurter wrote Black a conciliatory letter indicating that he "greatly regret[ted] the whole incident" and insisting that he had no "share in creating the situation whereby Bob felt it to be his duty to make clear the issue of qualification." But Frankfurter's feelings about Black were clearly ambivalent. On numerous occasions, he carefully drafted and filed, for biographers and other Court watchers no doubt, detailed and unflattering accounts of incidents in which Black was involved. Those corresponding with Frankfurter, moreover, apparently had no hesitation in referring to Black in disparaging terms. When, for example, Frankfurter declined to attend a 1945 dinner in Black's honor sponsored by the Southern Conference for Human Welfare—a controversial organization considered by its critics to be a hotbed of Communism—a friend had written Frankfurter "a word of appreciation," adding: "The perfume of public praise from people who ought to know better cannot eliminate the odor of the skunk. Official utterances may fool the public but there is still no substitute for character."[6]

On occasion, too, Frankfurter and Black had become involved in divisive personal disputes. When Justice Owen Roberts, who often had joined the Court's laissez-faire conservatives in striking down early New Deal legislation, announced his retirement from the bench in 1945, Chief Justice Stone prepared the customary farewell letter for his colleagues' signatures. Black, a harsh critic of the old Court's repudiation of the Roosevelt recovery program, objected to a passage in the letter which expressed the justices' regret "that our association with you in the daily work of the Court must now come to an end," and to the observation that Roberts had "made fidelity to principle your guide to decision." To secure unanimity, Stone had agreed to the Black deletions. When Frankfurter learned of them, however, he persuaded the Chief Justice to circulate the original letter among the brethren, with the passages to which Black had objected enclosed in brackets. In a brief letter to their colleagues, moreover, Frankfurter insisted that he could not be a "party to the denial, under challenge, of what I believe to be the fundamental truth about Roberts, the Justice,—that he 'made fidelity to principle' his 'guide to decision.' " "The upshot of the affair," Black's biographer Gerald T. Dunne has recorded, "was that Roberts received no letter at all, and the quarreling New Deal Court divided as bitterly on the issue of complimentary phraseology as it ever did on a question of substantive law. Douglas backed Black's position, and Murphy and Rutledge were willing to sign either draft. Frankfurter and Jackson dug in to fight to the end for the original version."[7]

The fundamental conflicts which the struggle over the Roberts retirement letter reflected did not end with President Truman's appointments to the Court; replacement of Stone, Rutledge, Murphy, and Roberts with Vinson, Minton, Clark, and Burton merely shifted the center of influence momentarily to the Frankfurter camp. And while Justice Jackson's death, Chief Justice Warren's considerable leadership skills, and Justice Black's 1957 marriage to his secretary Elizabeth DeMerritte—by all accounts a happy union—were to have a salutary effect on relations among the justices, the philosophical struggle between the Frankfurter and Black factions was still raging when Justice Harlan assumed his seat on the high bench. Although Harlan seemed destined by background and long association with the Hands and others of Justice Frankfurter's persuasion to join the restraintist bloc, Frankfurter left nothing to chance. Instead, he took advantage of every opportunity to win his new colleague's jurisprudential support and color Harlan's impressions of the Court's "liberal-activists."

In terms of their pre-Court connections, Frankfurter could not have asked for a more promising protégé. Harlan's first mentor, Emory Buckner, and Frankfurter had been close friends; indeed, Frankfurter was the first person with whom Buckner had lunched on his arrival in New York. When Harlan's father, in the spring of 1929, sought his son's advice about bringing Frankfurter, who was then teaching at Harvard, into some now obscure venture, Harlan had first discussed the matter with Buckner, then wrote his father that while Frankfurter was "[u]ndoubtedly . . . an extremely able and brilliant fellow," he was also "identified with the radical point of view in this country." "[A]s you will recall," he further observed:

> Frankfurter was very active in the Sacco-Vanzetti case, and publicly criticized the Courts for the way the case was handled. Frankfurter's activity in this case made him a lot of enemies among the so-called law and order and conservative groups, and it seems to me that this is a factor which you should take into consideration before making up your mind to use Frankfurter even if he turns out to be in sympathy with your plan. If the feeling in Chicago, particularly among the members of the Legislative Committee, is conservative, you might not want to run the risk of antagonizing them by introducing such a prominent radical.[8]

Harlan's advice to his father was as much evidence of his customary caution in dealing with potentially controversial issues as it was of his disagreement with Frankfurter's "radical" politics. Whatever misgivings Harlan may have had about Professor Frankfurter's political leanings were no doubt allayed by the restraintist posture he had assumed on the Supreme Court. The selective approach to enforcement of the Volstead Act which Buckner and Harlan had pursued, moreover, was similar to, and may have been patterned after, Frankfurter's own recommendations.[9]

Over the years prior to Harlan's elevation to the Court, he and Frankfurter had developed a reasonably close association. In 1947, Frankfurter sent his friend an inscribed copy of the published version of his Benjamin N. Cardozo lecture, "Some Reflections on the Reading of Statutes." Later, he favored his friend with a reprint of his entry on Justice Cardozo for the *Dictionary of American Biography*, inscribing it, "For John Harlan, who would have given comfort and pleasure to Cardozo, J." When Harlan was named to the Second Circuit, Frankfurter was effusive in his congratulations.

> Hardly a day passes that something does not turn up that makes me miss Buck. How he would rejoice to have you on the Court of Appeals! I do, because of my confidence that you will be worthy of the great

company of the past whom you are joining. . . . Is there a more goodly company to join! My years here have only increased my sense of the great place the Courts of Appeals have in our scheme of things, *provided* their judges are worthy of their functions and this Court is appropriately regardful of them.[10]

And when Frankfurter sent Harlan another "cordial and generous [and] heart-warming" letter on the occasion of his elevation to the Supreme Court, Harlan's response was equally enthusiastic.

> My dear Felix,
>
> I hope you won't mind my addressing you that way, for that is how I have always thought of you since the ERB [Emory Buckner] days. . . .
>
> While I was not so fortunate as to have sat at your feet at the Harvard Law School, I have always felt some sort of a special bond with you through our mutual and devoted friend ERB. Recent events have brought him much to mind. I am not sure that he would have welcomed such an honor for himself, but, as you say, I am sure that he would have rejoiced in it for one of his protégés—for an understanding of the other fellow's point of view and a generous impulse towards it was one of his strongest and most loveable traits.

While the nomination was pending in the Senate, moreover, Frankfurter provided Harlan with materials relative to the Court's work. "Since you are rolling up your sleeves, wisely, if I may say so," he added in a handwritten note to the nominee, "you might take a look at this—by way of 'background.' You see I treat you as one of the brotherhood in sending this for your confidential files."[11]

As his biographer H. N. Hirsch and others have pointed out, Frankfurter entertained serious doubts about Harlan's capacity as a justice and value as a jurisprudential ally. But Harlan surely must have looked more promising than other members of the Frankfurter bloc. And once Harlan was on the Court, Frankfurter became his new colleague's faithful correspondent, offering advice on a variety of matters, engaging him in friendly debate, and instructing him on the subtleties of his philosophical differences with Justice Black and his allies, as well as feeding him unflattering information about them. Some of what Frankfurter shared with the junior Justice had little to do with the substantive issues confronting the Court. When Frankfurter and Learned Hand became concerned, early in Harlan's tenure, for example, about their protégé's prodigious work habits, Frankfurter quickly sought to intervene. "An idle brain is, I know, the Devil's workshop," he wrote Harlan early in 1956.

> But is is no less true that all work and no play makes Jack a dull boy. To be . . . at it all the time and not to indulge in other interests, stifles the unconscious brooding faculties of man and strains his artistic faculties. For it—such exclusive pre-occupation with the immediate prob-

> lems of law—gives no opportunities for cultivating insight and imagination. And these lacks—insight and imagination—mark the essential differences between the great men in the Court's history and the ordinary and pedestrian.

While suggesting that Frankfurter and Hand were unduly concerned, that he had "[a]ctually . . . been doing no more than following the habits of a Wall St. lawyer in his approach to a new and challenging job," Harlan promised to follow a more deliberate pace, assuring his friend that the "last thing I want is to be the cause of any worry to you or . . . Hand."[12]

Frankfurter also expressed concern about Harlan's procedure for handling pending cases. The senior Justice believed that members of the Court should avoid reading the briefs filed in a case until its oral argument and chided Harlan for his "pre-argument brief reading." But Harlan was not dissuaded. "For myself," he rejoined,

> partly no doubt because I find it difficult to read and listen at the same time on the bench—pre-argument scanning of briefs is quite a "must" in my work habits. I have not experienced much danger from "prejudging," either from [the clerks'] bench memos [summarizing cases and suggesting a disposition] (of which I get very few) or from looking over the briefs. The rest of it—as well as your no doubt justified twitting on "misevaluation"—are habits which stem from Buck's "the extra 10%" formula which he burned into me as a youngster. And for which, perhaps to my own cost, I have always been professionally grateful to him.[13]

Perhaps because he too had experienced considerable difficulty in concluding that the Fourteenth Amendment's framers intended it to be a bar against segregated public schools, Frankfurter also began early in Harlan's tenure to share with his colleague his thesis that the first Justice Harlan would have voted to uphold segregation in education, despite his well-known *Plessy* dissent against segregated transportation. In a July 6, 1956, letter, Frankfurter reminded Harlan of an earlier conversation about Frankfurter's "belief that there is no evidence whatever that Harlan I thought that [school] segregation was unconstitutional and . . . my hunch that he would have sustained segregation, had the issue squarely come before the Court in his day."[14]

As evidence to support his position, Frankfurter cited the first Harlan's opinion for the Court in *Cumming* v. *Board of Education*, an 1899 case in which the justices had unanimously upheld the decision of a county board of education in Georgia to discontinue operation of its black high school for financial reasons in order to use the facilities for black elementary education, even though white high schools remained open. The black taxpayers who brought the suit had sought an injunction to restrain the school board from using county money to support the white high schools until equal facilities were also provided black students. Harlan I avoided discussion of the segregation issue in his opinion for the Court, focusing instead on the Court's conclusion that an injunction which would have the effect of closing the white schools would not provide relief for black parents and their children. In concluding his effort, however, the first Harlan emphasized that the management of public schools was a state matter in which the federal government could intervene only to prevent a "clear and unmistakable disregard" for constitutional rights. Frankfurter found it hard to believe that a judge who considered segregated education unconstitutional could have written the Court's opinion in the *Cumming* case, particularly since the trial judge in the case—"a true-blue southern Southerner"—had ruled against the segregation at issue there, only to be reversed by the Georgia supreme court.[15]

On returning to his Connecticut summer home after several days of golf at a New Jersey resort, "much troubled by that very beautiful but difficult . . . course," Harlan drafted a handwritten response. While recognizing the "inferences" which could be drawn from his grandfather's *Cumming* opinion, he could not share Frankfurter's central conclusion.

> I still think the most that can be said is that *Plessy* is little basis for thinking that the old boy would have voted against school segregation. While he did say in *Cumming* that a state system of education was a state matter, he also qualified it by stating that it could not run afoul of the Const[itution]—and earlier he went out of his way to note the anti-segregation argument—then left it open. I can't prove it but my instinct is that he would have been *against* segregation—voted against it, I mean. As you know, he did an about-face on the Civil War Amendments.
>
> Coming from a Southerner, the [trial court] opinion is interesting, but I don't read it, as your letter implies (unless I have misread your meaning) as being contra segregation, only pro separate *but* equal.[16]

Harlan's reference, of course, was to his grandfather's early opposition to adoption of the Reconstruction amendments, but later dissent from the Court's narrow construction of the Thirteenth and Fourteenth amendments in the *Civil Rights Cases*. Frankfurter, however, was not persuaded. "You and I are not in disagreement that Harlan's dissent in *Plessy* v. *Ferguson* gives no justification for assuming that he would have found segregation unconstitutional," he soon retorted. "While you say that's the most that can be drawn from his dissent, I would say that's the least that could be drawn from it." For Frankfurter, Harlan I's restriction of his opinion to *Plessy*'s facts—"about a score of times he referred to the fact that the segregation involved was discrimination on 'the public highway' "—was nearly conclusive.

> To me, his failure to refer to school segregation is significant, in view of the [*Plessy*] Court's reference [in its opinion] to school discrimination and the fact that Harlan was not, I believe, persnickety, as an ordinary rule, in restricting his opinions to the narrow scope of the facts of a case.

> I need hardly tell you that the notion is widely prevalent that Harlan anticipated striking down school segregation in his *Plessy* v. *Ferguson* dissent. That this isn't so is, of course, important as a matter of historic accuracy.[17]

Frankfurter also clarified the significance, for him, of the *Cumming* trial judge's position in the case. The trial judge's decision was based, he conceded, on the separate but equal doctrine, not on a finding that segregated schooling per se was invalid. "My point was, and I deem it important, that if a Georgia judge could have found in the *Cumming* case a violation of the equal protection of the laws, even though he based it on the separate-but-equal doctrine, it is rather surprising that Harlan should not have been at least as uncolor-blind as was the Georgia judge. I am not saying that the *Cumming* opinion result is not defensible. I am saying it is a casuistic bit of reasoning. Anybody who felt passionately against school segregation could easily have reached at least the result that the Georgia [trial] judge reached."[18]

When Harlan, either by a further letter or telephone conversation, persisted in his position, Frankfurter penned yet another defense of his stance. He could not "get away from the incongruity that a fellow who indulged in the broad rhetoric that the 'Constitution is color blind', should have sponsored such a narrow result in *Cumming*." Harlan I's *Plessy* and *Cumming* opinions "must be read in the light of the [Justice's] intellectual habits." Written by a Brandeis, "whose decisions practically always sailed close to the harbor of the specific facts of a case," the emphasis on the "public highways" in *Cumming* would carry no special import.

> But whatever virtues may be attributed to Harlan I, no one, I submit, would credit—or charge—him with having been a close reasoner, more particularly, a writer who strictly confined himself to the narrow limits of a particular case. And even when it comes to what might be called narrow adjudication, I submit that any judge who thought that the Constitution, as a legal proposition, is color blind, would at least have been able to reach the lawyer-like result . . . in not leaving colored high school children out in the cold.

Nor, Frankfurter asserted, would Harlan I's later embrace of the Reconstruction amendments after his initial opposition had "aroused hostility to his appointment . . . be a unique instance of a judge, who, by his opinions, contradicted, however unconsciously, the ground of opposition to him." Even in his dissent in the *Civil Rights Cases*, moreover, "the rights which he urged" involved equal access to transportation facilities, inns, and places of public amusement, not integrated schools.[19]

While the matter may have initially surfaced in a discussion of Justice Frankfurter's continued doubts about the constitutional—if not moral—status of segregated education, the Justice's debate with his junior colleague over the first Harlan's position on the issue was probably simply the sort of essentially academic exercise Frankfurter relished and not an effort to influence the direction of the younger Harlan's thinking on any element of the Court's current caseload. But on numerous occasions, especially early in Harlan's tenure, Frankfurter did attempt to clarify his colleague's thinking on a variety of issues confronting the Court and to convince Harlan of the wisdom of Frankfurter's position. He was particularly concerned that Harlan understand and appreciate the subtleties of his First Amendment jurisprudence and the relationship of the Bill of Rights to the states via the Fourteenth Amendment. To further this understanding, Frankfurter shared with Harlan letters he had written to Justice Black years before, challenging Black's broad, absolutist construction of the First Amendment as well as Black's contention that the Fourteenth Amendment's framers intended its provisions to incorporate the guarantees of the first eight amendments, thus making them fully applicable to state and local governments. Frankfurter also wrote Harlan numerous letters about those and related constitutional issues. In one letter, for example, he recounted for Harlan his debate with Black over the scope of the First Amendment in *Bridges* v. *California* and *Times-Mirror Co.* v. *Superior Court*, cases from 1941 in which the Court, speaking through Black, ultimately overturned contempt convictions imposed on publications deemed to interfere with the administration of justice. Initially, Frankfurter wrote Harlan, he had marshalled a narrow majority to uphold the convictions at issue in the cases, and had sent Justice Brandeis, then retired from the Court, a draft of his opinion. "Of course you have a unanimous Court," Brandeis remarked when he next spoke with Frankfurter. "Hardly that," Frankfurter prophetically replied. "I am very doubtful whether I will keep a Court. Black has a fierce dissent." To which, by Frankfurter's account to Harlan, Brandeis had vehemently retorted, "Black & Co. have gone mad on free speech!"[20]

Not surprisingly, Frankfurter also closely monitored the tenor of Harlan's opinions. When a Harlan effort appeared to embrace, in some slight degree, Justice Black's First Amendment views or incorporation thesis regarding the relation of the Bill of Rights to the Fourteenth Amendment, Frankfurter's reaction was prompt and predictable. When Harlan, for example, circulated a draft majority opinion in a minor 1957 case, which included the statement, "It is indisputable that the right to counsel in criminal cases is fundamental to our jurisprudence," Frankfurter quickly responded. Harlan's language could have been construed to conflict with *Betts* v. *Brady*, a 1942 case in which the Court, over Black's dissent, had held the Sixth Amendment right to counsel insufficiently "fundamental" to be federally required of states under the Fourteenth Amendment's due process clause. Frankfurter so reminded his junior colleague. "John, you can't use that phrase," he cautioned in a marginal notation on the Harlan draft. "I certainly cannot subscribe to it with *Betts* v. *Brady* on the books.

It would be quoted at once as indicating an invitation to ask us to overrule" *Betts*.[21]

Frankfurter voiced similar concerns about an early draft of Harlan's 1958 opinion for the Court in *NAACP* v. *Alabama*, which rejected the state's power to require disclosure of the controversial organization's Alabama members. An early draft of Harlan's opinion included the statement, "It is of course firmly established that the protection given by the First Amendment against federal invasion of such rights is afforded by the Due Process Clause of the Fourteenth Amendment against state action." By this point, Harlan had already made clear, via two obscenity cases of the previous term, *Roth* v. *United States* and *Alberts* v. *California*, his view that the Fourteenth Amendment's restrictions on state power over expression were not nearly so stringent as those imposed by the First Amendment on federal officials, even though the Court's own opinions had increasingly appeared to equate the two guarantees. As the Court's most vigorous opponent of incorporation, however, Frankfurter was alert to even the slightest deviation from the anti-incorporationist faith. "Why in heaven's name," he wrote Harlan,

> must we, whenever some discussion under the Due Process Clause is involved, get off speeches about the First Amendment? Why can't you . . . state in two or three sentences that to ask disclosure of membership . . . is, in the light of prior decisions, merely citing them, an invasion of the free area of activity under the Fourteenth Amendment not overcome by any solid, as against a very tenuous, interest of the state in prying into such freedom of action by individuals. . . .
>
> If you tell me that I am making a rather fastidious distinction of phrasing, I plead guilty. But it is this kind of talk that leads to the kind of guff argument that we get from [civil libertarians] at the bar. To me there is a lot of difference between your sentence and Cardozo's sentence [in *Palko* v. *Connecticut*], "The Due Process Clause of the Fourteenth Amendment may make it unlawful for a state to abridge by its statutes the freedom of speech which the First Amendment safeguards against encroachment by the Congress." These are delicate matters and therefore should be delicately phrased.[22]

In a later letter, Frankfurter conceded his "loose reference . . . years ago to the 'First Amendment' as a shorthand for freedoms protected against state action by the Fourteenth Amendment." Even so, he asserted that:

> Little did I dream in my early days when we were dealing with explicit curtailments of speech that loose rhetoric in the service of recently discovered doctrinaire views by members of the Court would be snowballed into a talismanic mouthing of "First Amendment" in dealing with state action, which only by the most indirect argumentation could be made to relate to utterance or refusal to utter, i.e. speech and its with-

> holding. It deserves repeating that the loose talk of this Court is responsible for, because it encourages and sustains, the kind of half-baked, flannel-mouthed talk that [civil libertarians] dish up to us in the confident belief that they have to get only one more "vote" to win their case. And so, by this process of building words on words, we have reached with reference to "First Amendment" precisely the same situation that led to . . . F.D.R.'s "Court packing plan," as a result of a series of decisions based on the destructive employment of "liberty of contract" [for laissez-faire ends].[23]

Despite the letters and a lengthy conversation with his colleague, Harlan continued to "have the most serious misgivings about" Frankfurter's suggestions for revising his opinion in *NAACP* v. *Alabama*. Even so, Harlan recast it in ways Frankfurter found acceptable. "Most of what I consumed at lunch was your *NAACP*," Frankfurter soon responded, adding: "You did indeed deal very open-mindedly with all my worries, very generously and I am intellectually appreciative. You have sufficiently met my main difficulty and I do not feel justified in asking for [more]. And so I shall join you."[24]

The revisions which had placated Frankfurter, however, had disturbed Justice Black. The draft, Black wrote Harlan, was "now written as though the First Amendment did not exist. In fact, this studious avoidance of any statement that might possibly imply a pertinency of the First Amendment leaves an impression on me that that basic provision of our Bill of Rights might be as contaminating as the leprosy." Black realized that unanimity was "essential" in racial cases and was "willing to go a long way to obtain such unanimity."

> If, however, agreement to Part III of your opinion is essential to get unanimous Court action, the price is greater than I am willing to pay. Personally, I do not believe that ignoring the First Amendment should be a *sine qua non* to unanimity here. If it is to be treated as having no effect in any cases, I believe it would be better to do so frankly, openly and without leaving anything to implication. I am not willing to do it either expressly or impliedly.

If a majority supported Harlan's revised draft, Black would submit a brief concurrence indicating his substantial agreement with the Court's judgment and opinion, but also stating his "belief . . . that the state has here violated the basic freedoms of press, speech and assembly, immunized from federal abridgement by the First Amendment, and made applica[ble] as a prohibition against the states by the Fourteenth Amendment." In support of his position, he would cite the "numerous" earlier cases "which relied on the First and Fourteenth Amendments to protect freedom of speech and press."[25]

Even before Harlan drafted the revisions in an effort to win Frankfurter's support for his *NAACP* opinion, Justice Douglas had objected to Harlan's treatment of the First and Fourteenth Amendments in his initial draft. Douglas detected in Harlan's effort the position he had advanced in *Roth* and *Alberts*, and he was not pleased. In Douglas's view, the Fourteenth Amendment incorporated the First "full-fledged, not watered down by some concept of due process."[26]

In the concurring and dissenting opinions Harlan had registered for *Roth* and *Alberts*, respectively, the obscenity cases to which Douglas was referring, he had argued that while the First Amendment imposed stringent restrictions over federal authority to regulate expression, state exercises of such power should be upheld under the free expression component of the Fourteenth Amendment due process clause if they had a "rational" basis. Douglas found the implications of such a position alarming, particularly if extended to racial cases. "If that is the test" under the Fourteenth Amendment, he asked, "why were we right in the Segregation Cases?"[27]

Douglas was particularly concerned with Harlan's suggestion that the NAACP (National Association for the Advancement of Colored People) could have been compelled to produce its Alabama membership lists had some legitimate state interest been cited to justify disclosure. Following a conference with his colleague, Harlan was able to soothe Douglas's concerns by including in the opinion the assertion that "state action which may have the effect of curtailing the freedom to associate is subject to the closest scrutiny."[28] Ultimately, too, Justice Black was persuaded to forego a separate opinion in the case, though, of course, the Court's debate over the relationship of the Bill of Rights to the Fourteenth Amendment was hardly over.

Justice Frankfurter not only attempted to mold Harlan's jurisprudence to the subtleties of his thinking, on occasion he also enlisted Harlan's assistance in converting new justices to their views. Frankfurter apparently had some difficulty convincing Justice Charles Evans Whittaker, who had replaced Justice Reed in 1957, of the need to avoid reference to the First Amendment in cases involving the Fourteenth. When, for example, Whittaker circulated a draft opinion for the Court in *Staub v. Baxley*, a 1958 case striking down a local ordinance which prohibited the solicitation of membership in dues-paying organizations without a city permit, Frankfurter questioned his new colleague's reference to both amendments in a state case, contending that the First Amendment "is not involved here and [reference to it] leads only to confusion of thought." Whittaker stood his ground, citing numerous earlier cases connecting the requirements of the two guarantees. But Frankfurter was persistent in his campaign. In 1960, on the eve of the incorporation revolution to take place in that decade, he apparently suggested that Harlan share anti-incorporationist literature with Whittaker, including Professor Charles Fairman's leading 1949 *Stanford Law Review* attack on Black's thesis that the Fourteenth Amendment's framers intended its provisions to apply the first eight amendments to the states. "In addition to Fairman's destruction of the Black claim," Frankfurter wrote Harlan,

> I suggest you ask Charlie to look at my supplementary materials in the Appendix to *Bartkus* [v. *Illinois*]. . . . It negatives the suggestion of incorporation, for it would imply that a good many of the ratifying States would have covertly amended their own Constitutions which were out of accord with the Fourth, Fifth and Seventh Amendments. By 1890 only eleven of the thirty ratifying States were in explicit accord with these provisions of the Federal Bill of Rights. Make Charlie consider what real hell would be raised in so many of our States by adoption of the incorporation theory—violative as that is of unbroken precedents, history and reason.[29]

Finally, whether out of a natural penchant for Court intrigue or as part of a conscious effort to drive a wedge between Harlan and the "liberal-activist" bloc, Frankfurter regularly fed his jurisprudential protégé with negative information and opinion about Justice Black and his allies. In early April of 1957, Frankfurter passed Harlan a handwritten note on the bench, then prepared for his files the following "almost verbatim recollection" of what he had written:

> After a good night's sleep I have resolved to tell you one of these days with details about the inner history of this Court since I came here. I shall do this for two reasons: (1) out of regard for your personal well-being (this is due to my feeling for you and it is confirmed by my devoted memory of two very beloved friends, Owen Roberts and Bob Jackson); (2) out of regard for the work of the Court and our responsibility toward it. This is a matter that is more important to me than the natural distaste of talking about colleagues.[30]

"Of course," Harlan soon replied, "I would welcome what you so generously offered in your letter." And what Frankfurter offered over the years was hardly confined to gossip about Justice Black's relations with Justices Roberts and Jackson. In 1958, Justice Clark was scheduled to participate on the program of the annual convention of the American Bar Association; several of the justices, including Black, a frequent critic of the organization's political leanings, had decided to attend the meeting as the association's guests. Frankfurter was alarmed that his brethren would even consider such an announcement and scornful of their asserted reasons for agreeing to attend. "For members and their wives," he wrote Harlan, "to go out there as the guests of the Association—except a Justice who had an active share in the program—strikes me as a bit shabby. And the excuse that their presence will generate good-will for the Court strikes me as reliance on a fatuous notion. The ultimate purpose is, of course, far different."[31]

Not surprisingly, Justice Black was the principal target of Frankfurter's wrath.

> I almost puked when I heard Hugo say that if it would be good for the Court, he'll go. Gosh! For nearly twenty years I have heard his uniform condemnation of the A.B.A. and his contempt for their views. And now, he puts on that noble act. The truth of course is, I have not a particle of doubt, that this will afford a pleasant trip for his young wife. He is not the only old Benedict I knew who is more eager to please his new bride than ever he was his first wife. (Josephine Black was an uncommonly lovely person.) I have little doubt that Hugo now believes that it "will help the Court," for he has infinite capacity—beyond anyone I've known—for self deception.
>
> If you find these observations too blunt, even acrid, don't blame the heat. Blame my nature.[32]

Initially, Harlan had been among those justices planning to attend the ABA gathering. Under pressure from Frankfurter, however, he began to have "second thoughts." In ultimately deciding not to attend, he wrote Frankfurter, he had explained to Justice Clark that he and Mrs. Harlan could not leave her ailing mother. But he had also told Clark, he assured Frankfurter, that he had "serious reservations anyway about one not, as he, performing a function, accepting such an invitation. The whole idea seems to me too goldfinery, although your 'shabby' is probably closer to it."[33]

While Justice Black was the principal target of Frankfurter's concerns, Frankfurter was also critical of other members of the "liberal-activist" bloc in his exchanges with Justice Harlan. When William Brennan replaced Justice Minton in 1956, Frankfurter had launched his usual campaign for his new colleague's jurisprudential soul. Brennan had been Frankfurter's student at Harvard, but he apparently did not appreciate his colleague's proselytizing efforts. Certainly, they had no noticeable impact on Brennan's voting patterns—at least not the sort of influence Frankfurter had intended. Brennan, Frankfurter decided, simply had an "ego" problem. "After sleeping on it," he wrote Harlan during the Court's debate over one 1958 case,

> I have decided to curb my temperamental spontaneity and not talk to Bill Brennan. "Too much ego in his cosmos." When [Harvard law professor] Paul Freund was here recently—and Paul Freund is as wise as any member of the profession whom I know—he asked, "Is my classmate Bill as cocksure as his opinions indicate?" Cocksuredness begets sensitiveness, and as his erstwhile teacher, I have to be particularly careful with Bill. He was plainly displeased at the thought of my writing anything before I saw what he will produce, on the assumption that he will take care of all there is to be said. Therefore, I do not think I ought to tell him what I think should be the conception and temper of our opin-

ion. All of this has nothing to do with my personal relations with him, which are as pleasant as they can be.[34]

Frankfurter also wished, he confided to Harlan, that Justice Douglas "were less shallow and thusly less cock-sure," although Douglas's "honesty cheers me much and gives me considerable hope." After reading Chief Justice Warren's draft opinion in the *Dixon-Yates* utility case, moreover, he wrote Harlan that while he doubted that Harlan's dissent in the case would shake his decision to join the Court's majority, Warren's "crude, heavy-handed, repetitive moralizing makes me feel like eating rancid butter, and there are things in it now that I will not swallow." Frankfurter was especially offended, he wrote, by the Chief Justice's "gratuitous" assault on the "whole 'business community.' " Charging Warren with the "bias of a sansculotte," the poorer class of French revolutionary, Frankfurter promised Harlan to undertake the "disagreeable task" of asking Warren "to take out his excessive moral (and some 'legal') baggage before I can join his opinion."[35]

In the main, Harlan would become Frankfurter's most loyal and effective ally. Little in Harlan's law practice had equipped him for the sorts of constitutional issues which form the most significant elements of the Supreme Court's work, and the new Justice no doubt appreciated—even though he did not always accept—Frankfurter's guidance. Not only would they come to share similar views regarding incorporation and other constitutional questions, they would also be in substantial agreement regarding matters of Court routine and procedure. In a significant 1958 address, entitled "Manning the Dikes," Justice Harlan sought to impress upon members of the Association of the Bar of the City of New York the legal profession's "sense of responsibility . . . in not cluttering up the courts with needless litigation." Since the Supreme Court's decision to grant or deny certiorari review of a case lay entirely within the Court's discretion, with reasons for its disposition rarely cited, Harlan could understand why it would be "difficult for a lawyer to withstand the normal impulse of a client to carry a hard-fought case through to the bitter end. For if a lawyer cannot assess with some degree of confidence the imponderables involved it is quite understandable that he should conceive it to be his duty to try for certiorari." Even so, "the time required to handle the certiorari work and that needed for the adjudication of cases, and more particularly for the writing of opinions, [were] coming into competition." The sheer number of certiorari petitions filed each year had convinced him that many lawyers had "a fundamental misconception as to the role of the Supreme Court in our constitutional scheme." Often, he observed, certiorari petitions reflected an assumption that the high Court possessed general review authority over the decisions of state courts, when in fact the Court could only review federal legal questions raised in such cases. Nor was the Supreme Court a general "court of errors and appeals in the same sense as most highest state courts." Instead, its review should properly be limited to the most significant cases.

The Court could help to limit the number of frivolous certiorari petitions filed each year, he asserted, by consistently refusing to grant review in minor or "uncertworthy" cases, "lest lawyers be led to believe that the rules governing certiorari are so capriciously applied that their only prudent course is to 'take a chance' that their petitions may find favor too." It might more frequently issue statements, too, regarding "the direction of its thinking as to the fitness for review of various recurring categories of issues." But the bar should also do its part, he concluded, to discourage "abuses of the certiorari procedure, whether born of ignorance of the nature of the process or of lack of responsible abstention on the part of lawyers in seeking to bring 'uncertworthy' cases to the Court." Harlan assured his audience that for the time being, the Court's certiorari work was being confined "within manageable proportions." Moreover, he opposed the division of the Court into two or more panels as a device for streamlining the process, or the imposition of penalties on those litigants who filed patently frivolous petitions. He considered it "shortsighted and unwise," however, for the Court and the bar "not to recognize that preserving the certiorari system in good health, and in proper balance with the other work of the Court, are matters that will increasingly demand thoughtful and imaginative attention."[36]

Harlan was also a vigorous opponent of the time-consuming federal court jurisdiction over disputes between citizens of different states, resolution of which involved application of the appropriate state law rather than federal statutes or administrative regulations. Such diversity of citizenship litigation, Harlan argued, should be eliminated from the federal courts' caseload "save in [those] instances where a 'foreign' litigant can show that he will not receive a fair hearing in the . . . courts" of the state in which the suit arose. At times, too, he expressed impatience, with indigent litigants who were permitted by federal law to file *in forma pauperis* petitions without representation by counsel or being required to follow the formal and relatively expensive procedures normally required for the filing of cases. In a 1961 memorandum to court and prison personnel in the Second Circuit, over which he exercised supervisory authority, he complained, for example, about the poor quality of indigent applications for an extension of the time allowed for the filing of petitions. Increasingly, he asserted, the applications he received from indigents in the Second Circuit were "so unilluminating as to make intelligent action thereon well nigh impossible." He agreed that indigents petitioning in their own behalf could not be held to the standards expected of litigants represented by counsel. But he found it "not too much to insist that applications made by unrepresented litigants should contain at least the minimal facts necessary for a determination as to the timeliness of their applications, the probable jurisdiction of this Court over the matter sought to be reviewed, and the reasons justifying an extension of time." Henceforth, he declared, he would entertain no applications not including such elements.[37]

Justice Frankfurter had long voiced the sorts of concerns which Harlan advanced. Following Harlan's address to the Association of the Bar of the City of New York, he shared with his colleague the impressions of one member of Harlan's audience, "not as a commentary on your lecture but as a commentary on the Court." "I discussed and heard a great many persons discussing Justice Harlan's talk," the friend had written, "and the most frequent remark I heard was that 'what Justice Harlan says may be fine, but so long as the Court does take some frivolous cases and is so unpredictable, I can't honestly advise clients that they have no hope of having certiorari granted, especially when the cost of preparing a petition is small compared to that of the whole litigation.' " At the bottom of Frankfurter's letter, Harlan penned his agreement: "Yes, and I would add that apart from this I am under no illusions as to the practical problems of the lawyer whose client asks him to try for cert. and is willing to pay for it."[38]

Justice Harlan in turn supported Frankfurter's continuing campaign to reform certain of the Court's procedures. In his annual letter of greeting to his brethren, Frankfurter regularly recommended changes in conference procedure, the Court's approach to opinion-drafting, and other reforms. He also criticized what he viewed as the Court's tendency to "mass" important cases for consideration at the end of each term. Following circulation of Frankfurter's 1957 effort, Harlan wrote his colleague that he was "strongly in favor of a full . . . discussion" of Frankfurter's suggestions at the term's opening conference of the justices, adding that if there were delay in dealing with the Justice's proposals, "I am very much afraid that there will be no discussion at all."[39]

On that occasion as on others, however, Harlan's support was to have little impact on the rest of the Court. After he reiterated his support for Frankfurter's position, and their discussion in conference, in a letter to Chief Justice Warren, the Chief Justice circulated a memorandum indicating that, at Harlan's suggestion, Frankfurter's views were to be discussed at the Court's next conference. Warren insisted, however, that "none of the controversy which the Court found itself in at the conclusion of last Term or any recent Term was due to 'massing.' " On a later occasion, moreover, Justice Douglas also opposed certain of Frankfurter's proposals, asserting that "To bring our flow of cases to a grinding halt due to rigid, arbitrary rules would, with all respect, be folly." In recent terms, Douglas lamented, the justices had "tended more and more to write a law-review-type of opinion," which Frankfurter and Harlan presumably favored. "They plague the Bar and the Bench. They are so long they are meaningless. They are filled with trivia and non-essentials." The opinions of Justice Holmes, written by the Justice while he stood at a desk, and thus noted for their brevity, should be the Court's model, Douglas contended, for they were "the most serviceable and the most enduring." The opinions in one recent coerced-confession case in which the restraintists had prevailed, he recalled, "were so long, and so discursive that one could find in them what he was looking for."[40]

While Harlan and Frankfurter shared essentially the same concerns regarding Court procedure, the nature of individual rights, and the role of the judiciary in the constitutional system, Harlan's relations with their colleagues were to be decidedly more harmonious and free of intrigue than Frankfurter's. Given Harlan's calm and unassuming personality, such a contrast was not surprising. Although usually gracious, he could be a cold and indifferent man. On one occasion, when a Root, Clark associate, devastated at his failure to make partner, sought Harlan's counsel, he was told that he might list his name with the bar association—a fate nearly worse than death for a young lawyer with more ambition than promise. In another case, his close friend Leslie Arps was disappointed and irritated at Harlan's failure either to help him secure a partnership in Harlan's firm or a military promotion during their World War II tour of duty. "I never mentioned it to him," Arps recalled several years after the Justice's death, but "I was very bitter at one time. . . . I cared for him a great deal, so it all disappeared. But it was an interesting aspect of his character that you would not see often." However, as Arps's remark suggests, such behavior was hardly typical. Whether as a conscious counterpoint to his bombastic father or as an intrinsic personality trait, Harlan was normally very sensitive to the feelings of others, both avoiding displays of temperament and repelled by them. Once during a telephone argument he had the temerity to hang up on his volatile sister Elizabeth. "Don't you dare ever hang up on me when I call you," she had soon written him. "That is not worthy of you, John. You should be willing to take criticism from your sister whether you like it or not. You *give* plenty when you want to." Harlan was characteristically penitent. Unable to reach Elizabeth by phone, he wrote her a note. "I do feel badly about, and apologize for, my abrupt ending of our telephone conversation earlier in the week. Such things ought not to happen between us, whatever the nature of our disagreement."[41]

Harlan was also a man of unusual patience. His sister Janet, a brilliant woman who had graduated Phi Beta Kappa from Smith College by age twenty, was to have three husbands, each of them "totally inferior" to her in the eyes of her family. Frequently over the years, usually in handwritten notes addressed to "Dearest Johnnie," she sought her brother's advice and, on occasion, his financial assistance. At times, she would strain his good humor. "Thanks for calling the other night," she wrote him on one occasion. "You sounded quite provoked with me, and I am sorry to keep bothering you." In the main, however, he was the loving and considerate brother, even when Janet's loans became gifts. "As to the money which I loaned you some years ago," he responded to one of her letters, "I would prefer to have you forget about it. Treat it as a contribution to [her son] Harlan's education." He even patiently considered the business propositions of Janet's third husband, a silversmith and inventor, which she channeled to him, including those bordering on the impractical. "I found myself getting quite snarled up in the operation when I tried to use it," he wrote her of the prototype for a bracelet cigarette lighter. "[M]ost men would not want to wear a bracelet," he added, and "lighting a cigarette from one's wrist might be hazardous to ladies' dresses, particularly ones with long sleeves." He doubted it could be patented.[42]

Such concern for the feelings of others and consummate skill at maintaining warm relations with family and associates would also characterize his relationships with his Supreme Court contemporaries. On rare occasions, he expressed private scorn at some action of the Court or an individual justice.

For example, when a majority reversed his victory in the Du Pont–General Motors antitrust suit, he could not contain his disappointment. Because he was a lawyer for the Du Pont brothers and certain of their corporate interests in the Du Pont–General Motors case, he was obliged to recuse himself from participation in the Supreme Court's review of the suit. When a majority voted to overturn the district court's dismissal of the case, Justice Frankfurter had sought to blunt the impact of the Court's action, urging Justice Brennan, who had been assigned to draft an opinion in the case, to avoid a ruling which required Du Pont to divest itself of its General Motors stock. The Clayton Act, Frankfurter wrote Brennan, merely permitted the government to institute injunctive proceedings in such cases; "[i]t does not provide for any consequence for a successful outcome of such proceedings." Specifically, he added, Congress had not provided that a violation of the law "demands unscrambling of the omelet."

> It would offend all the presuppositions in equity jurisdiction to make any particular remedy mechanically applicable to every situation presented by a violation of the Clayton Act. This would be a gross disregard of the very nature of equity, which rejects any mechanical application of a remedy, but demands an appropriate exercise of judicial power adapted to particular situations.
>
> Practically speaking, to impose this kind of "death sentence" on every violation of [Section] 7 would place such a situation as we have before us on a parity with a flagrant violation.[43]

In the Court's conference discussion of the case, Justice Brennan himself had argued that Du Pont and General Motors "tried hard not to abuse their relationship," and had agreed that divestiture should not be required in every case involving a violation of the Clayton Act. Apparently, Brennan's and Frankfurter's colleagues embraced the same position, for Brennan's opinion of the Court in the case imposed no specific remedy. Instead, it simply remanded the case to the district court for a hearing on "the equitable relief necessary and appropriate in the public interest to eliminate the effects of the acquisition."[44]

Brennan's opinion did make clear, however, that the Court rejected the defendants' assurances that Du Pont had viewed its purchase of General Motors stock as merely a "good investment." "[T]he wisdom of this business judgment," Brennan asserted, "cannot obscure the fact, plainly revealed by the record, that duPont purposely employed its stock to pry open the General Motors market to entrench itself as the primary supplier of General Motors' requirements for automotive finishes and fabrics." Harlan was incensed. Forbidden to participate in the case or to join justices Burton and Frankfurter in dissent, he penned Frankfurter a biting note while Brennan summarized the Court's opinion from the bench.

> Now that my lips are no longer sealed, if there was ever a more *superficial* understanding of a really impressive record, than Bill's opinion in duPont—I would like to see it. I hardly recognize the case as I listen to him speak. Harold's and your dissent at least puts on the Court's record something towards redeeming what (between you and me) for me has been the most disillusioning blot in the Court's processes.[45]

Despite his long career as a defender of corporate interests, Harlan the Justice would sometimes side with the government in antitrust and related cases. For example, when the Court upheld a decision of the Federal Trade Commission overturning a merger of Proctor and Gamble with the Clorox Chemical Company, he joined its decision. Generally, however, he sought to limit the impact of the antitrust laws and companion regulatory statutes. His frustration with the Du Pont–General Motors ruling was thus understandable, if uncharacteristic.[46]

Occasionally, too, Harlan and a colleague would become embroiled in a minor personal clash. Toward the end of Chief Justice Warren's last term, for example, a majority, over Harlan's objection, rejected retroactive application of the standards for police interrogation of suspects, as announced in the *Miranda* v. *Arizona* case, to confessions secured before the *Miranda* case was decided. While Harlan had vehemently dissented in *Miranda* and most other Warren Court holdings expanding the rights of criminal suspects and defendants, he also favored their retroactive application to all cases pending on appeal when a new procedural rule was announced. When Chief Justice Warren announced the Court's ruling rejecting retroactive application of *Miranda*, Harlan expressed hope from the bench that the issue might receive a new airing in the coming term. To Warren, Harlan's remarks smacked of satisfaction that the Chief Justice would soon leave the Court. "I got the message clear and loud, this morning," he caustically rejoined in a note to Harlan's chambers. A family member recalls that Harlan liked Warren personally but had little admiration for the Chief Justice's legal ability or preparation for service on the Court. His response to Warren's note, however, was prompt and characteristic:

> Dear Chief:
> I am distressed to learn that what I said in *Jenkins* this morning gave you offense. Nothing could have been further from my mind than what your note now conveys. I sincerely regret that anything I said should have lent itself to misinterpretation and ask you to accept my apologies.[47]

When Harlan read the *Washington Post*'s account of his remarks the next morning, he was even more distraught. " 'As we approach the new term,' said Harlan in an ad-libbed reference to the passing of the Warren era," the *Post* had reported, " 'I hope we can examine again the problem of when to apply new constitutional doctrines to old cases.' " "My distress over your note of yesterday," he assured the Chief Justice, "is enhanced by this morning's Washington Post's treatment of my Jenkins announcement. I simply want to supplement my note to you of yesterday by adding that it would grieve me very much were this unfortunate episode to leave scars on a professional and personal relationship with you that I have prized so highly."[48]

Such incidents were extremely rare, however. Harlan was generally successful in his efforts to maintain cordial relations with his brethren, including his and Frankfurter's principal jurisprudential antagonist, Justice Black. Initially, Harlan's relations with Black were apparently harmonious, but largely formal. Norman Dorsen, who clerked for Harlan during the 1957 term, recalls that "there wasn't much of a relationship" between the two justices during his clerkship. For several reasons, though, Harlan and Black grew closer over the years. First, Frankfurter and Black themselves enjoyed a warmer relationship during Frankfurter's last years on the bench and after his retirement. Frankfurter particularly approved Black's contention that civil rights demonstrators had no First-Fourteenth Amendment right to stage sit-ins on private property. After his retirement from the bench, and replacement by Arthur Goldberg in 1962, Frankfurter wrote Black a letter assuring him of his "esteem," applauding his colleague's sit-in stance, and urging him to file an opinion on the issue.

> I am dead certain that if you could write a separate little piece setting forth the essentials of what you told all of us twice at Conference—that you would never consent to any decision which held that the Constitution of the United States compelled you to do business with whom you did not want to do business, subject of course to two qualifications, that "your" business was really wholly your own and neither in its origin nor in its maintenance drew directly or indirectly on State or Federal funds and because of that factor no racial discrimination was permissible, and secondly, provided a specific case does not violate the Due

> Process Clause in its procedural aspects. . . . Even a few words of moderation along the lines I have tried to recall would have a powerful educative effect not only on the Negroes but also on whites. You could of course include an expression of your credo on the subject of racism, but were you also to add a moderating note it would be one of the greatest services you could render the nation and the Court.[49]

When Black did register such dissents, Frankfurter wrote again, praising his old adversary's "powerful" opinions. "More than a quarter of a century's close association," Black soon responded, "has enabled both of us, I suspect, to anticipate with reasonable accuracy the basic position both are likely to take on questions that importantly involve the public welfare and tranquility. Our differences, which have been many, have rarely been over the ultimate end desired, but rather have related to the means that were most likely to achieve the end we both envisioned."[50]

Given Harlan's high personal regard for Frankfurter, essential agreement with his jurisprudence, and appreciation for his counsel—even if he was at times bemused by the frequency with which it was offered—the mellowing of his mentor's relations with Justice Black probably improved Harlan's relations with the Court's senior Justice as well. So, too, no doubt, did the growing frequency with which Harlan and Black were allied on issues confronting the Court during their last years together on the bench. As they joined forces increasingly not only on sit-in cases but also on questions relating to the reach of "state" action subject to constitutional restrictions, the power of government over public property, the nonracial reach of the equal protection clause, and the nature of federalism, Harlan's appreciation for Black's role on the Court—if not for the subtleties of his jurisprudence—began to grow. At some point in Harlan's tenure, a dinner with his current and former clerks and their spouses had become an annual affair. For many years, Norman Dorsen recalls, the dinner had included Harlan's "extremely non-revelatory remarks" about the Court's work. Beginning in 1964, however, the Justice began to speak more frankly of his concerns about the directions of Warren Court decisions. "If it weren't for Justice Black," he added on one such occasion, "things would be in much worse shape." Harlan's clerks were amazed. "Yes," the Justice responded, "in every place there are institutional men, who care about the institution, and Black is one of them."[51]

Frankfurter undoubtedly realized the value of Harlan's personality in the politics of the Court's decision-making processes. "I strongly believe that a memo by you, to which I append agreement," he wrote his colleague during delicate negotiations in one case, "will carry with it the persuasiveness of your calm least discounted by my heat. I have a natural hesitation to put this on you, but my best hunch is that is the way we have the most promising chance." Frankfurter thus may have encouraged, to some degree, Harlan's ties to Black and their other frequent jurisprudential adversaries.[52]

Finally, of course, Harlan's courtly, gracious personality was undoubtedly more appealing to Black than Frankfurter's was likely to have been. Harlan, like Frankfurter, possessed the prestigious professional credentials Black lacked, although the backgrounds of Harlan and Frankfurter were poles apart. But Harlan was not the condescending "professor" Frankfurter was. Frankfurter's lectures to Black had even included an occasional spelling lesson. "Won't you please spell his name correctly," he had pleaded to Black at one point, "only one 'f,' viz CHAFEE." That simply was not Harlan's style. Also, Harlan was probably more "one of the boys" than Frankfurter could ever have been. Even though Harlan was a patrician—the only justice, a Washington newspaper once reported, with a box at the National Symphony—he also "had a side of him," his daughter has recalled, "that a lot of people didn't often see . . . a down-to-earth, sort of boyish simplicity. Once my present husband took my father for a ride in a racing car at about eighty miles an hour. My father was dressed only in trousers and an undershirt. Ethel McCall, his secretary, couldn't believe it. But around the house, he was a pretty simple man. He enjoyed a certain amount of bathroom humor; he loved practical jokes, gadgets." Occasionally, this element of his personality surfaced in the public Harlan. In a 1965 address to an association of law librarians, for example, he told the story of a judge who, while trying a bastardy case, became increasingly impatient with counsel for the mother. Following a lengthy luncheon recess, the lawyers in the case announced a settlement—the parties had decided to get married. The judge was pleased but told the mother, "It is my duty to advise you, young lady, that in the eyes of the law your child will unfortunately remain a technical bastard; do you understand that?" "Yes indeed I do, your Honor," the woman replied. "That is just what my lawyer has been telling me you were during these past few days." "In what follows," Harlan remarked to his audience, "I shall try to avoid earning a similar accolade at your hands." While probably more prudish than his colleague, Justice Black may have sensed, and appreciated, this element of Harlan's personality.[53]

Whatever the motivation, Harlan and Black were to become extremely close, especially during their last years on the bench, telephoning each other nightly to discuss issues facing the Court. "He thought the world of Hugo Black," Harlan's sister Edith has remarked. "My husband [Irwin Powell] was a good tennis player. John would take us over to the Blacks', and my husband and Justice Black would play tennis together. Black also used to come to dinner at my brother's home in Georgetown quite a bit. John frequently had twelve to eighteen people for dinner, and the Blacks often" were among the guests. According to Washington protocol, "any member of the Court present was to leave before anyone else could. When Hugo was there, he would leave about quarter of eleven, go around the block so that others could leave, then come back to continue his visit." Black was a great admirer of Harlan's grandfather, whose views on the application of the Bill of Rights to the states, congressional authority to protect civil rights, and related issues approximated Black's own; a portrait of Harlan I occupied a prominent place on the wall of Black's chambers. As a native of Harlan, Alabama, Black was convinced that he and Harlan were related. Following one trip to a cemetery where the original Alabama Harlans were buried, he excitedly reported his findings to his colleague. "All of this comes down to mean that while you and I are related only by marriage the Alabama Harlans and their descendants are a part of your Harlan family." And when Black's niece published a profile of her uncle, she inscribed Harlan's copy, "For Mr. Justice John Marshall Harlan—Because he is one of our relatives!" The Harlans were frequent dinner guests at the Blacks' Alexandria home, which was always well stocked with Rebel Yell bourbon, Harlan's favorite libation. Black also regularly favored the Harlans with figs, preserves, and other homegrown gifts. Often, too, the justices engaged in friendly debate over the many legal questions which continued to divide them. "I enjoyed our conversation last night," Black wrote his colleague after one lengthy telephone exchange from Harlan's Weston, Connecticut, home. "In fact it is better to talk perhaps than it is to write—at least on some subjects."[54]

For her part, Elizabeth Black wrote the Harlans numerous folksy letters, reflecting a strong friendship. When the Blacks made a trip to England, Harlan arranged for them to visit the House of Lords. While there, Elizabeth later reported to the Harlans, Justice Black appeared to be listening intently to a debate on abortion. Then he turned to his wife. "The Lady Lord sitting next to the man speaking," he whispered, "doesn't mind showing her knees, does she!" On another occasion, Elizabeth reported on an automobile racing film she and the Justice—whose own driving habits were notorious among their friends—had recently seen. "[T]o my horror we were in the driver's seat and could see the road coming up at us at a tremendous speed—it made me think of our drives to Florida!"[55]

Harlan's relations with the other justices—with the possible exception of Douglas, who seemed genuinely close to none of his colleagues—were also generally harmonious, whatever their philosophical leanings. When Justice Brennan expressed an interest in a nonresident membership in the Century Association, the prestigious New York club of which Harlan had long been a member, Harlan undertook a time-consuming effort in the Justice's behalf. He was also a constant source of encouragement to Justice Whittaker, who came close to suffering a nervous breakdown during his brief time on the Court. And when after his retirement Whittaker traveled about the country, giving strongly pro-capitalist, anti-union speeches, in which he accused the unions of having "acquired almost dictatorial power over wages," Harlan complimented his former colleague's efforts. Of one address Whittaker had given before a convention of the Kansas bar, Harlan remarked, "You have put some simple truths forthrightly and well." When Justice Harry Blackmun, appointed to the Court in 1970, had trouble adjusting to the Court's rigorous work schedule, Harlan was sympathetic, writing his new colleague, "I know what a difficult year of readjustment this has been for you, and all that I can say is that you are doing a superb job, and adding great strength to this institution." When Justice Douglas asked his colleague for a copy of an address Harlan had recently delivered at Princeton, noting that, according to one newspaper account, the Justice had "said some of us were amending the Constitution to suit our philosophical taste," Harlan promptly obliged. Once Douglas had read the address, he wrote Harlan, he concluded that the newspaper's reference "had no basis in fact."[56]

Unlike Frankfurter, not only were Harlan's contacts with his colleagues essentially cordial but he rarely engaged in gossip with or about other justices. Norman Dorsen was uncertain whether Harlan's restraint reflected breeding and self-control or only a "lack of passion, lack of real caring. If you really care about something, you get excited about it." Whatever the reason, Dorsen saw little of Frankfurter's intensity and temperament in the Justice he served.

> Harlan was the exact opposite. The entire year I was with Harlan I never heard him say a critical personal thing about another person. I regard that as an amazingly restrained quality. He was the most impersonal—if he had nothing good to say, he would say nothing. And Frankfurter, to put it mildly, was not that way. I think Harlan was a little amused by it and regarded Frankfurter as a force of nature from a different world—middle class, an intellectual. They had overlapping friendships with people like Buckner and a lot of the Harvard establishment, but they were not exactly soulmates.

Charles Fried, who clerked for Harlan during the 1960 term, found Harlan "such a likeable person, such a courteous and correct man," that the Justice's smooth relations with his colleagues seemed inevitable. But Fried sensed as well in Harlan a belief that such a position "was awfully good for the Court as an institution. . . . The idea that he work warmly and affectionately with the people he disagreed with—both the duty and the inclination—coincided." In Fried's judgment, Harlan did lack "political passion." But he believed deeply in the institution of which he was a part, and those feelings, Fried thinks, may have influenced his demeanor toward the other justices quite as much as the dictates of breeding and class.[57]

The Justice's sensitivity to the feelings and needs of others extended to subordinates. Whether out of a genuine concern or a sense of *noblesse oblige*, Harlan was unusually solicitous of household servants, often loaning them money, giving them Christmas gifts early when they were financially strapped, intervening in their behalf with the Internal Revenue Service (IRS) and public housing officials. When a creditor complained that Arlene Wardlaw, a faithful Washington servant, had failed to pay a bill, Harlan paid the account, with assurances that "Arlene had no intention of ignoring her obligation, but with her children growing up she has been hard pressed, and I am sorry I did not learn about the matter before." When Arlene became ill and unable to continue in the family's employ, Harlan sent her a monthly check. "Arlene was very dear to both of us," he wrote her husband following her death, "and we share your loss of her profoundly." When Harlan's sister Elizabeth notified him from New York that Elizabeth Middleton, a family servant of many years, had lost everything but her bed, cooking stove, and icebox in an apartment fire, he sent her a sizable check with the suggestion that she "might wish to discuss with" his sister "how you can best put the money to use." And when the IRS pressed Leanna Mitchell, the Harlans' Washington cook, about unpaid taxes, he wrote a lengthy letter in her behalf, explaining that she was making monthly payments under a prior agreement with the agency, arranged because of her husband's illness. Mrs. Mitchell took the Justice's letter with her to an interview with an IRS official, and the arrangement stood. He was equally solicitous of Elizabeth Morrow, a white woman who served in later years as Ethel Harlan's nurse-companion.[58]

Not surprisingly, given his personality, those in Harlan's employ proved exceptionally loyal. John Twarda, the caretaker at the Harlans' Weston house, first came to work for the family at age eighteen, just before the outbreak of World War II. Following military service, he returned to Weston, though factory work would have proved much more profitable, serving the Harlans as well as J. Edward Lumbard. After the Harlans' deaths, Twarda continued in the family's service as caretaker for their daughter, Eve. In the late 1980s, he was still putting in a few hours each week at Eve's Connecticut home.[59]

The Justice's Supreme Court staff were to be equally loyal. His secretary, Ethel McCall, remained with him throughout his tenure, his messenger Paul Burke almost as many years. "I admired and respected you, Mr. Justice," a member of the Court's secretarial pool once wrote him, "long before I came to work for the Court, but your kindness and graciousness . . . are the things that I will always remember."[60]

Perhaps Harlan was closest, however, to the young law graduates who served as his clerks. "I have always felt," his daughter has remarked, "that his law clerks were the sons he never had. He had a very warm relationship with them which continued throughout his life. He was interested in their families and what they were doing. I always felt he had only had the one daughter, and this made up for his not having sons of his own." In correspondence and at the annual dinners with his clerks and their families (affairs continued, albeit less frequently, after his death), the Justice kept abreast of their professional careers and personal lives. Their photographs and those of their families adorned the walls of his chambers. His loyalty and kindness to them were repaid. Given the insistence of Harlan the Wall Street litigator on knowing every detail about cases with which he was associated, it was not surprising that in the chambers of Harlan the Justice, as clerk Charles Nesson put it, "the work poured out." Justice Frankfurter joked, in fact, that Harlan ran a sweatshop. Even so, his clerks "felt anything but driven." Harlan, Nesson has observed,

> was not a taskmaster. He taught by example; a calm, gentlemanly man, hardworking, exceedingly warm and honest, with a capacity for absorbing and complementing the energies of others. He wanted his clerks to share fully in the job he was doing and in the pleasures he took from it. His great love was the craft of lawyering—breaking down a problem by research and analysis to uncover the essential questions which called for his judgment.[61]

Unlike Frankfurter and certain of his other colleagues, Harlan gave minor cases—"peewees" he called them—the same sort of close attention he devoted to the few particularly noteworthy cases reviewed each term. The pattern Harlan had his clerks follow in assisting him with the Court's caseload was typical of that employed by other justices. Each year the Court was obligated to review only a limited number of cases brought to it, while a decision to hear the overwhelming majority lay entirely within the justices' discretion. If four or more justices believed that a case merited review, the Court issued a writ of certiorari granting a hearing. If not, certiorari—and the Court's review—was denied.[62] When a petition for certiorari arrived at the Court, Harlan had one of his clerks prepare a memorandum, or cert. memo, summarizing the case and recommending a grant or denial of review. Particularly since many such petitions raised frivolous claims, or challenged economic controls or other government regulations long deemed largely, if not completely, outside the purview of the justices' concern, the cert. memos tended to be brief, most running a typed page, some only a sentence long. A large number of certiorari petitions were disposed of at each Friday's conference of the justices; the clerks were thus expected to have a week's batch of memoranda prepared by Wednesday evening or Thursday morning. In most cases, certiorari was denied. Once a case granted review had been scheduled for oral argument before the justices, however, the clerks sometimes prepared a bench memorandum, this time summarizing the case in some detail and normally recommending a particular decision for the justice's consideration. At times, each clerk would prepare a memorandum for the same case, with each recommending a different disposition. Following oral argument and conference discussion and votes, Harlan "debriefed" the clerks regarding the justices' deliberations. During the 1957 term, Norman Dorsen recalls, one of the Court's decisions was apparently leaked to the press in advance of its announcement by the justices. Harlan met with the clerks and cautioned them on the need for discretion. After that, Dorsen remembers, the justice shared less detail with the clerks regarding what went on in conference.

If Justice Harlan was assigned to write the Court's opinion in a case, or decided to file a concurring or dissenting opinion, a clerk was normally designated to prepare a draft. Virtually all the opinions he filed, however, bore the earmarks of the lawyerly style with which his opinions were to be associated. For the Justice reviewed each draft, usually making substantial modifications and occasionally rewriting the clerk's effort. The clerk would then prepare a revised draft, which the Justice would again review and revise. Once a Harlan draft opinion for the Court had been circulated among the other justices, he and the clerks would attempt to tailor the opinion to his brethren's suggestions, thereby retaining and perhaps expanding the number of justices willing to join his effort.

While a case was pending, particularly one of considerable significance, Harlan and his clerks frequently discussed and debated the issues raised. "I can remember spending hours in his office," Charles Nesson has remarked,

> arguing back and forth to get to the nub [of a case]. The Justice prepared for these discussions as he prepared for everything else. Quiet and measured in his approach to the cases, he would state his tentative conclusions and offer the framework of his analysis, then open each problem for response and discussion. When a case was particularly tough to crack, the Justice would take the briefs and memos home for the evening, assuring us that it would "succumb to a little bourbon." And inevitably it did.[63]

Harlan's discussions with his clerks reflected his practitioner background. "Usually," Norman Dorsen recollects, "it was not a . . . philosophical or theoretical discussion. He was not a philosophical man. He was a man who wanted to deal with the case the right way. He was a practical person." But such sessions did provide a forum for a thorough airing of the issues. Charles Fried remembers that:

> We had a lot of discussion. I can't remember the content of many of the discussions, but I remember the quality of the discussions. And the quality of the discussions was that they were quite free and fairly probing and that it was as if the Justice was in a way testing his conclusions and hoping to persuade us. It was almost as if we were the Justices and he the advocate for the position he had arrived at. And it was as if he hoped to persuade us that his position was correct. If he didn't persuade us, he was quite bothered.

Not that Harlan's clerks generally required much persuasion. The Justice recruited them with the assistance of law faculty who largely shared his jurisprudential philosophy—as the years passed, in fact, from his own former clerks who, after their service at the Court, had become professors at Harvard, Stanford, and other major schools. Paul M. Bator, who began teaching at Harvard after clerking for Harlan during the 1956 term, and who was working on a biography of the Justice until his untimely death, was a major source, for example, of Harlan clerks. When Bator suggested Charles Nesson for a clerkship, Harlan interviewed Nesson, then wrote Bator, thanking him for his recommendation. "If, when the time comes," the Justice added, "you decide to tap him for the 1964 Term, I am sure he would make an excellent Clerk. I should add that I told him that his ultimate selection, *vel non*, was entirely in your hands." Bator, in turn, was frank in his evaluations. The "most distinguished mind in the lot," he wrote of one prospect for the 1960 term, but "a mite inflexible."[64]

The ranks of Harlan's clerks would include a number of "liberal-activists," such as Norman Dorsen, who later would serve as a board member and president of the American Civil Liberties Union. But given the Justice's recruitment pattern, it was not surprising that many of his clerks, particularly in the early years, had already embraced the broad outlines of Harlan's thinking when they began their service in his chambers. Charles Fried, who was to pursue a conservative constitutional agenda as solicitor general in the Reagan administration, has observed:

> I came into the office, and Phil Heymann [Harlan's other clerk during the 1960 term] did, too, with a sort of Frankfurtian schooling in law. Phil had sat at the feet of Lon Fuller and Henry Hart. Henry Hart was sort of the reigning guru at Harvard, and I had had three different courses on constitutional law and the federal courts with Herbert Wechsler [at Columbia]. They were my teachers, my mentors, and they were in the same tradition as Frankfurter. . . . We [clerks] were all very close to each other philosophically, without even thinking of it. There was an assumption that Douglas was brilliant but irresponsible, that Black was brilliant, but that it didn't quite make sense. Learned Hand referred to [Black, Douglas, Warren, and Brennan as] the "Jesus Quartet," and that was something one would have heard from one's teachers, though Harlan would not teach in that way. That whole Learned Hand, American Law Institute group—those were Harlan's people. I would say that Herb Wechsler was a little bit more civil liberties minded than the Justice was, perhaps, and I was of [Wechsler's] mind, perhaps. But Wechsler was much more conservative than a Douglas. He was very troubled by "The Four." That was the general atmosphere of the thing, and so the discussions with the clerks were not ideological at all because I think we were all, in varying degrees and shadings, coming out of the same tradition—and weren't even aware we were.

As the 1960s progressed, the constitutional and judicial philosophy with which Justice Harlan and most of his clerks were imbued lost ground, gradually at first, then rapidly, obliging Harlan increasingly to assume the dissenter's role. It was a position Charles Nesson was never certain the Justice enjoyed.

> By nature he was a winner, bred in the traditions of Wall Street, entirely at ease with power, people and lawyerly competition, accustomed to having results respond to his ministrations. On Friday afternoons when he returned to chambers from the Court conference and reported the votes, I thought I sometimes caught a hint of resignation to the loneliness of his position—but just as many times I saw a gleam of mischief and fun as he mapped out a dissent. Never one to hold his fire or to play for alliances on the Court, he believed in stating his differences frankly, and was respected for it, even and perhaps especially by those with whom he differed most fundamentally.[65]

Whether or not Harlan relished the role into which circumstance had thrust him, Nesson, and presumably the Justice's other clerks as well, came to appreciate his impact on Warren Court decisional trends. In one of the first dissents Nesson was assigned, Harlan opened what his clerk regarded as "gaping holes" in the majority's draft opinion. When the draft was revamped to deflect Harlan's concerns, Nesson "felt frustrated and outmaneuvered. But not the Justice. Even though his truncated dissent would now carry less sting, he was pleased that our opinion had had effect, that the issue had been joined more closely, and that the dialogue of the Court had worked to produce a more substantial job." Harlan, Nesson found, was frustrated only when a majority draft had already been joined by at least four other justices, so that its author saw no need to answer Harlan's contentions. "The practice," Nesson has recalled, "offended the Justice's sense of craft—and, after some teaching from him, mine too."[66]

If his clerks appreciated Harlan's intellectual rigor and straightforward, guileless approach to the Court's caseload, they also admired what Charles Fried has termed his "enormous professional scrupulousness," and with good reason. Conscious perhaps of the embarrassing financial scandal in which his father and uncles had become embroiled, Harlan was determined to avoid any appearance of impropriety. Ever alert to any possible conflict of interest, he made it his policy to avoid participating in all litigation in which his old law firm represented one of the parties, even where he had never personally represented the client involved. On one occasion Justice Douglas wrote him that Chief Justice Stone had "always sat in Sullivan & Cromwell cases except (1) where his old client was involved & (2) where the business was pending when he was in the office." But Harlan made no exceptions. In 1962, for example, he recused himself from participating in litigation involving Pan American Airways, one of his old firm's longtime clients, even though some of the transactions at issue reached back as far as thirty-two years and Harlan had had nothing to do with them. Since creation of the New

York waterfront commission had been one result of the New York crime commission's work, he also refused to sit on cases involving that agency. He asked family members to alert him, moreover, about any case filed with the Court in which they had an interest. He declined requests to write articles honoring his sitting colleagues, even those with whom he was most closely allied. "I have strong convictions," he replied to one such invitation on the occasion of Justice Frankfurter's twentieth anniversary on the bench, "that sitting Justices ought not to be writing articles about each other." Following his appointment, he not only avoided all partisan political activity, he no longer even voted. And he was mildly amused when James Reston of the *New York Times*, seated next to Mrs. Harlan at a Washington dinner party, expressed surprise at the Justice's policy, assuring her that even "[W]e on the *Times* vote."[67]

Given Harlan's scrupulous regard for judicial propriety, an incident involving his daughter's first husband must have caused him considerable distress. After a brief stint at Radcliffe, Eve had married Wellington A. Newcomb. A Harvard law graduate, "Duke" Newcomb, as he was generally known, had been associated briefly with a New York firm, then became an assistant U.S. attorney when John Harlan's friend J. Edward Lumbard, a member of the same firm, became U.S. attorney for New York's southern district. By 1962, Newcomb, then thirty-eight, was attempting to establish a solo practice, but having difficulty building a clientele.

The Harlans were fond of their son-in-law, who had a charming personality, whatever the limits to his professional ambitions. In the spring of 1962, Justice Harlan discussed Newcomb's situation with Leo Gottlieb, a prominent New York lawyer who once had been a member of Harlan's firm and would later serve as Eve's counsel in her capacity as executor of her father's estate. In mid-July, Gottlieb mailed a letter and memorandum to partners in nine of New York's most prestigious firms, including David Peck, Leslie Arps, and other close friends of the Justice. "I am writing you," the letter began, "with reference to a most attractive young man by the name of Wellington A. Newcomb who happens to be a son-in-law of our mutual friend, John Harlan." Newcomb, Gottlieb explained, was "practicing law all by himself," and Gottlieb hoped that he, his friends, and their associates would recommend Newcomb for matters "we prefer not to handle or to act for another party in a situation we are in." Toward that end, Gottlieb had provided each lawyer in his firm with a copy of the memorandum which he had attached to his letter, setting forth Newcomb's background in greater detail. The memorandum, like the letter, noted Newcomb's relationship to Justice Harlan. In concluding the letter, however, Gottlieb stressed that "John Harlan has had nothing to do with stimulating my memorandum to our staff or this letter . . . the idea is entirely my own."[68]

Harlan had discussed Newcomb's situation with Gottlieb, but he had also understood that his name would not be brought into his former partner's efforts in Newcomb's behalf. When Gottlieb sent the Justice a copy of the memorandum—noting in a cover letter, "I would suppose that, after you have read this letter and the enclosures, you would tear them up"—Harlan was vacationing on a western ranch. "I am terribly sorry to say," the Justice responded immediately on receiving the materials from his chambers, "that I find your letter quite embarrassing from my standpoint since to an outsider what you have written might carry implications which you of course never intended." Harlan's first impulse had been to write each of the recipients personally, asking them to disregard Gottlieb's suggestion. But he quickly discarded that idea as "making a mountain out of a molehill." Instead, he asked Gottlieb to withdraw the original letter "in accordance with the suggested enclosed draft. I am quite embarrassed to ask you to do this," he added, "for I appreciate very much your interest in Duke. However I had not understood from our earlier conversation last Spring that Duke's relationship to me would be brought into your kind endeavors."[69]

With apologies to the Justice, Gottlieb promptly dispatched Harlan's draft over his signature.

> I find that I unwittingly caused embarrassment to John Harlan [the letter read] by having written you . . . regarding his son-in-law, Wellington Newcomb. John has written asking that I withdraw my earlier letter to you.
>
> While I know that you could not have regarded my letter as anything but an effort on my part to recommend a young lawyer whom I consider to be trustworthy and competent, nevertheless, in deference to John's wishes, I must ask you to consider my original suggestion withdrawn.

Within a few years, Newcomb and Eve were divorced. While they were still married, Harlan had honored his son-in-law's requests for advance sheets of the Supreme Court's decisions and opinions—though at one point he characteristically stopped sending Newcomb his cast-off copies of the official government edition of the reports, substituting instead a privately published version not "furnished me by the Government." Following the divorce, Newcomb asked Harlan whether the practice could continue. "I would like to accommodate you," the Justice replied, "but for reasons having nothing to do with you personally, I think it would be best not to resume the old arrangement."[70] Newcomb was to maintain amicable relations with his former in-laws, however, until the Justice's death.

Harlan's painstaking attention to judicial propriety would persist throughout his tenure. On two occasions toward the end of his life he was a target of crank petitions. He took each allegation, if not their sources, seriously. In 1969, a Chicago businessman denied certiorari by the Court charged justices Harlan, Douglas, and Abe Fortas with conflicts of interest, Harlan because of "his substantial ownership of General Motors stock . . . and financial interest in the New York-based Chase Manhattan Bank and other banks." The relationship of Harlan's alleged stock holdings to the case was remote at most. But the Justice promptly prepared a detailed memorandum for his files. He had, he asserted, never held any General Motors stock. He had held forty-five shares of Du Pont stock at a time when Du Pont also had substantial holdings in General Motors. But he had disposed of those shares by August of 1955. In 1962, his wife had received from her mother's estate ten shares of Du Pont stock and an equal number of General Motors shares, but that stock had been given to their daughter the following year. "So far as my records show," the Justice added, "neither I nor my wife have ever owned any stock in the Chase Manhattan Bank. Many years ago, when I was a director of the United States Trust Company, I did [own] a small number of qualifying shares [in that firm] . . . which I disposed of in the early 1950s, I think. So far as I can recall I have never owned any other bank stock and so far as I know my wife has never owned any bank stock."[71]

During the Justice's last term on the bench, one Roy Anderson, head of a group called the Christian Anti-Defamation League, appealed a case to the Court. Anderson had also filed a suit against judges of the Court of Appeals for the Second Circuit and Harlan, as the Supreme Court justice with supervisory powers over the circuit. In a letter to Harlan and the other justices on the circuit courts, Anderson proposed to conduct tours of the courts, providing they were first "cleared of homosexuals, alcoholics and drug addicts who serve as judges, law clerks, court clerks and personnel, so children may visit those courts without fear of molestation." Harlan sent his messenger a copy of Anderson's letter. "I'm thinking of making him," he wrote, "*Ass't* Messenger." But the Justice also sought the advise of his brethren as to "whether I should act on [Anderson's appeal] or recuse myself in light of an incomprehensible lawsuit in which I am named by Mr. Anderson as a defendant, together with most of the judges of the Second Circuit." Harlan's crusty Chief Justice was not so cautious. "I would not permit Mr. Anderson's past absurdities," Warren Burger promptly advised his colleague, to "affect your normal action on this matter. See Rule re 'Incomprehensibles and Crackpots.' "[72]

5

The Early Battles

If John Harlan's relations with his brethren were to be more harmonious and freer of intrigue than Justice Frankfurter's, the judicial and constitutional philosophy he would advance was to be decidedly Frankfurtian, albeit with its own special character and application. Among the most fundamental elements of Harlan's jurisprudence was the belief that the political processes and the principles of federalism and separation of powers ultimately were more significant safeguards of individual liberty than specific constitutional guarantees, as well as his corollary assertion that judicial interpretations of the latter must give due regard to the importance of the former in a free society. In a 1964 address, he would quote the provisions of the Bill of Rights, praising their "eloquent simplicity and clarity," but then remark:

> While these Amendments symbolize the respect for the individual that is the cornerstone of American political concepts, it would be a grave mistake to regard them as the full measure of the bulwarks of our free society. Except for the first three Amendments they are largely procedural protections against particular kinds of arbitrary governmental action and touch the activities of relatively few people; standing alone they do not account for the broad spectrum of freedoms which the people of this Country enjoy. They were indeed not a part of the original handiwork of the Framers of the Constitution.
>
> . . . They staked their faith that liberty would prosper not primarily upon declarations of individual rights but upon the kind of government the Union was to have. And they determined that in a government of divided powers lay the best promise for realizing the free society it was their object to achieve.[1]

In Harlan's judgment, the framers, as he perceived their motivations at least, were right. The imagination and resourcefulness of the people's elected representatives, and the diversity of approaches to individual issues which the federal principle permitted, were for him clearly preferable to a stultifying uniformity imposed by an appointed judiciary.

Throughout his tenure, Harlan would remain essentially faithful to this fundamental idea, deferring regularly, though not invariably, to federal and especially state authority. And while he spoke for the Court in a 1968 case upholding congressional power under the commerce clause to subject state and local governments to federal wage and hour standards, his opinion rested on firm precedent. During conference discussion of that case, moreover, he had expressed concern about the extent of federal intervention in state affairs at issue there, asserting at one point, according to Justice Brennan's notes, that "something should be said which recognizes the difficulties of possible interference with the functions of state governments." He was also quick to invoke the varieties of "abstention" doctrine, under which federal courts at times refuse to review state court decisions, as well as related doctrines designed to limit the reach of judicial intervention in the issues confronting the courts. And he was one of the strongest proponents of the "state action" concept, under which the reach of the Constitution's civil liberties guarantees is limited to state, rather than private, activity. When a majority held in 1963 that state defendants could file habeas corpus proceedings in a federal district court to challenge their criminal convictions, even when they had failed to comply with state procedural requirements, he vigorously dissented from the Court's significant relaxation of the abstention doctrine. He assumed the same stance two years later, when his brethren appeared to depart from the traditional rule that federal district courts must ordinarily abstain from issuing injunctions to stop state criminal prosecutions. And when a majority later reaffirmed the Court's traditional stance, he enthusiastically joined its decision. In numerous cases, he was to reject the Court's findings that state involvement in an ostensibly private action was sufficiently significant to trigger constitutional safeguards.[2]

Harlan's regard for the "passive virtues" did not mean that he was to have little personal sympathy for the plight of those seeking the Court's protection. As the following pages will reveal, he did not always find deference to governmental power over asserted constitutional rights an easy choice. Nor was rejection of civil liberties claims his inevitable response to their assertion. When the interests of the individual and the government clashed, however, he was normally to side with the latter.

But Harlan's jurisprudential philosophy would be characterized not only by deference to the dictates of federalism and separation of powers. Influenced no doubt by his Oxford experience, he was also a common law jurist who revered precedent, even those with which he strenuously disagreed. If able to distinguish the facts and underlying considerations governing a precedent he opposed, he naturally took advantage of the situation. When the Court in 1964, for example, extended its initial reapportionment decisions in *Reynolds* v. *Sims* and other cases, against which he had registered vehement dissents, to local units of government, he continued to dissent, challenging the majority's assertion that the earlier rulings justified the later ones. "I continue to think," he observed in one such case,

> that these adventures of the Court in the realm of political science are beyond its constitutional powers, for reasons set forth at length in my dissenting opinion in *Reynolds*. . . . However, now that the Court has decided otherwise, judicial self-discipline requires me to follow the political dogma now constitutionally embedded in consequence of that decision. I am not foreclosed, however, from remonstrating against this extension of that decision to new areas of government. At the present juncture I content myself with stating two propositions which, in my view, stand strongly against what is done today. The first is that the "practical necessities" which have been thought by some to justify the profound break with history that was made in 1962 by this Court's decision in *Baker* v. *Carr* [holding that malapportionment cases are subject to judicial review] . . . are not present here. The second is that notwithstanding *Reynolds* the "one man, one vote" ideology does not provide an acceptable formula for structuring local governmental units.[3]

Normally, however, Harlan was to follow even those precedents he most disapproved. "You are quite right," he wrote in response to one inquiry on the subject, "in saying that the practice has varied among different Justices. For myself I have so far endeavored to adhere to this general point of view."[4]

As a common law jurist, Harlan obviously recognized, and was sensitive to, the creative role which judges can play via their interpretive function. He believed, however, that adherence to abstention and related doctrines of self-restraint, rather than attempting what, to him, was a generally elusive quest for literal or historically intended meaning of the sorts Justice Black pursued, was the proper avenue for controlling judicial power. Similarly, he favored from the outset of his years on the bench narrow constitutional interpretations closely tied to the facts of individual cases and thus limited in their potential for extension to other contexts. His rejection of the Court's "one person, one vote" formula in the reapportionment field was motivated by such considerations, as was his opposition to the Warren Court's growing view that the equal protection guarantee, the principal vehicle for the Court's reapportionment decisions, required strict, and almost invariably fatal, judicial scrutiny of all laws based on "suspect" classifications or impinging upon "fundamental rights" not otherwise recognized in the Constitution. In the dissent he filed for *Shapiro* v. *Thompson*, the 1969 decision invalidating one-year residency requirements for welfare benefits, he would warn, for example, that every law affects important rights "in principle indistinguishable from those involved here," and that the Court's extension of strict review to laws affecting such interests would "go far toward making [it] a 'super-legislature.' "[5]

Finally, as U.S. Court of Appeals Judge Harvie Wilkinson, formerly a law professor at the University of Virginia, has pointed out, Justice Harlan became perhaps the "foremost practitioner of the Wechslerian ideal"—the view, espoused by Columbia law professor Herbert Wechsler, "that the main constituent of the judicial process is precisely that it must be genuinely principled . . . reaching judgment on analysis and reasons quite transcending the immediate result that is achieved." Justice Black frequently contended that the flexible approach to constitutional interpretation which Harlan and Frankfurter embraced was a veritable invitation to just such result-oriented decision making. Harlan was to argue, however, that judicial decisions should be based on "neutral" legal principles rather than appeals to "justice" or social utility. After a 1963 Harlan address to the American Bar Association, his friend Axel B. Gravem wrote the Justice that he had "particularly liked your allusion to Oliver Wendell [Holmes] who, when a chap started to talk about justice, 'got the heebie-jeebies.' " And when Harlan was invited to contribute a prefatory note to the Columbia law school's dedication of its 1965 class yearbook to Professor Wechsler, the Justice responded that "Wechsler's steadfast insistence that sound law reform should rest on sure-footed legal principle, and not proceed from legally unoriented, albeit socially praiseworthy, impulse, is a contribution to the Rule of Law of major and continuing importance."[6]

Harlan was particularly concerned that the Court avoid even the appearance of favoritism toward particular groups and causes. In October of 1956, very early in his tenure, he circulated among his colleagues a memorandum relative to *Hood* v. *Board of Trustees*, a South Carolina school desegregation case. The Court of Appeals for the Fourth Circuit had denied the *Hood* petitioners relief, holding that they must exhaust their administrative remedies under a recently enacted state law before pursuing a judicial challenge to segregated education. In urging the Supreme Court to reverse the Fourth Circuit's ruling, the petitioners pointed out that the South Carolina statute creating the "remedies" on which the appeals court had based its decision had been passed after a trial court had denied them relief. Far from a remedy, they complained, the law was actually simply a transparent device with which the state hoped to evade the Supreme Court's *Brown* mandate.

Harlan urged his brethren to deny certiorari, asserting:

> In effect, what we are being asked to do is to take judicial notice that South Carolina in all probability intends to use this statute as a means of evading the *Segregation Cases*. For my part, I think this would be a most unwise and lawless thing for the Court to do. Apart from all else it would fly in the face of the established tenet that this Court will not prematurely adjudicate cases presenting abstract, hypothetical, or remote questions. . . . This statute is not self-executing . . . and, without evidence, we are not entitled to speculate on how it will actually oper-

> ate. . . . Moreover, it is settled law that this Court will not look behind a statute to inquire into the propriety of the motives of the legislature.

In Harlan's judgment, it was imperative that the Court adhere to traditional notions of its powers and functions "as much [in] a case where a lower court decision has gone *against* colored folks as it does [in] one where the decision has been in their favor. Only by scrupulous adherence to this course will the Court's basic decision on segregation continue to be entitled to respect."

According to Justice Frankfurter's conference notes for *Brown* v. *Board of Education*, Justice Harlan had emphasized the need for unanimity—which he termed "vital"—during the justices' April 16, 1955, discussion of the sort of school desegregation decree to issue in the case. In *Hood*, however, he threatened to dissent. If the Court agreed to review the lower court's decision, he wrote his colleagues, the result could well be a divided decision—"a tragic thing in this over-all highly charged situation."[7]

Justice Harlan's emerging jurisprudential philosophy, then, included the belief that the political processes, federalism, and separation of powers were ultimately more valuable safeguards of freedom than specific guarantees to individual liberty, as well as the view that judicial constructions of such liberties should be conditioned by due regard for those important features of the American political and legal system. His philosophy was also characterized by a common law approach to judging which would emphasize precedent and flexible, evolving standards of constitutional interpretation; by recognition of the creative role judges play in the decision-making process and a belief that adherence to norms of judicial self-restraint was the proper way to constrain that creativity; by a preference for narrow constitutional constructions closely tied to the facts of individual cases and thus limited in their potential breadth; and by a commitment to constitutional interpretations based on "neutral" legal principles rather than on considerations of "justice" or social utility.

This judicial and constitutional philosophy would be developed and refined, of course, throughout the Justice's career, from his maiden opinion in the obscure *Society for Savings* v. *Bowers* to his forceful final dissent in the *Pentagon Papers Cases*.[8] Harlan's reaction to a number of issues confronting the Court early in his tenure, however, was to clearly reveal the broad outlines of his jurisprudence, as well as the internal conflicts between his general deference to government and his concern for the predicaments of individual litigants.

The Plight of Aubrey Williams

Although he was to file no opinion in the case, *Williams* v. *Georgia* was perhaps the first of many constitutional cases in which Harlan would play a prominent role. It was also to be among his most troubling. In March of 1953, a Georgia black named Aubrey Williams had been convicted of murder and sentenced to die in the state's electric chair. Two months later, the Supreme Court, in *Avery* v. *Georgia*, reversed the conviction of another black tried in the same Georgia county where Williams was convicted, holding that the method of jury selection used in the case had denied the petitioner equal protection of the laws. The same jury selection system—a tidy scheme in which the names of prospective white jurors were placed on white cards, while those of blacks went on yellow ones—had been used in Williams's trial. But the Georgia courts dismissed his appeal. A state law, it seemed, required that a defendant challenge his jury at the time it, to use the statute's language, was "put" on him, and Williams's court-appointed attorney had not challenged his client's jury on *Avery* grounds until eight months after his trial. By his lawyer's failure to follow proper procedure, the Georgia courts concluded, Williams had forfeited his right to challenge the constitutionality of a method of jury selection specifically repudiated by the Supreme Court.[9]

To encourage respect for state laws and procedures, the Supreme Court normally refuses to decide the federal claims of defendants who failed to follow state regulations applicable to their proceedings. Justice Harlan, of course, was to be a vigorous proponent of every variety of this abstention doctrine. But he found the *Williams* case deeply disturbing on a number of counts. For one thing, the state's own attorneys had conceded that the defendant was constitutionally entitled to a new trial, save for his lawyer's failure to follow proper procedure. The Justice found the quality of Williams's legal representation even more troubling. The Supreme Court had not handed down its *Avery* decision until after Williams's trial, but Georgia's highest court had made a ruling in the *Avery* case almost a year before Williams was tried. And while its decision had rejected Avery's claims, both the majority and dissenting opinions should have prompted "prudent" counsel, as Harlan later put it, to challenge Williams's jury at the time it was impaneled. The brief Williams's lawyer had filed in the case, moreover, had focused entirely on his client's *Avery* rights—rights the state's counsel were in no way disputing—while ignoring entirely the crucial issue of the timing of his challenge to the defendant's jury.[10]

Most damning of all in Harlan's eyes was that when the Supreme Court scheduled oral argument in Williams's case, the petitioner's lawyer had informed Georgia's attorney general that he probably would not participate in that important proceeding. And when the Supreme Court clerk wrote Williams's counsel that Chief Justice Warren "would appreciate your presenting oral argument if at all possible, particularly in view of the fact that this is a capital case," the lawyer complained of the financial burden a trip to Washington would impose. "This petitioner," counsel explained,

> has no money. His family have made contributions which have in fact paid actual expenses. At the present time, they have only paid one-half the cost of printing the brief, and in this situation, it appears that any expense connected with a trip to Washington will be out-of-pocket to me.
>
> In addition, I am sole counsel in a [divorce] suit in the Superior Court of Polk County, Georgia, on the calendar of that court for trial during the present week where my absence for any cause will have the result that payment of temporary alimony to my client will not be continued, which in turn, will have the result that I will lose the client.
>
> I have appeared in the Supreme Court of Georgia twice in this case and have pursued it thus far in the Supreme Court of the United States at a considerable sacrifice. It has been my intention to present oral argument if at all possible. In view of the foregoing, however, it simply does not seem that I will be able to.[11]

At this point, Chief Justice Warren appointed Eugene Gressman to represent Williams before the Court as an amicus curiae. The petitioner thus had the services of distinguished counsel at subsequent stages of the proceedings.

Justice Harlan was fearful, however, that what he would later term the original lawyer's "dismal record of gross negligence, if not worse . . . capped by [a] miserable brief," had done serious damage to Williams's case in the Georgia courts. He decided, therefore, to have his clerk Barret Prettyman undertake a thorough study of the case. Prettyman's research demonstrated to Harlan's satisfaction that in the Georgia courts a decision to deny an "untimely" motion for a new trial, based on defects in the defendant's jury, was a matter of judicial discretion, not an absolute rule. While traditionally disfavored, such motions had been granted in unusual cases, including several involving circumstances which, for Harlan, were less aggravated than those at issue in *Williams*. For example, in one 1937 death penalty case, the Georgia supreme court reversed a conviction by a jury on which an ex-convict, disqualified by law from jury service, had sat, even though the defendant's challenge was not until three months after the state high court had originally affirmed his conviction. In another case, a successful jury challenge was first mounted five months after the state supreme court initially upheld the defendant's conviction. The ground for the challenge in that case: the juror in question was related to the deceased wife of the prosecutor within the *ninth* degree, and several of the prosecutor's children had continued the kinship "by affinity." Numerous other similar cases were found. While none of them involved the precise issue of racial discrimination in jury selection, all suggested to Harlan that the Georgia high court could have ordered a new trial for Williams had its members been drawn to pertinent precedents and had they chosen to honor those precedents, especially since the defendant's lawyer had conceded his initial ignorance of the *Avery* case. Indeed, the fact that the

Georgia supreme court had stated that it did not credit the lawyer's assertion indicated to Harlan that, had its justices believed him, they would have ordered a new trial for Williams.[12]

The Georgia cases, it was true, had spoken of the challenge rule as discretionary only in cases involving objections to individual jurors. Cases dealing with challenges to an entire jury array, Prettyman reported, had "not talk[ed] in terms of discretion but rather in terms of waiver." Harlan's clerk was satisfied, though,

> that if the trial court *wanted* to grant the motion in a challenge-to-the-whole-array case, it could do it and the appellate courts would uphold it. In other words, despite the general policy against making challenges to the array after the jury is upon you, I think that the procedure is there for doing just [that] in extraordinary cases, even though it has not been done to date. However, I think it is at least arguable that the rule as to the whole array is an exception. The result is a little absurd: you can show the bias of a single juror but not that of the whole panel. But it is at least arguable, and I think myself that it is a sufficiently close question so that we cannot say as a matter of law that the state court evaded the federal question.
>
> . . .we are simply saying that the procedure is apparently there and that we are sending it back to give them another chance. We are perfectly within our rights in assuming this from the cases I cited.[13]

Justice Harlan agreed. In a memorandum circulated to his brethren on April 23, 1955, he summarized the case's "pretty lurid" facts, the performance of Williams's counsel, and the applicable Georgia precedents. "Where does all this get us?" he then asked.

> If we had power to review Georgia's discretion, I think it would not be difficult to hold that there was an abuse of discretion here. If counsel's explanation of his inaction be accepted as true—and I think it would be entitled to a strong presumption of truth—a new trial should have followed under the Georgia case referred to. If counsel was lying, then in the setting of this case I think it should have led the Court to further inquiry, and should not have been regarded, as it seems to have been, as a last minute effort to recant a choice already deliberately made as a matter of trial tactics.[14]

He and his brethren, Harlan conceded, were not at liberty to overrule the state court's exercise of discretion on a matter of state law, even where state judges had abused their discretion. At the same time, they could accept Williams's jury claim if satisfied "that in substance what Georgia did amounted to an 'evasion' of the federal right by means of a purported exercise of discretion on a matter of state law." Characteristically, however, the cautious Justice was reluctant to take "the bit in our teeth at this stage" of the proceedings in such an extreme fashion. Consistent with his clerk's recommendation, he suggested instead that the case be remanded to the Georgia courts so that they would have another opportunity to consider Williams's constitutional claim and the status of the state rule regarding jury challenges. "We can accompany the remand," he added,

> with a face-saving statement including Georgia's admission in this court of a clear violation of the petitioner's constitutional rights under *Avery*, and defense counsel's record of inaction in this Court. Surely on such remand there is some hope that the Georgia court would be constrained to reconsider its decision.
>
> I submit that we should find a way out of this smelly situation which, if not remedied, will be a blotch on this Court's ability to protect constitutional rights admittedly violated. And in this *sui generis* case I think we could take the course suggested without making bad law for the future.[15]

A majority of Harlan's colleagues were receptive to the junior Justice's strategy. In a six–three opinion which Justice Harlan joined on its second circulation among the brethren, Justice Frankfurter concluded that the Georgia courts had possessed the authority to grant Williams's motion for a new trial. "Since his motion was based upon a constitutional objection, and one the validity of which has in principle been sustained here," wrote Frankfurter, "the [state courts'] discretionary decision to deny the motion does not deprive this Court of jurisdiction to find that the substantive issue is properly before us." But since state officials had now acknowledged that the petitioner had been deprived of his constitutional rights, he added, the Court had chosen not to exercise its jurisdiction. Instead,

> orderly procedure requires a remand to the State Supreme Court for reconsideration of the case. Fair regard for the principles which the Georgia courts have enforced in numerous cases and for the constitutional commands binding on all courts compels us to reject the assumption that the courts of Georgia would allow this man to go to his death as the result of a conviction secured from a jury which the State admits was unconstitutionally impaneled.[16]

Frankfurter, like Harlan, was unduly optimistic. In a dissent joined by justices Reed and Minton, Justice Clark asserted that while he too was "not deaf to the pleas of the condemned," he would not "ignore the long-established precedents of this Court," adding:

> The proper course as has always been followed here, is to recognize and honor reasonable state procedures as valid exercises of sovereign power. We have done so in hundreds of capital cases since I have been on the

> Court, and I do not think that even the sympathetic facts of this case should make us lose sight of the limitations on this Court's power.[17]

While the justices of the Georgia supreme court may also not have been entirely indifferent to Aubrey Williams's plight, they were even more sensitive to traditional limits on the power of the U.S. Supreme Court than Clark and his fellow dissenters were. The Georgia court, wrote Chief Justice W. H. Duckworth for a unanimous tribunal, would bow to its federal counterpart on all questions of national law. It would "not supinely surrender," however, the state's sovereign authority. The federal high court, as Duckworth read its opinion, had conceded that he and his colleagues had decided the case "according to established rules of [state] law, and that no federal jurisdiction existed which would authorize that court to render a judgment either affirming or reversing the judgment of this court, which are the only judgments by that court that this court can constitutionally recognize." Duckworth reaffirmed his court's original decision, but solely for the record, and "[n]ot in recognition of any jurisdiction of the Supreme Court to influence or in any manner to interfere with the functioning of this Court on strictly State questions."[18]

Nor were the justices of Georgia's highest tribunal the only state jurists committed to Duckworth's thinking. In a letter to the Georgia chief justice, a copy of which was mailed to Earl Warren, Justice James B. McGhee of the New Mexico supreme court extended Duckworth his "hearty congratulations on the rebellion of yourself and associates against the usurpation of the rights and privileges of the people of the State of Georgia and its Court." McGhee had been "dumfounded," he wrote, by the Supreme Court's opinion "reversing the case on a challenge to the jury panel made by an experienced Georgia lawyer long after the trial." If Duckworth and company wound up in jail, the New Mexico jurist promised to pay them "a visit and bring you at least a package of cigarettes . . .[if] I do not myself get in jail for writing this letter."[19]

Following Duckworth's rebuff of Justice Harlan's efforts to strike a balance between deference to state authority and regard for constitutional guarantees, Williams's counsel petitioned the brethren for further review. In a memorandum for the conference, Justice Frankfurter assured his colleagues that "[i]f I had to do it over again, I would act now as I did before, both in granting the original petition and in disposing of the writ as we did. I was of course deeply torn in my mind about the problem raised by the case, but when Brother Harlan suggested, in the light of his investigation of Georgia decisions, a remand to the Georgia court for another look, I gladly fell in with his idea." Nor, by referring to Harlan's proposal, did he mean even "remotely to shirk my responsibility for what I wrote in the *Williams* opinion. . . . In a capital case I unblushingly confess that I conceive it to be my duty to exercise every resource of my mind to find a rational basis in support of vindicating a federal claim."[20]

Now, however, Frankfurter could see little basis for reversing the

Georgia supreme court's latest ruling. The violation of Williams's equal protection rights stood out "like the Washington Monument." But in its most recent pronouncement the Georgia court had asserted that the refusal of the state's courts to honor untimely challenges to a jury array was a binding procedural requirement, not a matter of discretion, and Frankfurter could conceive of no way "to make a case based on the ground that what the court said was the law of Georgia was a pretense and was not the law of Georgia." Nor had the petitioner's counsel been "so incompetent" that the Court could hold that Williams had in effect been denied the assistance of counsel necessary to assure him a fair trial in state capital cases. Thus, were the case to be decided on the merits, Frankfurter would be obliged to affirm the Georgia court.[21]

Frankfurter was, at the same time, deeply concerned by the tone of Duckworth's opinion. He agreed that he and his colleagues were "not censors of the manners of a lower court." But he found not only the tenor of the Georgia chief justice's rhetoric disturbing.

> Having reached the conclusion that I have on the merits, I would see no useful purpose to be served in voting to bring the case here had the Georgia court on remand of the case not challenged the jurisdiction we have exercised. I am no believer in answering a fool according to his folly. But this is too simple a dictum for a situation as complicated as this. The Georgia court was not merely childishly truculent. What really puts me in a quandary is the opening sentence of the Georgia opinion [which quoted the Tenth Amendment's reservation to the states of powers not delegated by the Constitution to the national government]. The Supreme Court there challenged . . . our right to do what we did. I think it is both appropriate and desirable to explain that what we did we had a right to do. Reliance on the Tenth Amendment as though that answers problems that are raised under the Fourteenth Amendment is a recurring manifestation of obfuscation by members of the profession on and off the bench who ought to know better. And resentment by States against employment by this Court of its jurisdiction in the protection of constitutional rights is nothing new.[22]

Frankfurter was prepared to vote to bring up the case for the purpose of making clear to "the Georgia courts and others by appropriately impressive language that the Fourteenth Amendment, as all other provisions of the Constitution in which federal rights are created, is a qualification of the Tenth and not the other way around." On this occasion, however, the Court decided, with Justice Harlan's acquiescence, simply to deny further review of the case. On March 30, 1956, Aubrey Williams died in Georgia's electric chair.[23]

The NAACP Versus Alabama

Conflict between Justice Harlan's deference to state authority and his regard for constitutional rights would also be reflected in the Court's protracted efforts to protect the National Association for the Advancement of Colored People from Alabama's officialdom. In the wake of the *Brown* decision, Alabama, like a number of other southern states, launched a campaign of harassment against the organization which had initiated and financed the attack on the region's segregated schools. The techniques employed varied. In Alabama, an attempt was made to force the organization to disclose its local membership lists, and thereby, state officials no doubt hoped, reduce its Alabama ranks of all but its boldest, or most foolhardy, members. Alabama's young attorney general, John Patterson, ably assisted by the state's judiciary, was to lead the attack. Initially, Patterson had planned to build his political base on a crime-busting image. He had quickly learned, however, that race was *the* issue in the post *Brown* South, and an assault on the NAACP seemed an especially promising ploy. John Harlan was to play perhaps the key judicial role in the nearly decade-long controversy Patterson's gambit spawned.

An Alabama statute required corporations chartered in other states to file a copy of its corporate charter with state officials, designate a place of business, and identify an agent qualified to receive service of legal papers. NAACP officials considered their organization exempt from the law and had never sought to comply with its provisions. For Attorney General Patterson, the organization's failure to comply with Alabama law was fortuitous, indeed. In 1956, Patterson went to the Montgomery County circuit court of Judge Walter Jones, seeking the NAACP's ouster from the state. On the day Patterson's complaint was filed, Judge Jones, a jurist of impeccable Confederate credentials, issued an ex parte order barring the association from further activities within the state and forbidding it to take steps qualifying it to do business there.[24]

NAACP attorneys moved to dissolve the restraining order, contending that the association was not subject to Alabama's law and that, in any event, the attorney general's suit infringed upon constitutional rights of speech and assembly. Before the date set for a hearing on the organization's motion, Patterson petitioned Judge Jones to order the association to produce a large number of its records and papers, including the names and addresses of its Alabama "members" and "agents." All such documents, he contended, were necessary to the state's preparation for the hearing. NAACP counsel objected to Patterson's move, but Judge Jones ordered the organization's officials to produce all the records Patterson had requested, including the membership lists, then postponed a hearing on the association's challenge to the restraining order until after the date set for production of the records.

While continuing to oppose Patterson's contention that the association was subject to the Alabama statute, NAACP officials offered to comply with the law if the restraining order were lifted. When they refused to obey the production order, however, Judge Jones held the association in civil contempt and imposed a $10,000 fine. If the organization complied with the production order within five days, the fine would be reduced or dropped. If not, it was to be increased to $100,000.

At the end of the five-day period, association attorneys produced substantially all the records stipulated in Judge Jones's order except the membership lists, divulgence of which, they again argued, would jeopardize rights under the First and Fourteenth amendments. They also moved to have the contempt citation modified, lifted, or stayed pending appeal of the case. Judge Jones denied the motions, declared the defendants in continuing contempt, and increased the fine to $100,000, as he had previously threatened. After Alabama's supreme court twice dismissed the association's request for review of Judge Jones's contempt citation, NAACP attorneys secured a writ of certiorari from the U.S. Supreme Court. Following the submission of briefs and oral argument in January of 1958, the justices voted in conference to reverse the Alabama courts.

In post *Brown* racial cases, the brethren had generally opted for brief, unsigned, or per curiam, opinions which contained little explication of their rationale for a particular ruling and thus permitted various facets of the segregation issue to jell in the lower courts with limited Supreme Court intervention. When Chief Justice Warren assigned Justice Harlan the task of drafting the Court's *NAACP* opinion, it was with the understanding that Harlan would adhere to that pattern. The Justice soon decided, however, that the *NAACP* case required a different approach. On April 22, 1958, he circulated a first draft of his opinion in the case. Accompanying his effort was a letter to his colleagues. "My work on this case," he wrote,

> has left me with the firm conviction that it would reflect adversely on the Court were we to dispose of the case without a fully reasoned opinion. In my view, the considerations here are quite different from those which have led us to *per cur* all of the cases in this field which have come to us since the original segregation cases were decided. Having found it impossible to write a satisfactory opinion within the normal compass of a *per curiam*, as originally proposed, I have ventured to prepare a full-scale opinion. In doing this, I have thought it important that the opinion should be written (1) with the utmost dispassion, (2) within an orthodox constitutional framework and (3) as narrowly as possible. You will be the judges of the extent to which these objectives have been attained.[25]

Harlan had no objection to the opinion he had drafted being issued as a per curiam, or even under another justice's name "if that be deemed wise." But he doubted the wisdom of issuing a per curiam of the length of the opinion he had drafted, or of registering a per curiam at all in the NAACP case.[26]

His colleagues agreed, and Harlan attempted to draft a signed opinion which they would also join. As noted in the previous chapter, that effort required him to strike a compromise between Justice Black's insistence that the Fourteenth Amendment rights at issue in the case be tied to the terms of the First Amendment and Justice Frankfurter's equally firm contention that the opinion make no reference to the specific safeguards of the Bill of Rights. Harlan was also obliged, it will be recalled, to satisfy Justice Douglas's concerns that the state be held to exacting requirements of judicial review in the case rather than merely to the lenient "rationality" standard Harlan was on record as favoring in state obscenity cases.

Ultimately, Douglas and Black were persuaded to join their colleague's opinion. In a May 8, 1958, note to Harlan, Black conceded that he "would prefer our holding be supported by different reasoning," but added, "should you write it to suit me in every respect there are others you could not get. In writing so as to get a court (if you do) you have performed a difficult task and rendered the Court an excellent service." Justice Frankfurter also eventually concurred with Harlan's efforts. But his recommendations went well beyond the case's relevance to the First Amendment. The NAACP's principal contention was that divulgence of its membership lists would provoke community reprisals against its Alabama members. In endorsing that claim, Harlan proposed adding the following sentence to the opinion: "We cannot blink the fact that strong local sentiment exists against the cause which petitioner espouses." Frankfurter promptly objected. "To my understanding, it does not add a jot or tittle to the legal argument of your opinion and gratuitously stirs feelings giving rise to irrelevant controversy, no matter how true I believe the statement to be."[27]

Anticipating Harlan's being "tempted" to cite a recent law review article on the "NAACP problem,'" Frankfurter also wrote his colleague

> to express the hope that you will not yield to the temptation. The old British rule against citing living authors was one unwise extreme. In recent years we have gone to the other extreme of citing every piece of junk that somehow looks in the direction of one's conclusions. Of course I don't mean to suggest that [this] article is junk, by any manner of means, but it has a lot of stuff in it that I certainly would not subscribe to and that I would not impliedly mean to approve by citation of the article.[28]

Whatever Harlan's initial intentions, his final opinion included no reference to recent law review pronouncements. Nor did the statement to which Frankfurter had objected find its way into the opinion.

There was little doubt that Frankfurter, Black, and Douglas would join the Court's judgment, if not Justice Harlan's entire rationale. One justice, however, threatened to register a dissent in the case. Justice Clark was concerned that the state's counsel had failed to set forth adequately Alabama's interests in acquiring the information it was seeking from the NAACP. He favored a remand of the case to the state courts for further proceedings on that issue before the Court reached a decision on the association's constitutional claims.

Since unanimity was considered crucial in racial cases, the possibility of a Clark dissent was a matter of considerable concern not only to

Harlan but to the other justices as well. On this occasion, Frankfurter would serve as Harlan's surrogate. In late June, as the Court's regular term was nearing an end, Frankfurter availed himself "of our long-standing freedom of telling each other what we think about things in the Court." In a letter to Clark, Frankfurter urged his colleague to reconsider his posture.

> If you were convinced that John's argument on the merits does not hold water and therefore felt compelled to dissent on the merits, that would be that. But for you to go on the kind of a ground that you thought was such a quicksand in *Williams* v. *Georgia* (the only justification for which was to avert an outright reversal) doesn't seem to me a good enough starting point for a break in the unanimity of the Court in what is, after all, part of the whole Segregation controversy. The sky is none too bright anyhow. The mere fact that you are dissenting on the ground that the State's interests have not been adequately put to us—though I thought at the time that the State's interests were put to us on the merits very effectively—would be blown up out of all proportion to what you yourself would subscribe to. . . . And so I wish you to consider whether the use that is bound to be made of what you have written is worth the price of registering what I will appreciate is a torturing difficulty for you in this particular case.
>
> Save your powder for the day—I hope it never may come, but it well may—that you will have to fire a real shot.[29]

Frankfurter's letter seemed to have had the desired impact. Five days after it was written, Clark withdrew his dissent and joined Harlan's opinion. Now the Court's decision, and the fruits of Harlan's diplomacy, could be announced.

To reach a decision upholding the NAACP's claims, Harlan had been obliged to overcome a number of preliminary hurdles. First, courts are traditionally expected to grant relief only to those whose rights are being personally injured, but the association's officials were claiming that Judge Jones's production order would infringe upon the rights of the organization's Alabama members, none of whom was a party to the suit. While normally insistent that the Court observe such restrictions on judicial power, Harlan had no difficulty, given the circumstances of the case, in permitting the organization's officials to assert its members' rights. The interests of the association and its members, after all, were inextricably intertwined; indeed, as Harlan put it, the organization "and its members are in every practical sense identical." More critically, he observed, requiring the members to defend their own rights in court obviously "would result in nullification of the right [to anonymous association] at the very moment of its assertion."[30]

Second, while the Court had long indicated, Justice Frankfurter (and his allies) to the contrary notwithstanding, that the freedoms of the First Amendment were binding on the states via the due process clause of the

Fourteenth Amendment, the First Amendment's language included no specific reference to a right of association. However, in a passage combining the flexible approach to the Fourteenth Amendment's general language, which he and Frankfurter favored, with the emphasis on the First Amendment's more specific terms, which Justice Black's incorporation thesis demanded, Harlan found a right of association to be implied by the Constitution's language.

> Effective advocacy of both public and private points of view, particularly controversial ones, is undeniably enhanced by group association, as this Court has more than once recognized by remarking upon the close nexus between the freedoms of speech and assembly. . . . It is beyond debate that freedom to engage in association for the advancement of beliefs and ideas is an inseparable aspect of the "liberty" assured by the Due Process Clause of the Fourteenth Amendment, which embraces freedom of speech. . . . Of course, it is immaterial whether the beliefs sought to be advanced by association pertain to political, economic, religious or cultural matters, and state action which may have the effect of curtailing the freedom to associate is subject to the closest scrutiny.[31]

Finally, there was a "state action" issue to be surmounted in the case. Like all other explicit constitutional guarantees except the Thirteenth Amendment's bar to slavery and involuntary servitude, the Fourteenth Amendment's provisions (as well as those of the First) restrict only governmental or "state" action. Yet the association was complaining that publication of the names of its Alabama members would result in private, community retaliation against them. Over the course of his years on the bench, as noted earlier, Justice Harlan was to insist that the reach of constitutional rights be limited to state action and those private activities truly permeated with state influence. Again, however, he had no difficulty finding the requisite state action in the *NAACP* suit.

> It is not sufficient to answer, as the State does here, that whatever repressive effect compulsory disclosure of names of petitioner's members may have upon participation by Alabama citizens in petitioner's activities follows not from *state* action but from *private* community pressures. The crucial factor is the interplay of governmental and private action, for it is only after the initial exertion of state power represented by the production order that private action takes hold.[32]

Having overcome these potential obstacles to a ruling on the merits, Harlan and the Court upheld the NAACP's constitutional claims with relative ease. Alabama officials had sought the association's membership lists and other records, the officials claimed, in order to determine whether it could qualify for doing business in the state. The association had not claimed an absolute immunity from state investigation. In fact, it had produced all the information demanded except the membership lists. But the Court, Harlan asserted, was "unable to perceive that the disclosure of the names of petitioner's rank-and-file members [had] a substantial bearing on" the purposes alleged to underlie the production order. In any event, whatever interest the state might have had was not "sufficient" to overcome the NAACP's constitutional concerns.[33]

Alabama tried to use legal precedent to bolster its claim. In a 1928 case, *Bryant* v. *Zimmerman*, the Court had upheld use of a New York statute to require a local Ku Klux Klan chapter to divulge the names of its members. But Alabama's officials could find no solace in that ruling. For one thing, the Klan had refused to furnish state officials with *any* information. More critically, the Court's opinion in the case had emphasized "the particular character of the Klan's activities, involving acts of unlawful intimidation and violence. . . . [T]he situation before us," asserted Harlan, was thus "significantly different from that in *Bryant*."[34]

Since Alabama had no basis in precedent or its asserted interests for requiring divulgence of the NAACP's membership lists, the contempt citation and fine, Harlan held, "must fall." The association had not yet been given a state court hearing, however, on the constitutionality of the "temporary" ex parte order, issued two years earlier, forbidding it to do business in Alabama. For that reason, the justices declined to review that issue. The NAACP, Harlan observed, must first appeal it through the state courts. "Only from the disposition of such an appeal can review be sought here."

Harlan's *NAACP* opinion was a collegial effort rather than a pure expression of the Justice's personal views. Even so, it was to become one of his most important efforts, cited and quoted frequently both as the leading precedent on the law of associational rights and as the model for judicial review of governmental action exerting an indirect impact on such freedoms. In a letter to the Justice, Dean Erwin Griswold of the Harvard law school found it "gratuitous to thank a Judge for doing his duty," but praised Harlan nonetheless for "a very workmanlike and judge-like job," adding:

> This was obviously a difficult problem. It was full of emotion, and could have been dealt with on an emotional basis, or with emotional overtone. But you avoided that completely. You have taken it up step-by-step, and have dealt fully and directly with the questions raised on a strictly legal basis. It is very impressive to see the way in which a strictly lawyer-like approach in such a case pushed back all other considerations, and leaves a very finished impression. Some people may not like the result, but it will have to be on a "don't like" basis. You have left no room for them to stand as far as law is concerned.

Other constitutional scholars, including Princeton's Edward S. Corwin, were equally effusive.[35]

Members of Alabama's judiciary, however, naturally did not share such impressions. Indeed, it was to be six more years before the NAACP was permitted to resume operations in the state. In his opinion for the Court, Justice Harlan had stated that the association had "apparently complied satisfactorily with the production order, except for the membership lists." But when he and his colleagues remanded the case to the Alabama supreme court for further proceedings "not inconsistent" with Harlan's opinion, the state court first delayed further action, then reaffirmed Judge Jones's contempt citation. Justice Harlan's ruling, the Alabama judges explained, had been based on the "mistaken premise" that, except for the NAACP's refusal to divulge its membership lists, the association had complied with every element of Judge Jones's production order.[36]

The Alabama supreme court issued its ruling on February 12, 1959. On June 8 of that year, the U.S. Supreme Court, in a brief per curiam opinion, summarily reversed the state court's ruling. After having first declined challenging the association's assertion that it had complied with every aspect of Judge Jones's order except that relating to the membership lists, the state's belated denial of the NAACP's contention, the Court held, had come "too late." If after a hearing the trial court found it necessary to issue a further production order, it could do so, if its order did not conflict with Justice Harlan's 1958 ruling. But the Alabama supreme court could not re-examine the status of the association's compliance with Judge Jones's original order.[37]

NAACP counsel had requested a decree ordering the Alabama judiciary to comply immediately with the 1958 ruling. On the assumption that the Alabama supreme court would "not fail to proceed promptly with the disposition of the" case, however, the Court again simply remanded the dispute into the hands of state jurists.

But again, the Court was to be unduly optimistic. When another year passed and the association was still unable to obtain a hearing in Alabama's courts, its attorneys sought an injunction from the U.S. district court in Montgomery. Mindful of the Supreme Court's traditional reluctance to permit federal district courts to intervene in pending state proceedings, the district judge dismissed the suit. When the NAACP's lawyers appealed that decision to the Court of Appeals for the Fifth Circuit in New Orleans, the Fifth Circuit panel agreed that the case should be litigated initially in the state courts, but ordered the district judge to retain jurisdiction in the event that the state courts did not act "with expedition."[38]

On October 23, 1961, the Supreme Court vacated the Fifth Circuit's decision, ordering it instead to instruct the district judge to proceed with a trial of the case "unless within a reasonable time, no later than January 2, 1962," the state courts had given the association a hearing. In December of 1961, over five years after he had "temporarily" ousted the NAACP from Alabama, Judge Jones finally conducted a hearing—and then entered a decree permanently enjoining the organization from doing "any further business of any description or kind" in Alabama or even attempting to qualify for doing business there. On February 28, 1963, Alabama's supreme court affirmed Judge Jones; Justice Harlan and his brethren again granted certiorari.[39]

By this point, the justices' patience had obviously been sorely strained. At a conference following further oral argument in the protracted litigation, one or more of Harlan's colleagues proposed that they depart from their usual practice of simply reversing the state courts and remanding the case "for further proceedings not inconsistent with our opinion," and issue instead an order instructing the Alabama courts "promptly to enter a decree, vacating in all respects the permanent injunction order . . . and permitting the Association to take all steps necessary to qualify it to do business in Alabama."[40]

Presumably, Justice Harlan had also lost patience with the intransigence of the Alabama judiciary. When in 1961, for example, the Court was reviewing the NAACP's petition for a federal district court review of its case, Justice Clark had circulated a memorandum opposing the association's desire to move the suit into federal court. "This we should not permit," Clark asserted, "so long as Alabama moves expeditiously, which its Attorney General has certainly impliedly, if not explicitly, said it is ready to do." By this passage on his copy of the Clark memorandum, Harlan had penned "Sure!"[41]

But Harlan's characteristic deference to state power and judicial propriety was to overcome his impatience. On his recommendation, the proposal that the Court itself fashion a forceful decree was not adopted. Instead, he drafted an opinion reversing the lower courts and once again remanding the case for further proceedings. On this occasion, however, he accompanied the remand with a warning: "Should we unhappily be mistaken in our belief that the Supreme Court of Alabama will promptly implement this disposition, leave is given the Association to apply to this Court for further appropriate relief."[42]

A few years later, in 1968, when the feelings of white Alabamians about Justice Black and his role in the dismantling of racial segregation had begun to mellow, a banquet was given in the Justice's honor during a visit to his native state. Later, Elizabeth Black wrote the Harlans that Alabama's chief justice J. Ed Livingston had made a number of offensive remarks at the banquet. A school slated for integration in Livingston's home county had been burned to the ground. Referring to Alabama governor George Wallace's infamous 1963 "stand in the schoolhouse door" at the University of Alabama, the chief justice had assured the audience, Elizabeth Black reported, that "he was to the right of Wallace. . . . Wallace only stood in the school house door . . . where he was from they burned them down." Earlier, Livingston had announced that Justice Black, the banquet's honored guest, "was just another man."[43]

In the *NAACP* case, however, Livingston and company had finally blinked. Several months after Justice Harlan's 1964 opinion was announced, the injunction against the association was dissolved.

Arkansas Versus the Federal Courts

Alabama, of course, was not the only southern state to adopt a posture of massive resistance in the wake of the *Brown* decision. Shortly after Justice Harlan announced his 1958 opinion in the *NAACP* case, Chief Justice Warren convened a special August term of the Court in an effort to resolve *Cooper* v. *Aaron*, the bitter dispute which had arisen over desegregation of Central High School in Little Rock, Arkansas. Three days after the Supreme Court's 1954 *Brown* ruling, the Little Rock school board announced its intention to comply with the Court's decision. Seven days after the second *Brown* decision, the board approved a plan for desegregating all grades of the city's schools by 1963, and seventeen black students were scheduled for admission to Central High for the 1957–58 academic year.

Ultimately, nine black students did attend the school during the fall term of that year, but only after federal troops dispatched by President Eisenhower overcame the obstructionist tactics of Arkansas governor Orval Faubus and other state officials, as well as the mob resistance those tactics helped to fuel. Amid continued local outcry against its decision, the school board, in February of 1958, asked the federal district court which had approved its desegregation plan to permit a two-and-a-half-year delay in the process of integrating the city's schools. A district judge upheld the board's request, and while the Court of Appeals for the Eighth Circuit overturned the district court's decision, the circuit panel also stayed execution of its decision pending Supreme Court review of the case. Following oral argument in the Court, justices Harlan and Frankfurter drafted a per curiam order lifting the Eighth Circuit's stay and affirming its decision rejecting the school board's request for a delay in implementation of the board's desegregation plan. The justices quickly issued that order but announced that an opinion setting forth their rationale would be released at a later date. Justice Harlan's role in that process would cast further light not only on his position in racial cases, but on his broader judicial and constitutional philosophy as well.[44]

Although Chief Justice Warren had assigned Justice Brennan the task of writing an opinion in the case, Justice Harlan also produced a draft opinion for the Court. His reason for pursuing such a course is unclear. Perhaps he simply wanted to clarify his own understanding of the facts and issues. He may have believed, however, that a somewhat more moderate opinion than Brennan could be expected to produce might be necessary to secure a unanimous Court. At one point, Justice Clark drafted a handwritten dissent in which he emphasized that he "adhere[d] steadfastly" to *Brown* but decried the speed with which *Cooper* v. *Aaron* was being decided. "[A]s I understood *Brown*," wrote Clark, "integration was not to be accomplished through push button action but rather by 'deliberate speed.' " The fact that certain southern states had resorted to "massive resistance," he added, gave the justices "no excuse to in turn strip [them] of those procedural safeguards that are the right of all other litigants." Clark's dissent went no further than an original longhand draft on two pages of a memo pad of the ABA's section on judicial administration, which the Justice then chaired. His concern, moreover, appeared to be purely over the Court's expedited handling of the case instead of with the merits of its decision. If Clark shared his misgivings with Harlan, that may have been what prompted his colleague to write an opinion which might be more palatable to Clark than Justice Brennan's effort.[45]

Whatever Harlan's motivation, the opinion he wrote differed in three important respects from Justice Brennan's initial draft. First, he omitted Brennan's reference to an oft-quoted passage from *Smith* v. *Texas*,[46] a 1940 jury discrimination case which construed the supremacy clause of Article VI of the Constitution to forbid both "ingenious" and "ingenuous" violations of constitutional rights. Second, and more critically, he avoided what was to become the most controversial element of the Court's ultimate opinion in the case—Brennan's discussion of *Marbury* v. *Madison*[47] and virtual equation of judicial interpretations of constitutional provisions with the Constitution, and thus the "supreme law of the land," itself. Instead, Harlan rested his position on the supremacy of national law and the obligation of officials to obey its commands. Finally, he sought to emphasize the Court's continued unanimous support for *Brown*, despite subsequent changes in its membership.

> The basic decision in *Brown* was unanimously reached by a Court, composed of Justices of diversified geographical and other backgrounds, only after the cases had been briefed and twice argued by lawyers of the highest skill and reputation, and the issues had been under deliberation for more than ____ months. Since the first *Brown* opinion three new Justices have come to the Court. They are at one with the Justices still on the Court who participated in the original decision as to the inescapability of that decision, believing that whatever history may be offered in justification of racial segregation, such discrimination in the public school systems of the States can no longer be squared with the commands of the Fourteenth Amendment that no State shall "deny to any person within its jurisdiction the equal protection of the laws."

Harlan circulated his draft only to Clark and Justice Frankfurter. He did, however, embody the substantive portions of his effort in a "Suggested Substitute" for the last six pages of Justice Brennan's draft. In a letter accompanying his suggestions, he explained that he had been "led to what you may consider an unusually tenacious course by the belief that you feel, I am sure, as strongly as I do, that the Court's ultimate product should be the best which the combined thoughts of the individual members of the Court can achieve." He had, he assured Brennan, "omitted no thought of substance contained in your draft." Instead, his concerns with Brennan's effort had "basically [been] one of organization of the opinion." To the extent there were differences in phrasing, he added, "I ventured to do it the way I did because in this case, surely form and substance are inseparable." Harlan had begun his full draft opinion with the sentence, "The opinion of the Court, in which (naming each justice) join, was announced by The Chief Justice," Over Justice Douglas's sole objection, the brethren had decided to make *Cooper* a joint opinion, and that decision, Harlan now explained to Brennan, had prompted his submission of the suggested substitute. "If this were an opinion under your sole authorship, I would not think of pursuing this course. In that situation, I would have joined the draft."[48]

Harlan shared his suggestions with Brennan and his other colleagues on September 23, the day before one of several conferences had been devoted to discussion of the case. Shortly before the justices convened, or at the conference itself, Justice Brennan circulated his reply. Harlan's draft, like Brennan's, was a forceful reaffirmation of *Brown* and the doctrine of national supremacy. While applauding the school board's good faith, for example, Harlan had found it "unthinkable" that the intransigence of state officials could be used to delay the "effectuation of . . . constitutional rights." State action, he asserted, could "not be so fragmentized." Justice Brennan agreed, moreover, that differences between his effort and the Harlan substitute were "largely entirely verbal." However, Brennan took issue with each of Harlan's proposed revisions. In Brennan's judgment, his draft's admonition against state attempts to circumvent *Brown*, "whether accomplished ingeniously or ingenuously," was "a vital statement very essential to the point we are making." So, too, was his reference to *Marbury* v. *Madison* and "detailed discussion . . . of this Court's responsibility for exposition of the law of the Constitution." Nor was Brennan sympathetic to his colleague's proposal that the joint opinion emphasize the adherence of the Court's newer members to the principles set out in *Brown*. "I feel," he wrote, "that any such reference . . . would be a grave mistake. It lends support to the notion that the Constitution has only the meaning that can command a majority of the Court as that majority may change with shifting membership. Whatever truth there may be in that idea, I think it would be fatal in this fight to provide ammunition from the mouth of this Court in support of it."[49]

Arguably, Justice Brennan's assertion that judicial constructions of the Constitution are analogous to the document itself was even more suggestive of the courts' creative role in constitutional explication than Harlan's reference to the postures of the Court's most recent arrivals. But their colleagues rejected Harlan's proposal to delete that portion of Brennan's draft containing the Justice's assertion, as well as the Justice's reliance on the rhetoric from *Smith* v. *Texas.* The brethern did decide to have Brennan add to the joint opinion, however, Harlan's references to the commitment of the Court's newest members to the *Brown* principles. And as Harlan had apparently been the first to propose, all nine justices signed the opinion which, following circulation of Brennan's fifth draft, they unanimously approved.

The Brennan draft was not to be the only opinion filed in *Cooper* v. *Aaron.* While Justice Frankfurter agreed to join Brennan's effort, he also decided to register a concurrence. Chief Justice Warren and Justices Black and Brennan were furious, particularly since the opinion their colleague planned to file added nothing of substance to what Brennan had written. "By now," as Warren's biographer Bernard Schwartz has indicated, the Chief Justice's "relations with Frankfurter had become too touchy for Warren personally to influence the Justice not to issue the opinion." But Warren did ask others, including Black, to talk with Frankfurter. And when Frankfurter, who had agreed to delay announcement of his effort until after issuance of the joint opinion, could not be deterred, Brennan and Black prepared a memorandum for their colleagues' consideration. Initially handwritten by Justice Brennan, the draft opinion stated that those who approved it "believe that the joint opinion of all the Justices handed down on September 29, 1958 adequately expresses the views of this Court, and they stand by that opinion as delivered. They desire that it be fully understood that the concurring opinion filed this day by Mr. Justice Frankfurter must not be accepted as any dilution or interpretation of the views expressed in the Court's joint opinion."[50]

The justices discussed the Brennan-Black proposal at their October 6 conference. In a memorandum prepared for his files after that session, Justice Frankfurter noted that he had been "ready to sign such a memorandum because to me it is impossible to conceive how any one can reasonably find that my concurring opinion constituted a 'dilution or interpretation of the views expressed in the Court's joint opinion.' " Following extensive discussion, however, the proposal was dropped. "It was the consensus of all the other six that it would be very unwise to file the proposed memorandum," Frankfurter wrote, "and after this sense of the meeting was expressed, Black and Brennan withdrew the memorandum."[51]

The decisive role in persuading the tenacious Brennan and Black, if not Frankfurter, to cease and desist may actually have been played by Justice Harlan. For Harlan—tongue firmly in cheek—submitted to his brethren the fruits of his own most recent labors in the case, a brief opinion which Justice Clark had agreed to join were the Black-Brennan proposal adopted, and which read as follows:

> MR. JUSTICE HARLAN concurring in part, expressing a *dubitante* in part, and dissenting in part.

> I concur in the Court's opinion, filed September 29, 1958, in which I have already concurred. I doubt the wisdom of my Brother FRANKFURTER filing his separate opinion, but since I am unable to find any material difference between that opinion and the Court's opinion—and am confirmed in my reading of the former by my Brother FRANKFURTER's express reaffirmation of the latter—I am content to leave his course of action to his own good judgment. I dissent from the action of my other Brethren in filing their separate opinion, believing that it is always a mistake to make a mountain out of a molehill. *Requiescat in pace.*

Harlan's "droll draft," Bernard Schwartz has suggested, "defused the conference tension. Though Frankfurter filed his opinion later that day, Black and Brennan withdrew their statement."[52]

A Proper Accommodation

If Harlan's participation in early racial cases at times reflected a struggle between his deference to governmental power and concern for the plight of individual litigants, his approach to issues of criminal procedure not tinged with racial elements rarely revealed such inner conflicts. Early in his Supreme Court career, as well as later, he generally sided with government over the criminal defendant. As in other civil liberties fields, he was particularly reluctant to disturb state criminal proceedings. In one of the first state criminal cases decided after his arrival at the Court, a majority overturned criminal contempt convictions growing out of an unusual Michigan arrangement. In the proceedings at issue, a state judge served as a one-man grand jury in investigating crime. Later, the same judge, after a court hearing, cited two witnesses for contempt for events which took place before him during the "grand jury" inquiry. A six–three Court, speaking through Justice Black, overturned the conviction on due process grounds.[53] When Black circulated a draft opinion in the case, his new colleague revealed, probably for the first time since his appointment to the Court, the sort of leeway to which he believed state courts were entitled under due process.

> I would very much like to see a statement in the opinion [he wrote Black] which recognizes that in reviewing state procedures under the due process clause we are more circumscribed than we are in reviewing such procedures in a federal case. In other words, that we recognize the due process clause leaves the States with wide latitude to determine their own procedures. This was the point that initially led me to think that we should probably affirm in this case, and it is the rub of the difference between the majority and the minority. I suggest therefore that the majority opinion should recognize the point.[54]

Apparently satisfied with revisions Black made in the opinion, Harlan, although initially inclined to vote to uphold the defendants' convictions, joined the majority. Normally, of course, Harlan voted to reject the criminal procedure claim in state cases, whatever the majority's rhetoric. At times, in fact, he assumed such a stance even when his mentor Frankfurter found a violation of constitutional rights. For example, in *Fikes* v. *Alabama*, decided early in the 1956 term, he and Frankfurter parted company when the Court, speaking through Chief Justice Warren, reversed the conviction and death sentence of an uneducated black of low mentality who had been found guilty of burglary with intent to commit rape. Two confessions admitted in evidence at Fikes's trial were obtained while he was held in a state prison far from his home, without the preliminary hearing required by Alabama law, or the advice of a lawyer, friends, or family. The first confession was secured after five days of intermittent questioning by police officers for several hours at a time, the second five days later following more such interrogation. Before the first confession, the defendant was allowed to see the sheriff of his home county and his employer, but not his father.[55]

In a concurring opinion, Justice Frankfurter stressed his view "that adequate power should accompany the responsibility of the States for the enforcement of their criminal law." But Frankfurter could see no "difference with respect to the 'voluntariness' of a confession, between the subversion of freedom of will through physical punishment and the sapping of the will appropriately to be inferred from the circumstances of this case. . . . No single one of these circumstances alone would in my opinion justify a reversal. I cannot escape the conclusion, however, that in combination they [brought] the result below the Plimsoll line of 'due process' " and offended "the civilized standards of the Anglo-American world." The conduct of state officials in the case, wrote Frankfurter, was not only inconsistent "with our professions about criminal justice, as against authoritarian methods that we denounce. It derives from an attitude that is inimical, if experience is any guide, to the most enduring interests of the law."[56]

Justice Harlan could not agree. In a dissent joined by justices Reed and Burton, he accused the majority of "overstep[ping] the boundary between this Court's function under the Fourteenth Amendment and that of the state courts in the administration of criminal justice," adding: "I recognize that particularly in 'coerced confession' cases the boundary line is frequently difficult to draw. But this Court has recognized that its corrective power over state courts in criminal cases is narrower than that which it exercises over the lower federal courts." The elements of coercion necessary to establish a state constitutional violation were, to Harlan's thinking, simply not present.[57]

Nor was Harlan convinced that Alabama officials had deliberately attempted to isolate Fikes from his family, counsel, and others interested in his welfare. After all, he had been permitted, "at his own request," to see the sheriff and his employer; and although his father had not been allowed to see the defendant before the first confession, he had seen him before authorities secured the second confession. Finally, while prison authorities had refused to honor a lawyer's request to see the petitioner, that attorney had been given "no authority from petitioner or his family to represent him" and state officials "evidently thought he was trying to solicit business." Such circumstances, Harlan concluded, quoting an earlier Frankfurter opinion, might "offend some fastidious squeamishness or private sentimentalism about combatting crime too energetically." But they did not amount to conduct which "shock[ed] the conscience." In his view, Fikes's treatment was thus beyond the proper reach of federal judicial scrutiny.[58]

Such thinking also permeated Harlan's early as well as later opinions for the Court in criminal procedure cases. In *Cicenia* v. *LaGay* (1958), for example, he employed the flexible, deferential approach to due process which then prevailed on the Court in upholding the murder conviction of a New Jersey man who had been denied an opportunity to talk with his attorney until he signed a confession, or to inspect his confession before entering what amounted to a guilty plea in the case. The petitioner, who was in custody seven hours before seeing his lawyer, charged in federal habeas corpus proceedings that he had been denied due process. Considering themselves bound by prevailing Supreme Court precedent, two lower federal courts denied him relief, but, as one put it, "without enthusiasm." In a dissent joined by Warren and Black, Justice Douglas decried the Court's continued failure "to bring our decisions into tune with the constitutional requirement for fair proceedings against the citizen."[59]

But again, Harlan had a different view. He and his colleagues, he assured readers, shared the lower courts' "strong distaste . . . over the episode. . . . Were this a federal prosecution," he added, "we would have little difficulty in dealing with what occurred under our general supervisory power over the administration of justice in the federal courts." He agreed, too, that the right to counsel enjoyed "a high place in our scheme of procedural safeguards." A general extension of that right to police interrogation of suspects, on the other hand, "in many instances might impair their ability to solve difficult cases." For that reason, he and his colleagues could not embrace the petitioner's claim, which, "in its ultimate reach, would mean that state police could not interrogate a suspect before giving him an opportunity to secure counsel." Instead, they would continue to "achieve a proper accommodation" of the competing social and individual interests at issue in such state cases by "determining from all the circumstances whether a conviction was attended by fundamental unfairness." To hold otherwise would impose "inflexible" national standards on "law enforcement problems [which] vary widely from State to State, as well as among different communities within the same State," thereby violating "the very essence of our federalism"—the principle "that the States should have the widest latitude in the administration of their own systems of criminal justice."[60]

When Harlan did join a decision overturning a state criminal conviction, he typically did so on narrow grounds. In *Payne* v. *Arkansas*, decided during the same term as *Cicenia*, the Court reversed the murder conviction and death sentence of a nineteen-year-old black who had confessed to the crime only after the local police chief told him that, otherwise, a mob "would [soon] be there to get him." Despite the mob atmosphere in which Payne's confession was induced, Justice Harlan, as he noted in a letter to Justice Whittaker, who had been assigned the Court's opinion in the case, initially could find "no vestige of a federal claim . . . on the coerced confession issue unless we are prepared to depart from settled precedent." Only after concluding that the police chief's own testimony "require[d] acceptance of petitioner's claim that the confession was induced through mob violence" did he drop plans to dissent in the case.[61]

While Harlan's flexible, "fundamental fairness" approach to due process can obviously be used to enlarge substantially the scope of individual constitutional guarantees, it was rarely to serve that function in Harlan's hands. In *Lambert* v. *California*, a five–four Court overruled on due process grounds a Los Angeles ordinance making it a criminal offense for convicted felons to remain in the city more than five days without registering with the chief of police, as applied to a woman who had no knowledge of her duty to register. Speaking for the majority, Justice Douglas agreed that "[t]he rule that 'ignorance of the law will not excuse' . . . is deep in our law." He asserted for the majority, however, that such a standard was inappropriate when applied to "a person unaware of any wrongdoing, [and] brought to the bar of justice for condemnation in a criminal case," especially where violation of the law at issue was "unaccompanied by any activity whatever." Were due process to permit such a law, he added, "the evil would be as great as it is when the law is written in print too fine to read or in a language foreign to the community."[62]

Although finding the case "extremely bothersome," Harlan ultimately joined Justice Frankfurter's *Lambert* dissent. Initially, he also prepared a dissent of his own. In that uncirculated draft, he indicated that he could find nothing "inherently unconstitutional about a criminal statute which punishes despite the lack of any 'wilfulness,' 'criminal intent' or 'scienter' on the part of the transgressor," at least in a "noninfamous" case. Certainly, conviction under such a law, in his judgment, would not violate any "fundamental" principle of justice. The local authorities had simply concluded that any "considerations of hardship to the individual" which the statute imposed were "outweighed by the added protection to the public which might flow from imposing on those concerned an unavoidable duty to register." Despite the difficulties the case posed for him, Harlan was unwilling to disturb that judgment.[63]

The Justice might have assumed the same stance in a federal case of the *Lambert* variety. While his deference to governmental authority was to be primarily evident in state cases, he was also to ascribe a flexible meaning to Bill of Rights safeguards at issue in federal criminal procedure contexts. In one 1957 case, the Court, speaking through Justice Black, reversed the murder conviction of a federal defendant who had been tried for first-degree murder, convicted of second-degree murder after the trial judge told jurors they had that option, then convicted of first-degree murder in a second trial after his first conviction was reversed on appeal. Finding the first jury's refusal to convict the defendant of murder in the first degree tantamount to an acquittal on that charge, Black concluded for the majority that the second trial for first first degree murder constituted double jeopardy forbidden by the Fifth Amendment.[64]

Justice Harlan joined Justice Frankfurter's dissent in the case. In *Palko v. Connecticut* (1937), the Court had upheld the first-degree murder conviction and death sentence of a defendant who had originally been convicted of murder in the second degree and given a life sentence, even though the state, not the defendant, had successfully appealed Palko's first conviction. In an important dictum which Frankfurter regularly applauded, the *Palko* Court, speaking through Justice Cardozo, had rejected the defendant's contention that the Fourteenth Amendment embodied the double jeopardy provisions of the Fifth, thereby making them applicable to state proceedings. Instead, Cardozo evaluated Palko's treatment under the flexible, "fundamental fairness" standard which the Court had long held to be implicit in the Fourteenth Amendment's due process guarantee. Now Frankfurter, joined by Harlan as well as Burton and Clark, argued that *Palko* should also be the Court's guide in *federal* double jeopardy cases and complained that the majority had "misconceive[d] the purposes of the double jeopardy provisons," thus making "an absolute of the interests of the accused in disregard of the interests of society."[65]

On the same day Justice Black registered the Court's opinion in the double jeopardy case, Harlan spoke for a majority in another suit with double jeopardy as well as self-incrimination overtones, but with the Court on this occasion siding with the government. In a federal jury trial, officials of the Shotwell Manufacturing Company were convicted of corporate income tax evasion. Between 1945 and 1952, however, the Treasury Department had followed a policy of not referring to the Department of Justice cases of intentional tax evasion where the culprits involved had made "a clean breast of things," as Harlan put it, prior to initiation of an IRS investigation. And the government's case against the Shotwell defendants was based in part on voluntary disclosures to Treasury officials. A court of appeals thus reversed their convictions. After petitioning the Supreme Court for certiorari, the government moved that the Court remand the case to the trial court for further proceedings before reaching the merits of the defendants' constitutional claims. Newly discovered evidence, government lawyers contended, had revealed that trial testimony concerning the timing and good faith of the defendants' disclosures was perjured and fradulent. The Court, per Harlan, honored the government's request.[66]

In a dissent joined by Warren and Douglas, Justice Black argued that the justices should have denied certiorari, thus permitting the case to go back to the district court for a new trial pursuant to the court of appeals' decision. During those proceedings, Black contended, the government could introduce any new evidence it wished. "The Court," he added, "now gives the Government an opportunity to introduce new evidence in an attempt to save a conviction it has lost in the Court of Appeals. If this does not technically infringe the protection against double jeopardy it seems to me to violate its spirit. . . . In fact it is even worse in some respects. Only the Government stands to benefit from this partial new trial while the defendants must fight to keep what they already have. Not a single case has been referred to or discovered where defendants have been subjected to such piecemeal prosecution. To my knowledge it is a new idea that the Government can supplement a trial record in order to retain a conviction which an appellate court would otherwise reverse."[67]

Speaking for the majority, Justice Harlan cited two recent cases in which the Court had refused to consider questions presented for review in the face of challenges to the integrity of their trial records. In both, however, government witnesses had perjured themselves. The differences between those cases and *Shotwell Manufacturing* were, Justice Black asserted, "manifest and crucial," since in each the Court had acted "to protect the rights of defendants, not as here to aid the Government." Given "our traditional methods of criminal justice," Black dryly observed, "this difference [was] not without importance."[68]

Harlan disagreed. Giving the government an opportunity to challenge the appeals court's suppression of evidence without risking a new trial which might end in the defendants' acquittal was, in his and the majority's view, merely consistent with the "fair" administration of justice. Acceptance of the respondents' petition, on the other hand, "would be tantamount to sanctioning a rule which would prohibit appellate review upon a record suspect of taint, if the taint might operate to the disadvantage of the defendants, but which would nevertheless require review if the taint might operate to their advantage." The Court, wrote Harlan, could not tolerate "that quixotic result. The fair administration of justice is not such a one-way street."[69]

Nor could Harlan accept Justice Black's contention that the Sixth Amendment right to trial by jury in "all criminal prosecutions" and Fifth Amendment guarantee to a grand jury extended to criminal contempt proceedings. In *Green* v. *United States*, decided in March of 1958, Harlan spoke for a majority in upholding contempt citations imposed on two of the defendants whose convictions under the Smith Act had been affirmed by the court in the *Dennis* case. In a vigorous dissent, Black charged that the power of judges to punish criminal contempt summarily was "an anomaly in the law" which was inconsistent with the Constitution's "sweeping unequivocal terms" and based on a historically inaccurate assumption that English judges had always possessed such authority. The early English cases which had laid the foundation for the power, wrote Black, uncharitably quoting from a treatise on the subject which Justice Frankfurter, a member of the *Green* majority, had once coauthored, had been decided "at a time when '[w]holly unfounded assumptions about "immemorial usage" [had] acquired a facitious authority and were made the basis of legal decisions.'. . . Later cases merely cite[d] the earlier ones in a progressive cumulation while uncritically repeating their assumptions about 'immemorial usage' and 'inherent necessity.' "[70]

Harlan contended, on the other hand, that recent historical research had revealed "no such clear error" but only that the precise nature of early English practice was "shrouded in much obscurity." Whatever its earliest status in Anglo-American law, he asserted, the summary contempt power had emerged in certain types of English cases at least by the early eighteenth century and had long been part of "our traditions," well grounded in American legal precedent. In any event, Harlan observed, recognition of the power did not mean that courts could abuse their discretion. As there are no congressional restrictions on their sentencing authority, judges had "a special duty to exercise such an extraordinary power with the utmost sense of responsibility and circumspection." Appellate courts were to uphold, moreover, only "reasonable" contempt citations. But the three-year contempt sentences imposed on the petitioners, to be served after completion of their five-year sentences for Smith Act violations, fell, in his judgment, within reasonable bounds.[71]

Harlan's adherence to flexible procedural standards of reasonableness and fairness, like Frankfurter's, was frequently to draw Black's scorn. And *Green* would be no exception. Harlan's assurance that contempt sentences must be "reasonable" was little consolation for Black, who thought "that irrepressible, vague and delusive standard . . . at times threaten[ed] to engulf the entire law, including the Constitution itself, in a sea of judicial discretion." In the *Green* context, it was to him a "trifling amelioration," which did "not strike at the heart of the problem and [could] easily come to nothing, as the majority's very approval of the grossly disproportionate sentences imposed on [the] defendants portend[ed]."[72]

Ironically, in applying the Fourth Amendment guarantee against "unreasonable" searches and seizures, the one Bill of Rights provision with language requiring judges to make judgments on the reasonableness of governmental action, Harlan early favored the establishment of clear legal standards. When a majority in 1956 held that evidence seized under an invalid federal search warrant could not be made available for use in a state trial, the Justice dissented from the restriction the Court had thus imposed on the so-called "silver platter" doctrine. Several years later, of course, he was also to dissent from the Court's extension of the exclusionary rule to state cases in *Mapp* v. *Ohio*.[73] Like Justice Frankfurter, however, Harlan generally favored a stricter reading of the Fourth Amendment right against unreasonable searches and seizures than he normally ascribed to Bill of Rights guarantees, and in an unfiled concurrence for a 1957 case, he urged establishment of clear guidelines for police in federal search and seizure cases.

The case was *Kremen* v. *United States*, in which the Court overturned the seizure of the entire contents of a cabin and their removal to FBI offices two hundred miles away for examination, pursuant to a warrant for the arrest of one of three persons apprehended at the cabin. Initially, Justice Douglas was assigned to write the Court's opinion. When the Douglas draft was circulated, however, Harlan prepared a concurrence in which he took issue with the majority's rationale. At one point in his draft, Harlan observed:

> The majority has here painted with such a broad brush that, in my opinion, federal officers are left in the greatest uncertainty as to what the law now is on this important aspect of law enforcement. It does such officers and the lower courts little good to be told that a particular search and seizure incident to an arrest is invalid because "unreasonable," with no content being given to that term. We have a responsibility in search and seizure cases, it seems to me, to establish rules which are comprehensible to the many officials of the Government who must comply with them day by day. An intolerable situation is created if we strike down action by Government in this area under rules so vague and so changeable that their meaning cannot be known until we ourselves, years after the event, have passed upon all the facts and circumstances of the particular case.[74]

Earlier cases involving warrantless searches incident to arrest had produced a confusing array of precedent. In *Harris* v. *United States*, a 1947 case, the Court had upheld as reasonable a search of a four-room apartment by police armed only with an arrest warrant, thereby broadly construing the permissible scope of warrantless searches incident to a valid arrest. The next year, however, the justices, in *Trupiano* v. *United States*, had struck down the warrantless seizure of a still on a New Jersey farm, even though it was in plain sight of the arresting officers. The police, the *Trupiano* Court explained, had had plenty of time to secure a warrant, yet had willfully disregarded the warrant requirement. Then, in 1950, the Court had appeared to swing back toward the *Harris* decision, upholding in *United States* v. *Rabinowitz* the warrantless search of a stamp dealer's one-room office after his arrest, and overruling *Trupiano* to the extent it conditioned the warrant requirement on the feasibility of securing one.[75]

Obviously attempting to accommodate the varying Fourth Amendment views of his colleagues, Justice Douglas had written a *Kremen* draft which invalidated the search at issue there on two grounds: first, that its unusually broad scope made it inherently unreasonable, and second, that the FBI agents had had "ample time" to obtain a warrant. In Harlan's judgment, Douglas was thus "perpetuat[ing]" the reasoning of *Harris*, under which "every search [was] to be treated on an *ad hoc* basis to see whether it is 'unreasonable' under a kind of floating standard," while at the same time reinstating *Trupiano*, and overruling *Rabinowitz*, *sub silento*. Harlan thought that Douglas should have made "more explicit" the Court's position regarding the status of those earlier precedents, "spell[ing] out governing principles for the guidance of law-enforcement officers and lower courts." Otherwise, the law of search and seizure was "left a shifting sand" and the justices had "fallen short of meeting [their] responsibilities."

Harlan's draft concurrence also made clear the stance he believed the Court should assume in such cases. On the other hand, he favored adoption of a rule narrowly limiting the scope of warrantless searches incident to arrest—one comparable, in fact, to that the Warren Court majority would embrace nearly a decade later.[76]

> I think we should return to the historic rule that searches incident to an arrest must, in the absence of highly unusual circumstances which necessitate further steps to save evidence from destruction, be confined to the person of the arrested individual and articles in his immediate control; and that seizures should extend no further than to implements or fruits of crime in plain sight at the scene of the arrest.

By rejecting such an approach and embracing "a concept of 'reasonableness-at-large,' so to speak," the *Harris* Court had allowed the reasonableness standard to become "little more than what a majority of this Court happen[ed] to regard as right or wrong in the particular case. After *Harris*, there was no longer any answer to the question, 'Reasonable in terms of what?" Now, Harlan argued, the Court should use *Kremen* as a vehicle for abandoning *Harris*. Such a posture would in no way compromise law enforcement. "To the contrary, I think it would promote it by making less likely the reversal of important and expensive trials like this one."

At the same time, Harlan rejected the *Trupiano* notion that warrantless searches incident to arrest are per se unreasonable if officers had "ample time" to secure a warrant. Such a standard had no "historical or constitutional pedigree." It was also "too artificial and difficult to apply." Harlan favored permitting the warrantless seizure of evidence "found on the person of the accused or in plain sight at the scene of the arrest," even if a warrant could have been obtained. After all, he asserted, such searches involved "no invasion of privacy other than that necessarily incident to the arrest itself."

When Justice Douglas read Harlan's draft, he was, he wrote his colleague, "greatly surprised and grieved" that Harlan had not shared his concerns with Douglas before circulating them among their colleagues. "I write as an agent of the group and am always anxious to accommodate as many views as I can." Without Harlan, Douglas added, he had no majority behind his opinion.

> Felix could not, in view of his intense hostility, ever join me in an important constitutional case. I had hoped you could. Certainly your arrival here seemed to bring a fresh breeze into an atmosphere where too much suspicion and distrust prevailed. . . . *Kremen* is utterly unimportant to me. . . . But human relations are terribly important to me. And it hurts me to see you play the game that has brought the Court into disrepute.

Douglas realized, he wrote, that certain members of the Court did not want an opinion in the case. "But that," he added, meaningfully, was "a two-edged sword. Everyone can play that game; and he who plays it is as often the victim as he is the beneficiary."[77]

Ultimately, only a brief per curiam opinion was to be filed in the case, and Harlan, not Douglas, would author it. Douglas had not been the only Justice to take issue with Harlan's draft concurrence. Justice Frankfurter, for example, virtually filled the margins of one page of his colleague's initial draft with his rebuttal of Harlan's rejection of the principle that warrantless searches were generally unconstitutional where officers could easily have satisfied the warrant requirement. But Douglas was never able to muster a majority for his efforts either. He had told Chief Justice Warren that "he should feel free to reassign it,"[78] and the Chief Justice gave the task to Harlan.

Despite his desire for an elaborate explication of a majority position on the issues raised, Harlan yielded to the inevitable and produced a per curiam which provided no explanation at all for the Court's conclusion that the *Kremen* search had been "unreasonable." "I have felt," he wrote Douglas in a letter accompanying his effort, "that the only hope in getting together on this course is for the opinion to say as little as possible." Toward that same end, he also omitted all citations to earlier precedents. Attached as an appendix to his ten-and-a-half page opinion was a single-spaced, eleven-page FBI inventory of items taken in the search. The defendants were targets of anti-Communist prosecutions, and Harlan hoped, he wrote Douglas, that "the inventory [would] have value to the group of readers who are always ready to criticize the Court for setting aside convictions, particularly in Commie cases."[79]

As noted earlier, the Justice's stance with regard to warrantless searches incident to arrest was to be an exception to his usual flexible posture in federal as well as state criminal procedure contexts, including those raising jurisdictional questions. Harlan was to prove extremely deferential to governmental actions in the fields of foreign affairs and national security. In 1958, for example, he would join a Frankfurter opinion upholding broad congressional authority to expatriate citizens. And when the Court, speaking through Justice Black, rejected such power in a 1967 case, Harlan would register a vehement dissent. It was not surprising, therefore, that in the last days of the Court's 1955 term, he joined a five–four majority in upholding the court-martial convictions abroad of two civilians sentenced to death for the murders of their servicemen husbands.[80]

Actually, though, Harlan had found the "Case of the Murdering Wives," as it came to be called, unusually troublesome. As the beginning of the 1956 term approached, he shared his concerns in two memoranda to other members of the original majority. "For my part," he wrote in one, "the trial of civilians by military courts is so obnoxious to our concept . . . that . . . I am most reluctant to regard it as satisfying procedural due process." Justices Burton and Minton responded with lengthy rebuttals, Minton asserting, for example, that while Congress could "not deny the essentials of a fair trial," it could "dispense with some of the trial methods which are guaranteed by the Constitution, such as trial by jury and indictment," and adding that courts-martial, in his judgment, met the "fundamental requirements of a fair trial." Harlan was not persuaded. Ultimately, he not only provided the crucial fifth vote supporting the grant of a rehearing in the case but also joined a new majority to overturn the earlier ruling.[81]

Characteristically, however, he refused to embrace a broad rejection of court-martial proceedings for all civilian defendants. Instead, he limited his concurrence with the Court's decision solely to capital crimes, leaving for another day the status of those charged with less serious offenses. "[W]e have before us a question analogous," he wrote, "to issues of due process; one can say, in fact, that the question of which specific safeguards of the Constitution are appropriately to be applied in a particular context overseas can be reduced to the issue of what process is 'due' a defendant in the particular circumstances of particular case." When a majority in 1960 rejected court-martial of civilians accused of noncapital crimes, he registered a dissent, joined by Justice Frankfurter, in which he emphasized "the awesome finality of a capital case, a factor which in other instances has been reflected both in the constitutional adjudications of this Court and in the special procedural safeguards which have been thrown around those charged with such crimes."[82]

An Added Advantage

Of early criminal procedure cases, however, *Griffin* v. *Illinois* would produce perhaps the clearest indication of what was to become Justice Harlan's normal approach to civil liberties issues. Griffin and a co-defendant named Crenshaw were convicted of armed robbery in an Illinois court. Following their convictions, they asked the trial judge to furnish them with a free transcript of the proceedings for use in preparing an appeal. They were, they claimed, "poor persons with no means of paying the necessary fees to acquire the Transcript and Court Records needed to prosecute an appeal." Under Illinois law, free transcripts were provided indigents only in death penalty cases, and the trial judge denied their motion without a hearing. The Illinois supreme court affirmed the trial court.[83]

At a December 9, 1955, conference, a majority of the brethren, including Harlan, voted to grant the petitioners relief, with the Justice stating that he would reverse the lower courts on equal protection grounds. Following that session, if not before, however, Harlan had begun to have second thoughts about the case, as had Wayne Barnett, one of the Justice's most conservative clerks, who found the case especially "troubling." Harlan and his clerk were particularly concerned about assertions that a transcript was absolutely necessary for an appeal of a criminal conviction in Illinois. Barnett did some "digging into Illinois" law. "I may have initiated that," he would later recall. "I would just think that someone was maintaining things that were not right, and I would go out and write a memo on it. Proponents of the petitioners were framing the issue as though it was impossible to appeal without a transcript, and it wasn't impossible. It seemed to me useful to find exactly what it was that Illinois procedure required, and I think I just started poking around." Barnett's initial research suggested to the Justice that Griffin and Crenshaw might "have obtained a review on the merits of their conviction by some mode short of including in their bill of exceptions a transcript of the stenographic minutes of the trial." If that proved to be the case, Harlan wrote his colleagues, "it seems to me to put a very different complexion on the case."[84]

When his clerk's further research confirmed Harlan's suspicions, he circulated a memorandum to his colleagues. In it, he challenged what he thought to be a key assumption of three opinions other justices were then circulating in the case—"that Illinois procedure afforded the petitioners no appellate review of trial errors in the absence of a stenographic transcript." In fact, Illinois precedents allowed appeals based on narrative accounts of trial proceedings drawn from any available source, including the notes or memory of the trial judge, counsel, or the defendant. Griffin and Crenshaw were present at their trials and thus "could take notes on the proceedings." Moreover, to all appearances they were "represented by counsel who could take notes." The issue in the case was thus, for Harlan, "simply whether an indigent defendant, in preparing his bill of exceptions to present an appeal, [was] constitutionally entitled to have furnished free to him the *added* advantage of a verbatim transcript which those who can afford it are able to purchase."[85] And that was an entitlement he was unwilling to accept.

Justice Black, who had been assigned to draft the majority opinion, quickly registered a biting rejoinder. The opinion which he had circulated in the case, asserted the Court's senior member, was "*not* based on the premise that a convicted defendant can *never* get full appellate review without a transcript, although there are statements in Illinois opinions broad enough to justify an inference of this kind. My opinion is based on the premise that in *many* cases it is impossible for a defendant to get full appellate review without a transcript." During oral argument, the veteran attorney for Illinois had remarked that "[t]here isn't any way that an Illinois convicted person in a non-capital case can obtain a bill of exceptions without paying for it." Under questioning from the bench, he had further conceded that there was no way for a defendant in such cases to have "any trial error reviewed, however, grave it is," if he was "too poor" to buy a transcript. Certainly, Black caustically observed, the state's counsel, who had "been arguing criminal cases for the State of Illinois for a great many years . . . should know more about the law of Illinois than can be readily obtained by a few quotations from a few state cases." Nor was the Justice impressed with Harlan's assertion that the defendants could have based their appeals on their own, or their counsel's, trial notes. "It would be incredible to hold," he exclaimed,

> that convicted persons could be deprived of rights accorded under law to other persons on the premise that defendants can always take notes sufficient to draw up a bill of exceptions. And I should think that defendants throughout the country would be in a very bad predicament if they had to depend on notes taken by counsel to draw up bills of exception to take advantage of all alleged trial errors. That may be good theory but it will not work in practice—at least, it will not work out so as to give a fair opportunity for appeal.

Indeed, it was not at all apparent that the defendants even had trial counsel. And, for Black, it seemed "clearly . . . improper to decide that they *could* not have needed a transcript, despite their allegations and the State's admission of this need, because they 'may' have had counsel present at the trial" to take notes for them.[86]

On this occasion as on many others, Black's logic had little discernible impact on the direction of Harlan's thinking. Harlan had circulated his memorandum on March 6. For several weeks thereafter, Justice Clark apparently attempted to persuade him to join Black's opinion. In a note attached to Black's March 20 circulation, for example, Clark reported to its author that his marginal notes reflected suggested revisions he had shared with Harlan. "I guess that I'm a fool to think anything can be done on Griffin," he wrote in another, unsigned note to Black, "but I really believe that something can be done to relieve this 4 opinion paradox. I hope so. If I fail I owe you an apology for holding you up."[87]

Black was to prove more perceptive than Clark. On April 6, Justice Harlan circulated a brief memorandum indicating that "[a]fter much thought," he had "decided to vote with the dissenters." Attached to the memorandum was a draft dissent. On April 23, 1956, Justice Black registered an opinion announcing the Court's decision, joined by the Chief Justice, Douglas, and Clark. Justice Frankfurter filed an opinion concurring in the Court's judgment. Justices Burton and Minton, joined by Reed and Harlan, registered a dissent. Justice Harlan also filed his dissent.[88]

Throughout Justice Black's career, the reach of the equal protection guarantee in nonracial contexts gave the Justice more difficulty than his published opinions revealed. In a forceful *Griffin* opinion, however, Black combined the enigmatic equal protection clause with the equally "vague contours" of due process in upholding the petitioners' claim and asserting that "[t]here can be no equal justice where the kind of trial a man gets depends on the amount of money he has." Black declined to hold that a free transcript must be provided every indigent defendant who sought to appeal his conviction. He insisted, however, that defendants given an opportunity under the law to file an appeal must be assured "adequate and effective appellate review"—the sort of review Griffin and Crenshaw, in his view, had been denied.[89]

Justice Frankfurter—who cast the crucial fifth vote in the case—concurred in the Court's judgment, but not in Black's entire rationale, primarily because of differences over the ruling's reach. For Black, judges were interpreters of the Constitution, not lawmakers. In the conference discussion of *Griffin,* he thus had argued that newly announced constitutional rules should be given fully retroactive, as well as prospective, application. And he refused to budge from that stance in his *Griffin* opinion. Frankfurter's concept of the judicial function was quite different, and he devoted a portion of his concurrence to rejecting Black's desire to have the Court "imprisoned within" what Frankfurter considered a "formal, abstract dilemma."[90]

Frankfurter had little difficulty, however, in endorsing Black's equal-protection-cum-due-process rationale. Those guarantees did not require the state to grant a right of appeal, nor did they forbid "reasonable" legal classifications. In his judgment, though, the discrimination at issue bore "no relation to a rational policy of criminal appeal" and instead "authorize[d] the imposition of conditions that offend[ed] the deepest presuppositions of our society."

> To sanction such a ruthless consequence, inevitably resulting from a money hurdle erected by a State, would justify a latter-day Anatole France to add one more item to his ironic comments on the "majestic equality" of the law. "The law, in its majestic equality, forbids the rich as well as the poor to sleep under bridges, to beg in the streets, and to steal bread.". . .
>
> The State is not free to produce such a squalid discrimination.[91]

Justice Harlan's posture in the case was Frankfurter's principal target. In his earlier memorandum, Harlan had opposed remanding the case to the lower courts for further proceedings to clarify the nature of the petitioners' claims and the requirements of Illinois law. Later, he urged just such a tack in an effort to forestall a ruling in the petitioners' favor. In his *Griffin* dissent, he contended that the Court's decision "should not be made upon a record as obscure as this, especially where there are means ready at hand to have clarified the issue sought to be presented." Even among the dissenters, however, he stood alone in favoring such disposition of the case.[92] He had thus reluctantly confronted the merits of the petitioners' constitutional claims.

Since the majority's ruling was "not—and on this record [could not] be—based on any facts peculiar to" the case, the proceedings raised, in Harlan's judgment, the following question: "Is an indigent defendant who 'needs' a transcript in order to appeal constitutionally entitled, regardless of the nature of the circumstances producing that need, to have the State either furnish a free transcript or take some other action to assure that he does in fact obtain full appellate review?" The Justice could find nothing in the Constitution's equal protection or due process guarantees which justified an affirmative answer to that question. Obviously, the equal protection clause would forbid a state to "discriminate between the 'rich' and the 'poor' in its system of criminal appeals." But Illinois had imposed no "arbitrary conditions," asserted Harlan, on the appellate process. "All that Illinois has done is to fail to alleviate the consequences of differences in economic circumstances that exist wholly apart from any state action." The Court was thus holding that, under equal protection, states had "an affirmative duty to lift the handicaps flowing from differences in economic circumstances" and give to poor defendants what it required others to purchase. Harlan could not tolerate such an "anomalous result." The "real issue" in the case, he contended, was "not whether Illinois *has* discriminated but whether it has a duty to discriminate." For Harlan, the answer to that question was clear.[93]

Indeed, in his judgment, the case did not even raise a legitimate equal protection issue. The typical equal protection case involved "the reasonableness of a 'classification' on the basis of which the State has imposed legal disabilities." *Griffin*, however, turned on "the reasonableness of the State's failure to remove natural disabilities," which, to Harlan, was essentially an issue of "fundamental fairness" governed by traditional principles of due process instead of equal protection. Yet, due process had never been construed to grant *any* right of appeal in criminal cases, and Harlan could find nothing "arbitrary or capricious" in Illinois' failure to provide indigent defendants free transcripts. "[W]hatever else may be said of Illinois' reluctance to expend public funds in perfecting appeals for indigents, it can hardly be said to be arbitrary. A policy of economy may be unenlightened, but it is certainly not capricious."[94]

Nor could he find Illinois' "failure . . . to provide petitioners with the means of exercising the right of appeal that others are able to exercise . . . so 'unfair' as to be a denial of due process." For one thing, he doubted whether "the non-arbitrary denial of a right that the State may withhold altogether could ever be so characterized." For another, he could not agree that a requirement could be imposed on the states merely because it was deemed to be "desirable" social policy. Due process required only "fundamental fairness," not an equalization of economic burdens, in the criminal appeal process.[95]

Harlan was not merely concerned with the Court's extension of equal protection and due process to the petitioners' claims. He was perhaps even more alarmed about *Griffin*'s ultimate potential impact. By the petitioners' own count, free transcripts were provided indigent noncapital defendants in no more than twenty-nine states. The Court's "sweeping pronouncement" would thus touch the laws of at least nineteen states and "create a host of problems affecting the status of an unknown multitude of indigent convicts." For Harlan, the decision had even more disturbing implications: "[i]f requiring defendants in felony cases to pay for a transcript constitutes a discriminatory denial to indigents of the right of appeal available to others, why is it not a similar denial in misdemeanor cases or, for that matter, civil cases?" Harlan's reluctance, as he put it, "to import new substance into the concept of equal protection" reflected also, then, his opposition to constitutional decrees with a potentially broad sweep.[96] And on this occasion, as anyone familiar with the ultimate directions of Warren Court decisions in the equal protection field is aware, his fears were to prove particularly prophetic.

Harlan had opened his *Griffin* dissent by emphasizing that he personally "would prefer to see free transcripts furnished to indigent defendants in all felony cases." Although his Wall Street career had afforded him little direct exposure to the plights of poor defendants, there was no reason to doubt the sincerity of his assertion. Harlan was long active in the work of the Legal Aid Society. In 1954, for example, he signed a fund-raising letter for the society in which he noted that 57,000 persons had been provided legal aid the previous year, then added: "None of these people could afford to pay a lawyer—all of them were entitled to equality under the law." In a 1957 address to the ABA's standing committee on legal aid, moreover, he would propose creation of an ad hoc committee to encourage large law firms in New York and elsewhere to assign some of their younger attorneys to indigent cases. The public defender system of attorneys paid by the state and the legal aid approach both had their place, he asserted, but he favored the latter as more nearly reflective of the spirit of American free enterprise. Nor, he observed, would the youth and inexperience of such counsel necessarily be an obstacle to their clients' effective representation. "Brains, energy and ambition," he asserted, "are a pretty good substitute for experience. As a matter of fact an experienced but dull lawyer is not as good as a young and ambitious man. In any case the judges are not going to let these young fellows be pushed around."[97]

While his proposal may have betrayed an undue optimism, if not naïveté, about the "spirit" of the free enterprise system, it also reflected genuine concern for poor litigants and a recognition, as he put it, that their "proper" representation was still "far, far away."[98] For Harlan, however, solutions to the special burdens confronting indigent litigants, like those to numerous other social problems, lay primarily with the political processes and an aroused citizenry, not with the courts.

John Marshall Harlan, 1899–1971. Courtesy Eve Harlan Dillingham

John Maynard Harlan, Justice Harlan's father. Courtesy Edith Harlan Powell

Harlan's mother Elizabeth, pictured here with young John and his eldest sister Elizabeth. Courtesy Edith Harlan Powell

A solicitious brother with his youngest sister Edith. Courtesy Edith Harlan Powell

A Harlan family portrait taken at the Murray Bay summer home of Harlan's grandfather, the first Justice Harlan, in Canada. Included in the photograph are, standing, John Maynard Harlan at the left; John Marshall Harlan's sister Elizabeth and her husband Roger A. Derby, third and second from right; and John Harlan, at far right; and seated, from the left, Harlan's sister Janet, his mother and three Derby children, and his sister Edith. Courtesy Edith Harlan Powell

Harlan's mother Elizabeth, pictured here with young John and his eldest sister Elizabeth. Courtesy Edith Harlan Powell

A solicitious brother with his youngest sister Edith. Courtesy Edith Harlan Powell

A Harlan family portrait taken at the Murray Bay summer home of Harlan's grandfather, the first Justice Harlan, in Canada. Included in the photograph are, standing, John Maynard Harlan at the left; John Marshall Harlan's sister Elizabeth and her husband Roger A. Derby, third and second from right; and John Harlan, at far right; and seated, from the left, Harlan's sister Janet, his mother and three Derby children, and his sister Edith. Courtesy Edith Harlan Powell

Harlan, standing second from right, with his prep school classmates at the Appleby School in Canada. Courtesy Eve Harlan Dillingham

Harlan, seated at far left, with Oxford classmates. Courtesy Eve Harlan Dillingham

The strikingly attractive Ethel Andrews, whom Harlan married in 1928.
Courtesy Eve Harlan Dillingham

Harlan with daughter Evangeline, the couple's only child. Courtesy Eve Harlan Dillingham

Harlan's mentor Emory Buckner, giving advice to a number of his "Boy Scouts." Standing between Harlan and Buckner, who are seated, is J. Edward Lumbard, one of Harlan's closest friends. Courtesy J. Edward Lumbard

Ella Wendel and Toby. In his first major civil case, Harlan successfully defended heirs to the eccentric Miss Wendel's enormous estate from more than two thousand claimants. Courtesy Drew University Archives

The Harlan country home at Weston, Connecticut. Courtesy John Twarda

Harlan with members of his World War II staff. Pictured from the left are Philip C. Scott, Joseph Labriola, Harlan, Louis Lusky, and Leslie H. Arps. Courtesy Louis Lusky

Shortly before his appointment to the Court of Appeals for the Second Circuit, Harlan represented Pierre and Irenee duPont in the massive GM-DuPont anti-trust suit. In this photo of the huge defense team organized for the case and their clients, Harlan is pictured standing in the center of the group. Courtesy Eve Harlan Dillingham

Harlan on the eve of his Supreme Court career, pictured with his daughter Eve, granddaughter Alice, Eve's first husband Wellington Newcomb, and Mrs. Harlan. Courtesy Eve Harlan Dillingham

Felix Frankfurter, Harlan's closest judicial ally on the Supreme Court. Credit: Collection of the Supreme Court of the United States, courtesy Supreme Court Historical Society

Hugo L. Black, Harlan's jurisprudential opponent but close personal friend, especially during their last years on the Court. Credit: Collection of the Supreme Court of the United States, courtesy Supreme Court Historical Society

Gatherings with his devoted clerks and their spouses became annual events during Justice Harlan's years on the bench. Courtesy Barrett Prettyman, Jr.

One of the last photographs of the Harlans, taken as they departed their Connecticut home following the Court's Christmas, 1970, recess. Courtesy John Twarda

6

The First Freedoms

In June of 1958, George Gray Zabriskie, a Wall Street acquaintance of John Harlan's, wrote Tom Dewey a letter lamenting what Zabriskie termed recent "pro-communist" decisions of the Supreme Court. "John Harlan," Zabriskie asserted, "must be nearly ready to throw up his hands in disgust at his futility in his present position. As far as I have followed his voting record, it has been pretty clean and he has been pretty consistent in siding with the anti-communist minority." But Zabriskie had a proposition for Dewey.

> Why don't you persuade [Harlan] to resign from the Court and run for the Senate, primarily on that issue. Being a gentleman, he would know how to put his message across without violent personal attacks on his present colleagues or other offensive McCarthyisms, as Nixon did in his early campaigns. At the same time he could make clear to the people the true concept of the Supreme Court and its great and . . . beneficient importance to the Republic. With a background of membership in the Supreme Court and anti-communism, I should think John would be the strongest candidate the Republicans could put up, unless General MacArthur could be drafted. . . . Moreover, unlike our present Senators . . . John might even show his independence of Big Labor. As things are now, both parties might as well acknowledge the unquestionable supremacy of Walter Reuther and his Unioneers by jointly nominating him for President in 1960, and thus save the country the expense and furor of a Presidential election.[1]

Zabriskie mailed a copy of the letter to Harlan's sister Elizabeth. "What do you think of this?" he asked in an accompanying note. "I don't suppose John would dream of doing it. I attached to the original a Daily News Editorial about the damage Warren and his pro-communist decisions have done & the need for the Butler-Jenner bill" limiting federal judicial power. Elizabeth in turn forwarded her copy to her brother with a question and comment of her own. "What do you think of this bright idea? I thought he was joking—but no indeed!"[2]

While the Justice no doubt found the suggestion as bizarre as his sister had, Zabriskie's enthusiasm for an anti-Communist Harlan Senate candidacy obviously reflected the general tenor of the Justice's position in cases involving government sanctions against American Communists. Harlan's posture in such cases was to be more complicated, however, than Zabriskie might have assumed. On more than one occasion, for example, the Justice was to indicate privately that he was "not an enthusiast for these Smith Act prosecutions" of Communist leaders, and several of his clerks left his service with similar impressions of his thinking. "The Justice," Charles Fried has observed, "viewed the McCarran Act and [other anti-Communist legislation] as McCarthyite garbage." Philip Heymann, who also clerked for the Justice during the Court's 1960 term, agrees. "I think that he had no sympathy for the statutes, that he thought they were dumb" laws. And Stephen Shulman, one of Harlan's clerks during the 1958 term, remembers that the Justice entertained doubts about the Smith Act's constitutionality. At the same time, Harlan's natural deference to governmental authority made him reluctant to erect broad First Amendment or related constitutional bars to anti-Communist sanctions, particularly where the degree of governmental interference with rights of association and expression in such cases seemed, to his mind at least, attenuated at best.[3]

Defanging the Smith Act

Harlan was to favor the tightest restrictions on governmental power in cases involving criminal prosecutions under the Smith Act for membership in the Communist Party and the advocacy of governmental overthrow by force and violence. In the *Dennis* case, the Court in 1951 had upheld the Smith Act against First Amendment and other claims by embracing Learned Hand's "gravity of the evil" variation on the "clear and present danger" test. During his brief tenure on the Court of Appeals for the Second Circuit, as was noted previously, Harlan had given the *Dennis* decision a broad reading in the *Flynn* case, holding that "Where a conspiracy to destroy the Government by force or violence is involved . . . the 'clear and present danger' concept . . . connotes no more than that the setting in which the defendants have conspired is such as to lead reasonably to the conclusion that their teachings may result in an attempt at overthrow." In two of his most important opinions for the Supreme Court, however, Harlan was to give the Smith Act's provisions an extremely narrow construction, which would make successful prosecutions under the law exceedingly difficult, if not impossible to mount.[4]

In the first case, *Yates* v. *United States*, fourteen California Communist leaders had appealed their Smith Act convictions to the Court. By June of 1957, when Harlan announced the Court's opinion in the *Yates* case, the government had already obtained 145 indictments and 89 convictions under the Smith Act. Given those figures and the *Dennis* precedent, Harlan was not about to agree with justices Black and Douglas, among others, that the statue should now be declared unconstitutional. He did hold for the Court, however, that the government was obliged in such cases to prove more than the mere "advocacy . . . of forcible overthrow as an abstract principle, divorced from any effort to instigate action to that end." The act's legislative history, he asserted, demonstrated "beyond all question that Congress was aware of the distinction between the advocacy or teaching of abstract doctrine and the advocacy or teaching of action, and that it did not intend to disregard it." Under the Smith Act, therefore, a defendant could be convicted only for "the advocacy and teaching of concrete action for the forcible overthrow of the Government, and not of principles divorced from action."[5]

Harlan's construction of the Smith Act hardly satisfied those, such as Black and Douglas, who embraced an absolutist or near-absolutist conception of the First Amendment. After all, the Justice read the law—and presumably the First Amendment—to permit prosecution of persons who advocated "the taking of forcible action in the future,"[6] rather than confining government's reach to the incitement of *imminent* lawless action. Even so, Harlan's *Yates* opinion was to have a dramatic impact on Smith Act cases. Based on his construction of the law, he and the brethren ordered the outright acquittal of five of the *Yates* defendants, holding the evidence "clearly insufficient" to justify their further prosecution. The cases against the remaining nine defendants were remanded for retrial. Ultimately, the government moved for dismissal of their indictments as well, since the evidence against them was largely of the doctrinal variety—and thus inadequate to satisfy the *Yates* standard. Following the decision, Smith Act prosecutions were drastically curtailed, then abandoned entirely.

The Court's ruling and its ultimate likely effect were not lost on the nation's McCarthyites. Critics scorned June 17, 1957, the date the *Yates* decision was announced, as "Red Monday." And temporarily at least, Justice Harlan, once a preeminent advocate for American capitalists, found himself the target of anti-Communist hate mail. "Just what does it take?" one of the Justice's new correspondents asked: "[D]oes a man have to have a bottle of Vodka in his hand—waving the Russian flag—saying to 'Hell with the U.S.' while standing on the American flag? Are you afraid of Russia? Why not recess until 1999." A "young patriot" charged that "the so-called Supreme Court is packed with traitors." An "American" asked, "What have the Commies got on you?" adding, "Your abstract opinion smells," while another writer labeled the Justice a "Rip Van Winkle," then complained, "Where have you been sleeping for the past twenty years? Don't you realize that the Communist Party is engaged in a great war to destroy the American system of government?" Many other cards and letters, mostly anonymous, expressed similar opinions.[7]

But Harlan and his brethren were not yet finished with the Smith Act. One provision of the law made it a criminal offense to knowingly be a member of any group which advocated the overthrow of government through force or violence. In 1955, Junius Irving Scales, scion of an aristocratic Greensboro, North Carolina, family, who had long been active in the southern wing of the American Communist Party, was convicted of violating the membership clause. The Supreme Court had first heard his appeal during its 1956 term. Only seven justices had sat in the case, however, and only four of that number, including Harlan, voted to uphold the clause's constitutionality. At the suggestion of Justice Frankfurter, the brethren scheduled the case for re-argument in the 1957 term, when a full Court could participate.[8]

On October 14, 1957, the government informed the justices that the FBI reports of two government witnesses had been withheld from the defendant and his counsel in violation of *Jencks* v. *United States*, a decision of the previous term which held that the withholding of evidence of possible benefit to an accused violated due process. The Court thus held that Scales was entitled to a new trial.

During the 1958 term, the Court again heard an appeal in the case, this time of Scales's second conviction, but then scheduled the case for re-argument in the 1959 term. When an appeal was filed that term in a related anti-Communist case,[9] however, the justices decided to hear both cases during the 1960 term. Following argument in October of that year, Chief Justice Warren contended in conference that the Smith Act should be construed to penalize only "active" membership in organizations dedicated to illegal overthrow and that the evidence against the accused was insufficient to establish such a tie on Scales's part to the Communist Party. Black, Douglas, and Brennan agreed with the Chief Justice. Harlan, Frankfurter, Clark, and Whittaker voted to affirm. Justice Potter Stewart, who had replaced Justice Burton in 1958, was the Court's newest member, and, as was often to be the case during the early years of his tenure, the critical fifth vote in the case, indicated that he was undecided, but leaning toward affirmance.

Justice Harlan ultimately drafted an opinion for the Court upholding Scales's conviction, but assigning the membership clause the narrow interpretation Chief Justice Warren had advanced in conference. Harlan's principal task was thus to convince Justice Stewart of the adequacy of the evidence which the government had presented against Scales. The Justice himself had long been convinced that the petitioner's conviction should not be reversed on grounds of insufficient evidence. In a June 29, 1959, memorandum on the evidence issue, for example, he had observed:

> Our function in determining the sufficiency of the evidence is simply to decide whether the facts shown are such as to justify the jury in concluding that petitioner was guilty under the Smith Act. We are neither called upon nor possessed of power to review the evidence as if we were the jury. And the desirability or wisdom of initiating this prosecution in the first instance is, of course, similarly beyond our province.
>
> Viewing the evidence in light of these limitations, we think it amply supports petitioner's conviction.[10]

While preparing for the October 1960, oral argument and conference in the case, Harlan had his clerk Charles Fried prepare a bench memo to which was attached a five-page, single-spaced summary of the *Scales* evidence and that presented in the *Yates* case. The *Yates* evidence, Fried concluded, had given "on the whole a very scattered and desultory impression instead of the focussed and to-the-point impression that one gets from *Scales*."[11]

In his own uncirculated memorandum, drafted some time after the October 1960, conference, however, Justice Stewart expressed doubt whether the evidence amassed against Scales was any more convincing than that found inadequate to support certain convictions at issue in *Yates*. After reviewing that memorandum, Charles Fried wrote Harlan that Stewart

> may have succeeded in convincing himself . . . that although the *Scales* evidence may be clearer and stronger, there is no such overwhelming *qualitative* difference [between *Yates* and Scales] that in one case the jury could not and in the other it could reach the conclusion to convict. His position is if anything, we were reading the record more permissisively than we should now when it is a matter of affirming a particular conviction—and not simply barring reprosecution.

But the clerk, too, and perhaps the Justice himself, also entertained such doubts. For Fried, who years later would recall being "bothered, but not very bothered," by *Scales*, added to his memo: "I must agree that it is hard to point to any really convincing evidence of a qualitative difference between the two records, and I take it that you feel this too. So the issue seems to be clearly drawn on whether this kind of comparison of the two cases is in order at all."[12]

But whatever Justice Harlan's personal views about the weight of the evidence in *Scales* relative to that in *Yates*, the Justice continued to press Stewart to vote for affirmance of the petitioner's conviction. In a letter responding to his colleague's memorandum, Harlan emphasized that the draft opinion he was then circulating in the case left "unimpaired both the [strict] *Yates* definition of Smith Act advocacy and its requirement of strict proof [of the law's violation]—two things that I have always considered were *Yates*' healthy contribution to this difficult field of law."

He also reminded Stewart of the Court's stance in *Noto* v. *United States*, another Smith Act membership case being decided along with *Scales*. At conference, according to Justice Brennan's notes, Harlan had indicated that he had "difficulty" with the *Noto* record and "at present would vote to reverse for insufficiency of evidence," adding: "The only evidence of 'purpose' here . . . is the testimony that Noto said something about 'Day will come when that kind of SOB will be up against wall & shot.' That's only evidence of his or party's kind of advocacy. Ought have high standard of proof in these cases & this is not enough." The Court had assumed the same stance, reversing Noto's conviction. As Harlan wrote Stewart, "[o]ur adherence to . . . *Yates* is surely made clear by the different conclusion we are reaching in *Noto*."[13]

Finally, Harlan appealed to his colleague's regard for precedent, observing:

> Although I am not an enthusiast for these Smith Act prosecutions, and believe that we should keep a tight rein on them, I must say that reversal here would be almost tantamount to overruling at least that part of *Dennis* and *Yates* which allowed the application of the statute to advocacy of unspecified future violence, and to the recruitment and readying of a group to engage in violence at the future direction of their leaders. For, within the substantive standards of *Dennis*, as refined and reaffirmed in *Yates*, I do not see how it can be said that there was not a jury issue here. Indeed, I find it difficult to see how the Government could be expected to make out a stronger case, again given the substantive standards of illegal advocacy established by *Dennis* and *Yates*.

If Stewart "remain[ed] unsatisfied," Harlan added, "I do hope you will give me a further chance to thrash this thing out with you in face to face discussion, as yours is the deciding vote."[14]

Ultimately, the Justice was able to convince Stewart to join him in affirming Scales's conviction; on June 5, 1961, the Court's decision in the case was announced over the vigorous dissents of Chief Justice Warren and justices Black, Douglas, and Brennan. In preparing an opinion in the case, Charles Fried, who wrote an initial draft following discussion with the Justice, recalls that Harlan decided to turn the case "into a conspiracy case, to say, look, this statute is terrible, but if you view it as an ordinary conspiracy statute and give the prosecution no more head than they would have in a conspiracy [case], then the question would be, 'was there enough evidence to affirm a conviction of conspiracy?'" Fried's co-clerk Philip Heymann has similar recollections. "He didn't like striking down a federal statute," Heymann remembers. "And what he did was a very clever technical job of making it into a conspiracy statute . . . to say that to be guilty of membership in the Communist Party, you had to have done what . . . an aider and abettor, an accessory, or a conspirator would have done with regard to violent action.

. . . I remember that he started by sort of forgetting all about the membership requirement, by saying, 'What could you make criminal?' And you could make criminal actively taking steps to engage in violence and . . . to urge other people to rather promptly take violent steps—you could make it criminal to be a conspirator. And he said that that's what membership [under the Smith Act] meant."[15]

The opinion which Harlan announced proceeded essentially along these lines. To convict under the act, the government was obligated to establish more than mere membership in the Communist Party, more than the defendant's knowledge of that organization's illegal goals—the only requirements a literal reading of the membership clause seemed to impose on such prosecutions. Instead, asserted Harlan, the clause reached only "active and purposive membership, purposive that is as to the organization's criminal ends." Only if Scales not simply knew of the Communist Party's illegal aims but also had a "specific intent" to accomplish those goals could his conviction be sustained. And for the majority, there was adequate evidence to satisfy that standard. An FBI undercover agent had testified, for example, that during "a compulsory recreation period" at a Communist training school run by Scales, an instructor had given "a demonstration," in Scales's presence, "of jujitsu and, explaining that the students 'might be able to use this on a picket line,' how to kill a person with a pencil."[16]

Nor did Harlan and company see any constitutional objection to the law or the petitioner's conviction. To Scales's claim that the membership clause permitted punishment of status alone and thus violated due process, Harlan countered:

> Any thought that due process puts beyond the reach of the criminal law all individual associational relationships, unless accompanied by the commission of specific acts of criminality, is dispelled by familiar concepts of the law of conspiracy and complicity. While both are commonplace in the landscape of the criminal law, they are not natural features. Rather they are particular legal concepts manifesting the more general principle that society, having the power to punish dangerous behavior, cannot be powerless against those who work to bring about that behavior.[17]

Given the *Dennis* and *Yates* precedents, the Justice added, the membership clause was also beyond the First Amendment's reach. Those cases had established that

> the advocacy with which we are here concerned is not constitutionally protected speech, and . . . that a combination to promote such advocacy, albeit under the aegis of what purports to be a political party, is not such association as is protected by the First Amendment. We can discern no reason why membership, when it constitutes a purposeful form of complicity in a group engaging in this same forbidden advocacy,

> should receive any greater degree of protection from the guarantees of that Amendment.[18]

Moreover, since the clause, as judicially construed, reached only those who knew of an organization's illegal aims and specifically intended to accomplish them by resort to force or violence, it could hardly be contended that the law's mere existence would chill the exercise of protected First Amendment rights.

Harlan's *Scales* opinion and the Court's decision to affirm a Smith Act conviction were well received, of course, in many quarters. Staunch anti-Communists flooded the Justice's chambers with letters praising the ruling and which supported registration, deportation, and worse for all Communists. For the four dissenters and civil libertarians generally, however, the majority's action was a bitter disappointment. Justice Douglas exclaimed in dissent, for example, that "[w]hen we allow this petitioner to be sentenced to prison . . . for being a 'member' of the Communist Party, we make a sharp break with traditional concepts of First Amendment rights and make serious Mark Twain's lighthearted comment that 'it is by the goodness of God that in our country we have those three unspeakably precious things: freedom of speech, freedom of conscience, and the prudence never to practice either of them.'"[19]

Such dismay was understandable. Junius Scales, whose aristocratic background bemused Justice Harlan, had been given a six-year sentence, the harshest ever imposed on a Smith Act defendant; he was to serve fifteen months in a federal prison before President Kennedy commuted his sentence to time served. Yet the evidence against him, like that against all persons prosecuted under the Smith Act, established only an affiliation and speech—often, in fact, the words of others instead of the defendants' themselves—divorced entirely from any illegal act. Paid undercover agents were the principal source of the evidence against Scales, moreover, and he has argued in his autobiography that their testimony was replete with exaggeration and distortions of the truth. In Harlan's opinion for the Court, for example, prominent play, it will be recalled, was given a prosecution witness' story that students at a Communist training school which the petitioner operated had been taught how to commit murder with a pencil. Following the agent's testimony at Scales's trial, in fact, a Greensboro newspaper had carried a headline declaring: "Communist School Taught Murder." In his autobiography, though, Scales gave this version of the incident:

> Childs testified at great length about a school I had run three years before on a farm. In addition to several North Carolinians, two women from Virginia had been present, along with Bob, the full-time Virginia Party functionary. One day (as I learned after the trial by consulting people present at the time), when classes had ended for the morning and the students were awaiting lunch, the Virginia women and a few

> others were chatting about street crime in their cities and how frightening it was to go out at night. Bob, eager to show off his World War II military training, launched into a demonstration of judo techniques, showed how a *New York Times* folded a certain way could become a club and how a sharpened pencil held in the palm could become a dagger.[20]

Scales obviously could not be considered an entirely disinterested chronicler, even of events which took place nearly forty years ago. But as a disillusioned former party member who initially saw the Communist movement primarily as a vehicle for improving the lot of American blacks, his accounts have the ring of truth and on the basis of such evidence he had been sent to prison with the Supreme Court's approval.

Even so, the surgery Justice Harlan performed on the Smith Act's membership clause, like that inflicted in *Yates* on its advocacy provisions, made successful prosecution under the act exceedingly difficult. Thus, although Junius Scales became a sacrificial lamb in the Court's effort to avoid a direct challenge to Congress' authority in a very controversial field, Smith Act prosecutions ceased altogether.

Loyalty-Security and the Constitution

Justice Harlan pursued a somewhat similar course in cases involving the denial of government jobs or other benefits on loyalty-security grounds. Particularly since the economic deprivation imposed by government in such cases was arguably less serious than the threat of imprisonment at issue in those of the *Yates* and *Scales* variety, he was somewhat more deferential to government in the former type of case than in the latter. As in *Yates* and *Scales*, he was reluctant to impose broad constitutional restrictions on loyalty-security and related programs. In one case, for example, an aeronautical engineer was fired from his job with a defense contractor after he lost his security clearance under regulations imposed by the secretary of defense without explicit authorization by the president or Congress and following administrative hearings in which he was denied access to much of the information adverse to him as well as any opportunity to cross-examine opposing witnesses. Harlan complained vehemently in conference of the engineer's treatment. "The set-up bothers me," Brennan's notes have him asserting, "the program recognizes implicitly that a guy can't be fired without knowing something about it and yet doesn't tell him. . . . [I]f this bastard form of due process is to be allowed, [it] ought to stem either from [the Congress] or the President." Yet when the Court touched on, though it did not decide, due process and related constitutional objections to the petitioner's treatment, Harlan filed a separate concurrence stating his preference for a decision in the petitioner's favor, but one based purely on the absence of congressional or presidential authorization for the regulation at issue in the case. Chief Justice Warren's opinion for the majority, he complained, "unnecessarily deals with the very issue it disclaims deciding. Ample justification for abstaining from a constitutional decision at this stage of the case is afforded by the Court's traditional and wise rule of not reaching constitutional issues unnecessarily or prematurely."[21]

At the same time, however, he also expressed disappointment at Justice Clark's treatment of the constitutional issues in the dissent his colleague registered in the case.

> It is regrettable that my brother Clark should have so far yielded to the temptations of colorful characterization as to depict the issue in this case as being whether a citizen has "a constitutional right to have access to the Government's military secrets." . . . Of course this decision involves no such issue or consequences. The basic constitutional issue is not whether petitioner is entitled to access to classified material, but rather whether the particular procedures here employed to deny clearance on security grounds were constitutionally permissible. With good reason we do not reach that issue as matters now stand. And certainly there is nothing in the Court's opinion which suggests that petitioner must be given access to classified material.[22]

As in *Yates* and *Scales*, though, Harlan was willing to assign a narrow construction to loyalty-security regulations which limited their impact. Consider, for example, his opinion for a divided Court in the 1956 case *Cole* v. *Young*, in which a food and drug inspector for the Department of Health, Education, and Welfare was summarily suspended from his position on charges of close association with Communists and a "subversive" organization. Cole had been dismissed under a 1950 law giving government agencies power to discharge employees when such action was deemed necessary to "the national security of the United States." Speaking for the Court, Harlan construed the law as reaching only those employees directly concerned with the protection of the nation from internal subversion or foreign aggression instead of those—such as Cole—who generally contributed to the strength of the nation only through their impact on the general welfare. Since no determination had been made that Cole's position was "one in which he could adversely affect 'the national security,'" Harlan held, his discharge was unauthorized.[23]

The Justice also insisted that agencies follow their own procedures in enforcing such regulations. Toward the end of the 1958–59 term, he spoke for the Court in overturning the discharge of William Vincent Vitarelli, a teacher employed by the Department of the Interior on the Pacific island of Koror. Since Vitarelli was not a military veteran or permanent civil service employee, he could have been discharged summarily without cause. In firing him, however, the Interior secretary purportedly followed procedures adopted for "security risk" cases. The secretary had first suspended Vitarelli and served him with written charges that his "sympathetic association" with Communists and their fellow travelers, as well as similar activities, tended to establish that his continued employment might be "contrary to the best interests of national security." At a hearing before a security board, no evidence or witnesses were produced in support of those charges. But Vitarelli and four witnesses who testified in his behalf were subjected to extensive cross-examination going well beyond the activities specified in the charges. He and the others were asked, for example, whether he was "scholarly," a "good administrator," careless or careful "with his language around" students, a "religious man," "an extremist on equality of races."

Following the hearing, Vitarelli was sent a notice of his dismissal "in the interest of national security." After he filed a lawsuit challenging his firing, he received a new dismissal notice, identical in form to the first, but omitting all reference to the reasons for his discharge or to pertinent security regulations.

Harlan, who was "disgusted" by Vitarelli's treatment, his clerk Henry Sailer has recalled, wrote a strong opinion detailing the numerous ways in which the proceedings at issue fell short of the Interior department's own regulations. Agency provisions stipulated, for example, that security hearings were to be "orderly" and that "reasonable restrictions shall be imposed as to relevancy, competency, and materiality of matters considered." But the Vitarelli hearing, the Justice asserted, had "developed into a wide-ranging inquisition into this man's educational, social, and political beliefs, encompassing even a question as to whether he was a 'religious man.'" Nor was Harlan impressed with the Interior secretary's claim that even were Vitarelli's original dismissal invalid, his subsequent notice, omitting all security references, had been valid. Although the Justice conceded that the secretary could have properly dismissed Vitarelli without cause at any time after the date of his first dismissal notice, Harlan and his colleagues found it impossible to separate the second notice from the first, particularly since the second notice, though not filed until October of 1956, was dated only ten days after the first notice, had been designated as a "revision" of the first dismissal, and contained a September 10, 1954, date for the termination of Vitarelli's employment—the same date on which Vitarelli was originally dismissed on security grounds.[24]

Even where governmental employees occupied positions relevant to national security interests, Harlan was among those on the Court who insisted that agencies remove alleged security risks only according to their own established procedures. When, for example, the justices reviewed the 1951 discharge by the secretary of state of veteran foreign service officer John S. Service as a security risk, despite the fact that the State Department's own loyalty board had repeatedly cleared Service of security allegations, Harlan spoke for the Court in overturning the secretary's decision. The Justice conceded that a federal law and several executive orders had clothed the secretary with "absolute discretion" to discharge security risks from the service. He concluded, however, that the department was bound to honor the procedural safeguards its own loyalty-security scheme embodied. Those procedures had been followed in Service's case up to the point of his discharge. Prior to the firing, moreover, President Truman had written Secretary of State Dean Acheson, emphasizing that the secretary's discretionary removal powers were to be exercised "without unduly jeopardizing the personal liberties of the employees within your jurisdiction."[25]

Justice Harlan refused, however, as noted earlier, to embrace broad constitutional objections to the denial of government benefits on loyalty-security grounds. In *Flemming* v. *Nestor*, for example, he spoke for a five–four Court in upholding the termination, under a 1954 law, of social security benefits to an alien who had been deported from the United States in 1956 for having been a Communist in 1933–39. In a biting dissent, Justice Brennan charged that the law under which the benefits were terminated amounted to a bill of attainder through which Congress had sought to punish without judicial hearing "aliens deported for conduct displeasing to the lawmakers." Speaking for the majority, however, Harlan found no "punitive design" in the "mere denial of a noncontractual government benefit," adding, "Judicial inquiries into Congressional motives are at best a haphazard matter, and when that inquiry seeks to go behind objective manifestations it becomes a dubious affair indeed."[26]

The Cold War Inquisitions

Justice Harlan was most reluctant to disturb those loyalty-security schemes which involved the attempts of governmental and quasigovernment agencies to acquire information from witnesses before legislative inquiries, bar admission committees, and related bodies—efforts the Justice apparently regarded as least intrusive upon individual freedom, and thus least deserving of close judical scrutiny. In the wake of Senator McCarthy's censure, congressional inquiries had substantially declined. But they had hardly disappeared, and much of the litigation such investigations spawned was still in the courts, along with the occasional new dispute. State legislatures also remained active, as had state bar associations and other groups anxious to uncover Communists.

During the 1956 term, the Court, in *Watkins* v. *United States*, reversed the contempt-of-Congress conviction of a university professor and labor organizer who had answered questions before the House Un-American Activities Committee (HUAC) about his own activities but refused to answer inquiries about former party members. Despite language touching on Watkins's First Amendment challenges to his conviction,

Earl Warren's opinion for the *Watkins* Court was ultimately cast in narrow, due process terms, the Chief Justice holding that HUAC's charge was so vague and broad that Watkins could not reasonably have been expected to know what questions were pertinent to the investigation and which were not. Justice Frankfurter joined the Court's decision, but on the limited ground that the questions at issue were not pertinent to the inquiry. Later, moreover, he would refer often to Warren's effort as that "god-awful *Watkins* opinion."[27]

Justice Harlan joined Warren's opinion in the *Watkins* case instead of Frankfurter's. In a letter to the Chief Justice, however, he had expressed "hope" that Warren and other members of the majority could "be persuaded to rest the decision solely on" pertinency grounds. Harlan also had "great difficulty" with the Court's opinion in *Sweezy* v. *New Hampshire*, which overturned a state attorney general's inquiry into "subversive" activities. Extremely reluctant to find the New Hampshire legislature's authorization of the investigation unduly vague, Harlan favored deciding the case, he wrote Warren, purely on First and Fourteenth Amendment expression grounds. When the Chief Justice's opinion rested the Court's decision on the absence of clear legislative authorization for the questions Sweezy had refused to answer, Harlan joined Justice Frankfurter's opinion "concurring in the result," based on a weighing of the competing governmental and freedom of expression interests at stake in the case.[28]

But *Watkins* and *Sweezy* were neither the Court's nor Harlan's last word on such inquiries. In the face of harsh congressional criticism of the rulings and the introduction in Congress of proposals to deny the Court jurisdiction in such cases, as well as other retaliatory measures, the Court retreated. In *Barenblatt* v. *United States*, decided in 1959, a five–four majority concluded that the charge of a HUAC subcommittee investigating Communist infiltration in education had been sufficiently clear to the witness, a college professor, and also rejected First Amendment and related constitutional challenges to his contempt conviction. A companion case, *Uphaus* v. *Wyman*, held, moreover, that the New Hampshire attorney general, whose efforts had been rebuffed in *Sweezy*, had power to force the director of a summer camp to turn over its guest list as part of the attorney general's effort to ferret out subversives. Justice Frankfurter, the senior justice in the majority, assigned Harlan the *Barenblatt* opinion.[29]

In *Watkins*, the Court had been able to avoid a direct ruling on the petitioner's First Amendment claims. In *Barenblatt*, Harlan could not. The *Dennis* Court had resolved the First Amendment issues at stake there by applying the "gravity of the evil" variation on the clear and present danger test which Learned Hand had advanced in the lower court. Despite his respect for Hand, however, Harlan preferred the balancing of interests approach for resolving First Amendment issues which Justice Frankfurter had invoked in his *Dennis* concurrence and other forums, including the *Sweezy* effort Harlan had joined. Stephen Shulman, the Harlan clerk who wrote the initial draft of the Justice's *Barenblatt* opinion, recalls that:

> Harlan was very unhappy with [the] whole line of congressional committee, Communist Party membership cases. Not necessarily with where they came out. He didn't like the way the law was going in that area. . . . [He considered the "gravity of the evil" approach] intellectually dishonest because the danger was always so damn big that there wasn't much of a way that you could realistically evaluate the individual's rights. Now, I'm not sure that the balancing test was a great leap forward in any way. But for some reason the Justice felt more comfortable with it. I think maybe it was that the concept of balancing the rights of the individual versus the needs of society was something that was more susceptible to honest intellectualization . . . because the notion of whether or not destruction of the republic is a serious evil had such a built-in answer.[30]

Following extensive discussion with the Justice regarding the need to incorporate the rhetoric of balancing of interests with other elements into the opinion, Shulman wrote a draft, devoting a week of a Court recess to the task. Harlan, Shulman recalls, made few revisions in his clerk's effort. Not so Justice Frankfurter. "I do feel strongly," he wrote his colleague,

> that at the very outset of your opinion you should have a few pungent paragraphs putting the case in its setting. Before the reader gets involved in the details of balancing, and in the necessary preliminaries as to the authority of the Committee, the scope of the Resolution [authorizing the investigation], its overwhelmingly established gloss through successive actions by Congress, he ought to have been made to realize the far-reaching power of Congress which we are asked to censor and curtail, while at the same time no doubt is left that we are on the alert in the protection of truly academic interests.

Nor, in Frankfurter's view, should Harlan

> shrink from saying quite outrightly that the Communist Party is not just another political party, from the point of view of national security, even though it may also sponsor some political reforms promoted by non-Communist parties. I do not see why you should shrink from saying, however mildly, that even this Court cannot be blind to our whole national policy during the last few years, and the vast burdens that these policies have entailed upon our whole Nation. If I were doing it, I would certainly refer to L. Hand's summary of this situation in his *Dennis* opinion.[31]

Not surprisingly, perhaps, Harlan adopted most of the proposed revisions which Frankfurter attached to his letter. "I am greatly indebted to you," he wrote his colleague, "for your suggestions . . . particularly the preamble [regarding the scope of congressional authority in the national security field], which I am taking over substantially intact." The balancing of interests formula Harlan was incorporating into the opinion had also originated with Frankfurter. His senior colleague's influence over the opinion did not mean, however, that Harlan was not personally committed to the substance, if not entirely to the rhetoric, of what he would ultimately produce. He clearly embraced the balancing of interests test. And after reading Justice Clark's draft opinion in the *Uphaus* case, he wrote Clark that he was "very much bothered by the absence of any 'balancing' treatment in your opinion," adding, "I think the opinion should show clearly why the constitutional rights asserted by the petitioner are overcome by a superior state interest in the production of the two items in question." At one point, he drafted a concurrence in which he balanced the competing interests at issue in *Uphaus*. Since the guests at the camp under investigation in the case had signed the camp register on their arrival, he asserted in the draft, they had thereby "made public the association they now wish to keep private." That did "not mean," he added, "that an interest in association privacy, once invaded, is forever lost. It does mean that an interest which begins and disappears at the same moment is clearly subordinate to a compelling interest, such as self-preservation, in the State."[32]

Harlan announced the Court's *Barenblatt* opinion on June 8, 1959. After rejecting Barenblatt's due process and related claims, he turned to the petitioner's First Amendment challenge to his conviction. "Where First Amendment rights are asserted to bar governmental interrogation," the Justice observed, "resolution of the issue always involves a balancing by the courts of the competing private and public interests at stake in the particular circumstances shown." Applying that standard to Barenblatt's case required a rejection of the defendant's claim. HUAC's power, after all, rested on "the right of self-preservation, 'the ultimate value of any society.'" And "[j]ustification for [the] exercise [of that power] in turn rest[ed] on the long and widely accepted view that" the Communist Party was no "ordinary political party," that its tenets "includ[ed] the ultimate overthrow of the Government of the United States by force and violence, a view which [had] been given formal expression by the Congress." Nor were the "strict requirements" of a Smith Act prosecution "the measure of the permissible scope of a congressional investigation into 'overthrow,' for of necessity the investigatory process must proceed step by step."[33]

The four dissenters on the Court were impressed with neither the majority's constitutional standards nor their application in Barenblatt's case. In a dissent which Warren and Douglas joined (Brennan filed a separate dissent), Justice Black accused Harlan of virtually rewriting the

First Amendment to "say 'Congress shall pass no law abridging freedom of speech, press, assembly and petition, unless Congress and the Supreme Court reach the joint conclusion that on balance the interest of the Government in stifling these freedoms is greater than the interest of the people in having them exercised.'"[34] Black further accused his colleague of balancing the wrong things—an exaggerated notion of threats to national security against the First Amendment interests of a lone petitioner. If any balancing were appropriate in such cases, the Alabama jurist contended, society's important interests in the First Amendment, not merely those of a single individual, should have been weighed against the government's claims.

Nor were the dissenters alone in their criticism of the ruling. Thurman Arnold, a prominent Washington attorney and Black's longtime friend, wrote Black praising his "magnificient dissent" and offering his own interpretation of Justice Harlan's opinion.

> That decision can only be defended upon the following grounds: The Supreme Court of the United States is essential as a bulwark of civil liberties. Without it civil liberties would soon go to pot and the First Amendment would become a dead letter. Therefore, any decision which puts the Court in an insecure position puts our entire civil liberties in an insecure position. A decision today upholding the *Watkins* case would endanger the security of the Court and would be, therefore, a blow to the cause of civil liberties. The rule should be, therefore, that the First Amendment should be suspended at any time when a decision upholding it encountered substantial public opposition with influence over Congress. Where no substantial opposition like this exists there is no reason why the First Amendment should not be applied as written. That seems to me the hidden rationale of the majority.

"[T]he more I contemplate the complex pressures of modern society," added Arnold, "the more convinced I am that it is utterly futile to get indignant about anything, and the more I contemplate that distressing reality the indignanter I get."[35]

In Harlan's judgment, however, government was entitled to broad latitude when it merely sought information from the subjects of its inquiries. He adhered to this stance even when witnesses were penalized following assertion of the privilege against self-incrimination. During his first full term, the Court, in *Slochower* v. *Board of Education*, overturned the discharge of a college professor fired for refusing on Fifth Amendment grounds to answer a congressional committee's questions concerning his 1940–41 membership in the Communist Party. The majority concluded that the privilege would be a "hollow mockery" were its exercise considered the equivalent of either a confession of guilt or a conclusive presumption of perjury. But Harlan concluded in dissent that Slochower's firing was based purely on "the exercise of the privilege itself . . . quite apart from any inference of guilt." The state, he reasoned, had simply made assertion of the privilege a ground for discharge, and he could find no constitutional objection to such a provision.[36]

Slochower had asserted his Fifth Amendment privilege before a federal legislative committee. When a New York City subway conductor refused on self-incrimination grounds to answer questions of a state official regarding his Communist membership, Harlan's position prevailed. Speaking for a majority in *Lerner* v. *Casey*, a 1958 ruling, he distinguished *Slochower*'s facts from *Lerner*'s and upheld Lerner's firing over the vigorous dissents of Warren, Black, Douglas, and Brennan. The Fifth Amendment, he pointed out, was not (yet) applicable to state proceedings, and the state could reasonably have concluded that Lerner's "failure to respond to relevant inquiry engendered reasonable doubt as to his trustworthiness and reliability."[37]

Harlan would be similarly deferential to bar admission committees. During the 1956 term, a majority voted to overturn the decision of the California Committee of Bar Examiners to deny Raphael Konigsberg a law license. The committee had found, according to the Court's reading of the record, that Konigsberg had failed to prove that he was of good moral character and did not advocate the forcible overthrow of government. Speaking for the majority, Justice Black concluded that neither the petitioner's past membership in the Communist Party; his attacks on U.S. participation in the Korean War, the policy positions of major political party leaders, the influence of "big business," racial discrimination, and the Supreme Court's anti-Communist rulings; nor Konigsberg's refusal to answer questions about his political affiliations and opinions rationally supported the committee's findings.[38]

In dissent, Justice Frankfurter argued that the petitioner's claims should be dismissed on jurisdictional grounds, a view also shared by Harlan. But Harlan, joined by Clark, dissented on the merits as well. Emphasizing that the case dealt with a sensitive area of federal-state relations "into which this Court should be especially reluctant and slow to enter," Harlan charged that the majority was acting as though it were a "super state court of appeals." Before the bar committee, the Justice asserted, Konigsberg had "made [an] unequivocal disavowal of advocacy of . . . overthrow." The committee's questions about his current or past Communist membership had been intended merely to test "the reliability of [the petitioner's] disavowal, and [his] moral character." Konigsberg's refusal to answer had thus obstructed the committee's inquiry, making "it impossible to proceed to an affirmative certification that he was qualified." That recalcitrance, rather than any committee finding as to Konigsberg's moral character, had been, Harlan charged, the sole ground for the committee's decision. And the Justice thought it "altogether beyond question that a state [could] refuse admission to its Bar to an applicant . . . who refuse[d] to answer questions reasonably relevant to his qualifications and which [did] not invade a constitutionally privileged area."[39]

Nor could Harlan accept the Court's assumption of judicial authority to second-guess the factual findings of state bar examiners.

> It is not only that we, on the basis of a bare printed record and with no opportunity to hear and observe the applicant, are in no such position as the State Bar Committee was to determine whether *in fact* the applicant was sincere and has good moral character. Even were we not so disadvantaged, to make such a determination is not our function in reviewing state judgments under the Constitution. . . . [W]hat the Court has really done, I think, is simply to impose on California its own notions of public policy and judgment. For me, today's decision represents an unacceptable intrusion into a matter of state concern.[40]

Although both Frankfurter and Harlan believed that the case should have been dismissed on jurisdictional grounds, in private, Justice Frankfurter vigorously disputed his colleague's assumption that he was obligated to reach the merits of Konigsberg's claims. "[D]o you really think that when one concludes that the Court is without jurisdiction," he wrote Harlan, "one is 'obliged' to deal with the merits because the majority finds jurisdiction?"[41]

Not surprisingly, Black and others of the *Konigsberg* majority also had concerns about Harlan's dissent. In one circulated draft of his opinion, Harlan had charged that the majority's position "would at least be intelligible if the Court were to hold that the Committee's questions called for matter privileged under the [free speech and association guarantees of the] First and Fourteenth Amendments." In a note to his colleague, Black promptly responded: "I only had time to read the last paragraph of your Konigsberg dissent but note that you regret to find what we say is 'unintelligible'—what's the matter? Are our words too big or something?" (Harlan then substituted "more understandable" for "intelligible.")[42]

Black was even more concerned about Harlan's quotation of lengthy excerpts from the *Konigsberg* record—excerpts used to support the contention that the committee's refusal to grant the petitioner a law license stemmed entirely from his refusal to answer its questions. "John's dissent," Black wrote Justice Douglas in a handwritten note, "accuses me of distorting the Konigsberg record & then picks out parts he likes to prove it. He has probably printed half the record & printed this way it gives a very unfair picture. It would be very unusual but I am wondering if we would not be justified in printing all the record as an appendix. In this way interested readers could determine for themselves who, if anyone, has misread the record."[43]

Douglas responded that he "would be inclined to rest on what you have," adding: "Harlan's opinion is too long for anyone to read. And those who will attack us will do so anyway." Justice Brennan concurred with Douglas. "[M]y own reading of John's dissent," Brennan wrote Black, "was that he buttressed rather than impaired the strength of the opinion—I said so to my boys this morning & for what it's worth, they say some of their colleagues think John has 'demolished' you." But Brennan could see no advantage in having the entire record printed. And while

Justice Burton thought "it might be well to print substantial material parts" of the record, adding, "I recall that I developed my convictions in the case *only after reading the entire record* which left no doubt in my mind as to [Konigsberg's] genuineness and moral character," Black ultimately heeded the Douglas-Brennan counsel. Harlan's final dissent, on the other hand, quoted extensively from the *Konigsberg* record.[44]

There was a limit, of course, even to the latitude Harlan was willing to extend bar examiners in cases of the *Konigsberg* variety. On the same day that case was decided, the Court overturned decisions of a New Mexico board and the state's supreme court denying on "moral character" grounds a law license to a man who had been a member of a Communist group in the 1930s. In a separate concurrence, Justice Frankfurter emphasized that a "wholly arbitrary" denial of bar admission violated due process, then concluded that the New Mexico authorities' assumption that the petitioner's youthful association "in and of itself made [him] 'a person of questionable character' [was] so dogmatic . . . as to be wholly unwarranted." Harlan joined what he termed, in a letter to his colleague, Frankfurter's "splendid" opinion.[45]

When Raphael Konigsberg was again denied admission to the California bar, however, Harlan stood by his original position in the case—and on this occasion, for a five–four majority. The bar committee's second decision, Harlan asserted for the Court, was based on the petitioner's refusal to answer questions regarding his membership in the Communist Party. That refusal, held Harlan, as he had in his earlier dissent, had thwarted a full investigation into the petitioner's qualifications. And neither the Fourteenth Amendment's protection against arbitrary state action nor the expression and associational rights the amendment embodied entitled Konigsberg to refuse to answer the committee's questions. In a companion case, Harlan, speaking again for the Court, accorded the claims of George Anastaplo, an unsuccessful applicant for admission to the Illinois bar, the same fate.[46]

By this point, Justice Harlan's files contained an extensive collection of materials attacking Justice Black's First Amendment jurisprudence—a collection which included, for example, the philosopher Sidney Hook's discourse on "Justice Black's Illogic." In elaborating on the Court's repudiation of Konigsberg's freedom of expression and association claims, Harlan vigorously rejected the absolutist construction of the amendment Justice Black had long embraced, declaring:

> At the outset we reject the view that freedom of speech and association . . . as protected by the First and Fourteenth Amendments, are "absolutes," not only in the undoubted sense that where the constitutional protection exists it must prevail, but also in the sense that the scope of that protection must be gathered solely from a literal reading of the First Amendment. Throughout its history this Court has consistently recognized at least two ways in which constitutionally protected freedom of

> speech is narrower than an unlimited license to talk. On the one hand, certain forms of speech, or speech in certain contexts, has been considered outside the scope of constitutional protection. . . . On the other hand, general regulatory statutes, not intended to control the content of speech but incidentally limiting its unfettered exercise, have not been regarded as the type of law the First or Fourteenth Amendment forbade Congress or the States to pass, when they have been found justified by subordinating valid governmental interests, a prerequisite to constitutionality which has necessarily involved a weighing of the governmental interest involved.[47]

Government attempts to collect information "of prior association, as an incident of the informed exercise of a valid governmental function," Harlan added, citing *Barenblatt* and other earlier cases, had traditionally been determined by such a balancing of competing interests. And "the State's interest in having lawyers who are devoted to the law in its broadest sense, including not only its substantive provisions, but also its procedures for orderly change, [were] clearly sufficient to outweigh the minimal effect upon free association occasioned by compulsory disclosure in the circumstances here presented."[48]

Justice Black had also long agreed that governmental regulations imposing only an "indirect" or "incidental" burden on expression could be subjected to a balancing test. But he favored reserving the balancing formula largely for regulations of the time, place, and manner of expression and believed that *Konigsberg* and *Anastaplo*, like *Barenblatt*, involved "direct," and thus absolutely forbidden infringements on the First Amendment. It was hardly surprising, therefore, that the Justice, joined by Warren, Douglas, and Brennan, registered forceful dissents in both *Anastaplo* and *Konigsberg*. And again, "the Four" were hardly alone in their dismay at the stance Harlan had assumed. "As one reads [Justice Harlan's] opinions," Black's friend Benjamin V. Cohen wrote the Justice, "one is depressed to think that young men so sensitive and conscientious as Konigsberg and Anastaplo should be excluded from the practice of law by those unable to appreciate and understand the finer qualities of mind and heart." "You have immortalized Anastaplo," added another friend of Black's, "and unfortunately for the *Five*, you have immortalized them also.[49]

Justice Frankfurter naturally had a different impression of Harlan's handiwork, especially his rejection of Black's absolutism. On one draft of Harlan's *Konigsberg* opinion for the Court, Frankfurter characteristically cautioned his colleague against equating the First Amendment and the Fourteenth, observing: "I strongly feel you should not—you above all—imply that the *First* Am't governs the States. All your e.g.s except [one] are XIV Am't cases. I urge an appropriate rephrasing." With Harlan's rejection of absolutism in another draft, however, Frankfurter penned, "Hooray!"[50]

Partly because of Justice Frankfurter's retirement from the Court in

1962, the leeway accorded government inquiries in cases of the *Barenblatt* and *Konigsberg* variety was to be short-lived. In two 1961 decisions, *Wilkinson* v. *United States* and *Braden* v. *United States*, both of which Harlan joined, the justices appeared to go even beyond *Barenblatt* in deferring to Congress' investigatory power; and in *Hutcheson* v. *United States*, decided in 1962, they upheld yet another federal contempt conviction. From that time on, in the main the Court began to overturn nearly every congressional citation growing out of loyalty investigations—albeit for the most part without challenging the scope of the investigatory power or probing the legislators' motives, but relying instead on strict enforcement of the requirement that questions asked be pertinent to the subject under inquiry and otherwise satisfy due process standards.[51]

When reversals of congressional contempt convictions rested on narrow grounds, Justice Harlan sometimes joined the majority, although still cautious about broad First Amendment constructions. On one occasion, he privately scorned the efforts of a civil liberties lawyer to read meaningful restrictions on the investigatory power into his *Barenblatt* opinion and Justice Stewart's opinion for the Court in the *Wilkinson* case, charging in a letter to Stewart that "it would be most unfortunate were Joe Rauh's fat red herring, fished up from the use of . . . phrases in our respective opinions, to succeed in persuading a majority of our Court to establish the ridiculous doctrine which he is advocating." But he also cautioned his restraintist brethren against intemperate attacks on the changing direction of the Court's decisions. When Justice Clark drafted a particularly stinging dissent for a number of contempt-of-Congress cases before the Court during the 1961–62 term, Harlan attempted to moderate Clark's tone. In a letter to his colleague he observed:

> In general, while I agree with much of what you have said regarding the motivations underlying the reversal of these cases, I feel quite strongly that the "general welfare" makes it unwise to say it, and especially at this stage when we are faced with a reconsideration of *Barenblatt, Wilkinson* and *Braden* next fall. I still have hope that a majority of the Court will not be so foolish as to say that Congress has no right to investigate in this field. But if I am wrong, that will be the time for both of us to write in strong protest, which I have every intention of doing if, unfortunately, occasion for that should arise. Meanwhile, I do press on you the undesirability of unnecessarily fanning emotions which may serve to embarrass the ultimate outcome which you and I feel so strongly about.[52]

Harlan again urged restraint when Clark asserted, in a draft dissent from the Court's 1964 decision overturning the denial of passports to Communists, that, as attorney general, he had found the American passport "[i]nvariably one of the most effective weapons in international intrigue, espionage, sabotage, [and] theft of government secrets." While

Harlan would join Clark's dissent, he wrote his colleague, he considered that passage "so personal to you, I feel it would be inappropriate for me to join in it. . . . I do think it lends itself to the criticism that it is somewhat 'dated.'" The passage was deleted.[53]

Balancing and Civil Rights

The Court never directly repudiated the broad reach of the congressional investigatory power Harlan had approved in *Barenblatt*. However, when a majority in 1963 imposed important First and Fourteenth Amendment restrictions on the scope of Congress' state legislative counterparts, the Justice registered a forceful dissent. The case involved was *Gibson* v. *Florida Legislative Investigation Committee*.

In this case, the president of the Miami branch of the NAACP was sentenced to six months in prison and a $1,200 fine when he refused to divulge his group's membership list. No evidence existed to suggest that the association or its Miami chapter was subversive or Communist influenced. But the Florida committee sought the branch's membership records in an effort to determine whether fourteen persons identified as Communists were part of the 1,000-member branch.[54]

In *NAACP* v. *Alabama*, Justice Harlan and the Court rebuffed that state's efforts to acquire the names of the association's Alabama members. At a conference following oral argument in the *Gibson* case during the 1961–62 term, Chief Justice Warren had argued that "[i]f this case [*Gibson*] stands it overrules *Ala.* v. *NAACP*," adding, "even under [the] balancing theory, [the] state has shown no adequate interest." But in this instance, Harlan saw the Florida investigation as "a bona fide inquiry into Communism . . . not a plot to destroy [the] NAACP." The committee was not attempting, he argued, "to get membership lists wholesale." Instead, the lists were to be used only to refreshen the memories of committee witnesses.[55]

Initially, Harlan's position in *Gibson* prevailed over the dissents of Warren, Black, Douglas, and Brennan. In fact, the Justice had been assigned to draft the majority's opinion. *Gibson*, he wrote, bore "no resemblance" to *NAACP* v. *Alabama* and other earlier cases in which the Court had "found lacking the compelling paramount state interest necessary to avoid bringing into play [the] constitutional protection" afforded associational rights by the Fourteenth Amendment. For in those cases, "no rational relation could be perceived between the compelled broad disclosure of the Association's members and the state concerns there involved." In *Gibson*, on the other hand, the state's interest in the membership lists purely for the limited purpose of refreshening witnesses' memories was "manifest." The petitioner, after all, had already indicated that he was prepared "to testify freely" about his own recollections. He was thus "in effect asking [the Court] to hold . . . that he had a constitutional right to give only partial or inaccurate testimony." Such a position, concluded Harlan, could "not be countenanced." Particularly in view of Gibson's willingness to testify from his own memory and the NAACP's own adoption of an "anti-Communist" resolution, Harlan found it "difficult to understand how [the committee's] limited use of the membership list could well be thought to have other than a minimal, if indeed any, additional adverse effect on the associational rights of other N.A.A.C.P. members or on the organization itself."[56]

Justice Frankfurter liked the Harlan draft, writing on his copy, "I'm for this as it is." In rejecting Gibson's contention that an investigating committee must develop evidence comparable to that needed to establish probable cause for issuing a search warrant before examining a particular organization's activities or summoning a particular witness, Harlan had asserted that "[s]uch a limitation upon the investigatory function is no more constitutionally imposed on legislative inquiries than it is on executive or judicial investigations." By that passage on his copy of the opinion, Frankfurter wrote, "Won't this rouse our libertarian watchdogs?"[57]

But the Court's first vote in *Gibson* was not its last. When Justice Whittaker resigned and Frankfurter suffered a collapse which would soon prompt his retirement, the Court decided to schedule the case for reargument during the 1962 term. Following that second hearing, the justices voted five–four to reverse the petitioner's conviction, Justice Arthur Goldberg, who had replaced Frankfurter, holding for the Court that the state had shown no substantial relationship between the Miami NAACP's membership lists and any overriding and compelling governmental interest. Joined in dissent by Stewart, Clark, and Byron White, another new addition to the Court, and largely tracking his earlier draft majority opinion, Harlan scorned what he saw as the Court's basic premise—the assumption that a government's interest in investigating "Communist infiltration *of* organizations" was less significant than its need to probe "Communist activity *by* organizations." Congress had long been held to have the authority to investigate Communist infiltration of "such diverse interests as 'labor, farmer, veteran, professional, youth, and motion picture groups.'" Evidence presented in the Smith Act cases had shown, moreover, "that the sensitive area of race relations [had] long been a prime target of Communist efforts at infiltration." Harlan thus found it "strange indeed" that the majority was prepared to deny state legislatures power to probe Communist penetration of civil rights groups and was in fact "requir[ing] an investigating agency to prove in advance the very things it [was] trying to find out"—the extent of Communist infiltration into a non-Communist organization.[58]

A political realist unencumbered by legal tradition might have dismissed the Florida inquiry, like the campaign against the NAACP in Alabama, as nothing more than harassment. But Harlan was always to be among those justices most reluctant to inquire into the motives underlying an ostensibly legitimate governmental action. Moreover, while he was willing on occasion as the Court's spokesman to use "compelling interest" rhetoric as the measure of government's burden in First and Fourteenth Amendment cases, it had already become clear when *Gibson* was decided that he favored extending government broad latitude in such litigation, even where no security interests were cited. In 1960, for example, the Court voted to overturn an Arkansas law requiring teachers in the state's public schools and colleges to file an annual affidavit on which they listed every organization to which they had belonged or contributed during the previous five years. The majority concluded that the law went well beyond any legitimate Arkansas interest in the fitness and competence of its teachers and was likely to inhibit a teacher's further association with controversial, but entirely legal, groups (such as the NAACP). Justice Harlan argued in conference, however, that the case should be distinguished from Alabama's protracted efforts to obtain the association's membership lists. "[The] essence of that case," he contended, according to Justice Brennan's notes, was that "there was no state interest of any kind let alone a superior one," justifying Alabama's scheme, whereas "here [the] question is whether in [the] field of education [a] state may inquire into one's associations." He agreed that the law could be struck down as applied if the state "fires or refuses to hire for [a reason] having no rational basis to teaching fitness." But he refused to presume that an illicit purpose underlay the law and found it impossible, as he would put it in a dissent filed for the case, "to determine *a priori* the place where the line should be drawn between what would be permissible inquiry and overbroad inquiry," adding: "Certainly the Court does not point that place out. There can be little doubt that much of the associational information called for by the statute will be of little or no use whatever to the school authorities, but I do not understand how those authorities can be expected to fix in advance the terms of their inquiry so that it will yield only relevant information."[59]

He assumed essentially the same stance when the Court overturned Virginia's application to the NAACP of its laws against barratry and related forms of improper litigative activity. Laws regulating unprofessional conduct by lawyers had been on the books in Virginia since 1849, albeit rarely enforced. Prior to 1956, no attempt had been made to apply them against the NAACP, though the association had conducted its activities openly in the state for many years. But in 1956—the year after the second *Brown* decision and during a period when the NAACP was sponsoring numerous civil rights suits—Virginia's legislature had amended its antibarratry regulations to reach any agent of an organization which retained a lawyer in connection with a suit in which the organization was not a party and had no pecuniary interest. That provision seemed clearly tailored for the NAACP.

In a 1959 case, Harlan spoke for a majority in abstaining from deciding a number of constitutional challenges to Virginia's statutes. In NAACP

v. *Button* (1963), however, the Court, per Justice Brennan, held that no compelling interest justified the laws' enforcement against the NAACP, an organization which employed litigation as a form of political expression rather than for private gain.[60]

Even so, Justice Harlan, joined by justices Clark and Stewart, registered a forceful dissent. State laws that were claimed to violate the Fourteenth Amendment, he reminded his brethren of the majority, should "be judged by the same basic constitutional standards whether or not racial problems are involved." He could find no "discriminatory purpose" underlying the statute's application, since the NAACP was "merely one of a variety of organizations that may come within the scope of the long-standing prohibitions against solicitation and unauthorized practice." If the association could establish that the regulations were being discriminatorily applied, it would be entitled to relief. "But," asserted Harlan, "the present record is barren of any evidence suggesting such unequal application, and we may not presume that it will occur."[61]

When regulation of the bar did not touch upon the sensitive issue of race relations, Harlan's posture was, if anything, even more deferential to governmental authority. In 1961, a badly divided Court upheld the constitutionality of Wisconsin's version of the "integrated bar" arrangement, under which all lawyers in the state were required to become members of its bar association and pay nominal annual dues. In a lengthy, forceful concurring opinion, which Justice Frankfurter, though joining it, characterized as an "assault on a mosquito with a machine gun," Harlan rejected the constitutional challenges raised against the system and decried as "most unfortunate" the "disquieting Constitutional uncertainty" the confusing array of opinions in the case would undoubtedly create. Not surprisingly for one who believed that programs of law reform should be the product primarily of the profession and the legislative arena instead of the courts, he found a "highly significant" state interest in the legal expertise and related services the integrated bar provided. Nor was he impressed with the First Amendment challenges raised against the system. Of the complaint that lawyers forced to join the bar and pay its dues were being subjected to what amounted "to a compelled affirmation of belief" in whatever the bar supported, he argued that their position was little different from that of a taxpayer forced to have his money used "for school textbooks or instruction which he finds intellectually repulsive." Of the contention that the integrated bar stifled dissent, he responded that "[b]efore the Constitution comes into play, there should surely be some showing of a relationship between required financial support of the opposition and reduced ability to communicate." And the nominal dues required—$15 annually in Wisconsin—did not, in his judgment, constitute such evidence. Indeed, he thought only those "ready to fall prey to what are at best but alluring abstractions on rights of free speech and association" could find "any solid basis for . . . Constitutional qualms."[62]

The Intractable Obscenity Issue

While Harlan accorded both federal and state governments wide latitude in cases involving government inquiries, regulation of the bar, and other, to his mind, "indirect" burdens on expression, the Justice was to pursue a somewhat different course in the obscenity field. Early in his tenure, his clerk Paul Bator offered Harlan two suggestions for handling such cases, both drawn from Justice Jackson. In a bench memo which Bator prepared for *Roth* v. *United States*, the first case in which the justices would embrace a definition of obscenity, the clerk wrote, "If, as had been suggested (among others by Jackson), the first amendment places more severe limitations on Congress in the speech area than the 14th does on the states, then . . . *Roth* should be weighed on its own merits." However, in a bench memorandum prepared for *Butler* v. *Michigan*, Bator advised:

> One more thought. Every case of this kind must necessarily depend on the particular book involved. But it would, I think, be unwise for the Court to make its decision rest too much on its judgment as to the value of [a] particular book. For to do so, as Justice Jackson said during the argument in the *Doubleday* case, would mean that this Court would make of the Supreme Court "the High Court of Obscenity." . . . In other words, endless litigation would ensue if this Court made the constitutionality of each application of the statute depend on the "value" of the book involved. For this reason I would recommend that the statute be treated rather abstractly and not too much be made to turn on how the Court reacts, subjectively, to the merits of this particular book.[63]

In the *Butler* case, a unanimous Court struck down as unduly sweeping a law forbidding the sale to anyone of material tending to corrupt the morals of minors, Justice Frankfurter declaring of such legislation, "Surely, this is to burn the house to roast the pig." By thus focusing on the statute's overbreadth, the justices were relieved of ruling on the obscenity of the book Alfred Butler had been convicted for selling. However, in *Roth* and other later cases, Harlan was to join most of his colleagues, disregarding Justice Jackson's counsel, and embark on a controversial campaign both to establish tests for what constituted the obscene and to apply them to specific books, films, and related fare.[64]

The cosmopolitan Harlan was no prude. He probably considered most obscenity controls silly, and he derived no little amusement from the Court's attempts to grapple with the issue. At one point, he was responsible for scheduling screenings in 22-B, the basement room of the Court used by the justices and their clerks, of such cinematic masterpieces as *A Woman's Urge*, *I, A Woman*, and *I am Curious (Yellow)*. In his memorandum announcing the viewing for *Language of Love*, Harlan noted that "No tickets are required." When he missed a screening, he took delight in probing his embarrassed clerks for detailed descriptions of the film at issue. Even in later years, after his eyesight had almost completely failed him, he still dutifully attended the showings, relying on the accounts of others for what he could no longer see. "Justice Stewart would sit next to Harlan and narrate," the journalist Nina Totenberg has written. "And about once every five minutes Harlan would exclaim in his proper way: 'By George, extraordinary!'" At the same time, the Justice would not deny government all power to regulate such material.[65]

Harlan naturally did agree with Justice Jackson, however, that the First Amendment placed greater restrictions over national authority in the field than those imposed on the states by the Fourteenth Amendment. As Justice Brennan was preparing to announce his opinion for the Court in the *Roth* case and its companion, *Alberts* v. *California*, in June of 1957, Harlan informed his colleague that he, too, might "want to write something in the two . . . cases" and asked that Brennan delay handing down the Court's decisions. When the cases went down ten days later, Harlan registered an opinion dissenting in *Roth* and concurring in the majority's disposition of *Alberts*.[66] Justice Brennan's opinion for the Court limited the reach of both federal and state authority in obscenity cases to material which appealed to the "average" person's "prurient interest." Such material, he added, was "utterly lacking" in any redeeming social importance. Brennan concluded, however, that the statutes at issue in the two cases satisfied that standard and upheld the petitioners' convictions without assessing the material on which they had been based.[67]

In his separate opinion, Justice Harlan raised three fundamental objections to the Court's approach. First, he questioned the majority's apparent assumption "that 'obscenity' is a peculiar genus of 'speech and press,' which is as distinct, recognizable, and classifiable as poison ivy is among other plants." For Harlan, the "obscenity" of a particular book or film was not really a question of fact. Instead, it was an issue "of constitutional *judgment* of the most sensitive and delicate kind." And he found the Court's failure to make such judgments about the material at issue in *Roth* and *Alberts* very disturbing.[68]

Harlan was also concerned by what he thought were meaningful distinctions between the language of the statutes the majority had voted to uphold and its own definition of obscenity. The Justice's primary objection to the Court's approach was directed, however, to its equation of federal and state power over obscene expression. Not surprisingly, he favored much greater deference to the latter than the former. Under the Fourteenth Amendment due process clause, he asserted, state regulations in the field need not be "wise, or . . . scientifically substantiated," but merely "rational." And it seemed "clear" to Harlan that it was "not irrational, in our present state of knowledge," to conclude that exposure to pornography could lead to dangerous sexual conduct or have an eroding effect on moral standards. He agreed that the consequences of exposure to pornography could not be precisely assessed, since "we deal here with an area where knowledge is small, data are insufficient, and experts are divided." Given the fact that "sexual morality" was "pre-eminently a matter of state concern," however, he thought the "Court should be slow to interfere with state legislation calculated to protect that morality."[69]

Not so with federal regulations. In dissenting from the Court's decision to uphold Roth's federal conviction for using the mails to distribute obscenity, Harlan acknowledged his view that "the historical evidence does not bear out the claim that the Fourteenth Amendment 'incorporates' the First in any literal sense." But he preferred to base his support of tighter judicial controls over federal obscenity regulations on what he termed "broader and less abstract grounds." For one thing, the national government, unlike the states via their police powers, had no direct authority over sexual morality, but only such "incidental" authority as it could derive from its postal powers. To Harlan, the national reach of federal censorship posed far greater dangers than state controls. The evil of such a regime for Harlan, however, lay not only, or perhaps even primarily, in its impact on expression. "The prerogative of the States to differ on their ideas of morality will be destroyed," he maintained, "the ability of States to experiment will be stunted."[70] Given the "attenuated federal interest" in obscenity, the "very real danger of deadening uniformity which [could] result from nation-wide federal censorship," and the First Amendment's provisions, Harlan favored limiting national authority in the field to "hard-core' pornography" and concluded that the federal obscenity statute could be constitutionally construed to reach only that class of material. Since the book and circulars Roth had been convicted of sending through the mails fell short, in Harlan's judgment, of that standard, his federal conviction should have been reversed and the indictment dismissed.

The Justice found nothing in the "broad and flexible command of the Due Process Clause," on the other hand, which would forbid California to prosecute those who sold books tending, as the state's statute put it, to "deprave or corrupt" a reader. Nor, after examining the material on which Alberts's conviction had rested, could Harlan "say that its suppression would so interfere with the communication of 'ideas' in any proper sense of that term that it would offend" due process. He thus joined the majority in upholding Alberts's state conviction.[71]

Had Justice Brennan been able to maintain majority support for his *Roth-Alberts* position, Justice Harlan's regard for precedent would probably have obliged him to join that majority in later cases. But after *Roth-Alberts*, as the Justice was quick to remind his clerks in later years, the Court was to muster no majority stance on the nature of obscenity for the balance of his tenure. He could thus continue to advance his own views in the field, relatively free of precedential restraints. In 1962, in fact, he even registered an opinion announcing the Court's decision in an obscenity case.

Manual Enterprises v. *Day* involved a challenge to a Post Office Department decision barring a shipment of homosexual magazines from the mails. Writing for what he hoped might become a majority, Harlan incorporated into his opinion the *Roth* "prurient interest" standard, but also characterized obscenity as material "so offensive on [its] face as to affront current community standards of decency—a quality that we shall hereafter refer to as 'patent offensiveness' or 'indecency.'" Since *Manual* and the other magazines covered by the Post Office's order were not such "obnoxiously debasing portrayals of sex," Harlan concluded, their distribution through the mails could not be suppressed.[72]

In an early draft of the opinion, Harlan had characterized obscenity as simply "prurient" and "inherently sexually indecent." Justice Stewart found the latter standard unsatisfactory. Stewart wrote his colleagues:

> Since this [phrase] is not a mere passing remark but the purported definition of a quality which must exist (in addition to "prurient interest") in order to render something obscene, I think considerable care should be given to the words ultimately chosen. At the moment I have no bright ideas about it, but perhaps a discussion among those who basically agree with your approach might produce the right phrase.[73]

Harlan's addition of the "patent offensiveness" standard to his opinion pleased Stewart, who somehow found the phrase "a better verbalization than any I have been able to think of up to now" and considered the revised draft "an improvement upon an already very good opinion." Ultimately, however, only Stewart would join Harlan's effort. In a June 9, 1962, letter to Justice Harlan, Brennan "lean[ed] to the idea that we ought let the widespread ferment continue a bit longer in legal periodicals and courts over the soundness and meaning of the *Roth* test before we re-examine it," particularly, he added, since "the Court [was] hopelessly divided in [the] area and there appear[ed] almost no prospect of an agreement of five of us upon anything."[74]

Brennan, unlike Stewart, was also troubled by the "patent offensiveness" element, which he thought might limit federal authority to "'hard core' pornography" alone, as Harlan had urged in *Roth*. "I have trouble defining 'hard core,'" wrote Brennan, anticipating Justice Stewart's virtually identical and oft-quoted observation by some two years, "although no trouble at all recognizing it when I see it." He questioned whether Harlan's elaboration would be an improvement upon his dissent in the *Roth* case, or might instead "only result in still further confusing an already confused subject."[75]

Harlan soon responded, expressing regret that he and Brennan were "so far apart in this case." Perhaps because he realized that a majority would never accept his advocacy of separate standards for federal and state obscenity cases, Harlan did not appear unduly disappointed with his colleague's reaction. "I am not at all sure," he wrote Brennan, "that separate writing is not the best way to inch along in this elusive field."[76]

Although a restrictive censorship policy in many states could itself have led to the rigid uniformity Harlan deplored, he would remain faithful to his obscenity stance for the balance of his years on the bench. In a dissent registered for the 1966 *Fanny Hill* case, for example, he characterized "hard-core" pornography as "that prurient material that is patently offensive or whose indecency is self-demonstrating," adding: "To be sure, that rubric is not a self-executing standard, but it does describe something that most judges and others will 'know . . . when [they] see it' . . . and that leaves the smallest room for disagreement." He thought it "plain," moreover, that since *Fanny Hill* did not fall within the ambit of such pornography, it could not be barred from the federal mails. He was equally certain, however, that "rational"—and thus, in a state case, constitutionally acceptable—standards had been applied by the courts of Massachusetts in finding the book obscene. "Some will think that what I propose may encourage States to go too far in this field," he further observed. "For myself, I believe it is the part of wisdom for those of us who happen currently to possess the 'final word' to leave room for such experimentation, which indeed is the underlying genius of our federal system."[77]

Given the latitude Harlan accorded states in the obscenity field, it was not surprising that when the Court in 1959 overturned a city ordinance making bookstore proprietors criminally liable for the books they sold, even if they had no knowledge of their contents, the Justice filed a partial dissent. "The question whether *scienter* [or proof of a knowing violation of the law] is a constitutionally required element in a criminal obscenity statute," he asserted, was "intimately related to the constitutional scope of the power to bar material as obscene, for the impact of such a requirement on effective prosecution may be one thing where the scope of the power to proscribe is broad and quite another where the scope is narrow." On the "meagre" data before the Court, he declined to decide whether the absence of the scienter element in the law at issue in the case imposed an unconstitutional chilling effect on the exercise of expression by limiting booksellers to material they had personally inspected. It was clear, however, that he favored a much more lenient scienter standard, if any at all, for state cases than that imposed in federal contexts. He also had no qualms about the state trial court's refusal in the same case to admit expert testimony regarding the obscenity of the material on which the appellant's conviction was based, declaring, "I know of no case where this Court, on constitutional grounds, has required a State to sanction a particular mode of proof." And while in the *Manual Enterprises* case he endorsed application of some "national standard of decency" in federal obscenity prosecutions, he no doubt favored for state cases the local community standards approach the Court would come to embrace after his death. Nor, of course, did he object to state laws forbidding the sale to minors of erotica, even that not considered obscene in the context of sale to adults.[78]

Harlan's stance did not mean, however, that he would approve every state regulation of such material. When the Court in 1959 struck down a New York law used to suppress a film which appeared to condone adultery, he rejected the majority's conclusion that the regulation, on its face, violated freedom of expression. But joined by Frankfurter and Whittaker, he did conclude that the film at issue depicted "nothing more than a somewhat unusual, and rather pathetic, 'love triangle,' lacking in anything that could properly be termed obscene or corruptive of the public morals." Although motivated more perhaps by regard for precedent than personal inclination, he also ultimately joined the Court in imposing strict procedural standards on state and local censorship codes. When the Court upheld a film review scheme in *Times Film Corporation* v. *Chicago* (1961), he joined the majority, albeit cautioning Justice Clark, the author of the Court's opinion, against "conveying the impression that we are saying that this sort of prior restraint is good in all circumstances, that is [,] whatever may be the character of the superior state interest, vis-à-vis First Amendment rights (e.g., obscenity, national emergency, subversive activity, etc.), and no matter what the subject matter of the restraint is (e.g., movies, newspapers, etc.)" Then he added, "I suggest that it would be well to make clear in the last paragraph that we are dealing only with obscenity and movies." While such a statement might have suggested that he would be less receptive to book, as opposed to motion picture, censorship, he did dissent several years later when the justices struck down a book screening system on procedural grounds. Ultimately, though, he would join the Court in *Freedman* v. *Maryland*, the important 1965 case imposing strict procedural requirements on motion picture codes, although at first he had dissented in the case. At the bottom of a bench memo prepared for the case, he had written, "Times Film surely controls, and I would dismiss." But after a recirculation of Justice Brennan's majority draft in the case, he wrote his colleague that although he had "voted the other way at conference, I am satisfied with the way you handled the matter and so join your opinion."[79]

Toward the end of his career, Harlan would also join Justice Thurgood Marshall's opinion for the Court in *Stanley* v. *Georgia*, which overturned on freedom of expression and privacy grounds a state's criminal prosecution for the mere possession of obscenity in the privacy of the home. *Stanley* was an egregious case in which federal and state agents armed with a warrant to search for gambling equipment found instead several obscene films which they proceeded to view, then confiscate. On a bench memo, Harlan had scrawled, "I'd limit to search & seizure, and would consider a summary reversal on that score." When some of his more liberal clerks later attempted to persuade him that *Stanley* provided a logical rationale for invalidating most obscenity controls, he proved unmovable. "We argued until we were blue in the face," one clerk has recalled. But the Justice insisted that *Stanley* "had nothing to do with obscenity. He was outraged at the search of a man's bedroom." Whatever his personal feelings, Harlan did join the Court's opinion in *Stanley* as well as its decision, though persuading Justice Marshall to delete language which seemed to suggest "a correlation between the right to distribute and the right to receive, [which] might carry implications of dilution with respect to our other obscenity cases (which are concerned solely with the right to sell)."[80]

Harlan later joined several opinions which narrowly limited *Stanley* to its facts—decisions prompting Justice Black to observe wryly, during their last term together on the bench, that "perhaps in the future" *Stanley* would "be recognized as good law only when a man writes salicious books in his attic, prints them in his basement, and reads them in his living room." In 1970, Harlan voted to uphold a federal law providing that persons receiving material which they regarded as obscene through the mail could demand removal of their names from the sender's mailing list. When Chief Justice Warren circulated a draft opinion in that case, however, Harlan responded that [y]our statement . . . to the effect that parents have an 'absolute' right to control the reading of their children in the home makes me a little gunshy," then added, "I have a distaste for absolutes and I can think of situations where a state might be able to enter the home in this realm."[81] At the end of his judicial career as near the beginning, then, he continued to draw distinctions between federal and state authority in the obscenity field, permitting the latter decidedly greater discretion than the former.

Indeed, when a majority in 1966 read a "pandering" element into the federal obscenity law, holding that distributors who pandered erotica could be convicted under the statute even in the absence of clear proof their products were obscene, he registered one of his most forceful dissents. Calling the Court's gloss on a 101-year-old statute "an astonishing piece of judicial improvisation," he complained that the majority's pandering rhetoric was "a mere euphemism for allowing punishment of a person who mails otherwise constitutionally protected material just because a jury or a judge might not find him or his business agreeable." He had "little" doubt that a state could enact such a statute; under its postal or commerce powers, Congress might "possibly" even have that authority. He was appalled, however, that the Court in effect had written "a new statute, but without the sharply focused definitions and standards necessary in such a sensitive area."[82]

Harlan would remain convinced, as he wrote a friend just months before his death, that the "obscenity problem [was] almost intractable, and that its ultimate solution must be found in a renaissance of societal values." He was equally certain, however, that given the difficulty of defining what many considered indefinable, his approach was the best means for striking an acceptable balance between authority and freedom in a complex field.

The Justice's friends wrote him frequently of their concerns about the dangers of pornography and their misgivings about the Court's approach to the issue. Based on the statements of FBI director "J. Edgar Hoover down to the local fellows," one New York cleric stated he was convinced of "an undoubted causal connection between this kind of literature and the unprecedentedly rapid" rise in sexual crimes. Harvard law professor Barton Leach suggested to his friend that the justices appoint masters to resolve particular cases "[u]nless you and your eight brethren are going to spend your time reading Fanny Hill, Naked Lunch, and a flock of these alleged 'scientific' manuals on sexual techniques 'in marriage.'" And when Harlan, in his *Manual Enterprises* opinion, described obscenity as offensive to "current community standards of decency," Dean Joseph O'Meara of the Notre Dame law school rejoined that the Justice's standard was "not at all clear to me. Indeed, I have the greatest skepticism as regards the possibility of identifying community standards or mores, that is, the public morality."[83] In his reply to Dean O'Meara, Harlan agreed that the "'community standards' test [was] of course far from ideal," but asserted that he had

> been unable to discover in any of the literature in this difficult field a more satisfactory yardstick for guiding the courts in their inescapable duty . . . of deciding the constitutionality . . . of the suppression of challenged material. The concept is not a novel one in our jurisprudence, as witness, for example, the prudent or average man test in the judging of conduct in negligence cases.

He also predicted that "much" of the difficulty the "community standards" test posed for O'Meara "would disappear were the Court ultimately to go, at least in federal cases . . . to a 'hard core pornography' test for the judging of obscenity."[84]

Although Harlan never made his position entirely explicit, it seems clear that while he accepted the responsibility of the courts to draw lines in the obscenity field, just as they were obliged to in other constitutional areas, he was also aware, as he noted in one letter, that such cases posed problems which were "among the most difficult, elusive, and delicate that the courts have to face."[85] He thus apparently saw his approach to the issue as not only consistent with the different scope he accorded the First and Fourteenth amendments, but also as a workable means by which the Court could partially extricate itself and inferior tribunals from a continuing constitutional quagmire. Under his hard-core pornography standard, federal obscenity controls would be presumed invalid and few, if any, prosecutions upheld. Given the broad leeway accorded states under his construction of the Fourteenth Amendment due process guarantee on the other hand, virtually no state obscenity convictions would be overturned. In neither federal nor state cases under Harlan's formula, therefore, would the outcome of individual disputes have turned on the sorts of subtle determinations the inherently vague obscenity formulae made it exceedingly difficult to make or predict. Such thinking would have been more characteristic of Justice Black's campaigns to limit the reach of judicial discretion than of Harlan's usual preference for case-by-case line-drawing. But it appears to have been at least partially the basis for his obscenity stance.

Whatever the thinking underlying his position, Harlan was to adhere to it until the end. At the conclusion of his last term on the bench, for example, he wrote a friend that "the preservation and assertion of state authority [held] the best promise for effective legal measures" in the obscenity area.[86]

Libel and Free Speech

Justice Harlan's preference for differential standards in federal and state obscenity cases was based in part, it will be recalled, on his belief that the national government's interest in such controls was attenuated at best, while the states enjoyed undoubted power over "sexual morality." In dealing with the law of libel, the Justice would ultimately rest his position on somewhat the same sort of balancing formula, albeit one perhaps less deferential to authority than he ordinarily embraced.

Speaking for a plurality in *Barr* v. *Matteo*, a 1959 ruling, Harlan had little difficulty extending absolute immunity from libel suits to all federal administrative officials for statements made within the "outer limits" of their duties, even though no constitutional provision specifically granted such a privilege. "[O]fficials of government," the Justice maintained, "should be free to exercise their duties unembarrassed by the fear of damage suits . . . which would consume time and energies which would otherwise be devoted to governmental service and the threat of which might appreciably inhibit the fearless, vigorous, and effective administration of policies of government." For good measure, he quoted at length from an opinion of Judge Learned Hand, which, he observed, "admirably expressed" the same sentiment.[87]

Although neither Harlan nor a majority of his colleagues was willing to extend the same privilege to journalists or other private citizens, in *New York Times* v. *Sullivan* (1964), he would join the Court in imposing a significant restriction on the power of government to penalize libelous comments about public officials.[88] And while at one point he threatened to register a partial dissent from Justice Brennan's opinion for the majority, his differences with his colleague were surprisingly minor, particularly in view of the latitude he normally accorded state tribunals.

New York Times v. *Sullivan* overturned the half-million-dollar judgment an Alabama jury had awarded Montgomery's commissioner of public safety for factual errors printed in a full-page advertisement which had criticized police handling of race relations in the "Cradle of the Confederacy." Given the nation's long tradition of robust, uninhibited debate on matters of public interest, as Justice Brennan concluded for the Court, such comment could be penalized under state libel laws only if made with "actual malice," that is, only if knowingly or recklessly false. Alabama's libel law required such proof for an award of punitive, but not general, damages; and since the jury's verdict had not differentiated between the two, the Court found it impossible to know whether the jury had found malice. The jury's judgment was thus reversed and the case remanded to the Alabama courts.

But Brennan did not stop there. Concerned that Sullivan might be given a new day in the state courts, he concluded for the brethren that the evidence presented by Sullivan "could [not] constitutionally support a judgment for respondent" under the actual malice test.[89]

Harlan "agree[d] entirely" with portions of Brennan's opinion announcing the "knowing or reckless falsehood" rule. He asked only that his colleague include a passage indicating that the justices had not yet been called upon "to delineate at this stage how far down the line of public officials this new constitutional doctrine would reach," adding, "I would not want to foreclose a cop, a clerk, or some other minor public official from ordinary libel suits without a great deal more thought."[90]

Even though Harlan questioned whether the Court should reverse and remand the case for further proceedings, he did conclude with the majority that the evidence was insufficient to justify a verdict for Sullivan. Initially—and uncharacteristically—he suggested via a proposed revision of Brennan's opinion that the Court enter an order completely terminating the litigation and thus foreclosing a further trial. But Justice Black was particularly unimpressed with that suggestion, and wrote Brennan: "I do not see how John could possibly adhere to that position on more mature reflection. I can think of few things that would more violently clash with his ideas of 'federalism.' . . . Construing the statute [Harlan proposed to invoke] as authorizing our Court to *overrule* state laws or to a right to new trial would undoubtedly raise constitutional questions, some of which as I recall were discussed in the famous *cause célèbre* Cohens v. Virginia."[91]

When it was discovered that the provision on which Harlan based his proposal had never before been applied to a state court, and after Brennan had shared with the Justice concerns about the statute's constitutionality "as applied to deny a state the right to apply its law governing new trials," Harlan withdrew his original suggestion. He next proposed, however, that since the *New York Times* jury's verdict could be, and was being, reversed without the Court's reviewing the evidence, the Court should make no statement at all regarding the sufficiency of the evidence under the actual malice standard. Brennan agreed to omit "everything which suggests that the respondent is not entitled to a new trial," but insisted on two grounds that his evaluation of the evidence be retained. First, he contended, such passages would alert the bar "that we are going to examine evidence in this area as we have in others." Second, the case could serve as an illustration of what evidence would be inadequate to support a libel judgment under the *New York Times* standard.[92]

Faced with Brennan's refusal to bend, Harlan wrote his colleague that he would file a short memorandum joining the Court's opinion but dissociating himself from its discussion of the evidence. The memorandum would go through three drafts. Consistent with the Justice's deep concern that the Court observe traditional rules of adjudication even in race-related cases, Harlan charged in the second draft that "[t]he Court's anticipatory assessment of the evidence is an unprecedented step which in my opinion does disservice in the long run to the great national interests which underlie this litigation." And while he softened "great national interests" to "basic constitutional concerns" in his final draft, he continued to insist that it was not "appropriate for the Court to examine the constitutional sufficiency of the evidence . . . since the judgments stand already reversed on other grounds."[93]

Although Justice Black was to file a separate concurrence favoring an absolute ban on libel suits, he would write Brennan "that despite my position & what I write I think you are doing a wonderful job in the Times case and however it finally comes out it is bound to be a very long step towards preserving the right to communicate ideas." Black expressed hope that Justice Harlan could be dissuaded from filing his memorandum. In his view, his colleague's statement would simply

> add to the idea which will likely be advanced that no one can actually tell what is decided. The addition in my judgment will have little if any effect on the course these litigants will follow hereafter. Besides, while I think your writing on the lack of evidence is fully justifiable, I would feel uneasy in doing so *at this time*. Unless the parties decide it would be judicially better to abandon their case, they are sure to keep on pursuing it and I think a later holding on the evidence question would be more easily understood.[94]

Under the pressure of such sentiment, Brennan finally came up with language acceptable to Harlan and other justices as well. On the recommendation of Justice Clark, who had also briefly threatened defection, Brennan revised the opening sentence of the section of the opinion to which Harlan had objected to read: "Since the respondent may seek a new trial, we deem that considerations of effective judicial administration require us to review the evidence in the present record to determine whether it could constitutionally support a judgment for respondent." Placing the discussion of the evidence in that light apparently satisfied Harlan. On Sunday evening, March 8, 1964, Harlan telephoned Brennan to report that he was withdrawing his memorandum. The next morning, just before Brennan's effort was announced as the Court's opinion, Harlan circulated a letter to the brethren informing them that he was "unreservedly joining the majority opinion."[95]

Early in the 1964–65 term, Harlan also concurred with Brennan in extending the *New York Times* rule to criminal libel contexts. *Garrison v. Louisiana* had first been decided the previous term. When Brennan produced a draft opinion for the Court which appeared to bar all such criminal prosecutions, however, Harlan had joined a dissent, which Justice Clark circulated. He had also written Clark a letter attacking Justice Byron White's conclusion in a separate opinion, also being circulated in the case, that while states could criminally punish "knowing or reckless falsehoods," they could not sanction comment motivated by "hatred, ill will or a wanton desire to injure," as "actual malice" was defined in Louisiana law. White's position, Harlan complained,

> would hold invalid a more rigorous standard than one which it believes valid. Negligent misconduct, even when it amounts to recklessness, is not ordinarily thought to be a greater wrong and more deserving of punishment than the deliberate infliction of harm; negligence has traditionally been regarded as a fault which, if carried to the extreme of recklessness, might in some cases *rise to* and be taken as *the equivalent* of actual malice. I cannot believe that the Constitution prevents a State from protecting its citizens against harm deliberately inflicted but not from harm occasioned by negligence. It seems obvious to me that our decision in the *Times* case should not be so construed.[96]

Harlan encouraged Clark to incorporate such concerns into his dissent and added that if White's effort, instead of Brennan's, became the Court's opinion, he planned to write a separate opinion embodying his own thinking.[97] But when Brennan, following re-argument of the *Garrison* case at the beginning of the 1964 term, held for the Court that criminal libel convictions must satisfy the knowing or reckless falsehood rule, Harlan joined his colleague's opinion without writing separately.

The Justice refused, on the other hand, to extend the *New York Times* rule beyond public officials to "public figures." Speaking for a plurality in two 1967 cases, he contended that a prominent citizen who was "not a public official . . . may recover damages for a defamatory falsehood . . . on a showing of highly unreasonable conduct constituting an extreme departure from the standards of investigation and reporting ordinarily adhered to by responsible publishers." The particular considerations or interests justifying a stricter standard of evidence from defamed public officials, he explained, did not apply to comment regarding public figures.

> These actions cannot be analogized to prosecutions for seditious libel [which had long been disfavored]. Neither plaintiff [a football coach and a retired general] has any position in government which would permit a recovery by him to be viewed as a vindication of governmental policy.

> Neither was entitled to a special privilege protecting his utterances against accountability in libel [as most government officials were].[98]

Public figures, he maintained, were thus deserving of greater protection from defamation than their official counterparts.

The Justice favored extending even greater protection to private citizens, including those involved in events of public interest. During his last term, when a plurality of justices extended the actual malice standard to such cases, Harlan dissented, charging that only "an undiscriminating assessment" of the First and Fourteenth Amendment values which underlay the *New York Times* decision could have led to its extension "in full force to all purely private libels." Citing particularly the relative ease with which public persons can gain "access to channels of communication sufficient to rebut falsehoods," he asserted that "countervailing state interests" justifying libel controls were considerably greater in cases involving private citizens than in those in which public persons were defamed. He concluded, therefore, anticipating by several years the position a Supreme Court majority would eventually assume, that "the States should be free to define for themselves the applicable standard of care" required in such cases, "so long as they [did] not impose liability without fault." Evidence of actual harm to the target of a defamatory publication or broadcast should be established, and the damages awarded should be related to the harm inflicted. Otherwise, the Constitution, in his judgment, imposed no substantive limitations on libel suits initiated by private citizens, even those involved in events of public interest.[99]

In the libel area as in other First and Fourteenth Amendment fields, then, Harlan was reluctant to paint with an unduly broad brush. He preferred instead to tailor constitutional standards to the competing interests evident in each category and subcategory of case. And as he moved from public officials, to public figures, to private citizens, he found the weight of "countervailing state interests" justifying such controls increasingly compelling.

The Religion Clauses

Justice Harlan's construction of the Constitution's religion clauses would also generally reflect the discerning, cautious, balancing approach which characterized other elements of his First Amendment jurisprudence. His grandfather, the first Justice Harlan, had witnessed firsthand the political divisiveness which church-state entanglements can provoke. When the first Harlan's intimate friend Alphonso Taft, father of the president and chief justice, had sought the Republican nomination for the Ohio governorship, charges that he was a Unitarian who denied the divinity of Christ fatally crippled his candidacy. Since Rutherford B. Hayes, the candidate nominated in Taft's place, had gone on to become governor and then president on the same sort of platform Taft had embraced, Harlan I had always thought the injection of religious bigotry into the Ohio campaign had cost his friend the presidency.[100]

Like his grandfather, Harlan II also feared the political friction a mixture of the secular and religious can generate. In an opinion registered the year before his death, he observed that "religious groups inevitably represent certain points of view and not infrequently assert them in the political arena, as evidenced by the continuing debates respecting birth control and abortion." He added, "Yet history cautions that political fragmentation on sectarian lines must be guarded against." It was thus not surprising that he joined the Court's decisions in *Engel* v. *Vitale* and *Abington* v. *Schempp*, overturning state-directed prayer and Bible-reading in the public schools, or that he agreed that an Arkansas law forbidding the teaching of evolution violated the establishment clause, voted to invalidate the more extreme forms of government aid to parochial schools, and agreed to uphold federal construction grants to church-related colleges only because Chief Justice Burger's draft opinion for the Court in the case at issue finally convinced him that there were "tenable distinctions" constitutionally separating colleges from their primary and secondary school counterparts. Nor was it extraordinary for him to join opinions stipulating that laws affecting religious institutions should have a secular purpose and a primary effect neither advancing nor harming religion, with all efforts made at avoiding excessive church-state entanglements. He also agreed that governmental interferences with religious liberty be invalidated unless found necessary to promote a legitimate and compelling government interest.[101]

Harlan defended the Court's most controversial religious rulings from the attacks of his friends. Following the *Engel* decision, a Princeton classmate had written the Justice that he was "shocked, ashamed and terrified" by the decision and added, "I thank God me and mine are Catholics and my kids are not only permitted, but are urged to pray." Later, the same longtime associate lamented that "[r]eligious intolerance has at long last made a full circle, from the horrible intolerance of all religions in the past, to the blessed tolerance that has existed for at least two centuries, to what we finally have today, the intolerance of the anti-Christ to those of us who believe." Others wrote to the same effect. Even the Justice's old friend Alexander Smith expressed concern that the decision seemed to indicate to the public "that the Court ha[d] repudiated the faith of our Fathers." Smith wondered, too, how the brethren could correct the impression that they were "non-believers in the basic Christian fundamentals," albeit assuring Harlan of his confidence that the Justice was "a man of deep Christian conviction."[102]

In his reply to Smith, as to others, Harlan politely but firmly denied that the prayer and Bible-reading opinions could "fairly be read as indicating an antireligious bias on the part of the Court," adding, "Had I thought that such was the case I can assure you that I never would have joined." He also assured his friend "from my own knowledge that none of the Justices is an irreligious person." He was certain that many of the Court's staunchest critics had never read the opinions—copies of which regularly accompanied his replies to complaints about them—and that they would "be the first to object to some other denomination's prayers being used in the public schools to which they send their children." And he raised a question as well. "Can it not be said that the very fact that these cases have stirred up so much controversy underscores the wisdom of a constitutional tenet that requires government to remain strictly neutral in religious matters?"[103]

As usual, though, Harlan's position was more complicated than such statements or his votes might suggest. He filed no opinion in *Engel* or *Schempp*. When, however, Justice Stewart, the lone dissenter in those cases, circulated a memorandum which would become his *Schempp* dissent, Harlan made brief but revealing notations on the Stewart draft. By his colleague's assertion that the Court erred if it did not recognize that religion and government "must necessarily interact in countless ways," Harlan wrote, "Yes." The Justice had "trouble," however, with Stewart's assertion that the prayer and Bible-reading cases raised "a substantial free exercise claim on the part of those who affirmatively desire to have their children's school day open with the reading of passages from the Bible." He placed a question mark by Stewart's assumption that the case "of course" posed no danger of official government support for religion. And by his colleague's conclusion that the ultimate question was whether children were coerced to participate, Harlan wrote, "I think this is the crucial issue, and that it must be resolved against the State." The Justice also joined a short concurring opinion filed for *Schempp* by Justice Goldberg, which embodied the essence of certain of Harlan's marginal notations on the Stewart memorandum and emphasized that "delineation of the constitutionally permissible relationship between religion and government is a most difficult and sensitive task, calling for the careful exercise of both judicial and public judgment and restraint."[104]

Harlan's stance in later establishment and free exercise of religion cases reflected the concerns Goldberg's *Schempp* concurrence, which he would frequently quote over the years, had embraced. He voted with the Court to uphold Sunday closing laws, but joined Felix Frankfurter's lengthy concurrence rather than Chief Justice Warren's majority opinion, perhaps because the Frankfurter effort arguably approached the issues raised somewhat more cautiously than the Warren opinion had. Moreover, when a majority found the Sunday closing rulings inapplicable to a later case and overturned South Carolina's denial of unemployment benefits to a Seventh Day Adventist unable to find a job not requiring Saturday work, he dissented. The majority, speaking through Justice Brennan, found no compelling interest, such as that in assuring a uniform day of rest used to uphold Sunday closing legislation, sufficient to justify South Carolina's decision. Harlan charged in dissent, however, that the state's policy of denying compensation to persons available for work was purely secular and that requiring the state to "carve out an exception to its general rule of eligibility" for religious reasons conflicted with the very neutrality the establishment clause had long been held to require. "Those situations in which the Constitution may require special treatment on account of religion," he asserted, "are, in my view, few and far between, and this view is amply supported by the course of constitutional litigation in this area."[105]

When the Court held that civil courts could not resolve essentially ecclesiastical questions arising from church disputes, he filed a brief concurrence, emphasizing what conclusions the justices were *not* making.

> I do not . . . read the Court's opinion . . . to hold that the Fourteenth Amendment forbids civilian courts from enforcing a deed or will which expressly and clearly lays down conditions limiting a religious organization's use of the property which is granted. If, for example, the donor expressly gives his church some money on the condition that the church never ordain a woman as a minister or elder . . . or never amend certain specified articles of the Confession of Faith, he is entitled to his money back if the condition is not fullfilled. In such a case, the church should not be permitted to keep the property simply because church authorities have determined that the doctrinal innovation is justified by the faith's basic principals.[106]

Toward the end of his career, Harlan also elaborated upon the sort of analysis he believed appropriate for determining whether laws affecting religious institutions met the requirement of neutrality. *Walz* v. *Tax Commission* upheld the extension of tax exemptions to property used solely for religious worship under a statute granting such privileges to religious, educational, and charitable organizations. In a separate opinion in the case, Harlan reasoned that judicial enforcement of the requirement that government be neutral in its contacts with religion required "an equal protection mode of analysis," explaining: "In any particular case the critical question is whether the circumference of legislation encircles a class so broad that it can be fairly concluded that religious institutions would be thought to fall within the natural perimeter" rather than being given the sort of special preference by government which the establishment clause prohibited. The statute at issue in *Walz* granted tax exemptions not only to religious property but to all institutions which furthered "moral and intellectual diversity." Harlan thus thought it consistent with the neutrality doctrine to grant exemptions to religious organizations promoting such goals as well as their secular counterparts. "As long as the breadth of exemption includes groups that pursue cultural, moral, or spiritual improvement in multifarious secular ways, including, I would suppose, groups whose avowed tenets may be antitheological, atheistic, or agnostic, I can see no lack of neutrality in extending the benefit of the exemption to organized religious groups."[107]

Harlan would always be aware that, as Justice Goldberg had asserted in *Schempp*, the resolution of religious liberty and establishment issues "presents no easy course." In fact, of all constitutional fields he would confront during his years on the bench, a protracted dispute mixing establishment and free exercise issues may have caused him the greatest difficulty.

In the 1960s and 1970s, conflict over the Vietnam war would bring numerous cases to the Court involving attacks on Congress' policy regarding conscientious objectors. Federal law conferred draft exceptions only on those pacifists who objected to war on grounds of "religious training and belief," specifically excluding those whose qualms flowed from "essentially political, sociological, or philosophical views or a merely personal moral code." During the 1964 term, the Court decided *United States* v. *Seeger* and other cases involving draftees who were neither members of orthodox pacifist religions nor willing to declare a belief in a supreme being—and thus had been denied conscientious objector (C.O.) status. In conference, Harlan had agreed with Justice Black that the government could force every one to fight, regardless of scruples. But when Congress granted exemptions from combat, added Harlan, it could not "pick and choose between religious beliefs," awarding C.O. status only to theistic pacifists.[108]

Later, however, Harlan wrote Justice Clark, who had been assigned to draft an opinion in the cases, that he was "presently of the view, contrary to the one I had at the Conference, that the 'Supreme Being' test [in the C.O. statute was] constitutional." Then, within a week of his letter to Clark, he drafted a dissenting opinion upholding the power of Congress to confer C.O. status only on theistic objectors and emphasizing the "pervasiveness" of congressional military power.[109]

The Justice agreed that statutes restricting First Amendment freedoms should be scrutinized more closely than other regulations. But he found little interference with Seeger's religious liberty flowing from Congress' policy that an admittedly constitutional flat ban on C.O. exemptions would not also inflict. There was slight danger, he thought, that the granting of objector status to theistic pacifists would prompt them to forego their own beliefs. Nor did he think the policy was any more likely to cause Seeger to develop feelings of separatism than those generated by government recognition of religious holidays, religious inscriptions on coins and public buildings, and religious references in the pledge of allegiance and other ritualistic recitations. Such "elements of establishment," he concluded, were "very far removed from what was realistically at the heart of the Establishment Clause." Viewed in isolation, the impact of the C.O. policy on Seeger "might be something more than a mere shadow," he concluded, "but when weighed against the tremendous congressional and national interest in accommodating religious free exercise and national defense, they [were] not . . . sufficient to render the . . . provision unconstitutional."

Despite its forceful language, Harlan ultimately withdrew his Seeger dissent and joined Justice Clark in an opinion of the Court construing the C.O. statute so broadly that Seeger and company fell within its scope, thereby relieving the justices from resolving the constitutional question Harlan had grappled with in his unfiled draft. As the discussion which follows indicates, however, the Justice was never comfortable with his decision to join Clark—or his conclusion that the C.O. statute was constitutional.

In Welsh v. *United States* (1970), a plurality, speaking through Justice Black, construed the C.O. law so sweepingly that it could be held to encompass even a draftee who had himself insisted that his opposition to war was not based on the religious training and belief the statute's language required. Justice Harlan cast the decisive vote to grant Welsh C.O. status. Unlike the plurality, however, Harlan also reached the constitutional issue which he believed the case "squarely present[ed]: whether [Section] 6(j) [the C.O. regulation] in limiting this draft exemption to those opposed to war in general because of theistic beliefs runs afoul of the religion clauses of the First Amendment." He had joined Seeger, he acknowledged, "only with the gravest misgivings as to whether it was a legitimate exercise in statutory construction." And he was now convinced that he had made a "mistake." Calling the plurality's sweeping construction of the law "a remarkable feat of judicial surgery . . . a lobotomy [which had] completely transformed the statute by reading out of it any distinction between religiously acquired beliefs and those deriving from 'essentially political, sociological, or philosophical views, or a merely personal moral code,' " he concluded, as he had in his unfiled Seeger dissent, that the law conferred C.O. status only on those whose pacifism flowed from their religious training and belief, in the more traditional sense of those words.

> Unless we are to assume an Alice-in-Wonderland world where words have no meaning, I think it is fair to say that Congress' choice of language cannot fail to convey to the discerning reader the very policy choice that the prevailing opinion today completely obliterates: that between conventional religions that usually have an organized and formal structure and dogma and a cohesive group identity, even when nontheistic, and cults that represent schools of thought and in the usual case are without formal structure or are, at most, loose and informal associations of individuals who share common ethical, moral, or intellectual views.[110]

Objectors of Welsh's persuasion, in Harlan's judgment, clearly fell within the latter category and were excluded from the C.O. statute's coverage.

Unable to avoid any longer a public analysis of the law's constitutionality, the Justice next turned to that issue. In his unfiled Seeger dissent, he had reasoned that Congress possessed authority to grant draft exemptions to religious objectors while denying them to other pacifists. Now, however, he reversed ground. Employing the essentially equal protection formula he had embraced the previous month in the *Walz* tax exemption case, he concluded that the C.O. statute "not only accords a preference to the 'religious' but also disadvantages adherents of religions that do not worship a Supreme Being," adding: "[This] constitutional infirmity cannot be cured, moreover, even by an impermissible construction that eliminates the theistic requirement and simply draws the line between religious and nonreligious. This in my view offends the Establishment Clause and is that kind of classification that this Court has condemned."[111] Harlan did not believe, however, that Welsh should be denied C.O. status. Since the statute had a broad severability provision stipulating continued enforcement of those sections not struck down in the courts, he favored simply extending the law's reach to those who had been unconstitutionally excluded in the past and whose commitment to pacifism was held with the "same intensity" that religious objectors display in clinging to theirs. Welsh's beliefs, he felt, satisfied that requirement.

Harlan realized that his stance necessarily allied his vote with those whose construction of the statute he had so vigorously scorned. He contended, however, that the policy's long history provided a "compelling reason" for "building upon" rather than eliminating a constitutionally offensive law. In the C.O. field as in other First Amendment areas, the Justice's stance reflected his traditional deference to authority, particularly in a field permeated with interests of national security.

7

The Second Reconstruction

Justice Harlan's secretary Ethel McCall and black messenger Paul Burke were the two permanent members of the Justice's staff. Mrs. McCall's tenure with Harlan apparently reached back to his service as chief counsel to the New York crime commission. Burke had joined him in 1957. "I would assume," he recently remarked, "that if he was still living, I would still be there in a wheelchair with him."[1]

The Justice's clerks recall Paul Burke with fondness and respect. They remember Mrs. McCall, however, as a "tyrant" who attempted to deny them access to the lavatory in the Justice's chambers and otherwise made life difficult. And while the recollections of most reflect the good-humored bemusement Marine recruits may have for their boot-camp drill instructors twenty to thirty years after the experience, others are less charitable. "Mrs. McCall," Robert Mnookin, one of Harlan's later clerks, has said, "was a terror. . . . She was controlling, bossy, actually did rather little work, was very protective of the Justice, and loved to lord it over the clerks."[2]

Mnookin could tolerate Mrs. McCall's treatment of him and the other clerks easily enough. "She lived at the Watergate. John Mitchell lived there, all these Nixon muckamucks. And we clerks used to tease her about that. We'd say, 'Mrs. McCall, come the revolution, Watergate's going to be the first place to go.' One day I came in and she says to me, 'Well, I had to tell them, Bob.' And I said, 'Tell who what?' And she replied, 'Well, you know, there've been bomb threats and the FBI came around door-to-door asking residents whether we had heard anything. And I had to tell them about our conversation.' To this day," Mnookin recalls with a laugh, "I don't know whether she did or not."[3]

But Mnookin was offended by Mrs. McCall's treatment of the Justice's black messenger. "She loved to lord it over Paul . . . more than the clerks. . . . She was very high-handed and abrupt, did not treat him with great respect, bossed him around mercilessly." Mnookin was perhaps even more disappointed that the Justice, for whom he had enormous respect and affection, "in no sense ever protected Paul. I thought Mrs. McCall was often quite cruel, and I think the Justice knew it and just kind of accepted it," perhaps because he "had an office routine that was working."[4]

At the time of Harlan's appointment, the messenger service at the Court still resembled in many ways the plantation system of the Old South. The positions often went to succeeding generations in the same families. Paul Burke's father, for example, had been a messenger for Chief Justice William Howard Taft. The father of Emerson Parker, Harlan's first messenger, whose death in August of 1957 had led to Burke's appointment, was a messenger for nearly forty years, first for Justice James McReynolds, and later for Justice Jackson. Parker himself had first become a messenger in 1938. Messengers were expected to perform a variety of personal chores going well beyond their official functions, and Burke was no exception. Early in his tenure as justice, Harlan had driven himself to work each day. "But we worked exceptionally long hours," Burke recalls, "and I would often have to drive him home. I got home the best way I could." When the Justice's eyesight began to fail him in the 1960s, his messenger took a bus to Harlan's Georgetown home each morning, then drove the Justice to and from his chambers. Still later, he simply kept Harlan's car at his own home, maintaining it, "as though it was my own." When the Harlans went out in the evening, to the Hugo Blacks' Alexandria home for dinner, for example, Burke typically was their driver. When the couple took a plane or train to their Connecticut home for the Court's summer recess, Burke drove their luggage up in the Justice's car.[5]

Particularly at the time of the 1954 *Brown* decision, critics frequently noted what they considered to be embarrassing conflicts between the Court's eloquent defense of racial equality and the treatment accorded its black messengers. Paul Burke's memories of his justice, however, have remained entirely favorable. "Through the years," he has said, "I was a little upset about some of the things I was required to do. . . . I practically did all the office work. I kept the Justice's docket book up to date. There were occasions before we had a secretarial pool when Mrs. McCall would be at lunch and I'd have to take dictation for memos the Justice wanted to get out to the other judges. Because I didn't take shorthand, he was very patient. But I was basically doing clerical work and almost an assistant secretary's work, which I felt I wasn't compensated for." He considered Harlan, however, "a true gentleman" with whom he had a "wonderful relationship from the very beginning." And his memories of Mrs. McCall, while mixed, are charitable as well. "We had our differences," he has recalled. "But I can't say that I was mistreated. She would jump on me just like she would anyone else. But one thing about her which I admired very much—she was not the type to carry a grudge. After I once was able to realize that Mrs. McCall was Mrs. McCall, she and I got along wonderfully, or fairly well." Nor would Burke attribute

Mrs. McCall's treatment of him to racial bias. And the Justice, in his view, "didn't have a racial bone in his body. He was very respectful. The policy at that time [meant] naturally that he would always call me by my first name. But from the first time he met my wife, it was always 'Mrs. Burke.' . . . He treated me, my wife, and my family as members of the family or as any other person. He treated us as equals."[6]

Whatever one may think of Justice Harlan's personal racial views or of his messenger's treatment, he had joined *Brown* II (1955) and written the major opinion for *NAACP* v. *Alabama*. In fact, according to Chief Justice Warren's clerk Gerald Gunther, Harlan contributed the most forceful sentence in *Brown* II—the Court's assertion that "it should go without saying that the vitality of these constitutional principles cannot be allowed to yield simply because of disagreement with them." In the succeeding years, moreover, he was to concur in most of the Court's decisions in race-related cases. But his regard for state authority, precedent, and traditional norms of judicial behavior, as well as his reluctance to probe the motives of state and local officials, would influence his position in those cases as much as such considerations permeated his thinking in every other constitutional field. As Henry Steiner, the clerk who worked with the Justice on his 1958 *NAACP* opinion, has remarked, Harlan had a "patrician's view" of the issue; he possessed "a non-cynical, genuine, and deep belief in the fundamental goodness of the country" and the basic decency of its officials. "He was shrewd enough to know what was happening in Alabama and the rest of the South. But he was also an 'all deliberate speed' person. He thought change should be accomplished in a 'gentlemanly' fashion, with all possible respect for state laws, procedures, and institutions. He had this deep sense of [the need to] do as little violence to the traditional forms of federalism as possible."[7]

Such caution was at times a disappointment to the Justice's clerks. During the 1964 term, for example, he joined *Swain* v. *Alabama*, in which a majority not only upheld an Alabama prosecutor's use of peremptory challenges to bar blacks from the jury in the trial of a black sentenced to death for the rape of a white woman, but also found the record insufficient to support a finding of systematic discrimination against blacks in jury selection, even though none had served on a trial jury in the county where Swain was convicted since about 1950. Earlier, moreover, he had favored denying certiorari in the case, writing at one point on a draft Goldberg dissent, "This opinion would require us to hold, in effect, that something akin to a proportional representation system is required in making up the grand jury list. And that peremptory challenges cannot be exercised for racial reasons." Charles Nesson, one of Harlan's clerks that term, had attempted to convince the Justice to join the *Swain* dissenters, but without success.

> No blacks had served on a petit jury there forever. And Harlan went along with a judgment that let them get away with it. . . . It was a

> classic situation of whether you would look through a superficial procedure to the substance underneath. . . . On the surface [the peremptory challenge] was a defensible procedure, and Harlan was not aggressive in looking through procedurally defensible arguments to get to the underlying substance. . . . He had the idea that the Supreme Court needed to move with very considerable caution in bringing about social revolution, and he had a quite fundamental disagreement with [Brennan and others] on the Court about its role in that regard. . . . Harlan had a very naturally conservative attitude toward [social] transformation in the courts.[8]

Nesson found the Justice's stance in another case decided that term equally disappointing, though hardly surprising. In *Fay* v. *Noia*, an important 1963 case, the Court had significantly expanded the power of federal district courts to hear habeas corpus challenges to state criminal convictions, Justice Brennan holding for the majority that a state defendant was entitled to file such a suit even if he had failed to comply with procedural requirements in the state courts. Relying heavily on the work of his former clerk Paul Bator, Harlan had registered a vigorous dissent in the *Fay* case, decrying the Court's dilution of the abstention doctrine and departure from long precedent. When, two years later, the Court approved a further relaxation of the doctrine in a case from the Mississippi supreme court involving civil rights leader Aaron Henry, Harlan again dissented, emphasizing once more the justices' need to encourage respect for state procedures, whatever the nature of the case before them. "Henry," Nesson recently remarked, "was a civil rights activist whom the police set up, but Harlan said we need to presume that the states are doing their job right unless it's perfectly clear that they're not. We can't simply assume they're screwing Aaron Henry. . . . Harlan saw procedural order as a [basic constitutional] value. Brennan was more realistic."[9]

Not only did Harlan pursue a characteristically cautious course in race cases, he also lectured his colleagues frequently about the need to avoid creation of a body of "Negro law" under which the civil liberties claims of black petitioners were given a more solicitous reception in the courts than those of other litigants. Earlier, Justice Frankfurter had raised such concerns himself. In conference discussion of one case during the 1962 term, for example, Frankfurter asserted that he could not "imagine a worse disservice" to the nation than for the Court "continuous[ly]" to act as "guardians of Negroes." Harlan was even more outspoken. The 1956 memorandum in which he had come close to threatening a dissent in the *Hood* case challenge to continued segregation in South Carolina's schools included such language, it will be recalled, as did his dissent from the Court's refusal, in *NAACP* v. *Button*, to permit Virginia to apply its barratry laws against the civil rights organization's lawyers.[10]

Nor were those the only such instances. In *Holt* v. *Virginia* (1965), a state judge had slapped two black attorneys with summary contempt citations and $50 fines. The judge had first refused to disqualify himself for bias from trying one of the lawyers for an alleged contempt growing out of a libel proceeding. Later, he denied a change of venue motion in which the second lawyer, representing the first, charged the judge with "acting as police officer, chief prosecution witness . . . grand jury, chief prosecutor and judge." Virginia's highest courts affirmed the convictions, holding that the language used in the motion violated a statute forbidding "[v]ile, contemptuous or insulting" attacks on a judge's official actions. But the Supreme Court reversed. Justice Black, no friend of summary contempt citations, held for a majority that "these petitioners have been punished . . . for doing nothing more than exercising the constitutional right of an accused and his counsel . . . to defend against the charges made."[11]

Justice Harlan dissented. "The only apparent reason for bringing this minor disciplinary contempt adjudication here for review," he scornfully lectured the brethren in an initial draft, "are intimations in the petition for certiorari that the matter has racial overtones, both petitioners being Negroes. Were those intimations borne out by the record, I would vote to reverse. But they are not. I am confident," he added, "that the Virginia Supreme Court of Appeals will remain alert to prevent any such perversion of the judicial process in the lower state courts."[12]

Harlan's earlier assertions along such lines had not gone unanswered. When the Justice circulated a somewhat similar initial draft in the *Button* case, for example, Justice Brennan protested, then predicted to Hugo Black, when Harlan agreed to modify his language, that the revised version "probably still [contained] a strongly suggested accusation that the Court is giving special status to Negro litigants denied to others." When Harlan circulated his one-paragraph *Holt* dissent, Justice Black also registered a quick rejoinder. In a "Dear John" letter apparently not circulated to their colleagues, Black expressed regret that his friend thought certiorari had been granted in the case purely because of its "racial overtones."

> This statement, I think, is not a correct one. That was certainly not my reason for voting to grant certiorari. Although I cannot speak for the others, I do not believe it was the reason for which they voted to grant certiorari. I think you are making a mistake in circulating a dissent on this basis because it brings in a question that I had hoped would not have to be treated. The probability is that others now will want to write on that subject. Whether they do or not, if you keep this dissent as it is, I shall be compelled to circulate an addition to my opinion with a footnote added substantially as follows: "The statement in dissent says that the only reason certiorari was granted in this case was because of 'racial overtones.' This statement is not correct. Certiorari was granted because [the case] raised [a] question concerning the rights of defendants to seek to escape trial of the contempt charges against them, either because of prejudice in the community or because of bias on the part of the judge."[13]

After receiving his colleague's letter, Harlan eliminated the language Black had found offensive. In a brief published dissent, however, he charged the Court with "set[ting] aside the trivial disciplinary penalty imposed [in the case] simply because in its view petitioners' conduct was not out of bounds," adding, "Believing that any differences over the professional propriety of petitioners' actions involve nothing of constitutional proportions, I would affirm" the lower court.[14]

Nor was the Justice willing to conclude that all racial classifications were *per se* invalid. Toward the end of his tenure, for example, Harlan concurred in the Court's decision to strike down an Alabama law requiring segregation in the state's prisons. But he and Justice Stewart also joined a separate statement in which Justice Black made explicit what the Court's opinion had, at most, only implied—"that prison authorities have the right, acting in good faith and in particularized circumstances, to take into account racial tensions in maintaining security, discipline, and good order." He then added, "We are unwilling to assume that state or local prison authorities might mistakenly regard such an explicit announcement as evincing any dilution of this Court's firm commitment to the Fourteenth Amendment's prohibition of racial discrimination."[15]

As in other fields, Harlan simply refused to paint with what he considered to be an unduly broad brush in racial cases, whatever his personal sympathies. Instead, he repeatedly urged resolution of such cases in the same way that other claims were confronted and with due regard for federal principles, precedent, procedure, and related traditional limitations on the pace and reach of judicial intervention—principles he thought it particularly important to honor in the most troubling and controversial issue areas. Such considerations pervaded his approach to all racial cases, but were especially evident in those growing out of three phases of the "Second Reconstruction" of the 1950s and 1960s—the civil rights protest movement, the revival of congressional activity in the field, and the battles over school desegregation.

Demonstrations, Sit-ins, and "State Action"

By the time of the Montgomery bus boycott of the mid-1950s and the civil rights sit-ins and mass demonstrations of the following decade, the Supreme Court had long recognized the right of Jehovah's Witnesses and other dissidents to distribute leaflets door-to-door and on the public streets and sidewalks, largely unmolested by local authorities. In *Marsh* v. *Alabama* (1946), in fact, the justices had even extended such guarantees to the business district of a company town possessing, asserted Justice Black for the Court, all the characteristics of any other community except for the fact of private title. But the Court had also long upheld the power of government to impose reasonable, evenhanded regulations of time, place, and manner on labor picketing and similar forms of demonstrative speech, and to punish expressions creating a clear and present danger to the public peace and order. When the civil rights demonstrators took to the South's streets, it was thus hardly surprising that southern officials responded with mass arrests and prosecutions for breach of the peace, trespass, obstruction of public passages, and a plethora of like offenses—prosecutions the Court was obliged to weigh against the First Amendment and related constitutional claims of those arrested.[16]

Since such protests included challenges to segregated lunch counters and related private facilities, the justices were also pressed repeatedly to rule on the extent to which such places of public accommodation might be covered by constitutional obligations. In *Shelley* v. *Kraemer* (1948), the Court had held that a state court's enforcement of a racially restrictive housing covenant against those no longer willing to obey its provisions violated equal protection. But *Shelley* had by no means resolved the constitutional status of a state's application of its trespass laws in behalf of a restaurant owner unwilling to serve black customers. Harlan and his colleagues were repeatedly pressed to resolve that complex issue.[17]

During the 1960s the Court handed down several important decisions involving civil rights demonstrations conducted on the streets and other public property. *Edwards* v. *South Carolina*, a 1963 ruling, overturned the breach-of-peace convictions of protesters who had staged a demonstration on the grounds of the state's capitol, Justice Stewart resting the Court's ruling partly on the event's peaceful character, but largely on the vagueness of the common law rule on which the convictions had been based. Two years later, in *Cox* v. *Louisiana*, the Court overturned another civil rights protester's Baton Rouge breach-of-peace conviction on vagueness grounds and also reversed his convictions under statutes forbidding the obstruction of public passages and picketing near a courthouse. The obstruction law, Justice Arthur J. Goldberg held, was susceptible to discriminatory application, and police had given Cox permission to lead the courthouse demonstration. In *Brown* v. *Louisiana*, handed down the next year, yet another set of protest convictions met the same fate. Overturning the breach-of-peace convictions of black youths who staged a sit-in in a small parish library to protest segregated library services, Justice Abe Fortas, who had replaced Justice Goldberg in 1965, found no evidence to support the charge, and held that the library was an especially appropriate, and constitutionally protected, setting for the expression at issue. But *Brown* was a five–four decision. Justice White, who had replaced Justice Whittaker in 1962, joined the majority only because he considered the prosecution racially motivated. Several months later, White joined the *Brown* dissenters to create a new majority for *Adderley* v. *Florida*, upholding trespass convictions growing out of a demonstration on the grounds of a jail. The Court's decision had largely turned on the state's special interests in jail security and an absence of evidence that other groups had been allowed access to the property in the past. And when Alabama's highest court upheld the conviction of black minister and civil rights leader Fred Shuttlesworth for parading without a permit following the famous Good Friday, 1963, civil rights demonstration in Birmingham, the Supreme Court reversed the convictions, citing the unbridled discretion given city officials under Birmingham's parade permit scheme.[18]

While Justice Harlan filed an opinion only in the *Shuttlesworth* case, that opinion and other materials provide a reasonably clear picture of the Justice's stance in such cases. In conference, he had originally voted to uphold the convictions at issue in *Edwards*. After further reflection, however, he wrote Justice Stewart, who had circulated a draft of the Court's opinion in the case, that he had become convinced that Stewart's "view of the matter [was] right" and he was "glad to join" his colleague's draft. When Justice Clark urged him to join his dissent in the case, Harlan responded:

> As I see it, the infirmity in the state court's opinion is that the Court did not judge the record by the requisite constitutional standard, viz., "clear and present danger." . . . Rather, as I read the state opinion, the court in effect simply held that the students had demonstrated long enough, and that in these circumstances disobedience to the police order made out a case of breach of the peace. I do not think that in the context of a general breach of the peace statute this avoids the Fourteenth Amendment.[19]

During conference discussion of the *Cox* case, the Justice had agreed that the police had, and could have, given the petitioner's group permission to conduct the courthouse demonstration. He then added, however, according to Justice Brennan's notes, that "from [the] time the police felt thing was getting out of hand [and] told them to go, there was a violation [of the law] when [they] refused to leave." Nor, he asserted, did he believe that a provision of the obstruction-of-public-passages statute exempting labor unions from its coverage make the regulation invalid. When the case was decided, Harlan joined a separate opinion by Justice White in which White agreed to the Court's reversal of the petitioner's breach-of-peace conviction on vagueness grounds, but dissented from the Court's decision to strike down the courthouse picketing conviction, largely for the reason Harlan had argued at conference, and found evidence that other marches had been permitted to obstruct Baton Rouge's public passages "very vague" at best.[20]

In a bench memo for *Brown*, the library sit-in case, Charles Nesson had recommended summary reversal, noting that the petitioners "were absolutely peaceful and quiet." Harlan noted on the memo that he, unlike his clerk, was "by no means sure that summary reversal is in order," but indicated that he "would be willing to reverse" on free expression grounds. Ultimately, however, the Justice joined Hugo Black's dissent in the case—a ringing denunciation of the majority's assumption that a breach of the peace in a library is to be measured by the same standards as those occurring in the streets as well as the notion that people have a right to expression wherever they happen to be. Their dissent also carried a vigorous plea for social change through the legislature and other traditional channels and warned that peaceful demonstrations can degenerate into violence and anarchy. While Harlan asked his senior colleague to modify language in the dissent smacking of the First Amendment's "incorporation" into the Fourteenth, he joined the revised version "with unreserved approbation," terming it one of his friend's "best opinions." When Black read portions of the opinion during a session of the Court, Harlan passed his friend a one-word note: "Amen!" A few months later, he was one of the four justices who joined Black's opinion upholding the trespass convictions at issue in the *Adderley* case, a vote which prompted a North Carolina lawyer to write, "Poor Grandpa Harlan, how he must suffer for such" a decision.[21]

Given the unlimited discretion to grant or withhold parade permits accorded city officials under the ordinance at issue there, *Shuttlesworth* may have seemed an easy case to most of the brethren. For Harlan, however, it presented "the difficult question [of] whether the Fourteenth Amendment ever bars a state from punishing a citizen for marching without a permit which could have been procured if all available remedies had been pursued." The Court, speaking through Justice Stewart, concluded that a violator of such an ordinance was protected from prosecution if those charged with enforcing it had given the regulation an unconstitutional construction. Harlan, by contrast, thought a person's right to ignore a law should "be made to turn on something more substantial than a minor official's view of his authority under" it. He realized, however, that it was "often necessary to have one's voice heard promptly, if it is to be considered at all" and that Shuttlesworth could not have exhausted the administrative and judicial remedies available to him under Alabama law and still engaged in the Good Friday protest on the significant date the demonstration had been scheduled. He thus voted with the *Shuttlesworth* majority. "I do not mean to suggest," he explained in a concurring opinion,

> that a state or city may not reasonably require that parade permit applications be submitted early enough to allow the authorities and judiciary to determine whether the parade proposal is consistent with the important interests respecting the use of the streets which local authority may legitimately protect. But such applications must be handled on an expedited basis so that rights of political expression will not be lost in a maze of cumbersome and slow-moving procedures. Neither the city of Birmingham nor the State of Alabama has established such expedited procedures.[22]

Two years earlier, though, Harlan had joined a different majority in affirming contempt citations issued against demonstrators who ignored a state judge's injunction against the Good Friday march. Dissenters on the Court charged that appeal of the order though the Alabama courts would have had the same impact as the permit ordinance on the critical timing of the demonstration. But Justice Stewart held for the Court that individuals must at least make some attempt to appeal a court order before defying it, without clear evidence of bad faith on the part of the trial judge.[23] Harlan obviously concurred in such thinking, choosing not to file a separate opinion in the case.

The Justice was to be more outspoken in cases involving sit-ins and related forms of protest on private property. During the 1961 term, the Court decided *Garner* v. *Louisiana* and two companion cases involving breach-of-peace convictions growing out of lunch counter sit-ins. In *Thompson* v. *Louisville*, decided in 1960, the justices had overturned the loitering and disorderly conduct conviction of an elderly black derelict who had shuffled to the music of a tavern jukebox, Justice Black holding for the Court that there was no evidence to support the charges. During conference discussion of the sit-in cases, Chief Justice Warren recommended reversal of those convictions on the same ground. Black, Frankfurter, and others agreed.[24]

Harlan, however, was reluctant to base his vote in the cases on *Thompson*. When Justice Black circulated his draft opinion for *Thompson*, Harlan had suggested addition of "a sentence or two . . . emphasizing that the record is 'completely devoid' of evidence—or some expression like that." Such language, he observed, would "fend against the future use of this opinion as a basis for due process attacks on grounds of mere 'insufficiency' of evidence." Following a telephone conversation, Black incorporated his colleague's suggestions into the Court's opinion. But although Harlan joined the Court's decision in *Thompson*, he remained concerned about the ruling's potential breadth and the notion of federal judges second-guessing the evidentiary findings of state courts.[25]

At the conference on the sit-in cases, the Justice informed the brethren that he could not go on the no-evidence argument but could agree that the statutes on which the petitioners' convictions rested were unconstitutionally vague. Citing *Cantwell* v. *Connecticut*, a 1940 case extending First and Fourteenth Amendment protection to expression on the public streets,[26] he also remarked, according to Justice Brennan's notes, that "there is a liberty here—whether speech or expression doesn't matter—[and a] state can't reach that conduct under a broad statute." When, despite his arguments, a majority decided to reverse the convictions on evidence grounds, he drafted a concurrence elaborating on the themes he had raised in conference.

In the *Garner* sit-in case, the Justice's opinion ultimately went through several drafts. But none satisfied his jurisprudential mentor. Felix Frankfurter thought it very important, as he put it in a letter to Chief Justice Warren, who had assigned himself the task of writing the Court's opinion, that the cases "be disposed of on the narrowest allowable grounds . . . not only deciding as little as possible but saying as little as possible in deciding it." He considered *Thompson* the appropriate model and urged Warren both to shorten his draft ("*Thompson* was disposed of in six pages while your draft opinion covers sixteen full pages") and to omit "reference to all the more far-reaching constitutional questions" raised in the cases, as well as the Chief Justice's "many references to 'color.' " In typically Frankfurtian fashion, he also shared with Warren "the kind of an opinion I have in mind and the kind of concurrence I would file if you are unpersuaded," albeit emphasizing that he did not "mean to suggest you should take over this draft of mine—nothing is further from my thought."[27]

Frankfurter also attempted to dissuade Harlan from filing his concurrence. In a letter to his colleague, Frankfurter reported that Harlan's draft "deeply disturbs me." Chief Justice Warren and justices Douglas and Brennan had begun to contend that places of public accommodation should be treated as quasi-governmental institutions with constitutional obligations, a position Douglas was to embrace in his own *Garner* concurrence. "If I entertained the extreme Warren-Douglas-Brennan constitutional views regarding sit-ins," Frankfurter wrote Harlan, "I would enthusiastically embrace your opinion."

> Starting with the premise that continuing to remain in what heretofore has been deemed to be "private" premises after a request to leave is a form of constitutionally protected free speech, no "trespassing" statute, no matter how narrowly drawn, will avail to have at least five members of this Court eventually, and I think very soon, hold that such a constitutionally protected right overbalances any claim of an exercise of property rights in an irrationally discriminatory way. More than that, such a premise opens up appealing contentions against irrational choices in the conduct of one's theretofore considered "private" affairs in matters involving the right of association, testamentory dispositions, etc., etc., that so offend against the increasingly permeating policy of not having such discriminating irrationality based on promotion of racial inequalities. *Cantwell* rests on a legally totally different starting point, namely the right of people on public streets [not on private property].[28]

"Of course," Harlan soon responded in a "candid answer" to Frankfurter's "candid letter," "I intended to espouse no such foolish doctrine as that the 'liberty' protected by the Fourteenth Amendment embraces activities on private property which the owner has the right to prevent or object to." Instead, he was convinced that in two of the cases, the refusal of store managers to serve the petitioners could not "fairly . . . be taken as a request that they leave such counters, still less the establishments themselves." It was more likely, he added, "that the management of these stores did not want to risk losing Negro patronage by making a request of that kind, preferring to rely on the hope that pangs of hunger, the irritations of white customers, or the force of custom would drive Negroes from the 'white' counters," particularly since the sit-ins were "entirely quiet and courteous." These petitioners not having been asked to leave the counters, he contended, they had a First and Fourteenth Amendment right under the *Cantwell* decision—which, he asserted, was "[s]urely . . . not limited to 'protected' activity occurring on the streets"—to remain there, free of arrest by police. In the third case, there was evidence that the petitioners had been asked to leave. But the breach-of-peace statute challenged there, like those in the other cases, was unconstitutionally vague, as he had contended in conference.[29]

Harlan agreed with Frankfurter that the cases should be closely limited to their facts and decided on narrow grounds. In his judgment, however, a decision based on the vagueness doctrine and the Court's recognition of a limited First and Fourteenth Amendment right of expression on private property, given the owner's consent, posed less daunting implications than an extension of the *Thompson* precedent.

> Like you [he wrote Frankfurter], I have always felt that the *way* in which these cases are decided is more important than their result. While I still stand ready to be corrected by your opinion when it arrives, I must say that I find the evidential approach not only untenable in this instance, but also one that forebodes trouble for the future.
>
> If we are ultimately to get a "trespass" case I can even now hear from some quarters of the conference table, "Well, we let those breach-of-the-peace fellows off, and we should not allow these poor little trespassers to go to jail"; and from other quarters, "Gosh, we'd better go along; if we don't, we're apt to get into a *Shelley* v. *Kraemer* situation."
>
> In other words, I see in the way these cases are being decided the early-flowering seeds of a body of "negro" law—something which would be *very* bad for the Court, and against which you and I, at least, have steadfastly stood shoulder to shoulder. That is why I have felt so strongly impelled to protest at this juncture and to warn for the future against the temptations of *Thompson* v. *Louisville* in cases of this genus. I have no regrets about *Thompson*, but it should be kept to size.
>
> As between expanding *Thompson* to serve as a hedge against the possibility of future extreme constitutional decision in this field, and running the risk of such a decision occurring, I would accept the latter course. If that kind of decision does eventuate, it will at least have the virtue of forthrightness.[30]

After reading Frankfurter's draft concurrence and letter to Warren, Harlan congratulated him on "a valiant effort to save the Court from a very bad opinion." With "regret," however, he added that he "could not possibly join what you have written. You will forgive me, I hope, if I say that I think it is a perfect autoptic profference . . . of the very fears I entertain about the *Thompson* approach in these racial cases." And when Justice Douglas circulated a concurrence in the cases, embracing the view, as Harlan's grandfather had in the *Civil Rights Cases*, that places of public accommodation have Fourteenth Amendment obligations, and noting that Justice Harlan shared that position, Harlan asked Douglas to make clear to which Justice Harlan he was referring. Douglas, of course, readily complied, but could not resist a touch of humor. "Your note . . . disappoints me, in one sense," he wrote the Justice. "Because before I opened the envelope I felt sure I would have a note from you saying 'Please state in reference to my grandfather that I too stand with you and him.' "[31]

The concurrence which Harlan ultimately registered in the cases largely tracked the sentiments he had expressed at conference and in his letter to Frankfurter. The Court, he observed, had "never limited the right to speak . . . to mere verbal expressions"; sit-ins and related activities also enjoyed constitutional protection. Moreover, while the Fourteenth Amendment obviously did not reach expression "conducted on private property over the objection of the owner . . . just as it would surely not encompass verbal expressions in a private home if the owner [had] not consented," the petitioners in two of the cases before the Court, in his judgment, had the owner's consent, or at least had not been asked to leave. And "[i]n the absence of any Louisiana statute purporting to express the State's overriding interest in prohibiting petitioners' conduct as a clear and present danger to the welfare of the community, [such a] peaceful demonstration on public streets, [or] on private property with the consent of the owner, was constitutionally protected." The petitioners' convictions in two of the cases thus violated their right to freedom of expression; and the statutes at issue in all three cases were unconstitutionally vague.[32]

Harlan continued in his refusal, however, to embrace the Court's extension of *Thompson*. Unless strictly limited to its facts, he warned, that decision was "bound to lead [the Court] into treacherous territory." And in *Garner*, the majority had taken that unfortunate step, using a precedent which stemmed from a "situation . . . unique in the annals of the Court" as a basis for moving "into the realm of reviewing the *sufficiency* of the evidence" needed to support a criminal conviction. Such intervention, he charged, was beyond the legitimate "purview" of the Court's authority.[33]

Harlan's public and private stance in the 1961 sit-in cases had made it abundantly clear that the Justice by no means agreed with his grandfather that people had a Fourteenth Amendment right of access to restaurants and other places of public accommodation, regardless of race or color. It was equally obvious that if confronted with a case involving a store owner who objected to the presence of blacks on his property, Harlan II would bow to state authority and the rights of private property, whatever the owner's racial views. In chambers and across the conference table, the issue was hotly debated, with Warren, Douglas, Brennan, and later Goldberg, who replaced Felix Frankfurter after the 1961–62 term, urging adoption of the first Justice Harlan's position, and Black and Harlan II, joined by Clark and White, the leading critics of that posture. But with Justice Stewart ambivalent on the issue, neither side had a majority. When the justices reviewed a number of sit-in trespass prosecutions during the 1962–63 term, they were obliged to rest their decisions on narrow grounds, thereby avoiding the core issue over which they were so deeply divided.[34]

Four of the five principal sit-in cases of the 1962–63 term involved prosecutions under trespass laws and similar statutes. In the fifth, Fred Shuttlesworth and another Alabama clergyman had been convicted of inciting, aiding, and abetting criminal trespasses. Even though the cases involved segregation by private establishments long held to be beyond the reach of the Fourteenth Amendment's equal protection guarantee, a majority found unconstitutional state action in each. In *Peterson* v. *Greenville*, *Gober* v. *Birmingham*, and *Avent* v. *North Carolina*, the existence of a segregation ordinance provided the requisite connection between state policy and the challenged prosecutions. In *Lombard* v. *Louisiana*, statements by the local mayor and police chief that sit-ins would not be tolerated enabled the justices to overturn the petitioners' convictions. And since, the Court concluded, no defendant could be convicted "for aiding and abetting someone to do an innocent act," the convictions in *Shuttlesworth* were also reversed, the justices noting that the trespasses the two ministers were accused of inciting had been overturned in the *Gober* case.[35]

For Harlan, however, the cases were not so simple. He joined the *Peterson* majority on the ground that the state had failed to offer any evidence to rebut the petitioners' charge of unconstitutional state influence, as evidenced by the segregation ordinance. But he rejected as "alluring but fallacious" the Court's assumption that the ordinance's mere existence alone established that "the discriminatory exclusion" at issue in the case was "in fact influenced by the law," and he favored a remand of *Gober* and *Avent* to the state courts for further proceedings along those lines. The Justice found "even more untenable" the Court's use of the statements of local officials as evidence of unconstitutional state influence. And while he joined the Court's reversal of the conviction of Shuttlesworth and his co-defendant on narrow grounds, he disputed the majority's "erroneous premise" that the petitioners had been charged merely with inciting the sit-ins at issue in *Gober*.[36]

Harlan also used the litigation as a forum for summarizing his position regarding the general reach of state power in such settings. "In deciding these cases," he asserted, citing the *Civil Rights Cases*, "the Court does not question the long-established rule that the Fourteenth Amendment reaches only state action. . . . And it does not suggest that such action, denying equal protection, may be found in the mere enforcement of trespass laws in relation to private business establishments from which the management, of its own free will, has chosen to exclude persons of the Negro race." He agreed that judicial enforcement of a property owner's private choice was state action, but insisted that "[t]he ultimate substantive question [was] whether there [had] been 'State action of a particular character' . . . whether the character of the State's involvement in an arbitrary discrimination [was] such that it should be held responsible for the discrimination." Not only did he agree that the mere enforcement of a trespass law in behalf of a bigoted property owner was permissible state action, but he also thought that the limitations on the Fourteenth Amendment's sweep recognized, despite his grandfather's dissent, in the *Civil Rights Cases* served "several vital functions," including the preservation of federal principles and a proper balance of the competing constitutional claims to liberty and equality.[37]

During the following term, the justices continued to debate the issue of state action, property rights, and the Fourteenth Amendment. When Justice Douglas was prevented by illness from attending an October 21, 1963, conference on several additional sit-in cases, he circulated a memorandum among the brethren reiterating his position that "the basic philosophy of the [*Civil Rights Cases*] was wrong." The question in such cases, argued Douglas, was not whether there was "state action but whether States, acting through the courts, can constitutionally put a racial cordon around businesses serving the public." Were the Court to forbid such discriminations, Congress could enact enforcement legislation. "But if," he added,

> we hold that this kind of discrimination is beyond the purview of the Fourteenth Amendment, there is nothing for Congress to "enforce" and the *Civil Rights Cases* are vindicated.
>
> An affirmance in these cases fosters apartheid tightly onto our society—a result incomprehensible in light of the purposes of the Fourteenth Amendment and the realities of our modern society.[38]

In *Griffin* v. *Maryland*, one of the cases decided that term, the justices overturned the trespass convictions of blacks who had staged a sit-in at a white-only amusement park. Since a park security guard arrested the petitioners in his capacity as a deputy sheriff, Chief Justice Warren concluded for the Court that the decision to make the arrests was permeated with the appropriate degree of state involvement. Warren found it immaterial that the deputy would have taken the same action in his purely private role as a park employee; whatever his authority as a park guard, he had acted as a state official in making the arrests.[39]

Harlan, joined by Black and White, dissented. The Justice could accept the Court's assumption that the security guard had made the arrests in his role as a sheriff's deputy. But he saw no difference between the character of the state involvement there and "what it would have been had the arrests been made by a regular policeman dispatched from police headquarters." Neither situation, in his view, constituted the sort of state action the equal protection clause prohibited.[40]

On the same day *Griffin* was decided, the justices also handed down a decision in *Bell* v. *Maryland*, a sit-in case involving no evidence of state influence over a property owner's decision to have Maryland invoke the trespass law against blacks he wished ejected from his restaurant. Initially, Black, Harlan, Clark, Stewart, and White had formed a majority to affirm the *Bell* petitioners' convictions. And Harlan had joined Black's draft opinion "with unreserved enthusiasm," calling it "a splendid job, and eminently right." He asked only that his colleague, in emphasizing that *Bell* had nothing to do with the scope of congressional power in the field, do so "without any qualifying caveat reference or even citation to the *Civil Rights Cases*."[41]

While Justice Black never explicitly said as much in an opinion, he believed that Harlan's grandfather had been largely right, and the majority wrong, in the *Civil Rights Cases*. Black agreed that the Fourteenth Amendment, as enforced by courts, prohibited only state violations of the rights it guaranteed. He also believed, however, that Congress had power to punish private as well as state interferences with those rights. Harlan II, on the other hand, obviously considered the *Civil Rights Cases* to have been correctly decided. There was thus a touch of irony in his suggestion to his colleague. Even so, Black readily complied.[42]

But the first vote in *Bell* was not the last. Following protracted and intense negotiation and in-fighting among the brethren, Justice Stewart defected from the Black-Harlan camp and Justice Brennan ultimately authored a majority opinion which avoided the basic constitutional issue and held instead that Maryland's recent passage of a public accommodations law required remand of the case to the state courts to determine whether the prosecutions should now be abated. Justices Douglas and Goldberg filed opinions advocating the extension of constitutional obligations to restaurants and similar facilities, and Chief Justice Warren joined Goldberg's effort. Justice Harlan had objected to the "unnecessarily harsh" tone of an initial dissent Black had circulated in the case before Brennan's approach emerged victorious.[43] When the Court's decision was announced, however, Harlan, along with White, joined an equally vehement Black opinion embodying the position both justices had long embraced.

If Harlan had any regrets about not writing in *Bell*, he soon had another opportunity to elaborate his stance. Late the following fall, the Court in *Hamm* v. *Rock Hill* cited the public accommodations title of the recently enacted 1964 Civil Rights Act in abating yet other sit-in trespass convictions and ordering the charges against the petitioners dismissed. In a brief yet pointed dissent, the Justice found "no support in reason or authority" for the Court's decision. Not surprisingly, given his regard for federalism, he was appalled that passage of a federal law could be held to abate state convictions. "Our federal system," he contended, "tolerates wide differences between state and federal legislative policies, and the presumption of retroactive exculpation that readily attaches to a federal criminal statute . . . unreservedly repeal[ing] earlier federal legislation cannot, in my opinion, be automatically thought to embrace exoneration from earlier wrongdoing under a state statute." "Until today," he added, the abatement doctrine had "always been applied only with respect to legislation of the *same* sovereignty." Nor, in his judgment, was Article VI, the provision of the constitution declaring national law supreme over state law, of relevance. "[T]here [was] not," he maintained, "a scintilla of evidence which remotely suggests that Congress had any such revolutionary course in mind" when it passed the Civil Rights Act.[44]

Harlan's dissent redeemed him with a Wall Street friend who earlier had complained to the Justice about his stance in the school prayer and Bible-reading cases. "I just read . . . your dissent in the 'sit in' decision," he wrote Harlan the day after the ruling was announced, "and, damn it, John, what you had to say will go down in history. Long, long ago I pinpointed you as the Greatest Dissenter of his day and age and, by God, you live up to it every blessed moment (you know the one case in which I disagreed with you!)."[45]

No doubt the friend was equally pleased with the Justice's later opposition to other forms of federal court intervention in such cases. During the 1964 term, the Court decided the case of James Dombrowski, head of a controversial organization active in a variety of southern civil rights causes. Louisiana authorities had arrested Dombrowski and other members of his group, raided their offices, and repeatedly threatened them with prosecution under state anti-Communist statutes. A Louisiana judge held the arrests and seizure of the organization's records illegal, but Dombrowski also sought an injunction from a federal district court, charging state officials with a campaign of harassment under statutes which were so broad and vague in their scope that their continued existence on the Louisiana law books imposed a "chilling effect" on the exercise of protected expression. When a three-judge district court denied relief and Dombrowski and his followers were indicted on state charges, they took their case to the Supreme Court.[46]

Traditionally, the brethren had permitted the federal trial courts to enjoin state judicial proceedings only in the face of clear evidence that the state courts were unwilling to protect a defendant's federal rights. Finding no such bad faith in *Dombrowski,* Harlan urged his colleagues at the conference table to "not jump" to a contrary conclusion. But to no avail. In a five–two vote, with Black and Stewart not participating, the Court, speaking through Justice Brennan, held that abstention was inappropriate when a federal trial court was confronted with a statute which was unconstitutionally broad and vague on its face. Such laws, concluded Brennan, imposed the sort of chilling effect on expression about which Dombrowski had complained and justified federal court intervention in cases in which they were the basis for a criminal prosecution.[47]

Harlan, joined by Justice Clark, filed a biting dissent from what he scorned as "a significant departure from a wise procedural principle designed to spare our federal system from premature federal judicial interference with state statutes or proceedings challenged on federal constitutional grounds." Few statutes, he contended, could not be challenged, "at least colorably," as unconstitutionally vague. Under the Court's ruling, many state prosecutions could thus be delayed pending "monitoring by the federal courts." Nor could the Justice accept the Court's major premise that state courts would not be as vigilant as their federal counterparts in "vindicat[ing] constitutional rights promptly and effectively." In *Dombrowski* itself, after all, the Louisiana courts had already struck down the seizure of the appellants' records, thereby honoring their Fourth and Fourteenth Amendment rights.[48]

The Justice also used the case as a vehicle for expressing his concerns about the Court's treatment of laws claimed to be unconstitutionally broad or vague "on their face." Because of the "chilling effect" they were claimed to impose on the exercise of protected rights, litigants were permitted to raise "facial" attacks against such statutes even if their own conduct was subject to regulation under a properly written law. Harlan found such an approach deeply disturbing.

> Interwoven with the vagueness doctrine is a question of standing. In a criminal prosecution a defendant could not avoid a constitutional application of this statute to his own conduct simply by showing that if applied to others whose conduct was protected it would be unconstitutional. To follow that practice in a federal court which is asked to enjoin a state criminal prosecution would, however, in effect require that the parties try the criminal case in advance in the federal forum . . . a procedure seriously disruptive of the orderly processes of the state proceedings. . . . [A]ppellants . . . able to reach a federal court before the state instituted criminal proceedings are now immunized with a federal vaccination from state prosecution.[49]

Dombrowski, of course, was not to be the last word on federal district court abstention. Following President Nixon's appointments in 1969 and 1970 of Warren Burger and Harry Blackmun, to replace Chief Justice Warren and Justice Fortas, respectively, the Court in *Younger* v. *Harris*, decided during Harlan's last term, gave *Dombrowski* a narrow reading and reaffirmed the traditional limits on federal court injunctions of state proceedings. Harlan helped to form the *Younger* majority. In 1966, the Justice joined a five–four Court in narrowly construing a Reconstruction-era statute which permitted the removal of state cases involving civil rights claims to federal court. In barring removal of a case in which state defendants contended that they had been arrested and charged solely because they were black or were assisting blacks to assert their federal rights, Justice Stewart asserted for the majority that the removal statute had not been intended "to work a wholesale dislocation of the historic relationship between the state and federal courts in the administration of the criminal law." Harlan clearly endorsed such thinking. In a letter to an Australian friend, he noted the recent effort "to permit more liberal removal" and applauded its failure. If that campaign had succeeded, he predicted, "federal courts would have been flooded with an unpredictable number of petty offenses—breach of the peace, trespass, obstructing the streets, etc.—which are properly the business of the state courts."[50]

Nor was the Justice willing to limit his traditional, relatively narrow conception of "state action" purely to the sit-in context. When a black filed a federal suit challenging the whites-only policy of a restaurant located in a Wilmington, Delaware, municipal parking building, a majority found a collection of ties between the restaurant and the government sufficient to trigger application of the equal protection guarantees. At conference, Harlan had first argued that he had found "no state action whatever. Not a hint of [an] effort on [the] part of [the] state to mask a discriminatory purpose" in the city's decision to lease the restaurant space to a private concern rather than operate it itself. He suggested that the case be remanded for further proceedings on the meaning of a state law authorizing restaurants and other places of public accommodation to refuse service to those who "would be offensive to the major part of [their] customers, and would injure [their] business." Were that law construed "to say [that] as [a] matter of law negroes as [a] class are offensive," he observed, the restaurant's exclusion of blacks could be condemned as forbidden state action without the Court being obliged to reach the broader issues which the case had raised. When the Court based its decision on those broader questions, he dissented, joined by Justice Whittaker. It was, he charged, "both unnecessary and unwise to reach issues of such broad constitutional significance as those . . . decided by the Court, before the necessity for deciding them [had] become apparent."[51]

When the Court confronted allegedly unconstitutional "state action" issues in later cases, Harlan either gave the concept a narrow construction or urged a decision based on other grounds. In 1966, the Court ruled that land left Macon, Georgia, by U.S. Senator Augustus O. Bacon as a park for whites, and so operated by the city for many years, had not lost its "public" character—and constitutional obligations—merely as a result of the recent appointment of private trustees. Thus the park was subject to the Constitution's guarantee of equal protection. Harlan, joined by Stewart, dissented, declaring the majority's "public function" rationale "as vague and amorphous as it is far-reaching" and condemning related grounds given for the ruling as well. When two years later the Court extended to shopping centers its 1946 holding in *Marsh* v. *Alabama* that the business district of a company town was subject to the

Constitution's commands, he again dissented. A Harlan clerk recognized the Justice's "apparent lack of enthusiasm for extensions of the preemption doctrine," the rule under which the federal government can exclude the states entirely from legislating in a matter subject to national control. Nevertheless, the clerk recommended reversal of a state court injunction against labor union picketing at a shopping center on the ground that such state regulations had been superceded by pervasive federal controls over labor-management relations. But since the union petitioners in the case had not properly brought the preemption question to the Court, Harlan argued instead that the case should be dismissed and declined a pronouncement on the state action issue. His distaste for what he termed the "rigid constitutional rule" the majority had established was clearly evident. And when the Court, during his last term, rejected "public function" and other arguments in refusing to order desegregation of Jackson, Mississippi, swimming pools which that city had turned over to a private group rather than integrate, the Justice joined the new majority.[52]

Harlan's opposition to the Warren Court's expansive notions of state action was most clearly reflected, however, in a 1967 California case, *Reitman* v. *Mulkey*. In 1964, California voters had approved Proposition 14, an amendment to the state's constitution which gave people an "absolute discretion" in housing transactions, thereby repealing existing California fair housing laws. California's highest court declared the amendment an unconstitutional governmental encouragement of racial discrimination in the housing market, and the Supreme Court initially refused to review the state court's decision. In an unfiled dissent against denial of certiorari in the case, Harlan decried what he claimed was the lower court's assumption that a state's mere repeal of civil rights legislation constituted state encouragement of discrimination prohibited by the Fourteenth Amendment's equal protection guarantee. "[T]his novel and potentially far-reaching constitutional theory," he exclaimed, "imperatively calls for review by this Court."[53]

Ultimately, the justices did grant certiorari in the case. Following review, however, they voted five–four to affirm the California supreme court's decision, Justice White agreeing with the state judiciary that the challenged provision's language and the anti–fair housing lobbying behind its adoption had justified the lower court's position. Joined on this occasion by Black, Clark, and Stewart, Justice Harlan again dissented. In his view, Proposition 14 in no way could be considered state encouragement of discrimination. California had simply "decided to remain 'neutral' in the realm of private discrimination" in the sale or rental of housing. He expressed concern, moreover, that the majority's decision, "salutary as its result may appear at first blush, [might] in the long run actually serve to handicap progress in the extremely difficult field of racial concerns." Any move to repeal fair housing or other civil rights laws, he reasoned, would naturally be promoted by their opponents, just as Proposition 14 had been. He thought it entirely likely, therefore, that the Court's decision would chill the prospects for future enactment of such laws since opponents could now argue that, once passed, they would be unrepealable.[54]

Congress and Civil Rights

While the Court attempted to delineate the reach of "state action" and the First and Fourteenth Amendment claims of demonstrators, Congress had begun to arouse itself from a nearly century-long civil rights slumber. The voting rights statutes enacted by Congress in 1957 and 1960 were more loophole than law. The Civil Rights Act of 1964, however, not only tightened the provisions of the earlier legislation; that landmark statute also erected bans to discrimination in employment, places of public accommodation, and federally funded institutions. In its 1965 and 1970 Voting Rights acts, Congress went even further. The 1965 law outlawed literacy and related voter tests in states and localities with a history of racial discrimination in suffrage and also imposed a "pre-clearance" requirement under which such jurisdictions were obliged to obtain the approval of the Justice Department or the District Court for the District of Columbia before enforcing new election laws. The 1970 counterpart extended the ban on literacy tests nationwide. Meanwhile, Justice Department lawyers resurrected largely dormant Reconstruction-era criminal statutes in attempting to combat racial violence, and private plaintiffs invoked other remnants of the first Reconstruction in civil suits attacking discrimination.

Had the public accommodations provisions of the 1964 Civil Rights Act been based purely on Congress' power to enforce the Fourteenth Amendment's equal protection guarantee, Justice Harlan undoubtedly would have been unwilling to support the amendment's use in an assault on private discrimination. But since the 1964 law, unlike its 1875 counterpart invalidated in the *Civil Rights Cases*, reached only businesses affecting interstate commerce, the Justice saw the regulation as a legitimate exercise of the commerce power. Even so, he pressed Justice Tom Clark, author of the Court's opinions upholding the act, to stress congressional findings that discrimination by such businesses actually reduced the flow of goods—contrary to the arguments of those who contended that compelled integration would harm, rather than promote, commerce. At one point, for example, he suggested that Clark add to his opinion in one of the cases the statement that "there was plentiful evidence of the fact that discrimination created profound and continuing unrest with a resultant reduction in sales by business in general."[55]

Given the abundant evidence that voter tests were often employed to assure a white, rather than a literate or educated, electorate, the Justice also considered Congress' ban on such regulations in areas with a history of racial bars to voting as a legitimate exercise of its authority under the

Fifteenth Amendment. While finding the issue "not free from difficulty," he agreed that the ban could be extended to the entire nation. "Despite the lack of evidence of specific instances of discriminatory application," he concluded in voting to uphold the literacy-test provision of the 1970 Voting Rights Act, "Congress could have determined that racial prejudice is prevalent throughout the Nation and that literacy tests unduly lend themselves to discriminatory application, either conscious or unconscious."[56]

But there were limits to the discretion Harlan was willing to accord Congress, even in the sensitive field of racial discrimination. One provision of the 1965 Voting Rights Act stipulated that no person who had completed six grades in a Puerto Rican school could be denied the vote because of an inability to read or write English. In a suit brought by New York voters, the Court, speaking through Justice Brennan, with Harlan in dissent, upheld the regulation as a means to secure nondiscriminatory treatment for Puerto Ricans in both the imposition of voting qualifications and the provision of government services—and thus as a valid exercise of the congressional power to enforce the equal protection guarantee.[57]

In *Lassiter* v. *Northampton County Board of Elections* (1959), the Court had held that a fairly administered literacy test did not violate equal protection. And Harlan had argued during conference debate over the voting rights law that *Lassiter* was binding on the Congress. "Congress can't define the [equal protection clause]," he exclaimed, "that's for us to say." When a majority disagreed, holding that Congress' enforcement authority permitted it to outlaw practices the Court had condoned where there was a "rational" basis for concluding that such practices could be used to deny equal protection, the Justice, joined by Potter Stewart, vigorously dissented. Under the doctrine of judicial review, he contended, judgments regarding the Fourteenth Amendment's "*substantive* scope" rested ultimately with the courts, not Congress. In the *Lassiter* case, the Court had held the English language literacy test to be a permissible exercise of state authority, and Harlan could not understand how a majority could now think that it was "open to Congress to limit the effect of that decision."[58]

The Justice readily conceded that the legislature's judgments and factual findings were "of course entitled to due respect." But, he charged, there was "simply no legislative record supporting" the conclusions underlying the challenged provision.

> [W]e have here not a matter of giving deference to a congressional estimate, based on its determination of legislative facts, bearing upon the validity *vel non* of a statute, but rather what can at most be called a legislative announcement that Congress believes a state law to entail an unconstitutional deprivation of equal protection. Although this kind of declaration is of course [also] entitled to the most respectful considera-

> tion, coming as it does from a concurrent branch and one that is knowledgeable in matters of popular political participation, I do not believe it lessens our responsibility to decide the fundamental issue of whether in fact the state enactment violates federal constitutional rights.

"At least in [an] area of [such] primary state concern" as the conduct of elections, he added, "a state statute that passes constitutional muster under the judicial standard . . . should not be permitted to be set at naught by a mere contrary congressional pronouncement unsupported by a legislative record justifying that conclusion." If Congress had power to enlarge upon judicial determinations of the equal protection guarantee's reach, Harlan could see no reason why it "should not be able as well . . . to dilute" the Court's decisions. "For if Congress by what, as here, amounts to mere *ipse dixit* can set that otherwise permissible requirement partially at naught I see no reason why it could not also substitute its judgment for that of the States in other fields of their exclusive primary competence as well."[59]

When Congress extended the scope of its authority over state election systems beyond the field of racial discrimination, the Justice greeted such control with even less enthusiasm. In dissents from the Court's use of the equal protection guarantee in *Reynolds* v. *Sims* and other cases to order reapportionment of state legislatures and attack other forms of nonracial classifications in the election process, Harlan argued that the Fourteenth Amendment's framers had not intended its provisions to reach state election practices. His reading of history and acceptance of historical records as a useful guide to constitutional meaning attracted considerable scholarly criticism, most notably from Duke law professor William Van Alstyne in a volume of the *Supreme Court Review*. Harlan sent a copy of Van Alstyne's article to Lloyd Weinreb, who had clerked for the Justice during the term the *Reynolds* case was decided and was then teaching at Harvard. "The piece strikes me as having labored long to produce a mouse," Harlan observed in a note accompanying the article. "What do you think?" Weinreb agreed. After discussing the effort with two senior faculty who shared his view that the Duke professor's assessment was wrong, Weinreb wrote a lengthy rebuttal of Van Alstyne's contentions—plus a footnote "pot shot," as he termed it, at another commentator who had scorned Harlan's "law-office history"—and sent a copy to the Justice. Weinreb proposed, he explained in an accompanying letter, to have it published in the *Harvard Law Review*, with a footnote indicating that he had served as Harlan's clerk but that the piece "represents the author's own views, which have not been discussed or in any way approved by Mr. Justice Harlan."[60]

Weinreb hoped that the Justice would not object to the rebuttal's publication. "I am not an avid mousehunter," he explained. "I do think, however, that for the sake of the historical record, Van Alstyne's piece should not be the last word on this subject. It would be a pity if the record of the past came to be regarded as too doubtful a source of enlightenment for reliance in constitutional matters."

In a telephone conversation with his former clerk, Harlan told Weinreb, according to the Justice's notes, that he "thought it best" the article not be published. The former clerk acquiesced, but Harlan continued vigorously to defend his own reading of the Fourteenth Amendment's history, and he was no more sympathetic to Congress' use of the amendment as a basis for voting rights legislation than he was to judicial decisions extending the amendment's reach to the election process. The 1970 Voting Rights Act not only outlawed literacy tests nationwide, it also imposed restrictions on residency requirements and the use of absentee ballots in presidential elections, as well as declared eighteen the minimum age for voting in both state and federal elections. When the Court, in *Oregon v. Mitchell* (1970), upheld the ban on literacy tests as an exercise of Congress' Fifteenth Amendment authority to forbid racial discrimination in voting, Harlan, as noted earlier, went along. But the Fifteenth Amendment's terms were limited purely to racial concerns. And the Justice vehemently rejected the contention that the Fourteenth Amendment had clothed Congress with further authority over the election process.[61]

Harlan's exhaustive study of records pertinent to the Fourteenth Amendment's adoption had convinced him that the amendment's history "with respect to suffrage qualifications" was "remarkably free of the problems which bedevil most attempts to find a reliable guide to present decision in the pages of the past. Instead, there [was] virtually unanimous agreement, clearly and repeatedly expressed," that its first section "did not reach discriminatory voter qualifications." He "confess[ed] complete astonishment," moreover, at those who argued, as did Justice Brennan, joined by White and Marshall, in a separate opinion in the case, that the amendment's history was no longer relevant and that its meaning must be adapted to changing social needs.

> It must be recognized, of course, that the amending process is not the only way in which constitutional understanding alters with time. The judiciary has long been entrusted with the task of applying the Constitution in changing circumstances, and as conditions change the Constitution in a sense changes as well. But when the Court gives the language of the Constitution an unforeseen application, it does so, whether explicitly or implicitly, in the name of some underlying purpose of the Framers. . . . This is necessarily so; the federal judiciary, which by express constitutional provision is appointed for life, and therefore cannot be held responsible by the electorate, has no inherent general authority to establish the norms for the rest of society. . . . When the Court disregards the express intent and understanding of the Framers, it has invaded the realm of the political process to which the amending power was committed, and it has violated the constitutional structure which it is its highest duty to protect.[62]

In short, he asserted, the Court had no business "substituting its own views of wise policy for the commands of the Constitution." And what the Court could not legitimately do, it should not permit Congress to do either, especially since the legislative branch was "subject to none of the institutional restraints imposed on judicial decisionmaking," but "controlled only by the political process."[63]

Harlan was not always willing to give the congressional products of the second Reconstruction the broad readings a majority of his colleagues supported. In *Allen* v. *State Board of Elections* (1969), the Court, speaking through Chief Justice Warren, construed the 1965 Voting Rights Act to require states and counties with a history of racial discrimination in voter registration to secure federal judicial or Justice Department approval before enforcing any new election law, not merely those imposing voter qualifications. In dissent, Harlan argued that the Court's construction conflicted with the act's language and legislative history. He noted, for example, that under the provisions at issue persons could not be "denied the right to vote for failure to comply" with any new state regulation for which federal "pre-clearance" had not been secured. He maintained that section 5 of the Voting Rights Act, the pre-clearance provision, was designed to prevent states from obstructing compliance with Section 4, the section of the law suspending literacy tests in jurisdictions with a discriminatory voter registration record.[64]

Under the Court's construction of Section 5, on the other hand, federal officials were now empowered to "determine whether various systems of representation favor or disfavor the Negro voter"—a task the Justice thought them ill-equipped to perform. He found the law's "regional application" equally troubling. It was one thing to ban voter tests in any region with a history of discrimination, but quite another to require federal approval in only one region of a problem "that is national in scope"—the impact of election systems on black voter influence. "I find it especially difficult to believe," asserted the Justice, "that Congress would single out a handful of states as requiring strict federal supervision concerning their treatment of a problem that may well be just as serious in parts of the North as it is in the South."[65]

Arguably, the Justice was even less receptive to expansive readings of text and history in construing Reconstruction-era statutes, and the constitutional powers on which they were claimed to rest, than he was in dealing with modern legislation. In 1961, the Court upheld a damage suit brought against Chicago policemen by black children and their parents under the 1871 Civil Rights Act, Justice Douglas declaring for a majority that a provision of the statute reaching acts committed "under color of law" included those engaged in by police acting without legal authority. Harlan joined that decision, but largely on the basis of what he considered to be controlling precedent. Without those earlier rulings, he would have considered the issue "very close indeed." And when the Court, in two 1966 cases, reinstated indictments against the alleged murderers of three civil rights workers in Neshoba County, Mississippi, and a black motorist in Georgia, the Justice dissented from one potentially far-reaching element of the Court's rulings.[66]

The Mississippi and Georgia cases involved criminal indictments under Sections 241 and 242 of Title 18 of the U.S. Code, modern counterparts of provisions in the 1870 and 1866 Civil Rights Acts. Section 241 prohibited conspiracies to violate rights "secured" under the U.S. Constitution and federal laws, while Section 242 punished deprivations "under color of law" of rights "secured or protected" by those provisions. Violations of Section 241 were punishable by sentences of up to ten years, $10,000, or both; Section 242 carried maximum penalties of only a year, $1,000, or both. Federal prosecutors thus sometimes preferred to secure indictments under Section 241 or under both provisions. But in the past, Section 241 and its predecessors had been construed to cover only a narrow category of national citizenship rights held to be implicitly protected by the Constitution, including the right of a registered voter to participate in federal elections and the right of a citizen to the custody of a U.S. marshal.[67]

In *United States* v. *Price*, the Mississippi case, the Supreme Court held that Section 241 could also be used to prosecute conspiracies to violate Fourteenth Amendment rights of equal protection and due process, such as those the eighteen suspects in the case were claimed to have violated by taking the lives of three civil rights workers and otherwise depriving them of their liberty without a trial or other constitutional essentials. The Court further ruled that Section 242 charges were permissible against all the suspects, not merely the three law enforcement officers who were among those indicted, since the others were acting in concert with the police and thus "under color of law." None of the defendants in *United States* v. *Guest*, the Georgia case, was a government official. But since the defendants were charged with having made false complaints to the police as part of their campaign of harassment against blacks, the Court found sufficient state involvement in the indictment's charge of violations of Fourteenth Amendment rights to avoid a confrontation with the *Civil Rights Case* position that congressional power under the amendment reached only "state" action. On the ground that the right of interstate travel was a privilege of national citizenship which Congress could protect against private as well as state interference, the Court also upheld a count of the indictment that charged interference with the victim's travel.

Justice Harlan joined the *Price* ruling and Justice Abe Fortas's opinion in the case. In a letter to his colleague, however, the Justice asked Fortas to delete language suggesting that Section 241 would reach private as well as government action. "Since this case does not face us with that question," he asserted, "I feel there should be no intimation on it one way or another."[68]

The Justice was also naturally willing to join Justice Stewart's strained effort to find unconstitutional state action—and thus avoid collision with the *Civil Rights Cases*—in counts of the *Guest* indictment involving Fourteenth Amendment rights. But he could not accept the majority's conclusion that congressional authority over interstate travel implied a guarantee from private interferences. Past cases recognizing a right of interstate travel had involved only "unreasonable *Governmental* interference" with the guarantee of travel. And the Justice thought it "unwise or impermissible" to extend the right's scope beyond such settings. Earlier rulings had also recognized congressional authority to protect certain privileges of national citizenship from private and governmental interference. But all those cases, asserted Harlan, had been based on narrow grounds and were "essentially concerned with the vindication of important relationships with the Federal Government." They should not be converted into a tool for an indefinite expansion of the scope of rights said to inhere in one's status as a U.S. citizen. After all, he observed, the framers had convened at Philadelphia "to establish a nation, not to reform the common law."[69]

Nor could the Justice agree that the "same considerations" which had led the Court to safeguard interstate movement from state infringement would justify its protection from "private impediments." "There is a difference in power," he contended, "between States and private groups so great that analogies between the two tend to be misleading. If the State obstructs free intercourse of goods, people, or ideas, the bonds of the union are threatened; if a private group effectively stops such a communication, there is at most a temporary breakdown of law and order, to be remedied by the exercise of state authority or by appropriate federal legislation." Refusal to permit Congress to protect the right of interstate travel from private interferences would not "render the Federal Government helpless." Under its commerce power, for example, Congress could have attacked numerous private interferences with interstate movement, including those relating to the enjoyment of civil rights. "Because Congress has wide authority to legislate in this area," he reasoned, "it seems unnecessary—if prudential grounds are of any relevance . . . to strain to find a dubious constitutional right."[70]

Harlan would adhere to this position for the balance of his career. In 1971, he joined the Court in reversing a district judge's dismissal of a civil suit brought under a Reconstruction-era statute by victims of a vicious Klan-style clubbing on a Mississippi highway. A 1951 ruling had limited the law's reach to conspiracies "under color of law." Speaking for the Court in *Griffin* v. *Breckenridge*, however, Justice Stewart construed the law to reach private action as well and held that Congress could authorize such suits under the Thirteenth Amendment and its power to protect the right of interstate travel. Harlan joined the Thirteenth Amendment portion of the Court's rationale, but found "it unnecessary to rely on the 'right of interstate travel' as a premise for justifying federal jurisdiction."[71]

There were limits to the Justice's willingness to uphold expansive constructions of the products of the first Reconstruction, even those enacted under the Thirteenth Amendment, which clearly reached private as well as governmental action. A provision of the 1866 Civil Rights Act gave all citizens the same rights as white citizens in property transactions. In *Jones* v. *Alfred H. Mayer Co.* (1968), the Court, speaking through Justice Stewart, upheld application of the law to the practices of a private real estate firm and ruled that Congress had power under the Thirteenth Amendment to impose such regulations. While the *Jones* majority's construction was consistent with a literal reading of the portion of the civil rights act at issue in the case, it was also an interpretation which had never before been accepted by the Court. According to Louis Cohen, a Harlan clerk during the term *Jones* was decided, the construction had originated with Laurence Tribe, who was clerking for Justice Stewart that year. "A lot of . . . people," Cohen remembers, "believed it was a joke that would not withstand analysis at all. After all, here we were talking about quite a dramatic, world-changing new meaning for a statute that was a hundred years old."[72]

Justice Harlan shared his clerk's skepticism. In a dissent joined by Justice White, he called the Court's extension of the law "to purely private action . . . almost surely wrong, and at the least . . . open to serious doubt." Section 1 of the original statute had recognized the right at issue in *Jones*, while Section 2 had provided that any violation "under color of law" of the rights granted in Section 1 would be punishable as a misdemeanor. For Harlan, Section 2 was strong evidence that the rights mentioned in Section 1 were rights protected only against state, not private, interference.

> [T]here is an inherent ambiguity in the term "right," as used in [Section 1]. The "right" referred to may either be a right to equal status under the law, in which case the statute operates only against state-sanctioned discrimination, or it may be an "absolute" right enforceable against private individuals. To me, the words of the statute, taken alone, suggest the former interpretation, not the latter.

But Harlan did not rest his stance on text alone. Quoting extensively from the debates over the statute's adoption, he also made a convincing argument that neither the civil rights law's supporters nor its opponents anticipated the expansive interpretation the Court was now advancing. The few earlier cases dealing with the law's meaning had consistently adopted the restrictive construction Harlan embraced.[73]

The Justice was not concerned solely with the majority's reading of text and history. He argued that Congress' recent passage of the 1968 Fair Housing Act had so diminished *Jones*'s significance that the case properly should be dismissed. Nor was it of consequence to him that the new statute was enacted only after oral argument in the case and thus "at a time when the parties and amici curiae had invested time and money in anticipation of a decision on the merits," or that the petitioners apparently would not be entitled to relief under the 1968 law. "I deem it far more important that this Court should avoid, if possible, the decision of constitutional and unusually difficult statutory questions than that we fulfill the expectations of every litigant who appears before us. . . . [I]f the petition for a writ of certiorari in this case had been filed a few months after, rather than a few months before, the passage of the 1968 Civil Rights Act, I venture to say that the case would have been deemed to possess such 'isolated significance,' in comparison with its difficulties, that the petition would not have been granted."[74]

But neither the majority nor Justice Harlan was to reverse ground on the matter. Early in the 1969 term, the Court extended *Jones*, which had involved an injunction action, to damage suits. Since the decision was handed down less than three weeks before the 1968 fair housing law became fully effective, Harlan found the majority "even more unwise than it was in *Jones*, in precipitately breathing still more life into [the 1866 statute], which is both vague and open-ended, when Congress has provided this modern statute, containing various detailed provisions aimed at eliminating racial discrimination in housing." He still spoke in dissent, of course. On this occasion, however, he picked up additional support for his stance—that of the Court's new chief justice, Warren Burger.[75]

The Demise of "Deliberate Speed"

While the justices were coping with civil rights demonstrations, the state action issue, and the reach of congressional power, they also began gradually to resume a prominent role in the continuing disputes over desegregation which the school decisions of 1954 and 1955 had generated. Not surprisingly, given the complexities of such cases and the emotions they aroused, the Court had avoided any major desegregation pronouncement for a decade after *Brown* I and *Brown* II, save its joint opinion in the Little Rock case. By the mid-1960s, however, the brethren's growing impatience with the slow pace of desegregation and the evasive tactics, or outright defiance, of southern officials was clearly evident. In *Griffin* v. *Prince Edward Co.* (1964), the Court rebuffed Virginia's scheme for maintaining segregation through public funding of "private" schools. *Green* v. *New Kent Co.* (1968) rejected a school desegregation plan which had resulted in virtually no integration and held that any plan, to be acceptable, must work. In *Alexander* v. *Holmes Co.* (1969), the justices called for desegregation "at once" and reversed the willingness of lower federal courts to permit yet another delay in the integration of more than thirty Mississippi school districts. And in *Swann* v. *Charlotte-Mecklenburg* (1971), decided during Justice Harlan's last term, the Court went even further, upholding the authority of trial judges to impose racial quotas, order the busing of students, and establish other devices for assuring meaningful desegregation. Meanwhile, the justices were also presiding over the dismantlement of segregation in virtually every other field of national life. In the aptly styled *Loving* v. *Virginia* (1967), for example, a state law forbidding interracial marriages met its demise.[76]

Justice Harlan joined these rulings as well as others of the same type. He displayed in the later desegregation cases, however, the same regard for traditional judicial norms, federalism, and comity his stances in *Hood*, the Little Rock controversy in *Cooper* v. *Aaron*, and other early cases had reflected. When Arthur Goldberg used the word "integration" in a 1963 case, for example, Harlan recommended a change of phrasing. "I prefer 'desegregation.' 'Integration' brings blood to southerners' eyes for they think that ['integration'] means just that—'integration.' I do not think that we ought to use the word in our opinions." Where elsewhere in his draft Goldberg used "immediate," Harlan recommended substitution of "prompt."[77]

Nor was this an isolated instance. When language in Justice Black's opinion for the Court in the *Griffin* case appeared to imply that states might have a constitutional obligation to maintain public schools, Harlan suggested to his colleague that "we should go [no] further, at least at this stage, than to authorize an injunction against the use of public funds for private tuition grants and against the granting of tax credits." He again intervened when Black circulated an opinion for the Court in the Montgomery County, Alabama, school desegregation case. Black's draft appeared to support deference for the factual findings of federal trial judges. The presiding judge in the case, U.S. District Judge Frank M. Johnson, Jr., had an excellent civil rights record. Harlan thought that Black's use of "the phrase 'by accepting the choice of the judge on the spot' might prove embarrassing to [federal appeals courts] in controlling District Judges who are not Frank Johnsons, and this certainly would be unfortunate." The fact that the Court of Appeals for the Fifth Circuit had been evenly divided in its review of Judge Johnson's decision seemed, to Harlan, a more appropriate and less potentially troubling basis for the Court's decision to uphold the district court.[78]

While during Harlan's tenure the Court was able to maintain unanimity in major desegregation cases, the Justice's regard for proper judicial procedure prompted him to register a dissent in one minor 1963 case. An Illinois public school had an enrollment of 251 blacks and 254 whites. With few exceptions, the black students attended classes in one section of the school, whites in another. Entrances and exits were also segregated. When a number of the black students challenged this arrangement, two lower federal courts dismissed their complaint, ordering them to exhaust administrative remedies available to them under Illinois law before seeking federal judicial relief. In *McNeese* v. *Board of Education*, the Supreme Court reversed the lower court rulings, Justice Douglas declaring for an eight-member majority that the exhaustion doctrine was inappropriate in such cases.[79]

In his lone dissent, Justice Harlan agreed with the lower courts. *McNeese*, he argued, was clearly not a typical desegregation case; the school's student body was composed of an almost equal number of blacks and whites, and no black student had been denied enrollment. The Justice was also impressed with the procedures Illinois had established for resolution of such complaints. There could be no "serious doubt," he asserted, "as to the efficacy of the administrative remedy which Illinois [has] provided." The Illinois procedure required at least fifty residents of a school district to file a complaint, or 10 percent of them if that was a lower number, to trigger pertinent provisions of the state law. Harlan thought that requirement could "hardly be deemed . . . untoward or unduly burdensome." Nor was the Justice bothered by the fact that the state superintendent of education could take no corrective action when confronted with a legitimate charge, but instead was obliged merely to "request" that Illinois' attorney general enforce the superintendent's findings through judicial proceedings. The action or inaction of both officials, after all, was also subject to judicial oversight. "And," added the Justice, "it must of course be assumed that these two responsible public officials will fully perform their sworn duty."[80]

For Harlan, Illinois' own record in the civil rights field was perhaps even more persuasive. "[W]e should be slow to hold unavailing," he observed, "an administrative remedy afforded by a state which long before *Brown* . . . had outlawed . . . racial discrimination in its public schools, and which since *Brown* has passed the further implementing legislation drawn in question in this litigation." The others could do what they believed they must do. But as for Harlan, he was "unwilling to assume that these solemn constitutional and legislative pronouncements of Illinois mean anything less than what they say or that the rights assured by them and by the Fourteenth Amendment will not be fully and promptly vindicated by the state if petitioners can make good their grievances."[81]

Although never registered in a published opinion, the stances Harlan assumed in two cases of desegregation, in Mississippi and Charlotte, were equally instructive. In the former, Nixon administration officials had joined Mississippi authorities in urging yet another delay in meaningful desegregation of that state's schools. Justice Black, a foe of "all deliberate speed" and continued obstruction of desegregation's pace, had been infuriated at the administration's position, which he viewed as nothing more than another cynical plank in the president's "southern strategy." At conference, the Alabamian angrily asserted that the Court should not even prepare an opinion in the case, but instead should issue a brief and sharply worded order rejecting any further delay and demanding immediate desegregation. If the Court deviated in the slightest from that posture, he warned, "I dissent."[82]

Ultimately, Black's stance largely prevailed. In a two-page *Alexander v. Holmes Co.* per curiam largely drafted by Justice Brennan and announced on October 29, 1969, the Court affirmed "the obligation of every school district . . . to terminate dual school systems at once and to operate now and hereafter only unitary schools." Issuance of that "unanimous" statement was preceded, however, by fierce in-fighting in which Harlan, characteristically, had sided with the Court's most moderate members. While the Justice agreed that inordinate further delay was unthinkable, he considered Black's insistence on "immediate" compliance unreasonable and unworkable. He also thought a fully reasoned opinion, as well as an order, critically important in such a significant case.

At Chief Justice Burgers's request, Harlan drafted an order in the case to be followed, he indicated, by an opinion of the Court. That draft then became the basis for an order which the Chief Justice, Harlan, and Justice White circulated among the brethren as "a 'passable' solution of the problem." In a cover memorandum, Burger noted that the three had "concluded, tentatively, to avoid fixing any 'outside' date" for compliance, adding, "I am partly persuaded to do this because of the risk that it could have overtones which might seem to invite dilatory tactics."[83]

Justice Black, naturally, was not impressed. After conferring with Douglas and Marshall, he began drafting his threatened dissent. "In my opinion," he wrote, "there is no reason why such a wholesale deprivation of constitutional rights should be tolerated another minute."[84] When Brennan, Marshall, and Stewart also circulated drafts, Harlan produced what he hoped would be an acceptable compromise, terming it "the most satisfactory" disposition of *Alexander* "from an institutional standpoint." The Justice's new draft which drew heavily on what Justice Marshall had written, proposed issuance of an order but no opinion and emphasized "that the phrase 'all deliberate speed' [was] no longer an acceptable formula for supplanting existing racially segregated school systems by unitary school systems in which neither race nor color plays any part in the attendance of pupils." It also stipulated that the court of appeals enter an order in the case no later than November 10 and require "termination of the dual school systems and the establishment of unitary school systems forthwith and in no event later than December 31, 1969." He preferred a listing of such "outside dates," he wrote Burger, because he thought they would "strengthen the hand of the Court of Appeals in resisting dilatory tactics on the part of any of the litigants."[85]

While Harlan and his new Chief were essentially in agreement on the approach the Court should take in the Mississippi case, he clearly favored broader remedial powers for federal trial judges in the desegregation field than Warren Burger preferred to accept. This was evident in the Charlotte case. In *Swann*, U.S. District Judge James McMillan had imposed racial quotas, ordered the busing of students, and invoked related devices in mandating meaningful desegregation of North Carolina's Charlotte-Mecklenburg school system. But the Court of Appeals for the Fourth Circuit, applying what it termed a "reasonableness" standard, overturned the portion of Judge McMillan's decision calling for the busing of elementary students, calling it "excessive" and thus beyond the reach of federal judicial power; the Charlotte-Mecklenburg school board had also raised numerous other objections to the order in its appeal of the case to the Supreme Court. Following oral argument in the case early in the 1970 term, Justice Harlan wrote a memorandum in the form of a draft opinion of the Court. In it, he rejected the appeals panel's rationale and the board's position as well.[86]

Attorneys for the school board had argued that its adoption of a student assignment system based on nonracially gerrymandered geographical zones fully satisfied its constitutional obligations. Harlan disagreed. "Racially identifiable schools," he observed in language which would have pleased his grandfather, were at the core of the system of education *Brown* I and II had condemned.

> Ostensibly justified under the "separate-but-equal" doctrine of *Plessy* v. *Ferguson*, in the interest of all the state's citizens, in reality segregation was the outgrowth of a political process in which the majority race—having entirely disenfranchised the minority race—forcibly confined the children of the black community to schools designated for their own race. In this circumstance, schools became racially identifiable as "white" primarily because of the existence of schools which were all black; or, to put the point another way, the central institution of the former dual system was really the "colored" school.

Thus, contended Harlan, while there was no "*substantive constitutional right*" to education in racially balanced schools, "the elimination of [racially identifiable] schools in actual fact [would] . . . serve to vitiate the . . . identifiability of schools as either 'black' or 'white.' " For that reason, trial judges, such as James McMillan, could consider the extent to which such schools had been eliminated in determining whether a system was moving toward compliance with its constitutional obligations; in fact they could impose racial quotas as a "remedial tool" for beginning the process of eliminating racially identifiable schools. That would not mean, in Harlan's judgment, that all schools entirely or predominantly of one race were unconstitutional. But any school board proposing to retain or create such an arrangement would bear a "heavy burden" of justification. Nor was he suggesting any "magic" in a particular "statistical mix of white and black students." Such determinations, he observed, should be left largely to "the district court's informed discretion."

Harlan was equally unimpressed with the appeals panel's conclusion that by ordering the busing of elementary students Judge McMillan had exceeded his constitutional powers, and with the school board's even broader assertion that the "resources and energies required by the District Court at all three levels of the [school] system" were unreasonably harsh. North Carolina law already provided for free busing of students living more than a mile and a half from their assigned schools. And

Harlan thought it could "hardly be maintained that a school board free to make" such arrangements to achieve certain policy goals could "at the same time . . . refuse to make the same sort of assignment in order to desegregate the school system." Moreover, while he conceded that there were obviously limits to the degree of busing which could be ordered in any given case, those limits, in his judgment, clearly had not been reached in *Swann*. The record of the case had revealed that children bused pursuant to Judge McMillan's ruling would not as a group travel as far as the 28,000 students already being bused at state expense. School boards also had to realize, concluded Harlan, that conversion to a racially unitary system was not merely a policy option but a constitutional obligation. "[W]hen some all-black schools remain under a proposed desegregation plan, school officials, as we noted in *Green*, bear a heavy burden of justifying this state of affairs."

Although the Justice did not circulate his memorandum among all the brethren, he did provide Burger with a copy, as well as Stewart and Marshall, who requested copies. Harlan also shared with his Chief his impressions about Burger's own drafts. "There is much in your opinion with which I could fully agree with some emendation," he wrote of a mid-February circulation. "More particularly, I agree with your basic proposition that as a *substantive* matter our past decisions in this field have never required integration or race-mixing." He did insist, however, that earlier cases had recognized "that mixing is a permissible, if indeed not a required remedial tool for the disestablishment of state-enforced dual school systems." And he thought that Burger's draft had "blur[red] this basic distinction." The Justice was primarily concerned, though, about Burger's failure, in his judgment, ever "to come to grips" with either of the lower court opinions in the case. Harlan thought Judge McMillan was right and should be affirmed, that the appeals court was wrong, and that differences in the two lower court opinions could not be dismissed, as Burger appeared to be attempting to, as issues of "mere terminology." All the justices had agreed, he reminded his colleagues, that *Swann* should be a vehicle for furnishing guidelines to the lower courts and that such an effort was "most important . . . at the present stage of this great problem." That goal could not be accomplished, he pointedly added, through "mere generalities."[87]

However unwillingly, the Chief Justice made revisions in his opinion along the lines Harlan and others suggested. After receiving Burger's third circulation in early March, Harlan wrote his colleague that, subject to the Chief's responses to certain further suggestions, he was now "prepared to join your opinion." First, Harlan was concerned that the Chief Justice was still offering the lower courts nothing "by way of an affirmative remedial standard." When that weakness was combined with other language in the opinion imposing "expressed limitations on the use of desegregation techniques going beyond contiguous zones," the result, Harlan feared, was to give the draft "a negative cast which might overshadow everything else we do." "To remedy this problem," Harlan proposed the addition of language clearly indicating that "the amount of actual desegregation of the races [was] certainly an appropriate consideration in assessing" a school board's compliance with the Constitution.[88]

Second, the Justice suggested a reorganization of a section of Burger's opinion dealing with "Racial Balances or Racial Quotas" and the deletion of certain language in the section. "I would find it very difficult," he observed of one passage he suggested omitting,

> to accept the proposition that district courts cannot—insofar as *the intermediate conversion phase from dual to unitary system* is concerned—command school boards who once submit a satisfactory student assignment plan at the start of the school year to demonstrate that they truly are operating without racial segregation in mind by continuing to assign students and pupils during the course of the school year with a view to maintaining whatever degree of actual desegregation the initial plan contemplates.

He shared Burger's hope "that the day will come when we judges can label a system 'unitary' and depart from the education business as such." But it was that hope, wrote Harlan, "that leads me to the view that we should (1) establish an affirmative presumption for assessing school desegregation plans in the first instance and (2) then permit district court judges to insist—as a matter of regulating the intermediate conversion phase—on continuing action to preserve the results the plan contemplates."

Ultimately, Burger produced an opinion Harlan and their colleagues could join. To a much greater degree than usual on the Supreme Court, that final product had been a collegial effort. Harlan's November memorandum and later suggestions may well have been the source of most of the opinion's key language.

As noted earlier, the Justice also joined each of the Court's extensions of *Brown* I to other forms of racial segregation—but always with the caution he displayed in every constitutional field. Consider, for example, *McLaughlin* v. *Florida*, decided early in the 1964 term. There the justices confronted a statute which prohibited an unmarried interracial couple from habitually living in and occupying the same room at night. Several years later, in the *Loving* case, Harlan would join the Court in overturning Virginia's ban on interracial marriages, and there was some sentiment on the Court for having the *McLaughlin* case eliminate bans on interracial couples. Harlan, however, thought *McLaughlin* "a very bad case," as he put it in a bench memo notation, "in which to decide the miscegenation issue." Concerned that the Fourteenth Amendment's framers might not have intended its provisions to be used for such a purpose, he had his clerk Charles Nesson conduct extensive research into the historical record. Nesson found "all sorts of evidence," he recently recalled, "that lots of people would have been amazed to think the amendment would void such laws." The clerk concluded in a memorandum to the Justice, therefore, that "[a]lthough the case for concluding that antimiscegenation statutes are not covered by the Amendment is not as good as that made in [your] dissent in *Reynolds* v. *Sims* for voting . . . the case is there." For Nesson, such a finding was "only the beginning of the problem. . . . The words of the amendment [were] broad enough to cover antimiscegenation laws. . . . Is 'equal protection' a principle which can grow? Or is it a fairly static principle which [nevertheless] applies differently as society changes around it? . . . [T]he division is not on what . . . history says, but on what its present force should be."[89]

While Harlan believed that the reach of the equal protection clause should be confined largely to its historic racial context, he probably agreed with his clerk that the types of racial classifications the Fourteenth Amendment prohibited were not necessarily limited to those envisioned by its framers. At the same time, the virtually complete lack of any evidence that the amendment was intended to eliminate miscegenation laws gave him pause. As Nesson has recalled, the Justice "thought [miscegenation] laws had to go, but he wasn't rushing in that direction. He would have been relieved if the historical record had not been absolutely clear."[90] Since, if anything, the available historical evidence offered support for such laws, Harlan did not believe the Court should move too quickly to a contrary decision, especially in a case which did not even directly raise the issue.

In a letter to Justice White, who had been assigned to draft the Court's opinion in the *McLaughlin* case, Harlan suggested use of a number of First and Fourteenth Amendment cases as a basis for invalidating Florida's cohabitation statute without, for the time being, disturbing its miscegenation law. Those cases had held, he asserted, that laws infringing upon "a constitutionally protected area" could be upheld only if "necessary, and not merely rationally related to, the accomplishment of a permissible state policy." Since Florida had offered no argument that its policy against interracial couples could not be as adequately served by its racially neutral laws forbidding illicit sexual behavior as by a law "which singles out the promiscuous inter-racial couple for special statutory treatment," the cohabitation statute could not be considered a "necessary," and thus constitutionally acceptable, adjunct to the state's miscegenation law, which the Court was assuming to be valid.[91]

Justice White agreed to incorporate Harlan's recommendations into his opinion. When he was later obliged to delete those passages under pressure from other justices, Harlan filed a concurring opinion. In a separate concurrence, Justice Stewart rejected as "invidious *per se*" any law which made "the criminality of an act depend upon the race of the actor." Harlan was not prepared to go that far. In his own concurrence, the Justice applied his "necessity" test to Florida's cohabitation law.

> If the legitimacy of the . . . statute is considered to depend upon its being ancillary to the anti-marriage statute, the former must be deemed 'unnecessary' . . . in light of the [state's] nondiscriminatory extra-marital relations statutes. If, however, the interracial cohabitation statute is considered to rest upon a discrete state interest, existing independently of the anti-marriage law, it falls of its own [racially selective] weight.[92]

Harlan was spared a number of particularly vexatious issues of the post second Reconstruction era, including those relating to the status of de facto segregation and affirmative action programs. Since he had suggested language in Chief Justice Burger's *Swann* opinion emphasizing that the case involved purely government-imposed or de jure segregation, rather than that caused entirely by housing patterns and other presumably private, de facto elements, it is likely that he would have joined the Burger Court's ultimate conclusion that de jure segregation alone was vulnerable to judicial oversight.[93]

There is even less basis for speculation about the stance he might have assumed in the affirmative action field. Whatever his views about the constitutional-legal merits of such programs, however, he had made his personal feelings reasonably clear just a few years before his appointment to the bench. In 1949, Harlan and an associate, acting as a subcommittee for the judiciary committee of New York City's bar association, had reviewed the credentials of a woman candidate for a federal district judgeship. "If the appointing power is determined to fill one of the vacancies . . . by appointment of a woman judge," they concluded in their report to the committee, she was "better qualified than any other woman whose name has been publicly suggested for such appointment. At the same time, there is a frequently expressed view that it is unfortunate that candidates should be selected for this high office on the basis of sex."[94]

8

Incorporation and Beyond

With rare if notable exceptions, Justice Harlan's stance in the race cases of the 1960s was consistent with prevailing trends on the Warren Court. His reaction to the Court's decisions in numerous other cases of that eventful decade was, of course, quite another matter. In 1960, he dissented when a majority, in *Elkins* v. *United States*, completed its dismantling of the "silver platter" doctrine under which the fruits of illegal searches by state authorities were admissible as evidence in federal criminal trials. Justice Frankfurter was willing to agree that evidence seized in violation of a state's own exclusionary rule, forbidding use of illegally seized evidence in its courts, should also be excluded from federal court. But Harlan, in a published memorandum joined by justices Clark and Whittaker, rejected even the "limited inroads" on the doctrine his mentor accepted and contended that "the nonexclusionary rule . . . [had] behind it the strongest judicial credentials, the sanction of long usage, and the support of . . . sound constitutional doctrine under our federal scheme of things."[1]

The next year the Justice dissented again when the Court overturned *Wolf* v. *Colorado*, one of Felix Frankfurter's most prized—and scorned—opinions. In *Wolf* and a number of subsequent cases, the Court had held that illegally obtained evidence could be used in state cases so long as the tactics of police were not particularly offensive. *Mapp* v. *Ohio*, a 1961 decision overturning *Wolf*, declared the exclusionary rule applicable to all state trials. Dolly Mapp had been convicted of violating a statute which made the mere private possession of obscenity a criminal offense, and at conference Harlan raised serious questions about the constitutionality of such a law. But he vigorously opposed use of the case as a vehicle for overturning *Wolf*. And when Justice Clark—whose defection from the Frankfurter-Harlan bloc produced a five-man majority for such a holding—circulated a draft opinion for the Court reversing Mrs. Mapp's conviction on that ground, Harlan attempted to persuade his friend to change his rationale.[2]

In a letter to Clark which he shared with Justice Frankfurter before delivering it to their colleague, but which he did not circulate to the other brethren, Harlan lamented Clark's choice of a basis for the Court's decision. The "whole Court," he predicted, would probably have agreed that criminal punishment for the mere possession of obscene material "impermissibly deters freedom of belief and expression, if indeed it is not tantamount to an effort at 'thought control.'" Extension of the exclusionary rule to the states, on the other hand, was "not only [a] highly debatable and divisive" ground for the Court's ruling, "but also require[d] the overruling of a decision to which the Court has many times adhered over the past dozen years." Nor was Harlan ready to accept Clark's conclusion that *Weeks v. United States*, the 1914 case which had first applied the exclusionary rule in the federal courts, had been based on the Fourth Amendment right against unreasonable search and seizure rather than an exercise of the Court's supervisory power over lower federal courts. Even if *Weeks* were constitutionally based, he added, the Fourteenth Amendment did not "incorporate" the Fourth Amendment "as such. *Wolf* itself . . . let alone the uniform course of the court's decisions, have laid that ghost at rest." Finally, the Justice rejected any suggestion on Clark's part that the *Wolf* Court's refusal to extend the exclusionary rule to state cases had rested "on mere 'factual considerations' devolving from the circumstances that most of the states at that time had no 'exclusionary' rule" and that the increasing number of state adoptions of the rule was thus a legitimate ground for *Wolf*'s reversal. "Rather, [*Wolf*] most certainly rested on the fundamentals of federal-state relations in the realm of criminal law enforcement." Also, if *Mapp* were retroactively applied to earlier cases, the ruling would lead, Harlan feared, to "a jail delivery of uncertain, but obviously serious, proportions" for state defendants imprisoned in violation of the rule—defendants now entitled to a new trial free of the evidence which led to their original convictions. "The upshot of all this," concluded Harlan, "is that I earnestly ask you to reconsider the advisability of facing the Court, in a case which otherwise should find a ready and non-controversial solution, with the difficult and controversial issues that your proposed opinion tenders."[3]

But Clark stood his ground. While conceding that *Wolf* had been followed in several cases, he insisted that "in each in which a full dress opinion resulted it was done grudgingly." He suspected, moreover, that "relatively few" defendants "before or since *Wolf*" had made "timely objections" to the use of illegal evidence at their trials—a necessary predicate, in his judgment, for a *Mapp* challenge to their convictions and the sort of "jail delivery" about which Harlan had warned. Most important, Clark could not ignore the inconsistency he perceived between the *Wolf* Court's recognition of a Fourteenth Amendment right of personal privacy against unreasonable searches and seizures and its rejection of the exclusionary rule in state cases. "[I]f the right of privacy is really so basic as to be constitutional in rank and if it is really to be enforceable against the states *(Wolf)*, then we cannot carve out of the bowels of that right the vital part, the stuff that gives it substance, the exclusion of evidence. It has long been recognized and honored as an integral part of the equivalent right against federal action." While Clark agreed that *Wolf* had rested in part on considerations of federalism, he thought the trend toward state adoptions of the rule had "dissipated . . . what, if any, pressure the federalism concept" had exerted on the *Wolf* Court. Whatever advantages federalism might offer, added Clark, extensions of the rule to the states would achieve "a necessary symmetry in our constitutional doctrine on both federal and state exercise of those powers incident to their enforcement of criminal law which deal most directly with individual freedom and pose perhaps its greatest threat." Besides, he pointedly observed, "I have a court and my theory at least has support."[4]

Harlan was not the only justice concerned with Clark's *Mapp* effort. Clark's draft referred to the Court's extension of "the Fourth Amendment's right of privacy" to the states. Justice Black promptly retorted that his willingness to join the opinion would depend "upon my understanding that you read *Wolf* as having held, and that we are holding here, that the Fourth Amendment *as a whole* is applicable to the States and not some imaginary and unknown fragment designated as the 'right of privacy.' " Black, the preeminent literalist for whom the exclusionary rule always posed enormous difficulty, ultimately filed a separate concurrence in which he reluctantly endorsed the rule and its application to the states, but based his position on the Fifth Amendment's guarantee against compulsory self-incrimination as well as on the right against unreasonable search and seizure. In his response to Black's letter, Clark had assured the Justice that the "gist" of his *Mapp* opinion viewed *Wolf* as holding "the entire Fourth Amendment to be carried over against the states through the Fourteenth." At the same time, he had sought to assure Justice Harlan that his opinion was no "windfall to 'incorporation' enthusiasts," albeit adding, "If it is then *Wolf* brought it on."[5]

But with Harlan as with Black, Clark's efforts were to no avail. When *Mapp* was announced, Harlan, joined by Frankfurter and Whittaker, registered a vigorous dissent elaborating on the objections he had raised in his letter to the ruling's author. The majority, he charged, had "simply 'reached out' to overrule *Wolf*" instead of basing its decision on the "simpler and less far-reaching" obscenity question—the principal issue decided by the lower court and briefed and argued before the brethren in the case. The "specifics of trial procedure," he added, were "within the sole competence of the States." For that reason, the "Court should continue to forebear from fettering the States with an adamant rule which may embarrass them in coping with their own peculiar problems in criminal law enforcement."[6]

In a later draft and the final version of his opinion, Justice Clark drew an analogy between coerced confessions and illegally seized evidence, concluding that the Court's policy of requiring the exclusion of all involuntary confessions, however reliable, logically would compel an identical holding for all illegal evidence, not merely that obtained through unusually offensive means, which *Wolf* and its progeny required. Harlan was not persuaded. The exclusion of illegal evidence was intended as "an appropriate remedy for what the police have done," while the exclusion of coerced confessions went "to the heart of our concepts of fairness in judicial procedure." The latter, he asserted, was "a *procedural* right," the violation of which "occur[red] at the time [an] improperly obtained statement [was] admitted at trial." Protection against such violation of the accused's constitutional rights thus could not be compared to the policy underlying the exclusion of illegal evidence. Harlan had no doubt that *Mapp*, like the coerced confession decisions, was designed to promote "the high purpose of increasing respect for Constitutional rights." He insisted, however, that "in the last analysis [the] Court can increase respect for the Constitution only if it rigidly respects the limiations which the Constitution places upon it, and respects as well the principles inherent in its own processes. In the present case I think we exceed both, and that our voice becomes only a voice of power, not of reason."[7]

Wolf and its progeny had been the targets of intense attack. Lower courts undoubtedly had found it difficult to predict what illegal seizures of evidence the Court would find "shocking to the conscience," and thus according to *Wolf* inadmissible in state cases, and which seizures did not encroach unduly on the privacy right *Wolf* had embraced. Harlan and Frankfurter could hardly have been surprised, therefore, that a majority of the Court would extend the exclusionary rule to all state cases.

The Court's further break with its past, decided the following term in *Baker* v. *Carr*, must have been a major shock to the two allies, however. That they ultimately stood alone in dissent from Justice Brennan's opinion for the *Baker* majority, which held that legislative malapportionment presented justiciable questions trial courts were obliged to review, was no doubt as alarming as it was deeply disappointing. For although Justice Frankfurter had spoken for only three members of the Court in rejecting a challenge to congressional malapportionment in *Colegrove* v. *Green* fifteen years earlier, no later case had challenged the Justice's assertion there that federal courts should avoid malapportionment's "political thicket." And *Baker* v. *Carr*, after all, involved the legislature of a sovereign state and thus issues of federalism the *Colegrove* Court had not confronted.[8]

Initially, it had appeared that Frankfurter and Harlan might muster a majority for their position. Following the first oral argument of *Baker* in the spring of 1961, Warren, Black, Douglas, and Brennan had voted to reverse the district court's dismissal of the suit, while Frankfurter, Harlan, Clark, and Whittaker favored affirmance, and Stewart passed. Victory for the Frankfurter-Harlan stance thus appeared entirely possible if the two could only win Stewart's vote and retain the support of Whittaker, who, while no enthusiast for *Colegrove*, was reluctant to see it reversed by a bare majority.[9]

Following re-argument but before a second conference in the case the next October, Justice Frankfurter circulated a sixty-page memorandum detailing his defense of *Colegrove* and the horrors awaiting the justices should they enter the reapportionment thicket. Frankfurter found it "necessary to state in comprehensive detail," he observed in a cover letter, "the problems involved in this case, the disposition of which has such far-reaching implications for the well-being of this Court." The four justices who favored intervention were unimpressed. Beside Frankfurter's assertion on the memo that Chief Justice Stone had agreed with his *Colegrove* opinion though he died before it was announced, Hugo Black, a *Colegrove* dissenter, penned on his copy of the memorandum, "He complained last year about my reference to inter-office communiations." Next to his colleague's assurances that "a court will always find the power to curb abuses," despite the "political question" on which Colegrove rested, Black noted, "There are abuses here." And where Frankfurter had emphasized that *Baker* was not a case in which a state had denied blacks, Jews, or redheads the vote, or given them only a fractional vote, Black retorted, "But it is a case in which a state has given persons—not only Negroes or Jews—¼ or 1/40th of a vote."[10] Frankfurter hoped, however, to persuade Stewart to embrace his thinking.

For his part, Justice Harlan wrote Stewart and Whittaker a lengthy, eloquent appeal. *Baker*, he asserted, was among the most important cases ever to come before the Court, "not excluding" *Brown*, and particularly so because of its implications for the Court's independence and "aloofness from political vicissitudes," which provides "the mainstream of its stability and vitality." The Court's insulation from the political processes, he added, was assured not only by constitutional and statutory safeguards "but also to a large extent, I believe, by the wise restraint which, by and large, has characterized the Court's handling of emotionally-charged popular causes." *Baker*, he warned, "threaten[ed] the preservation" of that independence.[11]

Harlan was in no way suggesting, he assured his colleagues, that any member of the current Court "or, hopefully . . . any future" justice, would yield to political pressure. "But," he asked, "is not the political aloofness of the Court almost as much a matter of appearance as of actual fact? And, were we now to enter this 'political thicket,' would we not inevitably be courting such appearances, however unfounded, as all manner and gradations of apportionment cases come to our door? The only sure way of avoiding this is to keep the gate to the thicket tightly closed." Nor, he added, should the justices "fall prey" to the soothing assurance that the states themselves will undertake the necessary reforms, if only the Court will "pronounce state apportionment to be a federal judicial concern. We should not . . . put our hand to the plow unless we are prepared to accept what may, and I predict is likely to, follow." Such concerns had guided the *Colegrove* Court, and Harlan considered that case, "its progenitors and offspring . . . among the wisest and [most] farsighted decisions of the Court." The "responsibility," he concluded, "is entirely in our laps, and to me it would be a sad thing were we by our own act to plunge this institution into what would bid fair, as time goes on, to erode its stature."

Justice Frankfurter applauded the "soul-searching" that must have preceded the normally taciturn Harlan's decision to write his colleagues and termed his letter an "important service to the Court, whatever the outcome." But neither the letter nor the two justices' other efforts would succeed. In February, Harlan shared with Stewart a *New York Times* editorial lamenting the partisan politics surrounding a Massachusetts congressional redistricting dispute and urged his colleague "to await (if your mind is still open)" a reading of an opinion Harlan was drafting "before casting what will be the decisive, and if I may say so, fateful vote in this case." "Feeling as strongly as I do about the shortsightedness and unwisdom of what is proposed to us" in Justice Brennan's draft opinion for the Court in the case, he added, characteristically, that he hoped Stewart would not think his request "presumptuous" or "unbrotherly." By that point, however, Stewart had already cast his lot with Brennan.[12]

The final tally was even worse. At conference, Justice Clark had voted to affirm the lower court, based on his conclusion that the *Baker* plaintiffs had failed to exhaust other avenues of relief before seeking a judicial remedy for their plight. But while preparing to write a dissent along those lines, at Frankfurter's suggestion, Clark discovered, as he put it in a letter to the Justice, that he could find no "practical course that the people could take in bringing [reapportionment] about except through the Federal Courts." Clark sent Harlan a copy of the letter. "I am sorry that I cannot go along," he penned at the top, "but it does not change the result anyway."[13]

Frankfurter could not conceal his frustration. "At the core of [this] sad performance," he wrote Harlan as the final fate of their position was becoming increasingly evident,

> was—is—a failure to appreciate the intrinsic and acquired majesty of the Court's significance in the affairs of the country and of the correlative responsibility of every member of the Court to maintain and further this significance.
>
> Why do I bother you with this? I suppose to prove the truth of a German saying that when the heart is full it spills over. And so it spills over on you—who alone gives me comfort.[14]

Harlan confined his own feelings largely to the pages of his published opinions. In his dissent, Frankfurter scorned the Court's assumption that judges had either the authority or the wisdom to determine what would constitute a "fair" system of representation. Harlan joined Frankfurter's effort, calling it "a remarkably fine document," and also filed one of his own. He thought it "beyond argument" that a system of representation could be based on other "factors . . . than bare numbers." Certainly, he argued, the equal protection clause demanded neither "mathematical identity [nor] rigid equality." Instead, it required only a "rational" basis, at most, for any apportionment scheme. And, to Harlan, a legislature could clearly reach the "rational" conclusion

> that an existing allocation of senators and representatives constitute[d] a desirable balance of geographical and demographical representation, or that in the interest of stability of government it would be best to defer for some further time the redistribution of seats in the state legislature. . . . [S]o long as there exist[ed] a possible rational legislative policy for retaining an existing apportionment, such a legislative decision [could not] be said to breach the bulwark against arbitrariness and caprice that the Fourteenth Amendment affords.

The issue, in short, was one of power, not wisdom or fairness.

> [O]ne need not agree, as a citizen, with what Tennessee has done or failed to do, in order to deprecate, as a judge, what the majority is doing today. Those observers of the Court who see it primarily as the last refuge for the correction of all inequality or injustice, no matter what its nature or source, will no doubt applaud this decision and its break with the past. Those who consider that continuing national respect for the Court's authority depends in large measure upon its wise exercise of self-restraint and discipline in constitutional adjudication, will view the decision with deep concern.[15]

Baker, however, was not to be Harlan's deepest disappointment during the Court's fateful 1961 term. On April 6, shortly after the decision was announced, Justice Frankfurter suffered a stroke while working in his chambers. All the brethren and their families were solicitous and encouraging. Justice Black advised Frankfurter to "not let Court business disturb you. In this way you can get back sooner and continue your long and highly useful public service." And Black's son, Hugo, Jr., expressed the hope that Frankfurter would soon be "back at the Court and debating with my father."[16]

But it was Harlan who was his mentor's mainstay. On April 25, Chief Justice Warren circulated a memorandum to Frankfurter's colleagues. In it, he complained of the justices' scant knowledge regarding Frankfurter's actual condition and the "critical" state in which his absence, as well as Whittaker's resignation and replacement by Justice White, had left the Court's docket. Warren declared that "the Court must know at least what the likelihood is of his returning before adjournment," then added, "I hesitate to say this because there is no one of us who would not do anything within his power to help Felix recover his health or to complete his work."[17]

The next day, Harlan visited Frankfurter's hospital room. "Justice Harlan was here yesterday," Frankfurter later noted in a letter dictated to a clerk, "and expressed himself very strongly, speaking both as a friend and a colleague, that my job was to concentrate on getting well and freeing myself of all Court burdens with which I am now concerned. Specifically he said it would be a personal favor to him if I allowed him to take over the legislative-v.-constitutional Court cases."[18]

Frankfurter accepted his friend's offer, and Harlan provided assistance in other ways as well. But two additional heart attacks made the probable inevitable. On August 28, Frankfurter sent President Kennedy a letter tendering his resignation from "the institution whose concerns have been the absorbing interest of my life."[19]

Frankfurter's formal separation from the Court did not end his efforts to influence Harlan or their other colleagues. In letters to Justice Black, the retired Justice Frankfurter urged his jurisprudential antagonist to register his views—and Frankfurter's—on the constitutional status of sit-ins. Before sending letters to other justices, Frankfurter sought Harlan's counsel. "Here is another one of those long ones," Frankfurter's secretary indicated in a note accompanying one such draft. "The Justice asks if you will read this and then call him to give him the benefit of your views."[20]

Harlan did his best to bolster his friend's spirits. "It's a real thrill," he wrote Frankfurter a month after his retirement, "to be getting this sort of thing again from you. Your handwriting is just as good as it always was, in fact more decipherable!!" But the cautious Harlan was unable to condone all his mentor's lobbying efforts. On one occasion, Frankfurter proposed circulating a law review article to the other justices. Harlan agreed that the piece was "impressive."

> Nevertheless, after reflecting overnight on our yesterday's conversation, I am still of the view that you should not send it to the Brethren. Although I cannot conceive of there being any impropriety in this one instance, it does seem to me that a recurring practice of this kind would be open to question. I therefore earnestly urge you not to "open the door," since it is bound to face you with troublesome decisions in the future. See *Baker* v. *Carr*. The best way, in my view, for the future is to handle your contacts with the Court on an informal and selective individual basis.[21]

Harlan may have found another Frankfurter campaign even more disturbing. During the term following Frankfurter's retirement, the Court reviewed *Gray* v. *Sanders*, a challenge to Georgia's "county unit" system, an electoral scheme deliberately designed to give rural voters control over the ballot box. Harlan was the lone dissenter from a ruling dismantling the system. In the summer before the term began, he had instructed his new clerks, David Shapiro and Richard Hiegel, to thoroughly familiarize themselves with various facets of the malapportionment issue and a lengthy memorandum a Frankfurter clerk had prepared on the subject.[22]

But Frankfurter was apparently uncertain, given Harlan's regard for precedent, about the Justice's continued commitment to their *Baker* stance. Or perhaps he feared that Shapiro and Hiegel might try to win Harlan over to the *Baker* majority's position. In any event, Frankfurter decided to lobby Harlan's clerks. To their considerable surprise, he invited Shapiro and Hiegel to his home for lunch. "When we arrived," Hiegel has recalled, "he instructed us to take notes, then proceeded to lecture us at length about *Gray* v. *Sanders*." The discussion was wide-ranging. At one point, Frankfurter asked Hiegel his impressions about a figure in the British labor movement. "It's a good thing," the retired Justice retorted when the clerk confessed he had never heard of the union leader in question, "that you didn't go to Harvard."[23]

Shapiro and Hiegel were shocked at Frankfurter's behavior. Harlan, Hiegel believes, was also offended, just as he was later that term when Justice Goldberg, Frankfurter's successor, attempted to lobby Harlan's clerks on other pending cases. It seemed likely that Harlan's feelings about Frankfurter were always, to some extent, mixed. As one of Harlan's early clerks has observed, "he obviously had enormous respect for Frankfurter. At the same time, one also sensed some kind of tension in the relationship. I mean, here was Frankfurter, who . . . was frequently lecturing, with this enormous sense of superior knowledge. . . . I wouldn't doubt that the Justice sensed some need to fight for his own independence," especially early in his tenure.[24]

Whatever his personal feelings, however, Harlan remained loyal and supportive of his colleagues to the end. Nor was his solicitude lost on Frankfurter's other friends. When University of Chicago law professor Philip Kurland, a Frankfurter clerk, was unable to attend a 1963 Harlan appearance at the school, he sent the Justice a letter of apology. "Presumptuous as it may be," wrote Kurland, "I wanted to tell you how grateful Mr. Justice Frankfurter's friends are for the very great kindnesses you have shown and are showing to him and to Mrs. F. In this most difficult of times for him, you give him the greatest consolation that he now has, not only by your attendance upon him, but because he regards you as the sole member of the Court dedicated by acts and not merely words to the proposition that the Supreme Court is a judicial body."[25]

Any doubts Justice Frankfurter might have had about the depth of Harlan's commitment to the jurisprudential philosophy they both embrace must have been resolved well before the Justice's death in 1965.

For Harlan continued after Frankfurter's retirement to be a forceful, eloquent critic of many Warren Court civil liberties trends, especially its extension of Bill of Rights safeguards to the states, expansive interpretations of the guarantees accorded criminal defendants, and enlargement of the equal protection guarantee well beyond that engimatic provision's historic racial context. Even before Frankfurter's death, Harlan had also begun to make clear his willingness to practice an element of Frankfurter's jurisprudence the elder Justice usually only preached—the notion that due process is an evolving concept which can expand, as well as contract, in meaning.

The Incorporation Revolution

By the time of Justice Harlan's appointment, if not long before, a majority of the Court had firmly embraced the claim that the Fourteenth Amendment imposed the same standards on the states as the First Amendment placed on federal officials. The justices had been decidedly more reluctant to extend the procedural safeguards of the Bill of Rights to state proceedings. In 1948, Justice Black had persuaded his brethren to guarantee state defendants a public trial. As the Court's spokesman, however, he had been obliged to hold only that public trials were a necessary ingredient of the procedural "fairness" demand of state tribunals by the Fourteenth Amendment's due process clause, drawing no connection between the Court's holding and the Sixth Amendment's specific guarantee of such trials in federal proceedings, much less to his broader thesis that the Fourteenth Amendment's framers had intended its first section to apply all the provisions of the first eight amendments to the states. Not until *Mapp* v. *Ohio* did the Court construe the Fourteenth Amendment to embody a single additional procedural guarantee equal in reach to one of those in the Bill of Rights. In its famous dictim in *Palko* v. *Connecticut*, the Court had concluded in 1937 that the Fourteenth Amendment's due process clause included within its meaning only those safeguards which were essential to liberty and justice. And the Court of the 1930s, 1940s, and 1950s had found only the guarantee to a public trial and the privacy right recognized in *Wolf* to be of so fundamental a character. The *Palko* Court had refused to apply the Fifth Amendment guarantee against double jeopardy to the states. *Betts* v. *Brady* (1942) rejected the claim that the Sixth Amendment right to counsel was essential to justice, at least in noncapital state cases. And in *Adamson* v. *California* (1947), a five–four Court rejected application to the states of the Fifth Amendment's safeguards against compulsory self-incrimination, as well as the "total incorporation" thesis Justice Black advanced in his lengthy *Adamson* dissent.[26]

But even before *Mapp*, a shift in the Court's position was becoming increasingly likely. In 1960, for example, the justices, with Potter Stewart not participating, divided equally on whether to sustain the constitutionality of an ordinance permitting building inspectors to conduct warrantless inspections. But in an opinion joined by Warren, Black, and Douglas (who had also joined Black's *Adamson* dissent), Justice Brennan not only indicated that he and the Chief Justice had "neither accepted nor rejected" incorporation of the entire Bill of Rights into the Fourteenth Amendment, but also repudiated the notion, basic to Frankfurter's and Harlan's thinking (though neither justice would have appreciated Brennan's language), that the due process test articulated in the *Palko* case was "a license to the judiciary to administer a watered-down version of the guarantee against unreasonable searches and seizures" to uphold warrantless administrative inspections.[27]

For the first several terms of the 1960s, Harlan was able to avoid a full-dress confrontation with the incorporationists. When Justice Black used such language in a 1961 ruling forbidding states to impose religious tests as a requirement for holding state office, Harlan joined only the Court's decision, not his colleague's opinion, "which I daresay," he wrote Black, "will not surprise you." When a Brennan opinion in an obscenity case appeared to suggest that the Fourteenth Amendment embodied the provisions of the First Amendment, he suggested that Brennan refer instead simply "to freedoms of thought and expression assured by the Fourteenth Amendment," without mention of its Bill of Rights counterpart. And he joined a 1962 opinion filed by Justice Douglas in a state case involving the obligations of government to provide "just compensation" when exercising the power of eminent domain only after Douglas modified language in his draft which, "read literally," as Harlan put it, "could be taken as 'incorporating' into the Fourteenth Amendment . . . the entire Fifth Amendment," not merely its just compensation provisions. He reminded his colleague, moreover, that an 1897 opinion extending the obligation to the states had "not refer[red] to the Fifth [Amendment], but only to the Fourteenth" Amendment's general protection against the taking of property without due process of law.[28] Largely because Brennan and certain other justices were still searching for a position on the issue, the debate had not yet come to a head.

Ironically enough, Harlan may even have been instrumental in securing a full Court review for *Robinson* v. *California*, the 1962 case in which the justices first forbade the states to inflict cruel and unusual punishments, which the Eighth Amendment barred federal authorities from imposing. Robinson was convicted of violating a state law prohibiting the use of narcotics or addiction to its use. Chief Justice Warren had placed Robinson's appeal on the special list to which cases meriting no review, in the Chief Justice's judgment, were relegated. Unless removed from the list at another justice's request, such cases were denied a full hearing without any discussion or vote at conference. Robinson's appeal was taken off the list. But that action meant only that it would be examined at conference. Removal from the list was not tantamount to a grant of review, much less a final victory for the appellant.[29]

When *Robinson* was brought up for discussion at conference, Harlan asked that a vote be delayed until he could examine the case further. Later, he circulated a memorandum to the brethren urging a grant of review. The Justice's reading of the trial record had convinced him that Robinson might have been convicted for his mere status as an addict rather than for any conduct on his part. For Harlan, such an expansive exercise of state power "raise[d] serious constitutional questions." At the very least, he added, the statute at issue was "capable of the most mischievous sort of abuse."[30]

When the Court not only agreed to a full review of Robinson's appeal but also reversed his conviction, Harlan joined the majority's decision, though not its opinion. With customary caution, the Justice indicated in a concurring opinion that he was not "prepared to hold . . . on the present state of medical knowledge" whether a narcotics addict could be held accountable to a state's criminal laws. Under the trial judge's instructions, Robinson's jury could have convicted him merely for his status. "Since addiction alone [could not] reasonably be thought to amount to more than a compelling propensity to use narcotics," he asserted, "the effect of the instruction was to authorize criminal punishment for a bare desire to commit a criminal act." Harlan could not tolerate such an "arbitrary" exercise of state power.[31]

But Harlan's concurrence in the *Robinson* decision was evidence neither that he embraced an expansive interpretation of the safeguard against cruel and unusual punishments nor that his resolve against incorporation, of whatever variety, was weakening. And while Justice Stewart's opinion for the *Robinson* Court had concluded that the conviction there violated the Eighth and Fourteenth Amendments, the opinion's language was reasonably consistent with Justice Frankfurter's conclusion in *Wolf* that the Fourteenth Amendment due process clause included within its reach safeguards comparable to the ones in the Bill of Rights, though not the express terms of those guarantees—the stance, of course, which Harlan also embraced. When, in *Powell* v. *Texas*, decided several years later, a majority initially construed *Robinson* to forbid the criminal prosecution of chronic alcoholics for public drunkenness, the Justice joined a Black dissent which drew a distinction between a state's power to punish conduct, at issue in *Powell*, and its prosecution of a mere status, as in *Robinson*. When the Court reversed ground and upheld Powell's conviction, Harlan joined the new majority.[32]

The lull in the storm was to be short-lived, however. The Court had held in *Betts* v. *Brady* that states were obliged to provide counsel for indigent defendants only where the "totality of the circumstances" of a particular case required appointment of an attorney to assure the accused a "fair trial." However, the Court had found such "special circumstances" in every case in which it had confronted the issue since 1950.[33] It appeared increasingly obvious, therefore, that *Betts* had been overruled de facto and that its formal repudiation awaited only the arrival of an appropriate case.

The appeal of Clarence Earl Gideon, an indigent Florida inmate convicted of breaking and entering under circumstances strikingly similar to those at issue in *Betts*, provided the vehicle. Justice Harlan apparently had sought to delay reconsideration of *Betts* as long as possible. For example, on a sheet of notations prepared for oral argument of *Conley* v. *Cochran*, decided on "fair trial" grounds during the 1961 term, he had noted that he did not "think we need reach overruling Betts v. Brady" in deciding the case. In the face of growing pressure from his colleagues and the close proximity of *Gideon*'s facts to those of *Betts*, however, he bowed to the inevitable. In a memorandum for the conference, he proposed that counsel in the case be

> requested to discuss the following question in their briefs and oral argument:
>
> "Should this Court's holding in *Betts* v. *Brady* . . . that the Fourteenth Amendment does not prescribe 'that, in every case, whatever the circumstances, one charged with crime, who is unable to obtain counsel, must be furnished counsel by the State' . . . be reconsidered?"[34]

But even the phrasing of Harlan's suggestion—unlike the brief, unelaborated question ("Should this Court's holding . . . be reconsidered?") actually submitted to the parties—reflected the Justice's concern about the impact *Betts*'s reversal would have on state proceedings. During oral argument in the case, he took issue several times with Gideon's Court-appointed counsel Abe Fortas and Fortas's characterizations of both *Betts* and the nature of the American federal system. When at one point Fortas appeared to disparage what he termed the Court's "understanding sensitivity . . . to the pull of federalism," an observer later reported that "[t]his usually gentle man [Harlan] visibly reddened, leaned forward and said very sharply, 'Really, Mr. Fortas, "understanding sensitivity" seems to me a most unfortunate term to describe one of the fundamental principles of our constitutional systems.' "[35] When *Betts* was overruled, it was thus not surprising that Harlan joined only the Court's judgment, not its opinion.

As the Court's spokesman in *Gideon* v. *Wainwright*, Justice Black was obliged to eschew invoking "total incorporation" rhetoric in defending the ruling—leaving that task to Justice Douglas via a concurrence which Black did, however, review and approve. Instead, he concluded that the Sixth Amendment guarantee to counsel was a "fundamental" right and therefore applicable to state proceedings through the Fourteenth Amendment due process clause. Nor, he observed, was the Court's conclusion a novel one. The justices had recognized counsel's fundamental character as long ago as *Powell* v. *Alabama,* the important 1932 decision reversing the conviction and death sentences of defendants in the infamous "Scottsboro trials" on counsel grounds. While the *Powell* Court, as the Court "frequently does," had limited its "holding to the [case's] particular facts and circumstances," it had also made "conclusions about the fundamental nature of the right to counsel [which were] unmistakable." Later cases, too, had recognized the guarantee's importance. *Betts,* Black concluded, had thus "made an abrupt break with [the Court's] own well-considered precedents."[36]

In his concurrence, Harlan agreed that *Betts* "should be overruled, but consider[ed] it entitled to a more respectful burial than" Black's opinion had given it. The *Powell* Court had found effective counsel "a necessary requisite of due process" in a capital case involving youthful, ignorant, and illiterate defendants tried in a hostile atmosphere. Those "limiting facts,' he insisted, "were not added to the opinion as an afterthought; they were repeatedly emphasized . . . and were clearly regarded as important to the result." When the *Betts* Court had held a decade later that appointed counsel was not required for state defendants in all cases, but only where necessary to assure a fair trial, it was following, not breaking with, the principles announced in *Powell.* In fact, observed Harlan, since *Betts* had recognized a state's obligation to appoint lawyers for indigent defendants in some noncapital cases, rather than capital cases alone, *Betts* "was in truth not a departure from, but an extension of, existing precedent."[37]

Harlan realized, however, that the *Betts* precedent was "no longer a reality." Even by the time it was announced, the Court had come close to holding that state indigents had an absolute right to counsel in capital cases. Numerous subsequent decisions had also "substantially and steadily eroded" the *Betts* "special circumstances" rule in noncapital cases, so much so, in fact, that a serious criminal charge alone had apparently come to constitute a special circumstance requiring appointment of counsel. "To continue a rule which is honored by this Court only with lip service," particularly when many state judges "charged with the front-line responsibility for the enforcement of constitutional rights" were not yet aware of *Betts*'s de facto demise, was, asserted Harlan, "not a healthy thing and in the long run will do disservice to the federal system."[38] For that reason, and perhaps that reason alone, he joined the Court's ruling.

The Justice emphasized, nevertheless, what he perceived to be the limits of the Court's ruling. *Gideon,* he maintained, applied only to cases involving "the possibility of a substantial prison sentence," leaving for another day the question "[w]hether the rule [it established] should extend to *all* criminal cases." Nor in his judgment did it disturb his reading of the *Palko* case. A holding by the Court that a particular guarantee of the Bill of Rights was, in the language of *Palko,* "implicit in the concept of ordered liberty," and thus applicable to the states, did not mean that the safeguard should have an identical meaning in both federal and state cases, including that established in earlier federal cases. "Any such concept," he observed, echoing his *Roth* opinion in the obscenity field, "would disregard the frequently wide disparity between the legitimate interests of the states and of the Federal Government, the divergent problems that they face, and the significantly different consequences of their actions." He had joined the Court's ruling in *Gideon*, he asserted, only because he understood that it had neither departed from the principles of *Palko* nor embraced "the concept that the Fourteenth Amendment 'incorporates' the Sixth Amendment as such."[39]

Again, as the Court's spokesman, Justice Black was hardly inclined to take issue with Harlan's reading of the ruling. Justice Douglas was not so inhibited. "My Brother Harlan," observed Douglas in his *Gideon* concurrence,

> is of the view that a guarantee of the Bill of Rights that is made applicable to the States by reason of the Fourteenth Amendment is a lesser version of that same guarantee. . . . But that view has not prevailed and rights protected against state invasion by the Due Process Clause of the Fourteenth Amendment are not watered-down versions of what the Bill of Rights guarantees.[40]

Over Harlan's protests, the view Douglas advanced would soon prevail. Three months after *Gideon* was announced, the Court held in *Ker v. California* that state search and seizure practices were subject to the same constitutional standards as federal practices. Harlan had thought an early draft of Justice Clark's disposition of the case had "handled the matter very well." But when a later draft "embrace[d] 'incorporation' in full-blown form," he parted company with Clark's opinion, expressing regret that his colleague had "felt constrained to depart from" his original stance. When the case went down, Harlan joined only the Court's judgment, stating his own views in a concurrence.[41]

In the past, he contended, federal searches and seizures had been governed by the standard of "reasonableness" required by the Fourth Amendment's language, while the practices of state law enforcement officers and courts were subject only to the "more flexible concept of 'fundamental' fairness, of rights 'basic to a free society,' embraced in" the Fourteenth Amendment due process clause—and "properly so," in Harlan's judgment. The *Ker* Court's rejection of that policy was both "uncalled for and unwise"—uncalled for because states were steadily improving their own procedures and the Fourteenth Amendment stood "as a bulwark against serious local shortcomings"; unwise because state variations in law enforcement problems should not be obstructed by a national "constitutional strait jacket," especially since those federal standards were "hardly notable for their predictability." He could see, concluded Harlan, "no good coming from [such a] constitutional adventure."[42]

The movement which Justice Black had long advocated now appeared irreversible, even if a majority was never to accept the complete incorporation of the Bill of Rights which Black favored, much less his reading of the intentions of the Fourteenth Amendment's framers. As late as 1961, Harlan spoke for the Court in upholding disbarment of a lawyer who had asserted his right against self-incrimination before a state court's investigations of professional misconduct in the legal profession, the Justice holding that the Fifth Amendment privilege did not apply to state proceedings and that the Fourteenth Amendment due process clause forbade only "irrational" state efforts to secure information through government inquiries. In *Malloy* v. *Hogan* (1964), however, a five–four Court reversed *Adamson* v. *California* and *Twining* v. *New Jersey*—which Justice Frankfurter had once termed "cloudless"—and held that the Fifth Amendment guarantee applied equally to state and federal cases.[43]

A Harlan clerk had urged the Justice to join the *Malloy* majority in this " 'pure vanilla' Fifth Amendment case" involving a petitioner jailed for civil contempt until he agreed to answer questions raised during a state gambling investigation. The draft opinion Justice Brennan had circulated in the case, the clerk conceded, had held "that the standards of self-incrimination applicable to the federal government [were also] applicable to the states." But Brennan had "expressly disclaim[ed] the incorporation theory," relying instead on "the fundamental fairness concept." A person, the clerk argued, should "not be held in prison until he talks; that violates my sense of fundamental fairness."[44]

Harlan could not agree. "I can only regard the Court's opinion as accepting in fact," he charged in a *Malloy* dissent, "what it rejects in theory: the application to the States, via the Fourteenth Amendment, of the [identical] forms of federal criminal procedure embodied within the first eight Amendments to the Constitution" and the judicial decisions construing them. The Justice agreed that the meaning of due process could expand over time, with the courts keeping it in step with the continuing "development of the community's sense of justice." He acknowledged, too, that both the Fifth and Fourteenth amendments prohibited some of the same practices. He vigorously rejected the notion, however, that the continuing judicial "re-examination" of the reach of due process, "including, of course, reference to the particular guarantees of the Bill of Rights" as an important guide to its meaning, could "be short-circuited by the simple device of incorporating into due process, without critical examination, the whole body of law which surrounds a specific prohibition directed against the Federal Government." Numerous earlier cases, including those raising Fifth Amendment self-incrimination claims, had repudiated, he asserted, such an approach. *Palko*, *Twining*, and other decisions had recognized that due process might include within its scope a particular Bill of Rights guarantee and that the language of the Bill of Rights "might provide historical evidence that [a right] . . . was traditionally regarded as fundamental." But they had also made clear that "inclusion of a [guarantee] in due process was otherwise entirely independent of the first eight Amendments."[45]

The fact that First Amendment rights had "generally been given equal scope" in federal and state cases was for Harlan "only tangentially relevant" to the basic issue.

> It is toying with constitutional principles to assert that the Court has "rejected the notion that the Fourteenth Amendment applies to the states only a 'watered-down, subjective version of the individual guarantees of the Bill of Rights.' " . . . What the Court has, with the single exception of the Ker case . . . consistently rejected is the notion that the Bill of Rights, as such, applies to the States in any aspect at all.

Nor was the Justice at all consoled that his colleagues were engaging in " 'incorporation' in snatches," rather than the total application of the Bill of Rights to the states for which Black and Douglas had campaigned. "If . . . the Due Process Clause *is* something more than a reference to the Bill of Rights and protects only those rights which derive from fundamental principles, as the majority purports to believe, it is just as contrary to precedent and just as illogical to incorporate the provisions of the Bill of Rights one at a time as it is to incorporate them all at once."[46]

But Harlan not only rejected the Court's application of identical self-incrimination standards in federal and state cases. While Malloy's treatment had affronted his clerk's "sense of fundamental fairness," the Justice had found no constitutional violation, whatever the standard employed. Noting that the statute of limitations had run out on any crimes Malloy might have committed during the time period about which he was probed, Connecticut's highest court had concluded that the petitioner had confused "vague and improbable possibilities of prosecution" with serious ones. In a separate dissent joined by Justice Stewart, Justice White contended that under the Court's own precedents, not even a federal witness' refusal to answer questions was "to be automatically . . . accepted." Harlan agreed on both counts. Given the unlikelihood that Malloy's response would actually have been used against him, his treatment, contended Harlan, was in no way "lacking in fundamental fairness." And the Court's reference to a federal standard was, "to put it bluntly, simply an excuse for [it] to substitute its own superficial assessment of the facts and state law for the careful and better informed conclusion of the state court."[47]

Harlan seemed clearly to have the language and holdings of *Palko*, *Twining*, and company on his side. But the incorporationists—"selective" and "total" combined, at least—had the votes. In *Pointer* v. *Texas* (1965), the Court extended to the states the defendant's Sixth Amendment right to confront accusers. *Klopfer* v. *North Carolina* and *Washington* v. *Texas*, two 1967 decisions, assumed the same stance with respect to the amendment's guarantees of a speedy trial and compulsory process for obtaining defense witnesses. In *Duncan* v. *Louisiana* (1968), a majority placed the right to trial by jury among the requisites of Fourteenth Amendment due process; and *Benton* v. *Maryland* (1969) overruled *Palko*, extending the Fifth Amendment guarantee against double jeopardy to state proceedings.[48]

Partly out of regard for precedent, partly because he considered certain of those guarantees compatible with his conception of due process, Harlan largely eschewed further extensive statements of his position in such cases. When, in the term following *Malloy*, the Court overruled *Adamson* v. *California* and forbade adverse comment by state prosecutors and judges on a defendant's refusal to testify, the Justice concluded that, given *Malloy*, he could see "no legitimate escape from today's decision," but joined it "with great reluctance, since [it] . . . exemplifies the creeping paralysis with which this Court's recent adoption of the 'incorporation' doctrine [was] infecting the operation of the federal system." That same year he concurred in the Court's *Pointer* decision, but only because he agreed that "in the circumstances" of the case, the petitioner's Fourteenth Amendment rights had been violated, and not because, as he put it, he sympathized at all with "this . . . [additional] step in the onward march of the long-since discredited 'incorporation' doctrine . . . which for some reason that I have not yet been able to fathom has come into the sunlight in recent years." He assumed essentially the same posture in voting with the Court in *Klopfer* and *Washington*, but registered no extensive opinion in either. And while he vehemently objected to the *Benton* Court's rejection of *Palko*—"one of this Court's truly great decisions"—he was obliged, "[u]nder the pressures of the closing days of the" 1968 term, to register only a brief, albeit scathing, dissent from the Court's ruling there also.[49]

Harlan departed from his usual pattern of brief rejoinders to further steps in the incorporation movement, however, in *Duncan* and other jury cases raising the issue. In fact, his *Duncan* dissent was to be the most elaborate expression of his position. In *Cheff* v. *Schnackenberg* (1966), the justices invoked their supervisory powers over lower federal courts to hold that jury trials were required in federal criminal contempt actions involving more than six months' imprisonment. Harlan, who had spoken for the Court in rejecting a constitutional challenge to summary contempt proceedings in the *Green* case less than a decade before, contented himself with a four-page challenge to the Court's ruling and the burden it posed for judges now obliged to speculate on the likely sentence to be imposed in a case prior to the presentation of trial evidence. But when a majority, two years later, not only extended the right of jury trial to state cases via *Duncan*, but also held in *Bloom* v. *Illinois* that jury trials were constitutionally required in serious state contempt proceedings, the Justice registered a lengthy challenge to both the majority's position and Justice Black's total incorporation thesis.[50]

The Court had to provide a justification for incorporation. Particularly, given the number of nations in which the right to trial by jury was largely or entirely unknown, the *Duncan* Court could hardly have declared it absolutely essential to liberty and justice, as the *Palko* dictum required. Whether certain other Bill of Rights safeguards recently applied to the states were also of that character was equally debatable. To provide a semantic rationale for its recent rulings, the *Duncan* Court, speaking through Justice White, thus held that a provision of the first eight amendments need be basic only to the "American scheme of justice" to qualify for inclusion in the Fourteenth Amendment. Finding jury trials such a fundamental to liberty, the majority overturned a provision of the Louisiana constitution granting jury trials only in cases carrying the death penalty or imprisonment at hard labor.

Justice Black, who obviously approved of "selective incorporation"—at least as practiced in the 1960s—as a satisfactory alternative to his support of the Bill of Rights' complete application to the states, originally drafted only a one-paragraph *Duncan* opinion reflecting his understanding that the majority was extending jury trials to state cases "because the guarantee appear[ed] in Article VI of the Bill of Rights and because the Court deem[ed it] implicit in the concept of ordered liberty." When Harlan circulated his elaborate *Duncan* dissent, however, the Alabamian filed a lengthy concurrence of his own, defending again, as he had in *Adamson*, his view that the Fourteenth Amendment's framers intended its provisions to totally incorporate the Bill of Rights, ridiculing his judicial and scholarly critics who had a contrary view, and charging that Harlan's "fundamental fairness" conception of due process, like Frankfurter's and the *Twining* Court's, was nothing less than an exercise in "natural law," enabling judges to graft their own ideas of justice, morals, and social utility onto the Constitution's text.[51]

In his dissent, joined "[a]fter considerable thought" by Justice Stewart, Harlan cited what he considered the "overwhelming historical evidence" challenging his colleague's reading of history. He also charged that the majority's approach lacked even the "virtue . . . of internal [logical] consistency" which Black's position at least possessed. Under Black's thesis, he observed, "we look to the Bill of Rights, word for word, clause for clause, precedent for precedent because . . . the men who wrote the Amendment wanted it that way." The majority, on the other hand, would accept neither "the total incorporationists' view of . . . history" nor "the task of determining whether denial of trial by jury in the situation before us, or in other situations, is fundamentally unfair." In short, the majority had "compromised on the ease of the incorporationist position, without its internal logic. It has simply assumed that the question" is whether a particular provision of the Bill of Rights "should be incorporated into the Fourteenth Amendment jot-for-jot and case-for-case, or ignored. Then [it] merely declares that the clause in question is 'in' rather than 'out.' "[52]

For Harlan, there was only one approach to determining the reach of due process which had history and precedent, as well as logic, on its side—the one he, Frankfurter, and, for most of the Court's history, a majority of its members had embraced.

> That is to start with the words "liberty" and "due process of law" and attempt to define them in a way that accords with American traditions and our system of government. This approach, involving a much more *discriminating* process of adjudication than does "incorporation" is, albeit difficult, the one that was followed throughout the 19th and most of the present century. It entails a "gradual process of judicial inclusion and exclusion," seeking, with due recognition of constitutional tolerance for state experimentation and disparity, to ascertain those "immutable principles . . . of free government which no member of the Union may disregard."[53]

Through this process, he added, the "Court [had] sought to define 'liberty' by isolating [substantive] freedoms that Americans . . . considered more important than any suggested countervailing public objective," as well as requiring states to guarantee each individual "fair and impartial procedures." The Bill of Rights, he asserted, as he had in earlier cases, was an important guide in the continuing search for such safeguards. But the due process clause was "meant neither to incorporate, nor to be limited to, the specific guarantees of the first eight Amendments." It was not "restricted" to rules fixed in the past, for that " 'would be to deny every quality of the law but its age, and to render it incapable of progress or improvement.' " Nor was it intended to impose "nationwide uniformity in details" on the states and the diversity the federal system was intended to promote.[54]

Applying his formula to the jury issue, and bolstered by a lengthy memorandum his clerk Louis Cohen had prepared, Harlan concluded that "it simply [had] not been demonstrated," nor, he thought, could "it be demonstrated, that trial by jury [was] the only fair means of resolving issues of fact." While he conceded that the jury was not "of course . . . without virtues," he contended that the abuses which had originally brought it into existence had "largely disappeared," while the "inherent defects" of this "cumbersome process" of decision making by "untrained" laypersons, particularly in complex cases, were obvious to all. Even if he could agree that trial by jury was a fundamental right in certain cases, he could see "nothing fundamental" in any inflexible rule the Court might devise for determining what crimes required such trials and which did not. Thus, he concluded, "quite without reason, the Court has chosen to impose upon every State one means of trying criminal cases; it is a good means, but it is not the only fair means, and it is not demonstrably better than the alternatives States might devise."[55]

Harlan's *Duncan* dissent had also reiterated a concern the Justice had frequently expressed in earlier cases—the "major danger," as he saw it, "that provisions of the Bill of Rights [might] be watered down [for federal cases] in the needless pursuit of uniformity" by a Court bent on applying the same standards to both federal and state proceedings, yet reluctant to bind states to "the sometimes trivial accompanying baggage of judicial interpretation" given "incorporated" rights in federal contexts. Two years after *Duncan*, the Justice's fears were realized, at least to his mind. In *Baldwin* v. *New York* (1970), the Court held that jury trials were required in all state cases in which a prison term of greater than six months was authorized. While Harlan rejected the idea that states should be subjected to such a standard, the rule imposed in *Baldwin* was at least that which had prevailed in federal cases. In *Williams* v. *Florida* (1970), however, the Court concluded that twelve-member juries were required for neither state nor federal trials, even though such proceedings had long been the norm in federal cases.[56]

Harlan vigorously dissented. He could understand why the incorporationists would wish to "allow the states more elbow room in ordering their own criminal systems." But he could not "possibly subscribe" to the notion that such a goal should be reached "by diluting constitutional protections" long applied in federal cases. For him, such thinking simply reflected a "constitutional schizophrenia . . . born of the [Court's] need to cope with national diversity under the constraints of the incorporation doctrine."[57]

The Court in 1972 finally saw Harlan's point and upheld nonunanimous state juries but endorsed the long-standing requirement of unanimity in federal trials. But by that time the Justice had died. The cases in which that decision was announced were already pending in the Court, however, during the Justice's last term, with four of his colleagues favoring unanimity for both federal and state juries, four supporting it in neither, and Harlan arguing that unanimous verdicts were required in federal cases under the Sixth Amendment, but not in state proceedings subject only to the requirements of "fundamental fairness." The triumph of those who would dilute the Sixth Amendment's historic meaning in order to avoid imposing jury unanimity on the states, asserted Harlan in a draft concurrence in the cases, "threaten[ed] . . . to 'chill' the Sixth Amendment out of existence" and "might well spell the demise—under the inescapable pressures of federalism—of many other provisions of the Bill of Rights belatedly funneled into the Fourteenth Amendment through the mysteries of 'selective incorporation.' " Extension to the states of all the obligations those guarantees had been construed to impose on federal proceedings would deny "the States of the Union the flexibility to develop criminal procedural systems in accordance with what local judgments determine to be local needs, as long as a defendant [was] afforded the procedural prerequisites of an essentially fair trial." Rather than dilute federal standards "where the price of incorporation [began] to loom too large," or ignore the dictates of federalism, the Court, maintained Harlan, should overrule *Duncan* and *Williams* and return to "the fundamental fairness approach of *Palko*."[58]

Even as he wrote, though, he must have realized that the chances of stemming the incorporation tide, in the near term at least, were slim at best. Several months after his *Williams* dissent appeared, Philip Heymann wrote the Justice for whom he had clerked that he "honestly" could not remember when he had "read a better reasoned or more articulately argued opinion." His Harvard law school colleague Paul Bator, reported Heymann, had "reacted with equal enthusiasm." "As you know," Harlan soon replied, "this whole business of incorporation is one about which I feel very strongly." "But," he added, "I am afraid the battle is a losing one."[59]

Law and Order

By that point, no doubt, the Justice had also come to consider his campaign against the Warren Court's rapid expansion of the constitutional rules governing criminal proceedings equally futile. Harlan, Louis Cohen has suggested, "had no fear of, or problem with protecting constitutional rights he considered fundamental from both state and federal violation. I remember thinking at the time I clerked for him, in fact, that I would rather trust my liberty to him than to Earl Warren, who, after all, sent Ralph Ginzburg to prison" for "pandering," while Harlan vehemently dissented from the Court's sweeping and novel construction of the federal obscenity statute in the *Ginzburg* case.

> But the Justice was also willing to trust the instruments of government to do their jobs. You get good results, he thought, by having people do their jobs, not by micromanagement. His real feeling in the criminal law area was that the Supreme Court simply couldn't micromanage the process, that it would never work. The cases that come before the Court are iceberg tips, anyway, and what's really important is the way people conduct themselves in everyday life. If the Justices got into the business of having the courts make every decision, they would absolve police and other people of that responsibility.[60]

When the Court attempted to "micromanage" police questioning of suspects, it was thus not surprising that Harlan vigorously objected, albeit rarely with any success.

For a time in the 1960s, the Court continued to adhere to constructions of the self-incrimination guarantee and its due process counterpart which Harlan embraced. In *Cohen* v. *Hurley* (1961), for example, he had spoken for a majority in upholding disbarment of a lawyer who had asserted the privilege before a state court inquiry into lawyer misconduct. When the *Shotwell Manufacturing Co.* case made a second appearance in the Court in 1963, he was again the majority's spokesman, affirming on that occasion the federal income tax evasion convictions of Shotwell officials, even though they had provided authorities with the evidence used to convict them through a "voluntary disclosure policy" under which delinquent taxpayers could escape prosecution by disclosing their derelictions prior to a criminal investigation of their conduct. Since the *Shotwell* petitioners had voluntarily furnished fraudulent information to officials in a scheme to reduce their tax liabilities, concluded Harlan, use of the information in their criminal prosecution had in no way violated their privilege against self-incrimination.[61]

Trouble for the Justice's flexible conception of the guarantee was already looming on the horizon, however. Justice Black registered a strong *Shotwell* dissent. When Harlan circulated a draft of his own opinion, moreover, Felix Frankfurter's replacement Justice Goldberg responded that "[i]n light of Hugo's dissenting views, [he was] concerned that [Harlan's] otherwise excellent draft . . . does not adequately express the view that the majority are here proposing no inroads whatsoever on constitutional rights." Goldberg thought it "essential" that the opinion emphasize the case's "total distinctiveness" from custodial questioning or offers of immunity to a suspect. "When a taxpayer, in voluntary action based upon a general offer of immunity, answers with a fraudulent scheme to avoid a greater tax liability," asserted Goldberg, "prosecuting him and using the incriminating statement against him violates no constitutional right." But such cases should be closely confined to their facts.[62]

Justice Brennan was also alarmed. "[Y]our treatment," he informed Harlan, "seems to suggest that incomplete truthfulness in a disclosure [alone] works a forfeiture of the Fifth Amendment privilege"—a position Brennan found "untenable." Nor could he agree with language in Harlan's draft suggesting that due process standards drawn from Fourteenth Amendment cases governed a Fifth Amendment self-incrimination claim. "However appropriate such nebulous concepts as 'official misconduct' and 'free will' may be in dealing with the Due Process Clause of the Fourteenth," contended Brennan, they "ought not to be unreflectingly carried over into cases invoking the Self-Incrimination clause of the Fifth." In Brennan's judgment, the latter required exclusion of any confession "induced by a promise of immunity . . . without regard to the quantum of 'official misconduct' or the degree to which 'free will' has been constrained." Particularly since *Shotwell* raised issues primarily under the Fifth Amendment self-incrimination guarantee, he observed in a later letter to Harlan, Brennan could see no "justifi[cation for] resort to Fourteenth Amendment concepts of self-incrimination which, under the present Court view, contrary to my own, are to be developed solely under the rubruc of due process, and without reference to the specific Self-Incrimination Clause."[63]

When Harlan made the modifications Goldberg and Brennan had suggested, the two justices joined his opinion. Brennan noted, in fact, that Harlan's revised draft was "just fine with me." By the end of the following term, however, Brennan and Goldberg not only helped to form a majority applying the Fifth Amendment's self-incrimination provision—instead of the "watered-down [due process] version" of the guarantee Brennan charged Harlan with favoring—to the states, they had also begun to lay down strict standards governing custodial police interrogation of suspects. For example, *Escobedo* v. *Illinois* (1964) required the assistance of counsel during any questioning initiated after an investigation had begun to focus on a particular suspect. And in *Miranda* v. *Arizona* (1966), a five–four Court went further, holding that, prior to any custodial questioning, a suspect must be informed of his right to silence, his right to counsel (and an appointed lawyer, if indigent) during any interrogation he chose to permit, and the consequences of cooperating with the police. Such warnings or comparable ones were necessary, observed Chief Justice Warren, to neutralize the "inherently coercive" nature of the custodial setting and to assure that suspects would be aware of, and free to exercise, their right against self-incrimination.[64]

On a clerk's bench memo for the *Escobedo* case, Harlan had written, "I am not ready to hold that there is an absolute right to counsel at this stage." And when the ruling was handed down, he filed a brief but pointed dissent, contending that police interrogations of suspects should continue to be governed by flexible "fundamental fairness" standards and charging that "the rule announced today is most ill-conceived and . . . seriously and unjustifiably fetters legitimate methods of law enforcement."[65]

The dissent which he registered in the *Miranda* case, however, was to be his most extensive and vehement assault on Warren Court procedural trends. The Fifth Amendment's self-incrimination provision, he charged, had never before been construed to apply to police questioning of suspects; the due process clause prohibited only "*undue* pressure," as he put it, on a suspect. "[T]he thrust of the new rules," on the other hand, was "to negate all pressures, to reinforce the nervous or ignorant suspect, and ultimately to discourage any confession at all. The aim in short is toward 'voluntariness' in a utopian sense, or to view it from a different angle, voluntariness with a vengeance." To the Justice, the ultimate likely impact of such "a strained reading of history and precedent" was obvious. The new rules would in no way protect against police brutality or the third-degree. Those who used such "tactics and deny them in court," after all, were "equally able and destined to lie as skillfully about warnings and waivers." Instead, the Court's new regime would "work for reliability in confessions almost only in the Pickwician sense that they can prevent some from being given at all," and thus would "impair, if they will not eventually serve wholly to frustrate, an instrument of law enforcement that has long and quite reasonably been thought [to serve a social interest] worth the price paid for it"—the effective prosecution of crime. "The foray which the Court makes today," he concluded, "brings to mind the wise and farsighted words of Mr. Justice Jackson . . . 'This Court is forever adding new stories to the temple of constitutional law, and the temples have a way of collapsing when one story too many is added.' "[66]

When the *Miranda* warnings were extended beyond the police station to any custodial setting, Harlan initially joined his fellow *Miranda* dissenters Stewart and White in challenging the majority's further inroads on police discretion. Ultimately, "and purely out of respect for *stare decisis*," or precedent, he "acquiesce[d]" in such decisions. He dissented, however, from other rulings expanding the reach of the Fifth Amendment and certain other procedural safeguards, including the majority's reversal of *Cohen* v. *Hurley* in a 1967 case. When the Court sided with the police, though, Harlan generally joined the majority's holding, if not always its rationale. He concurred, for example, with decisions upholding the authority of police to extract blood samples and other "physical" (as opposed to "testimonial") evidence from suspects, noting during conference discussion of one such case that police had a "right to use reasonable force in securing evidence." He was equally supportive of police discretion to conduct warrantless weapons frisks of suspects reasonably believed to be armed and dangerous. In conference discussion of a death penalty case, he appeared to favor the right of a defendant to demand that guilt and punishment be determined in separate proceedings, calling the failure to grant such an opportunity "one of [the] clearest cases of denial of fundamental fairness." During his last term, however, he spoke for the Court in upholding that such determinations could be made in a single proceeding as well as the authority of jurors to impose death or life imprisonment without statutory standards limiting their discretion. The Justice concurred, too, in the Court's 1970 decision upholding the power of trial judges to gag and bind, remove from the courtroom, or otherwise restrain unruly defendants. He asked that Justice Black remove a passage from his draft opinion for the Court in the case, because Harlan was "reluctant to subscribe to anything that casts doubt as to the permissibility of using civil contempt to deal with courtroom situations of this kind."[67]

Harlan's opinions in *Miranda* and many other such cases reflected his regard for federalism and state autonomy. As indicated earlier, he vigorously objected to the Court's 1963 relaxation of restrictions on the right of state prisoners to challenge their convictions through federal habaes corpus suits. He also favored a broad reading of the "harmless error" rule under which procedurally deficient convictions were upheld if the constitutional violation was found not to have contributed to the defendant's conviction. A majority of the justices were willing to apply the rule, but concluded in a 1967 case that a state must demonstrate "beyond a reasonable doubt" that a challenged procedural defect did not affect the accused's conviction before it could be dismissed as a "harmless error." Harlan argued, on the other hand, that he and his colleagues should ask only whether a state court's harmless error policy was "a reasonable one [and not] . . . applied arbitrarily to evade the underlying constitutional mandate of fundamental fairness." When the Court used the "beyond a reasonable doubt" standard to reverse, for example, a state court's finding of harmless error in a case in which the prosecutor and trial judge had made adverse comments on the accused's failure to take the witness stand, Harlan dissented. Evidence of the defendant's guilt, he asserted, was "admittedly extensive." Given that fact, the "jurors were certain to take notice of [his] silence whether or not there was comment since the evidence itself cried for an explanation . . . [T]his Court has confused the impact of the petitioner's silence on the jury with the impact of the prosecutor's comment upon that silence." Finally, Harlan was among those reluctant to have the Court begin to determine, as a matter of constitutional law, the nature and reach of the insanity defense. He agreed, for example, with a clerk's recommendation that certiorari be denied in one such case, writing on the clerk's memo, "We should still decline to get into McNaughten [versus] Durham rules" for determining insanity.[68]

The Justice's restraintist stance in numerous procedural contexts hardly tarnished his image, of course, with like-minded friends and supporters. The day after *Miranda* was announced, a Wall Street friend and frequent correspondent wrote him, "Thank God for your existence! The Supreme Court has made almost a fetish of pampering the un-religious, the unwashed, the un-educated, the un-moral and the un-American. . . . I hope to God before I die that one of our better writers will put together a book of the dissenting opinions of John Harlan." Another assured the Justice that "[y]our country will long remember your constant and intelligent campaign to keep the laws and traditions of the land from being altered by judicial rather than legislative process." And when the retired Justice Frankfurter asked J. Edward Lumbard, Harlan's longtime friend and chief judge of the Court of Appeals for the Second Circuit, to accept an award for Frankfurter from the National Association of District Attorneys, Lumbard's response reflected his sympathy for the criminal procedure view of both justices. "I shall do my best to convey to the Association," wrote Lumbard, "your ideas about prosecutors carrying on under the 'hot-air libertarianism' of today's majority on the Supreme Court."[69]

But Justice Harlan was by no means simply a knee-jerk vote for police and prosecutors in every criminal procedure context. He was primarily concerned with the broad reach and detail of the Court's new rules and the degree to which they restricted the discretion of federal and state authorities, as well as the ability of such officials to make their own reforms in the criminal justice system. When *Miranda* went down, for example, he noted in a letter to his Australian friend Sir Howard Beale that "[the] British of course have such a rule," but added, "like most British rules, they are attended by flexible administration which we are not so easily given to in the judicial system here." He also termed such decisions "the more unfortunate because they cut into massive criminal law reform investigations which are now in progress in this country, by casting the new rules in constitutional terms which renders change more difficult."[70]

Initially, in an effort to limit the impact of newly announced procedural rules, Harlan joined decisions holding that such procedural requirements should not necessarily be applied retroactively. And when the Court summarily ordered new hearings for indigent state defendants tried without a lawyer before the *Gideon* decision was announced, he dissented, charging that the question of *Gideon*'s retroactive application to earlier cases was "deserving of [a] full-dress consideration" and scorning as a "fiction" the notion "that the law now announced has always been the law." He later concluded, however, that every new procedural requirement should apply fully to all cases still pending on direct appeal when it was first announced, though not to habeas corpus challenges to criminal convictions previously upheld on appeal. And while his new posture may have been based in part on a belief that complete retroactivity for all the Court's new handiwork might inhibit the justices' zeal, he argued in dissent in one such case that "[i]f a 'new' constitutional doctrine is truly right, we should not reverse lower courts which have accepted it; nor should we affirm those which have rejected the very arguments we have embraced."[71]

Although Harlan was opposed to unduly detailed and inflexible procedural requirements, and especially their imposition on state authorities, he was never a certain vote for the government in such cases either. There were limits, for example, to the Justice's willingness to support state judicial findings of "harmless error." When the Court in *Bumper* v. *North Carolina* reversed a black defendant's conviction in a brutal rape case on illegal search and seizure grounds, Justice Black registered a vehement dissent in which he stressed the heinous nature of the petitioner's crime, disputed the majority's finding of a Fourth and Fourteenth Amendment violation, and concluded that, in any event, admission of the fruits of the search was constitutionally "harmless," given other evidence of the defendant's guilt. But in this case Harlan sided with the majority, overturning the lower court's ruling. In his concurring opinion, Harlan reminded his colleague that "the question [could not] be whether . . . the defendant actually committed the crimes charged, so that the error was 'harmless' in the sense that the petitioner got what he deserved." The improper admission of evidence seized in the illegal search could certainly have affected the result in the petitioner's trial. Its case thus could not be dismissed, asserted Harlan, as a harmless error.[72]

Nor, despite his opposition to the exclusionary rule's application per se to the states, was the Justice's vote to uphold the search and seizure claim at issue in *Bumper* terribly unusual. In an unfiled concurrence in the *Kremen* case early in his tenure, it will be recalled, Harlan had recommended meaningful restrictions on the permissible scope of the authority of police to conduct warrantless searches incident to a valid arrest. When the issue was again before the Court in the late 1960s, he initially voted in conference to uphold broad discretion for the police in such situations. Later, however, he reversed ground, joining a majority opinion in *Chimel* v. *California* (1969), which largely tracked the rationale of his *Kremen* concurrence. In another significant Fourth Amendment case, he also switched positions, first rejecting, then joining a majority in upholding the claim that the amendment conferred jurisdiction on federal trial courts to hear damage suits filed against police by the victims of an illegal search.[73]

In a number of cases, moreover, he took a strict view of the "probable cause" required for issuance of a search warrant. While he agreed, for example, that a warrant could be based on tips furnished by a "reliable" anonymous informer, he spoke for the Court in demanding more evidence of an informer's credibility than that based on mere casual rumor or general reputation. His imposition of such a standard on law enforcement officers prompted conservative columnist James Jackson Kilpatrick to lament, "[I]t is all the more disappointing to see that the majority opinion was written by Justice Harlan, who ordinarily is one of the soundest men on the Court. If Harlan has now gone over to the nit-pickers and bleeding hearts, one despairs of seeing a return to sanity in our criminal law."[74]

Ultimately, too, the Justice joined the Court, over Justice Black's lone dissent, in overturning *Olmstead* v. *United States* (1928), thereby subjecting police eavesdrop practices to the Fourth Amendment's warrant requirements. As late as the 1960 term, however, Harlan was recorded by Justice Brennan as remarking in conference that he could not "say that there [had] been indiscriminate lawlessness on [the] part of officers since Olmstead" and that "the world today [was] an unhappy time to" overrule that controversial decision. But in *Katz* v. *United States* (1967), he concurred in the reversal of *Olmstead* and its progeny and observed that, in the light of modern technological advances, those decisions were now "bad physics as well as bad law, [since] reasonable expectations of privacy may be defeated by electronic as well as physical invasion." And while he joined decisions upholding the use of undercover agents, even those carrying concealed recording devices, to elicit incriminating statements from suspects, he objected to the warrantless transmission of such conversations to the "surreptitious third ear." When a majority, for example, upheld the testimony of police who overheard an agent's conversation with a suspect by means of a transmitter concealed on the agent's body, the Justice dissented, finding a constitutionally relevant distinction "between the impact on privacy of single-party informer bugging and third-party" surveillance.[75]

On occasion, in fact, his *Escobedo* and *Miranda* dissents notwithstanding, the Justice supported Fifth Amendment claims. In 1967, for example, he was assigned to author the Court's opinion in *Marchetti* v. *United States*, in which the justices had voted to overrule *United States* v. *Kahriger*, a 1953 decision upholding a federal tax law which required gamblers to file information about their activities with federal tax officials, even though the data gathered were available for inspection by state and federal prosecutors. Justice Black objected to Harlan's assertion in an early draft of the opinion that the Court had a duty to "harmonize the individual's natural desire to find shelter in silence, free from the hazards and humiliations of self-incrimination, with the urgent governmental need for accurate and timely information." The Fifth Amendment's safeguard against compulsory self-incrimination, exclaimed the Alabamian in a letter to Harlan, was "an independent, specific, and special command that the Government shall not require such testimony, however much or however little the Government may need evidence concerning taxes or anything else. The Constitution there carves out a type of evidence *absolutely* forbidden." When Douglas and Brennan raised similar objections, Harlan deleted an entire section of the draft, although insisting that he in no way had intended to imply "that the taxing power may in some circumstances override the protections afforded by the Fifth Amendment privilege." When he continued to encounter difficulties in mustering a majority for his opinion, he withdrew from the assignment and asked that *Marchetti* be scheduled for re-argument the following term. In 1968, however, he again spoke for the Court in striking down the federal gambling statute.[76]

Not surprisingly, given his flexible conception of due process. Harlan was also willing to read into that enigmatic guarantee procedural rights mentioned nowhere in the Constitution's text. He joined the Court's general approach, if not always its specific holding, for example, in using the "fundamental fairness" conception of due process to extend certain procedural safeguards to juvenile proceedings, including those not specified in the Bill of Rights. In early 1970, he cautioned Justice White to revise language in an opinion to avoid any implication that the requirement that a defendant's guilt be established "beyond a reasonable doubt" was a "constitutional" command. Later that same year, however, he joined Justice Brennan's holding in *In Re Winship* that such a standard of guilt was one of the "essentials of due process and fair treatment" necessary in juvenile as well as other proceedings. And when Justice Black circulated a fierce *Winship* dissent scorning the majority's "natural law" approach to due process and contending that the guarantee required government merely to follow the "law of the land," that is, specific constitutional and legislative rules, in taking away a person's life, liberty, and property, Harlan added a lengthy footnote to his own concurrence in the case. He declared:

> I cannot refrain from expressing my continued bafflement at my Brother Black's insistence that due process . . . does not embody a concept of fundamental fairness as part of our scheme of constitutionally ordered liberty. His thesis flies in the face of a course of judicial history reflected in an unbroken line of opinions that have interpreted due process to

> impose restraints on the procedures government may adopt in dealing with its citizens . . . as well as . . . uncontroverted scholarly research . . . respecting the intendment of the Due Process Clause of the Fourteenth Amendment.[77]

At the same time, Harlan's constructions of due process, like his interpretations of more specific constitutional guarantees, reflected his customarily cautious approach to judicial review. In *Estes* v. *Texas*, for example, he dissented when a majority initially voted to reject a due process challenge to the televising of a criminal proceeding. When the Court reversed its position, he joined the new majority. He refused, however, to go along with the four other members of the five-man Court who supported a per se ban on broadcast coverage of criminal proceedings under all circumstances. For it was his view, as he wrote Justice Clark, author of the Court's opinion, "that in this novel field the [justices] should not decide or write more broadly than is necessary." While he also agreed that a criminal conviction could be overturned on a showing of massive prejudicial publicity against a defendant and the trial judge's indifference to neutralizing its impact, even without evidence that prejudicial publicity or the courtroom activities of the press had generated "specific prejudice" against the accused by the judge or jurors, he joined such rulings only in extreme cases. When the Court, for example, reversed the conviction of a defendant who had been denied a change of trial venue despite the fact that a film of his confession to the crime had been broadcast on local television, he joined Justice Clark's dissent. On a memorandum for the case, he noted that only three of the twelve jurors had viewed the interview, none of the three had testified to holding opinions about the accused's guilt, and the interview was broadcast two months before his trial. He had suggested, too, that Clark emphasize in his dissent "that in judging the 'fairness' of a particular juror—where demeanor, and not merely answers to questions, plays such an important part—we up here should be slow to overturn the findings of a trial judge."[78]

Whether sympathetic with a particular procedural ruling or not, the Justice always defended his institution from the charges of its critics. When the 1967 *Katz* decision extending the Fourth Amendment to government eavesdrop practices was announced, Chief Justice William H. Duckworth of the Georgia supreme court, who more than a decade before had rebuffed Harlan's efforts to delay Aubrey Williams's date with the electric chair, wrote the Justice to express his "highest regard for your superlative legal ability and competence"—and to excoriate the nation's highest Court. "By such nearsighted decisions," declared Duckworth, "you victimize the innocent public and force them to endure crime. . . . Concerned and thinking people throughout America are alarmed when our highest court constantly throws road blocks in the path of enforcing the law against criminals who respect neither the rights of the innocent people nor the majesty of the law, without which neither you nor I are safe from criminals even in our homes." Unless the courts fulfilled their "overriding duty . . . to preserve the government," all constitutional safeguards were "mere slips of paper." And there was more. Judges "willing to allow criminals to assault the bed-rock of our liberties which is our government on the flimsy pretense that the Constitution requires it . . . should resign," since "[o]nly a blind fool would think for one moment that either or all of our constitutional protections of individuals was intended to be protected at the price of destroying the very government that gave them." If Harlan and his colleagues would simply realize that state courts were "capable of honestly and intelligently enforcing criminal laws," that, in fact, "they know more than most of you about how to do it within the Constitution, the flood-tide of crime would abate." But until that day arrived, warned Duckworth, responsibility for that "flood-tide" would lie "primarily at the feet of the majority of the Supreme Court."[79]

An in-kind reply to the Georgia jurist's harangue would hardly have been in keeping with Harlan's personality. Had it come from a private citizen, in fact, it probably would have been filed unanswered. On this occasion, however, the Justice responded. He found the chief justice's "disapprobation" of *Katz*, he wrote Duckworth, "somewhat puzzle[ing]." The Court's ruling had made it clear, after all, that eavesdropping accompanied by a warrant, which the FBI agents could have secured in *Katz*, was "constitutionally permissible." And surely "[f]ew . . . would approve the indiscriminate use of electronic bugging, even in the field of criminal law enforcement." He had obviously opposed the Court's extension of the exclusionary rule to the states. But "the prevailing constitutional doctrine [was] now otherwise" in state cases, and the rule had been applicable in federal cases such as *Katz* since 1914. Thus, its application in *Katz* was "not something new." And while enforcement of the criminal law was indeed the "primary responsibility" of the states, that authority was subject to "overriding constitutional limitations." The debate over these limitations, which was then raging in the nation, was, in Harlan's judgment, primarily "the product of the extraordinary era in which we are living and not of any change in the basic point of view of the federal judiciary." "I have endeavored to reply to your letter," he concluded, "with the same frankness manifested in your letter to me."[80]

Substantive Equal Protection

The nation's Justice Duckworths reacted most vociferously to the Warren Court's forays into the criminal procedure field, and to its desegregation, school prayer, and obscenity rulings. Scholarly commentators found most interesting, however, the Court's growing willingness to read into the Constitution meaningful protection for personal privacy and other substantive rights not mentioned in the document's text, as well as for groups whose welfare, unlike that of the former slaves and their descendants, had not been a central concern of the Civil War and the Reconstruction amendments' chief architects.[81] If the Court's rulings in such cases were themselves intriguing, the stance Justice Harlan assumed in them proved even more fascinating.

During the pre-1937 heyday of judicial laissez-faire, a shifting coalition of justices had relied principally on the due process clauses as a basis for according constitutional status to "liberty of contract" and related economic freedoms in such controversial decisions as *Lochner* v. *New York* (1905) and *Adkins* v. *Children's Hospital* (1923). The language and early history of the due process guarantee suggest that it was originally intended to serve, largely or solely, a procedural function, requiring government merely to accord persons fundamentally fair proceedings when depriving them of life, liberty, or property. The justices of the *Lochner* era, however, had assigned due process a substantive meaning as well, holding that the guarantee also prohibited unreasonable government regulation of liberty and property. While the depression of the 1930s, growth of the modern administrative state, and changing personnel on the Supreme Court led the Court to repudiate the strict limitations on governmental authority over business and industry *Lochner* and its progeny had embraced, the justices had never completely dismantled the substantive due process rhetoric on which they were based. The dominant coalition of the 1960s was naturally reluctant, however, to invoke the chief doctrinal tool of the Court's most discredited era as a basis for a modern expansion of noneconomic personal rights, especially while Hugo Black remained on the bench. If anything, Black was even more opposed to the use of due process to grant protection to substantive rights than he was to its use as a vehicle for expanding the reach of procedural guarantees beyond those actually mentioned in the Constitution. He was thus alert to the slightest hint of such rhetoric in the Court's opinions. It was hardly surprising, then, that in the 1960s the Warren Court turned to the equal protection guarantee as a key vehicle for finding a constitutional basis for rights given no reference in the Constitution's text.[82]

Unlike the due process guarantee, the Fourteenth Amendment's equal protection clause had played only a minor role in the laissez-faire decision making of the pre-1937 period. Opinions in two cases of the World War II era also gave a possible doctrinal basis for that amendment's expansion beyond its historic racial context. In *Skinner* v. *Oklahoma* (1942) the Court, speaking through Justice Douglas, struck down a state statute which provided for the sterilization of certain habitual criminals, yet exempted others from its coverage. Such a law was probably vulnerable to condemnation under the traditional notion that even nonracial classifications must have some "reasonable" or "rational" basis. But Justice Douglas had announced in his *Skinner* opinion that Oklahoma's sterilization statute had interfered with the right of procreation, "a basic civil right of man," and that such laws were subject to strict judicial oversight. Two years later, in *Korematsu* v. *United States*, Justice Black spoke for the Court in upholding, on grounds of "military urgency," one of the many controversial wartime sanctions imposed on Japanese-Americans. Black had also observed, however, that racial classifications were "immediately suspect" and deserving of "the most rigid scrutiny."[83]

The use of such language in a case not involving discrimination against blacks arguably could provide support for the claim that discrimination against certain other groups might also be labeled "inherently suspect." Similarly, *Skinner*'s rhetoric offered possibility of precedent to those anxious to accord constitutional status to "rights" found nowhere in the Constitution's language. And in the 1960s the Warren Court made full use of both cases. In a dramatic expansion of equal protection's meaning, the Court developed what would be termed a "new" or "substantive" equal protection formula. Under it, laws which discriminated against members of a "suspect" class or infringed upon a "fundamental right" or "interest" no longer enjoyed the presumption of validity traditionally extended to nonracial forms of discrimination. Instead, they were to be presumed invalid and upheld only if government officials could convince the courts that they were not merely rationally related to some legitimate goal, but in fact "necessary" to the accomplishment of a "compelling" government interest—an especially onerous burden that only the regulation at issue in *Korematsu* would ever be found to satisfy.

The "fundamental rights" branch of the Warren Court's equal protection jurisprudence was first clearly reflected in its reapportionment opinions. But the justices also invoked it to justify strict scrutiny of the poll tax, voter requirements said to inhibit interstate travel, and laws interfering with the right to marry and safeguards said to flow from "intimate, familial" relationships. Language in the school desegregation opinions suggested, moreover, the existence of a fundamental right to an equal education, and Justice Brennan's opinion for the Court in *Shapiro* v. *Thompson* (1969), striking down a one-year residency requirement for welfare benefits, primarily on interstate travel/equal protection grounds, implied a constitutional right to the "necessities of life." Rhetoric in *Shapiro* and other opinions also appeared to add to the list of constitutionally suspect laws, such as those burdening the poor and persons of "illegitimate" birth.[84]

Justice Harlan vigorously opposed such extensions of equal protection's grip beyond racial classifications. In the reapportionment field, as noted earlier, he had challenged the majority's conclusion that the guarantee was ever intended to reach the electoral process. He also charged that, even were equal protection applicable in such cases, the guarantee prohibited only the "unreasonable" or "irrational" electoral scheme. He took the same position in other voting cases. In 1965 the Court, speaking through Justice Stewart, applied this traditional standard (of equal protection guaranteed by the Fourteenth Amendment) in striking down a Texas law denying most military personnel the vote in state elections.

Harlan argued in dissent that "any dispassionate survey of the past [would] reveal that the present decision is the first . . . to hold" the equal protection guarantee applicable to state voter qualifications. Even if the clause were so construed, he added, the challenged law had a rational basis.[85]

Harlan had the same reaction to the Court's treatment of the poll tax. When the justices initially voted in *Harper* v. *Virginia Board of Elections* to uphold the tax as a requirement for participation in state elections, he joined the majority; when the Court reversed its position, he filed a dissent. "[W]hether one agrees or not," he contended, "arguments have been and still can be made in favor of" poll taxes. And for Harlan that ended the matter. His colleagues had voted to strike such requirements down, he charged, merely because the poll tax was "not in accord with current egalitarian notions of how a modern democracy should be organized." And while a legislature could very properly make legal reforms based on "such changes in popular attitudes," it was "all wrong," in Harlan's judgment, "for the Court to adopt the political doctrines popularly accepted at a particular moment of our history and to declare all others to be irrational and invidious, banning them from the range of choice by reasonably minded people acting through the political process." In Justice Holmes's famous dissent from the Court's decision in *Lochner* v. *New York*, which rejected state authority to regulate the hours of labor of bakery employees, he had reminded his colleagues that the Fourteenth Amendment's due process clause did not embody any particular economic theory. Now, Harlan found it "appropriate to observe that neither does the Equal Protection Clause of that Amendment rigidly impose upon America an ideology of unrestrained egalitarianism." And when he later joined the Court in striking down a state law limiting the access of third parties and independent candidates to the ballot, he rested his concurrence on expression and association grounds, not equal protection.[86]

Nor was the Justice willing to expand the scope of "suspect classes" beyond the Fourteenth Amendment's historic racial setting. In *Levy* v. *Louisiana* and *Glona* v. *American Guarantee Co.*, a Court majority subjected to strict—and thus fatal—review Louisiana laws restricting the rights of illegitimate children and their parents. On his clerk's bench memo for the *Levy* case, Harlan had noted that a ruling invalidating such laws "would be pressing 'equal protection' to more than its outer limits." When a majority of the justices rejected that counsel, he instructed his clerk Louis Cohen to draft a dissent.[87]

"The Justice was, I now recognize," Cohen has remarked, "a splendid senior partner if you will, of a legal enterprise. He understood the theory of delegation, of pushing as much responsibility as possible down the ladder. So he got awfully good work from his clerks, and I came away feeling that I had done some of the best work of my career." Especially as the Justice's eyesight weakened, he had become even more inclined than in earlier years merely to discuss with his clerks the sort of opinion he wished to see written, then have them prepare an initial draft. In their discussions of *Levy* and *Glona*, Cohen remembers Harlan being "both amused and very troubled about where the law of equal protection seemed to be going." He considered the majority's position "silly" but also "very appealing. So his instructions to me, though not in so many words, were to be cute, to be light, to try to be persuasive. We probably had seen Douglas' effort [for the majority] by then. Harlan wanted to take that apart but in a way that would win the reader's sympathy rather than get his back up, which he knew was a danger"[88] in a case in which children were being penalized for the "sins" of their parents.

The statutes at issue in *Levy* and *Glona* limited the right of illegitimate children and their parents to recover for each other's wrongful death. In his draft, Cohen emphasized that such laws had traditionally been drawn along "highly arbitrary lines" based on legal relationships rather than biological ties or "questions of affection and nurture and dependence." A son might be permitted, for example, to recover for the wrongful death of parents he did not love, while a minor child cared for by loving relatives would have no standing to sue for their deaths. Cohen was "at a loss to understand" how such arbitrary rules would be "even marginally more rational" if based on biological instead of legal relationships, since neither was "indicative of the love or economic dependence that may exist between two persons," and thus even under the Court's standards, neither could be considered more "suspect" than the other.[89]

How well Cohen succeeded in producing a draft which would get no one's "back up" is debatable. Certainly, it had its lighter passages, including a humorous footnote allusion to a Shakespearean character. But he had also termed the majority's rationale an exercise in "brute force" and declared Douglas's suggestion that Louisiana had reduced illegitimates to the status of "nonpersons" as, "frankly, preposterous." Even so, Harlan was pleased. After reading Cohen's draft, the Justice added a one-sentence introductory paragraph, then instructed his clerk to send it to the Court's print shop. "These decisions," the opinion now began, "can only be classed as constitutional curiosities."[90]

But the dissent which the Justice registered in *Shapiro* v. *Thompson* and companion cases was his most elaborate critique of the "new" equal protection. Originally, the Court had voted six–three to uphold the welfare residency requirements at issue there, and Harlan had drafted an opinion concurring in that judgment. However, a dissent which Justice Fortas circulated in the cases persuaded Justice Brennan to change his vote, while Justice Stewart, who also had voted initially to uphold the regulations, later withdrew his vote, then, following re-argument of the cases the following fall, switched positions, creating a new majority to invalidate the laws at issue.[91]

In the draft dissent which he circulated after initial oral argument in the cases, Justice Fortas had argued that the residency provision interfered with both the right of interstate travel and equal protection. After reading the Fortas effort, Justice Brennan, who initially had voted to affirm the regulation, wrote his colleague that he could join "about everything you say that relates to burdens on the right to travel," but added: "I have a lot more difficulty . . . with affirming on the equal protection ground. If the cases can be disposed of on the burden argument, is there any necessity to add the additional support of a denial of equal protection." The opinion for the Court which Brennan ultimately produced in the cases, however, was a classic application of the "new" equal protection's "fundamental rights" doctrine. The challenged laws, he concluded, interfered with the fundamental right to interstate travel (and perhaps others relating to the "necessities of life"). They were thus to be struck down unless found "necessary" to the accomplishment of a "legitimate and compelling" government interest. Since the interests the welfare residency requirements were claimed to serve were either impermissible, susceptible to being served through means less restrictive of fundamental rights, insufficiently related to the regulation at issue, or less than "compelling" in importance, declared Brennan, they must fall.[92]

Much of Justice Harlan's dissent focused on what he termed "an equal protection doctrine of relatively recent vintage." Given the history underlying the Fourteenth Amendment's adoption, he considered the " 'compelling interest' doctrine . . . sound when applied to racial classifications." But its "more recent extensions," he declared, had been "unwise," especially those involving its "fundamental rights" branch.

> I think this branch of the "compelling interest" doctrine particularly unfortunate and unnecessary. It is unfortunate because it creates an exception which threatens to swallow the standard equal protection rule. Virtually every state statute affects important rights . . . in principle undistinguishable from those involved here, and to extend the "compelling interest" rule to all cases in which such rights are affected would go far toward making this Court a "super-legislature." This branch of the doctrine is also unnecessary. When the right affected is one assured by the Federal Constitution, any infringement can be dealt with under the Due Process Clause. But when a statute affects only matters not mentioned in the Federal Constitution and is not arbitrary or irrational, I must reiterate that I know of nothing which entitles this Court to pick out particular human activities, characterize them as "fundamental," and give them added protection under an unusually stringent equal protection test.[93]

The Justice did agree that the due process clause embodied an implied right to interstate travel. But while he was willing to label that guarantee a fundamental right, he would not subject regulations impinging on travel to the invariably fatal compelling interest standard. Instead, the decisive question for him in such cases was "whether the governmental interests served by [such regulations] outweigh[ed] the burden imposed." The residency requirement, in his judgment, had only an "indirect and apparently quite insubstantial" impact on interstate travel, while "the governmental purposes served by [them were] legitimate and real, and the residence requirements . . . clearly suited to their accomplishment." They were thus obviously constitutional; and the Court's holding to the contrary simply reflected, he asserted, "to an unusual degree the current notion that this Court possesses a peculiar wisdom all its own whose capacity to lead this Nation out of its present troubles is constrained only by the limits of judicial ingenuity in contriving new constitutional principles to meet each problem as it arises."[94]

A number of Harlan's clerks, among others, had difficulty understanding how the Justice could oppose equal protection's use as a vehicle for according unspecified rights constitutional protection while at the same time embracing a conception of due process which permitted precisely the same results. "I recall," Paul Brest, one of Harlan's clerks the year *Shapiro* was decided, has remarked, "some rounds of fairly fruitless arguments in which some combination of the three of us [clerks] would say that there is no difference between due process and equal protection. They are equally vague or not. He was just real stubborn about that. I think a lot of it had to do with the Frankfurter tradition, which was very deeply ingrained in Harlan." His position may also have reflected, says Brest, a "deep distrust of Justice Brennan and where he might be trying to take equal protection."[95]

For whatever reason, Harlan was convinced, as he put it in *Shapiro*, that the Court's "expansive view of 'equal protection' carrie[d] the seeds of more judicial interference with the state and federal legislative process, much more indeed than does the judicial application of 'due process' according to traditional concepts." And when changing membership on the Court began to lead, toward the end of his career, to a substantial curtailment of substantive equal protection, Harlan joined the new majority. He concurred, for example, with a 1970 decision upholding a monthly family ceiling on welfare allotments, rejecting the argument that such regulations interfered with a fundamental right that required their subjection to strict review. "Except with respect to racial classifications, to which unique historical considerations apply," he declared in a concurring opinion, the equal protection clause imposed only "a standard of rationality . . . that [did] not depend upon the nature of the classification or interest involved." When the Court upheld a Louisiana law restricting the inheritance rights of illegitimate children, he assumed the same stance, scorning the "extravagant notions" of equal protection's reach defended in a Brennan dissent. And while he had voted in 1969 to strike down a city charter provision requiring voter approval of all fair housing regulations, citing its discriminatory "racial and religious" character, during his last term he joined the Court in upholding a California constitutional amendment requiring voter referenda for new, low-rent housing projects.[96]

His posture did not mean that Harlan never joined decisions invalidating nonracial varieties of discrimination. But he invariably rested his vote in such cases on non–equal protection grounds. In *Williams* v. *Rhodes* (1968), for example, he agreed to strike down a law severely limiting the access of minor political parties and independent candidates to the ballot, but he did so on free expression grounds, not the equal protection rationale undergirding the Court's opinion. And while he dissented from the Court's holding in *Douglas* v. *California* (1963) that indigent defendants have a right to appointed counsel for the first appeal of their convictions, rejecting, as he had in the *Griffin* case early in his tenure, the notion that either equal protection or due process required states to eliminate "handicaps flowing from differences in economic circumstances," he joined, on due process grounds, a 1970 decision invalidating a sentencing system under which poor persons given a jail term and fine, but unable to pay the fine, were obliged to serve additional time in jail. In a concurring opinion for that case, he scorned the majority's equal protection analysis as "a 'wolf in sheep's clothing' . . . no more than a masquerade of a supposedly objective standard for *subjective* judicial judgment as to what state legislation offends notions of 'fundamental fairness.' " Such judgments could be more effectively made, he suggested, if the Court chopped its "rhetorical preoccupation with 'equalizing' " and focused instead on the "*rationality*" of challenged laws.[97]

Harlan's tenure ended before the Court began to augment the two-tiered equal protection formula of strict scrutiny and its lower-tier "rational basis" counterpart with a variety of intermediate standards of scrutiny for gender and other "quasi-suspect" bases of classification, as well as laws burdening personal interests considered important but not yet accorded status as a "fundamental constitutional right." It is doubtful, however, whether he would have joined that additional ripple on the modern equal protection doctrine, either. In 1961, he spoke for the Court in upholding a Florida law exempting from jury service all women who did not specifically request to have their names added to the jury roll. "Despite the enlightened emancipation of women from the restrictions and protections of bygone years, and their entry into many parts of community life formerly considered to be reserved to men," he had observed on that occasion, "woman is still regarded as the center of home and family life." He thus could not "regard it as irrational for a state legislature to consider preferable a broad exemption, whether born of the State's historic public policy or of a determination that it would not be administratively feasible to decide in each individual instance whether the family responsibilities of a prospective female juror were serious enough to warrant an exemption."[98]

Substantive Due Process

With notable exceptions in the reapportionment and criminal procedure fields, Hugo Black had joined Justice Harlan in rejecting substantive equal protection. Although Black had invoked such rhetoric as the Court's spokesman in *Williams* v. *Rhodes*, the 1968 decision striking down a state law limiting access to the ballot, he later explained that he sometimes had to "use words" to hold a majority.[99] But the Alabamian also hoped to live to see a complete repudiation of substantive due process. And on that score, he and John Harlan parted company.

In *Ferguson* v. *Skrupa*, a 1963 decision rejecting due process and equal protection challenges to a Kansas statute which limited the business of "debt adjustment" to lawyers alone, Black had declared for the Court, "We refuse to sit as a 'super-legislature to weigh the wisdom of legislation.' . . . Whether the legislature takes for its textbook Adam Smith, Herbert Spencer, Lord Keynes, or some other is no concern of ours." A draft opinion the Justice had originally circulated in the case had contained an even more clear-cut rejection of substantive due process in economic contexts. Justice Goldberg had found disturbing, however, the opinion's "many references to the idea that it is no longer this Court's function to pass upon the 'reasonableness' of a State's economic legislation" and asked that Black make revisions which would leave the justices "free to think in terms of 'unreasonableness' about the merits of conceivable extremes of state economic regulation when such cases arise." Black agreed to some of the modifications Goldberg recommended, but "with great regret. . . . With these changes," he lamented in a notation scrawled at the bottom of his colleague's letter, "we fail to administer the final fatal blow to the idea that this Court can overrule a legislature's belief of reasonableness."[100]

While Goldberg could now join Black's *Skrupa* opinion, Justice Harlan was unable to agree to even the watered-down version finally registered in the case. An April 10 circulation of a new draft suggested that courts no longer struck down "state laws which were thought unreasonable, that is, unwise or incompatible with some particular economic or social philosophy." A Harlan clerk had circled "or social" in that passage and cited in the margin of the draft those cases appearing to belie Black's assertion. "This opinion," the clerk warned, "almost does away entirely with the Due Process Clause. . . . [It] appears to do away even with the rational basis test."[101]

Black, of course, had little hope that his colleague would join such an opinion. "You were right in your preview of my reactions!" Harlan quickly responded, asking that Black "kindly add at the foot of your opinion" the statement that "Mr. Justice Harlan concurs in the judgment on the ground that this state measure bears a rational relation to a valid constitutional objective." Nor would a later draft circulation prove more appealing. "The word 'unreasonable' has been taken out," Harlan's clerk reported, "and this does improve the opinion." But the new version included "no discussion whatever . . . bearing on the question of [the law's] rational relation to a permissible objective."[102] Not surprisingly, therefore, Harlan stood firm in his original position in the case, joining the Court's decision but not the rationale of Black's opinion.

Justice Harlan remained a firm supporter of governmental authority over the economy. In fact, when the Court in 1957 handed down its only post-1937 decision invalidating on equal protection grounds a state economic regulation, and a grossly discriminatory one at that, Harlan had joined Justice Frankfurter's dissent, finding the statute at issue a "rational" exercise of state power.[103] But the Justice's refusal to endorse a total repudiation of economic due process (or equal protection) was no mere reflection of his likely conservative business leanings, despite his long and distinguished career as an advocate of such interests and preference for narrow readings of the antitrust laws. Instead, Harlan's acceptance of judicial oversight of the reasonableness of legislation—albeit an oversight conditioned considerably by deference to popularly elected officials, as well as the principles of federalism and separation of powers—was simply part and parcel of his broader due process philosophy, as his stance in Warren Court privacy cases made abundantly clear.

Two years before *Skrupa* was decided, the justices had confronted for a second time a Connecticut statute forbidding the use of contraceptives or medical assistance in their use, even in the marriage relationship. In 1943, the Court had dismissed a physician's challenge to the law, noting that he had claimed injury only to his patients' rights, not his own, and thus lacked standing to sue. In *Poe* v. *Ullman*, two patients as well as a doctor had challenged the statute. Emphasizing that the law had been used to prosecute only three persons since its enactment in 1879, and that those cases had been dropped once the Connecticut supreme court had upheld the statute's constitutionality, Justice Frankfurter had concluded for the *Poe* Court that those suits must also be dismissed.[104]

Not surprisingly, Justice Douglas registered a *Poe* dissent. The Fourteenth Amendment's due process clause included in its meaning, declared Douglas, not merely the explicit guarantees of the first eight amendments, but also those "emanat[ing]" from the specific safeguards, "from experience with the requirements of a free society," or "from the totality of the constitutional scheme under which we live." A right of privacy sufficiently broad to reach Connecticut's contraceptive statute lay, in Douglas's judgment, within those "emanations," and "to say that a legislature [could] do anything not within a specific guarantee of the Constitution [would] be as crippling to a free society as to allow it to override specific guarantees so long as what it does fails to shock the sensibilities of a majority of the Court." The pre-1937 Court, concluded Douglas, had not erred by "entertaining inquiries concerning the constitutionality of social legislation" under due process standards, but by the standards it applied and its failure to recognize that a "free society needs room for vast experimentation."[105]

In his conclusion, and substantially if by no means entirely in his rhetoric, Justice Douglas was not alone. Prior to oral argument of the *Poe* case, Harlan's clerk Charles Fried had prepared a bench memorandum urging the Justice to support relief for the patient plaintiffs, if not the physician. Fowler W. Harper, clerk and biographer of the late Justice Wiley Rutledge, one of the staunchest civil libertarians of the Roosevelt Court, was counsel to the plaintiff/appellants. Harper's brief, contended Fried, was "execrable," especially its assertion "that explicitly and specifically granted constitutional rights are absolute." But Fried was equally unimpressed with Justice Black's frequent warning that any departure from the "four corners of specifically guaranteed 'liberties' and 'rights' " would "inevitably" drive the Court "back [into] the morass of private judgment on the wisdom of legislation [in economic cases] from which Holmes, Stone, and Frankfurter [had] rescued it." Such a fear "assume[d] that merely because thinking has led to wrong conclusions in the past, all thought is a dangerous pastime. The way to avoid the errors of the past," wrote Fried, echoing Douglas, "is to be wiser than those who made them, not less bold."[106]

The critical question, to Fried, was not whether the Constitution included within its reach other guarantees than those given explicit expression in the document's language, but the standard to be applied in evaluating such rights. Since 1937, as Justice Stone's famous fourth footnote in the *Carolene Products* case of 1938 had suggested, the Court had drawn a distinction between economic liberties, on the one hand, and those which assured "that the political processes, on which everything else depends, [were] kept open and serviceable," on the other. Burdens on the former were evaluated under a lenient rationality standard, while restrictions on the latter were subjected to strict scrutiny. But, he asserted, neither the Court nor individual justices had restricted strict review to those substantive rights which were basic to the democratic process. Freedom of religion, for example, was another substantive right which enjoyed "a similar dignity." In *Meyer* v. *Nebraska* (1923) and *Pierce* v. *Society of Sisters* (1925), the Court had cited other such rights. And in his eloquent dissent from the Court's acceptance of warrantless wiretapping in *Olmstead* v. *United States* (1928), Justice Brandeis had referred to "the right to be let alone" as "the most comprehensive of rights and the right most valued by civilized men." Rights of marital privacy, argued Fried, were deserving of a comparable status.[107]

Justice Harlan substantially agreed. In conference he charged that the Court had "no business dismissing these cases" and condemned Connecticut's sweeping ban as "egregiously unconstitutional on its face." For Harlan, due process had a "substantive content . . . apart from incorporation of [the] first eight amendments." And while the state had broad power to regulate the public health, there were limits to its authority. The challenged law, unlike "ordinary statutes in this field," reached mere "use." It was thus, he asserted, "more offensive to [the] 'right to be let alone' than any [other regulation] possibly could be."[108]

The *Poe* dissent Harlan ultimately filed largely tracked his conference remarks and Fried's memo, as well as the approach to due process he would embrace in his attacks on the incorporationists. Following a convincing, point-by-point rejoinder to Justice Frankfurter's rationale for the case's dismissal, he turned to the appellants' constitutional claims. In ruling on the constitutionality of challenged legislation, the Court's approach should be a "rational one," drawing on "the text which is the only commission for our power[,] not in a literalistic way . . . but as the basic charter of our society, setting out in spare but meaningful terms the principles of government." Since the words and history of the Constitution's due process clauses cast "little light" on their meaning, a "rational" approach to constitutional construction was especially important in due process cases. "Again and again," asserted Harlan, the Court had "resisted the notion that the Fourteenth Amendment is no more than a shorthand reference to what is explicitly set out elsewhere in the Bill of Rights." Instead, due process reflected "a rational continuum which, broadly speaking, includes a freedom from all substantial arbitrary impositions and purposeless restraints . . . and which also recognizes, what a reasonable and sensitive judgment must, that certain interests require particularly careful scrutiny of the state needs asserted to justify their abridgment."[109]

Nor, he observed, as Justice Frankfurter had to Hugo Black's dismay so many times before, did such a conception of due process leave judges "free to roam where unguided speculation might take them." For the balance "struck between liberty and the demands of organized society" which such an approach required was actually "the balance struck by [the] country, having regard to what history teaches are the traditions from which it broke. That tradition is a living thing. A decision of this Court which radically departs from it could not long survive, while a decision which builds on what has survived is likely to be sound."[110]

When applying the "rational continuum" of due process to the issue at hand, Harlan found Connecticut's statute constitutionally deficient. He conceded that the moral judgment the law reflected was "no more demonstrably correct or incorrect" than those relating to "marriage and divorce . . . adultery, homosexuality, abortion, and sterilization, or euthanasia and suicide." But there was a critical difference. Like every other state, Connecticut recognized marriage as an acceptable legal relationship. Yet the contraceptive ban "allow[ed] the State to enquire into, prove and punish married people for the private use of their marital intimacy." It thus touched "a most fundamental aspect of 'liberty,' the privacy of the home in its most basic sense." For that reason, it was vulnerable to "a more rigorous constitutional test than that going merely to the plausibility of its underlying rationale." Instead, it should be "subjected to 'strict scrutiny' " and, under that standard, fall.[111]

Philip Heymann, the Justice's other clerk the term *Poe* was dismissed, recalls being "sort of skeptical," while Harlan and Charles Fried were "enthusiastic" in their belief that Connecticut's contraceptive law was unconstitutional. "Justice Harlan had a patrician manner about him, and he was outraged at this interference with personal privacy. . . . He just couldn't imagine such a law. It was government going into places it simply shouldn't." "Part of the energy in Harlan's *Poe* dissent" also came, Fried has remarked, "from the Justice's running battle with Black on incorporation. Part of the fun of *Poe* for the Justice was that his view of the Constitution was not necessarily more retrograde than Black's. It was a way of saying, 'Look, if you do it my way, it may look as though individual rights lose out every time, but that's not right. . . . By affirming non-incorporation, you sometimes knock down something the Bill of Rights does not.' "[112]

In the Court's final and decisive 1965 encounter with the Connecticut law, the Justice would say as much in a published opinion. Harlan—or Charles Fried—had rested the Justice's defense of stricter judicial protection for certain rights than others partly on *Skinner* v. *Oklahoma*, the 1942 sterilization case which became the key basis for the Warren Court's expansion of substantive equal protection. Despite his opposition to that development, however, Harlan would not abandon use of substantive due process as a vehicle for subjecting laws abridging privacy and related unspecified rights to meaningful review. And when the Court overturned the contraceptive law in *Griswold* v. *Connecticut* (1965), he registered a concurrence, which, unlike Justice Douglas's attempt in the Court's opinion to tie a right of marital privacy to the "penumbras" of specific Bill of Rights safeguards, grounded his vote squarely on the substantive due process rationale he had embraced in *Poe*.[113]

He took strong exception, moreover, to Justice Black's contention in a vehement *Griswold* dissent that a constitutional amendment, not judicial innovation, was the appropriate vehicle of constitutional change and that Harlan's "natural law" due process philosophy and related theories permitted judges to impose their personal predilections on the Constitution's text, the voters, and their elected representatives. For Harlan, the idea that "incorporation" could be used "to *restrict* the reach of Fourteenth Amendment Due Process" was as "unacceptable" as its employment to "*impose* upon the States all the requirements of the Bill of Rights." Nor could he agree that Black's approach was a more effective restraint of judicial discretion than his own. " 'Specific' provisions of the Constitution, no less than 'due process,' " he declared, "lend themselves as readily to 'personal' interpretations by judges whose constitutional outlook is simply to keep the Constitution in supposed 'tune with the times.' "[114]

Both justices would be dead before the Court held in *Roe* v. *Wade* (1973) that due process embodied an abortion right. In his *Poe* dissent, Harlan had included abortion laws among the reflections of a state's moral judgments he would be reluctant to disturb. Both Harlan and Black, moreover, had joined a decision rejecting a vagueness challenge to an abortion statute. But while Black had flatly opposed any constitutional recognition of such a right in conference discussion of that case, Harlan never fully revealed his position on the issue. And given his flexible approach to due process, he might well have accepted at least limited restrictions on governmental authority in that highly sensitive field.[115]

Griswold, however, was not to be the last scene of the Harlan-Black debates over the nature of due process and the judge's role in constitutional interpretation. Although a further expansion of due process' substantive component would await the *Roe* case, the Court invoked the guarantee several times in the last years of their tenure to accord protection to procedural rights not specifically mentioned in the Constitution's text. In the *Winship* case, proof of a defendant's guilt beyond a reasonable doubt had been held to be an implicit requirement of due process. *Goldberg* v. *Kelly* (1970) invoked due process in requiring that welfare recipients be given a hearing prior to termination of their benefits, and *Sniadach* v. *Family Finance Corp.* (1969) required notice and a hearing before a wage-earner's salary could be frozen pending garnishment proceedings. *Winship*, it will be recalled, occasioned a Harlan-Black debate over due process, and Harlan had joined the *Goldberg* and *Sniadach* majorities over Black's dissent. In a brief *Sniadach* concurrence, Harlan had insisted that his conception of due process was derived "from concepts which [were] part of the Anglo-American legal heritage—not . . . from the mere predilections of individual judges," while Black charged in dissent that it was precisely that sort of nebulous rhetoric which left judges "wholly free to decide what they are convinced is right and true," adding, "If the judges . . . are to be left only to the admonitions of their own consciences, why was it that the founders gave us a written Constitution at all?"[116]

But *Boddie* v. *Connecticut* (1971) was to provide the setting for the two justices' final public battle over the guarantee of due process. During the 1969 term, a majority had voted in *Boddie* to overturn the application to indigents of a state filing fee required for initiating divorce proceedings, and also agreed in *Sanks* v. *Georgia* to strike down a law under which a tenant wishing to challenge his eviction was forced to post a surety bond equal to double the amount of his rent, the bond going to the landlord if the tenant lost the case. Harlan was assigned to write the Court's opinions in the two cases. On the day before the last conference of the term, and after a majority had already joined Harlan's drafts, Black circulated a dissent in which he argued that the issues raised in *Sanks* could have become moot. At conference, Harlan indicated that the problem Black had raised was a minor one which could be answered in a footnote. But Black then persuaded their colleagues to have *Sanks*, and later, *Boddie* also, scheduled for re-argument the following term.[117]

The next fall, a majority did agree to dismissal of *Sanks*. With Harlan again the Court's spokesman, however, the justices also struck down the filing fee at issue in *Boddie*. And while a number of the brethren preferred a decision that rested on equal protection instead of due process, a clerk in Justice Marshall's chambers, at the urging of Thomas Krattenmaker, the Harlan clerk responsible for *Boddie* in the 1970 term, persuaded Marshall to agree to a due process holding, giving Harlan a majority for his rationale as well as the Court's decision. Emphasizing the state's monopoly over the dissolution of marriages, he concluded that Connecticut's exclusion of indigents from divorce proceedings was "equivalent [to] denying them an opportunity to be heard . . . and, in the absence of a sufficient countervailing justification for the State's action, a denial of due process." But to Justice Black, neither due process nor equal protection, as he put it in his *Boddie* dissent, "justifie[d] judges in trying to make our Constitution fit the times, or . . . [their] sense of fairness."[118]

Black, one of Harlan's clerks has remarked, "was one wily southerner. He would play procedural hardball in ways the Justice would never have contemplated. And Harlan was furious with Black for his shenanigans in *Sanks* and *Boddie*." But their philosophical and tactical differences would never overcome their friendship. After delivering to the brethren a scorching forty-five-minute courtroom lecture the day the *Griswold* decision was announced, Black entertained Harlan and others at dinner in his Alexandria home. And when reporters interviewed Black on the occasion of his eighty-fifth birthday in February of 1971, during his thirty-fourth year on the bench, Harlan sent his friend a congratulatory note. Earlier that term, in his capacity as supervisory justice over the courts of the Fifth Circuit, Justice Black had rejected due process and other constitutional challenges to a hair code for public school students, caustically observing that "[t]he only thing about [such claims] that borders on the serious to me is the idea that anyone should think the Federal Constitution imposes on the United States courts the burden of supervising the length of hair that public school students should wear." "I got quiet encouragement from your long-hair opinion," wrote Harlan in his note to his friend, "showing as it did that the Due Process clause does at least leave room for shocking the sartorial conscience. But I liked even more the 'Justices may come and go but Black goes on forever' theme of your press conference."[119]

9

Final Struggles

Their mutual affection and respect notwithstanding, the Harlan-Black jurisprudential differences during their last years on the bench would extend well beyond incorporation and due process. They also parted company on a variety of First Amendment questions, among other issues. And while the absolutist philosophy which Black embraced and Harlan disdained prompted the Alabamian's continued rejection of all obscenity controls, libel actions, and other "direct" infringements on freedoms the First Amendment guaranteed, Black's refusal to extend their reach beyond "speech" to demonstrative conduct, or to agree that people were free to express themselves wherever they happened to be, meant, ironically enough, that Justice Harlan at times assumed a more "liberal-activist" stance than his colleague in First Amendment cases.

Such contrasts in their positions emerged most clearly perhaps in a number of "symbolic speech" cases arising out of the social upheaval of the late 1960s. Both justices joined the Court in upholding a congressional statute forbidding the destruction of draft cards. In a brief concurring opinion, however, Justice Harlan indicated that his posture in the case might have been different had the petitioner been "entirely prevent[ed] . . . from reaching a significant audience with whom he could not otherwise lawfully communicate," adding, "This is not such a case, since O'Brien manifestly could have conveyed his message in many ways other than by burning his draft card." Black also publicly ridiculed the notion that school hair codes raised issues of constitutional significance, and Harlan observed on a clerk's memo in one such case that he could "see nothing whatever to this constitutional claim." But while Black rejected entirely the notion that free expression guarantees—"pure" or "symbolic"—extended to the public schools, Harlan characteristically assumed a more moderate stance.[1]

Consider, for example, their positions in *Tinker* v. *Des Moines Independent Community School District*, a 1969 case overturning the suspension of students who had worn black armbands to school as a symbol of protest against U.S. military policies in Vietnam, and permitting school officials to sanction only that student expression which substantially interfered with the educational process or school discipline. In a draft *Tinker* dissent, Justice Black declared that the Court's assumption of authority to review school disciplinary policies smacked of the "reasonableness due process test" which the justices had "unanimous[ly]" repudiated in *Ferguson v. Skrupa*, "except for Mr. Justice Harlan, who still, up to this day, adheres to the doctrine that judges have the power to hold laws unconstitutional upon . . . some. . . flexible [formula] without precise boundaries." In his own draft dissent, which he then circulated, Harlan observed, with "satisfaction," that the Court's opinion "had drawn from my Brother Black a dissenting essay . . . that again reveals to a remarkable degree his extraordinary capacities for vigorous expression and colorful self-mesmerizing characterization of the constitutional views of others."[2]

Black immediately went to his colleague, as he later noted on his copy of Harlan's draft, and explained that he "would take out my response to his [Harlan's] constitutional views if he preferred. He did and I eliminated that part of my opinion." The dissent which Black ultimately filed was a scathing rebuttal to the notions that First and Fourteenth Amendment rights extended to the schools and that the Court was an appropriate school board for the nation. In his own published dissent, Justice Harlan agreed "that school officials should be accorded the widest authority in maintaining discipline and good order in their institutions" and favored placing the burden on those challenging the authority of education officials to show that a particular regulation "was motivated by other than legitimate school concerns." Because he found nothing in the record "impugn[ing]" the good faith of school officials in the *Tinker* case, Harlan concluded that the Court should have upheld the suspensions at issue there. In his original draft dissent, moreover, he had noted that there was "much" in Black's dissent with "which I personally agree." Unlike Black, however, Harlan also insisted that school officials were "not wholly exempt from the requirements of the Fourteenth Amendment respecting the freedoms of expression and association."[3]

The justices' approach to cases growing out of unorthodox uses of the American flag reflected somewhat the same pattern. In *Street v. New York* (1969), a black, outraged by the shooting of civil rights activist James Meredith, had burned his flag on a New York street corner while shouting, "We don't need no damn flag. . . . If they let that happen to Meredith, we don't need an American flag." Sidney Street, a Brooklyn bus driver, was convicted of violating a state law which made it a misdemeanor to cast public contempt on a flag by "words or acts," and the New York courts rejected his claim that his act was a protest protected by the First and Fourteenth amendments. When the case reached the Supreme Court, Justice Harlan argued in conference that Street's jury could have convicted the petitioner for his "verbal expression," thus violating the defendant's freedom of speech, and not his conduct, and recommended that the conviction be reversed on that narrow ground, thereby enabling the brethren to avoid a ruling on the constitutional status of flag-burning. The justice's colleagues agreed, voting six–three to reverse along the lines he had suggested.[4]

With an "apology to Brother Harlan for inconstancy," Justice Fortas defected from the *Street* majority, concluding that the petitioner had been convicted for his conduct, not his speech. But Justice Black was the most vehement *Street* dissenter, rejecting both Harlan's rationale and the petitioner's assertion that the First Amendment covered flag-burning. Black found it beyond "belief," he asserted, "that anything in the Federal Constitution bars a State from making the deliberate burning of the American flag an offense." It is difficult to say what Justice Harlan's position on the issue of flag-burning was; his *Street* rationale had made it possible for him to avoid the issue there. However, in concurring with the Court's dismissal the following year of a case in which a defendant was convicted for wearing a vest fashioned from a cut-up American flag, he observed that the question "whether [such] symbolic expression . . . [was] protected from punishment by the Fourteenth Amendment" was one he could not "regard as insubstantial." And in his last term, he apparently remarked during conference discussion of another flag case that he could not "see how [it] can be said that [the] flag can't be used for protest which is anti-government."[5]

Nor were the Harlan-Black differences confined to the "symbolic" conduct arena. When one Paul Robert Cohen was convicted in California of disturbing the peace following his arrest in a courtroom corridor for wearing a jacket bearing the words "Fuck the Draft," Justice Black had initially favored summary reversal of the young man's conviction while Harlan had voted first to deny review, then to affirm the lower courts. Ultimately, however, Harlan spoke for a majority reversing Cohen's conviction, and Black dissented.[6] No doubt reflecting his own original impression of the case, Harlan began his opinion for the Court by acknowledging that *Cohen* v. *California* might "seem at first blush too inconsequential to find its way into our books," but immediately emphasized that the issue the case presented was "of no small constitutional significance." Cohen's conviction could not be defended, he asserted, as an obscenity regulation, for under the Court's many precedents in that troublesome field, "such expression must be, in some significant way, erotic." Since Cohen's epithet had been directed at no particular person or group, the case also did not involve an exercise of state power over face-to-face verbal assaults, or "fighting words." Nor did it present a legitimate "captive audience" situation. The Court, conceded Harlan, had long recognized the authority of government to protect "unwilling or unsuspecting viewers" from "otherwise unavoidable exposure" to offensive expression. But no evidence had been presented to indicate that "persons powerless to avoid [the] appellant's conduct did in fact object to it." Since Cohen had incited no one to imminent lawless action, and the statute under which he was convicted was not narrowly written to control the use of particular types of public property, those justifications for government interference with expression were, he added, equally inapplicable.[7]

Having surveyed "various matters" which, as he put it, "this record does *not* present," Harlan next turned to the basic question which *Cohen*, in the majority's judgment, did raise—whether a state could remove "one particular scurrilous epithet from the public discourse," either on the premise that "its use [was] inherently likely to cause violent reaction or upon a more general assertion that the States, acting as guardians of public morality," could cleanse the public vocabulary. The idea that government could eliminate certain language to prevent reaction to its display "by a hypothetical coterie of the violent and lawless" was, he asserted, "plainly untenable." While he found more plausible the notion that states had power "to maintain what they regard as a suitable level of discourse within the body politic," he rejected that defense of Cohen's conviction as well. After all, he observed, expression was intended to serve "emotive" as well as "cognitive" functions, and "one man's vulgarity [was] another's lyric." In fact, it was precisely because government officials could not make "principled distinctions" of that sort "that the Constitution [left] matters of taste and style so largely to the individual." There was the risk, too, he added, that government censorship of particular words could become a "convenient guise for banning the expression of unpopular ideas."[8]

Partly because he, too, was uncertain of the appropriate approach to the issues *Cohen* had raised, Justice Black filed no opinion. But he did join Justice Blackmun's dissent, which condemned Cohen's "absurd and immature antic . . . [as] mainly conduct and little speech." While Chief Justice Burger also filed no separate dissent in the case, he had circulated a brief opinion, indicating in an accompanying memorandum that his draft was "the most restrained utterance" he could manage. In that effort, Burger protested the Court's devotion of its "limited resources of time . . . to such a case as this," adding: "It is a measure of lack of a sense of priorities and with all deference I submit that Mr. Justice Harlan's 'first blush' was the correct reaction. It is nothing short of absurd nonsense that juvenile delinquents and their emotionally unstable outbursts should command the attention of this Court."[9]

Justice Harlan's *Cohen* opinion, as well as his willingness to join the Court's holding in *Stanley* v. *Georgia* that people have a right to possess obscenity in the privacy of the home, and his extension of the Fourth Amendment to eavesdropping in the *Katz* case, apparently convinced certain of Harlan's earlier clerks that some of their more liberal successors had somehow "gotten to" the Justice. Two of Harlan's later clerks had also clerked on the Court of Appeals for the District of Columbia when Warren Burger had sat on that bench. They were "not enamored with Burger," as one later commented, "and were eager to have [Harlan] think badly of the" new Chief Justice. But Harlan was "never very accommodating" on that score, for he had quickly decided that Burger ran a fairer conference than Earl Warren, who, the Justice had long suspected, had often allied with Justice Brennan to organize conference votes in advance of the brethren's discussion of pending cases.[10]

Several of Harlan's more liberal clerks have conceded that they did attempt to influence the direction of the Justice's votes in civil liberties cases and that while, as one put it, "the patient was already dead" on incorporation, reapportionment, substantive equal protection, and a multitude of other issues, they may have had some success in areas in which the Justice's position was not firmly fixed. Paul Brest, who served as one of Harlan's clerks in the 1968 term after working for the NAACP in Mississippi, and with whom Harlan was initially concerned that he might not be philosophically compatible, has suggested "that the later Harlan was more 'liberal' than the earlier Justice." But Harlan's later clerks have found it difficult to comprehend how any of their predecessors could ever have thought that a group of "young 'upstarts' " could exert an undue influence on the Justice's thinking. Instead, they attribute whatever impact they may have had to Harlan's own personality and tolerance of views which conflicted with his own leanings.[11]

Michael Boudin, who clerked for the Justice during the 1965 term, could hardly have been classified among Harlan's more liberal clerks, regardless of the political inclinations of his father, the noted civil liberties attorney. One of the things which struck Boudin most about Harlan "was how little he was given to pronouncements . . . or even to talking. He was unusual in the amount of listening he did. He struck me as someone so comfortable with himself and so self-confident that he found it easier than most people to listen. He was one of the relatively few people I've met who seemed to be completely comfortable, and in a way that relieved him of any obligation to always be explaining himself or proselytizing or pronouncing."[12]

According to other clerks, too, Harlan was an "amazingly tolerant" listener. "I remember," Paul Brest has remarked, "very long discussions, especially after conference. There would sometimes be really quite lengthy arguments, and he was amazingly tolerant of rather long attempts to change his mind." Bruce Ackerman, who was later to join the Yale law faculty, was one of Brest's co-clerks. "Ackerman, who was as bright and headstrong then as he is now, would go on at quite some length. . . . The Justice sometimes reacted to those discussions with bemusement. But I think that he thought the dialogue was valuable, and I think there were times when we changed his mind." Robert Mnookin, one of Harlan's clerks during the 1969 term, agrees.

> The wonderful thing about clerking for Justice Harlan was that he really believed in reasoned elaboration, all the stuff one was taught about how the judicial process ought to work. He really worked that way. He really believed in arguments, in meeting arguments. He believed in deciding things on the merits, explaining the real reasons for a decision, being candid about it. . . . And he always listened to your arguments. He never had any doubts about who had been confirmed by the Senate and whose values were going to ultimately prevail. But as a clerk you always had the sense that you were heard. And in fact we would occasionally feel that we had some impact on his thinking, because he was truly open to argument.[13]

There was a limit, however, to the degree to which even an "amazingly tolerant," open-minded jurist would yield to his clerks' efforts. They may have been a factor in his decision to reverse ground in the *Cohen* case; in fact, his oft-quoted assertion there that "one man's vulgarity is another's lyric," like most of that opinion's language, originated with a clerk. But he had resisted their efforts, it will be recalled, to persuade him to use the *Stanley* privacy rationale as a basis for rejecting most obscenity controls. And his clerks during the 1969 term were apparently unanimous in their opposition to his decision to join the Court in rejecting strict scrutiny of the discriminatory ceiling on welfare benefits at issue in *Dandridge* v. *Williams*. Whatever his clerks' leanings, moreover, he had dissented in 1967 when a majority, speaking through Justice Black, overruled Felix Frankfurter's opinion for the Court in a 1958 case which Harlan had joined, and held, contrary to long precedent and congressional practice, that Congress had no power to strip U.S. citizens of their citizenship. And his essentially restraintist positions in numerous other areas were firmly moored in his jurisprudence.[14]

For example, given the Justice's regard for the "passive virtues," it was not surprising that when the Court in 1968 relaxed its longtime ban on federal taxpayer suits in order to permit constitutional challenges to federal aid for parochial schools, he dissented. A 1923 decision had held that the financial burdens inflicted on individual taxpayers by federal spending programs were an inadequate basis for their being granted standing to attack such programs in the federal courts. In its 1968 decision in *Flast* v. *Cohen*, however, a majority, speaking through Chief Justice Warren, concluded that taxpayers, as taxpayers, had the standing to challenge exercises of Congress' taxing and spending powers claimed to violate a "specific" constitutional limitation on that power, such as the First Amendment's ban on laws respecting an establishment of religion.[15]

Harlan vigorously challenged the majority's rationale, arguing convincingly that the conditions the Court had announced for relaxing the ban on taxpayer suits had no bearing whatever on the degree of injury such plaintiffs had sustained—the critical element in determinations of standing. The Justice had little doubt of Congress' power to permit taxpayer suits. But his colleagues' grant of standing to litigants whose stake in a case was no different "from those of the general public" would, he warned, "go far toward the final transformation of this Court into the Council of Revision [with general power to review federal laws] which . . . was rejected by the Constitutional Convention."[16]

Most significantly, perhaps, Harlan continued late in his career as he had early in his tenure to endorse broad governmental power over speech and association in a variety of contexts, but especially in cases tinged with considerations of public safety. One notable exception was *Brandenburg v. Ohio* (1969), where he joined the Court in reversing the conviction of a Ku Klux Klan leader under a state criminal syndicalism act, holding with the Court that government could criminally punish those who advocated lawless action only where such advocacy would likely lead imminently to such action. Indeed, when Justice Fortas circulated a draft opinion for the Court very similar to the per curiam opinion ultimately filed in the case, Harlan wrote Fortas that he "entirely agree[d]" with his colleague's opinion, even though its language appeared to conflict with Harlan's opinions in the Smith Act cases and related litigation. But *Brandenburg* hardly raised issues of national security. And during his last term, the Justice joined a majority in upholding a state's power to require a loyalty oath from prospective lawyers and dissented from his colleagues' refusal to permit states to deny a law license to bar applicants who refused to answer questions about their personal beliefs or affiliation with allegedly subversive organizations.[17]

Finally, of course, there was his stance in the *Pentagon Papers Cases.* When the Court there rebuffed the Nixon administration's attempts to secure injunctions barring further publication of those controversial documents, Harlan joined Chief Justice Burger and Justice Harry Blackmun in dissent. Over the vigorous objections of Black and Douglas, who favored a summary rejection of the president's claims, the Court did hold oral argument in the cases—but not the sort of calm deliberation Harlan believed they warranted. In a brief but unusually caustic dissenting opinion, he lamented the "frenzied train of events [which had taken] place [in the cases] in the name of the presumption against prior restraints created by the First Amendment." His colleagues' "irresponsibly feverish" pace, he charged, had denied the Court the time necessary for "[d]ue regard [to] the extraordinarily important and difficult questions" the cases raised. It was, he added, "a reflection on the stability of the judicial process that these great issues—as important as any that have arisen during my time on the Court—should have been decided under the pressures engendered by the torrent of publicity that has attended these litigations from their inception."[18]

Since the majority had taken a position on the constitutional questions the cases had raised, Harlan considered himself compelled to reach them as well, albeit, he pointedly observed, "in telescoped form" in view of the Court's "precipitate timetable." On those issues, not surprisingly, he found the proper reach of judicial authority over "the activities of the Executive Branch of the Government in the field of foreign affairs . . . very narrowly restricted." A court, he asserted, could satisfy itself that "the subject matter of the dispute [lay] within the proper compass of the President's foreign relations power." It could also insist that determinations whether particular material should be kept secret be made by "the head of the Executive Department concerned." But beyond that the courts should not venture. A court could not "redetermine for itself the probable impact of [a] disclosure on the national security," for such determinations, he concluded, quoting Justice Jackson, had "long been held to belong in the domain of political power not subject to judicial intrusion or inquiry." Even if a court could sometimes overturn such judgments, he added, "the scope of review must be exceedingly narrow." At the very least, a judicial distaste for prior restraints should not be stretched to the point, declared Harlan, that it prevents "courts from maintaining the *status quo* long enough to act responsibly in matters of . . . national importance."[19]

Harlan's *Pentagon Papers* dissent had accorded government a greater degree of deference than his Smith Act opinions or even his stances in cases involving loyalty-security programs, bar admissions, and legislative inquiries ever had. That the cases involved purloined government documents undoubtedly was a factor in his position. But Thomas Krattenmaker, one of the Justice's last clerks, has suggested that Harlan's eyesight had deteriorated to the point at that stage of his life that he was simply overwhelmed by the pace of the litigation and the massive paperwork it generated. Krattenmaker considered the dissent the Justice's "worst opinion" and, along with his co-clerks, had attempted without success to persuade Harlan to change course. "Had I realized it was to be his last opinion," Krattenmaker later remarked, "I would have continued to press him."[20]

But neither the Justice nor Hugo Black, despite the sentiments of Harlan's congratulatory birthday note to his colleague the previous February, was to "go on forever." At eighty-five, Black's age alone made him a likely candidate for retirement, and he had suffered several recent strokes. As the 1970–71 term concluded, Harlan, at seventy-two, was in failing health. His dietary habits, for one, had always been suspect at best. Once when Ethel was to be away for the evening, she had carefully reminded her husband of the nutritious food stocked in their refrigerator, only to learn on returning home that he had consumed three boiled eggs and three martinis for supper! Such instances were not unusual. It was not surprising, therefore, that surgeons had removed half his stomach during ulcer surgery in 1961 and that the chronic chain-smoker of cigarettes was no longer the robust picture of health he once had been. At public events, he was now frequently seen leaning on Chief Justice Burger's arm.[21]

If anything, Harlan's failing eyesight, as Thomas Krattenmaker's explanation for his *Pentagon Papers* dissent suggested, had become an even greater burden to the Justice than the general deterioration of his health. At first he had resorted to stronger reading glasses, a substantial supply of new typewriter ribbons for his chambers, and large-print typewriters in an effort to compensate for his growing blindness. Later he had experimented with a number of special magnifying glasses, including one rectangular piece placed on the printed page, and a dictating machine he dubbed "The Robot," apologizing profusely to friends because he was now forced to send typewritten personal letters. Ultimately, however, he was obliged when reading, as one clerk put it, "virtually to put his nose to the page" and to rely increasingly on his clerks to read briefs, the draft opinions and memoranda of his colleagues, and other material to him. During Harlan's tenure on the Court, each associate justice was normally allotted two clerks. Beginning with the 1965 term, though, Harlan was assigned a third. In his last term, by one estimate, they were devoting up to sixty hours each week reading to the Justice.[22]

The nearly complete loss of his eyesight must have been a frustrating experience. Like Justice Black, he had always been fond of driving. In his younger years, John Twarda, the caretaker of the Harlan Weston, Connecticut, summer home, has recalled, he had cut a striking figure motoring off for a round of golf in a convertible. But following a serious collision with a truck in the mid-1960s, Twarda and the Justice's family had convinced him that he was no longer safe to himself or others to sit behind the steering wheel of an automobile. ("John," Twarda recalls Mrs. Harlan saying, "you tell my husband not to drive anymore. If he hears it from you, he'll listen. He won't listen to me.") From that point on, Twarda served as the Harlans' driver in Connecticut and New York, and the Justice's messenger, Paul Burke, was his Washington chauffeur. At times, too, the Justice would light the filter end of his cigarette. And one morning when his messenger was preparing to drive him to the Court, Burke heard Harlan greet someone, even though the sidewalk appeared deserted. "Damn, Paul!" the Justice then exclaimed, "I just said 'good morning' to a tree." While riding with Justice Douglas and his current wife on another occasion, he calmly flicked cigarette ashes into Mrs. Douglas's black-gloved palms, which he had mistaken for an ashtray. While working on an opinion at home with Louis Cohen on yet another day, the Justice poured his clerk an especially stiff portion of Rebel Yell sour mash—an act Cohen was uncertain whether to attribute to Harlan's blindness or simply to the Justice's personal preference.[23]

While one so proper as John Harlan would doubtlessly have been embarrassed by the incident with Mrs. Douglas, he took the other difficulties his blindness created for him largely in stride. "He laughed it off," Paul Burke remembers. "He knew he had failing eyesight, and he coped with it. . . . Nothing deterred him from doing what he had to do." That determination extended, of course, especially to his work as a justice. His office staff made certain to identify themselves and guests on entering his chambers. He began to carry with him to conference large charts bearing the names of pending cases and spaces for notations. At times, he would pen his nearly illegible observations in the wrong spaces, but the charts enabled him—and his clerks—to keep abreast of conference debates and the votes taken there. In the courtroom, he began to deliver opinions entirely from memory. While he drastically curtailed his speaking engagements, he memorized those addresses he did give as well. On the drive from Weston to one of his last such sessions, a speech to U.S. attorneys at the federal courthouse on Foley Square in Manhattan, John Twarda remembers that the Justice, normally a stickler for punctuality, played and replayed a tape recording of his remarks, cautioning Twarda to delay arriving at the courthouse until he had them committed to memory.[24]

Even though he now had to depend heavily on his clerks' eyesight, they in no way, they would later insist, controlled the flow of information to him. "This man," one of his last clerks has observed, "was a terrific manager of people. There was never any question that what he needed to have read to him was going to be read to him."[25] At the same time, the Justice's blindness and growing dependence on others must have exacted a tremendous emotional and physical toll.

If his failing eyesight posed special but surmountable burdens, however, his wife's declining health filled him with anguish. Although Ethel Harlan had always preferred the Connecticut countryside to Washington, she had been a tremendous asset to her husband through most of his years on the bench. Refined, attractive, and charming, she was the perfect capital hostess, and, like her husband, well-liked by all their associates. Gradually, however, she had grown increasingly dissatisfied with an environment in which most of the attention was focused on her husband. The Justice had a study constructed for her over the garage at their Georgetown home so that she could indulge her interest in writing. But nothing seemed to help. Furthermore, by the mid-1960s she had begun to exhibit the symptoms of arteriosclerosis or what later was to become widely known as Alzheimer's disease. John Twarda had first sensed that something was wrong when she began telephoning him and talking for hours "for no particular reason." Later, "she would forget she had a daughter or husband, and at times she felt persecuted. She would say, 'John, they can't do this to me. Why are they doing this to me?' She wasn't the woman that I had known." While the Harlans were attending the 1964 meetings of the American Bar Association in New York, she had become disoriented, unable to find her way back to their hotel.[26] When Harlan's clerks visited their Georgetown home for weekend work on pending cases, they began to notice that what she said often made no sense.

In January of 1970, the Justice discussed his wife's condition in a letter to a friend.

> Ethel is no longer the person you once knew. She has had almost a complete loss of memory, but is physically in very good condition. She is unable to sustain any social contacts, and we are leading a very quiet life with practically no social activities in which she is able to participate. There are days when she seems to be quite herself, and I daresay that if you happened to see her on one of those days you would not fully recognize her difficulties. I tell you all this because you and she are such old friends, but I hope that you will not intimate in any letter you write her, or to others, that you are concerned about her condition.[27]

From the time years before when he had written his mother of the "most wonderful girl" he planned to marry, Harlan had been devoted to Ethel. "There were always attractive ladies interested in him," his daughter has remarked. "But he was absolutely single-minded on that point as far as I know. When he was in England during the war, a lady tried to kiss him on the dance floor. Mother asked him how he had reacted." And he had replied, his amused eyes twinkling, "I deflected her." Watching his wife's memory deteriorate was, his daughter remembers, "very hard for him. . . . I don't see how he did it."[28]

As with his blindness, Harlan coped. Since he could not bear to have his wife institutionalized, he retained Elizabeth Morrow, a nurse, as his wife's constant companion. The Justice did his best to shield her from the indignities her condition would otherwise have inflicted upon her. During his clerkship, Louis Cohen lived in Georgetown and rode to the Court nearly every day with Harlan and Paul Burke. During coffee at the Harlans' one morning, the conversation turned to presidential wives, including Jacqueline Kennedy. "And Mrs. Harlan asked, 'Who is that, dear?' It was a painfully embarrassing moment. The Justice paused a minute, then said very gently, 'You remember, dear, Janet Auchincloss's daughter.' And Mrs. Harlan replied, 'Why yes, of course.' He should have been sent to Mars to show Martians what earthlings could be like."[29]

But at least Harlan was not obliged to face his burdens alone. On the Court, as Louis Cohen no doubt accurately summarized, this man who, as Justice Stewart put it, "could disagree without being disagreeable," would have "won any popularity contest hands down." Paul Burke, Elizabeth Morrow, and Ethel McCall remained completely devoted, as did the Justice's clerks. Over the years Harlan had continued to display a keen interest in his clerks and their families, and the affection was mutual. He presented the children of one or more of his clerks with an autographed copy of a children's book Ethel Harlan had written. When Paul Brest's three-year-old daughter visited the Court at the Justice's urging one Saturday morning, Harlan put her in the chief justice's seat, then went down to the lawyer's lectern and "argued" a case to her. When the clerks' wives or other family members attended sessions of the Court, he made certain they were given choice seats. "He treated his clerks," Brest has said, echoing numerous others, "like children or grandchildren. He was wonderfully warm. I can't remember his ever being even abrupt, let alone sharp or critical."[30] And as life became more complicated for the Justice, his clerks rallied to his special needs.

If anything, the Harlans' patrician manner had made them even more endearing to the Justice's clerks and their spouses. While Stephen Shulman was clerking for the Justice during the 1958 term, the Harlans had invited Shulman and his wife to join them in their box at the National Symphony. As the evening approached, Harlan suggested that while not required, his clerk might be "more comfortable" in black tie. Shulman, who had no tuxedo, rented one for the occasion. "And the Justice and I were the only people there in black tie." But proper was proper. When the Harlans were no longer able to attend the Symphony's concerts, the Justice offered the tickets to at least one of his clerks—suggesting that he, too, would find formal attire "more comfortable" for the occasion. Mrs. Harlan had eaten her first pizza at the Shulmans' home. Offered lox and bagels at another clerk's apartment, she was receptive but would take, she said, "only one 'lock.' "[31]

Particularly after Mrs. Harlan's memory began to decline, the couple seemed most content at their Weston, Connecticut, summer home. Their daughter, Eve, who lived in the area, had presented them with a grandson—John Harlan Newcomb—and four granddaughters; a sign along the long, stone circular driveway to the large, white house read, "Children at Play." The Harlans were very fond, too, of Eve's second husband Frank Dillingham, whose mechanical genius particularly impressed the Justice, who was notably lacking in such skills and frequently joked to his daughter, "Someday, I'm going to break everything in the house, put it all in the middle of the living room floor, and have Frank fix it." The Weston home had always been the site of casual entertaining with friends. In the 1950s, Harlan had fished with President Eisenhower, when the president made unpublicized visits to a West Point classmate in the area. Justice Black, Justice Brennan, Herbert Brownell, their spouses, and other friends visited Weston also, with Justice Black, at the time eighty, alarming his colleague one day when he failed to surface quickly from a dive into the swimming pool in which Harlan regularly swam morning laps. And a Christmas party for the J. Edward Lumbards and other area friends had remained an annual affair.[32]

But in Weston as in Washington, the Harlans were increasingly dependent on others, especially their faithful caretaker, John Twarda. As a teenager, Twarda had tended the gardens at the home of the mother of Horace Hitchcock, one of Emory Buckner's "Boy Scouts" and a close friend of Harlan. After Hitchcock's mother died, he introduced Twarda to the Harlans, whose Weston house was then under construction. With an apartment in the city, a new country home, a young daughter, and other servants, Harlan initially told Twarda he could not afford to pay the young man what both thought he was worth. Eventually, however,

Harlan agreed to Twarda's terms, giving his new gardener the keys to the house and telling him, "The place is yours." Years later, when Harlan was appointed to the Supreme Court, Twarda reminded the new Justice that "I got you to reverse yourself years ago." Harlan never regretted that decision. Twarda left the family for service in the Pacific during World War II and considered pursuing some other, more lucrative, occupation afterwards. But Harlan, he has remarked, "treated me like a son when I returned from the war, and his affection touched me. I went back to them and never left." Twarda became perhaps the Harlans' most devoted employee. Widely known as one of the Weston area's finer horticulturists, he painstakingly maintained the Justice's grounds and flowers. And when Harlan returned from a visit to Pierre Du Pont's Longwood estate, impressed with the elegant, terraced gardens he had seen there, Twarda immediately set to work landscaping the Harlans' grounds along the same lines, if on a smaller scale. When Harlan visited the Bridgeport federal courthouse for summer duties as the justice assigned to the Second Circuit, or made other official trips, Twarda served as his driver, as he did for the Harlans' personal trips.[33]

But Twarda was to become more than a caretaker and chauffeur. The Harlans treated him as a member of the family. Five or six times each year, the Justice invited him to their Georgetown home. During those Washington visits, Harlan introduced his caretaker to the brethren and other Washington dignitaries. When the Justice spotted him sitting in the public section of the courtroom during oral argument of a case, he had a messenger move him to the seating area reserved for the justices' families. In 1969, Twarda was the family's guest at Richard Nixon's inauguration. When, during their earlier years in Washington, the Harlans went out for the evening, the Justice left Twarda the key to their Georgetown home and a reminder that "the bar's open."[34]

Harlan's gracious manner of dealing with people extended to his caretaker. On occasion when Twarda drove the Justice into New York City, they had dinner at the Century Association. "He would say," Twarda recalls, " 'John, I'm going to have a drink'—he liked this Rebel Yell sour mash—'and you can have one, too. I'll leave it up to you since you're driving.' He obviously didn't want me to drink and drive, but he allowed me to decide."[35]

Twarda had thus watched with considerable alarm as the Justice attempted to deal not only with his near blindness and his wife's failing memory, but with a variety of other crises as well. One year, an interior decorator had fallen in the sunken living room of the Weston house, breaking a leg. During a Weston vacation Ethel McCall broke a leg and arm. A servant in the Harlans' Georgetown home also broke a leg. Earlier, the Justice had broken a leg in a fall from a horse at Justice Douglas's Goose Prairie, Washington, cabin. On one occasion, too, his daughter had been hospitalized in a New York hospital.[36]

Each such incident, Twarda could see, had taken its toll on the Justice. On the trip to Manhattan for his Foley Square address to U.S. attorneys, the caretaker was impressed with the precision of Harlan's directions and the skill with which he handled his audience. During the speech, the Justice had reminisced about his days as Emory Buckner's assistant in charge of prosecuting Prohibition cases. Afterwards, a young man asked him if he favored the legalization of marijuana. "The Justice," Twarda later recalled with a smile, "said a lot of words but never answered the question." When the Harlans prepared to return to Washington following their Christmas visit to Weston in 1970, their caretaker made certain to take numerous photographs of their departure. "I sensed that the Harlans were not going to be with us much longer."[37]

That March the Justice began to experience severe lower back pains. A "donut cushion" for his chair and similar remedies provided no relief. During the summer, he had entered a Connecticut hospital for tests. Physicians there discovered that one of his legs was slightly longer than the other and attributed his mounting discomfort to imbalanced vertebrae. But the pain persisted despite alterations in the heels and soles of his shoes. "To hell with this," the Justice finally told John Twarda, "I'm going back to Washington." Harlan's Washington doctor attributed his pain to a sacroiliac condition, but treatment for that diagnosis produced no noticeable results either. Earlier, physicians at Bethesda Naval Hospital had treated Justice Black successfully for a back ailment; on August 16, Harlan entered the Bethesda facility.[38]

Not long after his arrival there, Hugo Black was admitted to an adjoining suite in one of Bethesda's VIP towers. Despite continuing pain, Harlan remained in good spirits and continued to handle his Court duties. One or more times each day, Paul Burke visited with certiorari petitions, briefs, and other material from the Court. His clerks and other visitors came by regularly, too, and he spoke frequently by telephone with members of his staff and family, lawyers, judges, and old friends. Black, by contrast, wanted no visitors, rarely spoke, and then largely only to members of his immediate family and the hospital staff. Black's Bethesda physicians could find no sign of an illness. But the Alabamian, like Justice Harlan now nearly blind, was convinced he was dying, and he was to be as stubborn in that resolve as he had ever been in his controversial constitutional positions. When his son, Hugo, Jr., assured him he would soon be back at his chambers, the old man merely grinned and shook his head. "Face reality, Son." When presented with the optimistic reports of his doctors—"guessers," he called them—he replied with characteristic impatience, "They don't know what they're talking about. I'm finished, Son."[39]

In his reminiscenses of his father, Hugo Black, Jr., called the "intimate relationship" the younger Black developed with Justice Harlan during the two jurists' last days "one of the most treasured I have ever had with anyone," adding, "Even though he suffered excruciating pain in his back, was losing his sight, and no doubt was haunted by thoughts of imminent death, he possessed a wonderful sense of humor." Late each afternoon, Hugo, Jr., joined often by Justice Black's wife, Elizabeth, and other members of his family, enjoyed a cocktail with Justice Harlan. Often the conversation turned to Hugo, Jr.'s father—whether he ever had presidential aspirations, whether he wanted to remain on the bench at least another term, thereby breaking the Court's longevity record. "The biggest difference between your father on the one hand, and me and Justice Frankfurter on the other hand," Harlan told Hugo, Jr., one evening, "is the basic assumption we make about judges. Your father believes that you have to keep judges tethered—you can't trust their consciences loose without some kind of bridle." But the Justice also praised his colleague. "Nobody's judgment ever exceeded his—his is just the best."

Hugo, Jr., it appeared obvious, wished that his father could have been as optimistic and cheerful as Justice Harlan. But the senior Black—whose triumph over his humble origins had seemed as unlikely as John Harlan's professional success appeared foreordained—was determined to deal with death, as he had with life, on his own terms. And his dark mood even extended to his colleague. On one occasion, after Hugo, Jr., had shamed his father into taking walks in the hospital corridors to build up his strength, they passed Justice Harlan, leaning against a wall while smoking a cigarette. "Suddenly, without looking to the side," Hugo, Jr., later recalled, his father, himself a reformed smoker, "sniffed and said, 'John, you're smokin'.' " But Black resisted Harlan's efforts to draw him into conversation or bolster his spirits. Black had often remarked that under Harlan's construction of due process the guarantee was "nothing in the world but a shoot-the-works clause." One day, Harlan entered Black's room with a petition for certiorari which urged the brethren to strike down a state business regulation on due process grounds. "Here's a real candidate for the shoot-the-works clause." Harlan "was visibly disappointed," Hugo, Jr., later wrote, "when Daddy did not even respond."

While attempting to cheer his colleague, Justice Harlan was also becoming increasingly anxious about his own condition. Suspicious that he might have a spinal malignancy, his physician had removed a portion of his spine for analysis. That surgery, conducted on a Friday, had gone well. But the Justice, "on pins and needles," as Hugo Black, Jr., later put it, was obliged to wait until the following Monday for the test results. When doctors informed him that day that the specimen taken had been lost and that further surgery would be necessary once he had recovered from the first operation, "this gentle man," Hugo, Jr., recalls, "became infuriated." He and his partners would have fired any man in their firm who made such a mistake, he declared. He was leaving Bethesda, he informed Justice Black's son, and entering the hospital at George Washington University.

Citing the hospital's posh accommodations and the close attention given VIPs there, Hugo, Jr., and Elizabeth Black urged the Justice not to leave Bethesda. Also, Mrs. Harlan was under a nurse's care at their Georgetown home,[40] and the obligations of Eve Harlan's large family meant that her visits to her father, at that stage of his illness, were relatively infrequent. Justice Black's son, wife, and other members of the Alabamian's family, on the other hand, were at the hospital daily. Though the Blacks believed that they had probably derived more comfort from Harlan than he had from them, they told Harlan that they would no longer be able to "tend to" him if he left Bethesda.

But Harlan was determined. He transferred hospitals, and jokingly warned Hugo, Jr., "Just don't say anything," when his friend's son first visited the Justice's more spartan George Washington accommodations. George Washington's physicians confirmed what Bethesda's suspected. A hospital staff member's September 23 memorandum attributed the Justice's back pain to cancer in one of the bases of his lower spine.[41]

Rumors of Harlan's impending retirement had begun to surface in the press at least six years earlier, when the Justice's failing eyesight was first becoming a subject of Washington gossip. On reading one such report in a May 1965 column, his friend Barton Leach of the Harvard law school had written him, "If these stories are true, I would feel that the good Lord had not been very careful in his selection of those whom he would choose to afflict." In an effort to pressure Chief Justice Melville Fuller into retirement, Leach reminded Harlan, Theodore Roosevelt "inspired rumors that Fuller was to resign; whereupon Fuller, knowledgeable at the game, said, 'I am not to be paragraphed out of my place.' " The Coolidge administration had attempted the same ploy with Justice Holmes, again without success; and Leach apparently suspected President Lyndon Johnson's Democratic hand in the Harlan rumors. "My dear friend," he advised, "if you are ailing, quit while you're ahead. If you are not, ignore this crap."[42]

In his reply to Leach, Harlan emphasized that he was "*not* retiring." His eyes were giving him difficulty, he added, but "so far things have not become unmanageable." Of Leach's theory, he charitably wrote, "I am naive enough to think (or hope) that it was inspired by nothing more than a lust for gossip." But such rumors, like others about Justice Black, would persist. And in January of 1970, a columnist noted that neither Black "nor the ailing Justice Harlan" had interviewed prospective clerks for the 1970–71 term.[43]

But Harlan did continue on the bench that term, and although the last justice to do so, he also retained clerks for the 1971–72 term. The Justice, however, had always been a realist. On September 7, after three weeks at Bethesda, he had written Judge Henry Friendly, chief judge of the Second Circuit, that he would be unable to attend that year's circuit conference and that Justice Marshall had made the "nice gesture of substituting for me." His physicians, he reported, were "still baffled as to the source of the trouble," and while his pain was not yet "excruciating . . . it [was] enough to make me fidget like a jack-in-the-box, and interrupts my sleeping at night. . . . I hope the mystery will be cleared up before the open of Court in October," he added, "if it does not it will face me with some very difficult decisions"[44]

After his Bethesda physicians had begun to suspect cancer, Harlan queried Hugo Black, Jr., about his father's plans for retirement. He wanted to make certain, he explained to his friend's son and members of his own family, that his own retirement would not coincide with Justice Black's. "I do not want to do anything," he modestly, but characteristically, told Hugo, Jr., "to detract from the attention your father's retirement will get. . . . He is one of the all-time greats of our Court."

Justice Black had composed his own retirement messages even before his admission to Bethesda and persisted in his decision over the protests of his family, who still hoped, given the doctors' reports, that the Justice might yet recover. For a time, Hugo, Jr., and others had hit upon a successful stratagem for persuading his father to delay the announcement. Justice Black had long considered it improper for scholars to draw on the sketchy, cryptic, and often illegible conference notes of deceased justices in their research. He had been appalled, moreover, when political scientist Sidney Ulmer had recently concluded from his reading of Justice Burton's *Brown* conference notes that Black might have been willing to join a decision upholding segregated schools[45] ("Good Lord, Son," he exclaimed to Hugo, Jr., "You of all people know how false that is"). And he was now more determined than ever that his own papers not be used to distort history. Hugo, Jr., and other family members were thus able to convince him that their chances of honoring his wishes that his notes be destroyed might be jeopardized were he to retire prematurely.

When their task was completed, however, they could delay him no longer. On September 14, 1971, Black scribbled his signature on an updated set of retirement letters. "[A]nd I'll tell you something else," he had declared earlier, when he and Hugo, Jr., were arguing over his decision; "John Harlan can't see a thing. He ought to get off the Court too."

Hugo Black obviously held his colleague in high esteem and affection. When Harlan had first come to the Court, Black had recently confided to one of his colleague's clerks, the Alabamian had feared that the aristocratic Wall Street lawyer might be aloof and condescending toward "a backward country fellow," as Black often styled himself. He had been both pleased and relieved to learn, he added, that those concerns were wholly unfounded. Even as the two justices had become increasingly infirm, they still could be seen strolling down the Court's corridors, arms around each other. Following lunch one afternoon the previous term, they and their clerks had spent a pleasant afternoon drinking cognac and bourbon by the fireplace in Justice Harlan's chambers, the clerks listening fascinated as Harlan chided his colleague's support of Franklin Roosevelt's Court-packing plan, while Black offered up an equally good-humored rebuttal. His friend's illegible birthday greeting that year had brought tears to Black's eyes.[46]

Hugo, Jr., knew the depth of his father's feelings for his colleague and scolded him for presuming to suggest what Harlan should do. "You're right, Son," the old man replied. "I am tired."

With his physician's report in hand, Justice Harlan too realized what he must do. On September 23, a respectable ten days after Black's retirement and the day Harlan's doctors confirmed their diagnosis, the Justice sent his own messages to the president and the brethren. For weeks, journalists had pressed Court and hospital staffers and family members for information on the two justices' condition. On the morning after Harlan's announcement, Lyle Denniston of the *Washington Star* decried the Court's failure "yet to adopt candor as its practice in discussing judicial health." The statement Black had finally authorized, Denniston complained, gave "only the barest details." But Harlan's case, he declared, presented "an even more astonishing example of non-disclosure. He had been in the hospital a full month before word of it leaked out, and then the explanation was that he had a 'back ailment.' " The Justice's retirement letters were no more revealing. "I have reluctantly come to the conclusion," he wrote President Nixon, "that the time has arrived when, because of reasons of health, I can no longer carry on, to my own satisfaction, my full share of the work of the Supreme Court." His decision, he added, had been "a very difficult" one, but one "clearly called for [by] . . . the tenor of the medical advice I have received."[47]

Two days after Harlan's retirement, Hugo Black died—an act of will which surprised his doctors, but probably no one who knew him well. Justice Harlan was not to be so fortunate. As the weeks passed, his sister Janet moved into a Washington hotel and was at her brother's bedside daily. Edith and Elizabeth visited from New York each weekend, and toward the end Eve moved into her parents' Georgetown house. Justice Stewart made daily visits to the hospital. Chief Justice Burger also visited regularly, as did their colleagues, his secretary Mrs. McCall, former clerks, and old friends. Paul Burke, whom Harlan had arranged to have transferred to the clerk's office on the Justice's retirement, was there daily as well. And on one occasion, Harlan's first son-in-law, Wellington Newcomb, with whom the Harlans had maintained amiable relations following what the Justice had termed Newcomb's "civilized" divorce from their daughter, brought two of the Justice's grandchildren down for a visit.[48]

Harlan's condition steadily declined. One side of his body became totally paralyzed, the other racked with pain despite heavy sedation. At times his spirits faltered. When he and Charles Stewart, his assistant in the Du Pont litigation, were alone in his room one day, the Justice looked dejectedly at his old friend and asked, "Why did this have to happen to me?" "It was terrible," Stewart later remarked, "a very sad moment." But such lapses were rare. Especially before his clerks and members of his family he displayed remarkable resolve. When Henry Sailer, a Harlan clerk during the 1958 term, first learned that the Justice had been hospitalized, he telephoned Ethel McCall. "She was very evasive. . . . So Mike Boudin and I went over to see him. The change in the six weeks since I had last seen him was scary. He was almost unconscious and out of his mind with pain. . . . But he did take an interest in the new appointments to the Court. . . . Even in extremis, he was still interested in the Court as an institution." "He was in terrible pain," Charles Nesson has recalled of an earlier visit. "But he was immediately concerned about me. Here was this man in the most extreme situation, and yet he was still wide open to the people around him. As I spoke to him, I found it easier to focus on his paralyzed eye. Somehow I found myself resisting the fact that he was still an absolutely vital character; it was an act of will to engage him as a fully present person. Yet, despite excruciating pain and the hopelessness of his condition, that's the way he was engaging me. . . . It was a lesson in how to die bravely."[49]

Years earlier, Ethel Harlan had embraced the teachings of Christian Science. While Eve Harlan was married to Wellington Newcomb, whose mother was a Christian Science practitioner, Eve too had become a Christian Scientist. Eve credited her mother's faith for Ethel Harlan's recovery from a lingering illness which had left her a near-invalid through much of Eve's childhood, and she doubted the value of the exploratory surgery and related treatment to which her father was now being subjected. Aware of her feelings, Eve's aunts and at least one of the Justice's clerks feared that she might attempt to dissuade her father from pursuing every possible medical recourse. The Justice had insisted, however, that both Mrs. Harlan's deteriorating memory and his own condition be treated medically, and his daughter acquiesced in that decision. The physician's memorandum confirming spinal cancer had indicated that "[t]reatment was being initiated."[50]

But as Justice Black had scornfully reminded his son of the profession the elder Black had almost entered, medical science has its limits. Toward the end, the Justice's visitors, as Henry Sailer put it, could only kiss his forehead, offer words of encouragement they hoped he could hear, and sit at his bedside. Finally, mercifully, it was over. On December 29, Paul Burke drove Harlan's old and dear friend Leslie Arps from George Washington University hospital to the airport. When he returned, the Justice was dead. His daughter, his sisters, and Justice Stewart had been with him at his death.[51]

John Harlan had been as careful and methodical in preparing for his death as for every stage of his life. A few years earlier, while he and John Twarda were driving through the Weston countryside, they had passed Emmanual Episcopal Church, which the Justice occasionally attended. He planned, he told his caretaker, to be buried in the church's cemetery. In an October 11 memorandum and two supplements, he had dictated precise instructions for his funeral. His remains were to be cremated for burial in an urn which his daughter was to select. George A. Trowbridge, a New York cleric and Princeton classmate, was to conduct "a simple memorial service." His daughter was to notify Court personnel, family, servants, and friends, and host a buffet luncheon following the funeral. "Mrs. Harlan," who would remain at the Weston house until her death the following June, was, he added protectively, "not to be present at the house during the luncheon." John Twarda was to select flowers for the church.[52]

Twarda was a gardener, not a florist. He recalled, however, that years before, when Harlan had been in Europe on the date of Ethel Harlan's birthday or their wedding anniversary, he had telephoned Twarda, asking that his caretaker have a dozen long-stemmed red roses delivered to his wife with a note he would cable from Europe. On January 4, the day of the Justice's funeral, hundreds of red roses adorned Emmanuel Church's white interior as Harlan's family, all the Court's current and surviving former members with the exception of Earl Warren, staffers, servants, and friends braved a driving rain to pay the Justice final respects. Following a church service, the gathering assembled under umbrellas in the adjoining cemetery. There the Reverend Trowbridge gave thanks "for a life's task faithfully and honorably discharged; for good humor and gracious affection and kindly generosity; for sadness met without surrender, and weakness endured without defeat."[53]

Epilogue: Judge's Judge

Surveying a Supreme Court justice's life and analyzing his jurisprudence are comparatively easy tasks. Discovering the *why* underlying the judge's thinking is decidedly more difficult. In truth, of course, an incalculable number of factors exert varying degrees of influence on every jurist. Isolating and assessing them with anything approaching scientific precision is thus an impossible goal. At best, only crude and highly tentative conclusions can be attempted.

An explanation of Justice Harlan's judicial record is especially complicated. He was clearly devoted to the "passive virtues" he found implicit in the principles of separation of powers, federalism, majoritarian democracy, and precedent. But the same judge who opposed application of the Bill of Rights and the exclusionary rule to the states, court-ordered reapportionment, expansive notions of "state action," the *Miranda* warnings, and other broad constructions of the Fifth Amendment's guarantee against compulsory self-incrimination, and who yielded to governmental authority over expression and association deemed to threaten the nation's security, also voted to extend the Fourth Amendment's coverage to eavesdropping, joined decisions limiting the reach of warrantless searches, embraced the principles, if not always the pace, of the Court's desegregation decisions, rejected state-sponsored prayer and Bible-reading in the public schools, recognized the right to private possession of obscenity in the home and the public display of "one man's vulgarity," and publicly embraced a constitutional right of privacy four years before a majority of the brethren did so. Unlike Black, moreover, Harlan believed that the most effective safeguard against the abuse of judicial power lay in the individual judge's own commitment to self-restraint rather than in what he considered to be the inherent ambiguities of constitutional text and history. Harlan's "liberal-activist" votes in certain cases and "conservative-restraintist" leanings in others thus could not be attributed to the mixed signals the Constitution's language and the history surrounding adoption of its provisions presented Hugo Black.

Several elements in the Justice's background appear to have been reflected in, and to some extent helped to shape, his thinking in a variety of constitutional contexts. His prosecutorial experience surely must have had some appreciable impact. Even though they composed relatively brief episodes when viewed against the backdrop of his entire pre-Court career, Harlan's work as Emory Buckner's "Boy Scout" in charge of Prohibition enforcement, as his mentor's top assistant in the Queens sewer scandal prosecutions later in the 1920s, and as chief counsel to the New York crime commission shortly before his appointment to the federal bench no doubt helped to strengthen his regard for the role of the states in the federal system, as well as his support for flexible constitutional standards conditioned by countervailing social imperatives. Harlan's Prohibition efforts, as noted earlier, entailed frequent encounters with the then relatively new exclusionary rule and other procedural guarantees, including the right to trial by jury. In a courtroom attempt to take advantage of the "silver platter" doctrine, for example, he had sought to minimize his staff's contacts with the New York police, a major source of important, if often illegally procured, evidence, although neither he nor an assistant were able to cite a single instance when the police had not followed their "suggestions" in liquor cases. He was probably the author, moreover, of the memorandum Buckner submitted to the Senate judiciary committee, predicting the need for massive increases in the Prohibition budget were jury trials not suspended in such cases. Harlan's experience as Buckner's Prohibition chief may well have convinced him not only of the inherent futility of a national liquor policy but also of the wisdom of diverse state regulations in such sensitive areas. No doubt, it helped to nurture as well the sympathy for the special problems of law enforcement which was to be a common theme of his opinions. The death threats which he received during his work with the crime commission may also have had an impact on his thinking.

The Justice's World War II experiences, which he considered among the most significant and interesting episodes of his life, were also of undoubted relevance. The highly secret nature of his wartime activities probably contributed to the deference he was later to accord government in civil liberties cases with national security overtones. His suspicions of the Soviet Union and concern over "the tendency of higher [military] circles to play ball with the Russians" instead of his beloved Britain in the planning of Germany's postwar occupation, which feelings he expressed in his wartime diary, seem undoubtedly to have had an impact as well. The Justice had serious misgivings about the anti-Communist prosecutions of the Cold War era, and his clerk Charles Fried was no doubt correct when he recalled that Harlan considered the subversive advocacy and membership legislation of that era "McCarthyite garbage."

Moreover, his refusal during the 1952 presidential campaign to sign a lawyers' statement deploring the Eisenhower campaign's attempt to exploit his Princeton contemporary Adlai Stevenson's submission of a deposition in the Alger Hiss case was probably, as one of his closest friends has suggested, simply the act of a prudent Republican unwilling to be drawn into a controversial issue rather than a reflection of his own Cold War views. Even so, his wartime activities, and his disdain for the Soviets those experiences generated or intensified, may well have contributed to his reluctance as a Justice to second-guess the judgments of government officials regarding national security matters.

Harlan's affinity for the British is perhaps equally relevant to an understanding of his jurisprudence. When John Maynard Harlan enrolled his eight-year-old son in boarding school, he selected a Canadian school because the strict regimen and curriculum there closely approximated the English pattern. The younger Harlan had thrived in that environment; during his years as a Rhodes Scholar at Oxford's Balliol College, he had become a confirmed Anglophile. On one occasion late in his life, Chief Justice Burger shared with his colleague a draft of a speech he was preparing to deliver in London. "You are expert on all things British. Do you have any comments?"[1] Harlan's opinions even adopted British spellings, and his appreciation for the English clearly extended to their legal traditions.

Charles Fried, another Oxford product, doubts that Harlan found his years at Balliol an any more intellectually gripping experience than the year he spent at New York Law School in preparation for the state bar. But Harlan's Oxford experience seems certain to have influenced his flexible, essentially common-law approach to legal issues. In a 1958 piece for the *American Oxonian*, for example, he suggested that study at Oxford instilled in a person "respect for tradition and a lively and abiding appreciation of the importance of the Rule of Law in the workings of a democratic society," as well as a "broad-minded, but hard-headed, tolerance . . . an attitude of mind which tackles a problem with due account for differing views, which is free from the shackles of limiting preconceptions"—in short, the sorts of elements which appeared to permeate the Justice's jurisprudence. Throughout his adult life, moreover, he maintained close ties with British lawyers and jurists, as well as English conceptions of law and the judge's function. "The main point in my pamphlets," the Oxford scholar Sir Arthur L. Goodhart, whom Harlan had first met at a friend's Connecticut home in 1956, once wrote the Justice, "is that I believe the whole spirit of the common law is dead against 'absolute' rights. Its hero is the reasonable man."[2]

Harlan's social background and the corporate focus of his law practice were other strong influences on his jurisprudence, however difficult pinpointing their impact may be. Harlan's father, it will be remembered, was frequently in financial difficulty. When his son's law firm prepared his will in 1925, he had an estate of only $1,000. At his death less than ten years later, he had no real estate holdings and left only a gold watch, a pair of pearl studs and a scarf pin, and office and household furnishings totaling less than $500, plus nearly six thousand shares of stock in a Maine company whose charter had been suspended years earlier. At the time of Justice Harlan's appointment to the federal bench, the annual income from his law practice had reached an impressive $150,000. At his death, however, his wealth, excluding his two homes, was only in the low six figures.[3]

But Harlan and his family enjoyed impeccable social credentials, and his Princeton classmates, like many of his later social acquaintances, came from some of the nation's leading industrial and commercial families. His clients were drawn largely from the same background. From his first major civil case, in which he defended heirs to the estate of the eccentric and fabulously wealthy Ella Wendel against more than two thousand claimants, to his defense of the Du Pont brothers shortly before his appointment to the bench, his superlative legal skills were dedicated primarily to the protection of property from private and governmental interference.

There is evidence that Harlan personally sympathized with the interests he was retained to represent. For example, in his final argument to the district court in the Du Pont–General Motors antitrust case, he scorned the government for suggesting that huge holdings alone were illegal or socially undesirable and insisted that he had "been proud to represent these two distinguished men [the Du Ponts] to whom the government [had] so often turned in times when our country has been in peril." And when following his elevation to the Supreme Court, his brethren overturned the trial court's rejection of the government's case, he had vehemently complained to Justice Frankfurter about the majority's "*superficial* understanding of a really impressive record."

One could hardly suggest, of course, that Justice Harlan was at all inclined to resurrect the economic activism of the pre-1937 Court. He did vote regularly to limit the impact of antitrust legislation and related regulatory statutes. When Justice Black attempted to deal economic due process a final fatal blow in *Ferguson* v. *Skrupa*, moreover, he joined only the Court's ruling, not his colleague's rationale, even after the tone of Black's opinion had been substantially moderated. But he so routinely rejected substantive due process attacks on business regulations that his clerks rarely even prepared certiorari or bench memoranda in such cases. And he dissented from the Court's only post-1937 decision overturning a state economic control on equal protection grounds, even though the discriminatory features of the statute at issue appeared largely indefensible.[4]

What is evident is that Justice Harlan's close ties to corporate America may have made him somewhat more deferential to government in civil liberties cases than he might otherwise have been. When John Maynard Harlan had considered bringing Felix Frankfurter into some venture in 1929, as was noted earlier, his son had warned him that the Harvard professor was "identified with the radical point of view." Harlan's advice to his father was probably evidence more of his customary caution in dealing with potentially controversial issues than of his distaste for "radical politics. Norman Dorsen, one of the Justice's earlier and more liberal clerks, has remarked, however, that

> Harlan was part of the establishment, as close to an upper-class Justice we've had since [Charles Evans] Hughes. The thing that people from Wall Street, from that world, care about most is national security. That's at the core of their senses. They don't want to rock the boat. . . . Harlan was a true conservative. He was not a right-winger, certainly not a redneck in any way; he was an educated, upper-class internationalist with corporate clients that transcended the country. His main concern, his lodestar, was to keep things on an "even keel." He used that phrase many times to me in conversation. And one way to do that is to make sure that government has the authority to protect itself. . . . I don't think he believed there was a threat to the free enterprise, capitalist system in this country, but I also think he was not prepared to intervene when the government was taking steps to assure that there was no threat.[5]

Dorsen's observation may have captured a central element of Harlan's thinking—a mind-set which may have affected the Justice's reaction not only to government assertions of national security but to criminal procedure issues and other civil liberties claims as well.

If Harlan's aristocratic background, the associations it fostered, and the overwhelmingly corporate thrust of his law practice helped to shape his reaction to constitutional issues, so too did his judicial ties. Justice Frankfurter had begun campaigning for Harlan's jurisprudential soul even before the Senate had confirmed his nomination—writing and conferring with him frequently regarding the First Amendment, incorporation, and other concerns central to the Court's work, and also regularly feeding him negative information and gossip about Hugo Black and other members of the Court's "liberal-activist" bloc. Eve Harlan's first husband has recalled few occasions, in fact, when dinner at his in-laws' was not interrupted by Frankfurter's telephone calls—calls the gracious Harlan invariably took.[6] And while by this point in Harlan's career it was doubtful the senior Justice could have pushed his colleague in directions he did not wish to go, Frankfurter may have helped to refine Harlan's jurisprudential thinking. Judges Lumbard, Henry Friendly, Harold Medina (from whom Harlan had taken a bar review course while preparing for the New York bar years earlier), and other lower court judges with whom he was most closely associated also embraced the Frankfurtian tradition of self-restraint. Earlier in his career, moreover, Harlan's friends had included elder jurists of the same persuasion—most notably Learned Hand, who warned Harlan, shortly after his elevation to the Supreme Court, against "making the Bill of Rights in the form of LAW, instead of, like the British, thinking about it as 'cricket.' As a prelate of Balliol, you will know what I mean better than I do."[7]

Then, too, there was the Justice's relationship with Hugo Black. The two differed dramatically in their conceptions of the judicial role and responses to numerous constitutional issues. Both were bound together, however, by a deep concern about the potential for judges to abuse their authority. Their essential agreement on that fundamental point, as well as the obvious respect and affection these "wonderful old men of honor"[8] felt for each other, may have meant that each exerted subtle influences on the other, even on issues over which they most vigorously disagreed.

Of the claim of certain of Harlan's earlier clerks that some of their later counterparts may have pushed the Justice in "liberal-activist" directions, considerable caution is, of course, in order. It is only logical to assume that a Supreme Court justice's articulate, often brilliant, clerks—typically the "best" products of the "best" schools—should have some appreciable influence on the judge they serve; in fact, there is a crying need for a major study of the Court's clerks and their roles. The Justice—like Paul Bator and other major sources of his clerk candidates—clearly preferred those whose views were essentially compatible with his own generally restraintist philosophy. But the social and political changes of the 1960s dramatically increased the odds that the heroes of Harlan's later clerks would be Earl Warren and William Brennan rather than Felix Frankfurter, Learned Hand—or John Harlan.

As indicated in the previous chapter, several of Harlan's last clerks believe that their arguments may have influenced the Justice to assume activist positions on issues about which his mind remained open, and they are probably correct on that score. As several have readily conceded, however, they had virtually no impact on his thinking regarding incorporation, reapportionment, the "new" equal protection, obscenity, and many other questions on which his views were firmly fixed. The "liberal-activist" stances Harlan assumed in later cases, as well as earlier ones, were also for the most part narrowly confined to the facts at issue. While holding in the *Boddie* case, for example, that indigents must be exempted from filing fees in divorce cases, he based the Court's ruling there squarely on the absolute monopoly states possess over the dissolution of marriages—a factor the Court used after the Justice's death to restrict *Boddie*'s reach.[9] His willingness in the *Cohen* case to uphold a right to the public display of vulgarities probably rested primarily on his fear that any recognition of state authority to cleanse the public vocabulary would have been potentially limitless in its sweep. Thus, even where his clerks arguably effected a change in his position, their impact on the direction of the Court's rulings may have been negligible at best.

His clerks' memories of a Justice willing to listen to their arguments and give them due weight suggests an element of Harlan's makeup, however, which appears clearly to have contributed to his willingness to author the *Cohen* opinion, oppose broad federal censorship power, and embrace the Warren Court's privacy decisions. Harlan was not only open-minded and, as his son-in-law Wellington Newcomb put it, "undoubtedly the best listener I ever knew." The Justice and Ethel Harlan were cosmopolitan in taste and outlook. Ethel, especially, had a deep and enduring interest in art, music, and the theater. The couple's circle of friends included many from those backgrounds, among them the distinguished actor Raymond Massey, one of Harlan's Princeton contemporaries; the novelist Rumer Godden; and Cornelia Otis Skinner, who had been Ethel Harlan's childhood playmate in New Haven. Given their interests, neither the Justice nor his wife was probably comfortable with government-imposed censorship or intrusions upon personal privacy. It was thus hardly surprising that he would offer his services free to New York's board of higher education when a state judge, convinced that Bertrand Russell was bent on making "strumpets out of all our girls," barred the board's appointment of the renowned scholar to City College's faculty. Or that Harlan's failure to win a reversal of the judge's remarkable order on appeal would prompt a rare display of anger from this man for whom the charge that an adversary was "pontificating" was considered a harsh rebuke.[10]

The impatience with provincialism and intolerance that Harlan's stance in the Bertrand Russell affair reflected would persist throughout his life. "Although a patrician," one of his last clerks recalls, "he was not a snob at all and enjoyed all sorts of colorful people. I remember specifically his saying when the subject of homosexuality came up once . . . that he'd have no difficulty whatever having a clerk who was homosexual, which surely would not have been the case with certain of his 'liberal' colleagues. And I'm sure he had friends who were homosexual. . . . I remember thinking at the time that part of that no doubt reflected the Oxford upper-class experience, where it may have been more common and less stigmatized. He was very tolerant, quite cosmopolitan."[11] That attitude perhaps helps to explain his stance in the privacy cases and a number of First Amendment contexts as well.

Whatever the underlying keys to an understanding of his jurisprudence, however, Harlan's judicial record, the care with which he had developed it, and the grace he had invariably displayed in an era in which he, like his grandfather before him, had often written in dissent, impressed jurisprudential friends and foes alike. When Warren Burger first informed Richard Nixon of Harlan's hospitalization, the president sent the Justice a handwritten note of encouragement and praise. Harlan's continued decline and retirement had prompted similar messages from Nixon and others. At the Justice's death, the president had written Mrs. Harlan that her husband had "brought to our highest Court a measure of integrity, wisdom, compassion and sober good judgment that added luster to its record and provided a lasting source of strength to our society." In a statement to the press, Nixon called the Justice "one of the 20th century's . . . giants," while Chief Justice Burger praised his "careful, thoughtful opinions," Potter Stewart termed him "a human being of great worth," and journalists lamented the loss of a "lawyer's judge" and "judge's judge."[12]

An editor for the *Washington Post*, a frequent Harlan critic and one of the newspapers the Justice would have denied the right to publish the *Pentagon Papers*, suggested, however, that the Justice's own words furnished his best epitaph. When Justice Whittaker resigned from the Court a decade earlier, Justice Harlan had said of his colleague,

> Justice Whittaker was a prodigious worker who was satisfied with nothing less than full mastery of every record and brief. . . . While a man of intense convictions, he was always open minded, and in close cases one could never feel that he was beyond persuasion until the last word had been spoken or written on the issues. He had an innate sense of fairness but always strove against yielding up a sound legal conclusion to the compassionate circumstances of a particular case or to personal ideologies—temptations which make the art of judging the more exacting, and sometimes interrupt the even-handed application of the law.

To the editor, and many others as well, the Justice's description had been less accurate of Whittaker than of Harlan—the man whom Hugo Black's clerk John Frank had once characterized as an exemplar of "[d]isembodied, impersonal justice."[13]

Notes

Preface

1. Civil Rights Cases, 109 U.S. 3 (1883); *Plessy* v. *Ferguson*, 163 U.S. 537,560 (1896). For a contemporary examination of the first Justice Harlan's constitutional record, see Floyd B. Clark, *The Constitutional Doctrines of Justice Harlan* (Baltimore: The John Hopkins Press, 1915). For an excellent modern analysis of his thinking, see Henry J. Abraham, "John Marshall Harlan: A Justice Neglected," *Virginia Law Review* 41 (1955): 871.

2. *Hurtado* v. *California*, 110 U.S. 516, 538 (1884) (dissenting); *Patterson* v. *Colorado*, 205 U.S. 454, 465 (1907) (dissenting); *Lochner* v. *New York*, 198 U.S. 45, 65 (1905) (dissenting).

3. *Jones* v. Alfred H. Mayer Co., 392 U.S. 409, 449 (1968) (dissenting); *Bell* v. *Maryland*, 378 U.S. 226 (1964); *Duncan* v. *Louisiana*, 391 U.S. 145, 171 (1968); *New York Times Co.* v. *United States*, 403 U.S. 713, 752, 757 (1971).

4. *FTC* v. *Procter & Gamble Co.*, 386 U.S. 568 (1967); *United States* v. *Continental Can Co.*, 378 U.S. 441, 467 (1967) (dissenting); John M. Harlan to Hugo L. Black, April 11, 1963, Hugo L. Black Papers, Library of Congress, Box 372; *Ferguson* v. *Skrupa*, 372 U.S. 726 (1963); *Holden* v. *Hardy*, 169 U.S. 366 (1898).

5. *Reynolds* v. *Sims*, 377 U.S. 533, 589 (1964) (dissenting); *Harper* v. *Virginia Bd. of Elections*, 383 U.S. 663, 686 (1966) (dissenting); *Levy* v. *Louisiana*, 391 U.S. 68, 72 (1968) (dissenting); *Shapiro* v. *Thompson*, 394 U.S. 618, 655 (1969) (dissenting); *Perez* v. *Brownell*, 356 U.S. 44 (1958); *Afroyim* v. *Rusk*, 387 U.S. 253, 268 (1967) (dissenting).

6. *Griffin* v. *Illinois*, 351 U.S. 12, 29 (1956) (dissenting); *Mapp* v. *Ohio*, 367 U.S. 643, 672 (1961) (dissenting); *Miranda* v. *Arizona*, 384 U.S. 436, 504 (1966) (dissenting).

7. 175 U.S. 528, 545 (1899).

8. *NAACP* v. *Alabama*, 357 U.S. 449 (1958); *Poe* v. *Ullman*, 367 U.S. 497, 523 (1961) (dissenting); *Griswold* v. *Connecticut*, 381 U.S. 479, 499 (1965); *Roe* v. *Wade*, 401 U.S. 113 (1973); *Katz* v. *United States*, 389 U.S. 347, 360 (1967) (concurring); *Cohen* v. *California*, 403 U.S. 15 (1971); *Boddie* v. *Connecticut*, 401 U.S. 371 (1971).

9. Paul A. Freund, Foreword to *The Evolution of a Judicial Philosophy:*

Selected Opinions and Papers of Justice John M. Harlan, ed. David L. Shapiro (Cambridge, Mass.: Harvard University Press, 1969), pp. xiii–xiv. Professor Shapiro clerked for Harlan in the 1962 term.

10. Quoted in Lewis F. Powell, "Justice Harlan," *New York Law School Law Review* 31 (1986): 423–24.

11. *National Observer*, January 8, 1972.

12. Ibid.

13. Nathan Lewin, "Justice Harlan: 'The Full Measure of the Man,' " *American Bar Association Journal* 58 (June 1972): 580.

14. Charles Alan Wright, "Hugo L. Black: A Great Man and a Great American," *Texas Law Review* 50 (December 1971): 3–4.

15. The instructions, dated October 22, 1971, are on file in the John Marshall Harlan Papers, Seeley G. Mudd Manuscript Library, Princeton University, Box 547.

16. Lewin, "Justice Harlan," p. 580.

17. Edith Harlan Powell interview, May 12, 15, 1989, New York, New York.

18. *New York Times*, September 21, 1990.

Chapter 1. Buckner's "Boy Scout"

1. Except where otherwise indicated, this discussion is drawn from genealogical material, some of which presents conflicting accounts, in the Harlan Papers, Box 537, and from Clark, *The Constitutional Doctrines of Justice Harlan*, pp. 9–15.

2. Edith Harlan Powell interview.

3. Remarks of William Bradley, at memorial proceedings in the Supreme Court, December 16, 1911, quoted in Clark, *The Constitutional Doctrines of Justice Harlan*, p. 12. The case was *Taylor* v. *Beckham*, 178 U.S. 548 (1900). Characteristically, Harlan dissented, ibid., p. 585.

4. Edith Harlan Powell interview.

5. Harold L. Ickes, *The Autobiography of a Curmudgeon* (New York: Reynal & Hitchcock, 1943), p. 83.

6. Carter H. Harrison, *Stormy Years: The Autobiography of Carter H. Harrison* (New York: Bobbs-Merrill Co., 1935), p. 113.

7. Ickes, *The Autobiography of a Curmudgeon*, pp. 84–85.

8. Harrison, *Stormy Years*, p. 104.

9. Roger A. Derby, Jr., interview, May 17, 1989, New York, New York.

10. Ickes, *The Autobiography of a Curmudgeon*, p. 88.

11. Julius Barnard to John Marshall Harlan, November 10, 1954, Harlan Papers, Box 676.

12. Ickes, *The Autobiography of a Curmudgeon*, p. 87.

13. Ickes, *The Autobiography of a Curmudgeon*, pp. 84–88.

14. Barney Balaban to John Marshall Harlan, November 17, 1954, Harlan Papers, Box 676.

15. Ickes, *The Autobiography of a Curmudgeon*, pp. 88–89; Harrison, *Stormy Years*, pp. 104, 119; *Chicago Record*, April 6, 1897.

16. Ickes, *The Autobiography of a Curmudgeon*, pp. 96–107.

17. "Memorial of John Maynard Harlan," Harlan Papers, Box 547, written by Justice Harlan; *New York Post*, November 14, 1954; *New York Times*, March 24, 1934, May 24, 1924. For an example of his interest in international politics, see John Maynard Harlan to Nicholas Murray Butler, October 22, 1931, Harlan Papers, Box 547.

18. Edith Harlan Powell interview.

19. Ickes, *The Autobiography of a Curmudgeon*, p. 96.

20. Ibid., p. 112.

21. *New York Times*, March 24, 1934; Edith Harlan Powell interview.

22. Janet Harlan White interview, May 24, 1989, Reno, Nevada; Edith Harlan Powell interview.

23. Janet Harlan White interview; Malvina Shanklin Harlan, *Some Memories of a Long Life* (1915), an unpublished manuscript on file in the Library of Congress papers of the first Justice Harlan.

24. Paul M. Bator interview with Elizabeth Harlan Derby, undated, New York, New York, in the possession of Mrs. Paul M. Bator, Chicago, Illinois. I am grateful to Justice Harlan's daughter, Eve Harlan Dillingham, for a copy of her father's letter to his father.

25. J.S.H. Guest to R. M. Scoon, June 5, 1920, Harlan Papers, Box 481; Paul M. Bator interview with Elizabeth Harlan Derby.

26. Edith Harlan Powell interview; Paul M. Bator interview with David H. McAlpin, June 20, 1978, New York, New York, in the possession of Mrs. Paul M. Bator, Chicago, Illinois.

27. *Daily Princetonian*, January 13, 1920.

28. John Marshall Harlan interview, excerpted from Columbia University Oral History Project, Harlan Papers, Box 597.

29. J.S.H. Guest to R. M. Scoon, June 5, 1920, Harlan Papers, Box 481.

30. Edith Harlan Powell interview; Paul M. Bator interview with David H. McAlpin.

31. Ibid.

32. On Buckner's early life and career, see generally Martin Mayer, *Emory Buckner* (New York: Harper & Row, 1968); John Amber, "I *Shall* Keep My Oath," *Success*, July 1925, pp. 66–67, 116–17.

33. Amber, "I *Shall* Keep My Oath," pp. 116–17.

34. Mayer, *Emory Buckner*, p. ix. This statement is taken from Justice Harlan's introduction.

35. John Marshall Harlan to David H. McAlpin, June 19, 1964, Harlan Papers, Box 552.

36. Mayer, *Emory Buckner*; Paul M. Bator interview with Leo Gottlieb, May 14, 1980, New York, New York, in the possession of Mrs. Paul M. Bator, Chicago, Illinois.

37. Ibid., p. 144; John E. F. Wood, "John M. Harlan, As Seen by a Colleague in the Practice of Law," *Harvard Law Review* 85 (December 1971): 377.

38. Mayer, *Emory Buckner*, p. 143.

39. Remarks of Herbert Brownell, Memorial Proceedings in the Supreme Court, October 24, 1972, p. 10, William O. Douglas Papers, Library of Congress, Box 336. A portion of the proceedings appears in 409 U.S. v (1972).

40. Harlan to McAlpin.

41. Remarks of Herbert Brownell, pp. 110–11.

42. Emory R. Buckner to Felix Frankfurter, January 25, 1925, quoted in Mayer, *Emory Buckner*, p. 143.

43. *New York Times*, April 3, 1927.

44. Amber, "I *Shall* Keep My Oath," p. 66; Mayer, *Emory Buckner*, pp. 184–85; J. Edward Lumbard interview, May 17, 1989, New York, New York.

45. Edith Harlan Powell interview; *Scraps* (Special Edition), April 9, 1965, Harlan Papers, Box 487.

46. Ibid.
47. *New York Times*, March 6, 1925.
48. Ibid.; *New York Times*, March 7, March 15, 1925, April 3, 1927.
49. Ibid.
50. Ibid.
51. William G. Shepherd, "Flat-Wheeled Justice," *Collier's*, November 14, 1925, p. 8. The Buckner-Harlan memorandum is reprinted in *New York Times*, April 26, 1926.
52. 232 U.S. 383 (1914).
53. *New York Times*, June 18, 1926.
54. Ibid.
55. *New York Times*, November 14, 1925.
56. *New York Times*, October 9, 1925.
57. Ibid.
58. Emory R. Buckner to Felix Frankfurter, October 20, 1925, Felix Frankfurter Papers, Library of Congress, Box 31.
59. *New York Times*, November 17, 1925.
60. Ibid.; *New York Times*, April 12, April 15, 1926.
61. *New York Times*, November 18, 1925, April 12, 1926.
62. The letter was reprinted in *New York Times*, November 17, 1925.
63. Emory R. Buckner to W. B. Wheeler, October 7, 1925, Frankfurter Papers, Box 31.
64. Ibid.; *New York Times*, April 14, 1926.
65. *New York Times*, October 3, 1925, April 3, 1927.
66. *New York Times*, April 3, 1927.
67. *New York Times*, February 25, 1925.
68. Ibid.
69. *New York Times*, February 25, 1925, May 22, 1926.
70. *New York Times*, March 7, 1925.
71. *New York Times*, February 27, March 2, April 2, 1926.
72. Lewin, "Justice Harlan," p. 581; *New York Times*, May 21, May 22, 1926.
73. Ibid.
74. John Marshall Harlan to James H. Douglas, May 27, 1926, Harlan Papers, Box 600; *New York Times*, May 27, 1926.
75. Harlan to Douglas, ibid.
76. Ibid.; James H. Douglas to John Marshall Harlan, Harlan Papers, Box 600.
77. *New York Times*, May 26, 1926.
78. Ibid.
79. *New York Times*, May 27, 1926.
80. Ibid.
81. *New York Times*, May 26, May 28, June 4, 1926; Harlan to Douglas; Lewin, "Justice Harlan," p. 581.
82. *New York Times*, October 2, May 28, June 13, 1926.
83. J. Edward Lumbard, "John Harlan: In Public Service, 1925–1971," *Harvard Law Review* 85 (December 1971): 373.
84. Mayer, *Emory Buckner*, pp. 3, 264; *New York Times*, May 18, 1926.
85. *New York Times*, December 18, 1926, February 26, 1927.
86. *New York Times*, February 26, 1927. For examples of editorial praise of Buckner's handling of the case, see "Miller Guilty; Daugherty Free," *Literary Digest*, March 19, 1927, p. 11.

87. Ibid.

88. Mayer, *Emory Buckner*, pp. 252–53; *New York Times*, January 21, 1928; J. Edward Lumbard to author, December 12, 1989.

89. Mayer, *Emory Buckner*, p. 252; *New York Times*, April 6, 1928.

90. New York Sun, December 27, 1927; J. Edward Lumbard Interview; *New York Times*, April 1, 1928.

91. Mayer, *Emory Buckner*, p. 252; *New York Times*, May 20, 1928.

92. Lumbard, "John Harlan," p. 373; Lewin, "Justice Harlan," p. 58; J. Edward Lumbard interview.

93. This account is drawn from Mayer, *Emory Buckner*, p. 239, and from J. Edward Lumbard's somewhat more colorful description, which Harlan had related to him. J. Edward Lumbard interview.

94. Lumbard, "John Harlan," p. 372; Wood, "John M. Harlan," p. 378. John E. F. Wood joined Root, Clark in 1929 and later became a senior partner. Several years after his appointment to the Supreme Court, it might be noted, Justice Harlan gave an address to the University of Michigan law convocation on the subject, *Planning a Career at the Bar* (St. Paul, Minn.: West Publishing Co., 1960).

Chapter 2. Lawyer's Lawyer

1. Edith Harlan Powell to author, May 4, 1989.

2. Eve Harlan Dillingham interview, May 27, 1989, Redding, Connecticut.

3. Ibid.

4. Ibid. I am grateful to Eve Harlan Dillingham for a copy of her father's letter to his mother. An account of the wedding is contained in *The Bull*, November 17, 1928.

5. Edith Harlan Powell interview; Janet Harlan White interview; Paul M. Bator interview with Edith Harlan Powell, February 26, 1976, New York, New York, in the possession of Mrs. Paul M. Bator, Chicago, Illinois.

6. Ibid.; Roger A. Derby interview; Paul M. Bator interview with Elizabeth Harlan Derby.

7. Edith Harlan Powell interview; Roger A. Derby interview; *New York Times*, January 11, 1924. For an example of Richard Harlan's letter-writing, see *New York Times*, April 2, 1922.

8. *New York Times*, January 11, 1924; Roger A. Derby interview. Except as otherwise indicated, the following discussion is drawn from legal papers filed in a variety of lawsuits arising out of Richard Harlan's management of his wife's trust and from Margaret Harlan's testimony in one such suit. These papers and related materials were initially in Justice Harlan's possession but are now in the custody of the Justice's nephew, Roger A. Derby, the son of his sister Elizabeth, Warrenton, Virginia. Hereinafter these materials are cited as the Harlan Family Papers.

9. Adelaide Prouty Chrystie to Richard Harlan, January 28, 1911, Harlan Family Papers.

10. John Maynard Harlan to James S. Harlan, December 7, 1919, Harlan Family Papers.

11. The memoranda, dated January 4, 1919, December 31, 1919, and May 1920, are in the Harlan Family Papers.

12. Ibid.; *Harlan* v. *Harlan*, 281 Fed. 603 (1922), 163 U.S. 681 (1923).

13. *New York Times*, January 11, 1924.

14. Ibid.

15. Richard D. Harlan to John Maynard Harlan, undated, Harlan Family Papers.

16. John M. Harlan to Elizabeth Harlan Derby, undated, Harlan Family Papers; Robert Shanklin to John Marshall Harlan, May 14, 1931, Harlan Family Papers; Eve Harlan Dillingham interview.

17. Roger A. Derby interview; Edith Harlan Powell interview; John Maynard Harlan to John Marshall Harlan (the elder), April 27, 1907, Harlan Family Papers; Paul M. Bator interview with Edith Harlan Powell. Copies of John Harlan's telegrams and letters to his father are in the Harlan Papers, Box 547.

18. Elihu Root, Jr., to John M. Harlan, December 31, 1930, Harlan Papers, Box 590. The formal offer is on file in the same box.

19. Mervin Rosenman, *Forgery, Perjury, and an Enormous Fortune* (New York: Beach Hampton Press, 1984), pp. 1, 2, 17–26; *New York Times*, March 15, 1931. The Rosenman book is a brief but fascinating account of the Wendel case. For another entertaining account, see Cloyd Laporte, "John M. Harlan Saves the Ella Wendel Estate," *American Bar Association Journal* 59 (1973): 868. Laporte was a member of Harlan's law firm.

20. Rosenman, *Forgery, Perjury*, pp. 8–16; *New York Times*, September 29, 1931.

21. Ibid.

22. Ibid.

23. Ibid.

24. The provisions of Ella Wendel's will are itemized in ibid., ch. 4. See also *New York Times*, March 24, 1931.

25. Rosenman, *Forgery, Perjury*, ch. 4.

26. Ibid.; *New York Times*, March 15, 1931.

27. *New York Times*, March 24, March 28, 1931; Rosenman, *Forgery, Perjury*, pp. ii, 46.

28. Rosenman, *Forgery, Perjury*, p. 37. Friendly's remarks appear on the jacket to the Rosenman book.

29. *New York Times*, September 29, 1931.

30. Henry J. Friendly, "Mr. Justice Harlan, As Seen by a Friend and Judge of an Inferior Court," *Harvard Law Review* 85 (December 1981): 382; *Stansbury* v. *Koss*, 10 F. Supp. 477 (S.D.N.Y., 1931).

31. Friendly, "Mr. Justice Harlan," p. 382; Rosenman, *Forgery, Perjury*, p. 63.

32. These claims and many others are summarized in Rosenman, *Forgery, Perjury*, pp. 1–6.

33. *New York Times*, July 27, 1932. The Rosenman book examines Morris's claim in chs. 11, 15–19.

34. The letter and will are reprinted in *New York Times*, July 27, 1932.

35. Ibid.

36. Ibid.; *New York Times*, July 28, 1932; Arthur Garfield Hays, *City Lawyer: The Autobiography of a Law Practice* (New York: Simon and Schuster, 1942), pp. 322–25.

37. Hays, *City Lawyer*, p. 325; Friendly, "Mr. Justice Harlan," p. 383, n. 6; Lewin, "Justice Harlan," p. 581; Paul M. Bator interview with John E. F. Wood, December 17, 1979, and January 28, 1980, New York, New York, in the possession of Mrs. Paul M. Bator, Chicago, Illinois.

38. Hays, *City Lawyer*; Rosenman, *Forgery, Perjury*, p. 215.

39. Friendly, "Mr. Justice Harlan," p. 383; *New York Times*, July 28, 1932.

40. *New York Times*, November 18, 1932.
41. Rosenman, *Forgery, Perjury*, p. 151.
42. Hays, *City Lawyer*, pp. 329–30.
43. Ibid., p. 331.
44. Ibid.; Rosenman, *Forgery, Perjury*, p. 175.
45. Friendly, "Mr. Justice Harlan," p. 384.
46. Unknown to Emory R. Buckner, June 12, 1934, Harlan Papers, Box 488.
47. Lumbard, "John Harlan," p. 372; J. Edward Lumbard interview.
48. Ibid.; Eve Harlan Dillingham interview; John M. Harlan to Eustace Seligman, December 3, 1941, Harlan Papers, Box 596.
49. Mayer, *Emory Buckner*, p. 264; *The Bull*, July 16, 1932.
50. 43 N.E. 2d 43 (1942).
51. "Bertrand Russell Rides Out Collegiate Cyclone," *Life*, April 1, 1940, p. 24. For an excellent collection of essays and documents on the controversy Russell's appointment aroused, see *The Bertrand Russell Case*, eds. John Dewey and Horace M. Kallen (New York: Viking Press, 1941). Bertrand Russell, *Education and the Modern World* (New York: W. W. Norton, 1932), presents some of the philosopher's controversial views.
52. "Bishop v. Earl," *Time*, March 11, 1940, p. 54; *Kay* v. *Board of Higher Education*, 18 N.Y.S.2d 821 (1940); Barry Feinberg and Ronald Kasrils, *Bertrand Russell's America, 1896–1945* (New York: Viking Press, 1975), p. 156.
53. *New York Times*, March 28, 1940; Feinberg and Kasrils, *Bertrand Russell's America*, pp. 157–63.
54. Feinberg and Kasrils, *Bertrand Russell's America*, p. 158; Elmer Davis and Osmond K. Fraenkel, "Implications of the Russell Case," *Saturday Review of Literature*, April 13, 1940, pp. 8, 18; Horace M. Kallen, "Behind the Bertrand Russell Case," in *The Bertrand Russell Case*, pp. 23–24; Bertrand Russell, *The Autobiography of Bertrand Russell: 1914–1944* (Boston: Little, Brown, 1951), p. 335.
55. Kallen, "Behind the Bertrand Russell Case," p. 23–24.
56. Louis Lusky interview, June 19, 1989, New York, New York; Lauson Stone interview, July 14, 1990, New York, New York.
57. Ibid.
58. For rulings in the case subsequent to McGeehan's initial decision, see *Kay* v. *Board of Higher Education*, 20 N.Y.S. 2d 898, 23 N.Y.S. 2d 479, 20 N.Y.S. 2d 1016, 21 N.Y.S. 2d 396, 29 N.E. 2d 657 (1940).
59. *Judson* v. *City of Niagara Falls*, 140 App. Div. 62 (4th Dept., 1910), affirmed without opinion, 204 N.Y. 630 (1912); *Matter of Flischmann* v. *Graves*, 235 N.Y. 84 (1923).
60. E.g., *Gunnison* v. *Board of Education*, 176 N.Y. 11 (1903).
61. Brief of Respondent-Appellant and Intervenors-Respondents-Appellants, *Kay* v. *Board of Higher Education*, pp. 41–42.
62. Ibid., pp. 47–48.
63. Ibid., pp. 57–58, 63–64.
64. Ibid., p. 70.
65. Ibid., p. 88.
66. Louis Lusky interview; Louisville *Courier-Journal*, November 10, 1954.
67. This discussion is drawn largely from W. Barton Leach, "Meeting Ground of Law and Science in War: Operations Analysis in the USAAF, 1942–1945," *Lex et Scientia* 2 (July–September 1965): 163.

68. Ibid., p. 165.

69. Ibid., p. 166; Arthur Garfield Hays to John M. Harlan, October 20, 1942, Harlan Papers, Box 480. The secretary's note appears on a card Hays had enclosed with his letter.

70. Leach, "Meeting Ground of Law and Science," pp. 167–70. This discussion is also based upon a two-volume, handwritten diary which Harlan maintained during his tour of duty. I am grateful to his daughter for the opportunity to examine the diary.

71. Ibid.

72. Ibid.; Edith Harlan Powell interview; diary entries for July 22–25, 1944.

73. I am grateful to Eve Harlan Dillingham for the opportunity to examine a copy of the memorandum, which is dated May 1, 1944, and entitled, *Memorandum Concerning the Creation of the Air Ministry and the Royal Air Force as a Separate Branch of the British Military Services.*

74. Diary entries for March 18, 1944, May 11, 1943, August 6, 1944, August 20, 1944, November 10, 1944. Leach, "Meeting Ground of Law and Science," p. 169.

75. Diary entries for August 4, August 9, August 10, 1944.

76. Diary entries for August 7–8, 1944.

77. Biographical material in Harlan Papers, Box 563; Edith Harlan Powell interview; diary entries for November 27, 1944, December 10, 1944.

78. Eve Harlan Dillingham interview.

79. Ibid.

80. Ibid.; John Marshall Harlan to John D. Mailer, July 16, 1947, Harlan Papers, Box 479. Harlan resigned his membership in 1950, Edgar G. Crossman to John Marshall Harlan, June 2, 1950, Harlan Papers, Box 479.

81. Eve Harlan Dillingham interview.

82. Wood, "John M. Harlan," pp. 379–80; biographical materials, Harlan Papers, Box 483.

83. *DeBeers Consolidated Mines, Ltd.* v. *United States*, 325 U.S. 212 (1945); "John Marshall Harlan," *New York Law Forum* 1 (March 1955): 5–6.

84. *Cohen* v. *Beneficial Industrial Loan Corp.*, 337 U.S. 541 (1949).

85. *United States* v. *Imperial Chemical Industries*, 100 F. Supp. 504 (S.D.N.Y., 1951); 105 F. Supp. 215 (S.D.N.Y., 1952).

86. Unless otherwise indicated, this discussion is drawn from the opinions in *United States* v. *E.I. Du Pont de Nemours and Co.*, 126 F. Supp. 235 (N.D. Ill., 1954), 353 U.S. 586 (1957), and Charles Stewart interview, February 1, 1990, New York, New York. Stewart, who is now a federal district judge, was a close Harlan friend and professional associate.

87. *New York Times*, February 16, 1953.

88. Quoted in Lewin, "Justice Harlan," p. 582.

89. Eve Harlan Dillingham interview. I am grateful to Judge Stewart for a copy of Hotchkiss's statement.

90. *New York Times*, December 12, 1953.

91. *New York Times*, February 19, 1953.

92. A transcript of the final argument in the case is on file in the Harlan Papers, Box 516. Transcripts of other arguments are in Box 528.

93. *United States* v. *E.I. Du Pont de Nemours and Co.*, 126 F. Supp. 235, 242–43 (N.D. Ill., 1954). See also 126 F. Supp. 27 (N.D. Ill., 1954).

94. Jane Du Pont and Ada B. Sharp telegram to John M. Harlan, December 3,

1954, Harlan Papers, Box 516; George E. Thompson to John M. Harlan, November 24, 1952, Harlan Papers, Box 528.

95. Eve Harlan Dillingham interview; John M. Harlan to Irénée Du Pont, January 7, 1954, Harlan Papers, Box 528.

Chapter 3. The Appointments

1. U.S., Congress, Senate, Committee on the Judiciary, *Nomination of John Marshall Harlan, of New York, to be Associate Justice of the Supreme Court of the United States*, 84th Cong., 1st Sess., 1955, p. 166.

2. For an excellent general survey of the political backgrounds of Supreme Court justices, see Henry J. Abraham, *Justices and Presidents: A Political History of Appointments to the Supreme Court*, 2d ed. (New York: Oxford University Press, 1985).

3. Richard R. Heppner to John M. Harlan, January 18, 1939, Harlan Papers, Box 596. For a newspaper account of the Marcus controversy, see *New York Post*, January 18, 1939. For material on the organization and Harlan's involvement in it, see Albert E. Rorabeck to John M. Harlan, June 1, 1937, and other items in the Harlan Papers, Box 596.

4. For material relating to Harlan's involvement in the Bryan, Lumbard, Dewey, and Court of Appeals campaigns, see Harlan Papers, Boxes 487, 564, 512, and 487, respectively; *New York Times*, July 31, 1941.

5. For material relating to Harlan's bar and legal aid activities, see Harlan Papers, Boxes 567–70.

6. Whitney North Seymour to John M. Harlan, June 9, 1941, Harlan Papers, Box 481; John M. Harlan to Whitney North Seymour, June 13, 1941, Harlan Papers, Box 481.

7. Whitney North Seymour to John M. Harlan, August 26, 1942, Harlan Papers, Box 572.

8. Herbert Brownell interview, January 18, 1990, New York, New York. For material on Harlan's long association with Dewey and Brownell, see Harlan Papers, Boxes 487, 512.

9. A copy of the commission's charge is reprinted in *New York Times*, March 30, 1951.

10. Ibid.

11. *Nomination of John Marshall Harlan*, p. 159; *New York Times*, April 1, 1951.

12. *Nomination of John Marshall Harlan*, p. 37; Eve Harlan Dillingham interview.

13. Harry Weyher interview, July 17, 1990, New York, New York; Peter Magargee Brown interview, February 20, 1990, New York, New York.

14. Ibid.

15. Peter Brown interview.

16. Harry Weyher interview; Eve Harlan Dillingham interview; *Reports of the New York State Crime Commission*, January 23, 1953. I am grateful to Judge Robert Patterson, who served on the commission staff after Harlan's tenure as chief counsel, for a copy of the reports.

17. This discussion is drawn from the remarks of Harlan, Judge Proskauer, and Methfessel, as well as excerpts from the transcripts of the commission hearing and of disciplinary proceedings against Methfessel, in *Nomination of John*

Marshall Harlan, pp. 4–40, 55–61, 148–54, 159–64; and from *New York Times*, May 30, 1952.

18. Peter Brown interview.
19. Harry Weyher interview.
20. Ibid.; Peter Brown interview.
21. Peter Brown interview.
22. "Keith" to John M. Harlan, October 1, 1948, Harlan Papers, Box 512.
23. R. Keith Kane to John M. Harlan, September 16, 1952, Harlan Papers, Box 597.
24. J. Edward Lumbard interview.
25. *New York Times*, September 30, 1953, January 14, 1954; Theodore R. Kupferman to John M. Harlan, October 2, 1953, Harlan Papers, Box 482; John M. Harlan to Theodore R. Kupferman, October 6, 1953, Harlan Papers, Box 482.
26. Memorial Proceedings, p. 12.
27. "Arthur" to John M. Harlan, July 13, 1953, Harlan Papers, Box 482; Paul M. Bator interview with William Palmer, January 28, 1980, New York, New York, in the possession of Mrs. Paul M. Bator, Chicago, Illinois.
28. Undated, illegibly signed, handwritten letter to John M. Harlan, Harlan Papers, Box 482.
29. Henry H. Shepard to John M. Harlan, November 24, 1953, Harlan Papers, Box 482; John M. Harlan to Henry H. Shepard, November 25, 1953, Harlan Papers, Box 482.
30. John M. Harlan to Herbert Brownell, December 23, 1953, Harlan Papers, Box 482; *New York Times*, January 14, 15, 1954.
31. Edward J. Fox to William Langer, January 20, 1954, Harlan Papers, Box 482; John G. Buchanan to William Langer, January 21, 1954, Harlan Papers, Box 482; John M. Harlan to Herbert Brownell, January 28, 1954, Harlan Papers, Box 482; Axel B. Gravem to John M. Harlan, January 29, 1954, Harlan Papers, Box 482; William Langer to John M. Harlan, Harlan Papers, Box 482; *New York Times*, February 10, 1954.
32. See, for example, *Niles-Bement-Pond Co.* v. *Fitzpatrick*, 213 F. 2d 305 (1954); *Lupia's Estate* v. *Marcelle*, 214 F. 942 (1954); *Lewyt Corp.* v. *Commissioner of Internal Revenue*, 215 F. 2d 518 (1954).
33. *Constance* v. *Harvey*, 215 F. 2d 571 (1954).
34. *United States* v. *Wiesner*, 216 F. 2d 739 (1954).
35. *Newton* v. *Pedrick*, 212 F. 2d 357 (1954).
36. *Austrian* v. *Williams*, 216 F. 2d 278 (1954).
37. *United States* v. *H. Wool and Sons, Inc.*, 215 F. 2d 95 (1954).
38. *United States* v. *Chiarella*, 214 F. 2d 838 (1954).
39. *Airline Pilots Ass'n* v. *CAB*, 215 F. 2d 122 (1954).
40. *Hyam* v. *American Export Lines*, 213 F. 2d 221 (1954).
41. *United States* v. *Flynn*, 216 F. 2d 354 (1954); *Dennis* v. *United States*, 183 F. 2d 201 (1950), 341 U.S. 494 (1951).
42. *Schenck* v. *United States*, 249 U.S. 47 (1919); *Bridges* v. *California*, 314 U.S. 252 (1941); *Dennis* v. *United States*, 183 F. 2d 201, 212 (1950), 341 U.S. 494, 510 (1951).
43. 341 U.S. at 581.
44. *Flynn* v. *United States*, 216 F. 2d at 366–67. The trial judge, Edward J. Dimock, is quoted in 216 F. 2d at 367, n. 9.

45. 216 F. 2d at 360.

46. Ibid., p. 365.

47. Ibid., p. 373.

48. Ibid., pp. 374, 376.

49. Quoted in Eugene Gressman, "The New Justice Harlan," *New Republic*, April 4, 1955, p. 9.

50. Ibid.

51. *New York Times*, June 16, 1954.

52. *New York Times*, November 9, 1954; Herbert Brownell interview.

53. William O. Douglas, *Go East, Young Man—The Early Years: The Autobiography of William O. Douglas* (New York: Random House, 1974), pp. 329–30; Learned Hand to Dwight D. Eisenhower, October 22, 1954, Harlan Papers, Box 482.

54. Wellington Newcomb interview, June 29, July 9, 1990, New York, New York.

55. *New York Times*, November 9, 10, 14, December 10, 1954.

56. "The Supreme Court: A Real Pro," *Time*, November 22, 1954, p. 18; "Family Job," *New Yorker*, December 4, 1954, pp. 40–41.

57. Milton I. Hauser to John Harlan Amen, November 19, 1954, Harlan Papers, Box 482; John Harlan Amen to John M. Harlan, November 22, 1954, Harlan Papers, Box 482; Adlai E. Stevenson to John M. Harlan, November 11, 1954, Harlan Papers, Box 677; Pierre S. Du Pont, III, to John M. Harlan, November 22, 1954, Harlan Papers, Box 676; Harrison Parker to John M. Harlan, November 9, 1954, Harlan Papers, Box 677; "Lloyd" to John M. Harlan, November 10, 1954, Harlan Papers, Box 677; Louis Lusky to John M. Harlan, March 18, 1955, Harlan Papers, Box 677; Gene Tunney to John M. Harlan, November 26, 1954, Harlan Papers, Box 677; David Lindsay Keir to John M. Harlan, November 11, 1954, Harlan Papers, Box 677; Harold G. Brown, Jr., to John M. Harlan, November 23, 1954, Harlan Papers, Box 676; C. J. LaRouche to John M. Harlan, November 19, 1954, Harlan Papers, Box 677; Richard Joyce Smith to John M. Harlan, November 8, 1954, Harlan Papers, Box 677.

58. Harold Burton to John M. Harlan, November 12, 1954, Harlan Papers, Box 490; Earl Warren to John M. Harlan, December 14, 1954, Harlan Papers, Box 605; John M. Harlan to Barrett Prettyman, Jr., November 10, 1954, December 13, 1954, January 3, 1955, Barrett Prettyman, Jr., Papers, School of Law, University of Virginia, Box 2.

59. Dwight D. Eisenhower to John M. Harlan, November 15, 1954, Harlan Papers, Box 482; Harold Burton to John M. Harlan, November 12, 1954, Harlan Papers, Box 490; Tom C. Clark to John M. Harlan, November 15, 1954, Harlan Papers, Box 493.

60. *New York Times*, November 12, 1954.

61. William P. Rogers interview, January 19, 1990, New York, New York.

62. Ibid.; Abraham, *Justices and Presidents*, pp. 254–55; *New York Times*, November 20, December 3, 1954.

63. William P. Rogers interview; *New York Times*, November 20, 1954.

64. *New York Times*, November 23, 1954.

65. The *Tribune* observation was quoted in Irving Dilliard, "Warren and the New Supreme Court," *Harper's Magazine*, December, 1955, p. 60. The Lindley piece is on file in the Harlan Papers, Box 482.

66. *New York Times*, November 9, 1954.

67. Owen J. Roberts to John M. Harlan, March 29, 1952, Harlan Papers, Box 482; John M. Harlan to Owen J. Roberts, March 31, 1952, Harlan Papers, Box 482; Justin Blackwelder to John M. Harlan, January 6, 1955, Harlan Papers, Box 482; Justin Blackwelder to John M. Harlan, January 7, 1955, Harlan Papers, Box 482.

68. The statements are quoted in *Nominations of John Marshall Harlan*, pp. 113, 137.

69. Except as otherwise indicated, this discussion is drawn from *Rice* v. *Sioux City Memorial Park Cemetery*, 60 N.W. 2d 110 (Ohio Sup. Ct.), 348 U.S. 880 (1954), 349 U.S. 70 (1955).

70. *Shelley* v. *Kraemer*, 334 U.S. 1 (1948); *Barrows* v. *Jackson*, 346 U.S. 249 (1953).

71. 349 U.S. at 76.

72. See, for example, *New York Times*, November 20, 1954.

73. *Sunday Pioneer Press* (St. Paul, Minn.), February 13, 1955.

74. A copy of the letter, dated February 18, 1955, is on file in the Harlan Papers, Box 482; Wellington Newcomb interview.

75. Axel B. Gravem to Dwight D. Eisenhower, November 9, 1954, Harlan Papers, Box 482; Axel B. Gravem to William Langer, November 9, 1954, Harlan Papers, Box 482; Axel B. Gravem to Joseph C. O'Mahoney, February 14, 1955, Harlan Papers, Box 482; Axel B. Gravem to Harley M. Kilgore, February 14, 1955, Harlan Papers, Box 482.

76. David J. Winton to Hubert H. Humphrey, November 30, 1954, Harlan Papers, Box 482; Hubert H. Humphrey to David J. Winton, December 16, 1954, Harlan Papers, Box 482; Hubert H. Humphrey to David J. Winton, February 2, 1955, Harlan Papers, Box 482. Winton also contacted Minnesota Senator Edward J. Thye, who was also Winton's friend. David J. Winton to Edward J. Thye, November 30, 1954, Harlan Papers, Box 482; Edward J. Thye to David J. Winton, December 3, 1954, Harlan Papers, Box 482. V. Henry Rothschild to Herbert H. Lehman, November 22, 1954, Harlan Papers, Box 482.

77. Herbert H. Lehman to V. Henry Rothschild, November 27, 1954, Harlan Papers, Box 482; H. Alexander Smith to John M. Harlan, February 10, 1955, Harlan Papers, Box 482; John M. Harlan to H. Alexander Smith, February 17, 1955, Harlan Papers, Box 482.

78. Edward J. Fox to William Langer, November 16, 1954, Harlan Papers, Box 482.

79. Edward J. Fox to Harley M. Kilgore, February 2, 1955, Harlan Papers, Box 482; John G. Buchanan to Harley M. Kilgore, January 11, 1955, Harlan Papers, Box 482; John G. Buchanan to John M. Harlan, January 11, 1955, Harlan Papers, Box 482; John W. Davis to Harley M. Kilgore, February 8, 1955, Harlan Papers, Box 482.

80. *New York Times*, February 9, 12, 22, 1955.

81. Justin Blackwelder to John M. Harlan, January 6, 1955, Harlan Papers, Box 482; Simon E. Sobeloff to John M. Harlan, February 24, 1955, Harlan Papers, Box 482. For an excellent discussion of the role of the judiciary committee in the appointment process, see Abraham, *Justices and Presidents*, ch. 3, and Henry J. Abraham, *The Judicial Process*, 5th ed. (New York: Oxford University Press, 1986), pp. 78–88.

82. Earl Warren to John M. Harlan, December 14, 1954, Harlan Papers, Box 605; William O. Douglas to John M. Harlan, February 2, 1955, Harlan Papers,

Box 514; John M. Harlan to David J. Winton, February 7, 1955, Harlan Papers, Box 482.

83. H. Alexander Smith to John M. Harlan, February 10, 1955, Harlan Papers, Box 482.

84. *Nomination of John Marshall Harlan*, pp. 62, 54.

85. Ibid., pp. 70–71.

86. Ibid., pp. 2–3.

87. Ibid., pp. 78–79, 119, 125–26.

88. Ibid., pp. 99, 103; *New York Times*, February 26, 1955.

89. *Nomination of John Marshall Harlan*, pp. 4–6.

90. Ibid., pp. 34–36.

91. Ibid., pp. 55–60.

92. Ibid., pp. 60, 123.

93. Ibid., pp. 72, 123, 126.

94. Ibid., p. 103; Herbert Brownell interview.

95. *Nomination of John Marshall Harlan*, p. 23.

96. John M. Harlan to Justin Blackwelder, January 11, 1955, Harlan Papers, Box 482; *Nomination of John Marshall Harlan*, pp. 137–38, 142, 146, 171–72.

97. *Nomination of John Marshall Harlan*, pp. 138, 140, 141.

98. Ibid., pp. 140–41.

99. Ibid., pp. 147, 151, 161, 164; *New York Times*, February 26, 1955.

100. *Nomination of John Marshall Harlan*, pp. 164–65.

101. Unidentified note, December 7, 1954, Harlan Papers, Box 482; Porter R. Chandler to John M. Harlan, February 26, 1955, Harlan Papers, Box 482.

102. Except where otherwise indicated, this discussion is drawn from U.S. *Congressional Record* 101: 3011–36.

103. William P. Rogers to John M. Harlan, March 15, 1955, Harlan Papers, Box 482.

104. The Blackwelder memorandum, dated March 18, 1955, is on file in the Harlan Papers, Box 482.

105. John M. Harlan to Felix Frankfurter, March 5, 1955, Frankfurter Papers, Box 39; John M. Harlan to William T. Lifland, March 8, 1955, Harlan Papers, Box 482.

106. William T. Lifland to John M. Harlan, March 7, 1955, Harlan Papers, Box 482; William T. Lifland to John M. Harlan, March 11, 1955, Harlan Papers, Box 482.

107. Dwight D. Eisenhower to John M. Harlan, April 6, 1955, Harlan Papers, Box 482; Adlai E. Stevenson to John M. Harlan, March 23, 1955, Harlan Papers, Box 677.

Chapter 4. The Justice and Company

1. Eve Harlan Dillingham interview; Ethel Harlan to Marion Frankfurter, April 27, 1955, Frankfurter Papers, Box 39.

2. For a recent account of the Frankfurter-Black feud, see generally James F. Simon, *The Antagonists: Hugo Black, Felix Frankfurter and Civil Liberties in Modern America* (New York: Simon and Schuster, 1989).

3. Gerald T. Dunne, *Hugo Black and the Judicial Revolution* (New York: Simon and Schuster, 1977), p. 283; Robert H. Jackson to Hugo L. Black, September 10, 1937, Robert H. Jackson Papers, Library of Congress, Box 9; *Jewell Ridge*

Corp. v. *Local*, 325 U.S. 161, 176–78 (1945) (Jackson, J., dissenting); Hugo L. Black Memorandum to the Conference, May 5, 1945, Harlan Fiske Stone Papers, Library of Congress, Box 71; 325 U.S. at 897.

4. For one press account of the Black-Jackson dispute, see Doris Fleeson's column in the *Washington Star*, May 16, 1946. The text of Jackson's cablegram is reprinted in *New York Times*, June 11, 1946.

5. "John" to Hugo L. Black, June 11, 1946, Hugo L. Black Papers, Library of Congress, Box 61; "Gordon" to Robert H. Jackson, November 27, 1949, Jackson Papers, Box 26. The Jackson memoranda are on file in ibid.

6. Hugo L. Black to Felix Frankfurter, January 14, 1939, Frankfurter Papers, Box 25; Felix Frankfurter to Hugo L. Black, June 9, 1945, Stone Papers, Box 71; "Eddie" to Felix Frankfurter, April 12, 1945, Frankfurter Papers, Box 25.

7. Memorandum for the Conference, undated, Wiley B. Rutledge Papers, Library of Congress, Box 8; "F.F." to "Brethren," August 30, 1945, Rutledge Papers, Box 12; Dunne, *Hugo Black and the Judicial Revolution*, p. 231. I examined the Rutledge Papers in the Yale law library before they were organized and filed in the Library of Congress. The box reference is to the Yale collection.

8. John Marshall Harlan to John Maynard Harlan, April 27, 1929, Harlan Papers, Box 547.

9. Felix Frankfurter to Emory R. Buckner, February 8, 1925, Frankfurter Papers, Box 31.

10. Felix Frankfurter to John M. Harlan, January 26, 1944, Box 39. The inscribed reprints are in the Harlan Papers, Box 532.

11. John M. Harlan to Felix Frankfurter, November 11, 1954, Frankfurter Papers, Box 39; Felix Frankfurter to John M. Harlan, undated, Harlan Papers, Box 532.

12. H. N. Hirsch, *The Enigma of Felix Frankfurter* (New York: Basic Books, 1981), pp. 181–82; Charles Nesson, "Shaping Forces on Harlan's Legal Process," paper presented at New York Law School Centennial Conference in honor of Justice John Marshall Harlan, April 20, 1991, New York, New York (the proceedings of which are to appear in a forthcoming issue of the *New York Law School Law Review*); Felix Frankfurter to John M. Harlan, undated, Harlan Papers, Box 532; John M. Harlan to Felix Frankfurter, February 16, 1956, Frankfurter Papers, Box 39.

13. John M. Harlan to Felix Frankfurter, March 13 [no year indicated], Frankfurter Papers, Box 39.

14. Felix Frankfurter to John M. Harlan, July 6, 1956, Harlan Papers, Box 485.

15. Ibid.; *Cumming* v. *Bd. of Education*, 175 U.S. 528 (1899).

16. John M. Harlan to Felix Frankfurter, July 12, 1956, Frankfurter Papers, Box 39.

17. Felix Frankfurter to John M. Harlan, July 18, 1956, Harlan Papers, Box 485.

18. Ibid.

19. Felix Frankfurter to John M. Harlan, July 31, 1956, Harlan Papers, Box 485.

20. *Bridges* v. *California*, *Times-Mirror Co.* v. *Superior Court*, 314 U.S. 252 (1941); Felix Frankfurter to John M. Harlan, May 19, 1961, Frankfurter Papers, Box 66.

21. *Betts* v. *Brady*, 316 U.S. 455 (1942). The Harlan draft (for *Cicenia* v. *LaGay*) containing Frankfurter's notation is on file in the Harlan Papers, Box 533.

22. *NAACP* v. *Alabama*, 357 U.S. 449 (1958); Harlan opinion draft, Harlan Papers, Box 533; *Roth* v. *United States, Alberts* v. *California*, 354 U.S. 476, 496 (1957); Felix Frankfurter to John M. Harlan, April 23, 1958, Harlan Papers, Box 46.

23. Felix Frankfurter to John M. Harlan, April 24, 1958, Harlan Papers, Box 46.

24. John M. Harlan to Felix Frankfurter, April 24, 1958, Harlan Papers, Box 46; Felix Frankfurter to John M. Harlan, undated handwritten note, Harlan Papers, Box 46.

25. Hugo L. Black to John M. Harlan, May 2, 1958, Harlan Papers, Box 46.

26. William O. Douglas to John M. Harlan, April 22, 1958, Harlan Papers, Box 46.

27. Ibid.

28. *NAACP* v. *Alabama*, 357 U.S. at 461.

29. *Staub* v. *Baxley*, 355 U.S. 313 (1958); Felix Frankfurter to John M. Harlan, December 9, 1957, Harlan Papers, Box 610; Charles E. Whittaker to William Brennan, December 12, 1957, Harlan Papers, Box 486; Charles Fairman, "Does the Fourteenth Amendment Incorporate the Bill of Rights? The Original Understanding," *Stanford Law Review* 2 (1949): 5; Felix Frankfurter to John M. Harlan, January 12, 1960, Harlan Papers, Box 484.

30. Felix Frankfurter to John M. Harlan, April 3, 1957, Frankfurter Papers, Box 40, a typed, "almost verbatim recollection" of a handwritten note to Harlan.

31. John M. Harlan to Felix Frankfurter, undated bench note, Frankfurter Papers, Box 40.

32. Ibid.

33. John M. Harlan to Felix Frankfurter, July 18, [1958], Frankfurter Papers, Box 40.

34. Felix Frankfurter to John M. Harlan, September 12, 1958, Harlan Papers, Box 486.

35. Felix Frankfurter to John M. Harlan, undated but in a 1957 file, Harlan Papers, Box 532; Felix Frankfurter to John M. Harlan, undated, Harlan Papers, Box 533.

36. A copy of the address is on file in the Harlan Papers, Box 491.

37. John M. Harlan to Walter Bruchhausen, September 19, 1956, Harlan Papers, Box 513. The memorandum regarding indigent petitions is on file in the Harlan Papers, Box 543.

38. Felix Frankfurter to John M. Harlan, November 5, 1958, Frankfurter Papers, Box 40.

39. Felix Frankfurter to John M. Harlan, undated, Harlan Papers, Box 499; John M. Harlan to Felix Frankfurter, October 2, 1957, Harlan Papers, Box 499.

40. John M. Harlan to Earl Warren, October 3, 1957, Harlan Papers, Box 499; Earl Warren Memorandum for the Conference, October 7, 1957, Harlan Papers, Box 499; William O. Douglas Memorandum for the Conference, October 23, 1961, Harlan Papers, Box 499.

41. Roger A. Derby interview; Paul M. Bator interview with Leslie Arps, January 29, 1980, New York, New York, in the possession of Mrs. Paul M. Bator, Chicago, Illinois. Elizabeth Harlan Derby to John M. Harlan, undated, Harlan Papers, Box 512; John M. Harlan to Elizabeth Harlan Derby, November 21, 1969, Harlan Papers, Box 512.

42. Edith Harlan Powell interview. The correspondence between Harlan and his sister Janet, much of it undated, is on file in the Harlan Papers, Box 609.

43. *United States* v. *Du Pont Co.*, 353 U.S. 586 (1957); Felix Frankfurter to William Brennan, November 21, 1956, Frankfurter Papers, Box 30.

44. Frankfurter to Brennan, ibid.; 353 U.S. at 607.

45. 353 U.S. at 606; the note is on file in the Frankfurter Papers, Box 40.

46. *FTC* v. *Proctor & Gamble Co.*, 386 U.S. 568, 581 (1967) (concurring); *United States* v. *Continental Can Co.*, 378 U.S. 441, 467 (1964) (dissenting); *White Motor Co.* v. *United States*, 372 U.S. 253 (1963); *Brown Shoe Co.* v. *United States*, 370 U.S. 294, 357 (1962) (concurring and dissenting); *Klor's, Inc.* v. *Broadway-Hale Stores, Inc.*, 359 U.S. 207 (1959).

47. *Jenkins* v. *Delaware*, 395 U.S. 213, 222 (1969); *Miranda* v. *Arizona*, 384 U.S. 436, 504 (1966); Earl Warren to John M. Harlan, June 2, 1969, Harlan Papers, Box 606; John M. Harlan to Earl Warren, June 2, 1969, Harlan Papers, Box 606.

48. *Washington Post*, June 3, 1969; John M. Harlan to Earl Warren, June 3, 1969.

49. Norman Dorsen interview, May 24, 1989, New York, New York; Felix Frankfurter to Hugo L. Black, May 7, 1963, Black Papers, Box 60.

50. *Bell* v. *Maryland*, 378 U.S. 226 (1964); *Hamm* v. *City of Rock Hill*, 379 U.S. 306 (1964); Felix Frankfurter to Hugo L. Black, December 15, 1964, Black Papers, Box 60; Hugo L. Black to Felix Frankfurter, December 22, 1964, Black Papers, Box 60.

51. Norman Dorsen interview. For cases reflecting a growing Black-Harlan voting, if not jurisprudential, alliance during their last years, see, for example, *Harper* v. *Virginia Bd. of Elections*, 366 U.S. 663 (1966), on equal protection; *Reitman* v. *Mulkey*, 387 U.S. 369 (1967), on state action; and *Brown* v. *Louisiana*, 383 U.S. 131 (1966), on protest demonstrations.

52. Felix Frankfurter to John M. Harlan, undated, Harlan Papers, Box 534.

53. Frankfurter's admonition to Black appeared on Frankfurter's copy of Black's draft dissent in *Yates* v. *United States*, Black Papers, Box 334; *Washington Post Potomac*, October 31, 1965; Eve Harlan Dillingham interview. A copy of the address to law librarians is on file in the Harlan Papers, Box 491.

54. Edith Harlan Powell interview; Hugo L. Black to John M. Harlan, July 18, 1966, Harlan Papers, Box 484; Hugo L. Black to John M. Harlan, July 15, 1969, Harlan Papers, Box 484. Notes indicating Black's gifts to the Harlans are in the same container.

55. John M. Harlan to Edward, Lord Pearce, June 28, 1967, Harlan Papers, Box 484; Elizabeth Black to Ethel and John M. Harlan, August 3, 1967, Harlan Papers, Box 484; Elizabeth Black to Ethel and John M. Harlan, September 1, 1967, Harlan Papers, Box 484.

56. Copies of correspondence relative to Harlan's efforts in Brennan's behalf are on file in the Harlan Papers, Box 486; John M. Harlan to Charles E. Whittaker, March 18, 1963, Box 610; John M. Harlan to Harry Blackmun, May 20, 1971, Harlan Papers, Box 485; William O. Douglas to John M. Harlan, January 15, 1968, Harlan Papers, Box 514; William O. Douglas to John M. Harlan, January 15, 1968, Harlan Papers, Box 514.

57. Norman Dorsen interview; Charles Fried interview, May 26, 1989, Cambridge, Massachusetts.

58. John M. Harlan to Elizabeth Frizzi, June 9, 1965, Harlan Papers, Box 596; John M. Harlan to John W. Wardlaw, November 5, 1968, Harlan Papers, Box 596;

John M. Harlan to C. C. Lynch, December 6, 1965, Harlan Papers, Box 596. Other material relative to Harlan's treatment of household servants is also in this container and in Box 566.

59. Eve Harlan Dillingham interview.

60. Shirley Bartlett to John M. Harlan, December 30, 1965, Harlan Papers, Box 483.

61. Eve Harlan Dillingham interview; Charles Nesson, "Mr. Justice Harlan," *Harvard Law Review* 85 (December 1971): 390–91.

62. Except where otherwise indicated, this discussion is drawn from the Norman Dorsen and Charles Fried interviews, as well as case files in the Harlan Papers.

63. Nesson, "Mr. Justice Harlan," p. 390.

64. John M. Harlan to Paul M. Bator, June 26, 1963, Harlan Papers, Box 483; Paul M. Bator to John M. Harlan, November 10, 1959, Harlan Papers, Box 483.

65. Nesson, "Mr. Justice Harlan," p. 390.

66. Ibid., p. 391.

67. Charles Fried interview; William O. Douglas to John M. Harlan, March 24, 1961, Harlan Papers, Box 543; John M. Harlan to Earl Warren, November 6, 1962, Harlan Papers, Box 543; John M. Harlan to Henry F. Butler, May 31, 1963, Harlan Papers, Box 543; John M. Harlan to Alan V. Washburn, November 6, 1958, Harlan Papers, Box 533; Eve Harlan Dillingham interview.

68. Copies of the letter, dated July 17, 1962, and memorandum are on file in the Harlan Papers, Box 567.

69. John M. Harlan to Leo Gottlieb, July 24, 1962, Harlan Papers, Box 567. A copy of Harlan's suggested letter is is the same container.

70. John M. Harlan to Wellington A. Newcomb, August 21, 1962, Harlan Papers, Box 567; John M. Harlan to Wellington A. Newcomb, September 23, 1969, Harlan Papers, Box 567; J. Edward Lumbard interview.

71. A copy of the memorandum, dated June 5, 1969, is on file in the Harlan Papers, Box 479.

72. John M. Harlan Memorandum for the Conference, October 13, 1970, Harlan Papers, Box 481; Roy Anderson to John M. Harlan, et al., April 19, 1971, Harlan Papers, Box 481; Warren E. Burger to John M. Harlan, October 14, 1970, Harlan Papers, Box 481.

Chapter 5. The Early Battles

1. A copy of the address, entitled "The Bill of Rights and the Constitution," which was delivered at the dedication of the Bill of Rights Room in the United States Subtreasury Building in New York, August 9, 1964, is on file in the Harlan Papers, Box 544. See also his "Thoughts on a Dedication: Keeping the Judicial Function in Balance," *American Bar Association Journal* 49 (October 1963): 943.

2. *Maryland* v. *Wirtz*, 392 U.S. 183 (1968); Brennan's *Wirtz* conference notes are on file in the Brennan Papers, Box 414; *Fay* v. *Noia*, 372 U.S. 391, 448 (1963); see also *Henry* V. *Mississippi*, 379 U.S. 443, 457 (1965); *Dombrowski* v. *Pfister*, 380 U.S. 479, 498 (1965); *Younger* v. *Harris*, 401 U.S. 37 (1971); *Reitman* v. *Mulkey*, 387 U.S. 369, 387 (1967); *Burton* v. *Wilmington Parking Authority*, 365 U.S. 715, 728 (1961).

3. *Reynolds* v. *Sims*, 377 U.S. 533 (1964); *Avery* v. *Midland Co.*, 390 U.S. 474, 487–88 (1968).

4. John M. Harlan to Phillip E. Hassman, undated, Harlan Papers, Box 512.

5. *Reynolds* v. *Sims*, 377 U.S. at 589; *Shapiro* v. *Thompson*, 394 U.S. 618, 661 (1969); *Glona* v. *American Guarantee Co.*, 391 U.S. 73, 76 (1968) (dissenting); *Harper* v. *Virginia Bd. of Elections*, 383 U.S. 663, 680 (1966) (dissenting).

6. J. Harvie Wilkinson, III, "Justice John M. Harlan and the Values of Federalism," *Virginia Law Review* 57 (1971): 1185; Herbert Wechsler, "Toward Neutral Principles of Constitutional Law," *Harvard Law Review* 73 (1959): 15; Hugo L. Black, *A Constitutional Faith* (New York: Alfred A. Knopf, 1969), ch. 1; Axel B. Gravem to John M. Harlan, August 22, 1963, Harlan Papers, Box 654; John M. Harlan to L. Barry Schaefer, March 22, 1965, Harlan Papers, Box 544.

7. A copy of the Harlan memorandum is on file in the Harlan Papers, Box 494. Justice Frankfurter's *Brown* conference notes are on file in the Frankfurter Papers, Box 219.

8. *Society for Savings* v. *Bowers*, 349 U.S. 143 (1955). *New York Times Co.* v. *United States*, 403 U.S. 713, 752 (1971).

9. *Avery* v. *Georgia*, 345 U.S. 559 (1953); *Williams* v. *State*, 78 S.E. 2d 521 (1953).

10. This discussion is based on John M. Harlan, Memorandum for the Conference, April 23, 1955, Harlan Papers, Box 2.

11. Quoted in ibid.

12. Ibid.; *Wright* v. *Davis*, 193 S.E. 757 (1937); *Smith* v. *Georgia*, 59 S.E. 311 (1907). Other relevant cases are cited in the Harlan memorandum.

13. Barrett Prettyman to John M. Harlan, undated, Harlan Papers, Box 2.

14. Harlan, Memorandum for the Conference.

15. Ibid.

16. *Williams* v. *Georgia*, 349 U.S. 375, 391 (1955).

17. Ibid., p. 393.

18. *Williams* v. *State*, 88 S.E. 2d 376, 377 (1955).

19. James B. McGhee to W. H. Duckworth, August 3, 1955, Earl Warren Papers, Library of Congress, Box 427.

20. Felix Frankfurter, Memorandum to the Conference, undated, Frankfurter Papers, Box 222.

21. Ibid.

22. Ibid.

23. Ibid.; *Williams* v. *Georgia*, 350 U.S. 950 (1956); *New York Times*, March 31, 1956.

24. Except where otherwise indicated, this discussion is drawn from *NAACP* v. *Alabama*, 357 U.S. 449 (1958), 377 U.S. 288 (1964), and George R. Osborne, "The NAACP in Alabama," in *The Third Branch of Government*, ed. C. Herman Pritchett and Alan F. Westin (New York: Harcourt, Brace & World, Inc., 1963), pp. 148–203.

25. John M. Harlan, Memorandum for the Conference, April 22, 1958, Harlan Papers, Box 495.

26. Ibid.

27. Hugo L. Black to John M. Harlan, handwritten note, May 8, 1958; John M. Harlan, Memorandum for the Conference, May 23, 1958, Harlan Papers, Box 46; Felix Frankfurter to John M. Harlan, May 23, 1958, Harlan Papers, Box 46.

28. Felix Frankfurter to John M. Harlan, May 29, 1958, Frankfurter Papers, Box 40.

29. Felix Frankfurter to Tom Clark, June 25, 1958, Harlan Papers, Box 495.

30. *NAACP* v. *Alabama*, 357 U.S. at 459.
31. Ibid., pp. 460–61.
32. Ibid., pp. 462–63.
33. Ibid., pp. 464–65.
34. Ibid., pp. 465–66; *Bryant* v. *Zimmerman*, 278 U.S. 63 (1928).
35. Erwin Griswold to John M. Harlan, July 8, 1958, Harlan Papers, Box 538; Edward S. Corwin to John M. Harlan, July 7, 1958, Harlan Papers, Box 511.
36. 109 So. 2d 138, 139 (Ala. Sup. Ct., 1959).
37. 360 U.S. 240 (1959).
38. 190 F. Supp. 583 (M.D. Ala., 1960), 290 F. 2d 337 (5th Cir., 1961).
39. 368 U.S. 16 (1961); 150 S. 2d 677 (Ala. Sup. Ct., 1963).
40. A copy of the proposed decree is on file in the Harlan Papers, Box 203.
41. A copy of the Clark memorandum, with the Harlan notation, is on file in the Harlan Papers, Box 493.
42. 377 U.S. 288, 310 (1964). On his copy of the decree draft, which the justices had rejected at their May 29, 1964, conference, Harlan had written, "Not adopted, at JMH's Recommendation."
43. Elizabeth Black to Ethel and John M. Harlan, August 22, 1968, Harlan Papers, Box 484.
44. *Cooper* v. *Aaron*, 163 F. Supp. 13 (E.D. Ark., 1958).
45. Justice Harlan's draft opinion is on file in the Harlan Papers, Box 57. The Clark draft dissent is quoted in Bernard Schwartz, *Super Chief: Earl Warren and His Supreme Court—A Judicial Biography* (New York and London: New York University Press, 1983), p. 294.
46. 311 U.S. 128 (1940).
47. 1 Cr. 137 (1803).
48. Schwartz, *Super Chief*, p. 298; John M. Harlan to William Brennan, September 23, 1958, Harlan Papers, Box 486. A copy of his "Suggested Substitute" is on file in the Harlan Papers, Box 57.
49. A copy of Brennan's undated statement is on file in the William Brennan Papers, Library of Congress, Box 14.
50. Schwartz, *Super Chief*, p. 302. The handwritten copy of the Brennan-Black proposal, as well as typed copies, is on file in the Brennan Papers, Box 14.
51. The Frankfurter memorandum, dated October 6, 1958, is on file in his papers, Box 220.
52. Schwartz, *Super Chief*, p. 303. A copy of the Harlan opinion is on file in the Harlan Papers, Box 495.
53. *In Re* Murchison, 349 U.S. 133 (1955).
54. John M. Harlan to Hugo L. Black, May 11, 1955, Harlan Papers, Box 2.
55. *Fikes* v. *Alabama*, 352 U.S. 191 (1957).
56. Ibid., pp. 198–99.
57. Ibid., pp. 199–200.
58. Ibid., p. 201, quoting *Rochin* v. *California*, 342 U.S. 165, 172 (1952).
59. *Cicenia* v. *LaGay*, 357 U.S. 504, 512 (1958).
60. Ibid., pp. 508–10.
61. *Payne* v. *Arkansas*, 356 U.S. 560, 569 (1958); John M. Harlan to Charles Whittaker, April 29, 1958, Harlan Papers, Box 46. The *Payne* file, with pertinent Harlan notations, is in the same box.
62. *Lambert* v. *California*, 355 U.S. 225, 228–30 (1957).
63. A copy of the Harlan draft is on file in the Harlan Papers, Box 42.

64. *Green* v. *United States*, 355 U.S. 184 (1957).
65. Ibid., p. 216; *Palko* v. *Connecticut*, 302 U.S. 319 (1937).
66. *United States* v. *Shotwell Manufacturing Co.*, 355 U.S. 233 (1957).
67. Ibid., p. 250.
68. Ibid., p. 251, n. 3.
69. Ibid., p. 244.
70. *Green* v. *United States*, 356 U.S. 165, 193, 201, 196 (1958). The treatise quoted was Felix Frankfurter and James Landis, "Power to Regulate Contempts," *Harvard Law Review* 37 (1924): 1010, 1011.
71. *Green* v. *United States*, 356 U.S. at 185, 187, 188–189.
72. Ibid., p. 197.
73. *Rea* v. *United States*, 350 U.S. 214, 218 (1956); *Mapp* v. *Ohio*, 367 U.S. 643, 672 (1961).
74. *Kremen* v. *United States*, 353 U.S. 346 (1957). Harlan's draft concurrence is on file in the Harlan Papers, Box 28.
75. *Harris* v. *United States*, 331 U.S. 145 (1947); *Trupiano* v. *United States*, 334 U.S. 699 (1948); *United States* v. *Rabinowitz*, 339 U.S. 56 (1950).
76. *Chimel* v. *California*, 395 U.S. 752 (1969).
77. William O. Douglas to John M. Harlan, April 18, 1957, Harlan Papers, Box 514.
78. Ibid.
79. John M. Harlan to William O. Douglas, April 24, 1957, Harlan Papers, Box 514.
80. *Perez* v. *Brownell*, 356 U.S. 44 (1958); *Afroyim* v. *Rusk*, 387 U.S. 253, 268 (1967); *Reid* v. *Covert*, 351 U.S. 487 (1956).
81. Memoranda for Mr. Justice Reed, Mr. Justice Burton, Mr. Justice Clark, and Mr. Justice Minton, September 5 and 26, 1956, Harlan Papers, Boxes 484, 490; Harold H. Burton to John M. Harlan, September 7, 1956, Harlan Papers, Box 490; Sherman Minton to John M. Harlan, September 10, 1956, Harlan Papers, Box 565; *Reid* v. *Covert*, 354 U.S. 1 (1957).
82. *Reid* v. *Covert*, 354 U.S. at 75; *Kinsella* v. *Singleton*, 361 U.S. 234, 255 (1960).
83. *Griffin* v. *Illinois*, 351 U.S. 12 (1956).
84. Schwartz, *Super Chief*, p. 193; Wayne Barnett interview, January 20, 1990, Seattle, Washington; John M. Harlan, Memorandum for the Conference, February 27, 1956, Black Papers, Box 326.
85. John M. Harlan, Memorandum for the Conference, March 5, 1956, Black Papers, Box 326.
86. Memorandum by Mr. Justice Black, undated, Black Papers, Box 326.
87. Clark's notes are on file in the Black Papers, Box 326.
88. John M. Harlan, Memorandum for the Conference, Harlan Papers, Box 493.
89. 351 U.S. at 19–20. For discussions of Black's difficulties with equal protection, see, for example, Tinsley E. Yarbrough, *Mr. Justice Black and his Critics* (Durham, N.C.: Duke University Press, 1988), pp. 226–45, and commentaries cited there.
90. 351 U.S. at 25–26.
91. Ibid., pp. 21, 22, 23–24.
92. Ibid., p. 33.
93. Ibid., pp. 34–35.

94. Ibid., pp. 36, 37–38.

95. Ibid., pp. 38–39.

96. Ibid., pp. 33, 35.

97. Ibid., p. 29; John M. Harlan to Hugh Grant Strauss, January 7, 1954, Harlan Papers, Box 562; *New York Times*, July 16, 1957.

98. *New York Times*, July 16, 1957.

Chapter 6. The First Freedoms

1. George G. Zabriskie to Thomas E. Dewey, June 18, 1958, Harlan Papers, Box 512.

2. Ibid. Elizabeth's notation was penned on the back of the copy of the Zabriskie letter, which she had sent her brother.

3. John M. Harlan to Potter Stewart, February 13, 1961, Harlan Papers, Box 72; Charles Fried interview; Philip Heymann interview, February 8, 1990, Cambridge, Massachusetts; Stephen Shulman interview, January 20, 1990, Washington, D.C.

4. *Dennis* v. *United States*, 341 U.S. 494 (1951); *United States* v. *Flynn*, 216 F. 2d 354, 366 (2d Cir., 1954).

5. *Yates* v. *United States*, 354 U.S. 298, 318, 319–20 (1957).

6. Ibid., p. 324.

7. The notes and letters are on file in the Harlan Papers, Box 21.

8. This discussion is drawn in part from the excellent general survey of the *Scales* case in Schwartz, *Super Chief*, pp. 363–64.

9. *Communist Party* v. *Subversive Activities Control Board*, 367 U.S. 1 (1961).

10. A copy of the memorandum is on file in the Harlan Papers, Box 72.

11. The bench memo is on file in Ibid., Box 496.

12. Charles Fried to John M. Harlan, February 3, 1961, Harlan Papers, Box 598.

13. John M. Harlan to Potter Stewart; *Noto* v. *United States*, 367 U.S. 290 (1961); Brennan Papers, Box 407.

14. John M. Harlan to Potter Stewart, February 13, 1961, Harlan Papers, Box 72.

15. Charles Fried interview; Philip Heymann interview.

16. *Scales* v. *United States*, 367 U.S. 203, 209, 250 (1961).

17. Ibid., p. 225.

18. Ibid., p. 229.

19. Ibid., pp. 262–63. The correspondence is on file in the Harlan Papers, Box 105.

20. Charles Fried interview; Junius Irving Scales and Richard Nickson, *Cause at Heart: A Former Communist Remembers* (Athens: University of Georgia Press, 1987), pp. 275–76.

21. Brennan Papers, Box 405; *Greene* v. *McElroy*, 360 U.S. 474, 509 (1959).

22. Ibid., p. 510.

23. *Cole* v. *Young*, 351 U.S. 536, 544, 557 (1956).

24. Henry Sailer interview, February 1, 1990, Washington, D.C.; *Vitarelli* v. *Seaton*, 359 U.S. 535, 543 (1959); *New York Times*, June 2, 1959.

25. *Service* v. *Dulles*, 354 U.S. 363 (1957). President Truman's letter is quoted in ibid., p. 379.

26. *Flemming* v. *Nestor*, 363 U.S. 603, 617 (1960).

27. *Watkins* v. *United States*, 354 U.S. 178 (1957); Schwartz, *Super Chief*, p. 239.

28. John M. Harlan to Earl Warren, May 31, 1957, Harlan Papers, Box 29; *Sweezy* v. *New Hampshire*, 354 U.S. 234 (1957).

29. *Barenblatt* v. *United States*, 360 U.S. 109 (1959); *Uphaus* v. *Wyman*, 364 U.S. 388 (1959).

30. Stephen Shulman interview.

31. Felix Frankfurter to John M. Harlan, June 3, 1959, Harlan Papers, Box 533.

32. John M. Harlan to Felix Frankfurter, June 4, 1959, Harlan Papers, Box 61; John M. Harlan to Tom Clark, December 4, 1958, Harlan Papers, Box 493. The unfiled *Uphaus* draft is in the Harlan Papers, Box 61.

33. 360 U.S. at 126, 128, 130.

34. Ibid., p. 143.

35. Thurman Arnold to Hugo L. Black, June 10, 1959, Black Papers, Box 337.

36. *Slochower* v. *Board of Education*, 350 U.S. 551, 565–66 (1956).

37. *Lerner* v. *Casey*, 357 U.S. 468, 479 (1958).

38. *Konigsberg* v. *State Bar*, 366 U.S. 36 (1961).

39. Ibid., pp. 276–77, 280, 312.

40. Ibid., pp. 311–12.

41. Felix Frankfurter to John M. Harlan, April 26, 1957, Harlan Papers, Box 532.

42. Hugo L. Black to John M. Harlan, undated note, Harlan Papers, Box 540.

43. Hugo L. Black to William O. Douglas, undated note, Black Papers, Box 329.

44. William O. Douglas to Hugo L. Black, undated note, Black Papers, Box 329; William Brennan to Hugo L. Black, undated note, Black Papers, Box 329; Harold Burton to Hugo L. Black, undated note, Black Papers, Box 329.

45. *Schware* v. *Bd. of Bar Examiners*, 353 U.S. 232, 249, 251 (1957); John M. Harlan to Felix Frankfurter, April 17, 1957, Harlan Papers, Box 27.

46. *Konigsberg* v. *State Bar*, 366 U.S. 36 (1961); *In Re* Anastaplo, 366 U.S. 82 (1961).

47. 366 U.S. at 49–51 (footnotes omitted). Sidney Hook, "Justice Black's Illogic," *The New Leader*, December 2, 1957, pp. 17–20, as well as other commentary critical of Black's thinking, is on file in the Harlan Papers in Box 20 and other containers in the collection.

48. 366 U.S. at 52.

49. Benjamin V. Cohen to Hugo L. Black, May 24, 1961, Black Papers, Box 349. For discussions of Black's views, see generally James J. Magee, *Mr. Justice Black: Absolutist on the Court* (Charlottesville: University Press of Virginia, 1980), and Yarbrough, *Mr. Justice Black and His Critics*, chs. 4–5.

50. The drafts are on file in the Harlan Papers, Box 543.

51. *Wilkinson* v. *United States*, 365 U.S. 399 (1961); *Braden* v. *United States*, 365 U.S. 431 (1961); *Hutcheson* v. *United States*, 369 U.S. 599 (1962). Examples of cases limiting the reach of the investigatory power are *Deutch* v. *United States*, 367 U.S. 456 (1961); *Yellin* v. *United States*, 374 U.S. 109 (1963); *Russell* v. *United States*, 399 U.S. 749 (1962); *Slagle* v. *Ohio*, 366 U.S. 259 (1961).

52. John M. Harlan to Potter Stewart, December 6, 1961, Harlan Papers, Box 598; John M. Harlan to Tom Clark, May 17, 1962, Harlan Papers, Box 493.

53. *Aptheker* v. *Secretary of State*, 378 U.S. 500 (1964); John M. Harlan to

Tom Clark, June 17, 1964, Harlan Papers, Box 207. The Clark draft is in the same container.

54. *Gibson* v. *Florida Legislative Investigation Committee*, 372 U.S. 539 (1963).

55. Brennan Papers, conference notes, Box 409.

56. The draft opinion is on file in the Harlan Papers, Box 161.

57. Ibid.

58. 372 U.S. at 579–80.

59. Brennan Papers, Box 407; *Shelton* v. *Tucker*, 364 U.S. 479, 498–99 (1960).

60. *NAACP* v. *Button*, 371 U.S. 415 (1963); *Harrison* v. *NAACP*, 360 U.S. 167 (1959).

61. 371 U.S. at 448, 470.

62. *Lathrop* v. *Donohue*, 367 U.S. 820, 848–49, 857, 860 (1961).

63. *Roth* v. *United States*, 354 U.S. 476 (1957); *Butler* v. *Michigan*, 352 U.S. 380 (1957); undated bench memoranda, Harlan Papers, Box 22, 32.

64. 352 U.S. at 383.

65. John M. Harlan, Memorandum for the Conference, April 29, 1971, Harlan Papers, Box 499; Paul Brest interview; Nina Totenberg, *The Washingtonian Magazine*, January 1974, p. 42.

66. John M. Harlan to William Brennan, June 13, 1957. Harlan Papers, Box 486.

67. *Roth* v. *United States*, *Alberts* v. *California*, 354 U.S. 476 (1957).

68. Ibid., pp. 497–98..

69. Ibid., pp. 501–502.

70. Ibid., pp. 503–504, 506.

71. Ibid., pp. 507–508, 502, 503.

72. *Manual Enterprises* v. *Day*, 370 U.S. 478, 482–83.

73. Potter Stewart to John M. Harlan, June 5, 1962, Harlan Papers, Box 598.

74. Potter Stewart to John M. Harlan, June 11, 1962, Harlan Papers, Box 543; William Brennan to John M. Harlan, June 9, 1962, Harlan Papers, Box 486.

75. Brennan to Harlan, ibid.; Stewart made his well-known observation in *Jacobellis* v. *Ohio*, 378 U.S. 184, 197 (1964) (concurring).

76. John M. Harlan to William Brennan, June 11, 1962, Harlan Papers, Box 543.

77. *Memoirs* v. *Massachusetts*, 383 U.S. 413, 457, 460 (1966).

78. *Smith* v. *California*, 361 U.S. 147, 169–70, 172 (1959); *Ginsberg* v. *New York*, 390 U.S. 629, 704 (1968) (concurring).

79. *Kingsley Pictures Corp.* v. *Regents*, 360 U.S. 684, 708 (1959) (concurring); *Times Film Corp.* v. *Chicago*, 365 U.S. 43 (1961); John M. Harlan to Tom Clark, November 3, 1960, Harlan Papers, Box 113; *Bantam Books, Inc.* v. *Sullivan*, 372 U.S. 58, 76 (1963) (dissenting); *Freedman* v. *Maryland*, 380 U.S. 51 (1965); undated bench memo, Harlan Papers, Box 227; John M. Harlan to William Brennan, February 4, 1965, Harlan Papers, Box 227.

80. Bench memo, August 15, 1968, Harlan Papers, Box 545; Robert Mnookin interview, February 21, 1990, Palo Alto, California; *Stanley* v. *Georgia*, 394 U.S. 557 (1969); John M. Harlan to Thurgood Marshall, March 13, 1969, Harlan Papers, Box 565.

81. *United States* v. *Thirty-seven Photographs*, 402 U.S. 363, 382 (1971) (Justice Black, dissenting); *Rowan* v. *Post Office Dept.*, 397 U.S. 728 (1970); John M. Harlan to Earl Warren, April 23, 1970, Harlan Papers, Box 490.

82. *Ginzburg* v. *United States*, 383 U.S. 463, 495, 494 (1966).

83. John M. Harlan to Jarvis Cromwell, June 23, 1971, Harlan Papers, Box

547; Arthur L. Kinsolving to John M. Harlan, February 8, 1963, Harlan Papers, Box 543; W. Barton Leach to John M. Harlan, February 3, 1966, Harlan Papers, Box 562; Joseph O'Meara to John M. Harlan, August 30, 1962, Harlan Papers, Box 583.

84. John M. Harlan to Joseph O'Meara, September 19, 1962, Harlan Papers, Box 583.

85. John M. Harlan to Arthur L. Kinsolving, February 22, 1963, Harlan Papers, Box 543.

86. John M. Harlan to Jarvis Cromwell, June 23, 1971, Harlan Papers, Box 547.

87. *Barr* v. *Matteo*, 360 U.S. 564, 571 (1959).

88. *New York Times* v. *Sullivan*, 376 U.S. 254 (1964).

89. Ibid., p. 285.

90. John M. Harlan to William Brennan, February 26, 1964, Harlan Papers, Box 486.

91. Hugo L. Black to William Brennan, undated note, Brennan Papers, Box 107. For a general discussion of intracourt negotiations in the case, see Schwartz, *Super Chief*, pp. 531–44, on which the account here is partially based.

92. William Brennan to John M. Harlan, February 28, 1964, Harlan Papers, Box 486; William Brennan to John M. Harlan, March 2, 1964, Harlan Papers, Box 486.

93. The drafts are on file in the Harlan Papers, Box 194.

94. Hugo L. Black to William Brennan, undated notes, Brennan Papers, Box 107.

95. John M. Harlan, Memorandum for the Conference, March 9, 1964, Harlan Papers, Box 194.

96. *Garrison* v. *Louisiana*, 379 U.S. 64 (1964); John M. Harlan to Tom Clark, June 12, 1964, Harlan Papers, Box 217.

97. Harlan to Clark, ibid.

98. *Curtis Publishing Co.* v. *Butts*, 388 U.S. 130, 154–55 (1967).

99. *Rosenbloom* v. *Metromedia*, 403 U.S. 29, 62, 64, 70 (1971).

100. *New York Times*, August 3, 1924.

101. *Walz* v. *Tax Commission*, 397 U.S. 664, 695 (1970); *Engel* v. *Vitale*, 370 U.S. 421 (1962); *Abington* v. *Schempp*, 374 U.S. 203 (1963); *Epperson* v. *Arkansas*, 393 U.S. 97, 114 (1968) (concurring); *Lemon* v. *Kurtzman*, 403 U.S. 602 (1971); *Tilton* v. *Richardson*, 403 U.S. 672 (1971); John M. Harlan to Warren Burger, June 7, 1971, Harlan Papers, Box 499.

102. Baron Rothschild to John M. Harlan, June 27, 1962, Harlan Papers, Box 174; Baron Rothschild to John M. Harlan, September 25, 1962, Harlan Papers, Box 174; Alexander Smith to John M. Harlan, September 24, 1963, Harlan Papers, Box 596.

103. John M. Harlan to Alexander Smith, October 3, 1963, Harlan Papers, Box 596.

104. The Stewart memorandum is on file in the Harlan Papers, Box 598; *Abington* v. *Schempp*, 374 U.S. at 305.

105. *McGowan* v. *Maryland*, 366 U.S. 420, 459 (1961) (Frankfurter, J., concurring); *Sherbert* v. *Verner*, 374 U.S. 398, 423 (1963).

106. *Presbyterian Church* v. *Hull Church*, 393 U.S. 440, 452 (1969).

107. *Walz* v. *Tax Commission*, 397 U.S. at 696–97.

108. *United States* v. *Seeger*, 380 U.S. 163 (1965); conference notes, Brennan Papers, Box 411.

109. A copy of the draft dissent is on file in the Harlan Papers, Box 224, as is John M. Harlan to Tom Clark, February 8, 1965.

110. *Welsh* v. *United States*, 398 U.S. 333, 345, 344, 351, 354 (1970).

111. Ibid., pp. 357–58.

Chapter 7. The Second Reconstruction

1. Paul Burke interview, April 10, 30, 1990, Washington, D.C.

2. Robert H. Mnookin interview.

3. Ibid.

4. Ibid.

5. Paul Burke interview; *Evening Star* (Washington, D.C.), August 24, 1957, which contains an account of Emerson Parker's death.

6. Paul Burke interview.

7. Remarks of Gerald Gunther, prepared for delivery at the New York Law School Centennial Conference in honor of Justice John Marshall Harlan, April 20, 1991, New York, New York; *Brown* v. *Board of Education*, 349 U.S. 294, 300 (1955); Henry Steiner interview, January 20, 1990, Cambridge, Massachusetts.

8. *Swain* v. *Alabama*, 380 U.S. 202 (1965); Charles Nesson interview, February 1, 1990, Cambridge, Massachusetts. The Goldberg draft is on file in the Harlan Papers, Box 226.

9. *Fay* v. *Noia*, 372 U.S. 391, 448 (1963); Paul M. Bator, "Finality in Criminal Law and Federal Habeas Corpus for State Prisoners," *Harvard Law Review* 76 (1963): 441; *Henry* v. *Mississippi*, 379 U.S. 443, 457 (1965); Charles Nesson interview.

10. Frankfurter's conference remarks are drawn from Justice Brennan's notes for *NAACP* v. *Gray*, Brennan Papers, Box 409.

11. *Holt* v. *Virginia*, 381 U.S. 131, 138 (1965).

12. The draft is on file in the Harlan Papers, Box 234.

13. William Brennan to Hugo L. Black, January 9, 1963, Brennan Papers, Box 84; Hugo L. Black to John M. Harlan, May 10, 1965, Harlan Papers, Box 484.

14. 381 U.S. at 138.

15. *Lee* v. *Washington*, 390 U.S. 333, 34 (1968).

16. *Schneider* v. *Irvington*, 308 U.S. 147 (1939); *Martin* v. *Struthers*, 319 U.S. 141 (1943); *Marsh* v. *Alabama*, 326 U.S. 501 (1946).

17. *Shelley* v. *Kraemer*, 334 U.S. 1 (1948).

18. *Edwards* v. *South Carolina*, 372 U.S. 229 (1963); *Cox* v. *Louisiana*, 379 U.S. 536 (1965); *Brown* v. *Louisiana*, 383 U.S. 131 (1966); *Adderley* v. *Florida*, 385 U.S. 39 (1966); *Shuttlesworth* v. *Birmingham*, 394 U.S. 147 (1969).

19. John M. Harlan to Potter Stewart, February 5, 1963, Harlan Papers, Box 543; John M. Harlan to Tom Clark, February 20, 1963, Harlan Papers, Box 493.

20. Brennan Papers, Box 411; 379 U.S. at 591.

21. The Nesson memo is in the Harlan Papers, Box 544; John M. Harlan to Hugo L. Black, January 24, 1966, Black Papers, Box 387; John M. Harlan to Hugo L. Black, January 12, 1966, Harlan Papers, Box 24. The Harlan bench note is in the Black Papers, Box 387; Edmund W. Price to John M. Harlan, November 16, 1966, Harlan Papers, Box 596.

22. *Shuttlesworth* v. *Birmingham*, 394 U.S. at 159, 160, 163.

23. *Walker* v. *Birmingham*, 388 U.S. 307 (1967).

24. *Garner* v. *Louisiana*, *Briscoe* v. *Louisiana*, *Horton* v. *Louisiana*, 368 U.S. 157 (1961); *Thompson* v. *Louisville*, 362 U.S. 199 (1960). Conference discussion of the sit-in cases is based on Justice Brennan's notes in the Brennan Papers, Box 408.

25. John M. Harlan to Hugo L. Black, March 17, 1960, Harlan Papers, Box 484; John M. Harlan to Hugo L. Black, March 18, 1960, Harlan Papers, Box 484.

26. *Cantwell* v. *Connecticut*, 310 U.S. 296 (1940).

27. Felix Frankfurter to Earl Warren, December 4, 1961, Harlan Papers, Box 605.

28. Felix Frankfurter to John M. Harlan, December 1, 1961, Harlan Papers, Box 534.

29. John M. Harlan to Felix Frankfurter, December 4, 1961, Harlan Papers, Box 534.

30. Ibid.

31. John M. Harlan to Felix Frankfurter, December 5, 1961, Harlan Papers, Box 534; William O. Douglas to John M. Harlan, November 22, 1961, Harlan Papers, Box 514.

32. 368 U.S. at 201, 202, 206–207.

33. Ibid., pp. 190, 196.

34. For a thorough survey of the ongoing struggle, see Schwartz, *Super Chief*, chs. 10–12.

35. *Peterson* v. *Greenville*, 373 U.S. 244 (1963); *Gober* v. *Birmingham*, 373 U.S. 374 (1963); *Avent* v. *North Carolina*, 373 U.S. 375 (1963); *Lombard* V. *Louisiana*, 373 U.S. 267 (1963); *Shuttlesworth* v. *Birmingham*, 373 U.S. 262 (1963).

36. 373 U.S. at 251, 252, 254, 258.

37. Ibid., pp. 249–50.

38. William O. Douglas, Memorandum to the Conference, October 23, 1963, Harlan Papers, Box 497.

39. *Griffin* v. *Maryland*, 378 U.S. 130 (1964).

40. Ibid., p. 138.

41. *Bell* v. *Maryland*, 378 U.S. 226 (1964); John M. Harlan to Hugo L. Black, March 9, 1964, Black Papers, Box 377.

42. Author's interviews with Hugo L. Black, August 31, 1970, and July 6, 1971, Washington, D.C.

43. John M. Harlan to Hugo L. Black, June 2, 1964, Harlan Papers, Box 544.

44. *Hamm* v. *Rock Hill*, 379 U.S. 306, 322, 323–24.

45. Baron Rothchild to John M. Harlan, December 17, 1964, Harlan Papers, Box 544.

46. *Dombrowski* v. *Pfister*, 380 U.S. 479 (1965).

47. For a brief discussion of the Court's position in cases of the *Dombrowski* variety, see Tinsley E. Yarbrough, "Litigant Access Doctrine and the Burger Court," *Vanderbilt Law Review* 31 (1978): 56–69. The reference to Harlan's conference remark is based on Justice Brennan's notes, Brennan Papers, Box 411.

48. 380 U.S. at 498, 499.

49. Ibid., pp. 501–502 (footnote omitted).

50. *City of Greenwood* v. *Peacock*, 384 U.S. 808, (1966); John M. Harlan to Sir Howard Beale, June 29, 1966, Harlan Papers, Box 483.

51. Conference notes, Brennan Papers, Box 407; *Burton* v. *Wilmington Parking Authority*, 365 U.S. 715, 730 (1961).

52. *Evans* v. *Newton*, 382 U.S. 296, 322 (1966); *Marsh* v. *Alabama*, 326 U.S. 501 (1946); *Food Employees* v. *Logan Valley Plaza*, 391 U.S. 308, 337 (1968); *Palmer* v. *Thompson*, 403 U.S. 217 (1971). The clerk's bench memo is in the Harlan Papers, Box 314.

53. *Reitman* v. *Mulkey*, 387 U.S. 369 (1967). The Harlan dissent is in the Brennan Papers, Box 148.

54. 387 U.S. at 389, 387, 395–96.

55. *Heart of Atlanta Motel* v. *United States*, 379 U.S. 241 (1964); *Katzenbach* v. *McClung*, 379 U.S. 294 (1964); John M. Harlan to Tom Clark, November 30, 1964, Harlan Papers, Box 235.

56. *South Carolina* v. *Katzenbach*, 383 U.S. 301 (1966); *Oregon* v. *Mitchell*, 400 U.S. 112, 216 (1970).

57. *Katzenbach* v. *Morgan*, 384 U.S. 641 (1966).

58. *Lassiter* v. *Northampton County Bd. of Elections*, 360 U.S. 45 (1959); conference notes, Brennan Papers, Box 412; 384 U.S. at 668.

59. 384 U.S. at 669–71.

60. *Reynolds* v. *Sims*, 377 U.S. 533, 589 (1964); William Van Alstyne, "The Fourteenth Amendment, the 'Right' to Vote, and the Understanding of the Twenty-Ninth Congress," *Supreme Court Review* 1965: 33; John M. Harlan to Lloyd Weinreb, March 14, 1966, Harlan Papers, Box 531; Lloyd Weinreb to John M. Harlan, March 24, 1966, Harlan Papers, Box 531.

61. The notation, dated March 30, 1966, was penned at the bottom of Weinreb's March 24 letter; *Oregon* v. *Mitchell*, 400 U.S. 112 (1970).

62. 400 U.S. at 200, 201, 202–203.

63. Ibid., pp. 586–87.

64. *Allen* v. *State Board of Elections*, 393 U.S. 544, 585–86 (1969).

65. Ibid., pp. 586–87.

66. *Monroe* v. *Pope*, 365 U.S. 167, 192 (concurring); *United States* v. *Price*, 388 U.S. 787 (1966); *United States* v. *Guest*, 383 U.S. 745 (1966).

67. *Ex Parte* Yarbrough, 110 U.S. 651 (1884); *Logan* v. *United States*, 144 U.S. 263 (1892).

68. John M. Harlan to Abe Fortas, March 16, 1966, Harlan Papers, Box 531.

69. 383 U.S. at 763, 771.

70. Ibid., 772–73.

71. *Collins* v. *Hardyman*, 341 U.S. 651 (1951); *Griffin* v. *Breckenridge*, 403 U.S. 88, 107 (1971).

72. *Jones* v. *Alfred H. Mayer Co.*, 392 U.S. 409 (1968); Louis Cohen interview, February 4, 1990, Washington, D.C.

73. 392 U.S. at 452–53.

74. Ibid., pp. 478–80.

75. *Sullivan* v. *Little Hunting Park*, 396 U.S. 229, 241–42 (1969).

76. *Griffin* v. *Prince Edward Co.*, 377 U.S. 218 (1964); *Green* v. *New Kent Co.*, 391 U.S. 430 (1968); *Alexander* v. *Holmes Co.*, 396 U.S. 19 (1969); *Swann* v. *Charlotte-Mecklenburg Bd. of Education*, 402 U.S. 1 (1971); *Loving* v. *Virginia*, 388 U.S. 1 (1967).

77. *Watson* v. *City of Memphis*, 373 U.S. 526 (1963). John M. Harlan to Arthur Goldberg, May 20, 1963, Harlan Papers, Box 538.

78. John M. Harlan to Hugo L. Black, May 14, 1964, Harlan Papers, Box 208.
79. *McNeese* v. *Board of Education*, 373 U.S. 668 (1963).
80. Ibid., pp. 677, 678.
81. Ibid., pp. 679–80.
82. Unless otherwise indicated, this discussion is drawn from Bob Woodward and Scott Armstrong, *The Brethren: Inside the Supreme Court* (New York: Simon and Schuster, 1979), pp. 36–57.
83. Warren Burger, Memorandum to the Conference, October 25, 1969, Black Papers, Box 428. The draft order is on file in the same container.
84. Black's draft and notations regarding his reaction to the Harlan-Burger-White effort are in the Black Papers, Box 428.
85. John M. Harlan to Warren Burger, October 28, 1969, Harlan Papers, Box 606. The draft order is on file in the same container.
86. The memorandum, dated November 3, 1970, is in the Harlan Papers, Box 498.
87. John M. Harlan to Warren Burger, February 16, 1971, Harlan Papers, Box 490.
88. John M. Harlan to Warren Burger, March 11, 1971, Harlan Papers, Box 490.
89. *McLaughlin* v. *Florida*, 379 U.S. 184 (1964). Nesson's bench memorandum and a thick notebook summarizing his research are in the Harlan Papers, Box 218.
90. Charles Nesson interview.
91. John M. Harlan to Byron White, November 30, 1964, Harlan Papers, Box 218. The cases cited dealt largely with government's power to control expression in public places and included *Martin* v. *Struthers*, 319 U.S. 141 (1943); *Thornhill* v. *Alabama*, 310 U.S. 88 (1940); and *Schneider* v. *State*, 308 U.S. 147 (1939).
92. Byron White to John M. Harlan, December 1, 1964, Harlan Papers, Box 218; 379 U.S. at 197–98.
93. *Milliken* v. *Bradley*, 418 U.S. 717 (1974).
94. The report is in the Harlan Papers, Box 496. Florence Perlow Shientag was the judicial candidate, Mason H. Bigelow the other member of the subcommittee.

Chapter 8. Incorporation and Beyond

1. *Elkins* v. *United States*, 364 U.S. 206, 233, 251–52 (1960).
2. *Wolf* v. *Colorado*, 338 U.S. 25 (1949); *Mapp* v. *Ohio*, 367 U.S. 643 (1961); conference notes, Brennan Papers, Box 407.
3. John M. Harlan to Felix Frankfurter, May 1, 1961, Harlan Papers, Box 125; John M. Harlan to Tom Clark, May 1, 1961, Harlan Papers, Box 125. Frankfurter pronounced Harlan's letter "Good!" and uncharacteristically suggested few changes in its wording.
4. Tom Clark to John M. Harlan, May 4, 1961, Harlan Papers, Box 125. The case Clark specifically cited was *Irvine* v. *California*, 347 U.S. 128 (1954), in which Justice Jackson had indicated, as Clark put it, "that it was not then time to overrule or change" *Wolf*.
5. Hugo L. Black to Tom Clark, June 15, 1961, Black Papers, Box 349; for examinations of Black's difficulty with the rule, see generally Jacob W. Landnski, "In Search of Justice Black's Fourth Amendment," *Fordham Law Review* 45 (1976):

453; Yarbrough, *Mr. Justice Black and His Critics*, ch. 6; Tom Clark to John M. Harlan, June 15, 1961, Black Papers, Box 349; Harlan to Clark, May 1, 1961, Harlan Papers, Box 125.

6. *Mapp* v. *Ohio*, 367 U.S. at 674, 676, 681, 683.

7. Ibid., pp. 684–85, 686.

8. *Baker* v. *Carr*, 369 U.S. 186 (1962); *Colegrove* v. *Green*, 328 U.S. 549 (1946).

9. Schwartz, *Super Chief*, p. 412.

10. The Frankfurter memorandum, dated October 10, 1961, is in the Harlan Papers, Box 496. Black's notated copy is in the Black Papers, Box 353.

11. John M. Harlan to Charles Whittaker and Potter Stewart, October 11, 1961, Harlan Papers, Box 534.

12. Felix Frankfurter to John M. Harlan, October 11, 1961, Harlan Papers, Box 135; *New York Times*, February 8, 1962; John M. Harlan to Potter Stewart, February 8, 1962, Harlan Papers, Box 543; Schwartz, *Super Chief*, p. 419.

13. Conference notes, Brennan Papers, Box 408; Tom Clark to Felix Frankfurter, March 7, 1962, Harlan Papers, Box 943.

14. Felix Frankfurter to John M. Harlan, March 5, 1962, Harlan Papers, Box 534.

15. John M. Harlan to Felix Frankfurter, February 5, 1962, Harlan Papers, Box 135; 369 U.S. at 333, 334, 336–37, 339–40.

16. Hugo L. Black to Felix Frankfurter, April 19, 1962, Frankfurter Papers, Box 25; Hugo L. Black, Jr., to Felix Frankfurter, April 15, 1962, Frankfurter Papers, Box 25.

17. A copy of the memorandum, dated April 25, 1962, is in the Harlan Papers, Box 534.

18. Felix Frankfurter to Roland S. Homet, April 27, 1962, Harlan Papers, Box 534.

19. *New York Times*, August 30, 1962.

20. Elsie Douglas to John M. Harlan, undated note, accompanying draft of Felix Frankfurter to Hugo L. Black, May 6, 1963, Harlan Papers, Box 485.

21. John M. Harlan to Felix Frankfurter, September 28, 1962, Frankfurter Papers, Box 66; John M. Harlan to Felix Frankfurter, January 7, 1963, Frankfurter Papers, Box 66.

22. *Gray* v. *Sanders*, 372 U.S. 568 (1963). Harlan's memorandum to his clerks as well as the Frankfurter clerk's memorandum are in the Harlan Papers, Box 554.

23. Richard J. Hiegel interview, January 25, 1990, Cambridge, Massachusetts.

24. Ibid.

25. Philip B. Kurland to John M. Harlan, March 6, 1963, Harlan Papers, Box 534.

26. *In re Oliver*, 333 U.S. 257 (1948); *Palko* v. *Connecticut*, 302 U.S. 319 (1937); *Betts* v. *Brady*, 316 U.S. 465 (1942); *Adamson* v. *California*, 332 U.S. 46 (1947).

27. Ohio *ex rel. Eaton* v. *Price*, 364 U.S. 263, 275 (1960); William Brennan to Potter Stewart, May 23, 1960, Brennan Papers, Box 37; *Frank* v. *Maryland*, 359 U.S. 360 (1960).

28. *Torasco* v. *Watkins*, 367 U.S. 488 (1961); John M. Harlan to Hugo L. Black, June 13, 1961, Harlan Papers, Box 484; *Marcus* v. *Search Warrant*, 367 U.S. 717 (1961); John M. Harlan to William Brennan, May 31, 1961, Harlan Papers, Box

486; *Griggs* v. *Allegheny County*, 369 U.S. 84 (1962); John M. Harlan to William O. Douglas, February 20, 1962, Harlan Papers, Box 543; *Chicago, B. & Q.R. Co.* v. *Chicago*, 166 U.S. 226 (1897).

29. *Robinson* v. *California*, 370 U.S. 660 (1962); John M. Harlan, Memorandum for the Conference, November 15, 1961, Harlan Papers, Box 496.

30. Harlan, Memorandum for the Conference.

31. 370 U.S. at 678–79.

32. *Powell* v. *Texas*, 389 U.S. 810 (1968). A copy of the Black dissent is in the Harlan Papers, Box 313.

33. Apparently, *Quicksall* v. *Michigan*, 339 U.S. 660 (1950), had been the last case in which the Court had found an absence of any special circumstances requiring appointment of counsel in a state case.

34. The notation is in the Harlan Papers, Box 543; the memorandum, dated May 28, 1962, is in the same container.

35. This discussion is drawn from Anthony Lewis, *Gideon's Trumpet* (New York: Vintage Books, 1964), pp. 170–71.

36. *Gideon* v. *Wainwright*, 372 U.S. 335, 343, 344 (1963); *Powell* v. *Alabama*, 287 U.S. 45 (1932).

37. 372 U.S. at 350.

38. Ibid., p. 351.

39. Ibid., p. 352; *Palko* v. *Connecticut*, 302 U.S. at 325.

40. *Gideon* v. *Wainwright*, 372 U.S. at 346–47.

41. *Ker* v. *California*, 374 U.S. 23 (1963); John M. Harlan to Tom Clark, May 8, 1963, Harlan Papers, Box 493.

42. 374 U.S. at 44, 45, 46.

43. *Cohen* v. *Hurley*, 366 U.S. 117 (1961); *Malloy* v. *Hogan*, 378 U.S. 1 (1964); *Adamson* v. *California*, 332 U.S. 46 (1947); *Twining* v. *New Jersey*, 211 U.S. 78 (1908); Yarbrough, *Mr. Justice Black and His Critics*, p. 93.

44. The clerk's memo is in the Harlan Papers, Box 202.

45. 378 U.S. at 15, 16, 22.

46. Ibid., pp. 24, 27.

47. Ibid., pp. 31, 32, 33.

48. Pointer v. *Texas*, 380 U.S. 400 (1965); *Klopfer* v. *North Carolina*, 386 U.S. 213 (1967); *Washington* v. *Texas*, 388 U.S. 14 (1967); *Duncan* v. *Louisiana*, 391 U.S. 145 (1968); *Benton* v. *Maryland*, 395 U.S. 784 (1969).

49. *Griffin* v. *California*, 380 U.S. 609, 616 (1965); *Pointer* v. *Texas*, 380 U.S. at 408; *Benton* v. *Maryland*, 395 U.S. at 808.

50. *Cheff* v. *Schnackenberg*, 384 U.S. 373, 380 (1966); *Bloom* v. *Illinois*, 391 U.S. 194 (1968); *Duncan* v. *Louisiana*, 391 U.S. 145, 171 (1968).

51. The draft of Black's original *Duncan* opinion is in the Black Papers, Box 399.

52. Potter Stewart to John M. Harlan, May 7, 1968, Brennan Papers, Box 175; 391 U.S. at 176, 180, 181 (footnote omitted).

53. 391 U.S. at 176 (footnotes omitted).

54. Ibid., pp. 174, 176–77 (footnote omitted).

55. Ibid., pp. 187–88, 190, 193. The Cohen memorandum is in the Harlan Papers, Box 313.

56. Ibid., pp. 182, n. 21, 172; *Baldwin* v. *New York*, 399 U.S. 66 (1970); *Williams* v. *Florida*, 399 U.S. 78 (1970).

57. 399 U.S. at 118, 136.

58. *Johnson* v. *Louisiana*, 406 U.S. 356 (1972); *Apodaca* v. *Oregon*, 406 U.S. 404 (1971). The Justice's draft opinion in the cases is in the Harlan Papers, Box 441.

59. Philip Heymann to John M. Harlan, October 6, 1970, Harlan Papers, Box 554; John M. Harlan to Philip Heymann, October 14, 1970, Harlan Papers, Box 554.

60. Louis Cohen interview, February 4, 1990, Washington, D.C.

61. *Cohen* v. *Hurley*, 366 U.S. 117 (1961); *Shotwell Manufacturing Co.* v. *United States*, 371 U.S. 341 (1963). See also *United States* v. *Shotwell Manufacturing Co.*, 355 U.S. 233 (1957).

62. Arthur Goldberg to John M. Harlan, December 3, 1962, Harlan Papers, Box 543.

63. William Brennan to John M. Harlan, December 12, 1962, December 15, 1962, Harlan Papers, Box 486.

64. *Escobedo* v. *Illinois*, 378 U.S. 478 (1964); *Miranda* v. *Arizona*, 384 U.S. 436 (1966). Brennan penned his reaction to Harlan's revised draft in the margin of John M. Harlan to William Brennan, December 21, 1962, Harlan Papers, Box 486.

65. 378 U.S. at 493. The bench memo is in the Harlan Papers, Box 208.

66. 384 U.S. at 505, 516, 526.

67. *Mathis* v. *United States*, 391 U.S. 1, 5 (1968); *Orozco* v. *Texas*, 394 U.S. 324, 328 (1969); *Spevack* v. *Klein*, 385 U.S. 511, 520 (1967); See also *Garrity* v. *New Jersey*, 385 U.S. 493, 500 (1967); conference notes, Brennan Papers, Box 412; *Schmerber* v. *California*, 384 U.S. 757, 772 (1966); *Terry* v. *Ohio*, 392 U.S. 1, 31 (1968); conference notes for *Maxwell* v. *Bishop*, Brennan Papers, Box 416; *McGautha* v. *California*, 402 U.S. 183 (1971); *Illinois* v. *Allen*, 397 U.S. 337 (1970); John M. Harlan to Hugo L. Black, March 19, 1970, Harlan Papers, Box 484.

68. *Fay* v. *Noia*, 372 U.S. 391, 448, (1963); *Chapman* v. *California*, 386 U.S. 18, 55 (1967). The memo, for *Carter* v. *United States*, is in the Harlan Papers, Box 544. For another Harlan "harmless error" opinion, see *Fahy* v. *Connecticut*, 375 U.S. 85, 92 (1963).

69. Baron Rothchild to John M. Harlan, June 14, 1966, Harlan Papers, Box 565; Jarvis Cromwell to John M. Harlan, June 15, 1966, Harlan Papers, Box 565; J. Edward Lumbard to Felix Frankfurter, June 17, 1964, Harlan Papers, Box 535.

70. John M. Harlan to Sir Howard Beale, June 29, 1966, Harlan Papers, Box 483.

71. *Pickelsimer* v. *Wainwright*, 374 U.S. 2, 3 (1963); *Linkletter* v. *Walker*, 381 U.S. 618 (1965); *Desist* v. *United States*, 394 U.S. 244, 259 (1969). In *United States* v. *Johnson*, 457 U.S. 537 (1982); *Griffith* v. *Kentucky*, 479 U.S. 314 (1987), and in *Teague* v. *Lane*, 109 S.Ct. 1060 (1989), the Supreme Court appeared to adopt Justice Harlan's position; but see the remarks of Martha A. Field in the New York Law School Centennial Conference in honor of Justice John Marshall Harlan, April 20, 1991, New York, New York, to be published in a future issue of the *New York Law School Law Review*.

72. *Bumper* v. *North Carolina*, 391 U.S. 543, 553 (1968).

73. John M. Harlan to Byron White, June 10, 1969, Harlan Papers, Box 609; *Chimel* v. *California*, 395 U.S. 752, 769 (1969) (Harlan, J., concurring); *Bivens* v. *Six Agents*, 403 U.S. 388, 398 (1971) (Harlan, Jr., concurring).

74. *United States* v. *Spinelli*, 393 U.S. 410 (1969); undated and unidentified clipping, Harlan Papers, Box 484.

75. *Olmstead* v. *United States*, 277 U.S. 438 (1928); conference notes for *Silverman* v. *United States*, Brennan Papers, Box 407; *Katz* v. *United States*, 389 U.S. 347, 362 (1967) (Harlan, J., concurring); *Lopez* v. *United States*, 373 U.S. 427 (1963); *United States* v. *White*, 401 U.S. 745, 784, 792 (1971) (Harlan, J., dissenting).

76. *United States* v. *Kahriger*, 345 U.S. 22 (1953); Hugo L. Black to John M. Harlan, April 4, 1967, Harlan Papers, Box 484; John M. Harlan to Hugo L. Black, April 6, 1967, Harlan Papers, Box 484; John M. Harlan to Hugo L. Black, May 2, 1967, Harlan Papers, Box 484; *Marchetti* v. *United States*, 390 U.S. 39 (1968).

77. *In Re* Gault, 387 U.S. 1, 65 (1967) (Harlan, J., concurring and dissenting); John M. Harlan to Byron White, January 6, 1970, Harlan Papers, Box 609; *In Re* Winship, 397 U.S. 358, 359, 372–73, n. 5 (1970).

78. Schwartz, *Super Chief*, pp. 545–52; *Estes* v. *Texas*, 381 U.S. 532 (1965) (Harlan, J., concurring); *Rideau* v. *Louisiana*, 373 U.S. 723 (1963); John M. Harlan to Tom Clark, May 28, 1963, Harlan Papers, Box 493. The memo is in the Harlan Papers, Box 181. A draft dissent which Harlan wrote when the Court originally voted to affirm Estes's conviction is in the Harlan Papers, Box 230.

79. William H. Duckworth to John M. Harlan, December 28, 1967, Harlan Papers, Box 545.

80. John M. Harlan to William H. Duckworth, January 29, 1968, Harlan Papers, Box 545

81. See especially Kenneth Karst, "Invidious Discrimination: Justice Douglas and the Return of the 'Natural-Law-Due-Process Formula,' " *UCLA Law Review* 16 (1969): 716.

82. *Lochner* v. *New York*, 198 U.S. 45 (1905); *Adkins* v. *Children's Hospital*, 261 U.S. 525 (1923).

83. *Skinner* v. *Oklahoma*, 316 U.S. 535, 541 (1942); *Korematsu* v. *United States*, 323 U.S. 214, 216 (1944).

84. *Reynolds* v. *Sims*, 377 U.S. 533 (1964); *Harper* v. *Virginia Bd. of Elections*, 383 U.S. 663 (1966); *Kramer* v. *Union Free School District*, 395 U.S. 621 (1969); *Loving* v. *Virginia*, 388 U.S. 1 (1967); *Levy* v. *Louisiana*, 391 U.S. 68 (1968); *Shapiro* v. *Thompson*, 394 U.S. 618 (1969).

85. *Carrington* v. *Rash*, 380 U.S. 89, 97 (1965).

86. *Harper* v. *Virginia Bd. of Elections*, 383 U.S. at 684, 686 (1966); *Lochner* v. *New York*, 198 U.S. at 75–76; *Williams* v. *Rhodes*, 393 U.S. 23, 41 (1968) (Harlan, J., concurring). Materials relating to the shift in the Court's *Harper* position are in the Harlan Papers, Box 249.

87. *Levy* v. *Louisiana*, 391 U.S. 68 (1968); *Glona* v. *American Guarantee Co.*, 391 U.S. 73 (1968). The bench memo is in the Harlan Papers, Box 314.

88. Louis Cohen interview.

89. *Glona* v. *American Guarantee Co.*, 391 U.S. at 77, 79–80.

90. Ibid., pp. 76, 80; Louis Cohen interview.

91. *Shapiro* v. *Thompson*, 394 U.S. 618 (1969); Schwartz, *Super Chief*, pp. 725–32.

92. William Brennan to Abe Fortas, June 11, 1968, Brennan Papers, Box 179. The Fortas draft is in the same box.

93. 394 U.S. at 658, 659, 661–62.

94. Ibid., pp. 671, 674, 676, 677.

95. Paul Brest interview, January 28, 1990, Palo Alto, Calif.

96. *Shapiro* v. *Thompson*, 394 U.S. at 677; *Dandridge* v. *Williams*, 397 U.S. 471, 489 (1970); *Labine* v. *Vincent*, 401 U.S. 532, 540 (1971); *Hunter* v. *Erickson*, 393 U.S. 385, 393 (1969); *James* v. *Valtierra*, 402 U.S. 137 (1971).

97. *Williams* v. *Rhodes*, 393 U.S. 23, 41 (1968) (Harlan, J., concurring); *Douglas* v. *California*, 372 U.S. 353, 362 (1963) (footnote omitted), quoting *Griffin* v. *Illinois*, 351 U.S. 12, 34 (1956); *Williams* v. *Illinois*, 399 U.S. 235, 259, 260 (1970).

98. *Hoyt* v. *Florida*, 368 U.S. 57, 61–62, 63 (1961). For analyses of the Court's changing position after Earl Warren's retirement, see Wallace Mendelson, "From Warren to Burger: The Rise and Decline of Substantive Equal Protection," *American Political Science Review* 66 (1972): 1226; Ralph Winter, "The Changing Parameters of Substantive Equal Protection: From the Warren to the Burger Era," *Emory Law Journal* 23 (1974): 657; Tinsley E. Yarbrough, "The Burger Court and Unspecified Rights: On Protecting Fundamental and Not-So-Fundamental 'Rights' or 'Interests' Through a Flexible Conception of Equal Protection," *Duke Law Journal* 1977: 143.

99. Hugo Black interviews. For a discussion of Black's equal protection philosophy, see Tinsley E. Yarbrough, "Justice Black and Equal Protection," *Southwestern University Law Review* 9 (1977): 899.

100. *Ferguson* v. *Skrupa*, 372 U.S. 726, 731–32 (1963); Arthur Goldberg to Hugo L. Black, April 18, 1963, Black Papers, Box 372.

101. Drafts of Black's opinions, and the clerk's comments, are in the Harlan Papers, Box 172.

102. John M. Harlan to Hugo L. Black, April 11, 1963, Black Papers, Box 372.

103. *Morey* v. *Doud*, 354 U.S. 439 (1957).

104. *Tileston* v. *Ullman*, 318 U.S. 44 (1943); *Poe* v. *Ullman*, 367 U.S. 497 (1961).

105. 367 U.S. at 517–18, 521.

106. Fried's memorandum is in the Harlan Papers, Box 496.

107. *United States* v. *Carolene Products Co.*, 304 U.S. 144 (1938); *Meyer* v. *Nebraska*, 262 U.S. 390 (1923); *Pierce* v. *Society of Sisters*, 268 U.S. 510 (1925); *Olmstead* v. *United States*, 277 U.S. 438, 478 (1928).

108. Conference notes, Brennan Papers, Box 407.

109. *Poe* v. *Ullman*, 367 U.S. at 540, 541, 543.

110. Ibid., p. 542.

111. Ibid., pp. 547, 548.

112. Philip Heymann interview; Charles Fried interview.

113. 367 U.S. at 548; *Griswold* v. *Connecticut*, 381 U.S. 479 (1965).

114. 381 U.S. at 500, 501.

115. *Roe* v. *Wade*, 410 U.S. 113 (1973); *United States* v. *Vuitch*, 402 U.S. 62 (1971); conference notes, Brennan Papers, Box 417.

116. *Goldberg* v. *Kelly*, 397 U.S. 254 (1970); *Sniadach* v. *Family Finance Corp.*, 395 U.S. 337, 342–43, 351 (1969).

117. Robert Mnookin interview.

118. *Sanks* v. *Georgia*, 401 U.S. 144 (1971); *Boddie* v. *Connecticut*, 401 U.S. 371, 380–81, 394 (1971); Thomas Krattenmaker interview, January 25, 1990, Washington, D.C.

119. Robert Mnookin interview; *Karr* v. *Schmidt*, 401 U.S. 1201 (1971); John M. Harlan to Hugo L. Black, February 26, 1971, Harlan Papers, Box 484.

Chapter 9. Final Struggles

1. *United States* v. *O'Brien*, 391 U.S. 367, 388–89 (1968); *Karr* v. *Schmidt*, 401 U.S. 1201 (1971). The memo, for *Ferrell* v. *Independent School Dist.*, is in the Harlan Papers, Box 545.

2. *Tinker* v. *Des Moines School Dist.*, 393 U.S. 503 (1969). The draft opinions are in the Black Papers, Box 409.

3. 393 U.S. at 526. Black placed his summary of events on his copy of the original Harlan dissent in the case.

4. Conference notes, Brennan Papers, Box 415; *Street* v. *New York*, 394 U.S. 576 (1969).

5. Abe Fortas, Memorandum to the Conference, March 19, 1969, Black Papers, Box 408; 394 U.S. at 610; *Cowgill* v. *California*, 396 U.S. (1970); conference notes, Brennan Papers, Box 417.

6. *Cohen* v. *California*, 403 U.S. 15 (1971); Thomas Krattenmaker interview.

7. 403 U.S. at 15, 20, 21, 22.

8. Ibid., pp. 18, 22–23, 25–26.

9. Ibid., p. 27; Warren Burger, Memorandum to the Conference, May 27, 1971, Brennan Papers, Box 242. Burger's unfiled dissent is in the same container.

10. Paul Brest interview; Robert Mnookin interview.

11. Ibid., Louis Cohen interview; Thomas Krattenmaker interview.

12. Michael Boudin interview, February 1, 1990, Washington, D.C.

13. Paul Brest interview; Robert Mnookin interview.

14. Thomas Krattenmaker interview; Robert Mnookin interview; *Afroyim* v. *Rusk*, 387 U.S. 253, 268 (1967), overruling *Perez* v. *Brownell*, 356 U.S. 44 (1958). See also *Kennedy* v. *Mendora-Martinez*, 372 U.S. 144, 197 (1963) (Harlan, J., dissenting). Despite his regard for precedent, during his last term the Justice also joined a new majority in *Rogers* v. *Bellei*, 401 U.S. 815 (1971), which qualified the Court's ruling in the *Afroyim* case and upheld a regulation providing that persons born outside the United States of a citizen and an alien must satisfy a residency requirement in order to retain their U.S. citizenship. Moreover, he wrote Justice Black, *Afroyim*'s author and a vehement *Bellei* dissenter, he considered his "course wholly consistent with bowing to the basic holding in *Afroyim*." John M. Harlan to Hugo L. Black, Black Papers, Box 435.

15. *Flast* v. *Cohen*, 392 U.S. 83 (1968); *Frothingham* v. *Mellon*, 262 U.S. 447 (1923).

16. 397 U.S. at 129, 130.

17. *Brandenburg* v. *Ohio*, 395 U.S. 444 (1969); John M. Harlan to Abe Fortas, April 15, 1969, Black Papers, Box 404; *Law Students* v. *Wadmond*, 401 U.S. 1 (1971). See also *Cole* v. *Richardson*, 397 U.S. 238 (1970) (Harlan, J., concurring).

18. *New York Times Co.* v. *United States*, 403 U.S. 713, 753, 755 (1971).

19. Ibid., pp. 753, 756, 757, 758.

20. Thomas Krattenmaker interview.

21. Eve Harlan Dillingham interview; J. Edward Lumbard interview; Earl Warren to John M. Harlan, August 19, 1960, Harlan Papers, Box 605; Roger Derby interview; *New York Times*, September 19, 1971.

22. Thomas Krattenmaker interview; Paul Burke interview; Robert Mnookin interview; John M. Harlan to Mrs. Ernest Ives, July 21, 1965, Harlan Papers, Box 551.

23. John Twarda interview, June 16, 1990, Westport, Connecticut; Thomas Krattenmaker interview; Paul Burke interview; Louis Cohen interview.

24. Paul Burke interview; Thomas Krattenmaker interview; Louis Cohen interview; John Twarda interview.

25. Thomas Krattenmaker interview.

26. Eve Harlan Dillingham interview; John Twarda interview; J. Edward Lumbard interview.

27. John M. Harlan to Chi-Chen Wang, January 7, 1970, Harlan Papers, Box 603.

28. Eve Harlan Dillingham interview.

29. Ibid.; Louis Cohen interview.

30. Louis Cohen interview; Robert Mnookin interview; Paul Brest interview. The children's book Ethel Harlan wrote was *The Adventures of Little Man Coco* (Boston: Branden Press, 1966), originally written for her daughter. She also wrote unpublished poems and plays for children.

31. Stephen Shulman interview; Robert Mnookin interview.

32. Eve Harlan Dillingham interview; John Twarda interview.

33. Ibid.

34. John Twarda interview.

35. Ibid.

36. Ibid.

37. Ibid.

38. Ibid.; Paul Burke interview; John M. Harlan to Henry Friendly, September 7, 1971, Harlan Papers, Box 537.

39. Paul Burke interview; Allen R. Snyder interview, January 28, 1990, Washington, D.C. Snyder, who was one of Harlan's clerks for the 1971 term, continued in that position until the confirmation of Justice William Rehnquist, Justice Harlan's replacement. As had been the pattern since the onset of Harlan's difficulties with his eyesight, Martin Minsker, who had clerked for the Justice during the 1970 term, had planned to continue the next term also. James R. Bieke was Harlan's third 1971–72 term clerk.

Except where otherwise indicated, the discussion in this and the following paragraphs is drawn from Hugo Black, Jr., *My Father: A Remembrance* (New York: Random House, 1975), pp. 246–66, and from a June 22, 1990, telephone conversation with Mr. Black. I am very grateful to Mr. Black, who holds the copyright to his book, for his kind permission to draw extensively on his reminiscences.

40. Eve Harlan Dillingham interview.

41. Memorandum of Dr. George A. Kelser, September 23, 1971, Harlan Papers, Box 547.

42. W. Barton Leach to John M. Harlan, May 27, 1965, Harlan Papers, Box 562. A similar Drew Pearson column appeared in the *Washington Post*, August 7, 1965. Pearson, who years before had suggested that Harlan's appointment to the federal bench was designed to provide a vacancy for Tom Dewey in Harlan's law firm, now reported rumors that Dewey—who was then nearly seventy, had retired from public office in 1955, and would die before Harlan—might replace Harlan on the Court!

43. John M. Harlan to W. Barton Leach, June 1, 1965, Harlan Papers, Box 562; *New York Post*, January 5, 1970.

44. Thomas Krattenmaker interview; John M. Harlan to Henry Friendly, September 7, 1971, Harlan Papers, Box 537.

45. Hugo L. Black interviews.
46. Louis Cohen interview; Thomas Krattenmaker interview.
47. *Washington Star*, September 24, 1971; John M. Harlan to Richard M. Nixon, September 23, 1971, Harlan Papers, Box 547.
48. Janet Harlan White interview; Edith Harlan Powell interview; Eve Harlan Dillingham interview; Paul Burke interview; Wellington Newcomb interview.
49. Charles Stewart interview; Henry Sailer interview; Charles Nesson interview.
50. John Twarda interview; Eve Harlan Dillingham interview; Edith Harlan Powell interview; Henry Sailer interview; memorandum of Dr. George A. Kelser, on file in Harlan Papers, Box 547.
51. Henry Sailer interview; Paul Burke interview.
52. John Twarda interview. The memorandum and supplements, the latter dated October 15 and 22, 1971, are in the Harlan Papers, Box 547.
53. John Twarda interview; *Weston Forum*, January 5–11, 1972. A transcript of the Trowbridge prayer, partial list of those attending the funeral, and related items are in the Harlan Papers, Box 547.

Epilogue. Judge's Judge

1. Warren Burger to John M. Harlan, undated, Harlan Papers, Box 490.
2. Sir Arthur L. Goodhart to John M. Harlan, June 2, 1966, Harlan Papers, Box 538; Eustace Seligman to John M. Harlan, June 20, 1956, Harlan Papers, Box 596. A typescript of the *American Oxonian* piece is in the Harlan Papers, Box 658.
3. Edith Harlan Powell interview. The Justice's sister, a highly successful investment counselor, largely managed her brother's financial affairs. John Maynard Harlan's will and other material pertaining to his estate are in the Harlan Family Papers.
4. *Morey* v. *Doud*, 354 U.S. 439 (1957).
5. Norman Dorsen interview.
6. Wellington Newcomb interview.
7. Learned Hand to John M. Harlan, December 26, 1955, Harlan Papers, Box 539.
8. Paul Brest interview.
9. *United States* v. *Kras*, 409 U.S. 434 (1973).
10. Wellington Newcomb interview; J. Edward Lumbard interview. Godden mentions a visit to the Harlans' home in her autobiography *House with Four Rooms* (New York: Morrow, 1989).
11. Robert Mnookin interview.
12. Richard M. Nixon to John M. Harlan, September 16, 17, 23, 1971, Harlan Papers, Box 583; Richard M. Nixon to Mrs. John M. Harlan, January 3, 1972, Harlan Papers, Box 583; *New York Times*, December 30, 1971; *Washington Star*, December 30, 1971; Nina Totenberg, "John Marshall Harlan: A 'Judge's Judge,' " *National Observer*, January 8, 1972; "The Judges' Judge," *Time*, January 10, 1972, p. 14; David E. Rosenbaum, " 'A Lawyer's Judge': John Marshall Harlan," *New York Times*, September 24, 1971.
13. *Washington Post*, January 1, 1972.

Bibliographical Note

The John Marshall Harlan Papers in the Seeley G. Mudd Manuscript Library at Princeton University, the principal source of research for this work, reflect the exhaustive attention to detail and total mastery of subject matter which characterized Justice Harlan's career as lawyer and jurist. Voluminous and superbly indexed, with multiple copies of material appropriate for several files, the papers include extensive correspondence covering all phases of the Justice's life, transcripts and other material relating to important cases with which he was associated as one of the nation's most distinguished corporate attorneys, drafts of filed and unfiled opinions, conference notes, and the memoranda of individual justices and clerks, among other items. Harlan family papers, now in the possession of the Justice's nephew Roger A. Derby, were another excellent primary source, particularly of material relating to a financial dispute involving Harlan's father, John Maynard Harlan, and his father's two brothers, as well as other aspects of Harlan family life and the Justice's relationship with his parents. The unpublished memoirs of Harlan's grandmother Malvina Shanklin Harlan, entitled *Some Memories of a Long Life* and on file in her husband's papers at the Library of Congress, furnished additional insight into the family's history; and the papers of Chief Justice Earl Warren and justices Hugo L. Black, Felix Frankfurter, William O. Douglas, Robert H. Jackson, and William Brennan, also housed at the Library of Congress, were an excellent source of material relative to Justice Harlan's Supreme Court career and relations with his judicial colleagues. Other critical primary sources included the Justice's published opinions; his World War II diary, now in the possession of his daughter, Eve Harlan Dillingham; *Reports of the New York State Crime Commission*, January 23, 1953, on which he served as chief counsel; the hearings of the Senate judiciary committee on the *Nomination of John Marshall Harlan, of New York, to be Associate Justice of the Supreme Court of the United States;* the Justice's lectures and addresses, cited in the notes to the text; and relevant newspaper and magazine articles.

As important as the foregoing, however, were telephone interviews I recorded with members of the Justice's family and others familiar with his life and career. Family members with whom I talked were his daughter and her first husband, Wellington Newcomb, as well as his sisters Edith Harlan Powell and Janet Harlan White and his nephew Roger A. Derby. Lauson Stone and Louis Lusky discussed Harlan's appeal of a state judge's decision overturning the appointment of the controversial scholar Bertrand Russell to the faculty of New York's City College. Peter Magargee Brown, Harry Weyher, and Judge Robert Patterson shared with me their recollections of Harlan's work as chief counsel to the New York crime commission; and Judge Charles Stewart recalled the future Justice's handling of the Du Pont–General Motors antitrust litigation. Herbert Brownell discussed his long association with the Justice and Harlan's appointment to the federal bench, and William P. Rogers shared his memories of the Supreme Court nomination and Senate confirmation proceedings. Paul Twarda, caretaker of the Justice's Weston, Connecticut, country home for more than thirty years, and a close friend as well as employee, offered invaluable information and insights, as did Paul Burke, the Justice's messenger through most of Harlan's Supreme Court tenure. Extremely helpful, too, were many of the Justice's clerks, including William Lifland, who clerked for Harlan on the Court of Appeals for the Second Circuit as well as the Supreme Court, and the following Supreme Court clerks: Barrett Prettyman, Jr., Wayne Barnett, Norman Dorsen, Henry Steiner, Henry Sailer, Stephen Shulman, Charles Fried, Philip Heymann, Richard Hiegel, Lloyd Weinreb, Charles Nesson, Michael Boudin, Louis Cohen, Paul Brest, Robert Mnookin, Thomas Krattenmaker, and Allen Snyder. I was also given access to interviews that the Justice's clerk Paul M. Bator had conducted before his untimely death which are now in the custody of his widow, including interviews with Harlan's eldest sister Elizabeth Harlan Derby and with his friends and associates Leslie Arps, Henry Friendly, Leo Gottlieb, David McAlpin, Whitney North Seymour, William Palmer, and John Wood. No one with whom I spoke, however, was of more invaluable assistance than J. Edward Lumbard, senior chief judge of the Court of Appeals for the Second Circuit and Harlan's close friend for over forty years.

Relatively little scholarly research on Justice Harlan has appeared to date. The most insightful now available are Norman Dorsen, "The Second Mr. Justice Harlan: A Constitutional Conservative," *New York University Law Review* 44 (1969): 249; and J. Harvie Wilkinson, III, "Justice John M. Harlan and the Values of Federalism," *Virginia Law Review* 57 (1971): 1185. A superb collection of papers presented at the New York Law School Centennial Conference in honor of Justice John Marshall Harlan, held on April 20, 1991, will be published in a future issue of the school's law review. Among doctoral dissertations dealing with elements of the Justice's jurisprudence are John Corcoran Hughes, "John Marshall Harlan, the Warren Court and the Freedoms of Speech and Press" (New

School for Social Research, 1978); Howard Lowell Bennett, "Mr. Justice John Marshall Harlan and the Supreme Court, 1955–1971: A Study in Federalism and Judicial Self-Restraint" (Ohio State University, 1975); Patricia R. Nelson, "John Marshall Harlan: Twentieth Century Federalist" (Johns Hopkins University, 1971); and Imogene Gosnell, "The Judicial Philosophy of John Marshall Harlan in the Field of Civil Liberties" (Catholic University, 1970). A variety of additional secondary sources are cited in notes to the text. Among those of greatest value were Martin Mayer, *Emory Buckner* (New York: Harper & Row, 1968), the biography of Harlan's law associate and mentor; Mervin Rosenman, *Forgery, Perjury, and an Enormous Fortune: 2,303 Claimants to the Ella Wendel Estate (1931)* (New York: Beach Hampton Press, 1984), a fascinating account of Harlan's first major civil case; and Hugo L. Black, Jr.'s moving description of his father's and Justice Harlan's last days in *My Father: A Remembrance* (New York: Random House, 1975), pp. 246–66.

Index

Printed in the United States
77673LV00004BC/2

9 780195 060904